WRESTLING THE ANGEL

Wrestling the Angel

THE FOUNDATIONS OF MORMON THOUGHT:
COSMOS, GOD, HUMANITY

Terryl L. Givens

UNIVERSITY PRESS

OXFORD
UNIVERSITY PRESS

Oxford University Press is a department of the University of Oxford.
It furthers the University's objective of excellence in research, scholarship,
and education by publishing worldwide.

Oxford New York
Auckland Cape Town Dar es Salaam Hong Kong Karachi
Kuala Lumpur Madrid Melbourne Mexico City Nairobi
New Delhi Shanghai Taipei Toronto

With offices in
Argentina Austria Brazil Chile Czech Republic France Greece
Guatemala Hungary Italy Japan Poland Portugal Singapore
South Korea Switzerland Thailand Turkey Ukraine Vietnam

Oxford is a registered trade mark of Oxford University Press
in the UK and certain other countries.

Published in the United States of America by
Oxford University Press
198 Madison Avenue, New York, NY 10016

Library of Congress Cataloging-in-Publication Data
Givens, Terryl, author.
Wrestling the angel. Volume 1, The foundations of Mormon thought:
cosmos, God, humanity / Terryl L. Givens.
    p.   cm.
Includes bibliographical references and index.
Summary: "Wrestling the Angel, Vol. I is the first in a two part study of the foundations
of Mormon thought and practice, situated in the context of an overview of the Christian tradition.
The book traces the essential contours of Mormon thought as it developed from Joseph Smith
to the present. Terryl L. Givens, one of the nation's foremost Mormon scholars, offers a sweeping
account of the history of Mormon belief, revealing that Mormonism is a tradition still very much
in the process of formation."—Provided by the publisher.
ISBN 978-0-19-979492-8 (hardcover : alk. paper) — ISBN 978-0-19-979499-7
(ebook) — ISBN 978-0-19-937843-2 (online resource) 1. Church of Jesus Christ of Latter-day
Saints—Doctrines. 2. Mormon Church—Doctrines. I. Title.
II. Title: Foundations of Mormon thought.
BX8635.3.G58 2014
230'.93—dc23
                                                            2014001807

1 3 5 7 9 8 6 4 2

Printed in the United States of America on acid-free paper

To Tom Griffith
. . . the king's good servant, but God's first

A right faith is an excellent and valuable thing. But it is advantageous no further than it ... leads us to live an holy and godly life.

—JONATHAN MAYHEW

Contents

Preface

⌒————————————————————————————————

"WRESTLING THE ANGEL" seems an apt image for any mortal attempt to capture in finite time and in human language the essential propositions about the nature of God, his universe, and his creations. However, this book is not a work of either systematic or historical theology per se. It is, rather, the first volume in a two-part study of the foundations of Mormon thought and practice.

I situate these foundations in the context of an overview of the Christian tradition for a particular reason: Mormonism's status as a Christian faith, and its exact relationship to Christianity, continue to be subjects of longstanding dispute. As the prominent scholar Sydney Ahlstrom remarked of Mormonism in his celebrated *Religious History of the American People*, "one cannot even be sure if the object of our consideration is a sect, a mystery cult, a new religion, a church, a people, a nation, or an American subculture."[1]

The Catholic and mainline Protestant churches have declared, in recent years, that Mormonism "does not fit within the bounds of the historic, apostolic tradition of Christian faith."[2] By situating Mormon thought in the context of historic Christian doctrines, I hope to illuminate what is continuous with the Christian tradition and what is radically distinct from it. I particularly delineate Protestant antecedents and parallels, since that is the religious milieu in which Mormonism appeared and that strongly influenced Smith, by way of both imitation and reaction. This comparative method may not resolve the question of Mormonism's status, but it should better inform the debate.

Though Mormonism comes out of a biblical tradition, and was strongly influenced by nineteenth-century Restorationist thought, it propounded a theology that does indeed, in many cases, diverge radically from creedal Christianity. As I will argue, its substantive differences are most evident in, and largely attributable to, a unique underlying cosmic narrative. In addition to its temporally expansive purview, Mormonism posits a distinctive cosmology and metaphysics, in which it situates an unconventional narrative of human identity and a re-envisioned divine nature. For this reason, conventional theological categories do not always accurately translate from mainline Christianity to Mormonism, and do not effectively organize the field of Mormon thought. In what follows, I use the elaboration of Mormonism's underlying cosmic narrative as this study's framework, rather than employ a topical enumeration, on the one hand, or a strict chronology of Mormon doctrines, on the other.

I am here tracing what I regard as the essential contours of Mormon thought as it developed from Joseph Smith to the present, not pretending to address the many tributaries in and out of Mormonism's main currents. Following the major lines of development to the contemporary LDS Church will emphasize the priority of Smith and the founding generation of Mormon thinkers, but reveal significant developments in subsequent decades. Because Mormons believe in an open canon, and because extra-biblical pronouncements by prophets living and dead also constitute Mormon "scripture," Mormon doctrine is by definition impossible to fix; reflection on the meaning of this living, evolving tradition is, therefore, inescapably a lively and contested theological enterprise.

The Mormon faith tradition is a relative newcomer on the Christian landscape, and its academic study is in the process of significant shifts. Long considered an outlier to the standard Protestant narrative of American religion, Mormonism is increasingly seen as integral to our understanding of more than America's westward settlement or of the political management of religious difference. Enduring fascination with its social innovations (polygamy, communalism), its stark supernaturalism (angels, gold plates, and seer stones), and its most esoteric aspects (a New World Garden of Eden, sacred undergarments) has proved wholly inadequate for understanding Mormonism's status as an enduring—and thriving—belief system born of the nineteenth century's religious upheavals and innovations.

With this work, I hope to lend momentum to the growing effort to understand Mormonism in its historical and theological context. This volume focuses on Mormonism as a system of belief that engages, adapts, and redefines historic Christianity in ways that its adepts have found compelling. Theology is not the only—or even the principal—dimension of organized religion that constitutes a church's identity, or accounts for its success or failure; but it's an important one—one that in the case of Mormonism has historically been overshadowed by popular interest in the media-fed distractions already cited or obscured by Mormonism's own anti-creedalism and historical impatience with Protestant theology. Recent success in incorporating Mormonism into larger disciplinary narratives has done much to free the faith from a predicament similar to the Amish purgatory of simplistic horse-and-buggy caricatures. And a new generation of (primarily) young Latter-day Saint scholars have done significant work in demonstrating some of the intellectual richness and depth of Mormonism's theological heritage; this book builds on such work.[3]

For organizational simplicity, I lay out some conceptual preliminaries in section one, "Frameworks," before proceeding to Mormon thinking about the universe, Deity, and humanity in section two, "Cosmic Narratives." Additionally, it should go without saying (but perhaps does not) that I make no claim to present an official narrative or to speak authoritatively on Mormon doctrine. My study makes no attempt to be comprehensive, or to trace every byway and cul-de-sac of Mormonism's theological development. Neither does this volume pretend to capture the entirety of teachings that at various times have held sway. I am, rather, trying to trace the sources of those ideas that have come to constitute the essentials of Mormon teaching at the present moment regarding cosmology, the nature of the divine, and the anthropology and destiny of the human (a volume to follow will deal with ecclesiology, including such topics as authority, sacraments, spiritual gifts, and worship). Thus, I am not tracing every voyage of Columbus; I am focusing on the main currents that got him to the New World. To some degree, historical narratives are inevitably selective and implicitly interpretive, and this one is no exception. Other scholars would perhaps choose other logbooks to emphasize and doubtless would interpret them differently from how I have.

Acknowledgments

MUCH OF THE writing of this volume took place in conjunction with a series of graduate seminars sponsored by the Mormon Scholars Foundation. We struggled over several summers to make sense of the main narrative of Mormon theological development, while excavating parallel streams, opposing strands, permutations, and dead-ends. I therefore gratefully acknowledge debts that deserve more particular mention than memory permits. Especially helpful in reading drafts and providing criticism were Nathaniel Givens, Stephen Webb, Gerald Smith, Matthew Bowman, Steven Harper, Samuel Brown, Benjamin Huff, Rachael Givens Johnson, Joseph Spencer, Jonathan Stapley, Jacob Rennaker, David Golding, Benjamin Park, Richard Bushman, Max Mueller, Taylor Petrey, Boyd Peterson, Carl Cranney, and Spencer Fluhman. Special thanks go to Don Bradley, whose contributions were especially invaluable. As always, Fiona Givens was my first and last reader and guide.

WRESTLING THE ANGEL

Frameworks

THREE CONSTRUCTS FRAME the foundations of Mormon thought: history, theology, and restoration. Early Mormonism, like Christianity itself, unfolded as a series of historical, pivotal encounters with the Divine to which faithful believers assent. An alternating embrace of and hostility toward the theological enterprise informs Mormon attitudes about how those encounters are to be understood, elaborated, and interpreted authoritatively. And a particular understanding of restoration informs the manner in which Mormonism constructs itself as a synthesis of divine revelation, human instrumentality, and historical process.

History as theology is perilous.

—GRANT McMURRAY, past president of the Community of Christ (the former Reorganized Church of Jesus Christ of Latter Day Saints)

1

Historical Prelude

∽ ———————————————————————————————

ASSENT TO MORMONISM as a belief system is largely a matter of assent to several alleged historical events. This has typically been the case with Christianity in general. To be Christian has meant that one believes that a historical personage named Jesus was born of a virgin in Bethlehem some two thousand years ago, performed those miracles attributed to him at particular times and places, and rose from the dead precisely three days after his crucifixion in Jerusalem. However, some Christians believe that the extensive, complex transmission history of those foundational testimonies known as "the Gospels" allows for some degree of equivocation or mythologizing when it comes to the particular claims of the Christian message (such as a virgin birth or physical resurrection). Mormonism is similarly tied to a series of pivotal truth claims that form part of a historical record. But being more recent and well attested, the circumstances surrounding Mormonism's founding events admit less room for negotiation. A brief, chronological overview of those seminal happenings may be useful, as background to the theological developments on which this study will focus.

In 1820, fourteen-year-old Joseph Smith experienced a vision or visitation in which God the Father and Jesus Christ appeared to him, granted him personal absolution from his sins, and pronounced the Christian world to be in a state of apostasy. Three and a half years later, an angel self-identified as Moroni appeared to Smith, informed him that "God had a work" for the youth to perform, and went on to describe an ancient record "written on gold plates" that Smith was to translate using a set of "interpreters." On the fifth annual visitation from Moroni, Smith in the fall of 1827 retrieved the record and "interpreters" from a hillside in upstate New York. After several false starts and delays, employing those interpreters (which he also called Urim and Thummim), as well as a seerstone and later direct revelation, Smith dictated to a schoolteacher scribe, Oliver Cowdery, several hundred pages of text in the spring of 1829. In the midst of their work, a resurrected John the Baptist appeared to Smith and Cowdery and conferred upon them the Aaronic Priesthood, giving them the authority to baptize. (At a later, unspecified date, according to Smith, the apostles Peter, James, and John appeared to them and conferred the higher, Melchizedek priesthood, essential for other ordinances.) As the translation wound down, Cowdery, Martin Harris, and David Whitmer—the "Three Witnesses"—testified that an angel of God showed them the gold plates. Shortly thereafter, Smith revealed them to a group of Eight Witnesses who affirmed they had seen and handled the plates. In March 1830, Smith published his work as the Book of Mormon, and on April 6 formally organized the Church of Christ (later the Church of Jesus Christ of Latter-day Saints, or LDS).

It is common to think of Smith's prophetic career as advancing through several stages, each marked by substantial doctrinal developments of increasing boldness: the Smith of 1830, organizing a church and producing a Book of Mormon that both bear marks of his own Protestant background; a Kirtland, Ohio, period characterized by a new human anthropology and organizational developments; and finally the radical Nauvoo, Illinois, phase, where he introduced polygamy, human theosis, and a God who seems to be a highly evolved human. Several facts argue for a more nuanced approach to his doctrinal development. Most importantly, the seeds of almost all his furthest-reaching innovations are present as early as 1830, as this study will show. In the sphere of cosmology, both the Book of Mormon and Smith's 1830 biblical redactions challenge Christian dualism and suggest a different valuation of materiality. Regarding the human, Smith is in that same year already alluding to a pre-mortal creation and rejecting Calvinist conceptions of depravity and inherited sin. And the God he depicts in his personal encounters and 1830 scriptural texts is personal, passible, and embodied. Clearly his conceptions are in many cases tentative and incomplete. He is still fairly steeped in a contemporary religious vocabulary whose import he is already undermining—a fact ignored in a great many precipitous readings of Smith—and the details of his theology proceed by fits and starts. The process was irregular, uneven, and marked even in his lifetime by competing interpretations of Smith's pronouncements, which he seldom glossed himself.

Before his murder in 1844, Smith would dictate well over a hundred revelations, write doctrine-filled epistles, and give numerous sermons, expounding principles of a "restored gospel." He would describe other visions and angelic visitations, some associated with the bestowal of additional priesthood authority or "keys," and he would produce other scriptural writings later canonized by the Mormon Church. His successor Brigham Young and subsequent LDS prophets would add clarity and detail, occasionally propound new doctrines, and revise or even rescind old ones. However, with the death of Smith, virtually all theological foundations were in place, and the era of publicly declared visitations from the heavens to prophet-leaders came to a close.

We are now in the school of theology and making rapid progress in the study of this celestial science. I admit there are some few dunces in the school, some advance at the very slow pace, and some not at all.

—BRIGHAM YOUNG, 7 April 1852

2

Mormonism and Theology

⌒⎯⎯⎯⎯⎯⎯⎯⎯⎯⎯⎯⎯⎯⎯⎯⎯⎯⎯⎯⎯⎯⎯⎯⎯⎯⎯⎯⎯

THEOLOGIAN STEPHEN WEBB'S reference to "the informality of much Mormon theology"[1] would find a cheerful acknowledgment among most Latter-day Saints. This is because in the modern era Mormons have considered the very enterprise of theology to be largely a secular enterprise, a sign of true religion's failure, and not an activity worth pursuing with any energy. In the dichotomy of leading Mormon intellectual Hugh Nibley, theology is proof of the "Sophic's" triumph over the "Mantic": "The Sophic is simply the art of solving problems without the aid of any supernatural agency, which the Mantic, on the other hand, is willing to solicit or accept."[2] Early Mormons did not exhibit such an unqualified bias. Theology is, as the etymology suggests, reasoned discourse about God, and one of Joseph Smith's earliest projects was to organize a School of the Prophets and deliver there a series of "lectures on theology."[3]

For Mormons in the nineteenth century and beyond, the fortunes of the term *theology* shifted from period to period and leader to leader. Mormon Church authorities have been loath to propound creeds or catechisms to establish a baseline for orthodoxy. Smith's 1842 Articles of Faith—the closest thing Mormonism has to a creed—contain relatively few of Mormonism's key beliefs. They include some foundational tenets that situate Mormonism within historic Christianity (belief in God the Father, the Son, and the Holy Ghost, and in Christ as Redeemer). And they include some points that establish sharp distinctions from Christian tradition (the Book of Mormon as the word of God, no original sin). But they leave out completely such teachings as human pre-existence and possible divinization (theosis), eternal marriage, and God's corporeality.

The Articles of Faith, in other words, seem designed to find a balance between total conformity and radical difference in limning some of Mormonism's beliefs. They were designed for a general audience, in response to an inquiry by *Chicago Democrat* editor John Wentworth into the history and beliefs of the new church. They were not originally intended or used by the church in any devotional, liturgical, or normative way, though they have come to approach those functions;[4] children memorize them in the LDS Sunday School, and the church canonized the thirteen statements of belief in 1880. This is somewhat ironic, since their sparse representation of Mormon belief is also a reflection of early Mormonism's anti-creedal posture. In the 1830s, some Mormon leaders, like David Whitmer and William McLellin, even resisted the publication of Mormon scripture, reflecting their hostility to rendering doctrines of the latter-day "restoration" fixed or concrete.[5] The preface to the 1835 Doctrine and Covenants acknowledged the "aversion in the minds of many against receiving anything purporting to be articles of religious faith."[6]

This history, and the church's steadfast reliance on the principle of "continuing revelation," have resulted in a tradition of church teachings that is highly fluid and generally hard to pin down. No *Book of Discipline* or counterpart to the Roman Church's Catholic Catechism exists. At times, a prophet has denounced particular teachings from the pulpit, as Brigham Young did with Orson Pratt.[7] The First Presidency can also issue official statements, which they have done on numerous occasions. Finally, they may publish declarations or proclamations, which they have done a handful of times. However, the dominant mode is restraint from affirming or rejecting theologizing even by apostles whose teachings have been privately judged by the Presidency, as witness the case of Bruce R. McConkie (see below). Canonization is the most important vehicle for asserting the authority of church teachings or revelations, but even in a church that emphasizes its living prophets, such a step has occurred infrequently since Joseph Smith's era.[8] All of this makes the unfolding of Mormon thought a difficult process to track. It also makes for a dynamic, at times adventuresome, and ultimately uneven process—one which Smith himself generally applauded, encouraged, and practiced rather than lamented.

Joseph Smith, and this is not always fully appreciated within the tradition he initiated, did not feel that direct communication from God, gifts of seership, and an open, continuously expanding canon in any way obviated the need for theology. In one of the "Lectures on Theology" that he delivered in Kirtland, Ohio, he approved a contemporary definition of theology, with one crucial modification. Charles Buck had called it "that science which treats of the being and attributes of God, His relations to us, the dispensations of His providence, His will with respect to our actions, and His purposes with respect to our end." Smith defined it as that "*revealed science.*"[9]

When the church father Origen wrote one of the first treatises on Christian belief in the early third century, he noted that some articles of the faith were "delivered . . . with the utmost clearness on certain points which they believed to be necessary to every one."[10] Ever since, much of systematic theology has been concerned with articulating and elaborating those "certain points" that constituted core beliefs of the orthodox. A more recent authority, surveying the historical practice of theology, describes its parameters as "the whole complex of the Divine dispensation from the fall of Adam to the Redemption through Christ and its mediation to men by His Church."[11] Those parameters have often been recognized by poets and clerics alike. In the greatest Christian epic in the West, *Paradise Lost*, John Milton claimed to push the boundaries of "God-science" further than most when he determined to soar "above th' Aonian Mount," in order to pursue "Things unattempted yet in Prose or Rhime."[12] Yet even in his audacious claim to "justifie the wayes of God to men," he knew when to recognize the limits of appropriate inquiry. As Raphael counsels Milton's over-curious Adam,

> Solicit not thy thoughts with matters hid,
> . . . Heav'n is for thee too high
> To know what passes there; be lowly wise:
> Think only what concerns thee and thy being;
> Dream not of other Worlds, what Creatures there
> Live, in what state, condition, or degree,
> Contented [with what] thus far hath been revealed.[13]

From an early Mormon perspective, Christian theology was generally too reticent in probing beyond the bounds of the biblically revealed. What of the time *before* Creation? What was God doing then? Preparing Hell for such as would ask such impudent questions, was the answer Augustine recounted.[14] What of God's other dominions? Why is there man at all? For Milton, it was to compensate for the third of heaven's angels seduced by Satan;[15] the scriptures, however, are silent. What of human destiny in the worlds beyond? What are humans being saved *for*? Dante thought a state of eternal, rapturous contemplation, and few have proffered more specifics than that. Post-redemption theology seems an oxymoron.

Examples of more unfettered theologizing have appeared from time to time. Minister and amateur philosopher Thomas Dick defended his radically speculative *Philosophy of a Future State* (1829) as consistent with, if not always affirmed by, Holy Writ, and he took his fellow theologians to task for their reluctance to plumb "the nature of heavenly felicity, and the employments of the future world." He lamented "the vague and indefinite manner in which such subjects have been hitherto treated," and "the want of those expansive views of the Divine operations which the professors of Christianity should endeavor to attain."[16] A group of seventeenth-century clergy known as the Cambridge Platonists followed their namesake's example and wrote rather liberally about a time before the earth's creation.[17] Mormonism likewise expands its purview in both directions—pre-Creation and post-redemption. So it is that one of the distinctives that makes it difficult to align Mormon theology with the categories of Christian theology is the former's placement of the traditional "Fall to Redemption" narrative within a more ample three-act drama. As E. Brooks Holifield remarks, the scope of Joseph Smith's theological innovations leads to "realms of doctrine unimagined in traditional Christian theology."[18]

In addition to its expanded cosmic timeline, Mormonism is difficult to organize in traditional theological categories because it relies upon a vastly expanded scriptural canon. The Book of Mormon, Smith's first and major scriptural production, did not serve as the principal basis for Mormon theology. One well-informed commentator on Mormonism notes that by itself, "the Book of Mormon . . . may not have added enough doctrinal novelty to the Christian tradition to have made Mormonism more than a Protestant sect."[19] Smith, his adherents, and his detractors were united in seeing that work primarily as the evidence on which Smith's claim to divine authority rested. (It also magnified their sense of millennial urgency, a literal gathering of Israel, and Zion-building.) Smith virtually never preached from its pages, referenced its doctrines, or explicated its passages. However, as we will see, an impressive number of Mormon doctrines find their seeds, if not their elaboration, in those pages. Smith seems to have been at some level aware of the subtler doctrinal implications of the Book of Mormon, and his later work revising the record for republication in 1837 doubtless contributed to his ongoing elaboration of Mormon thought. It is also important to recognize that regardless of the truth value others imputed to his "golden bible," Smith was convinced it was the product of heavenly inspiration. As such, it is helpful in understanding Mormonism's evolution to recognize, in one writer's words, "that the Book of Mormon was not merely derivative from the prophet, but actually may have been formative on his life and work as a prophet."[20]

Smith's second scriptural product, the Doctrine and Covenants ("Book of Commandments" in its 1833, aborted incarnation[21]), represented a more self-conscious exposition of Mormon doctrine. In 1834, Smith appointed a committee, with himself as head, "to arrange the items of the doctrine of Jesus Christ, for the government of the Church."[22] The result was a compilation of most of his revelations received to date (which his fellow Saints publicly voted to "prize . . . to be worth . . . the riches of the whole earth"[23]), the "Covenants," prefaced by the Lectures on Theology, or "Doctrine" portion of the volume. Though the lectures were a joint production, with Sidney Rigdon a principal contributor, Smith's ideas found expression therein, and he approved the final product.[24]

The Lectures on Theology (subsequently called the Lectures on Faith) served as the text for the "School of the Prophets" which Smith organized in 1833, to instruct Mormon elders and to "prepare them to be messengers of Jesus Christ."[25] The lectures were written over the winter of 1834–35, and they laid important foundations. The core message of the lectures was the necessity of understanding the nature of God, in order to exercise salvific faith in him. Some of the teachings laid out were fairly novel (God himself created the world "by faith"); other doctrines were entirely conventional in their language (God was the "supreme governor, . . . omnipotent, omnipresent, and omniscient"; Jesus made salvation possible through his "atonement and mediation.") Significantly, virtually all the scriptural texts used for illustration are biblical ones, with many ideas lifted wholesale from Buck's dictionary.[26]

The seeds of two radical Mormon innovations are present in the lectures, but in muted form. The Father and Son are portrayed as separate personages, and salvation is defined as "the glory, authority, majesty, power and dominion which Jehovah possesses."[27] At the same time, these lectures reaffirm the pivotal principle of Smith's entire career and the church he founded: "How do men obtain a knowledge of the glory of God, his perfections and attributes? . . . Through prayer and supplication incessantly, until like Enoch, the brother of Jared, and Moses, they obtain a manifestation of God to themselves."[28]

However, even those supposedly theological lectures passed over most key LDS teachings (such as pre-existence, authority, eternal marriage) and were dropped from the scriptural volume in 1921. Smith would not attempt again anything substantial by way of systematic doctrine. His principal contributions came through those hundred-plus "revelations" generally delivered in God's voice, through numerous public sermons, and in a scattering of letters and via private councils. Shortly after overseeing the lectures, Smith authored an essay designed to aid missionaries "in a measure, in doctrine."[29] It consisted largely of a biblically based exposition of repentance, baptism, and the gift of the Holy Ghost. This focus could be construed as strategic: Mormons then as now emphasize Christian commonalities before proceeding to the unfamiliar. Or, it could be seen as reflecting Smith's theological background: largely conservative and Protestant. In truth, the essential core of Mormonism has always been faith, repentance, and baptism. The enlargement of Mormon theology to encompass a materialistic cosmology, Adamic gospel, anthropomorphic God, pre-existent humans, and post-mortal families was rooted in the 1830s, but waited upon others than Joseph Smith for its full elaboration.

Although Smith is considered by Mormons to be the first in a continuing line of modern prophets (as Catholics consider Peter to be the first in a continuing apostolic succession), his status and influence far transcend chronological primacy. At the assembly convened to determine his successor subsequent to his murder, a virtually unanimous vote rejected any individual's attempt to inherit Smith's title or role. Young took the reins as chief of the Quorum of Twelve Apostles, not as the new Mormon prophet.[30]

Smith's commanding role as restorer of the gospel (and his continuing designation as "*the* prophet" rather than "the first prophet") explains why, even before Smith's death, his colleagues had begun this work of explicating and organizing his teachings. Foremost in this regard was Parley Pratt, who published his hugely influential *Voice of Warning* in 1837. In 1870, Mormon dissident Edward Tullidge commented on the influence of the Pratt brothers:

> Ask the people what brought them into the church, and you would hear from every direction Parley Pratt's "Voice of Warning" or "Orson Pratt's Tracts," until it would almost seem to you that the Pratts created the church. Indeed the best part of Mormon theology has been derived to a great extent from them, and so it may be said that they also, to a great extent, originated Mormonism.[31]

While the first half of Tullidge's statement would have gratified Parley Pratt, he likely would have objected to the claim that he had "created" or "originated" Mormonism. Though manifesting a fiercely independent streak, Pratt consistently demonstrated his commitment to the revelations and teachings of Joseph Smith, whom he revered as a prophet and restorer of ancient truths. Only once, in a personal dispute over a failed business transaction in 1837, did he clash openly with Smith, and even then he reiterated his devotion to Mormonism's scriptural canon. Pratt saw his role not as innovator but as systematizer and popularizer. His *Voice of Warning* was largely polemical and missionary oriented. A book of fervent millennialist expectation, it laid out Mormonism's claim to be the gospel restoration of prophecy.

Pratt defined the essential features of the Kingdom of God as comprising the basic principles Smith defended, and confirmed its organization and offices as consistent with the New Testament pattern. He added a disquisition on the necessity for authority, spiritual gifts, and the continuing revelation manifest in the production of the Book of Mormon. He situated Mormonism in the context of a full-blown dispensationalism, and affirmed literalism as the proper mode of scriptural exegesis. A year later, he moved beyond synthesis to produce more speculative writings that pushed Mormon thought in new directions.

Pratt's writings and interactions with Smith illustrate this more nuanced and convoluted process of doctrinal development; Pratt combined materials from both

Smith and the cultural background to produce his own syntheses. He ranged freely within the broad parameters of Smith's revelations, but also extended the boundaries of Mormon thought and elaborated doctrines in ways that usually, but not always, received the imprimatur of Smith and subsequent prophets. In general, Pratt's extensive writings were seen as systematizing, expanding, and making more accessible Smith's teachings. They illustrate in this way a crucial stage of most new religious movements: the explication, organization, and popularization of a theological system based on a founder's scattered corpus of writings and pronouncements.[32]

Significant changes and developments to Mormon theology occurred immediately upon Smith's death. Pratt in fact announced this next phase as a self-conscious operation. "The chaos of materials prepared by [Joseph Smith] must now be placed in order in the building," he wrote less than a year after the martyrdom.[33] He and his brother Orson played principal roles in this process, though Orson went further afield than Parley and was subjected to the censorship of the Mormon Church's second president, Brigham Young, as a result. At the same time, the Pratts played little role in key doctrinal developments of Young's administration regarding an evolving temple and adoption theology, which Young spearheaded. On another front, Parley produced in 1855 his summa theologica, *The Key to the Science of Theology*, the first attempt at a truly comprehensive treatment of the Mormon theological system. Among other achievements, his *Key* completed the task he began in 1838 of developing a comprehensive naturalistic cosmology based on Smith's materialist conception of Deity.

Its impact was unparalleled. One nineteenth-century memoirist wrote, "We had every encouragement to read the Church publications: *The Voice of Warning*; The Pearl of Great Price; and *Key to Theology*."[34] That only Pratt's writings would be on equal footing with the Pearl of Great Price, canonized in 1880, suggests the special status his works held in the minds of early LDS leaders and laity. His corpus was a virtual fifth scriptural volume of the church. Thomas D. Brown, in fact, claimed that Joseph Smith had pronounced *Voice of Warning* a standard work;[35] in 1864, it was one of two works Brigham Young recommended to a correspondent for an overview of Mormon doctrine.[36] In 1875, it was the very first title mentioned in the LDS *Deseret News* list of "Books worth Reading" (Pratt's *Key to Theology* was next).[37]

Meanwhile, Smith's successor, Brigham Young, was continuing to carry theology's torch. "Our favorite study," he proclaimed, "is that branch which particularly belongs to the Elders of Israel—namely, theology. Every Elder should become a profound theologian—should understand this branch better than all the world."[38] He inaugurated theology courses in the church's Brigham Young Academy (where a theological department was still flourishing at the turn of the twentieth century).[39] Though Young added virtually nothing to Smith's scriptural corpus, he set about expanding and elaborating Smith's vision of the centrality of temple worship, with its rituals of eternal sealing and aspirations to expand endlessly a heavenly human family, linked back to Adam and unfolding into an infinite future. Many of Young's doctrinal innovations faded into obscurity, met with little acceptance, or were subsequently repudiated or reversed: blood atonement (a belief that one's own blood must be shed to atone for certain sins), Adam-God theory (a teaching that Adam is the creator of human spirits and to be identified as the God humans worship), and a racially based priesthood ban. Still, the Young era saw substantial development of many of Smith's ideas. One can gauge how far emphasis had shifted from the church's early days to Young's presidency, when considering the periodical that Young commissioned the church's leading intellectual, Orson Pratt, to publish as a defense of Mormon doctrines—principally plural marriage. Named *The Seer* (1853–54) in commemoration of Smith, it promised to "illucidate" three teachings, none of which had even been mentioned in Smith's earlier Articles of Faith, or received substantial attention in Smith's revelations: "the ancient Patriarchal Order of Matrimony, or Plurality of Wives, . . . The Celestial origin and pre-existence of the spirits of men . . . and their final redemption and exaltation, as Gods."[40]

After Young—and perhaps in partial reaction to Young's unpopular innovations, but also reflecting intellectual as well as geographical isolation from a larger, unsympathetic host culture—succeeding generations of leaders did little to mask their contempt for theology. John Taylor, Brigham Young's successor, had earlier referred to sectarian theology as "the greatest tomfoolery in the world."[41] Now, the self-conscious project of Mormon theologizing shifted direction. With the 1890 manifesto ending polygamy, the status of an important component in Mormonism's doctrinal system was suddenly thrown in doubt; emphases shifted from the relational to the personal, from the other-worldly to the proximate, even while, as part of Mormonism's quest for Americanization, consolidation and elucidation of the basics rather than expansion and speculation became the rule.

As a consequence, with a few important exceptions, a growing distinction appears in the Mormon consciousness between "doctrine" as true, inspired, and authoritative teachings, on the one hand, and theology as the purely human pronouncements associated with an apostate Christendom, on the other. Theology, in this later view, is what happens when revelation fails. Sadly, perhaps, the shift reflects a diminishing excitement about the unbounded range of Smith's vision. Parley Pratt, for example, reveled in the way Smith ruptured traditional Christian categories of thought:

What a glorious field of intelligence now lies before us, yet but partially explored. What a boundless expanse for contemplation and reflection now opens to our astonished vision. What an intellectual banquet spreads itself invitingly to our appetite, calling into lively exercise every power and faculty of the mind, and giving full scope to all the great and ennobling passions of the soul. . . .[42]

The contrast is stark with Taylor's successor Wilford Woodruff, who was a long way removed from the heady visions of Joseph Smith and speculations of Young. In response to the controversies over Young's Adam-God theology, Woodruff urged commonality and unanimity of belief:

I want to say this to all Israel: Cease troubling yourselves about who God is; who Adam is, who Christ is, who Jehovah is. For heaven's sake, let these things alone. Why trouble yourselves about these things? . . . God is God. Christ is Christ. The Holy Ghost is the Holy Ghost. That should be enough for you and me to know. If we want to know any more, wait till we get where God is in person. I say this because we are troubled every little while with inquiries from elders anxious to know who God is, who Christ is, and who Adam is. I say to the elders of Israel, stop this.[43]

A generation later, a brief efflorescence of Mormon thought emerged when three luminaries produced intellectually rigorous attempts to systematize and elaborate a comprehensive theology—with mixed acceptance by church leadership and membership. Church apostle James E. Talmage (first Mormon to receive a doctorate) published under church sponsorship the *Articles of Faith* in 1899, the only officially sanctioned treatise covering the fundamentals of LDS belief; and the church's definitive study of Christology, *Jesus the Christ*, in 1915 (employed to teach adult priesthood holders the next year). The church's official imprimatur marked these works as authoritative teaching rather than speculative theology. Ranging rather more broadly, John Widtsoe published at least half a dozen church manuals, including *Rational Theology* in 1915, along with several other works that argued the reasonableness of Mormon doctrine and its compatibility with modern science; finally, the prolific autodidact B. H. Roberts was called upon by church leadership to prepare myriad manuals for the instruction of LDS youth and adults alike, including a five-volume *Course in Theology* (1907–11).

In addition, Roberts hoped to cap his thirty odd works with a magnum opus called *The Truth, The Way, The Life: An Elementary Treatise on Theology*. This masterwork on Mormon thought was finished in 1928, but he was unwilling to make changes to accommodate a church committee that reviewed it, and it was never published in his lifetime. The disputed passages consisted largely of the doctrinal speculations and conceptual bridges that he found necessary to achieve his preferred synthesis of the LDS scriptural corpus with the science—especially paleontology—of his day.[44] Those few caveats only serve to emphasize the influence wielded by this array of writers, under the auspices of the Mormon leadership's sponsorship and sanction. But the committee's effective veto of Roberts's publication project could be seen as marking another significant watershed in the history of Mormon thought. As the church grew more bureaucratically sophisticated, populous, and geographically diffuse, the maintenance of orthodoxy through centralized correlation and control became a more urgent concern. In this light, we might see Roberts, with his more ambitious and speculative bent coming up against a cautious and conservative leadership, as marking the end of a period of theological expansiveness. The work of Widtsoe and Talmage, by contrast, set a precedent for what would become, increasingly, a doctrinaire bent to publications emanating from the leadership.

A new direction in church orthodoxy was more clearly signaled in the 1930s. Roberts and Talmage died in this decade (Widtsoe would pass in 1952); the staunchly conservative and highly influential J. Reuben Clark was called into the First Presidency of the church in 1933. Higher Criticism dates back to the eighteenth century (or earlier, by some definitions), but it produced mid-twentieth-century reverberations that appear to have impacted Mormon leadership in particularly powerful ways. The Fundamentalist-Modernist Controversy of the 1920s and '30s marked a critical juncture in the split of American Presbyterians into liberal and conservative wings, but the strife and division spread throughout Protestantism. More locally, the LDS Church experimented with sending several of its educators to study theology at the University of Chicago in the 1920s. When some of the Chicago program alumni returned to the church's university, espousing their newly acquired liberal viewpoints, conservatives in the LDS hierarchy became reactionary.[45] There followed a period of retrenchment, of growing unease with worldly learning and with intellectualism generally. The synthesis of secular and spiritual that was the hallmark of the School of the Prophets was challenged in Clark's landmark address to church educators, wherein he warned that "the things of the natural world will not explain the things of the spiritual world; that the things of the spiritual world cannot be understood or comprehended by the things of the natural world; that you cannot rationalize the things of the spirit." Clark warned about "special training" in the academy and the infiltration into church education of the "most modern views" in particular.[46]

Over the next decades, two apostles would assume dominant influence over the articulation of Mormon doctrine: Joseph Fielding Smith and his son-in-law Bruce R. McConkie. Smith expressed alarm over the "dangers lurking in modern thought,"[47] and forcefully argued for a literal reading of scripture that was incompatible with modern science. His most controversial contribution, *Man: His Origin and Destiny*, was quickly withdrawn as a training manual soon after its introduction, but its authoritative tone and authorship lent it great influence. Much more enduring in its impact was a volume published by McConkie in 1958, entitled simply

Mormon Doctrine. It was, the author said, "the first major attempt to digest, explain, and analyze all of the important doctrines of the kingdom . . . . [T]he first extensive compendium of the whole gospel—the first attempt to publish an encyclopedic commentary covering the whole field of revealed religion."[48]

Two apostles assigned to review the book for church president David O. McKay recommended over 1,000 corrections, and McKay suspended its republication "even in a corrected form."[49] Nevertheless, after making several changes, McConkie republished his book in 1966, and the church's publisher marketed the immensely influential title all the way until 2010. Official reservations notwithstanding, church publications have quoted from the book prolifically in lesson manuals and teaching materials. Though a member of the First Council of the Seventy (just below the president and apostles in authority) at the time of *Mormon Doctrine*'s publication, after his 1972 call to the Quorum of the Twelve Apostles, McConkie came to be considered by the general church membership as the church's foremost scriptural scholar and theological expert. The book's enduring success, in spite of its contested authority, is perhaps a testament to the human proclivity for dogma. Mormonism has no creed. But at McConkie's hands, Mormon doctrine was authoritatively declared, neatly encapsulated, unambiguously defined, and alphabetically arranged. But it also revealed another fact, and that was the near total absence of a competing model. Pratt's 1855 *Key to Theology* was by 1958 an archaic work, and Talmage's 1899 *Articles of Faith* made no attempt to be comprehensive ("grace" does not even appear in the index). In this vacuum, McConkie, disapproving review committee notwithstanding, did far more to shape popular conceptions of Mormon teaching than any figure of the twentieth century's second half, achieving what one scholar calls a "near-canonical status that McKay had fought unsuccessfully to avoid."[50]

It may be no coincidence that in the immediate aftermath of the controversial books by Joseph Fielding Smith and Bruce McConkie, the church moved to centralize and coordinate all church programs and curricula in a massive "correlation program," under the leadership of Harold B. Lee. A primary impetus was Paul H. Dunn's doctoral project, which established that "what the Brethren thought ought to be taught, and what was actually being taught, . . . were miles apart."[51] One consequence of Lee's reform was to move beyond simple coordination of curricula, to centralize church authority in the Quorum of the Twelve Apostles to an unprecedented degree. The pervasive taboo against "teaching outside the manuals" dates to this period. Efforts by General Authorities (LDS leaders with worldwide jurisdiction) to launch independent forays into doctrine or theology became well-nigh impossible.

After McConkie's passing in 1985, no particular church authority emerged with a comparable—or comparably expressed—sense of theological vocation. ("It is my province to teach to the Church what the doctrine is" he had said.[52]) Though

Mormons believe in an open canon and continuing revelation, their scriptures have undergone only three additions in the last century, and only one of those derives from a post-World War I revelation. The most authoritative bases of Mormon theology, in other words, were laid in the early nineteenth century, and the following few generations saw the majority of the tradition's most ambitious and sustained attempts to explore and develop those foundations. Annie Clark Tanner, a Mormon who grew to maturity in the latter half of the nineteenth century, considered that she had herself lived through a shift in church emphasis from the theological and theoretical to the ethical and practical; speaking of her childhood, she noted that "belief in the theological doctrine was more emphasized in the Church, at that time than practical application of ethical teaching."[53]

This historical corroboration of Webb's impression about the informality of Mormon theology—and its shifting fortunes—explains a conundrum not unique to the Mormon faith tradition: how to know what constitutes "official" doctrine. A substantial literature within Mormonism debates whether there even is, in fact, anything that can be called Mormon theology, and how it might be ascertained. James Faulconer has famously referred to Mormonism's "atheological" character, "without an official or even semi-official philosophy that explains and gives rational support to [its] beliefs and teachings."[54] He cites in support Smith's assertion that "The Latter-day Saints have no creed, but are ready to believe all true principles that exist, as they are made manifest from time to time."[55] Nevertheless, it is obvious that a body of teachings and propositions and beliefs *have* arisen in the Mormon faith tradition, and the question is how to establish general grounds for their relative authority. A framework common to many models, and endorsed by the LDS Church itself, gives priority to the four "standard works" of the Mormon scriptural canon, discourses of the leadership delivered in the church's semi-annual General Conferences, and church handbooks and curricular materials.[56] As many critics of such a model point out, interpretation complicates simple appeals to canon, the thousands of conference sermons are rife with mutually incompatible views, and teachings are constantly evolving.[57] In this study, I will use such sources and many others, from pamphlets and tracts to privately published works, of both LDS ecclesiastical leaders and lay men and women who have exerted conspicuous influence on Mormon thought. Although my intention is primarily descriptive, my judgments are obviously selective and subjective.

The four aptly named "standard works" have paramount authority in shaping Mormon teachings and grounding their authority. These consist of the Bible (in the King James Version), the Book of Mormon (comprising largely writings by purported ancient American prophets Smith published in 1829–30), the Doctrine and Covenants (a compendium of 138 revelations, almost all of which Smith received between 1823 and 1843), and the Pearl of Great Price, an amalgam of additions to Genesis, writings attributed to Abraham, emended portions of Matthew, and some of Smith's autobiographical writings. The Bible is perhaps the most ambiguously authoritative, since an article of faith acknowledges its inspiration has been diluted by translators (or "transmitters," as Smith seems to have understood the concept of translation); even so, LDS biblical interpretation has tended more toward fundamentalist literalism than historically nuanced or figurative readings. This is largely a product of Mormonism's origins in a time when Common Sense theology was dominant; Timothy Dwight, one of the most influential churchmen of the era, hammered home its relevance to religious discourse and scriptural interpretation: "Our Savior treats every subject in the direct manner of Common Sense," he taught. "By the first third of the nineteenth century," writes another historian, "Common-sense habits of mind were axiomatic."[58] Parley Pratt set the tone for Mormon scriptural exegesis with recurrent attacks on those who would "spiritualize" the Bible, rather than read in the plain, literal sense.[59]

Complicating the bases of Mormon theology further, Mormons expand not only the scriptural canon but also the definition of scripture itself. Regarding verbal pronouncements, a revelation declares that anything spoken by priesthood leaders "when moved upon by the Holy Ghost shall be scripture"[60]—which of course is of little help to academics and observers trying to sort doctrine from opinion.

In the first generation of the Mormon Church, the picture is especially complicated, for several reasons. First is because Smith hated dogma and tests of orthodoxy. A revelation declared him "a seer, translator, and prophet," but his *calling* as a prophet was some years morphing into the virtual *office* of Prophet. (The first was a function of his revelatory experience; the second was an institutionally defined position in an ecclesiastical hierarchy.[61]) Joseph Smith was as likely to promote openness as to exert his authority. He severely rebuked his own brother Hyrum for performing unauthorized rituals.[62] But in another case, he "did not like the old man being called up for erring in doctrine" when a council met to discipline Pelatiah Brown for speculating on the meaning of portions of the book of Revelation. "It looks too much like methodism and not like Latter day Saints. Methodists have creeds which a man must believe or be kicked out of their church. I want the liberty of believing as I please, it feels so good not to be tramelled."[63]

Second, Smith seldom exerted editorial control over the publications of church members. Associates, missionaries, editors of church newspapers, and apostles like W. W. Phelps, Orson Pratt, and Parley Pratt printed broadsides, pamphlets, and in some cases books with no supervision. When several reviewers referred to Parley Pratt's *Voice of Warning* as a standard work along with Mormon scriptures, neither he nor Smith corrected the perception.[64] Smith allowed a virtually unconstrained flowering of Mormon theology, as his colleagues enthusiastically joined in vigorous exploration, elaboration, and conjecture, constituting a communal project of religion making.[65] It was not until months after Smith's death, in the face of schismatic fracturing, that Parley Pratt established the Quorum of the Twelve Apostles' editorial control over publishing of Mormon teachings.[66]

Finally, Smith himself freely mingled oracular pronouncement with vigorous speculation, repeatedly insisting that he did not always speak as a prophet. A popular joke has more than a hint of truth to it that Catholics espouse papal infallibility, but no Catholic believes in it. Joseph Smith espoused prophetic fallibility, but no Mormon believes in it. Smith lamented before he was even dead, with his features marbleized and his flaws airbrushed by his followers, the cumbersome myth of his infallibility and ready access to unfiltered truth. To one of his friends, he complained that "he did not enjoy the right vouchsafed to every American citizen—that of free speech." Smith added that "when he ventured to give his private opinion on any subject of importance, his words were often garbled and their meaning twisted, and then given out as the word of the Lord because they came from him."[67] Yet Smith's successors were themselves divided on how inspired some of Smith's pronouncements were, as is evident in the oscillating fortunes of the April 1844 General Conference address Smith gave, called the King Follett Discourse, his most famous and controversial sermon. It is the principal source for some of Mormonism's most radical conceptions of God (though most all of them had been raised earlier, some as far back as 1830). But the sermon's status as officially recognized doctrine had some bumps in the early twentieth century and again at the century's end.

The church paper *Times and Seasons* published the text in August 1844, mere weeks after Smith's death, and Smith had intended its wider publication and dissemination; it appeared in pamphlet form the next year. But Charles Penrose opposed its publication. George Albert Smith, an apostle in 1912, said he and others of the leadership "feared that it contained some things that might be contrary to the truth," and it was excised from the official *History of the Church* published that year.[68] In the 1950 and subsequent editions, it was reinserted. In 1998, a magazine interviewer asked LDS president Gordon B. Hinckley directly about the current status of portions of the King Follett Discourse dealing with God's human embodiment. Hinckley replied, "I don't know that we teach it. I don't know that we emphasize it. . . . I understand the philosophical background behind it, but I don't know a lot about it, and I don't think others know a lot about it."[69] In later remarks to church members, he seemed to reaffirm his commitment to the doctrine in question.[70] Under Hinckley's tenure, the doctrine appeared conspicuously in church manuals.[71]

The shifting fortunes of the King Follett Discourse are but one instance of a problem not as unique to Mormonism as some observers believe: how to reconcile evolving doctrine and abandonment of precedent, on the one hand, with claims of prophetic authority and oracular power, on the other. Mormonism's historical suspicion of theology is born of the sentiment that God's word is eternal and his prophets reveal it through clear channels of communication; theology, by contrast, is a negotiation involving reason, politics, social pressures, and evolving human values.

Fourth church president Wilford Woodruff famously assured his members that the Lord would never permit the president of the church "to lead [the people] astray."[72] But that guarantee was of course circular: it was only comforting to those who already believed a prophet's word was categorically valid. Mormonism's namesake scripture defines God's word as both canonical and fluid: an iron rod, and a text to be adapted to particular time and place;[73] in another revelation God claimed the prerogative to "command and revoke, as it seemeth me good."[74]

Young's Adam-God theory was taught for a generation or two; polygamy came and went; the priesthood ban forbidding ordination of blacks to the priesthood was implemented and rescinded. It is true that these developments have moved Mormonism toward the theological and cultural mainstream, and thus seem particularly "convenient" instances of revelation. What they actually suggest is that Mormonism, with its espousal of "continuing revelation," living prophets, and an open canon, is not all that far removed from Catholic conceptions of an original deposit of faith given to the apostles that the church must teach and protect, even while acknowledging that said deposit of faith unfolds and develops over time, subject to the Holy Spirit's guidance.

In Catholic and Protestant, as well as Mormon traditions, the legitimacy of change is the fulcrum on which larger questions of authority hinge. As the Jesuit John Courtney Murray put the case,

> the parting of the ways between the two Christian communities [Catholicism and Protestantism] takes place on the issue of development of doctrine. *That* development has taken place in both communities cannot possibly be denied. The question is, what is legitimate development, . . . and what, on the other hand, is accretion, additive increment, adulteration of the deposit, distortion of true Christian discipline? . . . Perhaps, above all, the question is, What are the limits of development and growth—the limits that must be reached on peril of archaistic stuntedness, and the limits that must not be transgressed on peril of futuristic decadence?[75]

Mormonism, like Catholicism and some varieties of Protestantism, claims that doctrine not only can but must evolve as a living tradition and that its spiritually inspired stewards respond to changing needs, capacities, and conditions. Mormonism differs in its conception of the "keys," or priestly authority its stewards hold as "prophets, seers, and revelators," and in one entirely crucial regard: Mormonism asserts that the original deposit of faith is itself expanding—that is, the canon is never closed. But some openness to change is shared with all but the most recalcitrant fundamentalists. Mormonism's ninth Article of Faith, which affirms belief "that God will yet reveal many great and important things," is similar in spirit to the words of the Congregationalist minister George MacDonald: "To the man who would live throughout the whole divine form of his being, . . . a thousand questions will arise to which the Bible does not even allude. . . . They that begin first to inquire will soonest be gladdened with revelation; and with them he will be best pleased, for the slowness of his disciples troubled him of old."[76]

Mormonism's great nineteenth-century challenge to prophetic infallibility was the revocation of the practice of plural marriage. The splintering of several self-identified fundamentalist Mormon groups was occasioned by their perception that John Taylor's successors had betrayed the unalterable doctrine of plurality, and thus fell from their calling. Less culturally and emotionally disruptive, and confounding to some of the faithful in a different way, has been the LDS Church's 1978 revocation of the racial ban on priesthood. This is because polygamy's inception and discontinuance were both written with the scriptural finger of God, even if the latter occurred in the context of enormous political pressure. A revelation was claimed for both moments in Mormon polygamy's history.[77] It turns out the origins of the priesthood ban have no such claim to a revelatory foundation, and Young's dual position as territorial governor and Mormon prophet at the time of its implementation, along with readily available nineteenth-century racist theologies of the era, further impugn its original authority. And so the current church hovers uneasily on the brink of considering the century-long practice a terrible human tragedy; as long ago as the 1930s, influential apostle Hugh B. Brown believed that the denial of priesthood to blacks was wrong and worked to reverse it. LDS president David O. McKay famously referred to the ban as a policy rather than a doctrine.[78] But it was March 2013 before the church formally denied record of any authoritative origin to the practice.[79]

The case of the priesthood ban is important not only for the inherent gravity of what's at stake in personal costs—generations of African-American members deprived of dignity and full participation in the church and all it offers temporally and spiritually, owing to a leader's culturally inherited misconceptions—but also because the ban represents a crucial moment of the LDS Church's self-understanding and self-definition as a human institution of divine origin, a church staffed by fallible men but rooted in the notion of inspired, authoritative, and prophetic leadership. Gary Wills has referred to the difficulties entailed by the Catholic Church's doctrine of papal infallibility: it fostered structures, rather than individuals, that were prone to deception. Doctrinal modifications or corrections are virtually impossible because, in the absence of mechanisms for dealing with revelatory failure, "it would shake people's faith in the church for the papacy to reverse its course."[80]

Wills also writes that Catholic painters painted and Catholic preachers preached many versions of a common topos: "a figure wearing the papal crown in the fires of hell, presenting the Pope as a terminal sinner damned forever." He then wisely notes, "This was . . . a lesson of the faith, not an attack on it."[81] The same principle is found in Mormon scripture, though it hasn't fully permeated Mormon culture. God chose Joseph Smith not in spite of but because of his weakness; it was designedly through the instrumentality of such a flawed vessel, he was told by revelation, that God "might show forth [his] wisdom through the weak things of the earth."[82] The LDS Church has no doctrine of infallibility, but it is characterized by a church culture that elevates the prophet and his mantle to near infallible heights. (Mormons regularly sing an anthem to Joseph Smith in worship services, and by tradition sing a hymn in praise of modern prophets when the current office holder enters large assemblages.) The challenge of Mormon leadership is how to balance Woodruff's assurance that the leadership will never lead members astray, with the empirical and doctrinal reality of prophets designated by the voice of revelation as "the weak things of the earth." In the case of the priesthood ban, how Mormon leaders will finally resolve the possibility of a colossal mistake countenanced by ten LDS prophets remains to be seen, but if a resolution appears, it will signal a seminal moment in the Mormon theological tradition.

One Mormon apostle recently reminded the church that "not every statement made by a Church leader, past or present, necessarily constitutes doctrine."[83] Scripture, apostolic pronouncements, First Presidency statements, writings of scores of Mormons that have fed into the stream of Mormon belief through the years—all make up a still evolving and sometimes inconsistent amalgam. All attempts to capture the essence of Mormon thought, as is true of any living tradition, are limited and provisional.

All things had under the Authority of the Priesthood at any former period shall be had again—
bringing to pass the restoration spoken of by the mouth of all the Holy Prophets.
—JOSEPH SMITH, 5 October 1840

3

The Meaning of Restoration

FOR ALMOST TWO thousand years Catholics, and later many Protestants, held that orthodoxy was defined by chronological precedence. The "primum" is the "verum," in church father Tertullian's formulation. Most Protestant reformers (other than Luther) based their revolution on this premise, asserting their duty to return Christianity to the "unsullied and undefiled" original teachings of Jesus and the apostles. Puritans built on the same foundations, believing, in William Bradford's words, that the "churches of God" should "revert to their anciente puritie; and recover their primitive order."[1]

By the nineteenth century, growing numbers of Americans in particular believed it apparent that Christian teachings and practice had everywhere undergone radical and continuous change in preceding centuries. Neither Catholics nor mainline Protestants could by that time convincingly maintain they were replicating New Testament forms and practices. They could forgo that appeal, join the throngs of Seekers and Restorationists, or give new emphasis to the concept of the "original deposit of faith" and its development.[2] In 1843, Anglican churchman John Henry Newman (soon to be Catholic and eventually cardinal) did just that. In his "Essay on the Development of Christian Doctrine" he forcefully defended the evolution of church forms and teachings: "From the history of all sects and parties in religion, and from the analogy and example of Scripture, we may fairly conclude that Christian doctrine admits of formal, legitimate, and true developments, that is, of developments contemplated by its Divine Author."[3]

Newman's influential formulation was timely. The English-speaking world had for a few decades been awash in a religious sea change that was transforming the spiritual and denominational landscape even more dramatically than the Great Awakening of the eighteenth century. In America, at least, sanctifying rather than denying change provided a reasonable alternative to the persuasive force of an appeal to primitive Christianity, whereby the mainline churches suffered a distinct disadvantage. Varieties of Seekers, Primitivists, and Restorationists roamed the religious landscape with the greatest competition coming from each other. The deficiencies of contemporary Christianity implied in their insistent questions found a large audience: Where were the gifts of the early church? Where were the plain and simple doctrines? Where were the lay ministry, immersive baptism, and a dozen other principles and practices seen in the New Testament? Newer movements that emulated early Christian forms and practices grew like weeds. As historians have argued, "those churches that prospered in the westward-moving, primordial nation were those churches that depicted most vividly the ancient primordium to a primordial people."⁴ Prominent in this array of primitive denominations was Mormonism, or what came to be called the Church of Jesus Christ of Latter-day Saints. Any account of its origins and early development must therefore situate its driving teachings within this larger, evolving framework of tradition and restoration.

RESTORATION IN THE NINETEENTH CENTURY AND EARLIER

Versions of restorationism go back centuries. Christian Humanism, Continental Reformation thought, and Tyndale's covenant theology gave powerful impetus to the idea of primitivism—or return to an original state perceived as pure—in the sixteenth century, and as Richard Hughes and Leonard Allen suggest, primitivism and restorationism are mutually implicating enough to be virtually synonymous.⁵ Leaders across the spectrum of Christian reform movements envisioned restoration as a return to practices more in harmony with the New Testament model. John Calvin certainly considered he was engaged in a Restoration movement,⁶ and his archrival Michael Servetus titled his major theological work *The Restoration of Christianity* (*Christianismi Restitutio*).

In the early nineteenth century, however, the term was appropriated and expanded by a group of dynamic reformers. Barton Stone in Kentucky and Thomas Campbell operating in Pennsylvania and Virginia spearheaded movements that emphasized several inherited restorationist ideas, especially a return to a purer Christianity. Campbellites themselves could be simply indifferent to non-scriptural practices, but as the ideal was translated in practice by Restorationists like the later Churches of Christ, Christians must eliminate any belief or practice not scripturally sanctioned.

Restorationists took this principle also to entail the avoidance of denominational titles (hence their self-labeling as Christians and Disciples of Christ, respectively), and were possessed of an urgent sense of mission to prepare for, or actively hasten, the millennium. Their merger constituted the foundation of the American Restoration Movement.

Restorationists generally considered the Bible sufficient as a source of both authority and doctrine. Some Seekers, on the other hand, anticipated a restoration of some kind of authority to administer the church and its ordinances of salvation. Joseph Smith's mother, Lucy Mack Smith, described her brother as just such a Christian: "he became what is called a seeker. . . . He held that there was no church in existence which held to the pure principles of the Gospel but labored incessantly to convince the people that by an exercise of prayer the blessings and privileges of the ancient disciples of Jesus might be obtained and eventually would be."[7]

Lucy Smith similarly revealed the fundamental Primitivist assumptions that underlay the religious values of her world: "I then proceeded to relate the substance of what is contained in the Book of Mormon, dwelling particularly upon the principles of religion therein contained. I endeavored to show them the similarity between these principles, and the simplicity of the gospel taught by Jesus Christ in the New Testament."[8] This is precisely what Sidney Mead referred to in describing this era as a contest among denominations for each "to justify its peculiar interpretations and practices as more closely conforming to those of the early church as pictured in the New Testament than the views and policies of its rivals."[9] The religious ferment sweeping the upstate New York countryside of the early 1800s was saturated in this language of restoration, and it pervaded Smith's household and his own rhetoric. His personal quest for religious truth was largely shaped by these cultural shifts. To the natural religious sensitivities of this teenager were added both the fuel of fiery revivalism and his own family's religious divisions.

Even as a boy Smith was disturbed by the verbal violence of ardent preachers contending for converts in successive waves of camp meetings and Sunday sermons. Whether Smith was at this time simply an open-minded, unchurched youth or a more religiously sophisticated seeker is difficult to say, since two different accounts of his first visionary experience suggest two different answers. In the church's canonical rendering of Smith's "First Vision," he was frankly perplexed by the competing claims of the Presbyterians and Methodists, and went to the woods to put his simple question to God: "which of all the sects was right," and then he added a highly significant, "for at this time it had never entered into my heart that all were wrong."[10] Six years earlier, however, his recollection was that he had in fact been persuaded by his own reading of the Bible, and doubtless by the seeker rhetoric of his region, that truth was nowhere on the earth. "By searching the scriptures," he insisted, "I found that mankind did not come unto the Lord but that they had apostatised from the true and liveing faith and there was no society or denomination that built upon the gospel of Jesus Christ as recorded in the new testament."[11]

Regardless of any predisposition he might have had entering the woods, both accounts confirm his new understanding upon leaving the grove of trees. In response to his prayerful petition, Jesus Christ appeared in a shaft of blinding light and told him, "The world lieth in sin at this time and none doeth good no not one. [T]hey have turned asside from my gospel." Or in his later words, "they were all wrong, and . . . their Creeds were an abomination in his sight, . . . They teach for doctrines the commandments of men." If he had previously inferred a universal apostasy, his belief was confirmed. If the idea had never entered his heart, it was permanently entrenched there now. The new question looming was, what exactly did this "apostasy" entail?

APOSTASY

Apostasy, as generally used in Smith's day, had several meanings. The influential theological dictionary of Charles Buck defined *apostasy* as a falling away of truth that was Adamic (as in original sin), national (as in idolatrous Judah), or personal (as in Judas).[12] Protestant Restorationists sometimes used the term to refer to the corruption of the Roman Church and its successors. In Smith's thought, there was no question that what he called "an apostacy . . . from the Apostolic platform" had occurred.[13] He used that expression in early 1833, and a church newspaper article first employed the term "Great Apostasy" shortly thereafter.[14] But with Smith, the term assumed very early a distinctive meaning. "We can never understand precisely what is meant by restoration, unless we understand what is lost or taken away," Parley Pratt would write in 1837.[15] His point may seem obvious, but it actually represents a particular variety of Restorationist thinking. Pratt is already referring to apostasy as loss or diminution, which is how Mormons today think of the term. Restoration conjures up the image of repairing, reconstituting, or replacing what was lost. But the dominant meaning that apostasy, or corruption of the original *kerygma*, had for Pratt's contemporaries was the virtual opposite: unwarranted accrual, and restoration would signify a cleansing or reduction. That is how the term is generally used in art and architectural restoration alike, where restoration generally involves peeling away layers of accretion: lacquers, dirt, and grime that have accumulated, or partitions, paneling, and paint that were deliberately imposed on an original structure. That was the sense in which many religious restorationists understood the term, as suggested by the simple motto of the age's most prominent restorationists, Alexander Campbell and Barton Stone: "Where the holy Scriptures speak, we speak; and where they are silent, we are silent."[16] Ethan Smith, another contemporary, quoted the maxim, "Divinity consists in speaking with the scripture; and in going *no further*" [original emphasis].[17]

Important exceptions to reform by reduction existed—especially in the frequent refrain: where have the spiritual gifts gone? Early Methodists, for example, noted their widespread absence and found visions, prophetic dreams, and even healings to be evidence of God's presence. The Methodist pursuit of such gifts led one scholar to refer to their "militant supernaturalism."[18] But time and again, the language of reformers and Primitivists, as with the moniker "Puritan" itself, suggest purification and its synonyms. And purification works by subtraction, not addition, as in the expunging of unauthorized musical instruments, singing, stained glass, or sacraments. "Spiritual building" has gone too far, complained the translators of the Geneva Bible, for "how can it be lawful to procede . . . any other waies, then Iesus Christ the Sonne of God . . . hath commanded by his worde?"[19] Or as Cromwell's chaplain John Owen had it, invoking the familiar analogy of art restoration, "paintings, crossings, crucifixes, . . . altars, tapers, wafers, organs, anthems, litany, rails, images, copes, vestments, what were they but Roman varnish" on religion, in need of removal.[20] Restoration, in other words, usually represented a return to a fixed point in the past, an "original purity."[21] It intended the systematic removal of what Christ had never inaugurated and the New Testament had never authorized.

Like his contemporaries, Smith believed the absence of spiritual gifts was visible evidence of a decisive rupture with the church of the New Testament. But spiritual gifts were only the superficial manifestation of a much greater challenge to the integrity of the Christian religion, one that was the core of his thinking about apostasy. The point was made most clearly by Benjamin Winchester, an important early leader in the LDS Church. In his influential *History of the Priesthood* of 1843, he wrote: the "Holy Priesthood . . . is the channel through which all the spiritual gifts, such as miracles, revelations, visions, &c., flow or are obtained; . . . . When it ceases to exist on earth, the church falls into darkness, and ultimately degenerates into apostasy." In this view, the priesthood was not just the source of spiritual gifts, which were signs of grace; more importantly, priesthood was the source of the sacraments, which were the vehicles of grace—the indispensable means by which the salvation of the human family was effected. The most important deficiency in the modern church, Smith wrote, involved the original "Laws," "ordinances," and "covenants" of the gospel.[22] Consistent with period usage, Smith originally used the term *ordinance* in a generic way to denote God's laws and statutes as well as divinely prescribed rites and ceremonies. Gradually, the term came for Mormons (as for low-church Protestants) to signify what Catholics would call "sacraments." An ordinance was "an institution of divine authority relating to the worship of God; such as baptism, . . . the Lord's supper," and so on, according to a theological dictionary Smith relied upon.[23] Smith comes to use the term in essentially the same way.

"They have strayed from mine ordinances," reads section 1 of the Doctrine and Covenants, the manifesto of Smith's new church, given in 1830. As the designated preface for his collection of revelations, this section laid down the essential rationale behind the Mormon restoration. In the ordinances, Joseph would write in 1835, is the power of godliness manifest. With the authority of the priesthood, he continued, we access those powers of godliness.[24] When Smith recast his account of his First Vision, he used language that linked precisely those priesthood powers and ordinances to God's own language describing the essence of Christian apostasy. The purveyors of contemporary religion, he records the divine personage as explaining, have "a form of Godliness, but they deny the power thereof."[25] The 1787 Methodist *Discipline* indicated a similar concern: the Church "has lost the . . . Power of Religion," it declared.[26] Wesley and his Methodist followers were convinced that Methodists "uniquely possessed both the form of godliness and the power of true religion."[27] But whereas Wesley would find that power in "the therapeutic nurturing of holiness," Smith would emphasize authority derived from God channeled through saving ordinances.[28] Smith believed that in his day neither the proper ordinances nor the authority to perform them was to be found on earth. This Mormon understanding of apostasy was concretized fairly early. Restoring this loss of priesthood authority, and consequently of the proper forms of "true order" and "true worship," was the great project Saints understood as the purpose of Smith's ministry.[29]

Accordingly, the central purpose of the gathering and temple building—practices at the core of Smith's religion-making, was stated in an 1841 revelation: "that [God] may [again] reveal mine ordinances therein, unto my people."[30] So Smith clearly conceived of apostasy as primarily the corruption of ordinances, and loss of the priesthood authority to perform them. "All the known world have been left for centuries without . . . a priesthood authorized of God to administer ordinances," as Orson Pratt summarized, writing in 1840 that this belief in "a general and awful apostasy from the religion of the New Testament" was a pivotal principle of the LDS Church.[31]

Given this conception, the crucial components of the restoration, the priesthood and the ordinances, could only be restored by reestablishing a direct line of authority; this required angelic visitations and the transfer of what Smith called "keys."

RESTORATION

Predicated on a foundation of priesthood authority that Smith believed he had received by the hand of angelic messengers, the Restoration could proceed apace.[32]

As the restoration of authority and associated ordinances suggested, Smith's work was emphatically expansionist rather than reductive. The first inkling Smith would have that the Christian error he would principally address was insufficiency, rather than surplus, actually came in 1823. Mormon scholars are virtually unanimous in pointing out that Smith's 1820 "First Vision" did not mark the launch of any restorationist scheme. If he planned or intuited any future role for himself as a religious innovator or instrument of divine operations, he gave no evidence of such an understanding. This theophany was not like the calling of Moses or of Abraham or Isaiah. It was not a calling at all. Joseph was a fourteen-year-old sinner and seeker, not a boy prophet. His experience had no biblical parallel, insofar as a private individual's yearning for personal redemption and illumination was the object, and no fate of any covenant people or Christian community was implicated in the heavenly response. His experience was, in this regard, of a piece with many kindred experiences described by his contemporaries.[33]

Likewise, on a September evening in 1823, Smith was seeking personal consolation for his self-doubt, not guidance in any larger project, when the light descended upon him for the second time, as he described the visit of the angel who identified himself as Moroni. Two momentous developments emerged out of this encounter. First, Moroni informed Smith that "God had a work for [him] to do." In clarifying what this work would entail, Moroni turned Smith's understanding of restoration inside out. "He said there was a book . . . written upon gold plates, giving an account of the former inhabitants of this continent."[34] Here is no simple paring away, no mere stripping back to essentials, but the prelude to a vast expansion. In Smith's agenda about to unfold, any return to fundamentals or New Testament forms heralds not an end point but a new beginning; more rather than less is the result, as Moroni introduces the first of many new scriptures into Mormonism's version of Christianity in a process that would rupture the concept of *sola scriptura*, enlarge the scope of Christ's earthly ministry and words from one hemisphere to two, and signify boundless expansion rather than studied contraction of sacraments, ordinances, and scripturally authorized practices. In other words, in Smith's scheme of restoration, any pruning of accretions is meant to clear the way for the tree's trunk to reattain the fullness of its original foliage.

The Book of Mormon did this by its form as much as by its content. In its position as a third testament, its real burden was to provide a new and compelling genealogy, not of Christ back to Abraham, or the human family back to Adam. It attested to its own provenance, in a chain of authenticity traceable from God's first command to the original record-keeper Nephi, through a thousand years of providential history in the New World, to a hillside in upstate New York, when a young Joseph Smith resurrected the record from its stone tomb. Like the poet George Herbert's

silken twist let down from heaven, or like Jacob's ladder along which angels ascended and descended, the Book of Mormon served believers as a concrete conduit
that connected them to a divine source, along which sacred energies flow in both
directions. As such, it functioned—and still does—not just as witness but also as
tangible embodiment of God's living word, manifest in the continuing production
of scripture through prophets who still walk the earth.

The second development to emerge on that September night appeared when
Moroni quoted from Malachi, but significantly, "with a little variation from the way
it reads in our Bibles." The Bible, in other words, was depicted as neither complete
nor accurate. Nor was it sufficient. As Parley Pratt would later develop the concept
with vibrant but controversial imagery, Mormon thought demoted scripture to the
status of stream rather than fountain. Pratt conceded that "the scriptures are . . .
useful in their place." But "they are not the fountain of knowledge, nor do they
contain all knowledge." Their greater value lies in the way "they point to the fountain, and are every way calculated to encourage man to come to the fountain and
seek to obtain the knowledge and gifts of God."[35]

God's utterance preceded, and superseded, its incarnation as holy writ, tainted as it
was by the flawed conduits of human understanding and fractured language. Even
believing himself to be the Lord's oracle, Smith would simultaneously deliver revelations in the voice of God and lament, "Oh Lord God, deliver us from this prison, . . .
of a crooked, broken, scattered and imperfect language."[36] And he would spend his
entire life revising and recasting the words he gave his people as scripture, struggling to
claw his way through irredeemably fallen human language to its perfect divine source.

By general Christian consensus, special revelation to the biblical prophets, the
incarnation and ministry of Christ, and the canonized Old and New Testaments
provide sufficient basis for knowledge of saving truths. Joseph Smith, like other figures ranging from the French Prophets to Anne Hutchinson to Ann Lee and myriad
others, disagreed. "I have learned for myself," he said to his mother upon returning
from his first supernatural encounter with Deity. Joseph Smith would claim, as both
office and spiritual gift, but also as Christian believer, the right to immediate revelation from God. Before he translated the first word of the Book of Mormon, Joseph
Smith had already stepped outside prevailing understandings of restoration.

It is true that his emphasis on recuperating the elegant simplicity of the New
Testament's teachings had enough precedent for Smith to be persuasively labeled a
plagiarist by Alexander Campbell.[37] And his emphatic declarations of priesthood
and a prophetic commission conferred upon him by heavenly beings appealed
powerfully to others of his age seeking such clear signs of divine authority.[38] But in
essential ways, Smith had more in common with the secular apostles Walt Whitman and Ralph Waldo Emerson than with a Stone or Campbell. As David

Holland has recently demonstrated, Smith was one of many American religious figures who resisted the strictures of a closed canon; he just happened to be more successful than most in creating "a Bible with the back cover torn off."[39]

Whitman considered his mission to be "the Great Construction of the New Bible,"[40] and Emerson urged Harvard graduates to consider "that God is, not was; that He speaketh, not spake."[41] But even Emerson, like the Restorationists, would have balked at Smith's drastic redefining of primitive Christianity and its tangible, speaking God. Smith effectively asked his contemporaries how deeply and how literally they believed their own rhetoric. As Richard Bushman phrased it, Smith's life "posed the question, Do you believe God speaks?" He challenged Christianity's notion of a "single revelation serving for all time" as well as Emerson's "mild sort of inspiration seeping into the minds of all good people" and advocated instead "specific, ongoing directions from God to his people."[42] The texts of Smith's revelations at times sound like the voice of God orienting a lost pedestrian to the site for New Jerusalem.

Conventional Protestant notions of a Christian apostasy—or falling away from Christian truth—began with the premise that Christ had established his true church in Palestine, only to have errors and corruptions creep in with the passage of time. In the course of the Reformation, the question was only how far those corruptions extended and how drastic the required remedies were. It became imperative, for instance, "to distinguish between corrupt Churches & false Churches," since, as the nonseparating Puritans would argue, "the corruption of a thing doth not nullify a thing."[43] But in the course of measuring current institutions against past incarnations of truth, the more liberally minded turned also to another destablizing question: what eternal truths might have been known to the ancients?

Some posited that in addition to an original gospel dispensation, foreshadowings and fragments of the true gospel were evident among a variety of peoples scattered through time. Jonathan Edwards, like many of the church fathers believed that God had in fact imparted to several ancient peoples essential gospel truths that were subsequently lost. Much earlier, Augustine expressed a version of this idea when he wrote in his *Retractions,* "What is now called Christian religion has existed among the ancients, and was not absent from the beginning of the human race, until Christ came in the flesh: from which time true religion, which existed already, began to be called Christian."[44] But such thinkers granted mere smatterings of eternal principles in the religions and philosophies of antiquity; only the Bible represented the full and complete account of God's revelation. (Speaking of the Jews, for instance, a commentator contemporary with Edwards wrote that "we have the gospel as well as they [had], and in greater purity."[45])

Prisca theologia, as this doctrine came to be called,[46] (which means ancient theology), or "fulfillment theology" as the doctrine is called in recent formulations, was useful both to account for prevalent archetypes (such as animal sacrifice and the idea of a divine incarnation) that could otherwise impugn the uniqueness and hence the validity of Christian doctrines, and to assert God's justice and mercy in dispensing truth to Christian, Jew, and pagan alike. Previous thinkers had emphasized the piecemeal nature of prior revelation and its final consummation in modern scripture. Augustine, for example, saw pre-Christian fragments of truth as typological, pointing to a future fulfillment rather than revealing a lost plenitude. Smith pushed the principle of *prisca theologia* in the other direction. "From what we can draw from the Scriptures relative to the teaching of heaven," he said, "we are induced to think that much instruction has been given to man since the beginning which we have not."[47] As Smith's popularizer Parley Pratt put it with his typical self-assurance, "we have only the old thing. It was old in Adams day it was old in Mormons day & hid up in the earth & it was old in 1830 when we first began to preach it."[48]

Smith's production of the Book of Mormon was the first and most conspicuous instance of this radical paradigm. The ancient Israelites described in that book arrived in the Americas, worshiped Christ, and taught his gospel six hundred years before the advent of the Christian era. They lived the law of Moses, but taught faith in Jesus, preached repentance, and baptized in his name.

A further development in Smith's understanding of restoration, one that pushed his purview back beyond the New Testament, through the Old Testament, and to the very beginnings of the human race, came in the months after the Book of Mormon was published. By late 1830 Smith had dictated a series of purportedly lost revelations of Moses and Enoch, which were distilled into one distinctive idea by the church's newspaper, the *Evening and Morning Star*, in 1833: "Adam was the first member of the church of Christ on earth," the summary read; "the plan of salvation was revealed to Adam," noted a subsequent treatment.[49] According to this scriptural emendation, after the Fall God himself taught Adam that he must

> turn unto me, and hearken unto my voice, and believe, and repent of all thy transgressions, and be baptized even by water, in the name of mine Only Begotten Son, which is full of grace and truth, which is Jesus Christ, the only name which shall be given under heaven, whereby salvation shall come unto the children of men. . . . And thus he was baptized, and the Spirit of God descended upon him, and thus he was born of the Spirit, and became quickened in the inner man.[50]

As Smith (or a subordinate) elaborated in a church editorial in 1834, "Abel was taught of the coming of the Son of God . . . [and] of his ordinances. . . . Perhaps, our friends will say, that the gospel and its ordinances were not known till the days of John. . . . We cannot believe, that the ancients in all ages were so ignorant of the system of heaven as many suppose."[51] On another occasion Smith said that God not only revealed all the ordinances of salvation to Adam, but intended them "to be the same forever, and set Adam to watch over them [and] to reveal them from heaven to man or to send Angels to reveal them" in the event of their loss.[52] As a consequence, Smith came to envision restoration as a dynamic process involving the interaction of angels and men, resurrected beings and earthly prophets, crisscrossing time and dispensations, in the fluid, perpetual reconstitution of gospel entropy.

Smith described a recurrent process, in which key figures in one dispensation would convey lost teachings and ordinances to another. Generations after Adam, Enoch became a ministering angel appearing to Jude, and later Abel performed a similar ministry to Paul, Smith said.[53] But Smith described a crescendo of heavenly voices, visitations, epiphanies, and revelations that marked this as the final dispensation, the dispensation of the fullness of times:

> And again, what do we hear? Glad tidings from Cumorah! Moroni, an angel from heaven, . . . A voice of the Lord in the wilderness of Fayette, Seneca county, . . . ! The voice of Michael on the banks of the Susquehanna, . . . The voice of Peter, James, and John in the wilderness between Harmony, Susquehanna county, and Colesville, Broome county, on the Susquehanna river, . . . And again, the voice of God in the chamber of old Father Whitmer, in Fayette, Seneca county, and at sundry times, and in divers places through all the travels and tribulations of this Church of Jesus Christ of Latter-day Saints! And the voice of Michael, the archangel; the voice of Gabriel, and of Raphael, and of divers angels, from Michael or Adam down to the present time, all declaring their dispensation, their rights, their keys, their honors, their majesty and glory, and the power of their priesthood; giving line upon line, precept upon precept; here a little, and there a little; giving us consolation by holding forth that which is to come, confirming our hope![54]

Adam would seem to be as far into the distant past as one could go, in reconstituting what Pratt had referred to with wry understatement as "the old thing." But a few years after his recuperation of the Moses material with its exposition of Christian principles and ordinances going back to Adam, Smith pushed the temporal parameters of the gospel even further back, when he produced a description of the Great Council in Heaven—a scriptural work apparently inspired by ancient papyri. These Abrahamic writings, like the recuperated Genesis material with its restoration of the Prophecy of Enoch, the Zenos parable from the Book of Mormon, missing texts of John the Beloved that Smith recovered,[55] and a "transcript from the records of the eternal world" describing the afterlife and its various kingdoms[56]—all of these form a grand project that constitutes a major idea in its own right. The cumulative weight of these experiences seems to have created in Smith's mind a wholesale inversion of the traditional model of biblical fullness and *prisca theologia*. Rather than finding in the pagans and ancients foreshadowings and tantalizing hints of God's revelation which will culminate in the Christian canon, Smith was to work, with growing momentum, backwards and outwards, as if he gradually conceived of his objective as nothing less than a totalizing recuperation of gospel fullness that transcended and preceded and encompassed any one particular incarnation, the Bible included. Crucially, Smith conceived of restoration as going beyond recuperation of lost truth and authority. The project also envisioned, as the ninth Article of Faith's cited above portended, "many great and important things pertaining to the kingdom of God" that he would "yet reveal." Restoration was an open, not a closed system. This is the sense in which, as Richard Bushman notes, Smith "did not think of himself as going back to a primordium of Christianity, as the Puritans did. . . . [Smith] saw himself as completing a work that had never been completely realized."[57]

INSPIRED SYNTHESIS

This project of restoration presupposed, of course, a longstanding pattern of deviation from the true standard. In the twentieth-century Mormon narrative, this Great Apostasy often suggested an abrupt darkness descending on the early church within a generation or two of Christ's death. That did not appear to be Joseph Smith's understanding, which was in part shaped by his reading of the Revelator's allegory of the "woman in the wilderness" and its contemporary interpretations. In 1795, the Scottish minister Alexander Fraser published his *Key to the Prophecies*, which included a gloss of a passage from the book of Revelation: "And the woman fled into the wilderness, where she has a place prepared by God, . . . where she is nourished for a time."[58] In Fraser's interpretation, this refers to the time when, "as the visible church declined from the doctrines and precepts of Christianity, the true Church of Christ gradually retired from the view of men, till at length, . . . the true church of Christ, considered as a community, wholly disappeared."

This was not, Fraser believed, an unmitigated calamity. For the church in the wilderness, according to the words of prophecy, is "fed by the word and Spirit of God, without the outward ordinances, . . . which . . . were defiled."[59] In his vision, then, the "true church of Christ" is rendered invisible, protected, nourished, and preserved—while it awaits the restoration of properly administered ordinances or sacraments. Popular writer Joseph Milner, read by early Mormons, similarly wrote of the flight of "the faithful servants of Christ 'into the wilderness'" and advocated the need "to search out the real Church from age to age, . . . indeed a work of much labour and difficulty. . . . The ore is precious, but it must be extracted from incredible heaps of Ecclesiastical rubbish."[60] Indeed, he proclaimed an "apostacy" from the Church of Christ complete by the seventh century, believing the "visible church" was fallen into ruin, but he persisted in his "search after the scattered fragments of the true church."[61] All this language, from the focus on corrupted ordinances to the preservation of precious fragments, also appears in Smith's corpus of thought.

Fraser drew a further moral from his reading of the allegory in Revelation. When any church becomes "visible as a society, she shall not be safe, but be corrupted more or less by the same artifices which overwhelmed the [first] great body of professed Christians." New reformations can occur, but inevitably the process of corruption will continue "ad infinitum" he writes. At least, until the time of the prophesied years of exile come to an end. Then, and only then, will the church become "visible as a community, extended over the whole earth, 'clear as the sun, fair as the moon, and terrible as an army with banners.'"[62] (This is a pairing of the Revelation allegory with Song of Solomon's reference to the terrible army, which Smith will also replicate.[63])

A few decades later, in 1825, an article appearing in an independent religious journal *The Telescope* picked up Fraser's interpretation of the woman's flight into the wilderness. "Whenever a people become organized into a visible body," it agreed, "they are no longer the true church of Christ but fall in with the grand apostasy."[64] Observing the condition of Protestant Christianity, the author agreed with Fraser's maxim that conspicuous organization was only an invitation to new apostasy, and even quoted as corroboration the lament of John Wesley and John Fletcher that the Methodists had themselves so quickly fallen into strife and excess.

Some nineteenth-century interpreters believed that with the abdication of Austrian Emperor Franz II in 1806, and the dissolution of the Holy Roman Empire, the wilderness sojourn of the church was at an end. In 1806, David L. Rowland published "An Epitome of Ecclesiastical History" according to which in or about 1800, the dominion of anti-Christ would end and the church would enter a "happy state."[65] William Coldwell wrote in 1831 that, according to promise, the church had not been "devoured; it was wounded and driven from the temple, but not slain. God himself prepared a refuge, and amidst that refuge . . . [protected] the Church in the wilderness." But the era of its deliverance had begun.[66] Jonathan Edwards, working with the same year of 1260 as the period of apostasy intimated by the Revelator, had predicted an end to exile in 1866.[67]

Such glosses did not merely corroborate Smith's conviction that he had been called by God's authority to fulfill the restoration prophesied in the book of Revelation; the details of the allegory suggested something of the process by which restoration would unfold. We do not know when Joseph Smith first conceived his work as entailing the formal organization of an actual church. The directive to organize one may have come as an unwelcome surprise at the very moment when the already onerous task of producing a five-hundred page text, under vexing opposition and skepticism, had become overwhelming. In one and the same revelation, given March 1829, Smith is told he may desist from the translation until rescue arrives, but he is as the same time told of an even larger enterprise soon to unfold.[68] The revelation's focus is on the Book of Mormon and its preparatory function of effecting what it called "a work of reformation," the putting down of "all lyings and deceivings and priestcrafts." In sum, says the voice of God, "I will *establish my church* [emphasis added], like unto the church which was taught by my disciples."[69]

This first reference to a church to be established, recorded in 1829, is published in 1833. This first version of the revelation, however, is not what appeared in the 1835 Doctrine and Covenants. In the interim, apparently taking to heart the allegory of the Revelator and perhaps contemporary glosses of it, Smith recast his language accordingly. This significant redaction now refers to the "beginning of the rising up and *coming forth of my church out of the wilderness* [emphasis added]."[70] Subsequently, Smith dictates other revelations that employ that very language. One refers to the restoration as "this church I . . . called forth out of the wilderness;" another expresses the hope that "thy church may come forth out of the wilderness of darkness, and shine forth fair as the moon, clear as the sun, and terrible as an army with banners."[71]

Smith is reading his own moment in history as fulfilling a particular process or event described allegorically by the Revelator. The biblical prophecy reads more fully that "there appeared a great wonder in heaven, a woman clothed with the sun, and the moon under her feet, and upon her head a crown of twelve stars. . . . And there appeared another wonder in heaven; and behold a great red dragon. . . . And the dragon stood before the woman which was ready to be delivered, for to devour her child as soon as it was born. And the woman fled into the wilderness, where she hath a place prepared of God, that they should feed her there a thousand two hundred and threescore days."[72]

In the LDS edition of the Bible, the heading identifies the woman in this allegory, as have virtually all Protestant commentators, as a representation of the primitive church, whose flight before the forces of Satan portends the Great Apostasy. But like Fraser, Smith seems to have noticed the crucial detail that this woman is not banished from the earth—she retreats into the wilderness. There she does not perish. On the contrary, she is nourished for a prolonged period of time. Smith's invocation of the language of this allegory suggests a view of church history in which many teachings and principles of the original church survived more or less intact, though clearly remote from the mainstream—underground, or on the peripheries of orthodoxy. As his subsequent work was to prove, Smith came to envision the Christian church as in retreat, not in oblivion. He did not interpret this coming out of the wilderness as an abrupt event but, rather, as a gradual process of assimilation, differentiation, and development. As a revelation *prior* to the church's formal 1830 organization indicated, the Lord's church already existed, constituted of the repentant; Smith reassured its members in the voice of God that he was about to "bring [a new] part of my gospel to the knowledge of my people."[73] Fittingly, the Nauvoo Temple exterior, in which Smith's work found its fullest expression, was ornamented like the wilderness woman in John's vision: with sun, moon, and stars. And Smith had said, the temple, broken down at Jerusalem's destruction to be rebuilt later, was a "Type of the church."[74]

In 1832, Smith gave his fullest account of how this modern day restoration would unfold, as the beginning of a process rather than as a discrete event, in glossing the parable of the wheat and tares.[75] Contamination drove the church into the wilderness, he wrote, the tares of priestcraft growing prolifically among much wheat of truth. Yet even now, two years after the incorporation of the church, the process of "bringing forth the word" was just beginning, the revelation declared. Joseph's own work, as he read in the Book of Mormon, was to bring "to pass *much [but not all] restoration.*"[76]

Smith's predecessors and contemporaries believed the church in the wilderness symbolized the reality of an invisible church, where righteous individuals, their spiritual gifts, and godly principles and practices persisted. (Two of many examples would be John Calvin, who contrasted the invisible church, consisting of "the elect who have existed from the beginning of the world," with "the whole body of mankind scattered throughout the world, who profess to worship one God and Christ;" Jacob Boehme, who spoke of the *Kirche ohne Mauer* [church without walls] as a heavenly community distinct from the tainted and unstable institutional church.[77]) Smith likewise was given to understand that God recognized an enduring spiritual church that existed prior to and independent of any temporal form. This was the purport of the 1829 revelation cited just above. Christ's invisible church (which the Book of Mormon in 1 Nephi 14 referred to as "the church of the Lamb of God") was ever present. Its members, who already "belongeth to my church . . . need not fear," Christ was about "to build it up" by means of the Restoration, not "destroy that which they have [already] received."[78]

One of the clearest confirmations of Smith's understanding of a holy church in the wilderness that had never fully disappeared came in a May 1831 revelation, when the Lord revealed that in the background, independent of the Latter-day Saint restoration, God had reserved unto himself "holy men" about whom Joseph knew nothing.[79] This echoes, of course, the idea of the invisible church, and an earlier revelation to Smith that in the latter days the Lord's work would be temporal before it was spiritual, suggesting the temporal institution must not be confused with the spiritual church.[80] Smith's task would involve neither simple innovation nor *ex nihilo* oracular pronouncements upon lost doctrines alone, but also the salvaging, collecting, and assimilating of much that was mislaid, obscured, or neglected. This would include doctrines, practices, sacraments, rituals, even blueprints for brick-and-mortar Zions, and temples with baptisteries modeled on Solomon's temple with its brazen sea.

A recent biographer of the great philosopher Spinoza wrote, "He rejected the orthodoxy of his day not because he believed less, but because he believed more."[81] Smith had a similar propensity to range widely and freely in appropriating truths as and where he found them. "Mormonism is truth; and every man who embraced it felt himself at liberty to embrace every truth: consequently the shackles of superstition, bigotry, ignorance, and priestcraft, falls at once from his neck; and his eyes are opened to see the truth."[82] Mormonism, as he saw it, was about removing rather than imposing boundaries. "I stated that the most prominent difference in sentiment between the Latter-day Saints and sectarians was, that the latter were all circumscribed by some peculiar creed, which deprived its members the privilege of believing anything not contained therein, whereas the Latter-day Saints have no creed, but are ready to believe all true principles that exist, as they are made manifest from time to time."[83]

Joseph Smith said late in his ministry, "If the Presbyterians have any truth, embrace that. If the Baptists and Methodists have truth, embrace that too. Get all the good in the world if you want to come out a pure Mormon."[84] Elsewhere, he called it "the first and fundamental principle of our holy religion" to be free "to embrace all, and every item of truth, without limitation or without being circumscribed or prohibited by the creeds or superstitious notions of men, or by the dominations of one another."[85] Smith was always pushing in the direction of expansive addition rather than contracting reduction: "we don't ask any people to throw away any good they have got we only ask them to Come & get more."[86]

This catalog of his liberal statements on religious truth suggests that Smith's prophetic practice was neither the unstudied and erratic plagiarism of his caricaturists nor always the epiphany-driven receipt of "vertical revelation" imputed to him by his devoted followers. Many modern Mormons imagine a relatively linear process of doctrinal development in the church's early years, with Smith revealing each new doctrine to the church in orderly sequence. Smith, however, viewed himself as both revelator and inspired synthesist, pulling truths not only from heaven but also from his culture, his background, and his contemporaries, as we shall see. It's not that Smith's attempt to reconstitute a perfect theology happened to be impaired by his humanity; his vision of prophets as flawed and fallible vessels, and of restoration as an untidy and imperfect process involving many sources, varying degrees of inspiration, and stops and starts, *was itself* a theological proposition with him. God's authorship of the work of restoration was only evident if the vehicle of that restoration was conspicuously flawed like himself. In a revelation as much about striking self-disclosure as God-disclosure, he wrote of the Lord saying to him that "unto this end have I raised you up, that I might show forth my wisdom through the weak things of the earth."[87] On another occasion he insisted, "A Prophet is not always a Prophet, only when he is acting as such."[88] Smith believed himself to be an oracle of God, subject to moments of heavenly encounter and the pure flow of inspiration. But he also was insatiably eclectic in his borrowings and adaptations, with an adventuresome mind, prone to speculation and fully comfortable with the trial and error of intellectual effort.

Most of the teachings Smith would pronounce upon were to be found in contemporary or ancient thinkers. Some precedents he did not acknowledge and may have been unfamiliar with—such as the pre-mortal existence of humans or post-mortal theosis, or divinization. Other teachings he likely adapted from contemporary sources—such as the Revelation-inspired model of restoration we have seen and his rationale for viewing eternal punishment as God's punishment rather than as endless punishment (see chapter 20). For yet others, he invoked precedents or parallels, such as the eternity of matter and of heavenly education seen in the writings of Thomas Dick (chapters 5 and 21). Two other examples suggest how self-conscious he and his associates were about this strategy of inspired eclecticism, or restoration as gathering truths in from the wilderness. In 1843, the church came under attack for its doctrine of baptism for the dead. "You are as bad as the papists," said some, detecting a suspicious similarity with the doctrine of purgatory. Rather than distance the practice from what contemporaries labeled an apostate papist teaching, the editor Thomas Ward responded: "We believe, that fallen as the Roman church may be, she has traces of many glorious principles that were once in the church of Christ, of which . . . the protestant world knows nothing."[89] Smith affirmed, in his last recorded sermon, that "the old Catholic Church is worth more than all" the other sects.[90] In the same regard, as we will see in chapter 20, Universalism provided rationales for redeeming the dead that Smith would appropriate virtually verbatim.

A second example is Smith's borrowings from Masonry. According to Benjamin Johnson, Smith "told me Freemasonry, as at present, was the apostate endowments, as sectarian religion was the apostate religion."[91] Masonry is to the endowment, Smith reasoned, as sectarianism is to religion generally: not to be discarded wholesale. Smith joined the Masons, found much of value there, and modified and recontextualized what he had found. His expressed theological rationale seems exactly modeled on Augustine's gloss of the Old Testament story of the spoiling of the

Egyptians. On the night of their exodus, the children of Israel "appropriated to themselves" their enslavers' riches, "designing them for a better use." Just so, Augustine argued, the "heathen" have truths which, like gold and silver, they are "perversely and unlawfully prostituting to the worship of devils." It is the task of the Christians to "take them away from them, and to devote their proper use in preaching the gospel."[92] Smith readily assimilated—often explicitly and transparently—the scattered truths and practices he found, whether from contemporary writers like Thomas Dick or groups like the Masons, and "put them to their proper use." His open reliance on Charles Buck, mentioned in connection with his Lectures on Faith, further attests his willingness freely to appropriate teachings conformable to his syncretist vision.[93]

Smith's understanding of restorationism involved both inspiration and experimentation. "By proving contraraties, truth is made manifest," he wrote on another occasion.[94] That the final result of his labors was a product of providential intent and guidance, he had no doubt. As he wrote about his first vision, "why does the world think to make me deny what I have actually seen, for I had seen a vision, I knew it, and I knew that God knew it."[95] At the same time, there was more than a note of jest in his telling remark to detractors that "I had rather be a fallen true prophet, than a false prophet."[96] His prophetic vocation, in other words, involved visions, borrowings, re-workings, collaborations, incorporations, and pronouncements, with false starts, second-guessings, and self-revisions. Smith experimented with polyandry, then ceased; he implemented, then suspended a communalistic mandate; he dictated revelations, then subjected them to sometimes substantial, repeated revision. His self-understanding as a prophet included the ever present sense of his own fallibility, the need for intellectual struggle, an indebtedness to other flawed but gem-laden religious traditions, and inspiration as a continual wrestle with heavenly powers. He saw himself as neither the deluded charlatan of his detractors nor the airbrushed Moses of his latter-day adherents. As he so well captured his synthetic approach, context and history might provide him with "all the truth" but he had "an indepen[den]t rev[elation]n in the bargain."[97] In other words, he clearly claimed the right to look to the present and the past, but also to reveal things never before a part of human knowledge. Restoration was an open-ended receptivity to all that God had ever revealed, and all that he would yet reveal.

A scholar has written that "during the formative period of The Christian Church orthodoxy resembles a symphony composed of various elements rather than a single melodic theme, or a confluence of many tributaries into a single stream rather than a river which pursues its course to the sea without mingling with other waters."[98] Mormonism was both like and unlike Christianity in that regard. Mormon thought, in fact, may be best understood in terms of paradox. Founded on the radical premise that direct revelation is the province of every individual, Mormonism quickly ordered the flow of revelation in a kind of federal channeling of prerogatives that remain rigidly hierarchical even as every person is invited to seek unmediated access to God.

The formation of Mormon teachings in many instances looks like early Christianity's gradual development of doctrine that only assumed definitive form at the intersection of passing time and forces from inside and outside the movement. Joseph Smith's sense was that he was recuperating Christianity from its exile in the wilderness, reassembling it by gathering truth, restoring broken covenants, and adding new revelations. He would help "bring to light the things that have been revealed in all former dispensations, also other things that have not been before revealed."[99] This process was not always linear or tidy; many of Smith's associates contributed to the growth and elaboration of doctrine alongside Joseph Smith, as well as sharing in his spiritual gifts. Smith's authority to dictate revelation for the entire church was clearly established in September 1830,[100] but he seldom invoked that authority to impose his theological understanding. "It does not mean that a man is not good because he errs in doctrine," he said of a Mormon rebuked by others for his preaching. "It feels so good not to be trammeled."[101]

What this means is that Smith's self-understanding of the prophetic role encompassed earnest effort, seeking, speculating, and ranging freely in search of truth. He could speak authoritatively at times, but he was seldom dogmatic and frankly acknowledged the project of restoration involved a "broken language" and much human weakness—including his own. "He said he was but a man and they must not expect him to be perfect. . . . If they would bear with his infirmities . . . he would bear with their infirmities."[102] And so, the work of interpreting the revelations of God and creating a coherent system of belief proceeded apace. Rigdon and the Pratt brothers, in particular, joined in the enterprise of theologizing, speculating, interpretation, and systematizing. What they all shared was the firm belief that an original church, "once indeed beautiful, pure, and intelligent;—clothed with the power and spirit of God," by their day was "a picture of ruin and desolation." It now lay "in broken fragments scattered, rent, and disjointed; with nothing to point out its original, but the shattered remnants of its ancient glory."[103] For those with eyes to see, however, the world was replete with these scattered "fragments of Mormonism."[104] This, ultimately, was the meaning of Smith's notion that the temple of Jerusalem, its destruction and rebuilding, was a type of the church. With the temple, as with the metaphorical "ancient palace" now reduced to ruins, to which they also compared the primitive church, the work of restoration would entail bringing together the new and the old, the excavation and assemblage of what was sound and the replacement and incorporation of what had been irredeemably lost or corrupted from Eden forward.[105]

Cosmic Narratives

MORMON THOUGHT POSITS an unconventional cosmos, a reconfigured godhead, and a radical human anthropology. The universe, in Mormon thought, is eternally existent rather than a product of divine summoning out of nothingness. Dualism is rewritten as two-tiered monism (spirit as more refined matter), and laws are themselves as eternal as God. The godhead consists of three separate and distinct deities (two of them embodied), with an unembodied Holy Ghost. But Mormon thought encompasses a seldom discussed Feminine Divine as well. Human beings, meanwhile, come to earth "trailing clouds of glory" from a premortal state, carry within them the seeds of divinity, and aspire to become—through the atonement of Christ—full "partakers of the divine nature."

The plan of salvation with its three divisions is rather like a grand three act play. . . . You are a member of the cast on stage in the middle of it all.

—LDS teaching video

4

A Short Primer on Mormonism

THE ESSENTIAL OUTLINES of Mormon theology constitute a fairly simple—if unfamiliar—story. God is the supreme intelligence in the universe, but he is not the source of all being, or even the creator of that which constitutes the human soul. Men and women have existed from eternity as uncreated intelligence. A Heavenly Father (and Mother) fashions that intelligence into spirit form (or in another reading of Smith's original understanding, adopt preexisting intelligences/spirits into familial relationship). Through untold eons of pre-mortal existence, these spirits, by the exercise of their moral agency, acquire knowledge and attributes of godliness under the loving tutelage of their Heavenly Parents. God's self-designated purpose is eventually to shepherd these spirits toward his own exalted condition. At a decreed point in humankind's eternal progress, God orchestrated the creation of this world, in preparation for the human family's ascent (not fall) into mortality.

In God's conception of human existence, moral agency is the bedrock value, and the capacity for independent virtuous activity is a crucial part of eternal moral development. This stage of mortal incarnation is, therefore, shrouded by a veil of forgetfulness, that individual choices might be the more freely rendered. A universal human endowment of the Light of Christ, or vestigial intimations of eternal realms and values manifest as conscience, counterbalance to some extent the countervailing influences of environment and heredity.

Embodiment itself is not a temporary degradation from spiritual existence, but a step upward, since God himself is embodied and the highest form of existence is the unification of a spirit and a glorified body. Birth into a physical body and earthly environment does not entail inheriting an original sin, but it does involve an array of factors that challenge and tax our moral faculties. Overcoming these obstacles is essential to the development of the spirit as well as the perfecting of the body.

Sin is therefore inevitable, but also an important part of our moral education. We can only know good from evil, and the relative value of each, by personally experiencing their consequences. That is how we learn to love and strive for the one and shun the other. At the same time, sin—the willing choice to violate moral law—alienates us from God and produces a spiral that leads us further and further away from him and his influence. This process of self-damnation, and the impossibility of self-elevation from sin and death, makes some kind of intervention by a higher power necessary. Yet that intervention must occur without destroying our agency. In other words, our freedom to choose—which entails the freedom to bear the consequences of those choices—must not be nullified by an outside Savior.

Jesus Christ mediates the collision of these two principles—God's loving mercy and human freedom. His atonement, in which he takes upon himself the pain and experience of human sin, enables and motivates the repentant individual to use his freedom to better ends—to re-choose, in other words. This process of repentance, re-choosing, continually self-correcting and re-orienting one's life, continues until one finds oneself in harmony with God and the eternal laws that undergird the universe.

Heaven consists of more than reunion with God. The highest salvation, or "exaltation," involves participation in the divine nature. This necessarily involves divine indwelling. "As man expands toward divinity, more and more of the divine enters into his being, until he attains a fullness of light and truth."[1] But the heavenly condition, in addition to an indwelling of divinity in the sanctified individual, entails an endless life comprising divine activities and mode of being. These include the enjoyment of eternal relationships, encompassing both the perseverance of one's earthly family and the ongoing creation (or adoption) of new posterity.

God desires to save and exalt the entire human family. Smith's restoration represents his vision of the process and means for so doing, assembled from restored scripture, revealed truths, and the scattered shards that litter history and culture. The priesthood authority Smith claimed entails the authority to perform those sacraments (or ordinances) which were foreordained as the mechanisms by which individuals manifest their desire to be full participants in the process. Baptism, the Sacrament (the Eucharist), the Endowment—all represent various levels of covenant making that mark stages in one's progress toward the divine nature. The highest of those ordinances, performed in temples, enacts the supreme end and object of salvation: the binding (or "sealing") of the human family to each other and to God.

This story, itself an unfamiliar narrative in Christian history, unfolds in a radically reconceived framework of a dynamic and still evolving universe, an embodied God of body, parts, and passions, and an eternal human spirit. These Mormon fundamentals did not emerge at once, or in logical order. What is surprising is the fact that the framework for these fundamentals was in place, at least in outline, within the first five years of the church's existence. In fact, by the end of 1830, thanks largely to the prophecy of Enoch that Smith produced in December of that year, Mormonism was already teaching a personal and passible, weeping God, the doctrine of human pre-mortality, an unflinchingly revisionist and optimistic version of Adam and Eve's fall, and a doctrine of deification whereby humans could participate fully in the divine nature and enter into a sociable heaven.

Cosmology

He is the alone fountain of all being.

—Westminster Confession of Faith

Element had an existence from the time He had. The pure principles of element are principles
which can never be destroyed; they may be organized and re-organized, but not destroyed. They
had no beginning and can have no end.

—JOSEPH SMITH, King Follett Discourse

5

Eternalism

⌒

IN 1789, AS revolutionaries in France were reshaping the political order, the leading astronomer of the age, William Herschel, was shifting the cosmic paradigm. His
paper on "The Construction of the Heavens," published by the Royal Society in
1785, effected a change in the Western world's cosmic vision more dramatic than
Copernicus's replacement of an earth-centered system by a heliocentric one. For
generations of thinkers, God's supreme perfections had suggested that the universe
he created was likewise flawless and complete when he laid down his celestial instruments. When he pronounced his labors good and rested from his efforts, the perfectly ordered cosmos had naught to do but hum along in sublime harmony until
the end of time.

At first, Herschel's astronomical observations through his telescopes of unprecedented power and precision only confirmed the infinitude of God's domain, revealing star systems beyond star systems in unending procession. But Herschel
quickly perceived that he was observing a universe in the process of continual dis-
ruption, upheaval, and transformation on a colossal scale. He described "extensive
combinations," stars in process of "condensation," others in retreat or in collision.
"When, at the same time that a cluster of stars is forming in one part of space, there
may be another collecting in a different, but perhaps not far distant quarter, which
may occasion a mutual approach towards their common center of gravity. . . . As a
natural consequence of the former cases, there will be formed great cavities or va-
cancies by the retreat of the stars towards the various centers which attract them."

The whole was a scene of such violent contestation that he admitted surprise that the entirety did not "tend to a general destruction, by the shock of one star's falling upon another."[1] Indeed, as one writer has summarized the import of Herschel's startling discovery, he "completely overturned any residual idea of a stable, over-arching, temple-like universe, created once and for all by the great Celestial Archi-tect," and replaced it with a dynamic cosmos of waxing and waning worlds, "fluid movements and changes."[2]

Being versus Becoming, Process versus Perfection, Creation, Time, and Eternity—on diverse interpretations of such principles hang theologies, cosmologies, and philo-sophical systems. Five years after Herschel's essay, William Blake gave the new age its master key when he wrote that "without contraries is no progression."[3] The long nineteenth century would see Blake's assertion elaborated across the entire span of intellectual achievement. The Great Chain of Being—unchallenged paradigm of a static, orderly, and harmonious universe—was buried beneath the emergent model of chaos, flux, radical transformation, and conflict. Thomas Malthus wrote in 1798 that human populations and natural resources were in perpetual collision, resulting in a planetary legacy of famine, disease, and calamity. G. W. Hegel made the violent confrontation of a thesis with its antithesis the interpretive key to human history. (Marx made matter rather than spirit the foundational principle, and transformed Hegel's dialectic into the most influential political theory of succeeding generations.) Darwin rewrote human understanding of the natural world, and God's place in it, by accounting for the diversity and splendor of all creation in terms of unremitting competition within and between species. If there was one prevailing sense in which Joseph Smith was a child of his age, it was in the avidity with which he reflected this dynamic, fundamentally Romantic view of the world, an orientation that suffused his cosmology, his human anthropology, and even his doctrine of deity.

In the spring of 1833, the Mormon Church was three years old. Smith was settled in Kirtland, Ohio, teaching in his School of the Prophets, a type of adult education class for church leaders that mingled scriptural study with academic subjects. Smith was at this time winding down his "translation" of the scriptures, by which he meant an inspired redaction of the King James Bible, moving through the Apocrypha (then included in that version) in early March. The next month, he adjourned the school, and on April 30 convened a conference of high priests. We don't know what particu-lar questions or concerns were on his mind in the next few days, but on May 6 he produced one of his theologically richest revelations, one that covered an array of topics and gave radical redefinition to the universe as well as the Creator, the crea-ture, and their relationship. Human pre-existence, original innocence, the glorious destiny of humans, and more are touched upon. It was the first revelation to provide a metaphysical framework for the work of restoration he was already undertaking.

With this revelation, which assimilated the dynamism and commotion and flux of Herschel's cosmology into the theological realm, outlines of the essential range and contours of Joseph Smith's theology emerge for the first time. In espousing the eternity of matter in particular, the revelation lays the groundwork for a whole cosmology. "The elements are eternal," the revelation stated, adding that man, as spirit or intelligence, was also "in the beginning with God," and such intelligence "was not created or made, neither indeed can be."[4] Smith's eternalism—the belief that the content of the universe is uncreated and unending—can be dated to this 1833 pronouncement.[5] Of course, "eternal" may connote "endlessly enduring," as well as "without beginning or end of existence." Smith clarified the point six years later, with a clear public rejection of creation *ex nihilo*: "anything created cannot be Eternal, and earth, water &c—all these had their existence in an elementary State from Eternity."[6] A year later, in 1840, Smith was discoursing on "the eternal duration of matter."[7] That particular expression was the title of an essay Parley Pratt had composed a few years earlier, wherein he defined "eternal" unambiguously. "Matter and spirit are of equal duration; both are self-existent,—they never began to exist."[8]

One scholar of religion notes that today, "the doctrine of creation *ex nihilo* is regarded as the linchpin of Christianity, the truth on which theism stands or falls."[9] Mormonism's emphatic rejection of this tradition may be why one theologian calls Mormonism, "of all the branches of Christianity, . . . the most imaginative, and . . . intellectual[ly] audaci[ious]."[10] Mormonism's underlying materialist cosmology, he believes, offers a vigorous challenge to a Christian orthodoxy rooted in a metaphysics of spirit. If it is correct that creation *ex nihilo* is Christianity's linchpin and the foundation of its theism, then its displacement would have the most profound implications for a new faith tradition. Indeed, one Mormon writer has summarized four radical theological propositions that Joseph Smith's eternalism of matter entails. "Unlike the Necessary Being of classical theology, who alone could not *not* exist and on which all else is contingent for existence, the personal God of Mormonism confronts uncreated realities which exist of metaphysical necessity. Such realities include [1] inherently self-directing selves (intelligences), [2] primordial elements (mass/energy), [3] the natural laws which structure reality, and [4] moral principles grounded in the intrinsic value of selves and the requirements for growth and happiness."[11]

CREATION

In the early Christian centuries, Neoplatonist, Gnostic, and Hebraic conceptions of how the world was created vied for supremacy, with early church fathers divided on the issue. Justin Martyr's position was, for a time, the standard Christian line:

"we have been taught that He in the beginning did of His goodness, for man's sake, create all things out of unformed matter."[12] Justin found comfortable congruence between Platonic conceptions of creation involving preexisting materials and a reading of Genesis that emphasizes creation as a reordering of chaos (the six periods all emphasize separation rather than formation, for example). The opposite view, that God created the universe out of nothing (*ex nihilo*), has long been the standard Christian position, but is considered by most scholars today to have emerged only a few centuries after Christ.[13]

A number of reasons converged to make this latter dogma the normative one. The older creation *ex materia* seemed to early Christian thinkers to imply a God who was just a glorified craftsman, a doctrine dangerously close to Gnostic conceptions. Considering God the mere manipulator of matter, some Fathers argued, seems to "exclude the idea of the almightiness of the creator."[14] A God who could not just instill order, but who could also summon material reality itself into existence, was self-evidently superior. Athanasius (ca. 293–373) put the case simply: "If He is not Himself the cause of the material, but makes things only of previously existing material, He proves to be weak, because [he is] unable to produce anything He makes without the material."[15] In addition, a God who shared his eternal nature with other objects or entities in the universe seemed diminished thereby. Still, it was not until 1215 that the Fourth Lateran Council definitively declared for creation *ex nihilo*. Over the subsequent Christian centuries, virtually no significant challenge to the doctrine would emerge.

Creation *ex nihilo*, so long the bedrock of Christian belief, was being called into question by scientists and churchmen alike, with the dawn of the nineteenth century. At the very time Herschel was revealing the chaotic processes of star formation, Antoine Lavoisier was proving that the elements of those stars could be recombined in endless configurations, but were neither created nor destroyed. He published his law of conservation of mass in 1789. Such scientific challenges to conventional ways of thinking about creation preceded a flurry of reconsiderations by religious writers. The Anglican John Mason Good asked in writing: "has [matter] existed from all eternity? or has it been called into being by the voice of an Omnipotent Creator?"[16] He concluded it was created, perhaps because he understood that the alternative was tantamount to atheism in a popular view. For, if matter was independent of God, what need of a Creator?

That fear was pointedly expressed by Richard Watson in his 1824 *Apologies for Christianity*: "If . . . we have recourse, as many of the ancient philosophers had, to the independent existence of matter, then we must admit two self-existing principles, which is quite inconsistent with genuine theism." Only atheists, in other words, would hold such a view.[17] But some felt an accommodation was possible. An 1824

New York almanac published in Smith's county described the theory of Isaac Orr "that matter has been eternal, and still perfectly dependent on the Deity for its existence and properties."[18]

The eternalism of matter was also suggested by a Scottish lay philosopher/theologian tremendously popular in America, Thomas Dick. In 1826, he published his *Christian Philosopher,* which attempted to synthesize theology with contemporary science. He expressly challenged the earth's creation *ex nihilo*, insisting that Moses's "sole intention" was to detail the process of creation "from the chaotic materials which previously existed."[19] But he goes no further than to suggest an indefinite past existence for those materials. With his subsequent work, *Philosophy of a Future State*, he denied anything material could be destroyed, and described creation as essentially mixture and recombination, but didn't assert eternity of matter.[20] Still, he wrote, only "changes and revolutions," but no annihilation, was observable in the universe.

If science was on the mind of these churchmen, it was probably the voice of Georges Cuvier, not Lavoisier, they were hearing—or perhaps that of his poetic popularizer, Lord Byron. In his biblical drama *Cain* (1821), Byron presented a version of earth creation based on the geological catastrophism of the French paleontologist. In Byron's drama, Lucifer shows Cain the phantoms of the planet's earlier inhabitants. "Was [my earth] theirs?" Cain asks. "It was," Lucifer responds, "but not as now. . . . *Their* earth is gone forever—so changed by its convulsion, they would not be conscious [of] a single present spot of its new scarcely hardened surface." Cain's present world has been re-created, in other words, after "a most crushing and inexorable destruction and disorder of the elements, which struck a world to chaos. . . . Such things, though rare in time, are frequent in eternity."[21]

Cuvier had written in 1813 that the earth suffered cataclysmic upheavals in a process marked by recurrent apocalyptic destruction. Byron's adaption of Cuvier's catastrophism and Herschel's dynamic cosmos to the creation story was seconded by Dick, who was quoted in the Mormon newspaper: "The work of creation is still going forward, . . . and . . . the Creator is replenishing the voids of space with new worlds and new orders of intelligent beings."[22] By this time, Smith had already written in the Lord's voice, "as one earth shall pass away, and the heavens thereof, even so another shall come, and there is no end to my works."[23]

So when Joseph Smith declared in 1833 that "the elements are eternal," and that creation was always recombination, he was not alone in challenging centuries of Christian cosmology.[24] That the world in its eternal materiality was subject to larger cosmic processes than merely local catastrophes, Smith left no room for doubt: "this Earth has been organized out of portions of other Globes that [have] been Disorganized," he said. "Organized and formed out of other planets which were [broken] up and remodeled and made into the one on which we live." "This earth was not the first of God's work," he added, and clearly it would not be the last.[25]

The first exception to creation *ex nihilo*—and indicated above as a corollary to eternalism, the belief that the human soul existed long before earthly creation—was common among Jews, Platonists, and Christians.[26] In Greek thought, objects were "meant to be ennobled" by their pre-existence. They were independent and self-existing. Early conceptions of human pre-mortality in the Jewish tradition, by contrast, emphasized God's omnipotence and sovereignty over present and future alike. The pre-existence of the human soul was therefore seen as reflecting on God's glory, not man's.[27] But the positioning of God and human on the same eternal scale of existence caused considerable concern among some early Christian writers. "What could be worse pride," asked the convert Augustine, "than the incredible folly in which I asserted that I was by nature what [God is]?"[28] So while pre-mortal existence was common in the early Christian centuries, it was exiled from the orthodox mind by the sixth. Mormonism asserts the eternal identity of the human as an essential part of the eternal universe Smith described. The fuller implications of this eternalism for understanding the exact nature of the human and our relationship to the Divine will be explored in chapter 17.

God, the father is material.

Jesus Christ is material.

Angels are material.

Spirits are material.

Men are material.

The universe is material . . .

Nothing exists which is not material.

—PARLEY PRATT

6

Monism

⌐͜—————————————————————————————————————

ASSERTING THE CO-ETERNAL nature of spirit as well as matter, indicated by Pratt's naming of both as "self-existent," suggested a second cosmological principle. This is the position that matter and spirit are not just similarly eternal; they are ultimately two manifestations of the same reality or substance. The consequence in Smith's thought is a collapse of the radical divide between body and spirit, the earthly and the heavenly. From Plato through Paul and to Descartes, a thoroughgoing dualism has prevailed in Western metaphysics. Smith rejected this entire heritage, though he was not the first to question the radical opposition of matter and spirit. Early Greeks and Roman Stoics had reduced the universe to one underlying substance, but few thinkers had in the centuries since. In the modern world, a seventeenth-century Jew from Amsterdam, Baruch Spinoza, "drove a stake through the heart of two millennia of religion and philosophy," writes one scholar, when he dissolved all such polarities into one, single thing he called "Substance."[1] God and the world, mind and body, thought and extension, spirit and matter—all pertained to the same realm of substance.

Thomas Hobbes had less influence on theology, but he, too, asserted a thoroughgoing materialism while yet professing belief in God. In a passage on what he considered logically absurd formulations, he wrote that some philosophers make "insignificant sounds," such "as this name, an *incorporeal body*, or . . . an *incorporeal substance*." Such "contradictory and inconsistent" use of language he thought was meaningless, "signify[ing] nothing at all."[2] The obvious applicability of such a test to language about God convinced some people then and now that Hobbes was an atheist. He was not; he simply believed that an incorporeal substance was an absurdity, so God must be a material being.[3]

This rejection of metaphysical dualism had been contemplated by a few other religious thinkers of the same era. In England, as the Cambridge Platonists revisited the doctrine of human pre-existence, they also questioned the immateriality of spirit. Joseph Glanvill thought it might be reasonable to conceive of pre-mortal spirits as being in a "purer state of Life, . . . joyn'd only to such a refined body, which should have been suitable to its own perfection and purity?"[4] (According to Anatole France, "several of the Fathers, such as St. Justin, Tertullian, Origen, and Clement of Alexandria thought that the Angels were not purely spiritual, but possessed a body formed of some subtile material.")[5] Glanvill's mentor Henry More had been emphatic in arguing, against Descartes, that if spirit were not extended, if it could not be located in space, then it could not exist. Spirit must be material, therefore.

The poet John Milton, writing in the same era, similarly propounded monism, holding that a single material substance that is "animate, self-active, and free" composes everything in the universe; "spirit is rarefied matter," and "all things, from insensate objects through souls are manifestations of this one substance."[6] A century later, the poet William Blake—influenced by the Swedish mystic Emanuel Swedenborg—stated emphatically, "Man has no Body distinct from his Soul; for that call'd Body is a portion of Soul discern'd by the five Senses."[7] But all such deviations were anomalies and heresies.

Spinoza was excommunicated from his synagogue as a heretic, the Cambridge Platonists passed from the scene with little lasting influence, and mystics Swedenborg and Blake, like the poet Milton, have by and large been deemed theological eccentrics. Samuel Coleridge, influential poet and armchair theologian, replied to such monistic conceptions of the universe on behalf of millions when he wrote that "The very ground of all Miracle is the heterogeneity of Spirit and Matter."[8] The basis of religion, in the West at least, is generally inconceivable apart from otherworldliness, a transcendent realm beyond the fleeting and frail stuff of material reality—spiritual, ineffable, supernatural.

Mormonism virtually eliminates the divide. Smith's 1833 pronouncement was vigorously elaborated and defended by Parley Pratt in 1838, when he produced the faith's first theologically radical essay: the *Treatise on the Regeneration and Eternal Duration of Matter*. It was there that Pratt moved beyond asserting the self-existence of matter and spirit, to claim their effective conflation. "Eternity is inscribed in indelible characters on every particle," he wrote. They are alike in their origin and in their immortal nature. They were equally affected by Adam's transgression, and will be equally regenerated by Christ's atonement.[9]

Joseph Smith stated definitively in 1842 that the cosmos was ultimately constituted of matter only. As he wrote in a church editorial:

> The body is supposed to be organized matter, and the spirit by many is thought
> to be immaterial, without substance. With this latter statement we should beg
> leave to differ-and state that spirit is a substance; that it is material, but that it
> is more pure, elastic, and refined matter than the body;-that it existed before
> the body, can exist in the body, and will exist separate from the body, when the
> body will be mouldering in the dust; and will in the resurrection be again
> united with it.[10]

He reaffirmed the ontological sameness of matter and spirit in an 1843 statement
later canonized as scripture: "There is no such thing as immaterial matter. All spirit
is matter but it is more fine or pure."[11] Pratt, typically, states the most radical implications of this new cosmology, when he celebrates Mormonism's uncompromising
materialism: "God the Father, is material. Jesus Christ is material. Angels are mate-
rial. Spirits are material. Men are material. The universe is material. . . . Nothing
exists which is not material. . . . Immateriality is but another name for nonentity—it
is the negation of all things, and beings—of all existence."[12] In fact, he wrote in his
Key to Theology, "to a mind matured, or quickened with a fulness of intelligence . . .
there is no use for the distinction implied in such terms" as "Physical and Spiritual,"
"because all things which do exist are eternal realities, in their elementary
existence."[13]

Smith's conflation, like those unorthodox forays that preceded him, does away
with the longstanding dichotomy of the world into radically distinct, incommensu-
rate spheres, of a privileged mind and inert matter, or mind and body (in Descartes's
language, a privileged thinking substance [*res cogitans*] and an inert corporeal substance [*res extensa*]). In all its forms, Platonic privileging of intellect over physicality,
Pauline elevating of spirit over flesh,[14] or Descartes's mind in opposition to matter,
Western dualism has divided the universe in twain, to the advantage of the former
categories and to the disadvantage of the latter.

The privileging of spirit over matter seems a natural, intuitive response to matter's
inertness, as well as its association with corruptibility and instability. In the early
Christian centuries, the Gnostic fear that God would be debased and contaminated
by his interaction with a material universe led to a theory of creation *ex nihilo* to
begin with.[15] Similar, more modern, prejudices against materiality partially explain
Christian discomfort with Darwin and naturalistic accounts of human origins. The
appearance of humans only at the end of a protracted process mired in materiality
and natural laws seems to some incompatible with the human's privileged place

in God's plan. Random processes acting upon inert matter seem an affront to a more intentional, meaning-laden origin.

As Jane Bennett notes, however, "the problem of meaninglessness arises only if 'matter' is conceived as inert, only as long as science deploys materialism whose physics is basically Newtonian. . . . [But] matter has a liveliness, resilience, unpredictability, or recalcitrance that is itself a source of wonder for us."[16] Smith's materialism is rooted in a similar elevation of matter to unorthodox capacities and constitution: "Hence we infer that God had materials to organize the world out of chaos—chaotic matter, which is element, *and in which dwells all the glory*. Element had an existence from the time He had [emphasis added]."[17]

Further evidence that Mormonism had erased materiality's inferior or subordinate status came in Smith's Abrahamic writings, the first of which he produced in 1835. In Smith's revised account of creation, the Gods utter their commands and then "watched those things which they had ordered until they obeyed."[18] The Pratts took this to mean that the elements in their most fundamental aspect exhibit a degree of intelligence, or agency, and are therefore responsive to the Divine Will. Orson Pratt held that "an unintelligent particle is incapable of understanding or obeying a law, while an intelligent particle is capable of both understanding and obedience. It would be entirely useless for an Intelligent Cause to give laws to unintelligent matter."[19]

Contra Newton, Pratt's metaphysics rested in part on his belief that it made more sense to attribute to a body self-motion than attraction, an active rather than a passive principle (rather like Joseph Priestly). "How much more absurd would be the idea of a substance so entirely inert that it could not move itself, but yet able to move a universe of substance toward itself," he reasoned.[20] Equally absurd, in his view, is the idea that intelligence can be bestowed upon matter by another being: "To say that some being gave this property to atoms is to admit the prior existence of a being with intelligence. . . . Reason has demonstrated, that the intelligence of every atom must either be without beginning, or else be the result of contact and combination."[21]

Parley Pratt wrote that "these eternal, self-existing elements possess in themselves certain inherent properties or attributes, in a greater or less degree; or, in other words, they possess intelligence, adapted to their several spheres."[22] That last sentence was removed from editions of Pratt's work subsequent to his death; but Brigham Young went on to express a kindred view in 1856, preaching that "there is life in all matter, throughout the vast extent of all the eternities; it is in the rock, the sand, the dust, in water, air, the gases, and in short, in every description and organization of matter, whether it be solid, liquid, or gaseous, particle operating with particle."[23]

As Sterling McMurrin has remarked, the Pratts' views are rather like those of Leibniz, "who held that all reality consists of mind atoms that are living centers of force." Though Mormonism has never officially embraced the Pratts' reading of eternalism, McMurrin is right that the LDS conception of matter is "essentially dynamic rather than static, if indeed it is not a kind of living energy, and that it is subject at least to the rule of intelligence."[24] This position is very much like the Process Theologians' view that "actual entities at every level embody an element of self-determination."[25]

John Widtsoe echoed the Pratts' language in 1908, writing that "Life is nothing more than matter in motion; that, therefore, all matter possesses a kind of life. . . . Matter . . . [is] intelligent . . . hence everything in the universe is alive."[26] Like the Pratts, he believed intelligence was a precondition of adherence to law. Nevertheless, twentieth-century Mormonism resisted affirming such a virtual panpsychism. By 1915, Widtsoe had himself retreated: "that a degree of intelligence is possessed by every particle of . . . matter cannot be said," he wrote. "Nor is it important."[27]

Such extrapolations from Smith's radical materialism may be mere speculation. But the fundamental claim of a thoroughgoing materialism gave indelible definition to the Mormon theological landscape. The divine, the human, and the nature of salvation are reconceptualized in accordance with those foundations. Out of these two principles, eternalism and cosmic monism, Smith elaborated a vision of God, the human, and the universe, unlike anything known in the Christian world of his day.

Even God himself should He act upon this principle He would cease to be God for the principles that Sustain him & his Throne would forsake him & he would cease to be God. For light & truth & every other good principle cleaves unto itself. And these all sustain the throne of God & He sustains them.

—BRIGHAM YOUNG, 27 February 1853

7

Laws Physical and Spiritual

FAR MORE WAS at stake in Smith's new cosmology than the age of the earth's primal elements or the ongoing creation of sister planets. With the advent of creation *ex nihilo*, God, rather than the natural world, came to be the ground of all reality: One historian of philosophy describes the implications of that development in early Christian thought: "in order that God's power would be absolute, nature had to lose its necessity and eternity.... A world where things have their proper natures and proper modes of actualization seems to place undesirable limits on God."[1] That is why most Christians now consider God, as the Westminster Confession states, to be "the source of all being"—meaning the source of the natural world and the laws that govern it. But if, as Joseph Smith taught, matter is as eternal as God, the question is raised: Are the laws that govern an eternal material universe, or the moral laws that govern the interactions of eternal spirit beings, eternal and independent of God as well?

One version of the dilemma raised by such a question was first posed by Plato in his dialogue the *Euthyphro*. In modified form, the question is: "Does God command what is morally good because it is morally good, or is what is morally good morally good because God commands it?" Put another way, the question is: Do some values, absolutes, principles, or laws exist independently of God? Is God the author of cosmic law, or not its author but its master? Certainly classical theism sees God as the source of all that exists, including law, but in some contemporary theologies, God is the "chief exemplification" of deep metaphysical principles which even he is not able to "freely cancel or interrupt," whereas so-called laws of nature are only contingent.[2]

More commonly, however, the Christian God stands outside the universe of space and time, and frames the laws that govern it. As one scholar describes the implications for ethics and theology, "nothing is right or wrong in itself. God could easily have decided to denominate 'anything we call good' into evil, and vice versa."[3] Not all theologians agree with this version of "divine command theory"—though it has been common in the West. As God is generally seen as the author of all physical reality, so he would also be the founder of all values, all morality, all meaning, that we find in the cosmos. As one example of how this works, Thomas Aquinas wrote that "when we say 'God is good' the meaning is . . . 'whatever good we attribute to creatures pre-exists in God,' and in a higher way. . . . He pours out goodness in things because He is good."[4] Everything, then—all beings, creatures, values, meaning, and truths—have their origin and existence and subsistence in God.

But if the content of the universe is co-eternal with God, what of other parts of reality's fabric—like those laws? In a monistic scheme, where spirit and matter are two manifestations of the same substance, it is a small step to hold that physical and moral laws are also but two manifestations of universal law. Timothy Keller refers to the "ancient understanding" that "there was a transcendent moral order outside the self, built into the fabric of the universe. If you violated that metaphysical order there were consequences just as severe as if you violated physical reality by placing your hand in a fire."[5] Parley Pratt took such thinking a step further. He considered the moral and physical orders to be fully subject to the same eternal laws. In the *Treatise on the Regeneration and Eternal Duration of Matter*, for example, he argued that as sin introduced calamity to the world, "in a physical as well as moral point of view," it "materially affected the earth itself." So also, Pratt argued, does Christ's atonement function equally to redeem man and the physical world; "all things, . . . animal and vegetable."[6] And those laws, like the elements to which they pertain, are eternal.

Of Sir Isaac Newton's momentous decipherment of the laws of the universe, the French scientist Pierre-Simon de Laplace famously told Napoleon, in his philosophical euphoria, that he no longer had need of God to make sense of creation. Secular science could henceforth exile God from his universe. In Joseph Smith's conception, by contrast, naturalism and God co-exist. There is room, in a cosmos of self-existent, universal, eternal laws, for a God who is divinely supreme. Self-existent principles, he argued, underlie the very structure of the universe and exist independently of God, though he is our source for knowing them. "Every principle proceeding from God is eternal," Smith declared, "eternal and self-existent." Recognizing this fact is not just important, it is "the first step in the salvation of men."[7]

Parley Pratt took this to mean that not just humans but God as well must fully recognize and embrace those laws. In Pratt's theological euphoria at Smith's eternalism, God was re-inscribed in Laplace's universe of natural law, as a part of it rather than outside it. In embracing a universe of things that co-existed with God, Pratt inferred that the laws and principles which defined relations and interactions among such elements were also of eternal duration. The consequence, he reasoned, was that God is himself subject to law. It is impossible, he wrote in his 1838 essay, "for God to bring forth matter from nonentity, or to originate element from nothing," because "these are principles of eternal truth, they are laws which cannot be broken, . . . whether the reckoning be calculated by the Almighty, or by man."[8]

Pratt expounded this doctrine more fully in his *Key to the Science of Theology*. Even the Father and Son, he declared, being part of an eternal and physical universe, are "subject to the laws that govern, of necessity, even the most refined order of physical existence." Because "all physical element, however embodied, quickened, or refined, is subject to the general laws necessary to all existence."[9] Not only laws of self-contradiction demarcate the limits of divine power, but so do scientific laws of the type Lavoisier propounded in laying the foundations of modern chemistry on the law of conservation of mass. It is as if Christianity's worst fears of the Gnostics are borne out; in Pratt's explication, God is part of the universe, master architect but not master magician. In this conception, miracles do not represent, as they traditionally have, "the intervention of God in the natural order" or "the suspension of the natural order."[10] They represent, as they did for C. S. Lewis, the operations of God within a natural order imperfectly comprehended by humans.[11] John Widtsoe agreed; God was "part of [the] universe"; his "conquest over the universe" was a function of his "recognition of universal laws" and "the forces lying about him."[12]

As was so often the case with Smith's theology, the seeds of this radical repositioning of law relative to God were in the Book of Mormon. Though Smith seldom connected his teachings explicitly to the scripture he had produced in 1830, he may have thought that volume hinted at such a perspective. The prophet Alma taught that those who "are without God in the world . . . have gone contrary to the nature of God; therefore, they are in a state contrary to the nature of happiness."[13] He continues, intimating that happiness has preconditions with which God is in perfect harmony, and that God must himself abide the requirements of justice or forfeit his identity as God: "Mercy could not . . . destroy the work of justice. Now the work of justice could not be destroyed; if so, God would cease to be God."[14] The later Nephite prophet Mormon echoes this formulation, writing that God "changeth not; if so he would cease to be God."[15]

In the modern church, there has been limited resistance to this idea. In its 1929 response to B. H. Roberts's masterwork which propounded these views of the independent existence of universally valid law, an apostolic committee objected that God "is the author of law," and cited LDS scripture ("he hath given a law unto all things") in support.[16] However, such a proof text is at best ambiguous (the context suggests more cosmic ordering than universal law: God "hath given a law unto all things, by which they move in their times and their seasons"). By and large, the momentum of Smith's teachings has been irreversible. Most Mormons understand that the process by which humans acquire the divine nature is the same by which God maintains his: conformity to the eternal laws that govern the realm of spirit and matter, the physical and the interpersonal, alike. Brigham Young, in referring to the ostensibly miraculous resurrection of humankind, insisted that "all God's creation is a natural philosophy, and the only miracle there is, is to see the effect without a cause, and yet there is a natural law for all things."[17] As Mormon philosopher Kent Robson notes, "although there has been a lot of discussion about the laws, it seems to me that [in Mormon thought] they are clearly independent of God and to some extent out of God's control."[18]

The Divine

Neither this Act nor any Clause Article or Thing herein contained shall extend or be construed to extend to give any ease benefit or advantage to any . . . person that shall deny in his Preaching or Writing the Doctrine of the Blessed Trinity.

—An Act for Exempting their Majestyes Protestant Subjects dissenting from the Church of England from the Penalties of certaine Lawes, 1688

I have always declared God to be a distinct personage, Jesus Christ a separate and distinct personage from God the Father, and that the Holy Ghost was a distinct personage and a Spirit: and these three constitute three distinct personages and three Gods.

—JOSEPH SMITH, 16 June 1844

8

The Godhead

OF THE INNUMERABLE tenets over which Christians may disagree, none has been so central to the question of orthodoxy as the doctrine of the Trinity. And few, since the formation of creedal Christianity in the fourth century, have found such enduring consensus. Christianity would fracture into broad divisions, then splinter ever more finely into hundreds of denominations and sects, over the role of grace, ecclesiastical governance, the number of sacraments, the mode of baptism, and a hundred other issues; but adherence to a core Trinitarianism would remain a virtual constant among the vast majority to the present day. Its preeminence as the non-negotiable core of Christian dogma was reaffirmed in the English Toleration Act of 1688. By this piece of legislation, dissenters were at last protected in the exercise of their religious freedom—as long as they did not go so far in their heresy as to deny "the Doctrine of the Blessed Trinity."

In significant ways, the last three centuries have changed nothing in this regard. By way of illustration of this fact, in May of 2000 the United Methodist Church passed a resolution asserting that the Church of Jesus Christ of Latter-day Saints "does not fit within the bounds of the historic, apostolic tradition of Christian faith." First cited by way of explanation was Mormonism's "radically differing doctrine on . . . the nature and being of God." The Presbyterian Church (U.S.A.) and the Southern Baptist Convention passed similar resolutions[1] followed by the Vatican, which declared Mormon baptisms invalid in 2001.[2]

Trinitarianism is a position that is not explicit within the New Testament, but emerges from a series of ecumenical councils convened to resolve doctrinal disputes in the fourth century. An early edition of the *Catholic Encyclopedia* asserts that "the various elements of the Trinitarian doctrine are all expressly taught" in the New Testament, while a subsequent edition holds that "among the Apostolic Fathers, there had been nothing even remotely approaching such a mentality or perspective."[3] "One does not find in the NT the trinitarian paradox of the coexistence of the Father, Son, and Spirit within a divine unity," agrees the *Anchor Bible Dictionary*.[4] The impetus behind the development of the doctrine was twofold: first, the need to rationally accommodate belief in a Father, Son, and Holy Ghost—three apparent divinities—to an unflinching monotheism; and, second, to define God in terms that do justice to both his transcendence and his humanness, his eternal existence outside of time and his historical incarnation and participation within time. In the second and third centuries, a number of theories began to take shape that defined the roles and interrelationships of the two principal members of the godhead (as well as the Holy Spirit), and tried to do so in a way that safeguarded an essential unity.

Irenaeus (d. ca. 200) had articulated an emerging consensus about the roles associated with each member of the godhead, but had not addressed the problem of their ontological unity. "The rule of our faith," he wrote, was belief in "one God, the creator of all things," "Christ Jesus our Lord, . . . through Whom (i.e. the Word) all things were made" and who lived and died to "produce perfect reconciliation between God and man," and "the Holy Spirit," a guiding influence "poured out . . . upon all mankind in the earth."[5] This lack of a clear statement defining the nature of divine unity opened the way for a variety of doctrines that attempted to resolve the issue.

A group now labeled Dynamic Monarchianists, for example, emphasized the unity of God by arguing that a divine element or power had entered into the man Jesus, working through him to accomplish God's plans. Modalistic Monarchianists, by contrast (also called Sabellians or Patripassianists) held that Father, Son, and Holy Ghost were different names given to the one God, or different manifestations (modes) by which he operated at different times. Influential Fathers like Tertullian (160–225) and Origen (184–253) refuted these positions, but no clearly defined orthodoxy had appeared by the end of the third century.

By the fourth century, the main point of controversy concerned the relationship of the Son to the Father. Followers of Arius (250–336), an Alexandrian presbyter, argued that Jesus Christ was created by the Father and therefore implicitly subordinate to the Father. This position (Arianism or subordinationism) was a logical way to maintain monotheism in the face of an incarnate, divine son. As Arius explained in his statement of belief, "[The Son] is not eternal or co-eternal or equally self-sufficient with the Father, nor does He have his being alongside the Father . . . thus postulating two self-sufficient first principles."[6] Arius's position was construed by many as qualifying Christ's full divinity. As a consequence, he wrote in another letter, "We are persecuted because we say that the Son has a beginning, but that God is without beginning."[7]

The position had significant support, but was opposed by most bishops of the era. Emperor Constantine convened an assembly of bishops to settle the matter, and the result was the Nicene Creed, which solved the difficult problem by employing a nonbiblical term—homoousios, or "of the same substance"—to definitively establish co-equality of Father and Son. The resultant creed defined Jesus as "the Son of God, the Only-begotten begotten from the Father, that is from the substance of the Father, God from God, light from light, true God from true God, begotten not made, consubstantial with the Father."[8]

It was at this same time that Alexander of Alexandria, ardent foe of Arius, emphasized the beginnings of an apophatic theology—that is, one which concedes the incomprehensibility of the divine: the Son is begotten, Alexander writes, "but in an unutterable and inexplicable fashion, . . . since his substance defies investigation . . . just as the Father himself defies investigation."[9] Arianism was vanquished in the Councils, but the label would hover in the backgrounds of subsequent history, available as a damning accusation against those inclined to see hierarchy in the godhead.

The Trinitarian doctrine received fuller elaboration from Augustine, among others, who emphasized not just the consubstantiality of the three members of the Trinity (that they were all of the same substance or essence) but also the full equality of each, by attaching the full range of the divine attributes to each;[10] this is the position reflected in the later Athanasian Creed (5th–6th c.), which affirms that "such as the Father is, such is the Son, such also the Holy Spirit," therefore "in this Trinity there is nothing before or after, nothing greater or less, but all three persons are coeternal with each other and coequal." But this creed goes further, expressing the essential mystery of Trinitarianism, referring to the object of worship as "one God in Trinity, and Trinity in unity, without either confusing the persons or dividing the substance."[11]

Through centuries of Christian orthodoxy and into the Reformation, the Trinitarian formulae would remain one of the few constants in Christendom, with only minor episodes of dissent emerging now and then. One tragic instance involved Michael Servetus, who went to the stake in 1553 for his treatise "On the Errors of the Trinity." A more serious challenge came from the Socinians of the same era, who denied not the Trinity per se, but only the existence of a Trinity before Christ was born in the flesh. However, virtually no enduring sect would emerge to challenge core Trinitarian dogma until the Unitarians gained traction in the early nineteenth century (the American Unitarian Association was formed in 1825). William Ellery Channing virtually defined the movement with an 1819 sermon laying out "the distinguishing opinions" of the movement.[12] Primary among these was the insistence that "the Father alone is God" and that the doctrine of the Trinity was "irrational and unscriptural."[13]

Mormonism's rupture with traditional Trinitarian thought, like Unitarianism, represents a rejection of the Nicene solution. But it does so by moving in the direction opposite to Unitarianism. Instead of reducing the Trinity to one, Mormons expanded the "Unity in Trinity" to three physically distinct, fully individuated persons. Mormons trace their doctrine of deity to Smith's 1820 theophany, in which he claimed to personally behold God himself, who appeared in a shaft of light and "did in reality speak to me."[14] Mormons, however, may see in this visionary episode more theological illumination than the young Smith did. They emphasize, for example, a radically new conception of divinity revealed at this time. Smith here learned "the Father and the Son are real, separate beings with glorified bodies of flesh and bones."[15]

Actually, it is difficult to know exactly what Smith concluded about the nature of the godhead from this experience. In one of his very few subsequent references to the vision, the only import it registered was the assurance "that he had received a remission of his sins."[16] That Smith did not even reflect immediately on its bearing on the Trinity is evident in his lack of attention to the very question of number when describing his experience. In his earliest, 1832 account, he recorded that "the Lord opened the heavens upon me and I saw the Lord and he spake unto me saying Joseph my son they sins are forgiven thee," leaving unclear whether his two uses of "Lord" referred to one personage or two, in succession.[17] In his 1838 retelling, and all other first and second-hand accounts, Smith more clearly indicated that he "saw two personages, . . . one of [whom] spoke unto me calling me by name."[18]

Smith claimed at the end of his life that he had "always decl[are]d God to be a distinct personage, J[esus] C[hrist] a sep[arate] & distinct personage from God the Fa[the]r, [and that] the H[oly] G[host] was a distinct personage . . . & these 3 const[itute] 3 distinct personages & 3 Gods."[19] By "always," he meant since 1830, he clarified. Such a conclusion, he implied, was a simple matter of experience. "Any person that had seen the heavens opened knows that there is three personages in the heavens holding the Keys of Power," he said in an earlier sermon.[20]

In addition to his own visitation, he may have had in mind the New Testament account of the martyr Stephen's vision, wherein he saw Christ on the right hand of God. But few Christians have concluded from this report anything about the nature of those heavenly beings, or infer therefrom a physical distinctness of persons in accord with the description (else Trinitarian thought would have been dead in the cradle). That's because Trinitarianism is a religious mystery, not a dogma perceptible to the senses. Few Trinitarians deny that God the Son was born, lived, and resurrected as a physically incarnate, differentiated individual. That no more disproves the consubstantiality of three divine persons than the wafer of flour in the Eucharist disproves transubstantiation.

At the same time, in the grammar of New Testament language, the Father and Son are clearly represented as two different individuals. A separate Father and Son appearing in his vision would not have surprised Smith—after the shock of the vision itself had receded. If this encounter provided the basis of his later rejection of Trinitarianism, it was because his commonsense experience of two deities became the ground for his later theological reflection on the godhead—but at the time it is unlikely that it would have struck the boy as a theological novelty or an upsetting of Christian dogma. By his own and his family's accounts, it was the message, not the persons of the vision, that presented him with a new religious understanding on the occasion of his 1820 vision. His sins were forgiven him, and no true church was to be found on the earth.

When Smith supervised an 1834 series of theological lectures, his stance on divine embodiment was not clear. The language, which was not Smith's, was in many ways conventional. God is "the only supreme governor," and is "omnipotent, omnipresent, and omniscient."[21] At the same time, the word *trinity* nowhere appears. "There are two personages" who are members of "the Godhead," the Father, who is a "personage of spirit," and the Son, who is a "personage of tabernacle." If the Holy Spirit, which is the "mind" of God informing both, be considered, then the godhead may be said to consist of those three.[22] Though Smith would develop and clarify the sense in which he considered the Father to be a Being of spirit, the distinctness of the three divine persons remained a constant emphasis. In 1841 he affirmed that the "Godhead . . . was not as many imagined—three Heads & but one body, he said the three were separate bodys."[23]

Asserting a godhead comprising three distinct persons, as Smith did, reopened the ancient dilemma the Nicene doctrine had resolved: how to reconcile three divine persons with monotheism—or belief in the One God. The Book of Mormon in some ways compounded the problem. As one philosopher has noted, "the Book of Mormon is even more express than the Bible in teaching that the Father, Son, and Holy Spirit are one God." Thus Mormons actually "face the same original puzzle as traditional Christians of explaining how this is."[24] This is a puzzle to which most Mormons appear oblivious or indifferent, since the radical distinctness of the three persons is now a Mormon commonplace. But in the church's early years, the Book of Mormon conundrum provided the occasion for Orson Pratt especially to embark upon theological speculations that would reconcile the paradox. He wrote that not the Eternal Father, but the omnipresent substance of which he is an individuation, is the divine power or God which "governs and controls all organization by wise and judicious laws."[25] In another version, he wrote that "the Unity, Eternity, and Omnipresence of God, consisted in the oneness, eternity, and Omnipresence of the attributes, such as 'the fullness of Truth,' light, love, wisdom, & knowledge, dwelling in countless numbers of tabernacles in numberless worlds; and that the oneness of these attributes is what is called in both ancient & modern revelations, the One God."[26] That had the virtue of reconciling monotheism with plurality, but it was going too far for Brigham Young, who saw this as portending the worship of godly attributes rather than God himself. He ordered the excision of this idea from Pratt's collected pamphlets.

In his own references to the godhead, Smith articulated a version of divinity similar to what now goes by the name of social Trinitarianism.[27] Smith referred to what he called the office or "provence of the Father to preside as the Chief or President" of the three deities.[28] Another second-hand account of Smith's version refers to an "Everlasting covenant [that] was made between three personages before the organization of this earth, and relates to their dispensation of things to men on the earth: these personages . . . are called God the first, the Creator; God the second, the Redeemer; and God the third, the witness or Testator."[29] Their oneness is therefore more than a solidarity of shared purpose: it is a covenantal relationship of unity, in which each has separate functions but each can—and does—represent the whole.

This understanding has persisted with little substantial variation. As B. H. Roberts later elaborated, "by appointment, any One of Three of the unit Intelligences may become the embodiment and representative of all the power and glory and authority of the sum total of the Divine Intelligences; in which capacity either the One or the Three would no longer stand only in their individual characters as Gods, but they would stand also as the sign and symbol of all that is divine—and would act as and be to all intents and purposes *The One God*."[30]

If Smith's initial treatment of the godhead employed some conventional categories and language, subsequent developments more emphatically differentiated Mormonism from other Christian denominations. With time, the seeds planted in Joseph Smith's first theophany developed into three interrelated hallmarks of Mormon doctrine about deity. First, God's personal responsiveness to human prayer; second, his passible nature (i.e., his susceptibility to be moved by emotion); and third, his physical embodiment. One other theistic development—a Heavenly Mother—has remained mostly at the peripheries of Mormon doctrine, while a fifth—the conflation of Adam and God—had a brief flourishing, then disappeared almost entirely.

If thou shalt ask, thou shalt receive revelation upon revelation, knowledge upon knowledge, that thou mayest know the mysteries and peaceable things—that which bringeth joy, that which bringeth life eternal.

—Evening and Morning Star, July 1832

9

Revealer God

ᴏF THE MANY improbabilities narrated in the Old Testament, Balaam's speaking ass is surely among the furthest removed from the world of normal experience. But from one perspective, more surprising than a talking animal may be the fact that Balaam was quicker to argue with the creature than marvel at its sudden talkativeness. Young Smith's encounter with Deity was marked by a similar disproportion between the grandeur of his experience and the first response it elicited. "I had actualy seen a light, and in the midst of that light I saw two Personages, and they did in reality speak to me," he later recorded. But at the time, in reply to his mother's query about his shaken condition, he merely replied, "I have learned for myself that Presbyterianism is not true."[1]

In Christian theology, revelation has had many meanings. The principal models described by one historian of the subject include revelation considered as God's revealed word—that is, the Bible, revelation as God's acts in history, and revelation as "inner experience."[2] While countless Christians believe that God is mighty to answer prayers, instill comfort, and guide the seeker, theology has to some extent abandoned the idea that God issues specific, content-laden (propositional) responses to individual, prayerful queries. As one historian notes, the emphatic anti-anthropomorphism (resistance to imputing human characteristics to the divine) of Christianity is largely responsible for this development, which renders the continuing use of the term "revelation" problematic: "To claim that God reveals Himself to man but to reject the [belief that] He reveals Himself by speaking to man is to so whittle away the analogy on which the concept of divine revelation is built that it must be seriously asked whether the concept of divine revelation has enough content to license its continued use. Revelation in the fully personal sense characteristic of personal agents has been abandoned."[3] Doubtless numerous Christians, especially evangelicals, would consider such a claim an overstatement—but few would deny the general tendency it describes. Nor would they respond to the trend in the way of Mormonism has, with a more literal anthropomorphizing of God.

Individualized, propositional, personal revelation has proved a perennial powder keg. If revelation is available to everyman, what is to prevent Christianity from becoming holy anarchy? One of the earliest church controversies was one in which church father Tertullian found himself on the losing side, supporting the proponents of the "new prophecy" promulgated by the late second- and early third-century followers of Montanus, a man gifted with "special revelations," against the bishops who did not recognize his authority.[4] Not coincidentally, Tertullian has been called the "first Protestant," and in the centuries since, sporadic claims for special revelation have recurrently proved destabilizing to Christian orthodoxy.

English Familists of the sixteenth century (an offshoot of Anabaptists) claimed immediate revelation, and in the seventeenth century French prophets (Camisards) claimed they heard the voice of God. So did Anne Hutchinson, in colonial America, who suffered banishment as a result. Her interrogators asked her, "'How do you know that was the Spirit?' She replied 'How did Abraham know that it was God that bid him offer his son. . .?' 'By an immediate voice,' Thomas Dudley replied, meaning the direct voice of God, unmediated by Scripture or a minister. 'So to me,' Anne Hutchinson said."[5] "The ground work of her revelations," Governor John Winthrop pronounced at her 1637 trial, "is the *immediate* revelation of the spirit and not *by* the ministry of the word" (emphasis in original). Unfortunately for Hutchinson, as her biographer notes and the verdict revealed, "professed direct revelation from God . . . [was] an ecclesiastical crime."[6] Calvin, after all, had held that "the Spirit never dispensed revelations independent of the Word."[7] Abraham might not have been the most prudent example for her to cite, since his voice led him to attempt human sacrifice.

The history of Christianity reveals a consistent, inverse relationship between a religious group's majority status and its championing of personal revelation. In Hutchinson's case, the fear of the authorities was that her claim to personal revelation was a form of antinomianism—that is, it made obedience to moral as well as civil laws subordinate to personal conscience, as shaped by direct communication from God. The irony, one historian notes, is that her case showed that "What was once a Protestant orthodoxy when the Puritans were a persecuted minority in England, contending with the episcopacy, had become a heresy when they were the majority in control of the government and churches of New England. The corporate decision, not the individual's, came to matter."[8]

A hundred years later, Jonathan Edwards issued his own warning against personal revelation's subversive potential: "If this be supposed, that God does now in these days give to some revelations to be declared to others, let us consider what will be the consequence.... What a door is open to Satan! How the church of God is like a city broke down and without walls."[9]

One church that went further than others in elevating personal revelation to a cardinal position was the Quaker faith. According to one sympathetic observer, Quakers believed the Protestant reliance on "private judgment" in matters of belief, if divorced from belief in personal revelation, was "absurd and monstrous." For them, the ground of faith must be "the testimony of the spirit within—divine, inward revelations from God." Not coincidentally, of course, Quakers were persistently viewed as a subversive and dangerous sect. They recognized the necessity to distinguish "true revelations . . . from false," and asserted "conformity with the Holy Scriptures" as a guide.[10] But the synthesis is inherently unstable. Belief in personal revelation—that God would dispense knowledge or truth to individuals in extra-canonical ways—would seem to suggest either revelation's redundancy or scripture's insufficiency. The inevitable consequence, as a historian noted in this case, was that "Quakers undermined the very concept of canonicity in order to weaken its control over the Inner Light."[11] The Hicksites, Quaker followers of Elias Hicks, explicitly privileged the Inner Light over the scriptures. And Shakers, another branch of Quakers, were even "more radically open about their conceptions of revelation."[12]

Given the destabilizing potential of personal revelation, many ministers reacted warily to revelatory expectations. Wrote an Edinburgh cleric in 1830, "I am aware that prayer for the outpouring of the Holy Spirit has been, and may be recommended in terms which Scripture sobriety does not justify. Some have spoken of this divine gift as if they expected something actually miraculous, something altogether new to the church in the present day, conferred independently of the word, and in a manner almost perceptible to the senses."[13]

The dangers of extra-scriptural revelation seemed everywhere apparent in the nineteenth century, in a number of ill-fated contemporary movements led by charismatic "prophets." Robert Matthews, the self-styled "Matthias" ended up accused of feeding his dwindling flock poisoned blackberries; John Christopher Hartwick, an eccentric Lutheran clergyman, obtained over twenty thousand acres along the Susquehanna River in New York to establish a town to be called New Jerusalem, but his dreams never got off the ground. He had no disciples, was dropped as minister by several congregations, and found no one willing to accept his spiritual oversight (he disliked women and bathing alike, tempering his appeal significantly).[14]

Another "prophet" led a small group called the Pilgrims in upstate New York to don bear pelts, forgo bathing, and wait upon him as God's mouthpiece. A much-abused visitor concluded the sect was "a striking exhibition of the melancholy consequences which naturally result from *leaving the Scriptures to seek for new revelations.*"[15]

Another proof of revelation's simultaneous appeal and anarchic potential is the example of the American Transcendentalists. The movement grew rapidly in the 1830s, organized around a central principle that "man has ideas, that come not through the five senses, or the powers of reasoning" but result, rather, from "direct revelation from God [or] his immediate inspiration." To these views was added "a universal law of access"—the point that revelation should be available to all in a democratizing of religion.[16] These Transcendentalists shared the goal of unmooring revelation from the church and bringing everyone to the mountaintop.[17]

In the early nineteenth century, an era dominated by millennial expectations and hopes, many looked to new revelation, not for fresh knowledge or personal edification, but for affirmation that God still spoke and was acting in preparation for his Son's return. "The air was thick with rumors of a 'new Religion,' a 'new Bible,'" writes one historian of the Campbellite movement.[18] Even Christians who were not millennialists were open to evidence, in Emerson's words, "that God is, not was; that He speaketh, not spake."[19]

In addition to Quakers and Hicksites, the Swedenborgians as well as Native and African-American religions shared this same goal of democratizing or personalizing revelation. It was against this history and background that Mormonism appeared as something both novel and entirely familiar. Smith's personal claim to his 1820 theophany and to a series of angelic visitations over the next several years had numerous contemporary parallels.[20] But by 1830, his claims took more concrete and destabilizing forms. The twin concepts of personal revelation and an open canon intersected with the publication in that year of the Book of Mormon. Smith's 1820 experience of seeking God and finding himself rewarded with a personal visitation had found reaffirmation in 1823 when, he wrote, "I betook myself to prayer . . . for a manifestation to me that I might know of my state and standing before him. For I had full confidence in obtaining a divine manifestation, as I had previously had one."[21] On that occasion, the angel Moroni appeared and told Smith that he would be instrumental in translating an ancient record written on gold plates and buried nearby. After seven years of what he described as angelic apprenticeship, delays, and translation efforts, 5,000 copies of the Book of Mormon were published.

The Book of Mormon made a far greater impact through the story of its origins and production than through any new theology it contained. As we noted, Rodney Stark has observed that "the Book of Mormon . . . may not have added enough doctrinal novelty to the Christian tradition to have made Mormonism more than a

Protestant sect." That claim is both true and misleading.[22] Adherents and opponents almost universally saw in the Book of Mormon echoes of familiar New Testament teachings. The most important religious principle the Book of Mormon conveyed was a point the text enacted as well as explicitly taught: God's highly personal
involvement in human life and his revelatory responsiveness to individual prayer in
a manner that might be called dialogic revelation.[23] Through thematic structure,
numerous textual examples, and a final, concluding instance of readerly invitation,
the volume hammers home the insistent message that God will personally deign to
reply to the lowliest seeker of truth.

Its most insistent instance of the principle unfolds when Nephi, the son of a
prophet and patriarch, prays to have the same vision his father had described. An
angel appears, and asks him if he does not believe the words of his father. The implication seems to be, as the Old Testament suggests, that "prophecy was preeminently
the privilege of the prophets."[24] And indeed, virtually no OT instances exist of personal revelation bestowed upon individuals who are *not* prophets or patriarchs.[25]
When Nephi acknowledges that he doubts nothing his father has said, implicitly
conceding he is simply requesting his own, personal revelatory experience, the angel's response is not reproof, but heavenly exultation: "Hosanna to the Lord, the
most high God; for he is God over all the earth, yea, even above all. And blessed art
thou, Nephi, because thou believest in the Son of the most high God; wherefore,
thou shalt behold the things which thou hast desired."[26] Nephi is commended for
seeking access to the mysteries of heaven for personal, rather than public, edification. The story seems to be cast as a deliberate and decisive break with biblical and
conventional Christian notions alike about what degree of revelatory interaction
with God is possible and for whom.

As a particularly successful embodiment of the growing democratization of
Christianity, the Book of Mormon was both celebrated and derided for its populist
appeal. "Ask God, the Eternal Father, in the name of Christ, if these things are not
true," invited its self-identified concluding editor, "and if ye shall ask with a sincere
heart, with real intent, having faith in Christ, he will manifest the truth of it unto
you, by the power of the Holy Ghost. And by the power of the Holy Ghost ye may
know the truth of all things."[27] To which the book's first published critic responded,
"If there was anything plausible about Smith, I would say to those who believe him
to be a prophet, hear the question which Moses put into the mouth of the Jews, and
his answer to it—'And if thou say in thine heart, How shall we know the word
which the Lord hath not spoken?'—Does he answer, 'Ask the Lord and He will tell
you?'. . . Nay, indeed."[28] But many responded as did convert Eliza R. Snow: "The
voice of God revealing to man as in former dispensations was what my soul had
hungered for."[29]

As surely as the Catholic Church grounded its claims of authority on the rock of Peter, so did Mormonism ground its own on personal revelation.[30] In fact, Smith insisted that the rock Jesus referred to in the exchange reported by Matthew *was* the rock of revelation.[31] "Take away the Book of Mormon and the revelations, and where is our religion? We have none," he said in another setting.[32] In Mormonism's first generation, revelation was frequently understood in those dramatic terms that the Book of Mormon described and Smith himself experienced: full-blown theophanies, angelic appearances, the voice of God, visions, "pure intelligence" flowing into a receptive mind, creating "sudden strokes of ideas."[33] Smith wanted a church full of prophets and revelators (as long as they did not usurp his prerogatives). As one Mormon scholar remarked: "Joseph Smith was the Henry Ford of revelation: he wanted everyone to have one."[34] Mormonism's own St. Paul, Parley P. Pratt, was especially fired by the near access to God that Smith had promised the faithful:

> for My Part I never can rest untill My Eyes have seen my Redeemer until I have gazed like Nephi upon the gloryes of the Celestial world until I Can Come into full communion and familiar Converse with the angels of glory and the Spirits of just men made Perfect through the Blood of Christ and I testify to All Both Small and great, Both Male and female that if they stop short of the full Enjoyment of these things They Stop Short of the Blessings freely offered to Every Creature in the Gospel.[35]

Nevertheless, early in Smith's own prophetic career he found it necessary to dampen enthusiasm for revelations that imitated his own. Hiram Page was one of the eight men who saw and handled the gold plates, and his name is appended to an affidavit prefacing the Book of Mormon, to that effect. Some five months after the Mormon church's organization, he began to make use of a seer stone, through which he claimed to receive revelations for the nascent church, prompting Smith to produce a revelation that established the principle of the presiding spiritual authority in the church. The revelation, by declaring that "no one shall be appointed to receive revelations and commandments [for] this church excepting my servant Joseph Smith, . . . until I shall appoint . . . another in his stead,"[36] effectively transformed the role of a prophet into the office of Prophet. Henceforth, Mormonism would distinguish between personal revelation pertaining to an individual and her stewardship, and revelation as a prophetic prerogative that authoritatively expresses God's will to the church as a whole.

At the same time, Smith understood revelation as spanning a spectrum from the dramatic to the subtle, ranging from virtual transcripts of heavenly communication (or dictations *from* heavenly transcripts) to utterance that is authoritative by virtue of the speaker's status alone. Smith recorded as revelation some words that he claimed to hear from the mouths of angels or even Deity himself. At other times, he saw and heard things in a kind of trance, while others present in the room felt and saw nothing.[37] But several personal letters were later canonized and the majority of his revelations were apparently pronouncements that he uttered while feeling himself under the influence of spiritual guidance, but in the absence of supernatural manifestations.

Ten years after the death of Smith, Brigham Young still affirmed the doctrine of personal revelation in official pronouncements: "It is not only the privilege but the duty of every individual to so live in accordance with the light and requirements of the gospel as to be able to ask and receive revelation from the Almighty at all times and under all circumstances."[38] But by then, a new model of revelation, one that informs Mormon religious culture to the present, had become dominant. In attempting to help translate the gold plates, Oliver Cowdery had been instructed "that you must study it out in your mind; then you must ask me if it be right, and if it is right I will cause that your bosom shall burn within you: therefore, you shall feel that it is right."[39] Such subjective feelings, rather than propositional content, had become by Mormonism's second generation the normative model for Latter-day Saint revelation. (Modern LDS prophets typically counsel that "we hear the words of the Lord most often by a feeling. If we are humble and sensitive, the Lord will prompt us through our feelings."[40]) Smith, by contrast, had emphasized an intellectual component as a hedge against emotionalism. He characterized revelation as "pure intelligence flowing into you," and another scripture he dictated suggests the spirit will manifest itself "in your mind and in your heart."[41]

The dialogic revelation from God modeled in the Book of Mormon—and common in the church's first generation—persists as a theoretical possibility. But what Max Weber called "the routinization of charisma," has produced in the Mormon case two consequences: first, as in the New Testament church, Pentecostal manifestations evident in the founding years taper off, becoming less dramatic, more private, and more subjective. Second, smoothly functioning institutional structures and councils, guided by "inspiration," fill the function earlier served by Smith's charismatic leadership. Smith himself fostered this transition, writes one historian, saying he "intended the revelatory power to pass from himself to the councils of the church which were organized in 1834 and 1835. In making these changes, Smith not only shifted the responsibility for revelation from himself to the councils, he also moved the locus of revelation from the individual prophet to the church's administrative bureaucracy."[42]

Young himself reported no theophanies or voices from heaven, and few visions, but claimed the same priesthood keys as those bestowed upon Joseph Smith. This has been the case, with a few exceptions in the case of visions, for Young's successors. Each has proclaimed the same unceasing access that prophets and laity alike have to God's mind and will, the same right to inspiration to execute one's personal or priestly duty. But the scriptural canon, ruptured by the Book of Mormon, has settled into relative stability with the additional supplements of the Doctrine and Covenants (last modified in 1981) and the Pearl of Great Price, added to the Standard Works in 1880. With a few exceptions, the only statements in the post-Joseph Smith era publicly accorded the status of revelation were ones that stipulated the cessation of prior practice (polygamy and the priesthood ban), not the introduction of new doctrines or policies.[43] Some leaders have downplayed expectations that revelation occurs with any regularity. B. H. Roberts said as long ago as 1905 that "not even good men, no, not though they be prophets or other high officials of the Church, are at all times and in all things inspired of God. It is only occasionally and at need that God comes to their aid."[44]

In the life of Mormons generally, and in the conversion process particularly, the assurance of a God dispensing personal revelation is still absolutely fundamental—if its charismatic varieties have largely disappeared, at least from public discourse.[45] In a significant twist on the witnessing of evangelicals, the moment of conversion for Mormons is not generally seen as the recognition of one's sinful nature and transformation to a state of grace, but the moment of one's spiritual confirmation of a particular set of propositions about God and his work of modern restoration. The moment of illumination Smith experienced in a personal encounter with Deity remains a template for the religious experience Mormons aspire to generally. The emphasis, however, is not on manifestations of parallel drama, but on the experience of comparable certainty. It may be, as James indicated, that the just shall live by faith. But Mormonism is so replete with aspirations to epistemological certainty that more than one observer has labeled the tradition "gnostic."[46] Book of Mormon prophet Alma teaches that faith can develop in the faithful into "perfect knowledge"; Moroni assures readers of his testimony that "through the power of the Holy Ghost, ye may know the truth of all things."[47] The consequence is a Mormon culture saturated with the rhetoric of certainty, in spite of scriptural assertion that mere belief is a gift of equal standing with spiritual knowledge.[48]

Not only are the heavens endlessly open to human inquiry, but Smith imagined God as so engaged as dispenser of revelation that it takes an act of will to resist him. "As well might man stretch forth his puny arm to stop the Missouri river in its decreed course, or to turn it up stream, as to hinder the Almighty from pouring down knowledge from heaven upon the heads of the Latter-day Saints."[49] The most significant doctrinal point emerging from Joseph Smith's first vision, which Mormons consider the inaugural event of a new dispensation, was what he learned about God as "the Lord, the Revealer."[50] The salient moral he drew from his theophany was the astonishing fact of God's appearance in answer to a personal prayer. "I had found the testimony of James to be true, that a man who lacked wisdom might ask of God, and obtain, and not be upbraided."[51] That principle became the intellectual engine behind the movement, soon made into a maxim. "Man, being created but little below the angels, only wants to know for himself," proclaimed the first issue of the church newspaper, which Smith oversaw.[52] The Hidden God of Aquinas and Luther became, in the system of Joseph Smith, the Revealed and Revealer God.

How is it that thou canst weep?

—Evening and Morning Star, August 1832

10

Vulnerable God

◦⌐ ───────────────────────────────────

"WE ARE NEVER so defenceless against suffering as when we love," Freud writes.[1] In his *Great Divorce*, C. S. Lewis imagines a time when love will no more exact such a desperate price as now it does. In heaven, the Bright Lady queries her former lover, "Can you really have thought that love and joy would always be at the mercy of frowns and sighs?" Pity, she explains, could in this sense be used "for a kind of blackmailing. Those who choose misery can hold joy up to ransom, by pity."[2] What is true of lovers, Lewis writes, is also true of God. To imagine a God literally troubled or grieving for His wayward creatures would be monstrous, because it would make God hostage to the whims of those creatures. It would allow darkness to "infect" the light. To be susceptible to emotion is also to be vulnerable to external events and conditions, to be subject to change. For all those reasons, Christian orthodoxy has long insisted on a God who is not subject to the vagaries of emotion, and therefore neither vulnerable nor changeable. As the embodied God, Christ clearly experienced the full extent of human suffering, throughout His mortal life, and to infinite degree through the process of His atonement and death. God the Father, however, was held to be beyond the vicissitudes of pain—directly or indirectly.

The basic position was historically so uncontroversial, notes one scholar, that no challenge to the doctrine emerged between its defense in the third century by Gregorius Thaumaturgus (*Ad Theopompum*), and assorted critiques of the position in the late nineteenth century.[3] Another scholar agrees: "the idea that God cannot suffer, [was] accepted virtually as axiomatic in Christian theology from the early Greek Fathers until the nineteenth-century."⁴

Scholars have generally assumed the influence of Greek thought in the Christian doctrine of God's impassibility (literally the non-experience of emotion, but more generally understood in theology as God's imperturbability or lack of change in the face of emotion, pain, or suffering). "For the Greeks, God cannot be passive, He cannot be affected by something else, He cannot (in the broad sense) 'suffer' (*paschein*), because He is absolutely self-sufficient, self-determining and independent," writes one.⁵ Church fathers and Reformers alike emphasized God's imperviousness to the vicissitudes of human-like emotions. There were some exceptions, such as Origen, who asked, "The Father, too, himself, the God of the universe, 'patient and abounding in mercy' and compassionate, does He not in some way suffer? Or do you not know that when He directs human affairs He suffers human suffering?"⁶

Origen was swimming against the current. Augustine flatly rejected the notion of God's suffering ("who can sanely say that God is touched by any misery").⁷ Aquinas would later write with equal emphasis that even though we associate mercy with God, it is the "effect" of mercy, not the feeling or suffering ("affection of passion"), that is meant; this is because "to sorrow . . . over the misery of others belongs not to God."⁸ In this way, many theologians admitted that God could feel love or other emotions; but they did not affect him as passions, or perturbations of his perfect equanimity. The possibilities of his being affected by human suffering, in other words, were seen as constrained by the absoluteness of his perfections. By the Reformation, Luther quotes Erasmus as saying that "God is represented as being angry, in a fury, hating, grieving, pitying, repenting, neither of which, nevertheless, ever takes place in him." Luther agrees, saying "these things are no more than grammatical particulars, and certain figures of speech, with which even schoolboys are acquainted."⁹ It is not the possibility of God having emotion per se that causes theological complications; it is the association of passion with change. Susceptibility to shifting emotional conditions seems antithetical to God's absolute perfection. As Plato had reasoned, in terms and with a logic that Christian monotheism embraced, "whatever is . . . good . . . admits least of being changed by anything else." And since a god is in every way perfect, "if he's changed at all . . . it would have to be into something worse . . . for surely we can't say that a god is deficient."¹⁰

In 1563, building upon the Augsburg Confession, the Anglican Thirty-Nine Articles added "passions" to the attributes God did not possess, thus turning the inherited tradition of impassibility into an explicit creedal statement. "There is but one living and true God, everlasting without body, parts, or passions," affirmed the very first article. The Westminster Confession of Faith, approved by the English Parliament in 1648, established the basis of Reformed theology embraced by the Puritans and the Presbyterians. This document, which served as the basis of Baptist and Congregationalist theology as well, confirmed the impassibility of God and added the phrase "a most pure spirit, invisible" to the formula of the Articles.

When Methodists broke with the Anglican creed, Wesley's 1784 Articles of Religion affirmed belief in the "one living and true God, everlasting, without body or parts," omitting the "passions."[11] But the Methodists were clearly unsure about the passibility of God. The 1801 Book of Common Prayer restored the term "passions," and the American branch of Methodism (the Protestant Episcopal Church of America) also reaffirmed the precise, earlier language in its 1801 Articles of Religion. "There is but one living and true God, everlasting, without body, parts, *or passions.*"[12] However, the Methodist Book of Discipline of 1808 again omitted passions, describing "one living and true God, everlasting, without body or parts, of infinite power, wisdom, and goodness."[13] Then the *Methodist Magazine* reverted to the older form (God is "without body, parts or passions"),[14] and the formula persisted into the twentieth century. In 1831, the Presbyterian Daniel M'Calla still spoke for most Christians when he held in public debate "We never believed that God could suffer."[15] A few generations later, however, the doctrine had very few defenders.

As one scholar writes, "toward the end of the nineteenth century a sea of change began to occur within Christian theology such that at present many, if not most, Christian theologians hold as axiomatic that God *is* passible, that He does undergo emotional changes of states, and so can suffer."[16] Theologians refer to the surge in "theopaschism" (a suffering god) as a "revolution," a "structural shift in the Christian mind," and opine that "we have only begun to see where systematic theologies rooted in the suffering God might lead."[17]

In fact, writes another scholar, there is now "a remarkable consensus" behind the claim that "God suffers."[18] Indeed, nothing could be easier than to align pre-nineteenth-century formulations and contrast them with recent developments. Aristotle's "unmoved Mover," Augustine's "impassible God," and the creedal formulation of a God "without body, parts, or passions," stand in dramatic contrast to Abraham Heschel's invocation of God as "the Most Moved Mover," and recent book titles like "the God who risks," and "the Suffering God."[19]

Mormonism's break with the creedal God in this regard is emphatic; it embraces the suffering God without trying to salvage any remnants of the historical doctrine of impassibility. From the first months of the church's organization, Smith portrays not just a passible Jesus but a God the Father whose love causes him to suffer, grieve, and even weep in divine empathy with the human. The first such depiction comes with the Book of Mormon itself. In an allegory attributed to one Zenos, the chronicler Jacob relates the story of a servant who labors incessantly to preserve a dying olive tree. The servant's intercessory role, pleading to forestall the tree's burning, identifies him as the Christ; the Lord of the vineyard who sends him, watching the object of his care fall into ruin, is a clear representation of God the Father. Seeing the fruitlessness of his servant's efforts, "the Lord of the vineyard wept, and said unto the servant: What could I have done more for my vineyard?"[20]

Months after the Book of Mormon's publication, Smith further develops this motif of the weeping God. In mid-1830, he begins a revision of the Bible that results in a text that in significant ways is more doctrinally foundational than the Book of Mormon he had just published. Most prominent in this regard is an ascension narrative in which the prophet Enoch is taken into heaven and records his ensuing vision. He sees Satan's dominion over the earth and God's unanticipated response to a world veiled in darkness: "The God of heaven looked upon the residue of the people, and he wept; and Enoch bore record of it, saying: How is it that the heavens weep, and shed forth their tears as the rain upon the mountains? And Enoch said unto the Lord: How is it that thou canst weep?"[21]

The question here is not about the reasons behind God's tears. Enoch does not ask, Why do you weep? but, rather, How are your tears even possible, "seeing thou art holy, and from all eternity to all eternity?" Clearly, Enoch, who believed God to be "merciful and kind forever," did not expect such a being could be moved to the point of distress by the sins of his children. And so a third time he asks, "How is it thou canst weep?" The answer, it turns out, is that God is not exempt from emotional pain. As the Lord explains to Enoch, "unto thy brethren have I said, and also given commandment, that they should love one another, and that they should choose me, their Father; but behold, they are without affection, and they hate their own blood . . . and misery shall be their doom; and the whole heavens shall weep over them, even all the workmanship of mine hands; wherefore should not the heavens weep, seeing these shall suffer?"[22] In other words, it is not their wickedness but their "misery," not their disobedience but their "suffering," that elicits the God of Heaven's tears. This motif of the weeping God appears in other ancient traditions.[23] In one Talmudic text, the passage made famous by Handel's *Messiah* is markedly recast to suggest that God, burdened by the sins of the world, appeals to his people to console him, not the other way around ("Comfort me, comfort me, my people," the text reads.)[24]

The possibility of God's condition or mood or emotional state changing was reasonably deemed implausible since all change must be either for the worse or for the better. Neither kind of change could be posited of a perfect God. But Enoch's weeping God the Father is in no way immune to the vicissitudes entailed by his immersion within a web of human relationships, rather than position outside them. He participates in rather than transcends the ebb and flow of human history, human tragedy, and human grief. Furthermore, his distress at the predicament humans have brought upon themselves clearly evidences a disappointment, a regret, at the course of events—which can only mean they are not consistent with his will. We are here at almost the furthest remove imaginable from the God of Augustine and Calvin, who predestines even the inheritors of eternal damnation. Mormonism's God, by contrast, does not control events, predetermine outcomes, or effect a universe totally in harmony with his will.

It might be true, as Smith learned before the church was organized, that "the works, and the designs, and the purposes of God cannot be frustrated, neither can they come to naught."[25] But those works, designs, and purposes include the guarantee of our moral agency, not of our role in such plans. It would seem, in the Mormon conception, that it is not God's mastery over history, as much as his response to its ebb and flow, that defines his divinity. In his omniscience, he has made provision for the eventual triumph of his plans. But no actor in the script is indispensable. God reserves the right to appoint replacements for those who fail,[26] even as he can turn setbacks and afflictions to gain.[27]

If the heavens wept over Lucifer at his fall, as Smith declared,[28] it was plausible to insist that God's heart beat in sympathy with those of his creation who remain within the orbit of his divine influence. God's response to the manifold creatures by whom he is surrounded, the movement of his heart and will in the direction of those other beings, establishes the pattern of his divine activity. As Smith's Book of Mormon pronounced, "He doeth not anything save it be for the benefit of the world; for he loveth the world." And an 1830 text elaborated, "For this is my work and my glory, to bring to pass the immortality and eternal life of man."[29] For Mormons, it is God's freely made choice to inaugurate and sustain costly loving relationships that is at the very core of his divine identity.

That which is without body or parts is nothing.

—JOSEPH SMITH, 5 January 1841

11

Embodied God

⟋

SMITH FAMOUSLY REPORTED God as telling him Christian "creeds were an abomination," but what creeds was he referring to? Mormons tend to see the Protestant Reformation as preparatory to the Restoration, and a partial corrective to the Great Apostasy of the Roman Church.[1] But the creedal formulation most attacked by early Mormon writers, and defended by their antagonists, had nothing to do with the Athanasian or Nicene debates; it was the Protestant wording of the Anglican Thirty-Nine Articles (1563) that was the epicenter of controversy. Some of the older Christian creeds imply an ethereal, bodiless God, but the Articles made it explicit: "There is but one only living and true God, everlasting, without body, parts, or passions [*incorporeus, impartibilis, impassibilis*]."[2]

As we saw above, a God subject to passions would risk, by definition, being a God who experiences change. He would therefore exist in time rather than in eternity. And he would seem to come perilously close to the human in his nature and mode of existence. These considerations go a long way toward explaining what is at stake in the humanizing of Deity, and why writers have often referred to "the philosophical horror of anthropomorphism."[3] As Marcel Sarot has argued, "we are then confronted with the choice to give up passibilism, or to accept that God is, in a sense embodied."[4] Another theologian suggests that "every Christian doctrine must be recast in the light of the modern assumption that God's being is a suffering being," but the implications have only been tentatively explored.[5] It is in recognition of the slippery slope of passibilism—belief in God's susceptibility to emotion—that even

the advocates of a more feeling God were anxious to qualify just what kind of emotion God can feel, and how. If they did not read his emotions figuratively, they often
read them in a way that did not require bodily experience.

In other words, a human-like susceptibility to the passions is questionable enough;
an actual bodily nature, which passions can suggest, seems self-evidently beyond the
pale. Some few theologians, however, embrace the full consequences of their openness to passibility. For them:

> passibility is closely connected to corporeality, and . . . if God is passible, . . . he
> should be corporeal as well. . . . Christian theology does not exclude in advance
> all possible forms of divine embodiment, and . . . it seems possible to develop a
> theory of divine corporeality that both admits divine passibility and is com-
> patible with the basic tenets of Christian theology. It cannot be denied that
> the position arrived at this way is rather uncommon.[6]

Extremely uncommon would be more accurate, though in addition to his own,
Marcel Sarot surveys three recent theories of divine embodiment, those of Charles
Hartshorne, Luco van den Brom, and Grace Jantzen.[7] Another scholar notes that
"the pendulum has swung so far away from the invisibility of the Hebraic portrait of
God that some scholars take God's body for granted," and cites Daniel Boyarin and
Benjamin Sommer as examples.[8] Nevertheless, anthropomorphism is one of the
most perennial dangers to orthodoxy against which the Christian church has historically guarded itself. Trinitarian thought has long used the terms "persons" to
refer to the members of the godhead. But as the Puritan John Norton warned, "persons" was a similitude and should not mislead Christians by its erroneous connotations.[9] How the ancients understood the personhood of God is not altogether clear.
It is common for moderns to say, with inordinate confidence, that "religious discourse was not intended to be understood literally" by premoderns.[10] The Bible itself
sends mixed messages on the subject. Numerous passages affirm an essential physical likeness between God and humankind; Seth's similitude to Adam parallels
Adam's to God; Israelites see God's feet; Moses sees his back; he is "seen face to face"
by his people, and so on.[11] At the same time, as the *Encyclopedia Judaica* notes, "both
personifications of the deity as well as attempts to avoid them are found side by side
in all parts of the bible."[12] Some exponents of the generally accepted "documentary
hypothesis" (which attributes the Torah or first five books of the Old Testament to
four authors or groups of authors) denominate as "H" a fifth author, one who "reper-
sonalizes [God], deliberately reintroducing anthropomorphism."[13]

Judaism's "basic opposition" to those verses that emphasize his corporeality is
based on the Decalogue, and its condemnation of images based on any creaturely

likeness. Belief in God's "absolute transcendence" is simply "axiomatic" in Jewish thought.[14] Noting the several strains of anthropomorphic thought in the Bible, some historians write that "over the course of its history, Israelite religion reduced anthropomorphic depictions of Yahweh."[15] The Genesis account of man's creation "in the image and likeness of God," according to some scholars, already represents a movement away from an older, even more anthropocentric tradition. (In Genesis, for instance, no actual description of the divine is given.[16])

In the New Testament, Jesus himself affirms that "God is spirit,"[17] and the omnipresence and omnipotence of God seem too antithetical to flesh and bones to admit any debate on the point. As the *Catholic Encyclopedia* avers, "this tendency [toward anthropomorphism] is strongly manifested in primitive heathen religions."[18] However, that characterization overlooks a more complicated history of the idea in the first Christian centuries. Tertullian (ca. 160–225), for example, referred to God's body (*corpore*), imputing to it a distinct materiality and "even a certain tangibility."[19] In fact, as David Paulsen has convincingly demonstrated, and theologian Stephen Webb acknowledges, "divine embodiment would have been part of the theological mainstream prior to Origen and Augustine."[20] The idea reappeared with the Audians, a Christian sect in the fourth century who espoused the human form of God, as did others at the turn of the fifth. In response, Cyril of Alexandria wrote that "God cannot be embodied or exist in any bodily form . . . Deity is without dimensions or configurations."[21] Since the Middle Ages, however, and like the Trinity itself, God's non-bodily and non-material nature was essentially a settled question throughout Christian history.

By the close of the eighteenth century, enough hints of anthropomorphism were emerging in religious discourse that clerics were suddenly taking greater pains to preempt the imputation of human attributes, including bodily form, to the Deity. In the eighteenth century, an Anglican writer was so repelled by "the old Heresie of the Anthropomorphites" that he condemned even the visual representation of God ("how shall I excuse the Papists, who have God the Father represented, as an old Man in their Churches as I have with Horror seen and beheld!"[22]). A few years earlier, Stephen Charnock had agreed that any corporeal representations of God were "a disgrace to His nature" and found it necessary to spend two chapters in his *Several Discourses Upon the Existence and Attributes of God* (1682) refuting a God of body or parts.[23]

The precautions were timely. John Hargrove, in 1800, unleashed his challenge to orthodoxy, asking, "if the Divine being is divisible, Is He not material? If He has NO body, how can He be substantial? and, if He has no PARTS, how can He BE or EXIST, at all? What difference can there be between saying God has NO BODY; and flatly declaring that He is NO-BODY? . . . and therefore, I cannot perceive wherein this doctrine of God's having no body differs from ATHEISM."²⁴ (Parley Pratt makes the identical charge in 1845.²⁵) The allegation of atheism may seem ironic, given that the target of the label are the mainstream believers in God. However, this irony is precisely the point intended by orthodoxy's critics and will become common in nineteenth-century debates on the subject.

By 1829, Hargrove was joined by William Kinkade, an independently minded ex-Presbyterian:

> The Presbyterian confession of faith says, "God is without body, parts, or passions." In my view this is equal to Atheism; because if we divest him of these, there is nothing left that would constitute being, or that would be perceptible to the mind. Ears, hands, and eyes are parts of an intelligent ruler, and if God has none of these, He cannot hear, handle, nor see us. If He is without passions, He has no mercy, love, nor anger, and therefore cannot forgive, us, love us, nor be angry with us, because if He has not these passions, He cannot exercise them. If it were possible for the divine Being to exist without body, parts, or passions, He would be to us neither desirable, dreadful, nor useful.²⁶

Besides, he argues, "the Bible represents God as a real person. It . . . ascribes to him nearly all the members of the human body."²⁷

As the next decade opened, the purported materiality of God became a debating point between contending clergy. In 1831, a celebrated debate took place between Daniel M'Calla, a Presbyterian defender of the Trinity, and William Lane, a Universalist of the "Christian Connexion." Most of the audience of course supported M'Calla, who began with a curious history of the "Christians," characterizing those Restorationists originating with Barton Stone and the Alexanders as "worshippers of a material God, having form, eyes, ears, hands, and feet."²⁸ M'Calla accused Lane of assenting to the material God of the Unitarians ("described by Kinkade [and Joseph] Priestly"). Lane replies that his beliefs were personal conclusions, not Unitarian or "materialist." Some observers believed that in this debate, Lane was driven "to the acknowledgment that God the Father was a *material* being, and then after receiving the awful castigation which such a sentiment deserves, . . . he denied that he said so, and though he described God as a being who has 'a real body and parts, a location, a centre and a circumference,' yet he would deny him to be material."²⁹

The confusion and seeming self-contradictions of Lane's position are terribly important, pointing as they do to the difficulties and complications resulting from a vocabulary not thoroughly adequate to the kinds of distinctions some religious thinkers were attempting to draw in this era. To most people, *material*, *physical*, *corporeal*, and *bodily* seem safely interchangeable terms. Lane, like Kinkade, could well have believed he was self-consistent in denying a God who filled infinite space, even while maintaining that he was not a materialist, and that God was "a Spiritual Being."[30] Lane's quandary foreshadows the many misreadings of Joseph Smith's position by modern scholars who see contradictions and abrupt change rather than ambiguity and semantic inadequacy at work. Smith, too, struggled for an adequate vocabulary as he worked to develop a conception of God, one that rejected inchoateness and ineffability while stopping short of crude human materiality.

Several contemporaries were likewise affirming a bodily God while hedging on the question of what that implied by way of materiality. Reverend H. Mattison associated such beliefs with the Campbellites, Hicksites, New Lights, Universalists, and Mormons.[31] In addition to Kinkade and Jabez Chadwick, who said he was "prepared to defend" the materialist position, Mattison quotes one L. Perry ("I believe He is a body") and G. Fancher ("God has a body, eyes, ear, hand, feet, &c., just as we have") as partaking of the heresy.

Most of the early Unitarians in the controversy were emphasizing the materiality of the incarnate Christ, not the Father. They were nonetheless an important link to early Mormon thought about the nature of God. From its inception, as William Channing acknowledged in his historic sermon on the movement, American Unitarianism harbored "a difference of opinion . . . among us in regard to an interesting part of Christ's mediation; I mean, in regard to the precise influence of his death on our forgiveness."[32] Most Unitarians, in other words, rejected orthodox versions of Christ's role as Savior and Mediator. Even so, while emphasizing Christ's physical distinctness from God, many Unitarians nonetheless emphasized his divinity, thus effectively espousing two separate deities (in a move that anticipated the social trinity of Mormonism). Chadwick, for instance, one of the better known anti-Trinitarians, began as a Baptist, but came to believe that Jesus Christ was "next in dignity to the Father, but unquestionably inferior and dependent," even if he was "the Son of God, begotten or created before all worlds."[33] Lane similarly insisted that Jesus was "a divine person."[34]

Clues to Joseph Smith's thinking about the Trinity and divine materiality, or at least divine embodiment, emerge even prior to 1830. If his first vision did plant the seeds of God and Christ's corporeal distinctness, the Book of Mormon may have confirmed the view. The climactic event in that scripture occurs when a physically embodied, post-ascension Christ appears to vast multitudes among the ancient Americans.[35] More strikingly, in his translation of the Book of Mormon, Smith depicts a visitation of the pre-mortal Christ to the prophet Ether. In that scene, Christ emphasizes the corporeal nature of his pre-mortal self. "Seest thou that ye are created after mine own image? . . . Behold, this body, which ye now behold, is the body of my spirit; and man have I created after the body of my spirit."[36] (Smith's contemporary William Kinkade likewise taught that "Jesus Christ in His pre-existent state . . . has always been in the shape of a man."[37]) Such a pre-mortal bodily spirit would seem to challenge traditional Trinitarian conceptions, by extending the embodied form of Christ backward in time. Smith's language is also significant for bringing together seemingly antithetical terms: a body, but a body made out of spirit.

Shortly thereafter, in late November 1830, Smith was emending the creation account in Genesis, during his work on the Bible's "retranslation." He inserted a crucial clarification to Genesis 5:1–2: "In the day that God created man, in the likeness of God made he him; in the image *of his own body*, male and female, created he them" (emphasis added).[38] As David Paulsen notes, "evidently, Joseph added the clarifying phrase, 'of his own body,' to distinguish his understanding of the text from any incorporealist construction. From Joseph's revision of these biblical texts, it appears clear that in 1830 he understood that both the Father and Son are embodied and that man's body was made in their image."[39] In 1833, Smith suggested he had more in mind than a spiritual body in the case of the Deity. After indicating the "elements" are the counterpart of spirit, and pronouncing those elements to be eternal, he declared that "the elements are the tabernacle of God."[40]

It is certainly the case that years before the Nauvoo era, Smith's followers were already focusing on Christianity's bodiless God as a hallmark of its apostate condition. Warren Cowdery criticized the Methodists for believing in a deity "without body or parts" in an 1836 church article.[41] While Cowdery wrote in a Mormon periodical for a Mormon audience, others seem to have been listening; in that same year, a Presbyterian minister from Kirtland wrote that Mormons believed in a "material being, composed of body and parts."[42] A body would naturally seem to imply a physical body, but it was some time before Mormons clarified exactly what they meant by an embodied God. The 1834 Lectures on Faith, for example, specify the Son as being a "personage of tabernacle," but the Father as being "a personage of spirit."[43] He was still identified in those terms in an 1841 Mormon periodical.[44]

Even Parley Pratt, most prolific at theological exposition in these years, appears to have been uncertain of the terminological distinctions. In 1838, he repeated Cowdery's criticism of other Christians for belief in "a God without body or parts." Why worship a God, he wondered, "who has no ears, mouth, nor eyes," adding with humorous sarcasm, "that we do not love, serve, nor fear your God; and if He has been blasphemed, let him speak and plead his own cause: but this He cannot do, seeing He has no mouth. And how He ever revealed His choice of La Roy Sunderland, as a 'Watchman' for His Zion, I am at a loss to determine." On the other hand, Mormons, he affirmed without apology, "worship a God, who has both body and parts; who has eyes, mouth, and ears, and who speaks when He pleases."[45]

However, when Mormons were criticized in 1840 by William Hewitt for believing in a God in human form rather than a God of spirit, Pratt insisted Hewitt was jumping to unwarranted conclusions. A spirit, Pratt replied, does indeed have "eyes, mouth, ears, &c." Nevertheless, a divine body is "not composed of such gross materials as flesh and bones."[46] Pratt may have sincerely believed that was the Mormon position, since it would be another year before Smith would state in public that "There is no other God in heaven but that God who has flesh and bones."[47] Weeks later, Smith repeated the idea that "the Son Had a Tabernicle & so h[a]d the father."[48] The move from ascribing a tabernacle only to the Son in 1834, to making the Father like him in that regard by 1841, apparently came with Smith's understanding that a tabernacle need not imply flesh and blood.

This defining step in the refinement of Mormon conceptions of a corporeal God was the distinction between such a body of flesh and blood, which is mortal and human, and a glorified body of flesh and bones, which is immortal and divine. Flesh and blood cannot inherit the kingdom of heaven, Smith quoted Paul as saying, because "blood is the part of the body that causes corruption." In God, by contrast, as in resurrected humans, blood is replaced by "the Spirit of god flowing in the vains."[49] The clarification came with Smith's 1843 pronouncement, later canonized, declaring the Father and Son both to have "a body of flesh and bones as tangible as man's."[50] The distinction between spirit or blood coursing through a divine body of flesh may be a theologically esoteric point, but it reconciled what had appeared to be contradictions in the tangled development of Mormon ideas about God's embodiment.

OMNIPOTENCE, OMNIPRESENCE, OMNISCIENCE

Among the many reasons for orthodoxy's "horror of anthropomorphism" is the belief that a bodily conception of God threatens to diminish God, by virtue of its inherent materiality and finitude. As we saw with Mormon cosmology generally, Smith denied any necessary inferiority attached to material existence. In fact, he emphatically privileged materiality *above* merely spiritual existence. He insisted on the general principle that "they who have tabernacles have power over those who have not."[51] It is not clear, in Mormon thought, why this is so. Brigham Young taught in reference to embodiment that "attributes can be made manifest only through an organized personage. All attributes are couched in and are the results of organized existence."[52] By the catchall "attributes," Young meant both the physical and mental powers familiar to us as mortals, and the virtues of divine excellence, like wisdom, intelligence, and honor.[53] Not only power and attributes are dependent upon corporeality, in Mormon thought, but eternal happiness is as well. Only "spirit and element, inseparably connected, receive a fullness of joy," Smith pronounced in 1833.[54] Pratt writes in his "Materialism" essay that "the spirits and bodies of men are of equal importance and destined to form an eternal and inseparable union with each other."[55]

Another way in which Mormonism circumvents traditional objections to anthropomorphism is by contracting the "omnis" of divinity, rather than expanding the virtues of the bodily. Mormons effectively reinterpret the three infinites of orthodox theism: omnipresence, omnipotence, and omniscience. Influential writer Orson Spencer, in his Letter Eight, "The True and Living God," 13 September 1847, argues that God is a corporeal, anthropomorphic being, whose "holy dwelling place, is literal, local, real and to its occupants, it is visible and tangible."[56] God's omnipresence is accomplished through the unembodied Spirit of God, or Holy Ghost. As John Jaques's catechism, a phenomenally popular and respected compendium of Mormon doctrine in the early Utah period, rehearsed: "Q. If God is a person, how can He be everywhere present? A. His person cannot be in more than one place at the same time, but He is everywhere present by His Holy Spirit."[57] God's omnipresence, in other words, is operative through the agency of the Holy Ghost (or the Light of Christ, in more contemporary Mormon discourse; see chapter 15).

As for God's omnipotence, Mormon leaders have differed over the years as to the implications of that term. Hyrum, Joseph's brother and church patriarch, insisted that "Our Savior is competent to save all from death and hell. . . . I would not serve a God that had not all wisdom and power."[58] A conservative strain of thinking has followed that trajectory, arguing that God is perfect in the conventional sense, and progresses only in the sense of adding to his creations, not in any sense of personal evolution in knowledge or power. In the twentieth-century church, Joseph Fielding Smith and apostle Bruce McConkie were adamant in condemning as heresy any divergence from Hyrum Smith's position. B. H. Roberts intended to include in the 1912 official church history he edited Smith's King Follett Discourse, which defined God as a glorified, exalted human. But as we noted above, he was overruled, the sermon excised, and not reinserted until 1950.[59] Brigham Young, on the other hand, explicitly read Joseph Smith's King Follett sermon to mean that in the sphere of "knowledge and power . . . God . . . is progressing eternally."[60] Whether growth in dominions and creations and posterity constitutes advancement or progress may be little more than a semantic question. However, it is clear that given God's relational nature, and his infinitely creative capacity and activity, he is a being whose orbit of relationships and mode of existence are therefore, in the Mormon conception, ever expanding, dynamic, and open.

The crucial role of choice or agency in the Mormon view of God's nature further complicates the question of his omnipotence. Positing the independent existence of eternal law suggests that God may be divinely perfect as a consequence of his deliberate, willful embrace of, and compliance with, those laws. Some theologians have faulted Mormonism for believing in a God who is good by choice—that is, by conformity with law rather than by nature.[61] Some Mormon thinkers have responded that a God who is good by nature rather than choice cannot deserve our praise, since he cannot act otherwise than according to that nature.[62] In addition, it is hard to see how terms such as "love" or "trust" could define a relationship to such a deity. As Blake Ostler has argued, "trust presupposes the ability to refrain from doing as trusted."[63] (We rely on the law of gravity to function consistently; we trust friends and spouses to be faithful.) Only a God who *chooses* to love us and honor his promises can elicit trust and love in return.

Such a deity would have the option and possibility of choosing contrary to moral goodness, and that is hardly compatible with conventional ideas of God. It is true that a God who exists independently of moral absolutes, who exists in willful conformity with them rather than as their source, may seem too unstable an entity to be a source of absolute trust and faith. Most Mormons have clearly chosen to value choice and moral freedom—even in the divine—over necessary attributes or nature. To the objection that such a view of deity risks the logical possibility of a fallible God incapable of guaranteeing his promises, one Mormon philosopher responds that he trusts God "because He's told us that he can. My faith in God is grounded in His self-disclosures, not in logical inferences from philosophically constructed premises."[64]

As for God's omniscience, Mormonism provides no clear dogma. For centuries, the term has meant to most Christians that God's knowledge encompasses all that was, all that is, and all that yet will be. If, in fact, God exists outside of human categories of space and of time, then the future is indeed eternally present to him. It is not that he *fore*sees the future; he sees the future as he does the present. The seeming conflict between an all-knowing God and the free actions of humanity is one of theology's oldest dilemmas.[65] If God knows you will eat roast beef tomorrow, the argument goes, then how can you be free to eat fish, in contravention of God's certain knowledge? Boethius replied to this question in the sixth century. First, he said such fatalism was to mistake cause and consequence. God knows what will happen because it will happen; it doesn't happen because God foreknows it. Explained in different terms, Boethius argues that existing *outside* time, God's foreknowledge cannot be dependent on what happens *in* time; so neither can his knowledge from *outside* time predetermine what happens *in* time.[66] God's foreknowledge, he added, does not come from the necessary unfolding of events. "Just as knowledge of things in the present conveys no necessity on them as they happen, so the foreknowledge of future things places no necessity on them to make them come about."[67]

Following in Boethius's wake, most Christian theologians have agreed that God's omniscience and free will are reconcilable—even if only with difficulty. And such omniscience has traditionally been taken to include future events of every sort. So Aquinas, for instance, writes that God knows the future not just based on causal inevitability; "God sees all things in His eternity, which . . . embraces all time." And by "all things" he means "even casual and chance events" of the future.[68] In the words of one scholar, "the question is not *whether*, on a Christian view, God has knowledge (timelessly or otherwise) of future events, but merely *how* he has such knowledge."[69] Some exceptions to this view exist, however, calling into question the scope and meaning of omniscience. In the eighteenth century, English poet Christopher Smart wrote a lyric celebration of God's omniscience, praising his "wondrous, uncircumscribed" knowledge that encompassed the past, present, and future of the poet's entire soul: "all her future workings, every thought, and every faint idea yet unform'd."[70] A few decades later, Scottish philosopher and poet Thomas Brown hinted at an alternative view when he defined omniscience as God's "knowing every relation of every thing *existing*" (my emphasis).[71]

This is the tack taken by some philosophers of religion. As W. S. Anglin puts the case, one could define God's perfect knowledge this way: "if any proposition is true, then God knows it is true." Not being yet determined, one might argue, any statement about the future is not a true proposition and therefore not part of God's perfect knowledge.[72] For most theists, such a view produces a God too limited to serve as the object of complete confidence. But limited omniscience does not preclude God's envisioning and anticipating every possible contingency, only the particular form every human decision will take.

Smith originally used conventional categories of timelessness with regard to God; in the winter of 1834–35, he employed (or countenanced) traditional theological language in the second of the Lectures on Faith, teaching that God was omniscient, as well as omnipotent and omnipresent (he dwells in an eternal present).[73] As a result God would be omniscient in conventional ways—that is, knowing past, present, and future without hindrance. Smith's personal experience translating the Book of Mormon must have confirmed to him God's foreknowledge of the future down to the most minute details. After losing the first 116 pages of his translation, Smith discovered that the ancient American prophet Nephi had made provision for just such an event. Nephi recorded on the gold plates a second account of his history according to God's command, "for a wise purpose in him, which purpose I know not."[74] Smith apparently saw the providential preparation for his own misstep twenty-five hundred years later as a clear sign of an omniscience that included future actions.[75]

After his 1830s employment of the term, *omniscience* drops from Smith's vocabulary (if it was *his* term in the Lectures on Faith) and is absent from Young's. At the same time, Smith was already defining eternity as endless temporality, not as atemporality. Eternity was simply time "without beginning of days or end of years," or as he emphasized later, "Eternity means that which is without beginning or end."[76] As

Young would put it, "we are all in eternity, and out of it we can never get, it is bound-less, without beginning or end, and we have never been out of it. Time is a certain portion of eternity allotted to the existence of these mortal bodies."[77]

As a result, in Mormon thought God comes very early to be firmly situated within the same ontological *and* temporal realms as the human. Instead of dwelling outside of space and time, he inhabits the same universe of materiality and temporality as we do. The contrast with most Christian thought could not be more stark.[78] As the great Anglican theologian Austin Farrer wrote, "Deity . . . is defined as Timeless Life, though with us all life is temporal process, and cannot be imagined otherwise, and all that is timeless is lifeless abstraction and cannot be imagined otherwise."[79] Believing God to be a part of the temporal universe, as Mormons do, has clear impli-cations for the meaning of his omniscience. Young took Smith's teachings to mean that if God exists in and through time, his knowledge must grow in some sense. In one of his many disputes with Orson Pratt, Young condemned Pratt's position that "the Father and Son do not progress in knowledge and wisdom because they already know all things past, present and to come."[80] In a sermon, Young claimed that "there never will be a time to all eternity when all the God[s] of Eternity will cease advanc-ing in power knowledge experience & Glory for if this was the case Eternity would cease to be & the glory of God would come to an End but all of celestial beings will continue to advance in knowledge & power worlds without end."[81]

Pertaining to the scope of his knowledge in particular, a fraught issue is the ques-tion of whether God's knowledge encompasses the present *and future* of all God's creations (or whether his children, as independent agents, are even part of his "cre-ations"), on the one hand; or whether the reality of human agency means the future is undetermined and therefore unknowable even to God, on the other. As early as 1855, a Mormon catechism for children carefully hedges the question:

"1. Q. Does God know all things *pertaining to the workmanship of His hands?* [my emphasis]

A. Yea. Nothing escapes His knowledge," the text declares, quoting a scripture with an implicit caveat, "Known unto God *are all His works*, from the begin-ning of the world [my emphasis]."[82]

B. H. Roberts also equivocated on this question. In one context, he held that the Bible made "foreknowledge of future events . . . an incommunicable attribute of Je-hovah."[83] In his summative work, however, he held that God was "not . . . omniscient up to the point that further progress in knowledge is impossible to him; but that all the knowledge that is, all that exists, God knows. All that shall be He will know. . . .

Much more is yet to be. God will know it as it 'becomes' or unfolds."[84] James Talmage recognized the challenge omniscience could present to agency, but dismissed it. He wrote in 1915 that "God's foreknowledge as to what *would be* under any given conditions is [not] a determining cause that such *must be*."[85] Later he returned to the theme: "Foreknowledge [is] not a determining cause," he maintained. "He, with His omniscience, knows what is to come to individuals and nations." But it is "most irrational and illogical" to take this as warrant for denying personal accountability.[86]

The *Encyclopedia of Mormonism* states that "Latter-day Saints differ among themselves in their understanding of the nature of God's knowledge. Some have thought that God increases endlessly in knowledge as well as in glory and dominion. Others hold to the more traditional view that God's knowledge, including the foreknowledge of future free contingencies, is complete."[87] But it is hard to find in Mormon writings either any apostolic pronouncement that limits God's knowledge of the future or the opinion that divine omniscience would be an impediment to free will. Smith denied the assumption that God's omniscience must condition at least a limited predestination. He asserted simply, "I believe that God foreknew everything, but did not foreordain everything; I deny that foreordain and foreknow is the same thing."[88]

A God who is absolute and transcendent, who stands outside the flow of time and is the source of all reality, represents a severe challenge to the doctrine of free will. Such a God would present us, as Sterling McMurrin argues, with an "immutable reality." In this view, a God who is outside the flow of time would inhabit a perspective, a privileged perspective, from which the future is already a given—fixed and immutable. By placing God within history, as a part of the ongoing processes of the universe, and limited to knowledge of the present and past, McMurrin thinks Mormonism avoids this predicament. "The ultimate immutability of reality is thereby denied . . . and human freedom take[s] on new meaning, for the future is real and unique, not merely from the perspective of men, but as well from the perspective of God."[89]

It may be the case, as another Mormon philosopher argues, that the language of omnipotence, omnipresence, and omniscience is an inappropriate infiltration of orthodox Christian vocabulary into Mormonism: "Mormons should consistently renounce such attributes or at least make very clear the distinction between Mormon usage and Catholic-Protestant usage."[90] And indeed, Smith's early use of those terms (if indeed it was his language), as was occasionally the case with Smith's religious vocabulary, was likely more an instance of uncritical cultural absorption than studied theological reflection. In any event, there is available in Mormonism a plausible way to accommodate all three "omnis": God has all the power there is, consistent with his respect for free will and the laws of self-contradiction; God is everywhere present through the medium of the Light of Christ; and God is possessed of all the knowledge there is.

If Mormon theism is nonetheless unconventional in its anthropomorphic God, it does find some modern parallels in the finitism some would read there. William James also famously proposed a religious paradigm that avoided the materialist/supernaturalist alternatives. Scientific naturalism is inadequate, he concludes, because "there are resources in us that naturalism with its literal and legal virtues never recks of, possibilities that take our breath away, of another kind of happiness and power ... and these seem to show a wider world than either physics or philistines can imagine."[91] On the other hand, he argues, the problems with positing a God equivalent to the Absolute is utterly untenable. (Among other problems, satisfying as the concept of the Absolute is, it satisfies only intellectual rationality. It does not successfully address what he labels aesthetic or moral rationality.) The only solution, James finds, would be a God who is in some sense finite—that is, a God who is in the universe and subject to its laws. He believes, in accordance with biblical theism but at variance with creedal Christianity, that it would be hard to "conceive of anything more different from the absolute than the God, say, of David or of Isaiah. *That* God is an essentially finite being *in* the cosmos, not with the cosmos in him. . . . If it should prove probable that the absolute does not exist, it will not follow in the slightest degree that a God like that of David, Isaiah, or Jesus may not exist, or may not be the most important existence in the universe for us to acknowledge."[92]

Mormons are in agreement with James, but most avoid the language of finitism out of fear of misunderstanding. One prominent LDS religious scholar, for example, insists that "Evangelicals are convinced, wrongly, that Latter-day Saints believe in a finite, limited or changeable god, even though that notion is repugnant to us."[93] The simple truth is, Mormons are divided on more than the question of language. That God has a body of finite dimensions; occupies space, rejoices and weeps; and adds continually to his posterity and creations, while bringing about human salvation subject to the constraints of moral agency, elicits no disagreement. Whether these conditions add up to a finite, limited God who is "progressing" is still a subject of debate.

Mormons and William James are of course not the only ones to reconceive the Divine in ways that break with conventional omnipotence. In the mid-twentieth century, Alfred North Whitehead and then Charles Hartshorne argued that God is in some sense involved in temporal processes, and therefore mutable and passible. Mormons would not embrace their entire agenda, but certainly would affirm Whitehead's claim that God "does not create the world [in the sense of *ex nihilo*], He saves it; or, more accurately, He is the poet of the world, with tender patience leading it by his vision of truth, beauty, and goodness."[94]

Many theologians subsequently aligned themselves with this "process theology." Sterling McMurrin wrote in 1965 that "finitistic theology has lost much of its attractiveness,"[95] but his obituary was premature. He may be right that "the word 'finite' stirs nothing in the soul of the worshipper,"[96] but then a God without body, parts, or passions, who exists outside of human time, does not exactly thrill the heart, either. Process theology continues to win adherents, and in the 1980s a new form of finitism emerged, with many of its propositions overlapping with Mormon positions. Advocates of "Open Theism" argued that the future is not yet determined and cannot therefore be an object of divine knowledge. God, they held, is passible in the sense of being susceptible to influence through human prayers and actions.[97]

Ultimately, Mormon theism can be almost unrecognizable to other Christians because it might be said to begin with what the philosopher Thomas Nagel calls the datum of the human soul in a universe where a transcendent God is not an a priori condition.[98] Reversing the usual sequence, Mormonism makes the spirit prior to the world, co-eternal with God. The human soul is, in this case, not the emanation, not the temporal or logical consequence of a creator God. It is the starting point for the development of a cosmology, but it also—via Joseph Smith's King Follett Discourse—creates a point of departure for the most radical conjectures about the nature of God.

Certainly Joseph Smith's most startling theology concerned the apparent oxymoron of an eternal God's origin. And it is doubtless this speculation that has occasionally caused LDS unease with the King Follett Discourse. Or with its most radical and startling proposition: "He once was *a* man like one of us and . . . God Himself, the Father of us all, once dwelled on an earth the same as Jesus Christ himself did in the flesh." In a midrash-like gloss, Smith had Christ declare:

> I saw the Father work out His kingdom with fear and trembling and I am doing the same, *too*. When I get my kingdom, I will give it to the Father and it will add to and exalt His glory. He will take a higher exaltation and I will take His place and I am also exalted, so that He obtains kingdom rolling upon kingdom. . . . So that Jesus treads in His tracks as He had gone before and then inherits what God did before.[99]

Smith took the idea a step further in his last recorded sermon on the "plurality of gods." Therein he referred to "a God above the Fa[the]r of our L[or]d J[esus] C[hrist]," referencing the Revelator's allusion, in the King James rendering, to "God and his Father." "We shall see as we are seen," he continued, "& be as God—& he as the God of his Fa[the]r."[100] Smith did not extrapolate from the KJV reference, but claimed his insight derived from the Abrahamic text he began to translate back in 1835, wherein he learned that whenever two spirits exist, "there shall be another more intelligent than they."[101] Intelligences exist one above anot[he]r," he glossed that passage, "that there is no end of it."[102]

Smith had hinted at this conception of Deity in an 1841 sermon, where he said, without elaboration, that "God the father took life unto himself precisely as Jesus did."[103] Even earlier, in 1840, future LDS prophet Lorenzo Snow learned—by a personal revelation he said—that "as man now is, God once was. As God now is, man may be."[104] The second part of that couplet, Smith had himself suggested without comment in 1832, when he said heirs of salvation would be "gods, even the sons of God."[105] Given Snow's understanding that humans may progress to become gods, Snow may have found the couplet to be a reasonable inference. But it is clear that in this case, as in so many others, Smith's Nauvoo theology was elaboration of rather than rupture with his earliest theology.[106]

Most Mormons have taken the Snow formulation to mean that the Father, like mortals who are exalted, began as a man but acquired his divinity after a process akin to earth embodiment and probation. Orson Pratt's reading was typical: Joseph Smith challenged the Christian fundamental "that God the Eternal Father, whom we worship . . . was always a self-existing, eternal being from all eternity, that He had no beginning as a personage."[107] And it is this reading that gives the idea its blasphemous edge, reducing God to the status of successful earth pupil. However, as Christ was fully divine before his incarnation, some Mormon writers have found it more reasonable to take Smith to mean that the Father, also, was God before, not after, he took upon himself physically incarnate form at some point in his eternal existence. He may have experienced mortality, in other words, but not as a step toward divinity—which he always possessed.[108] But that is not the way Smith or his successors seem to have understood the principle. Smith did not just claim that God was once embodied, but that this phase was part of the story of "how God came to be God," for we have falsely "imagined" that he was "God from the beginning of all eternity."[109]

The Mormon theologian who pursued Smith's King Follett ideas most doggedly was Orson Pratt. "We are compelled to believe," he wrote, that the Father, Son, and Holy Ghost "must have had a beginning, for inasmuch as they indicate a design there must have been an anterior designer—this designer must have been a self-moving intelligent substance capable of organizing itself into one or more most glorious personages."[110]

In 1915, the apostle John Widtsoe, a scientist and leading church intellectual, was charged with writing church manuals. One result was his attempt to demonstrate that Smith's teachings "were in full harmony with the most advanced scientific thought, and that he anticipated the world of science in the statement of fundamental facts and theories of physics, chemistry, astronomy and biology."[111] So, like Pratt, Widtsoe emphasized the scientific appeal of Smith's materialism and the logical—if not religious—appeal of an evolved God: "It is only logical to believe that a progressive God has not always possessed His present position," he wrote.[112] "By the persistent efforts of will, His recognition of universal laws became greater until he attained at last a conquest over the universe, which to our finite understanding seems absolutely complete. We may be certain that, through self-effort, the inherent and innate powers of God have been developed to a God-like degree. Thus He has become God."[113]

Joseph F. Smith's First Counselor, Anthon H. Lund, expressed some unease on the point. He objected to this idea of "the origin of God, which [Widtsoe] makes an evolution from intelligences and being superior to the others He became God." He added, "I do not like to think of a time when there was no God."[114] But even Lund had been a signatory to the First Presidency statement declaring God "an exalted man, perfected, enthroned, and supreme."[115] In other words, he may have been objecting not to the idea that the God we worship was once man but to the suggestion of a time before *any* God presided over the universe.

James Talmage defended Smith's view of God as a perfected man by recourse to a New Testament epithet for Christ. Bypassing traditional interpretations of the expression, and its extensive use by Ezekiel, in *Jesus the Christ* Talmage argued that the significance of Jesus's self-identification as "The Son of Man" "lies in the fact that He knew His Father to be the one and only supremely exalted Man." Therefore, the title was "applicable to Himself alone, He was and is the Son of the 'Man of Holiness,' Elohim."[116] In a sermon, Talmage elaborated his argument with the point that Christ's own words (which Smith had quoted to similar effect) revealed that he did only what he had seen his father do. Talmage concluded: "it necessarily follows that the Eternal Father once passed through experiences analogous to those which His Son, the Lord Jesus, afterward passed through." He "had experiences incident to the mortal state."[117] The text was approved, but after delivery as a sermon it was reprinted as a pamphlet with important omissions. Charles Penrose of the First Presidency spoke for many when he warned, "the widespread publicity of this doctrine would cause difficulty to elders in the field, who . . . would be confronted with the charge that we as a people worship a man."[118]

Current LDS reticence on the doctrine seems a product of both feared misunderstanding and some uncertainty. It is not just that emphasizing such a teaching ill serves the needs of an evangelizing church; Mormon prayer, worship, and references to Deity are for all practical purposes thoroughly and genuinely conventional. Mormons worship a being they recognize, regardless of speculations regarding his origin, as "the Most High God," "the supreme Governor of the universe" and "the Father of mankind."[119] Hence Church President Gordon B. Hinckley's words on the subject when queried in a *Time* magazine interview, "Is this the teaching of the church today, that God the Father was once a man like we are?" He answered, "I don't know that we teach it. I don't know that we emphasize it."[120] Similarly, he was asked by the *San Francisco Chronicle*, "Don't Mormons believe that God was once a man?" He responded, "I wouldn't say that. . . . That gets into some pretty deep theology that we don't know much about."[121]

Truth is reason—truth eternal
Tells me I've a mother there.
—LDS Hymn

12

Mother God

ᕲ _____

THE MORMON ANTHROPOMORPHIC (humanlike in shape) and anthropopathic
(humanlike in feeling) God is, quite unmistakably, a male God in his role and characterization as the Eternal Father. But Mormonism incorporates in its concept of
deity the Divine Feminine as well. Pre-exilic Israel is now widely regarded as wor-
shiping a female consort of Yahweh called Asherah; William Dever, for example,
considers her to have been extremely important in Israel's folk religion, basing his
argument on biblical references to "Asherah" and "Asheroth," graffiti mentioning
"Yahweh and his Asherah," and archaeological evidences.[1] Worship of the deity is
condemned in Jeremiah, and her priests are mentioned alongside Baal's in the story
of Elijah's contest at the altar.[2] (Though, intriguingly, they are not destroyed alongside the priests of Baal.) Apparently, her worship was widely tolerated until the re-
forming kings of the seventh century.[3] Eventually, of course, Hebrew monotheism
was purged of competing gods as well as putative consorts. Perhaps as an echo of this
earlier trajectory, Mary's role as mother of Christ gave her a privileged status in
Catholic thought, and she was often called "heavenly mother" as a consequence.[4]
Julian of Norwich did refer to Christ as "our heavenly Mother," but meant the expression figuratively.[5] A female God has never been a part of orthodox Christian
belief.

In the seventeenth century, the Quaker Isaac Penington was influenced by the
eighth Proverb that depicted pre-existent Wisdom ("Sophia" in Greek) as God's companion in a time before creation. Accordingly, he referred to a "heavenly mother . . .

of all that are born of the Spirit;" "Wisdom," he elaborated, is "the heavenly mother of all the living. . . . The Spirit which begets all, who are truly begotten to the Lord."[6] The Shakers took this idea of a heavenly mother a step further in their earliest publications. Shakers were more famous for their belief that Ann Lee was a female embodiment of Christ, but their foundational gender innovation was the inference, from Genesis 1:26 ("in the image of God he created them; male and female he created them"), that God was both male and female. In 1823, they asserted that Jesus "received the elements of eternal life from his *Eternal Parents*" (emphasis original) and that he yielded to the will of those same "heavenly Parents."[7] Frederick Evans similarly made explicit the biblical connection Penington had implied, writing that "those who reject their *Heavenly Mother*, do thereby reject *true wisdom*," and referred to the "true order of the *Godhead* as Male and Female,—an *Eternal Heavenly Father, and an Eternal Heavenly Mother*."[8] Such parental imagery came very close to anthropomorphic literalism. "The Deity consists of *two*," wrote Shaker medium Paulina Bates, "male and female; . . . the Eternal Father and [His] co-worker, Holy and Eternal Mother Wisdom."[9] Ultimately, however, the duality sounded more mystical than literal: Before "the Mother spirit was brought forth," wrote Bates, "the essence of eternal male and female principles existed in the first source of all existence."[10] And the earliest Shaker writings refer to spiritual rebirth as involving a "spiritual union of [the convert's] heavenly parents, in the work of regeneration."[11]

Early Mormons had close connections to the Shakers; Jesse Gause, Joseph Smith's First Counselor in the Presidency had been a Shaker. Parley Pratt, the St. Paul of Mormonism, lived near the Shaker community at New Lebanon, New York, and his extended family "was shot through with Shakerism."[12] Another principal Shaker community, North Union, was close to Kirtland, early center of Mormon conversion. Though the Mormons explicitly condemned Shaker beliefs as heresy ("the Son of Man cometh not in the form of a woman"),[13] the Shaker attempt to propound a female principle in the makeup of divinity was the contemporary theological expression closest in spirit to Mormonism's subsequent direction in this regard. The Moravians had propounded similar theologies the century before, making "Jesus and other persons of the Christian deity female."[14] But they had little lasting influence.

Other contemporaries were also challenging the orthodox monopoly of divine masculinity. As the century progressed, influential Unitarian Theodore Parker began praying in public to the "Heavenly Father and Mother."[15] At times he singled out the "Infinite Mother,"[16] but his general usage suggested he was, Shaker-like, urging a conception of the divine that incorporated both masculine and feminine principles. The flowering of feminist theologies in recent decades has included several strategies to redress the historical exclusion or subordination of the feminine from divine constructions; some follow Parker in reinterpreting God and Christology alike with more room for feminine aspects in both, some have worked to recuperate the Sophia tradition, as a neglected entity in the heavenly triad, and some promote a language and a theology that move beyond gender altogether.

Tracing the origins of Mormon belief in a Heavenly Mother is difficult, but may have developed out of language appearing in Smith's revelation on celestial marriage. Though not published as part of the scriptural canon until 1876, his 12 July 1843 pronouncement on the subject contains the promise that in the eternal worlds, married and sanctified women who enter into their exaltation in the highest kingdom of heaven will "bear the souls of men."[17] The syntax of the sentence makes the meaning a little ambiguous. The wives referred to "are given unto [a husband] to multiply and replenish the earth . . . and for their exaltation in the eternal worlds, that they may bear the souls of men." Whether the bearing refers to replenishing *this earth*, or an activity *"in the eternal worlds,"* is unclear.[18] In any case, the same revelation guaranteed to the exalted "a continuation of the seeds forever,"[19] which Mormons have consistently read as a reference to post-mortal procreation.[20] And listeners at the time believed Smith was teaching a doctrine of spirit procreation. Franklin D. Richards reported on a sermon a few days later, wherein Smith referred to "eternal contracts" that led to "the multiplication of Lives [in] the eternal worlds." Richards concluded, "I deduce that we may make an eternal covenant with our wives and in the resurrection claim that which is our own and enjoy blessings & glories peculiar to those in that condition even the multiplication of spirits in the eternal world."[21] If Smith in this revelation and thereafter linked the bearing of souls, or a continuing progeny (seed) in the eternal worlds, with the condition and status of "gods," the implication is present that humans were themselves conceived and created as the spirit progeny of just such a Heavenly Mother. Though Smith was apparently referring at the time of his death to spirits and intelligence as likewise eternal and uncreated, he was also giving signals of a conception of spirits as begotten by God. Pratt and others may have found in the clear allusion to heavenly births the basis for a new understanding of spirit origins and parentage.

The idea of a Heavenly Mother first appears in print in a letter of W. W. Phelps, where he exclaims, "O Mormonism! Thy father is God, thy mother is the Queen of heaven, and so thy whole history, from eternity to eternity, is the laws, ordinances and truth of the 'Gods'-embracing the simple plan of salvation, sanctification, death, resurrection, glorification and exaltation of man, from infancy to age, from age to eternity." That Phelps's reference to a Mother in Heaven is literal is clear in the tableau that follows, describing Jesus Christ's pre-mortal designation as Savior: "he was anointed with holy oil in heaven, and crowned in the midst of brothers and sisters, while his mother stood with approving virtue and smiled upon a Son that kept the faith as the heir of all things."[22] Phelps was Smith's close associate and occasional ghostwriter in this period and, as Samuel Brown has written, he tended to publicize key Mormon developments years before they were officially announced or developed.[23] In this case, Phelps cited as proof text for his assertion the references in Jeremiah to the Queen of Heaven (though in that context her worship is condemned).[24] He followed that exposition up several months later with a hymn sung at the December 1844 dedication of the Nauvoo Seventies Hall, which announced "the myst'ry that man hath not seen; Here's our Father in heaven, and Mother, the Queen."[25] And in this case, Phelps acknowledged Smith as the idea's source in his very title: "A Voice from the Prophet." Shortly thereafter, Phelps sketched a speculative reconstruction of the earth's—and humanity's—prehistory as a short story, wherein he referred to Adam's pre-mortal existence as "a child with his father and mother in heaven."[26]

The idea's most popular and enduring formulation in Mormonism was also poetic: Eliza R. Snow wrote a poem in late 1845 she called "My Father in Heaven," though it became known as "O my Father." Snow's marriage to Joseph Smith as a plural wife is often cited as evidence that he was personally teaching the idea to a small, intimate circle. Susa Young Gates reported that Zina D. H. Young and Eliza both learned the doctrine of a Heavenly Mother directly from Joseph Smith.[27] Snow expounded the teaching as an intuitive truth:

> I had learn'd to call thee Father,
> Through thy Spirit from on high,
> But, until the key of knowledge
> Was restor'd, I knew not why.
> In the heav'ns are parents single?
> No, the thought makes reason stare!
> Truth is reason—truth eternal
> Tells me I've a mother there.[28]

The poetic form as well as idea may have been influenced by the Shakers; Shaker preacher Richard McNemar wrote similar lines in 1835:

> To whom does woman owe her birth?
> Did she originate
> From nothing but her mother earth,
> In her primeval state?
> Can any one suppose she was,
> From Adam's rib alone,

Without a corresponding cause,
From the eternal throne?[29]

A literal Heavenly Mother, who bears human souls, clearly suggests a literal Heavenly Father who sires them. As we will see in chapter 17, Smith expressed views that alternated between spirit adoption and literal spirit birth; however, within months of his death, God's fatherhood becomes literalized in tandem with the development of the theology of a Heavenly Mother. That step was apparently taken—or made public—by the Pratts, who were always opposed to "spiritualizing" the scriptures, in any case. They elaborated a version of literal spirit birth that Brigham Young and subsequent Mormon leaders endorsed.

Given this new genealogy of the human spirit, it was inevitable that Mormon descriptions of Deity would assume a dualistic nature. And so we find Orson Pratt teaching from the Tabernacle in 1871: "When we get there we will behold the face of our Father, the face of our mother, for we were begotten there the same as we are begotten by our fathers and mothers here, and hence our spirits are the children of God, legally and lawfully, in the same sense that we are the children of our parents here in this world."[30] A few years later, he was referring to the process of exaltation as one in which earthly children grow to the likeness of their parents in an echo of adults growing into the knowledge and likeness "of our Heavenly Parents."[31]

By 1884, the language was even more anthropomorphic: counselor in the First Presidency, George Q. Cannon, wrote that "God is a married being, has a wife" and "we are the offspring."[32] In 1885, apostle Erastus Snow echoed the teaching: "it is not said in so many words in the Scriptures, that we have a Mother in heaven as well as a Father. It is left for us to infer this from what we see and know of all living things. . . . The idea of a Father suggests that of a Mother."[33] Snow took the additional step of effectively redefining "God" in the language of heavenly marriage: "'What,' says one, 'do you mean we should understand that Deity consists of man and woman?' Most certainly I do. If I believe anything that God has ever said about himself, and anything pertaining to the creation and organization of man upon the earth, I must believe that Deity consists of man and woman. . . . I have another description: There never was a God, and there never will be in all eternities, except they are made of these two component parts; a man and a woman; the male and the female."[34]

It should not go unnoticed here that, perhaps ironically, Mormon theology anticipated some contemporary theologies by reinscribing the patriarchal God of history in a dualistic cosmos, one that has always included a divine—if unheralded—feminine component. "What we have taken as absence was presence all along, but we did not have the eyes to see it," notes V. H. Cassler in regard to the Mormon conception of God as dual.[35] The teaching of a Heavenly Mother arose in the context of the generation of human souls, and that role has been at the center of the church's teachings on the subject. In 1909, the church officially and clearly proclaimed that "the undeveloped offspring of celestial parentage," humans are "begotten and born of heavenly parents," and "all men and women are in the similitude of the universal Father and Mother and are literally the sons and daughters of deity."[36] Again in 1916, the First Presidency affirmed that we are born of "glorified parents [who] have attained exaltation."[37]

However, David Paulsen and Martin Pulido find abundant evidence of historic Mormon "portrayals of Heavenly Mother as procreator and parent," but also "as a divine person, as co-creator of worlds, as coframer of the plan of salvation."[38] Several LDS leaders affirmed that the female divinity is a being worthy of adoration in Her own right, an example of a being who progressed from "womanhood to Godhood," in Orson Whitney's words, a "mother who possessed the attributes of Godhood," in John Widtsoe's language.[39] In a foretaste of late twentieth-century feminist controversies in the church, First Presidency member George Q. Cannon warned such language had a dangerous potential for diverting us from God the Father as the true "object of our worship."[40] Still, teachings on her equal divinity with the Father persisted. In recent years especially, Mormon leaders have emphasized the radical position articulated by early Mormon feminist and intellectual Susa Young Gates, who ascribed to "the divine Mother, side by side with the divine Father, the equal sharing of equal rights, privileges and responsibilities."[41] That these powers clearly transcend the domestic sphere of this or any other home was taught from Brigham Young to the present. Women who inherit celestial glory will, presumably like their Heavenly Mother, "be prepared to frame and make . . . worlds," said Young; they will have "power to create or organize worlds," confirmed Elder Milton R. Hunter.[42]

In recent decades, to the chagrin of Mormon feminists and progressives, LDS references to a heavenly mother have been more muted—in part a reaction to feminist initiatives in the church to include the Heavenly Mother in prayer and worship. Nevertheless, the church officially reaffirmed the doctrine as recently as 1995, in its "The Family: A Proclamation to the World," which affirms that all men and women are beloved children "of heavenly parents."[43]

We went to conference again. President B. Young delivered an interesting discourse concerning Adam's being the father of our spirits as well as bodies.

—WARREN FOOTE JOURNAL, 8 October 1854

13

Adam-God

THE DEVELOPMENT OF Mormon theology was not always linear, and along the way some paths turned out to be dead-ends. One of these was the set of ideas that constitute what came to be known as the Adam-God doctrine. Joseph Smith had denied the principal Christian teachings about Adam—that he was the primal villain in the tragedy of human history—and replaced them with a set of propositions that accorded the founding patriarch uncommon prestige and honor, extending all the way back to a pre-earthly past.

In revising the Old Testament after publishing the Book of Mormon, which celebrated Adam's fall as a sacrifice that made possible a human posterity, Smith produced a fuller account of Adam's post-garden life than Genesis provided. In this version, the Lord expressly forgives Adam for his "transgression," and teaches Adam the gospel, who is then baptized with water and the Holy Ghost.[1] A few years later, Smith referred in a revelation to Adam as "Michael, . . . the father of all, the prince of all, the ancient of days."[2] The ancient of days, an expression from Daniel 7, was traditionally understood to refer to God. Here were already seeds of a growing conflation Young would develop. By Michael, Smith meant the pre-existent archangel of great authority, he later clarified.[3] This is the same Michael who, as God's chief lieutenant, led the hosts of heaven against Satan in Christian tradition.

In 1838, Smith named a major Missouri Mormon settlement after the patriarch, Adam-ondi-Ahman, prophesying it was the place where Adam would come at a future day "to visit his people."[4] Months later, he described that occasion as a grand council wherein Adam, as the supreme priesthood authority in the human family holding "the keys of the universe," would personally deliver up his stewardship to Christ preparatory to the second coming.[5] That stewardship, he later clarified, involved his presidency over the dispensation of the fullness of times; Adam, in other words, possessed the fullness of priesthood keys (or authority) to administer the ordinances of salvation. And to him was given responsibility to reveal to humankind those ordinances of salvation at the appointed times, either in his angelic role as Michael or through the intermediary of other celestial messengers.[6]

Within months of Smith's death, Brigham Young further developed a unique theology of Adam. He may have felt an early kinship with the biblical patriarch, since in his first meeting with Joseph Smith, Young prayed in tongues and Smith identified the language as Adamic.[7] Two years before his martyrdom, Smith had begun administering religious rituals he called an "endowment" in the upper rooms of his store. He directed Brigham Young to more fully "organize and systematize all these ceremonies,"[8] which he did as they moved into the Nauvoo Temple. Records from 1845–46 indicate that by then, an enacted creation narrative involved three characters: God the Father, the Son, and Michael/Adam.[9] In this temple ritual in which Smith tutored Young, in other words, Adam constitutes the third member of a creator trinity.

Over the next six years, Young came increasingly to conflate the persons of God and Adam. He had an array of reasons to do so. There was available to him a substantial body of contemporary biblical interpretation that conflated Michael the Archangel and God, but without identifying, as Mormonism, did, Michael with Adam. William Kinkade believed that Christ "must be Michael the Archangel," and noted that "most of the principal writers of the Trinitarian school" agreed with him.[10] He cites John Brown's *Dictionary of the Holy Bible* to this effect (a copy of which Joseph Smith donated to the Nauvoo library),[11] along with a host of other commentators ("Butterworth, Cruden, Taylor"). Young was also doubtless influenced by Smith's reference to Adam holding "the keys of the universe," and by his King Follett sermon, wherein he suggested a plurality of perfected celestialized humans, or gods. In addition, Smith suggested that those perfected humans go on to produce their own posterity on worlds of their own creation, and that each new world will have its own "Adam."[12] Finally, since in the theology of temple sealing each patriarchal unit was presided over by a preceding patriarchal figure, Adam would not illogically be considered the great King of Kings.[13]

In 1847, Young already hinted that he was understanding Adam to be more than the first man; his role as progenitor of the human race made him a father without parallel, and that function evoked in Young's mind only one possible conclusion; referring to his own role as adoptive father to other Saints, he said "I do not consider that I am worthy of that appellation. Father in the priesthood implies the Great Head. The term would be proper to Father Adam. Jesus had reference to the same thing when he told his disciples not to call any man on earth their father, for their father was in heaven."[14] While he was bringing together Adam's and God's roles as supreme Fathers, he was at the same time finding a striking confluence between Adam and Christ. In remarks about the resurrection, he finds their roles, if not their identities, the same in crucial regards. "Michael the archangel or Adam holds the keys of the resurrection and after a man is raised from the dead, has an immortal body and receives an ordination to hold the keys of the resurrection from under the hands of Michael or those having authority, he then has power to raise the dead, and not before. Jesus was the first fruits of the resurrection."[15] Furthermore, in the logic of resurrection, which Mormons believed would be effected by fathers raising their own descendants from the grave, Adam would necessarily be the first in the process.[16]

Young was clearly following what he saw as a logical trajectory that led him from Adam as God's pre-mortal lieutenant, to Adam as a participant in Creation, to Adam as the Great Head of the human family, to Adam as possessor of the keys to the resurrection, to Adam as a god presiding over this human world under the superior provenance of Elohim. He announced the culmination of his speculations in a bombshell sermon on 9 April 1852. After reminding his congregation that Adam was "Michael, the Archangel, the Ancient of Days," he went on to declare that "HE is our FATHER *and our* GOD, *and the only God with whom* WE *have to do.*" He further proclaimed that Jesus was begotten by "the same character that was in the garden of Eden, and who is our Father in Heaven." In the same remarks he affirmed that "the earth was organized by three distinct characters, namely, Eloheim, Yahovah, and Michael," doubtless leaving many confused as to exactly how these relationships were to be sorted out.[17]

The church newspaper in England published Young's sermon the next year, in November 1853. Two issues later, the editor attempted to make sense of it. The writer reasoned that "Adam is really God" in the sense that "there are Lords many and Gods many," and that "we are under obligations to our father Adam, as to a God," given his eating of the fruit that made possible the birth of the human race. So "why may not Adam be a God, as well as any of his sons, inasmuch as he has performed the work to which the Great Eloheim appointed him."[18]

Meanwhile, Young continued, intermittently, preaching his Adam as God doctrine. "Adam and Eve . . . had been on an earth before," he said in 1853.[19] Then in February 1854 he reaffirmed the core ideas of Adam-God: "Who did beget [Christ]? His Father, and his father is our God, and the Father of our spirits, and he is the framer of the body, the God and Father of our Lord Jesus Christ. Who is he? He is

Father Adam. Michael, the Ancient of Days."[20] Later that year, he complained that Orson Pratt "could not believe that Adam was our God or the father of Jesus Christ,"[21] and a few days later he repeated his teachings. But uncharacteristically for Young, on this occasion he qualified his remarks by employing the phrase "I think" or "I guess" or "I reckon" eight times.[22] He then added that "I do not pretend to say that the items of doctrine, and ideas I shall advance are necessary for the people to know, or that they should give themselves any trouble about them whatever. . . . These are my views."[23]

Throughout his ministry, digressions on Adam-God notwithstanding, Young continued at the same time to employ the language of more conventional Mormon (and Christian) theism. "Christ is the author of this Gospel, of this earth, of men and women, of all the posterity of Adam and Eve," he said on one occasion.[24] "The Lord sent forth His Gospel to the people; He said, I will give it to my son Adam," he preached on another.[25] Young continued to believe in the veracity of his Adam-God teachings, but he was willing publicly to acknowledge his theological limitations: "I do not know every thing. There is a mystery Concerning the God I worship which mystery will be removed when I Come to a full knowledge of God."[26] Still, before he died he directed the doctrine be part of the "lecture at the veil," a message pronounced at the conclusion of the Mormon temple endowment ceremony. According to Young's secretary, the discourse affirmed that "Adam was an immortal being when he came on this earth," Eve was "the mother of all living [in that she] bore those spirits in the celestial world," and Jesus was "Father Adam's oldest son."[27]

After Young's death, the teaching drifted in stages to the realm of nonbinding speculation. George Q. Cannon wrote without criticism, mere months after his passing, that "Some of my brethren . . . did have feelings concerning his course. . . . [S]ome even feel that in the promulgation of doctrine he took liberties beyond those to which he was legitimately entitled."[28] Others at both official and lay levels continued to affirm the value of Adam-God ideas, however, creating mixed messages as to whether the doctrine was false or simply beyond the comprehension of the average member. In these years, the temple lecture included as part of the ritual continued to make reference to elements of the teaching. By 1891, some leaders in outlying areas of Utah were seeking official guidance on the "diverse and unreconciled views prevailing" in the wards.[29] The First Presidency's response was to admonish the church "to worship . . . and to always pray to the Father in the name of His Son Jesus Christ." Rather ambiguously, counselor George Q. Cannon said "it was not necessary that we should [teach] or endorse the doctrine that some men taught that Adam was the Father of Jesus Christ."[30]

A decade later, the doctrine as a whole was emphatically repudiated. In 1902, soon-to-be apostle Charles Penrose wrote in the church periodical *Improvement*

Era that "The Church of Jesus Christ of Latter-day Saints has never formulated or adopted any theory concerning the subject treated upon by President Young as to Adam. . . . Michael the Prince, the Archangel, the Ancient of days, will sit on his throne and receive the allegiance of his innumerable sons and daughters, over whom he will preside by virtue of his patriarchal and royal authority. But he himself will be subject to the great Elohim, the Lord God Almighty, the Supreme Ruler."[31] If he meant the doctrine was never canonized or affirmed by revelation or official proclamation, he was correct. However, his remarks—like those of many successors—conveyed the impression that Young had never promoted the Adam-as-God theology, when in fact the idea was held tenaciously by Young until his death and then by many others into the twentieth century. If the First Presidency's early twentieth-century proclamations on the nature of God and Talmage's authoritative work on *Jesus the Christ* weren't sufficient to lay the teachings firmly to rest, church president Spencer W. Kimball put the nail in the doctrine's coffin when he stated definitively at a 1976 Church General Conference, "We denounce [the Adam–God] theory and hope that everyone will be cautioned against this and other kinds of false doctrine."[32]

[Jesus Christ] died, was buried, and rose again the third day, and ascended up into heaven; and all other things are only appendages to these.

—JOSEPH SMITH, July 1838

14

Christology

"IN ISRAEL OF the biblical tradition," writes one scholar, "only one name of God was cultically appealed to: Yahweh" (or Jehovah, as it has long been rendered in English). Originally written as YHWH, the name appears some 6,000 times in the Old Testament, and has been dated to the eleventh century BCE.[1] The first verse of the Bible, however, employs a different name for the divine being—Elohim. The fact that Elohim appears as the divine name in the oldest portions of the Bible suggests its origin (and that of its root, *El*) in pre-Israelite traditions, and Canaanite religion in particular. To virtually all biblical scholars and lay readers, Yahweh and El, or Jehovah and Elohim, are different appellations for the one God of Judeo-Christianity. The different designations appear to suggest different contexts and emphasis: Jehovah was understood as a "primarily national" God of Israel; Elohim, with its plural *-im* ending, may have been employed to emphasize his status as "God of gods," or "The highest God."[2]

However, some scholars now see the two names of the divine as deriving from two originally distinct divinities. "The original god of Israel was El," writes Mark Smith, and Yahweh was a separate deity. In fact, as he reads Deuteronomy 32:8–9, Yahweh was early on considered to be a son of El.[3] Another scholar points to Psalm 82, with its reference to a divine council, as another trace of their original distinction.[4] In this line of thinking, "the Israelite conception of Yahweh eventually absorbed the functions of El and, by the tenth century BCE, King Solomon's day, had come to be identified with him."[5] Margaret Barker has pushed this thesis the furthest, arguing that until the Babylonian captivity, the Jewish people considered Elohim to be the Most High God and Jehovah to be one of his sons, the God of Israel. Enough remnants of the original system remained in Jewish culture and mentality, she believes, to have facilitated early Christian acceptance of Christ as Jehovah, son of Elohim. She goes so far as to suggest that Paul himself saw Yahweh as "the pre-existent Christ," a separate person from God the Father, in a way that was inconsistent with monotheism. Even the early Father Justin likewise saw biblical appearances of Yahweh as manifestations of the pre-existent Christ, "and *proof that there was a second God mentioned in the Scriptures*" (her emphasis).[6]

Numerous nineteenth-century Christian commentators associated Jehovah with Christ, but in the sense of Jehovah being God, and Christ that God incarnate. Thus Edward Andrews writes that "Jesus is called Jehovah" while asserting that the Scriptures declare Jehovah to be a "Triune God."[7] Similarly, Richard Watson could argue that "Jesus Christ [is] the Jehovah of the Old Testament," even as he calls Jehovah, like "God," one of the "Divine appellations."[8] Within Trinitarian theology, in other words, the identification of Christ with the God of the Old Testament cannot be taken to mean a literal distinction among the persons of the godhead, or of a Jehovah separate and apart from Elohim. Some writers in this era, however, did suggest that Jehovah was not simply one of God's appellations, and therefore interchangeable with others.

In 1814, the Calvinist Ethan Smith wrote a treatise arguing that Christ's sonship did not in any way imply subordination or derivation from the Father (the old Arian heresy). The Son was not, he thought, "literally propagated by the Most High, in some period before the creation of the world."[9] That was conventional enough; but he goes on to assert that God and Christ are "abundantly noted" as separate persons in the Old Testament, fulfilling separate roles, even before the incarnation. He emphatically identifies this pre-mortal Son—whom he designates Jehovah—with the second of "the first two Persons in the Godhead." Those biblical passages which speak of Jehovah, he writes, "are to be applied to Christ." "Jesus Christ," not "God the Father," appeared to Moses, wrestled with Jacob, and is "the Lord God of the holy prophets," the "Jehovah of hosts" himself.[10]

Realizing his challenge to conventional Trinitarian thought, Ethan Smith can only reassure the reader that "the Father is not absent" in these representations, even though "God and Christ are, in some mysterious sense, two.... There is a real, though mysterious, personal distinction between the Father and the Deity of Christ." Even so, he reverts to an orthodox formulation at the end, not wholly convincing in light of his prior assertions: "they are not two distinct Gods; they are one God."[11]

Joseph Smith, we have seen, did not hesitate to assert the utter distinctness of the three members of the godhead. And he eventually added to the nomenclature employed by Ethan Smith, which equated Christ the Son with Jehovah, the name employed in earliest Israelite religion, Elohim, to designate the Father. Initially, however, Smith and his colleagues used both titles to refer to God the Father. The church newspaper affirmed that Mormons believed "in God the Father, who is the Great Jehovah and head of all things, and that Christ is the Son of God, co-eternal with the Father."[12] The next year, Smith used the terms interchangeably in a prayer addressed to "thou eternal, omnipotent, omnicient, and omnipresent Jehovah, God; thou Eloheem...."[13]

By 1844, however, there are hints that Smith was beginning to see Elohim as the more proper title for God the Father in his capacity as "the God of all Gods" who presided over the Divine Council.[14] (However, in his last sermon, he would pluralize "head of Gods" into heads of Gods, indicating his belief in Gods more supreme than the one Christians worship.[15]) With the inauguration of the endowment ceremony of the temple, part of which reenacted the planning and execution of creation by a divine council, "Eloheem" and Jehovah referred to the two gods who participated with Michael/Adam in the project.[16] Those designations would eventually be clarified as corresponding to the Father and Son of contemporary Mormon theology, although usage continued to be uncertain and irregular in succeeding decades. Though Young affirmed the simple formula: "Elohim [and] Yahova ... were father [and] Son,"[17] it is not clear he meant *the* Father and *the* Son. With John Taylor, the terminology is still inconsistent. He clearly indicated that Christ "is not only called the Son of God, ... [but also] Jehovah, the I Am," in an 1882 doctrinal treatise he authored. Yet, he also refers to Christ as carrying "out the designs of Jehovah."[18] Some of this inconsistency may be attributed to ingrained Protestant habits, the inherited vocabulary and practice of Trinitarian thought (the first five LDS prophets were all adult converts from Protestant faiths), and some to a still evolving understanding of Deity.

The picture began to resolve in the late 1800s. By then, George Q. Cannon was identifying Jesus as "the Being who spoke to Moses in the wilderness and declared, 'I am that I am,'"—that is, as Jehovah.[19] James Talmage then more definitively clarified LDS Christology when he wrote in his tome on the subject in 1915 (under First Presidency assignment and the church's imprimatur), "God the Creator, the Jehovah of Israel, the Savior and Redeemer of all nations, kindreds and tongues, are the same, and He is Jesus the Christ."[20] That seemed to confuse more than clarify, since his statement left unresolved the problem of reconciling his picture of the Old Testament Creator God as the second member of the Trinity—the Son—with the consistent scriptural references to the Fatherhood of the biblical God. In 1916, the church produced a "Doctrinal Exposition" that set forth the nature of Christ's fatherhood: Christ was the Creator, our spiritual Father, and also, in an effectual nod toward Trinitarianism, Father by divine investiture.[21] As Bruce McConkie read the statement, it meant that "nearly all the passages of scripture, both ancient and modern, which speak of God as our father and of men on earth being the sons of God . . . teach . . . that Jehovah is our Father and . . . we become his children by adoption."[22] Of course, by making recourse to the principle of divine investiture, Mormonism diminishes somewhat its own distance from Trinitarian thought. For it is saying that effectively, or in practice, the distinctions between the members of the godhead disappear, since one can seldom be certain who is really speaking or being scripturally identified in any given instance.

Talmage's identification of the biblical God with Jesus Christ involves sharp distinctions from the Athanasian Creed of Christendom. Rather than asserting the essential equality of the Son with the Father, Talmage affirms that the Son is subordinate to the Father, as Smith had declared in 1843 ("3 personages—in heaven who hold the keys.—one to preside over all.")[23] Still, Talmage essentially codified the Mormon idea that the Father is effectively eclipsed by the Son in the biblical record. In Talmage's reading, which remains authoritative in the LDS Church, virtually all biblical references to God, or to Jehovah, are references to the pre-mortal Son. He is, effectively, the God of this world, directing and presiding over the affairs of the human family under the Father's supervision. When the Father does appear in cosmic history, it is generally to bear witness of the Son (as at his baptism, or in Joseph Smith's First Vision).

Mormonism is sometimes charged with Arianism, because of this clear primacy accorded the Father. However, Arianism involved several other claims not applicable to Mormons (such as holding Christ to be a creature rather than fully divine), so the label is inaccurate. The question of how Christ could be fully divine pre-mortally, and at the same time literally begotten in the spirit by the Father, has never been fully resolved in Mormon doctrine. This problem is only compounded by a revelation of Smith that declares Christ "received not of the fulness at the first, but continued from grace to grace, until he received a fulness: and thus he was called the Son of God, because he received not the fulness at the first."[24] Talmage read this as suggesting that His divinity is not here referred to; rather, as a mortal man, Jesus experienced a "graded course of growth and development," growing into full "knowledge" of himself and his mission. However, the same revelation promises to the obedient the same inheritance of the Father's "fulness" that Christ obtained, and an eventual "glorifi[cation] in" Christ, as he is glorified "in the Father." It draws a linguistic parallel, in other words, between Christ receiving a fulness, but not "at the first," and humans receiving an eventual fulness. The phrasing, therefore, might be construed as indicating—in contradistinction to the council of Chalcedon's pronouncement that Jesus was fully human and fully divine at birth, and "perfect in his divinity"²⁵—a process of total divinization, or Christ's receipt of the Father's fulness, finally achieved through the experience of mortality. This may explain Talmage's own guarded phrasing, when he indicates that the mortal Jesus's "graded course of growth" notwithstanding, the fact that he "had been *associated* with the Father from the beginning" is never in doubt.²⁶

At the same time, Mormons believe there is no diminishment to Christ's divinity in asserting the precedence of God the Father. Mormons worship the Father, in the name of the Son, while holding both to be God:

> In all His dealings with the human family Jesus the Son has represented and yet represents Elohim His Father in power and authority. This is true of Christ in His preexistent, antemortal, or unembodied state, in the which He was known as Jehovah; also during His embodiment in the flesh; and during His labors as a disembodied spirit in the realm of the dead; and since that period in His resurrected state. To the Jews He said: "I and my Father are one." ... Yet He declared "My Father is greater than I." ... Thus the Father placed His name upon the Son; and Jesus Christ spoke and ministered in and through the Father's name; and so far as power, authority and Godship are concerned His words and acts were and are those of the Father.²⁷

Their effective equality still leaves unresolved the question of how a being who is coequal with the Father can also be his "firstborn." Here, Mormon theology is just as imbued with seeming contradiction as the creedal Christ who is "begotten not made." For Mormons emphatically declare Christ to be an eternal God, without beginning or end. At the same time, they take literally Christ's biblical status as "the first born of all creation."²⁸ Smith in fact has Christ confirm that designation, wherein he declares "I was in the beginning with the Father, and am the Firstborn,"²⁹ though Smith never clearly indicated what that meant. A possible clue is found in Smith's recasting of the language of John's first chapter: "the word was with God and the word was God" became "the Son was with God and the son was of God."³⁰

Most Mormons, following developments after Smith's death, have taken this to mean, in line with their conception of pre-mortal existence, that all beings have existed eternally as either spirit matter or "intelligence."³¹ Then, at some point in the distant past each was begotten, sired, fashioned, or advanced into the condition of a spirit being—Christ included. In this scheme, of all the spirit children that the Father begat (or adopted, in some readings of Smith's thought), Christ was "the first born, or begotten of the Father," and therefore "Eldest Brother" to the rest, as Smith called Him as early as 1833.³² (Protestants had long used the term, but hardly with the same significance.) Young taught the same months after Smith's death—and the doctrine is now confirmed in the LDS Bible Dictionary.[33] References to Jesus as humankind's "Elder Brother" were officially sanctioned in 1919.[34] The First Presidency at that time affirmed "the literal relationship of Father and Son between Elohim and Jesus Christ. Among the spirit children of Elohim the firstborn was and is Jehovah or Jesus Christ to whom all others are juniors."[35]

Talmage had affirmed this view in his *Jesus the Christ*, where he wrote that Christ's designation as "firstborn" signified that he was the first intelligence "among all the spirit-children of the Father" to become a spirit entity.[36] Whether this mode of creation was more analogous to human conceiving or human adoption, Talmage does not say, and Smith himself never addressed the question of Christ's spiritual begetting. Both, however, taught that Christ *became* divine at some point in the distant pre-earth past. John's words, "'In the beginning,'" Talmage asserts, mean only "a time antecedent to the earliest stages of human existence upon the earth."[37] Still, clearly at some point before the world's creation Christ was divine, because identifying him with the Jehovah of the Old Testament makes his position as God unequivocal. James Talmage in 1915 declared unambiguously that "Jesus Christ . . . was with the Father in that beginning and . . . was Himself invested with the powers and rank of Godship."[38]

The problem this presents for Mormon theology has to do with the relationship between divinity and incarnation. As we saw with Smith's King Follett teachings, the general LDS teaching has been that even God the Father experienced mortality at some point. Only "Spirit and element, inseparably connected, receive a fulness of joy," Smith's revelation declared.[39] Given the emphasis on the Father's embodiment, the implication is that Christ himself experienced mortality not just as a transcendent instance of condescension, not just to achieve full empathy and unity with a suffering humanity along the path to atonement, but as a necessary stage in his own fully realized divinization. The question, then, pertains to how he could have been divine *before* he was embodied in a physical body. One hint of an answer is given in the Book of Mormon. With one conspicuous difference from his similar pronouncement in the Sermon on the Mount, a *resurrected* Christ enjoins the Nephite people to "be perfect, even *as I*, or as your Father in heaven is perfect."[40] One possible reading of this distinction is to suggest that while yet in the spirit, Jesus achieved perfect conformity with eternal law, a fullness of virtue and wisdom that made him divine. Yet his acquisition of a glorified body represented the unqualified culmination of that process. The Greek word translated as "perfect," *teleios*, implies just such a condition, a process come to total completion and fruition.

Mormons thus embrace a Christ who is fully divine, God from before the world was created, and add that he was literally foreordained in a pre-mortal council to be the savior of the human family. In the presence of myriad spirit beings, God the

Father asked for a volunteer to redeem mankind, and Jesus responded, "Here am I, send me. And another answered and said: Here am I, send me. And the Lord said: I will send the first."[41]

As for the manner of Christ's earthly conceiving, Mormons "affirm the virgin birth but reject the traditions of the immaculate conception, of Mary's perpetual virginity, and of her 'assumption.'"[42] The Christian dogma of virgin birth is founded in the words of Luke, who wrote that the angel Gabriel said to Mary, "The Holy Spirit will come upon you, and the power of the Most High will overshadow you; therefore the child to be born will be holy; he will be called the Son of God." Matthew's account says more simply, Mary "was found to be with child from the Holy Spirit."[43] The principal force of the Christian teaching is that Christ was not a mortal son of mortal parents. He was truly man and truly God, conceived and born of woman but in some sense progeny of a divine Father. Mormons embrace the same truths, but see in that Father a glorified personage of flesh and bones. In an era when Mormon thinkers were prone to analogical reasoning, Young could speculate that "the Father came down and begat him, the same as we do now," but his ideas were rejected by subsequent prophets like Harold B. Lee.[44] Joseph Smith said nothing on the subject, and the church's official teaching treats the subject with the reverence and reticence due the topic, saying simply, "Elohim is literally the Father of the spirit of Jesus Christ and also of the body in which Jesus Christ performed His mission in the flesh. . . . No extended explanation of the title 'Son of God' as applied to Jesus Christ appears necessary."[45]

Our faith is concentrated in the Son of God, and through him in the Father; and the Holy Ghost is their minister to bring truths to our remembrance, to reveal new truths to us, and teach guide, and direct the course of every mind, until we become perfected and prepared to go home, where we can see and converse with our Father in Heaven.

—BRIGHAM YOUNG

15

Holy Ghost

ᕱ ────────────────────────────

"THE EARLY [CHRISTIAN] church found itself puzzled by the Spirit and unable to make much in the way of theological sense of this area of doctrine."[1] Christian doctrine on the Holy Ghost, or Holy Spirit, was relatively late in developing. One of the earliest Christian creeds, perhaps dating to the second century, is the Apostles'. It affirms belief in God the Father and in Jesus Christ the Lord. The Holy Ghost is acknowledged only incidentally, as the power by which Christ was conceived. Over the next centuries, the focus remained on the Father and Son, since their exact relationship within the framework of monotheism was the principal theological preoccupation of the era. The Nicene Creed (325 CE) established the status of the Holy Ghost as a member of the godhead, who "is worshipped and glorified." The Athanasian Creed of the sixth century establishes the essentials of Trinitarian thought, bringing all members into full equality: "the Godhead of the Father, of the Son, and of the Holy Ghost, is all one; the Glory equal, the Majesty coeternal."[2] The biblical basis for such a triune formula is indicated in Christ's Great Commission, when he charges his apostles to baptize "in the name of the Father and of the Son and of the Holy Spirit."[3]

While the doctrine of the Holy Spirit has not generated anywhere near the controversies and heresies and debates that swirled around the other two persons of the Trinity, the roles and functions associated with the Holy Spirit have been manifold. In the Old Testament, the term is employed with a possessive as another name for God himself, as when "his holy spirit" is grieved; or as a synonym for God's presence, as when the Psalmist pleads, "Cast me not away from thy presence; and take not thy holy spirit from me."[4] In the New Testament, the terms emphasize a particular endowment of divine influence or inspiration. Christ is "led by the Spirit" in the wilderness;[5] "The Holy Spirit will teach" disciples at the appropriate moment "what you ought to say";[6] and disciples "speak in other languages" under its influence.[7] John, in particular, associates the Spirit with the role of advocate or comforter.[8] Paul expands the Spirit's purview beyond Pentecostal speaking in tongues to include an array of other "spiritual gifts."[9] He also emphasizes the role of the Spirit in the sanctifying of the devout disciple.[10] In light of this vast array of manifestations, functions, and signs of the Spirit's activity, the Christian tradition says relatively little about the Holy Spirit considered as a member of the godhead.

Mormon understanding of the Holy Ghost itself, apart from its gifts and manifestations, has evolved through varied stages of development. One difficulty presented by Mormonism's embodied God was that it seemed to disallow the omnipresence that a deity worthy of the name was thought to require. And though Smith never referred to the Holy Ghost as physically embodied (he thought it might be one day, according to one source[11]), he did call it a personage, seeming therefore to compromise its ability to be everywhere present. In fact, he was reported to say in 1843 that "the Holy Ghost is a personage, and a person cannot have the personage of the H[oly] G[host] in his heart."[12] Brigham Young may have found Smith's remarks misleading or misrecorded, saying in 1857 that the Holy Ghost was a personage, but *not* "a personage having a tabernacle like the Father and Son,"[13] and Smith's words, by way of correction or revision, were changed accordingly in the church's official history (and consequently in the scripture drawn from it and canonized in 1876). The passage now indicates that since the Holy Ghost "is a personage of Spirit," it can indeed "dwell in us."[14] According to the Book of Mormon, the Holy Ghost can appear in the form of a man, as it does in an encounter with the prophet Nephi.[15]

The Pratts recognized early on that the Holy Ghost, construed as the only unembodied member of the godhead, offered a solution to the limitations of a corporeal God. They defined the Holy Ghost, or Holy Spirit, as an intelligent, cosmic ether, virtually limitless in extension. In this regard, the Holy Ghost could be infinite in the range of its influence. To explain how the Spirit could also be accurately referred to as individuated in personal cases, they speculated that it could effectively resolve into a form that corresponded to every person's endowment of "the spirit," or the "gift of the Holy Ghost": "When organized, in individual form," it serves as the animating power in intelligent beings; but there are "vast quantities of this spirit or element not organized in bodily forms, but widely diffused among the other elements of space."[16]

Speculating even more boldly, both Pratts imputed to the Holy Ghost a foundational role as a kind of ground out of which all self-awareness, sentience, and God himself emerged. As Orson argued, the original divine entity was not God the Father; rather, "the Great First Cause itself" consisted of "conscious, intelligent, self-moving particles, called the Holy Spirit."[17] It is the "grand moving cause of all intelligences, and by which they act," agreed Parley.[18] Such theories went a step too far for Young to countenance. Like Orson's essay on "The Great First Cause," Parley's passages were edited out of later editions of the influential *Key to the Science of Theology*.

The Pratts were effectively developing the implications of a revelation wherein Smith had introduced to Mormonism a concept complementary to the Holy Ghost. "The Light of Christ" in Smith's hands became a solution to the theological demand for divine omnipresence. The phrase "Light of Christ" had long been in circulation by poets and churchmen (both Philip Sidney and John Foxe used the term, for example[19]), but usually in reference to a kind of general Christian enlightenment (as opposed to pagan benightedness). Others were using the term to refer to conscience, and Quakers used the term synonymously with their more famous expression, the "inner light."[20] Smith in an 1832 revelation described the Light of Christ more expansively as a principle or power, encompassing "the light of the sun, . . . the light of the moon, . . . the light of the stars, and the power thereof by which they were made . . . which light proceedeth from the presence of God to fill the immensity of space." More than a simply physical medium, this light was also expressly defined as "the light which is in all things, which giveth life to all things, which is the law by which all things are governed, even the power of God."[21]

At the time, neither Smith nor his contemporaries seemed to hold that what the revelation described was separate and distinct from the Holy Ghost in nature or function. It appears that in their descriptions of the Spirit as a universal ether, the Pratts were assuming the Light of Christ was another name for the Holy Ghost, since their language frequently echoed this revelation, as when Parley wrote that the Holy Ghost "penetrates the pores of the most solid substances, pierces the human system to its most inward recesses."[22]

Both Pratts were attempting to fit a doctrine of the Holy Ghost into their grand plan of creating a "scientific" theology, one amenable to contemporary standards of scientific understanding. For Parley this meant going so far as to find a physiological explanation for the interaction of spirit and body. At the same time, merging the two into a single theory would mitigate—if not solve altogether—the longstanding Cartesian mind-body problem (how can body and spirit interact if they occupy different planes of reality?). Smith had essentially collapsed the dualism that created the problem, when he defined spirit as highly refined matter.

Two philosophers write that this form of "non-Cartesian dualism" is unconventional in the Christian past, but has "more going for it than its critics typically admit."²³ Lacking a genuine ontological distinction, or what their contemporary S. T. Coleridge called "the heterogeneity of spirit and matter," body and spirit conceived of as different manifestations of a single substance would not have to interface across an ontological gap. As Parley Pratt explained the case, "that substance called the Holy Spirit . . . like all others, is one of the elements of material or physical existence, and therefore subject to the necessary laws which govern all matter."²⁴ So it was only reasonable to conjecture, as he did, that "the usual channel for all spiritual fluids . . . in their operations upon the human system, or in their passage from one animal body to another, is the nerves."²⁵ Building on Pratt's ideas, Lorenzo Snow preached in 1860 that "the nervous system seems to be a sort of connecting link between our spirit and our tabernacles."²⁶ B. H. Roberts softened Pratt's mechanistic paradigm only slightly: "to impart a portion of the influence of the Holy Spirit by the touch or by the laying on of hands; or to impart a portion of the element of life from one animal body to another . . . is as much in accordance with the laws of nature as for . . . heat and electricity [to be their] own medium of conveyance."²⁷

Talmage also found Pratt's integration of the Holy Spirit into the physical operations of the universe both theologically and scientifically sound. "The Holy Ghost directs and controls the numerous forces of Nature, of which indeed a few . . . have been made known to the human mind. Gravitation, sound, heat, light, and the still more mysterious, seemingly supernatural power of electricity, are but the common servants of the Holy Spirit in His operations."²⁸ The language is important for its tone more than its theology. Talmage, as the highest ranking scientist of the church of that era, was becoming the point man for defending the compatibility of the gospel with advances in science, and the LDS First Presidency used him to counter the dogmatic hostility to evolution, pre-lapsarian death, and the earth's antiquity, that other Christians—including some in the Mormon leadership—were exhibiting.²⁹ Given the general acceptance at that time of a "luminiferous ether" that pervaded the cosmos, the Mormon conception of a spirit-like fluid that filled the universe seemed a plausible marriage of faith and science. So thought John Widtsoe, writing that there was "no grander or more fundamental doctrine in science than that of the ether," and finding it anticipated Smith's revelation on "the light which . . . proceedeth forth from the presence of God to fill the immensity of space."³⁰

The later nineteenth century saw both a tempering of Mormonism's quasi-scientific language and a rejection of the priority of the Holy Ghost in the godhead (which Orson had tried to champion). In 1860, Orson was still asserting this supreme status of the Spirit, as the only solution to the felt need for divine omnipresence. "The Holy Spirit 'is in all things and round about all things,'" he preached. "Go where you will, through endless space, and you will find the Spirit there, and consequently, when we speak of the omnipresence of God, we have reference to his

Spirit." He took his point much further in attempting again to position that spirit as the core and foundation of divinity, as he had in his "Great First Cause." Referring to Smith's ideas about a plurality of gods, Pratt insisted that "there is but one God, and He is in all worlds, and throughout all space, wherever the same identical light or truth is found." Hence, when we worship, we "worship that Holy Spirit or intelligence," for we are worshipping the attribute that constitutes divinity.[31]

It was a solution of sorts, but Young rejected it,[32] and another resolution eventually emerged to resolve the problem of omnipresence while maintaining the preeminence of the Father and the status of the Holy Ghost as a distinct personage. A gradual separation of two doctrinal principles developed: the Holy Ghost and the Light of Christ. In the latter nineteenth century, Mormons used the term "Light of Christ" frequently but with inconsistent meaning. Young most often used it in its modern LDS sense as a universal endowment, "that lighteth every man that cometh into the world." He preached that "no son or daughter of Adam ever lived on the earth, or ever will, but has had or will have the Light of Christ within them."[33] Elsewhere he uses it interchangeably with the Holy Ghost, the endowment of personal revelation, and the guidance that believers enjoy.[34] He also suggests it is the spark of divinity in all humans, that may blossom forth into godhood, but seems to be referring to Smith's description of the Light of Christ in particular when he teaches that "God is in all—the light of all, through all, and is soul of all that he has."[35]

By 1894, counselor in the First Presidency George Q. Cannon lamented "the ambiguity in our printed works concerning the nature or character of the Holy Ghost . . . . However the Presidency deemed it wise to say as little as possible on this or other disputed subjects."[36] Even with the publication of Talmage's *Articles of Faith* (1899), a hard-and-fast distinction between the Holy Ghost as an unambiguously finite personage and the diffuse influence of the Light of Christ is not definite: The former "is a being endowed with the attributes and powers of Deity, and not a mere force or essence," Talmage wrote. He is "capable of manifesting Himself in the form and figure of man," (as evidenced in the Book of Mormon, 1 Ne. 11) but not in the form of a dove.[37] (Not the Holy Ghost but "a natural dove descended on the head of the Lord Jesus, in . . . sign that the Holy Ghost was given to him," said Young.[38]) In an indication that the Light of Christ was not yet clearly defined or differentiated from the Holy Ghost, Talmage never even used the former term in his classic work. He only alluded to Smith's 1832 language when he referred to "the power of life" as "an emanation from the spirit of God."[39] Even so, Pratt's chapter on the Holy Ghost, with its ether-like descriptions, had by now been excised from his *Key to Theology*.

Soon thereafter Joseph F. Smith moved toward present LDS teaching. He wrote that though the Holy Ghost was sometimes used interchangeably with the Light of Christ, "the Holy Ghost is a personage of the Godhead, and is not that which lighteth every man that cometh into the world."⁴⁰ From that point on, Mormons have more generally understood the Holy Ghost to be a distinct being within the social Trinity; the Light of Christ is seen as a divine influence or power that pervades the universe, and is manifest at the personal level as conscience, or a universal moral faculty, in a kind of concession in the face of Mormonism's particularism. In other words, since Mormon thought confines the *gift* of the Holy Ghost to those who receive a properly administered and authorized priesthood ordinance, the Light of Christ becomes a comparable spiritual endowment given to each human being at birth. Put more simply, the universal human possession of "conscience is a manifestation of the Light of Christ."⁴¹ At the same time, in its ether-like ubiquity, it "fills the immensity of space and emanates from God,"⁴² for once and for all creating an omnipresent divine influence.

An additional theological advantage accrues from the articulation of the Light of Christ as a universal human endowment, not dependent on authorized bestowal as is the gift of the Holy Ghost. Mormons lack any concept of prevenient grace, an idea that Arminians like John Wesley employed to solve a catch-22: Humans are fallen and mired in sin. To be saved they need to respond to Christ's offer of salvation. But having the Holy Ghost would seem to be a prerequisite to choosing to respond to the Spirit, which the unregenerate don't have until *after* they respond to its promptings. (It seems a "gross blasphemous absurdity" to expect "the Holy Ghost to direct a man who knows he has not this faith," Wesley wrote. It is like asking a faithless man to pray for faith when faith is the precondition for getting what we pray for.⁴³) One solution to this dilemma was to propose a provisional grace that God sends not in *response* to seeking but to *prompt* the seeking of the unregenerate individual.⁴⁴

Wesley said this unsought and undeserved heavenly gift was "frequently termed 'natural conscience,' but more properly 'preventing grace.'" It was characterized by "all the drawings of the Father; the desires after God, which, if we yield to them, increase more and more;—all that light wherewith the Son of God 'enlighteneth every one that cometh into the world.'"⁴⁵ For Mormons, the Light of Christ performs comparable theological work, explaining how any human remote from God's presence, mired in sin and a fallen world, can recognize and respond in the affirmative to the Spirit's first invitation to come unto Christ. Clearly, the connection that was explicit in Wesley is implicit in Mormon theology: the Light of Christ, or conscience, is God's guarantee that the fall into mortality does not utterly alienate humankind from his voice.

He remarked that . . . the organization of the spiritual and heavenly worlds, and of spiritual and heavenly beings, was agreeably to the most perfect order and harmony—that their limits and bounds were fixed irrevocably, and voluntarily subscribed to by themselves.
—JOSEPH SMITH, 9 October 1843

16

Other Beings

SATAN

IF ANY MYTH can make a claim to near universality among the cultures and religions of the world, it is probably the primeval conflict between good and evil. Christianity has long contended with scattered, cryptic, biblical allusions to a conflict in the celestial realms that antedated even the creation of the earth. "And there was war in heaven," says the writer of Revelation in the most prominent example, "Michael and his angels fought against the dragon; the dragon and his angels fought back, but they were defeated, and there was no longer any place for them in heaven."[1] But a war is just the latter stage of a conflict unresolved by other means. What was the conflict itself about, and who was involved?

The Jews had only recently elevated Satan to the role of presiding high priest of evil among the angels, when Jesus said, "I watched Satan fall from heaven like a flash of lightning."[2] In so doing, Jesus established for early Christians a mythology of Satan as a fallen angel. The Jewish philosopher Philo, contemporary with Christ, understood the Bible to suggest that some heavenly souls "migrated to earth . . . because they were unable to endure the satiety of divine goods."[3] Probably influenced by Philo, the early Father Origen similarly held that some of God's angels, through "satiety" of blessedness, regressed to become demons.[4] One of these spirits was Satan, whom he identified as a fallen Lucifer rather than an originally evil being. He based his reading on scripture and etymology: If, Origen reasoned, he was a dark and fallen creature, why was he once called Lucifer, which means "light bearer"? Certainly that "being [did] once exist as light before he went astray, and fell to this place, and had his glory turned into dust."[5] Tertullian (ca. 160–225 CE) and Jerome (347–420 CE) articulated the simplest explanation: Lucifer, the "light bearer," was a principal archangel before his fall, at which point he became Satan the adversary.

John Milton found the cause of Lucifer's demotion to be rooted in his almost-primacy. "O had his powerful destiny ordained me some inferior angel," the fallen angel complained, "I had stood then happy; no unbounded hope had raised ambition."[6] Origen found the key to Lucifer's fall in an Isaiah passage about overweening pride, reading a reference to the king of Babylon as an allegory of pre-mortal events: "How you are fallen from heaven, O Day Star, son of Dawn! How you are cut down to the ground, you who laid the nations low! You said in your heart, 'I will ascend to heaven; I will raise my throne above the stars of God; I will sit on the mount of assembly on the heights of Zaphon; I will ascend to the tops of the clouds, I will make myself like the Most High.' But you are brought down to Sheol, to the depths of the Pit."[7]

Although this genealogy is not universally accepted in Christendom, it has been a common reading historically, waning over time. Some commentators, like Adam Clarke, profess astonishment than anyone could believe the Holy Spirit would "call this arch-enemy of God and man the *light-bringer*."[8] But until the devil became increasingly demythologized in the modern era, an early nineteenth-century standard reference work could matter of factly define the devil as "Satan" or "Lucifer," "a fallen angel, especially the chief of them."[9]

In Mormon cosmology, evil is traced to a primeval conflict over how to secure humanity's destiny. Joseph Smith embraced this early Christian narrative, which the Book of Mormon affirmed: "an angel of God, according to that which is written, had fallen from heaven; wherefore he became a devil."[10] Smith further filled in the background story, relying upon two sources: his revision of the book of Genesis (1830) and his production of texts he associated with the patriarch Abraham, which Smith first generated in 1835 inspired by papyri that he acquired from one Michael Chandler.[11] In Smith's version, as in ancient Near Eastern traditions, God convenes a divine council before the creation of humans.[12] There he stands in the midst of many "noble and great" spirits, and declares an ambitious plan. "We will go down, . . . and we will make an earth whereon these may dwell; and we will prove them herewith, to see if they will do all things whatsoever the Lord their God shall command them." In response, "one among them that was like unto God" offers himself as executor and instrument of the Father's plan, apparently indicating a willingness to expiate the sins that will inevitably accrue to all mankind in the wake of such a probationary scheme.[13]

It is at this point, according to a revelation Smith had published in 1830, that a second figure steps forward with a competing proposal. Referring to Satan, God tells the prophet Moses that

> He came before me, saying—Behold here am I, send me, I will be thy Son, and I will redeem all mankind, that one soul shall not be lost, and surely I will do it; wherefore, give me thine honor. But, behold, my Beloved Son, which was my Beloved and Chosen from the beginning, said unto me—Father, thy will be done, and the glory be thine forever. Wherefore, because that Satan rebelled against me, and sought to destroy the agency of man, which I, the Lord God, had given him; and also, that I should give unto him mine own power; by the power of mine Only Begotten, I caused that he should be cast down; and he became Satan, yea, even the devil, the father of all lies, to deceive, and to blind men, and to lead them captive at his will.[14]

The critical action in this scene unfolds while Satan is yet Lucifer, an angel of "authority in the presence of God," the Bearer of Light, as his name signifies. In this story, the devil was of the same order as humans—an unembodied spirit being— though along with his name Lucifer there are other hints he may have attained to a position of elevated stature. He alone challenges the Father, and presents himself as a potential savior in the model of the Son. W. W. Phelps, writing in Smith's name (and presumably with his blessing), refers to Lucifer's fall "from his Godified state."[15]

It is also noteworthy that this primeval contest is not about good and evil per se. It is only after the Father says "I will send the first" that Lucifer becomes angry and rebellious, and is cast out, becoming Satan. That Satan was not always the embodiment of evil is confirmed by virtue of the fact that "the heavens wept over him" upon his exile.[16] So in the logic of the scriptural narrative, Lucifer's proposal was not obviously and self-evidently evil. In Mormonism's cultural grammar, Lucifer's plan has often been associated with coercion. A common version of the story holds that his intention was simply to "force" people to be righteous, or to keep the commandments. The expression "sought to destroy the agency of man" has in common parlance been equated with a strategy of compelling human beings to do the right thing. Such a reading is problematic, for reasons besides its naiveté. (It is hard to see how an appeal to force could be persuasive with a substantial proportion of the heavenly hosts.) Clearly, there are far more subtle and sophisticated ways to "destroy the agency" referred to in the scriptural passage—principal of which is the simple tampering with the consequences of choice.

If every choice a person made resulted in totally unforeseen and unpredictable consequences, one would be inhabiting a realm of chaos. Agency would be meaningless and freedom effectively nonexistent if no reliable principles existed by which to make choices that were attached to the particular ends desired. This is what the Book of Mormon prophet Lehi suggests in his great sermon on freedom, when he says that "men are instructed sufficiently," "and the law is given to men," and that as a result they are "free forever, . . . to act for themselves and not to be acted upon, save it be by the punishment . . . according to the law."[17]

By this logic, an undeserved punishment *or an unqualified reward* is an equal threat to the idea of moral agency; in both cases the meaning of one's choice has been nullified and freedom vacated. That insight produced in early Mormonism a different conception of "Satan's plan" than commonly obtains in current Mormon discourse. Only a few writers like third president John Taylor assumed the devil "probably intended to make men atone for their own acts by an act of coercion."[18] But others came to believe that the Luciferian proposal may very well have hinged on the promise that regardless of human choices in a mortal probation, salvation would be assured. In this view, the perils of mortality were too high to enforce accountability for human choice. (This was Congregationalist theologian Edward Beecher's understanding of the war in heaven: "From pleasure, of course, there was no temptation to revolt, but from a discipline of suffering, such as they needed to fit them to be the founders of the universe with God, they could be tempted to revolt."[19])

So according to Lucifer's proposal, humans wouldn't be forced to make the right choices. Any choices they made would suffice. Which is the same thing as saying, no choice they made would have mattered. If choice doesn't matter, then moral agency is an empty cliché. That would offer a plausible scenario by which Lucifer sought to destroy the agency of man, in a strategy as tempting then as it is now: eat, drink, and be merry, and tomorrow you repose in paradise. This is how many first-generation Mormons understood the War in Heaven. In the Book of Mormon, the belief that one may be saved regardless of one's choices is associated with two anti-Christs. The first preaches unconditional universalism. (Churches often differentiate themselves most vehemently from those closest in nature to them; Mormonism is quasi-universalist and drew early converts disproportionately from universalist backgrounds.) Nehor teaches the universalist tenet that "all mankind should be saved at the last day."[20] The second anti-Christ, Zeezrom, disputes with the missionary Amulek, claiming that he denies to God the power to save people "in their sins." Amulek counters that, since "no unclean thing can inherit the kingdom of God," even God cannot save a person in his sins.[21] The distinction is more than a quibble over semantics. Amulek is implying that a salvation effected *in spite* of choice ("in sin") would violate God's guarantee of human agency, whereas a salvation effected through choice ("from sin") would not.

Most early Mormons apparently saw Satan's pre-mortal assault on agency in just these terms, as a denial of consequence rather than an effort at coercion. W. W. Phelps, in an 1844 letter, notes that Zeezrom's (and Nehor's) conceptions were akin to the devil's. Then he draws the specific parallel: "Lucifer lost his [first estate] by offering to save men in their sins," he wrote.[22] Orson Pratt initially disagreed with Phelps, writing that redeeming humankind "from the effects of their sins without any exercise of their agency in the act of repentance or reformation" would destroy justice, "but not destroy the agency of man."[23] By 1880, however, he came to see that Satan's plan to "destroy the agency of man" did indeed entail redeeming "them all in their sins."[24]

George Q. Cannon, Brigham Young's counselor, taught the same principle from the Tabernacle to an audience of Latter-day Saints: "Satan desired that man should be saved through the taking away from him of his agency. He would save everybody regardless of their own acts."[25] In the twentieth century, J. Reuben Clark returned to the theme while considering the more facile version of coercion also possible: "Satan's plan required one of two things: either the compulsion of the mind, the spirit, the intelligence of man, or else the saving of men in their sins."[26] To some significant degree, it would seem, saving anyone *in his sins* would be a misnomer in any case. As we will see, the Mormon conception of salvation is emphatically existential. So any salvation that does not involve sanctification would represent a human destiny far short of its divine potential. Granting the possibility of such a heaven open to all comers—it would not be the heaven that God envisioned.

Christian assent to the reality of Satan was largely unquestioned until the modern era—but persists as a majority view among believers. A poll taken in 2005 showed that 68 percent of Americans believed in the devil, including 55 percent of people with postgraduate degrees.[27] Mormonism, too, affirms the reality of Satan as a spiritual being (though the belief had ebbed in the early twentieth century).[28] In the Mormon version of events, according to the verse succeeding the scriptural reference to Lucifer's thwarted efforts in the heavenly council, the newly christened Satan resorts to the earth, where he seeks "to lead [mankind] captive at his will."[29] Failing to get official sanction for his plan to destroy agency, in other words, he prosecutes it as an unsanctioned renegade. Rather than remit the consequences of choice (his rejected plan), he works to impair human capacity to choose wisely, according to the Book of Mormon: "At that day shall he rage in the hearts of the children of men, and stir them up to anger against that which is good. Others will he pacify, and lull them away into carnal security, that they will say: All is well in Zion; yea, Zion prospereth, all is well—and thus the devil cheateth their souls, and leadeth them away carefully down to hell. And behold, others he flattereth away, and telleth them there is no hell; and he saith unto them: I am no devil, for there is none—and thus he whispereth in their ears, until he grasps them with his awful chains."[30] A substantial number of early Mormons were converts from Methodism, and their staunch Arminian tendencies already predisposed them to a theology that celebrated the role of individual will in personal salvation. (Jacob Arminius argued, contra Calvinism, that the individual was free to choose or reject salvation. Grace alone saved, but it was not irresistible, hence election was not unconditional; John Wesley became the most prominent champion of his views.)

Mormonism's unique cosmic drama added new theological weight to that perspective, and goes far toward explaining what one philosopher calls Mormonism's "almost obsessive Mormon concern for free moral agency."[31] Accordingly, impairment or denial of freedom would be the greatest of evils. In the same year that Smith produced his first Abrahamic narrative, his wife Emma Smith compiled the church's first hymnbook. Given pride of place as hymn number one was "The Freedom of the Will," an unabashed paean to individual agency:

> Know this that ev'ry soul is free,
> To choose his life and what he'll be' . . .
> For this eternal truth is given,
> That God will force no man to heaven.[32]

In Mormonism's conception of the grand struggle for the souls of humankind, Satan is not simply the great Tempter, enticing with all the allures sin can present. He is the great Counterfeiter, who offers captivity and bondage where the gospel offers liberty and life. Sin is the instrument rather than the final form of damnation.[33]

FALLEN ANGELS

Christ's triumph in the War in Heaven, according to John the Revelator, was engineered by Michael the Archangel, whose victory was historically celebrated on the feast day known as Michaelmas. The losers, we read, were "thrown down to the earth" as fallen angels.[34] Biblical allusions to celestial creatures who have fallen appear as early as the sixth chapter of Genesis, which refers to *Nephilim* who are associated with the co-mingling of "sons of god" with the "daughters of humans." As Moses Aberbach holds, misleading translations (such as the King James and other versions that render *Nephilim* as "giants") and official targums cannot entirely obscure a "'fallen angels' tradition which exploited the plain etymology of the word, from *npl* 'to fall.'"[35]

Both the first and last books of the Bible, then, bear evidence of this "fallen angel" motif.[36] The second epistle of Peter also refers to sinning angels that God cast into hell, and Jude alludes to angels who failed to "keep their own position but left their proper dwelling."[37] Early church fathers, like Tertullian, also believed in "certain spiritual essences," who from angelic status, "fell of their own free-will," and now walk the earth as demons, where "their great business is the ruin of mankind."[38]

In recent centuries, the theme of Lucifer and myriad angels who rebelled, were defeated, and now harry the human race has been more prominent in literary than in theological circles. Dante gave them a prominent place in hell; those fallen angels who "once had reigned from heaven" are now guardians of hell's lowest regions.[39] John Milton, like Tertullian, made them a potent presence in the world. Exiled to hell, they are soon led forth "triumphant out of th[e] infernal pit" by their captain, and are suffered instead, with Sin and Death, "to waste and havoc" an earth once "fair and good."[40] In hundreds of morality plays, Faust stories, and folk legends, Satan and his fallen followers are a semi-serious counterweight to myriad angels of light.

Within this cosmology, the biblical cases of demonic possession appear as but the most dramatic manifestation of the malign reality of these fallen beings. Such interpretations continued through the medieval era and into the modern, often mingled with charges of witchcraft and sorcery along the way. In America at least, fears of possession persisted another century after witchcraft paranoia faded, but by the late eighteenth century, among the Methodists, at least, "the condition resembling demonic possession required healing rather than exorcism." And while Methodists continued to affirm belief in a literal devil, "the Evil One's role was generally that of the harasser who assaulted, challenged, and haunted, rather than possessed."[41] At the same time, the Catholic practice of exorcism, popularized by Hollywood, has kept alive a tradition of belief in demonic possession.

Smith's theology of Satan and his legions, like so much else in his theology, grew inexorably out of his insistent materialism. Just as physical embodiment of our pre-mortal spirits was the principal purpose of earth life (and the effective reward for those pre-mortal spirits "who kept their first estate"), denial of embodiment was the punishment visited on those who opposed the Father's plan. "The Devil has no body," Smith repeatedly taught, "and herein is his punishment." This version of cosmic prehistory gave particular cogency to one New Testament account in particular. As Smith continued, the devil "is pleased when he can obtain the tabernacle of man and when cast out by the Savior he asked to go into the herd of swine showing that he would prefer a swine's body to having none."[42]

Smith was convinced of the reality of Satan and his cohort of evil spirits the same month he organized the church. He was visiting the Joseph Knight family in Colesville, New York, when a report came to him that Newel, Knight's twenty-year-old son, had grown increasingly agitated and distressed after failed attempts to pray.

[Smith] went and found him suffering very much in his mind, and his body acted upon in a very strange manner. His visage and limbs distorted and twisted in every shape and appearance possible to imagine; and finally he was caught up off the floor of the apartment and tossed about most fearfully. . . . [Smith] rebuked the devil, and commanded him in the name of Jesus Christ to depart from him; when immediately Newel spoke out and said that he saw the devil leave him and vanish from his sight.[43]

From that day to the present, Mormons have taken the presence of Satan and his fallen hosts of heaven as real entities who work to disrupt the Lord's purposes. Though the belief is out of harmony with more liberal trends in contemporary religion, Mormons find in the Book of Mormon an anticipation of such skepticism about the devil's reality: "And behold, others he flattereth away, and telleth them there is no hell; and he saith unto them: I am no devil, for there is none—and thus he whispereth in their ears, until he grasps them with his awful chains, from whence there is no deliverance.[44] However, the LDS belief in fallen entities is counterbalanced by a view of manifold angelic beings who ply the earth.

POPULOUS HEAVENS

In Judaism and early Christianity alike, God inhabits a populous abode. Several biblical passages describe a heavenly assembly, with various orders of beings. Psalm 82, for example, describes how

> God has taken his place in the divine council;
> in the midst of the gods he holds judgment:
> How long will you judge unjustly
> and show partiality to the wicked? . . .
> I say, "You are gods,
> children of the Most High, all of you;
> nevertheless, you shall die like mortals,
> and fall like any prince."[45]

The translation and meaning of this psalm, which was invoked by Jesus in the New Testament and apparently refers to a plurality of deities, is vigorously disputed. Accused by his Jewish audience of making himself the equal of God, Jesus responds by saying, "is it not written in your law, 'I said, you are gods.' If those to whom the word of God came were called 'gods,' . . . can you say that [I am] blaspheming because I said, 'I am God's son?'"[46] The exact significance of Jesus's allusion to gods is unclear, but in context this citation of the passage can only be effective if he is affirming the Psalmic reference to other gods or godlike beings.[47] Otherwise it would hardly serve to soften or justify his own claim to divinity. The identity of these pre-mortal sons of God—the *bene elohim*—is far from clear, however.

The sons of God appear in another pre-mortal scene, in which Job is asked where he was when God "laid the foundation of the earth," "when the morning stars sang together and all the heavenly beings shouted for joy."[48] Another vivid description of a divine assembly in the Hebrew Bible is found in the story of the wicked King Ahab (871–852 BCE) in the book of Kings. A prophet named Micaiah appears before the king and forecasts divine retribution for Ahab's misdeeds. He describes the remarkable conditions under which God decreed Ahab's fate:

> I saw the Lord sitting on his throne, with all the host of heaven standing beside him to the right and to the left of him. And the Lord said, "Who will entice Ahab, so that he may go up and fall at Ramoth-gilead?" Then one said one thing, and another said another, until a spirit came forward and stood before the Lord, saying, "I will entice him." . . . Then the Lord said, "You are to entice him, and you shall succeed; go out and do it."[49]

Similar, though less detailed, scenes appear when God countenances the temptation of Job in another convocation of the court of heaven involving the "sons of God" (*bene elohim*) along with "the accuser" (*ha-satan*, Job 1), and when, surrounded by several "attendants," God asks for a volunteer to go forth to his people, and commissions Isaiah, after asking, "Whom shall I send, and who will go for us?"[50] Other heavenly characters are intimated in the words of Moses, who speaks of how

> The Lord came from Sinai,
> and dawned from Seir upon us;
> he shone forth from Mount Paran.
> With him were myriads of holy ones;
> at his right, a host of his own.[51]

Theodore Mullen argues that these "Holy Ones . . . are the members of Yahweh's court" whom one also sees in Psalm 68:18 and in several other Old Testament scenes.[52] In addition to these "holy ones" (*qedosim*), other terms for the various members include "sons of gods/gods" or "sons of El," (*bene elim*) "sons of the Most High/Elyon" (*bene elyon*), and "sons of God" (*bene ha elohim*).[53] Against the background of the Heavenly Council, such beings provide the basis for what Mullen calls "the development of an elaborate angelology wherein there were specific ranks and hierarchies of divine beings."[54]

Such references to angels, and sons of God—as well as to fallen ones and morning stars—are but ghostly remnants of an entire cosmology now mostly lost to us. Moshe Halbertal and Avishai Margalit point out that in early monotheistic traditions, "the gap between God and human beings is filled by the intermediary forces of angels, constellations, and demons. The world of divinity becomes a kind of complex bureaucratic system, or an emanated chain of being."[55] But most biblical translations render a vast array of differentiating terms as "angels," blurring these distinctions and collapsing an intricately tiered and variously populated heaven into a monochromatic landscape. Some writers asserted a more ordered gradation through the Christian centuries. Clement of Rome named eleven, but others, like the writer of the apocryphal Testament of Adam, identified nine orders of heavenly powers: angels, archangels, archons, authorities, powers, dominions, thrones, seraphim, and cherubim.[56] Pseudo-Dionysius followed suit with his influential *De Coelesti Hierarchia* in the fourth or fifth century; a host of others modified or repeated this hierarchy, through Thomas Aquinas in the thirteenth century.[57]

Because of their presence in both Old and New Testaments, their persistent portrayal through centuries in high and low culture alike, and their myriad appearances in personal narratives and experience, angels have never gone out of fashion. In 1826, an editor of a book on the subject noted that while "the visible Ministry of Angels was always rare," it was only "*nearly* discontinued since the completion of written Revelation." One of their prophesied functions, the author wrote, is "to assist in the solemn transactions of the last day."[58] It would be a mistake, he continued, to relegate them to the past, since "they are equally beneficent of the human race at this day, as in generations of old; and are still sent forth by the great Father of Spirits on the same gracious errands." But their ministry, he assumed as a matter of fact, was through "their invisible agency on our souls."[59] A modern scholar of the subject agrees. "Angels are the unseen forces in the creation," she writes.[60] They are the invisible portion of God's creation, and even biblical angels are generally "perceived but not seen."[61]

Smith's career as prophet—and, one could argue, Mormonism itself—might be said to begin not with a theophany, as many Mormons believe, but with an angelic visitation, from a very visible angel. By the early twentieth century, Joseph Smith's 1820 vision of God and Christ had acquired its current designation as his "First Vision," and is portrayed as the inaugural event in his religious mission. But Smith himself dated his ministry to 1827, which is when the angel self-identified as Moroni delivered to Joseph Smith the gold plates.[62] It was this same angel who, four years previous, had first informed young Smith that God had a special "work for [him] to do."[63]

Over ensuing years, Smith would make direct and oblique references to a panoply of angels by whom he was visited. After Smith's death, President John Taylor stated:

"the principles which [Joseph Smith] had, placed him in communication with the Lord, and not only with the Lord, but with the ancient apostles and prophets; such men, for instance, as Abraham, Isaac, Jacob, Noah, Adam, Seth, Enoch, and Jesus and the Father, and the apostles that lived on this continent as well as those who lived on the Asiatic continent. He seemed to be as familiar with these people as we are with one another."[64] One Mormon contemporary of Smith reminisced that Joseph Smith came to know angelic visitors so well he could identify them by voice before he saw their faces.[65]

Smith's description of Moroni in particular signaled an important and alienating feature of his religious thinking. One scholar has sympathized that Smith's was "the perennial despair of visionaries striving how to say the unsayable" and goes on to describe him and his peers (Jonathan Edwards, Emerson) as "nearly blinded by God's waylaying light, [turning] to analogy and metaphor, finding in nature 'images and shadows of divine things.'"[66] But this is to miss the essential core of the Mormon heterodoxy: the conflation of heaven and earth into the same material universe. Smith forsakes the nebulousness of the mystics for the simple literalism of the Old Testament. Like the angels who visit and eat with Abraham, apparently indistinguishable from desert travelers, so do Smith's angelic ministers take the form of ordinary men. Of Moroni he wrote that "His hands were naked and his arms also, a little above the wrist, so, also were his feet naked, as were his legs, a little above the ankles. His head and neck were also bare. I could discover that he had no other clothing on but this robe, as it was open, so that I could see into his bosom."[67] We can contrast his description with Rudolf Otto's pronouncement: "A spirit or soul that has been conceived and comprehended . . . ceases to be of interest for the psychology of religion."[68]

In fact, Smith would articulate the interpenetration of earthly and heavenly ministries as a general principle: "there are no angels who administer to this earth but who belong or have belonged to this earth."[69] By that he meant that an angel is a mortal who had died and "advanced farther—their light and glory being tabernacled, and hence [they] appear in bodily shape," either in a "resurrected or translated body."[70] Elsewhere he said more simply, "Angels are beings who have bodies and appear to men in the form of man."[71] Disembodied spirits of the deceased may be called to be angels of a different sort "visiting and ministering to disembodied spirits" as Christ did during his three days of entombment.[72] In this rewriting of the traditional Chain of Being, angels are not a special creation, existing from eternity to eternity. The term, in Smith's scheme, simply denotes human souls at different stages in their progression, or acting in the performance of special assignments.

Moroni's visit to Smith served to collapse the heavenly and the earthly in yet another way. Not only did he identify himself as a man who had lived in the Western

Hemisphere where he now ministered, but his message also pertained to a set of gold plates "giving an account of the former inhabitants of this continent."[73] Most angels bring knowledge of heavenly things, or of divine activity about to unfold. This angel, himself one of those "former inhabitants," instead directed Smith to events that were local, earthly, and human. In the person of Moroni, Smith found the physical embodiment of a bridge between earth and heaven, the human and the divine. Consistent with this initial event, Smith went on to insert even those angels of biblical renown into an earthly genealogy. The ancient patriarch Noah, Smith declared, subsequently performed angelic ministry as Gabriel, and Michael the Archangel was the angelic name of Adam, for example.[74]

Early Mormons expected angelic ministrations, not just at the pivotal Restoration events, where John the Baptist, and later Peter, James, and John, appeared in resurrected form to ordain Joseph Smith and Oliver Cowdery to the Aaronic and then the Melchizedek priesthood. Smith's scriptural language and sermons alike were replete with promises that angels would minister to the faithful. The Doctrine and Covenants references angels some fifty times, affirming that holders of the priesthood possess the keys of the ministering of angels, and assuring missionaries of the presence of "mine angels round about you to bear you up."[75] Women as well were included in such promises: "If you live up to [your] privileges," Smith told the women of the church in 1842, "the angels cannot be restrained from being your associates."[76]

GUARDIAN ANGELS

From describing angels as prior inhabitants of the earth to identifying them as beings formerly known to us as friends or kin is a small step. So did Joseph F. Smith reason:

> When messengers are sent to minister to the inhabitants of this earth, they are not strangers, but from among our kindred, friends, and fellow-beings.... Our fathers and mothers, brothers, sisters and friends who have passed away from this earth, ... may have a mission given them to visit their relatives and friends upon the earth again, bringing from the divine Presence messages of love, of warning, or reproof and instruction, to those whom they had learned to love in the flesh.[77]

At the funeral of Seymour Brunson, Heber C. Kimball declared that he was ushered across the veil by his friend David Patten, who had died two years before. In fact, Kimball wrote, the "room was full of Angels that came after him to waft him home."[78] Kimball's language could have been adopted from period hymns that invoked similar images of the good death. "They came to waft him home," went one version, "on downy wings of love."[79] "Blessed then is he," in the words of another, "for ever blessed, Whose guilt is purged, whose soul is clear, . . . and waits for wings to waft him home."[80]

While angels who serve as God's messengers are a staple of both the Old and New Testaments, the idea that angels are assigned to watch over particular individuals is more tenuously grounded. The Greeks believed in *daimons,* lesser divinities who sometimes attended upon mortals. (Socrates referenced his personal *daimon* on the occasion of his trial.[81]) Church father Jerome, no friend of the philosophers, may have found his support for the same idea in those biblical passages where angels protect Lot or Moses, or in Jesus's words in reference to little children, that "their angels continually see the face of my Father in heaven."[82] In any case, Jerome taught that "from birth each one has an angel assigned to him for his protection."[83] The same idea was taught in the apocryphal Testament of Adam: "one angel from this lowest order accompanies every single human being in the world for his protection."[84]

Few Christian beliefs were so universally embraced, so widely depicted in art, so fertile a source of folk traditions, and so enduring to the present day as belief in these heavenly shepherds. Calvin believed they "regard our safety, undertake our defense, direct our ways, and exercise a constant solicitude that no evil befall us,"[85] and nineteenth-century editions of the Book of Common prayer petition God that "St. Michael and all Angels . . . may succor and defend us."[86] Some late Victorian writers narrowed down their purview, referring to "those heavenly angels which God gives to every man baptized in His name. We each have one who follows all our steps, who comforts us and upholds us."[87]

Joseph Smith was insistent that the veil was more permeable, and the worlds of the living and the departed more continuous, than we recognize. The ancient patriarchs, our fathers, "are in heaven, but their children are on Earth. Their bowels yearn over us. God sends down men for this reason."[88] Combining the idea of this porous membrane with prevalent Christian notions, early Mormons spoke matter of factly about guardian angels. Smith referred to seeing his guardian angel in a dream,[89] and being protected only while it was in attendance. In apparent commentary on those words, the church newspaper remarked after Smith's death that "while the angel that administers to man is still in attendance, his life is protected, for the guardian angel is stronger than death; but when he is withdrawn humanity is easily overcome."[90] Mormonism's first theologian, Parley Pratt, referred to guardian angels who "hover about [their kindred] with the fondest affection and the most anxious solicitude."[91] Brigham Young himself declared, "All people have their guardian angels," but probably with Pratt in mind said, "Whether our departed dead guard us is not for me to say."[92]

In the nineteenth century, references to guardian angels appeared frequently in Mormon patriarchal blessings,[93] and were common in Mormon preaching. Heber C. Kimball affirmed their role in his mission: ("our guardian angels were there to assist us, and they delivered us out of . . . danger"[94]), as Orson Hyde did of mission work generally ("your guardian angels have [spoken] to you in dreams and in visions"[95]). One twist the theme took in Mormonism was the belief, alluded to by John Taylor, that certain people, at least, made "a covenant" in the preexistence "with one of thy kindred spirits to be thy guardian angel while in mortality."[96]

Orson Pratt confirmed a prior speaker's assertion that "each person upon the face of the whole earth [has] his guardian angel from the time that he comes into the world." At the same time, Pratt laid the foundations for a movement away from the belief, when he pointed out in his typically rationalist manner, that

> there are a great many places where those angels cannot be present, [while] the Holy Spirit is omnipresent is in every place at the same moment of time, regulating the seasons, and governing the planets in their courses. There would have to be a vast number of angels to be present in every place at the same instant of time, directing the movements of each particle of matter throughout the vast extent of space; consequently this is attended to by that All-powerful Spirit that exists in inexhaustible quantities throughout the universe.[97]

Neither Smith nor subsequent leaders invoked revelations or particular insights to justify what was a widespread belief, relying upon the same sources Christians had for generations. In the late nineteenth century, George Q. Cannon used in support the same proof text employed by Jerome: "The Lord Jesus plainly informs us concerning certain agencies which the Father uses to watch over his little ones-guardian angels, who always behold His face in heaven. They watch over those who are put in their charge."[98] The general belief in guardian angels persisted, even attaining First Presidency support in a 1941 pronouncement that "Your guardian angels stand by you to see that no harm shall touch you, no evil thought disturb you."[99]

Two short years later, the tide was turning against the notion. Harvard graduate and Mormon apostle John Widtsoe wrote that "the common belief . . . that to every person born into the world is assigned a guardian angel to be with that person constantly, is not supported by available evidence. . . . The constant presence of the Holy Ghost would seem to make such a constant, angelic companionship unnecessary." At the same time, he acknowledged that "angels often guard us from accidents and harm, from temptation and sin."[100] Given the fact that LDS scriptures clearly confirm this function ("I have given the heavenly hosts and mine angels charge concerning you"[101]), it would seem that Widtsoe, like some of his contemporary successors, was resisting a concession to angel sentimentalism more rooted in Victorian culture than in theology. In addressing the question of guardian angels, more recent church publications cite Widtsoe's comment, before adding Bruce McConkie's dismissal of personal guardian angels as "counter" to the way God exercises his watchfulness.[102] "The term 'guardian angel' is not used in the scriptures," reminds the church's youth magazine.[103] Still, Mormons continue to affirm their belief in the reality, and the real ministry, of heavenly messengers of light. Elder Jeffrey Holland devoted a General Conference talk to Mormonism's abiding faith in the doctrine, noting that "from the beginning down through the dispensations, God has used angels as His emissaries in conveying love and concern for His children. . . . Our own latter-day history [is] filled with accounts of angels ministering to those on earth. . . . It is rich doctrine and rich history indeed." But that history is an ongoing story, he insisted. "Seen or unseen they are *always* near."[104] At the same time, Mormons are today far more likely to ascribe heavenly intervention to "the spirit" than to angels. It is hard to say if that represents a genuine shift in thinking or simply a more culturally decorous language.

The Human

Whoever says or thinks that human souls pre-existed, . . . but that, satiated with the vision of God, they had turned to evil, . . . and had been condemned to punishment in bodies, shall be anathema.

—EMPEROR JUSTINIAN, 6th century

Man was also in the beginning with God. Intelligence, or the light of truth, was not created or made, neither indeed can be.

—1835 D&C 82:5 (D&C 93:29)

17

Life Before Birth

"CREATION OUT OF nothing," one religious scholar writes, "represented a fundamental change in the Christian understanding of both God and the world." Foremost among these consequences was the radical divorce of Creator and creature: "Creation *ex nihilo* tore the universe away from God." The universe at that point became "of an entirely different nature (*ontos*) from the substance of the living God."[1] The cost of such a transition was a profound alienation: "The doctrine of creation *ex nihilo* implies that the most fundamental ontological divide is between God and the created order. . . . The soul has nothing in common with God; there is no kinship between it and the divine. Its kinship is with its body, in virtue of their common creation, rather than with God."[2] A breach of immense ontological distance replaced the prior intimacy between God and the human known to Plato, Plotinus, and some of the early Christians.

Another consequence of the embrace of creation *ex nihilo* is that for most of Christian history, radical dualism has been a virtual given: "Christians believe in two levels of existence, the level of God's existence as self-contained and the level of man's existence as derived from the level of God's existence," writes a systematic theologian.[3] Mormonism turns Christian theology on its head and reintegrates the Creator and his creature into one unitary realm. It does this by asserting not just the eternity of matter but of spirit as well. Or, rather, of spirits.

Of all the Christian doctrines Mormonism purported to restore, few have been so thoroughly eclipsed in Christian history as the soul's pre-mortal existence. Both

Semitic and Greek sources fed into early church traditions of ante-mortal humans that were widespread though not universal. The pseudepigraphal *Prayer of Joseph* (first century CE) refers, as do other Jewish sources, to the pre-mortal existence of Israel's patriarchs.[4] From the same era, the *Apocalypse of Abraham* (70–150 CE) describes "a multitude of tribes who existed previously" along with "the ones I have prepared to be born of [Abraham] and to be called my people."[5] Even more authoritative— especially in the early Christian centuries—was the *Wisdom of Solomon*, dating from the first or second century BCE, and included in the first known listing of Christian canonical writings, the Muratorian Canon of the second century. The author notes that "As a child I was naturally gifted, and a good soul fell to my lot; or rather, being good, I entered an undefiled body."[6]

In the New Testament itself, the apostles assumed pre-mortal existence, in querying Jesus about the possibility of a blind man sinning before conception (John 9). In addition to Jewish and Platonic precedents, the preexistence of Christ, who was humanity's exemplar, may have led some early Christians to assume such a prior state was true of themselves as well.[7] Since the biblical allusions to preexistence, however, were at best cryptic and scattered, three theories of the soul's origin circulated in early Christian thought: creationism (creation by God at conception, quickening, or birth), traducianism (creation by parents at conception), or preexistence (an eternal or ancient existence before birth). The Father often considered the church's first theologian, Origen (185–254), was in no doubt as to which best explained a cosmos populated by a variety of good and evil beings. Since God would not have created anything inherently evil, and since such creatures are rational and free, he argued, their present status and positions must be the consequence of choice made long ago.

> Some sinned deeply and became daemons, others less and became angels; others still less and became archangels; and thus each in turn received the reward for his individual sin. But there remained some souls who had not sinned so greatly as to become daemons, nor on the other hand so very lightly as to become angels. God therefore made the present world and bound the soul to the body as a punishment.[8]

Origen's position was opposed by his younger contemporary Tertullian (160–ca. 220), who feared that making souls pre-existent imputed to the human "so large an amount of divine quality as to put it on a par with God." His strategy to avoid such an error was to "reckon the soul as very far below God: for we suppose it to be born."[9] An additional problem with attributing to the soul an inherent immortality was the implication that its continuing existence would not be contingent on God's grace. Immortality was at that time held to be an attribute of the divine alone, unless the spirit's subsistence was, as in the case of humans, sustained by God's active will. (Our finite spirits "are created anew every moment" according to Jonathan Edwards.[10])

This scheme reinforced a stable hierarchy in which only God was self-existent. If any created thing was thought to have the appearance of immortality, it is only because through God's grace, "they have been privileged to remain the same through countless ages, though by nature they are fleeting, and liable to dissolution."[11] In fact, the Catholic Church would not make the soul's immortality into dogma for a thousand years.[12] So the dispute over human origins left subsequent Christians in a quandary that went unresolved for another few centuries. The Father Arnobius of Sicca (died ca. 330) was unsure. He inclined to preexistence believing that "either sent forth from Him, or having fallen from Him, we are confined in the darkness of this body."[13] But he confessed he was simply unable to say for sure. "By what sire have [souls] been begotten, and how have they been produced? . . . We, too, admit that we are ignorant of this, do not know it; and we hold that, to know so great a matter, is not only beyond the reach of our weakness and frailty, but *beyond that* also of all the powers which are in the world."[14]

A full century later, the church was no closer to resolution. Augustine (354–430) typically pronounced upon disputed matters of doctrine with a commanding authority, but in this case, he too was unsure. The "obscurity of this darkest question," he wrote to a correspondent, simply does not admit of a clear solution.[15] Years later, still struggling with the issue, he noted there are

> four views about souls: (1) they come into being by propagation [traducianism]; (2) they are created individually for each person who is born [creationism]; (3) they already exist somewhere and are sent by God into the bodies of those who are born ["sent" preexistence]; (4) they sink into bodies by their own choice ["fallen" preexistence]. It would be rash to affirm any of these. For the Catholic commentators on Scripture have not solved or shed light on this obscure and perplexing question.[16]

The problem was, each theory came with vexing difficulties. Creationism, belief that God created each soul at conception or birth, made God complicit in all violent or depraved acts of procreation, and left unanswered the problem of how a soul fresh from God's hand could be tainted by Adam's sin. Traducianism, the view that parents created the spirit in tandem with the body, seemed beyond merely human powers of generation and was inconsistent with the nature of spirit, which was seen as "indiscerptible," or incapable of division.

Preexistence avoided these problems, and had several advantages which appealed to Augustine, as he discussed across a variety of texts. Foremost of these, the paradigm accounted for the human longing for God and heaven. As he asked rhetorically, "where and when had I any experience of happiness, that I should remember it and love it and long for it?"[17] Eventually, Augustine became distracted with fending off the heresies of Pelagius regarding free will and original sin, and abandoned his support of preexistence. Meanwhile, the other dominant churchman of his era, Jerome, admitted to identical consternation. In 410 or 412, he wrote to the bishop Marcellinus, "I well remember your little problem about the [origin] of the soul; although I ought not to call it little, seeing that it is one of the greatest with which the church has to deal."[18] And the church did deal with the issue.

Beginning in 400, synods and councils begin to condemn figures associated with Origen—who taught other doctrines like universal salvation, that were even more controversial than preexistence. Other considerations factored into the shift as well: the emergent doctrine of creation *ex nihilo* required that no thing or entity compete with God's primal existence. The Gnostics had long affirmed their own versions of preexistence, another strike against the doctrine. And in the early Middle Ages, Plato declined in importance as Aristotle surged, removing a principal pillar of intellectual support for preexistence. In the mid-fifth century, Leo the Great was explicitly rejecting human preexistence as "blasphemous fable."[19] The final blow came in the sixth century, when the Emperor Justinian declared that "whoever says or thinks that human souls preexisted, . . . shall be anathema."[20] Subsequent councils confirmed his edict.

For the next thousand years and more, pre-mortal existence circulated at the peripheries of Christian doctrine, or completely submerged, erupting only briefly now and then for reconsideration by the orthodox and those who considered the soul's origin still an unresolved issue. One account relates that Anselm of Canterbury (1033–1109), the greatest Christian philosopher of his age sometimes credited as the founder of Scholasticism, expressed a deathbed wish to "settle a question about the origin of the soul, which I am turning over in my mind, . . . for I do not know whether anyone will solve it when I am dead."[21]

In the late Middle Ages, persistent Neoplatonic threads hinting at preexistence appeared in the literature of mystics like Hildegard von Bingen and Julian of Norwich.[22] In the Renaissance, Marsilio Ficino popularized the *Corpus Hermeticum*, esoteric teachings including preexistence attributed to ancient Egyptians, while other humanists like Pico della Mirandola revived the work of Origen, who was then enthusiastically rehabilitated by a group of seventeenth-century clergymen philosophers known as the Cambridge Platonists.

Benjamin Whichcote, Nathaniel Culverwell, George Rust, Henry More, one of England's first women philosophers, Anne Conway, and several others made it their mission to promote humankind's "natural light," perfectibility, and preexistence. Rabbinical and kabalistic traditions kept preexistence alive while Christian leaders pronounced anathemas, and the Cambridge group imbibed these influences along with "that miracle of the Christian world—Origen."[23] An ardent disciple of Descartes and Newton, More in particular promoted two foundational principles for understanding the universe: "those two dazeling Paradoxes of the Motion of the Earth [Copernicanism] and the Præexistance of the Soul."[24]

A century later, the influence of the Cambridge group had faded enough that an English philosopher could almost consider with justice that the doctrine of preexistence was "universally exploded," but the idea still had some life in the Christian world.[25] In America, Benjamin Franklin noted that the doctrine was at least well-intentioned, aiming "to save the honor of the Deity, which was thought to be injured by the supposition of his bringing creatures into the world to be miserable, without any previous misbehavior of theirs to deserve it."[26] In philosophy, the idea was taken up by the greatest intellectual of the age, Immanuel Kant, who invoked several reasons to advocate a version of preexistence. He found preexistence useful to explain the intuition of universals, and a more appealing basis for human identity than the vagaries of sexual passion. But most importantly for his system, only by taking the soul outside the temporal chain of causality could he find a convincing ground for human freedom.[27]

By the nineteenth century, a number of theologians in Germany and America were anxious to base the Christian doctrine of sin on a more rigorous theory of human freedom and accountability. William Benecke (1776–1837) wrote an influential commentary on Romans, asking how or when humans born without a divine law could have transgressed one, to incur condemnation. Allowing such premises, he asked, "can any other answer be given than that which I have drawn from them; namely, in an ante-human existence?"[28]

German theologian Julius Müller (1801–1878) followed similar reasoning all the way to a eureka moment. If humans are guilty of sin, they must be possessed of what he called an actual, unconditioned "freedom of the first decision." But where can we find a moment before we are shaped and determined by environment, heredity, and bodily disposition? "The course of our inquiry compels us TO LOOK BEYOND THE REGION OF THE TEMPORAL IN ORDER TO FIND THE ORIGINAL SOURCE OF OUR FREEDOM," he wrote. "Human freedom must have its beginning in a sphere beyond the range of time, wherein alone pure and unconditioned self-determination is possible. In this region we must seek that power of original choice."[29]

Responding to the temper of the times, the great Calvinist theologian Charles Hodge (1797–1878) admitted that preexistence offered a more equitable scheme of human choice, justice, and accountability, but insisted that it was unnecessary as a theory since God's condemnation was based on Adam's sin and not on "the voluntary act of each individual man."[30]

Joseph Smith was most likely unfamiliar with the debates in philosophical idealism or German theology; neither is it likely that he was aware of the popularity of preexistence among his British literary contemporaries. Thomas Taylor (1758–1835) had just made all the works of Plato available in English for the first time, and among the Romantics, a frenzied revival of the philosopher—and his ideas about preexistence—followed. William Blake imagined a pre-existent realm in *Thel* (1789); Samuel Taylor Coleridge imagined his baby son to be "a spirit, to this nether sphere Sentenc'd for some more venial crime to grieve,"[31] and defended the idea to his friend John Thelwall, insisting that "if you never have had [intimations of preexistence] yourself, I cannot explain [them] to you."[32] His mentor William Wordsworth gave the idea its most famous poetic expression of the era when he wrote that

> Our birth is but a sleep and a forgetting
> The soul that rises with us, our life's star
> Hath had elsewhere its setting, and cometh from afar
> Not in entire forgetfulness, and not in utter nakedness,
> But trailing clouds of glory do we come from God who is our home.[33]

He, too, defended the principle, saying to Isabella Fenwick, "let us bear in mind that, tho' the idea is not advanced in revelation, there is nothing there to contradict it, and the fall of Man presents an analogy in its favor." Even if his orthodoxy precluded an unqualified endorsement, he insisted that "the notion of preexistence [has] sufficient foundation in humanity for authorizing me to make for my purpose the best use of it."[34]

Closer to home, few poets in Joseph Smith's America appropriated the idea until the Transcendentalists came on the scene a few years later, but the idea was not unknown. Dr. Ashbel Green (1762–1848), minister and president of Princeton University, had propounded in an 1825 issue of the *Christian Advocate* a defense of preexistence. "The safest and MOST RATIONAL" version of the soul's origin, he had argued, is "to suppose that ALL souls were created at the beginning of the world; that they remain in a *quiescent* state *till* the bodies which they are to inhabit are formed."[35] "We know not whether to smile or frown," minister and author George Duffield had responded in print in 1832. The editor of the *Christian Observer* (where Duffield's article appeared) was less restrained: "monstrous hypothesis," he remarked. "Most monstrous speculation, unscriptural, anti-scriptural, and absurd," fumed a reader.[36]

Where Smith first encountered or entertained the possibility of a human preexistence is impossible to say. Orson Pratt thought the idea first appeared in the Book of Mormon, where the "brother of Jared" sees the pre-existent Christ in bodily form, and learns that men were "created after the body of my spirit." This meant, in Pratt's reading, that "all the human family . . . were created in the beginning, after the image of that body; that is, . . . a pure spiritual body."³⁷

Clearer indications came, Pratt notes, in the summer or fall of 1830, when Smith worked on his revision of the Old Testament. One of the first significant emendations he introduced involved the second account of creation (Gen. 2). After the passage in which God explains that he made every plant and herb "before it grew," Smith added the phrase, "For I the Lord God, created all things, of which I have spoken, spiritually, before they were naturally upon the face of the earth."³⁸ In this same period, he sketched a chapter of pre-mortal history that he may or may not have taken to include the human race. In an 1830 text, he records God's lament that "A third part of the hosts of heaven [Satan] turned away from me because of their agency."³⁹ That these hosts included pre-mortal humans becomes rather clearer in November or December of that year, when continuing his work on the Old Testament, Smith has the patriarch Enoch learn in a vision about "the spirits that God had created," and discover that God "made the world, and men before they were [in the flesh]."⁴⁰ The appearance of those ideas in the Enoch text was decisive, though this would not be clear for some time.

In March 1831, another of Smith's revelations referred to the earth as being "filled with the measure of man, according to his creation before the world was made."⁴¹ But little note was made of these references, by Smith or anyone else, and he may have followed some Jewish commentators in seeing such references as implying an "ideal creation" in the mind of God only. In any case, we have no record of his broaching the subject in public or with associates in these first years. The 1830 revelation was not published until September 1832 (and section 49 months later), and the reference to creating men "before they were in the flesh" also did not appear in print until March 1833 (Moses 3 would not see publication for several decades).

The idea acquired fresh and decisive impetus from two other revelations that occurred in the meantime. The first, dated to March 1832, was "A Sample of Pure Language," in which the name of God is given as Awman, or "the being which made all things in its parts." And the "children of men," it went on to say, are "the greatest parts of Awman."⁴² The phrasing might not of itself have suggested a pre-mortal genealogy. Together with a second revelation, however, the text points quite clearly to a conception of human spirits as emanating from God. Little is known of the context in which the related revelation, dated 27 February 1833, was pronounced. One source indicates the original version was "sung in tongues by Elder D. W. Patton . . . and interpreted by Elder S[idney] Rigdon."⁴³ Recorded in the hand of Frederick G. Williams, the revelation was apparently influenced by the Enoch text already mentioned. In this song sung in tongues by Patton and rendered in English by Rigdon, Enoch "saw the begining the ending of man he saw the time when Adam his father was made and he saw that he was in eternity before a grain of dust in the ballance was weighed he saw that he emenated and came down from God."[44]

The likelihood that the Awman revelation and the Enoch hymn were together pivotal in concretizing the idea of preexistence is supported by the fact that when an anonymous poet, perhaps W. W. Phelps, published in the church paper a poetic celebration of preexistence in May 1833, it bore the marks of these two sources.[45] Tellingly, Smith unambiguously affirmed the eternal preexistence of human spirits early this same month, declaring that "Man was also in the beginning with God. Intelligence, or the light of truth, was not created or made, neither indeed can be."[46] Yet Phelps published his poetic declaration based, not on the definitive revelation of Smith, but on the hymn of Enoch:

> Before the mountains rais'd their heads
> Or the small dust of balance weigh'd. With God he[Enoch] saw his race began
> And from him emanated man,
> And with him did in glory dwell
> Before there was an earth or hell....[47]

The importance of the Awman and the Enoch texts (Moses 6–7 and the subsequent tongue-singing revelation) in founding the first clear understanding of preexistence is further evident in the fact that Parley Pratt invoked both the language of the Enoch hymn and the imagery of the Awman revelation in his 1838 linkage of theosis and pre-mortality, wherein he argued that "the redeemed . . . return to the fountain, and become part of the great all, from which they eminated."[48] (Such language also suggests that Pratt is already taking the idea of emanation and Smith's reference to the eternity of "intelligence" in the singular to mean that human spirits evolve—or are fashioned by God—from undifferentiated divine spirit into individuated entities, a two-stage preexistence which Smith never describes but which becomes normative in Mormon thought.)

All these developments illustrate that Smith was developing a conception of human preexistence gradually but consistently from the year the church was organized. After the 1832 and 1833 developments, a significant expansion occurred when Smith began studying papyrus scrolls that he acquired in 1835 along with several Egyptian mummies. Working with these papyri, he claimed another burst of inspired revelation and produced writings attributed to the biblical patriarch Abraham. The first chapter begins as a more ample retelling of the story of Abraham's flight from Ur to Canaan, briefly sketched in Genesis 1:31–12:4. By the third chapter, however, Smith conveys an unambiguous Mormon doctrine of fully individuated, pre-mortal humans:

> Now the Lord had shown unto me, Abraham, the intelligences that were organized before the world was; and among all these there were many of the great and noble ones. And God saw these souls that they were good, and he stood in the midst of them, and he said: These I will make my rulers, for he stood among those that were spirits, and he saw that they were good; and he said unto me: Abraham, thou art one of them; thou wast chosen before thou wast born.

And those spirits—or at least some aspect of them—are emphatically uncreated: "If there be two spirits, . . . notwithstanding one is more intelligent than the other, have no beginning; they existed before, they shall have no end, they shall exist after, for they are . . . eternal."[49]

This picture was published in March 1842 in the church's *Times and Seasons*. By then, however, Smith was openly teaching the doctrine in public. "The Spirit of Man is not a created being; it existed from Eternity & will exist to eternity." Along with the elements, "all these had their existence in an elementary State from Eternity," he pronounced in August 1839.[50] In February of the next year, he proclaimed the doctrine in Washington, D.C. At least one auditor found the idea strikingly novel. "I believe that the soul is eternal," Smith was reported as saying, "and had no beginning; it can have no end. Here he entered into some explanations, which were so brief that I could not perfectly comprehend him. But the idea seemed to be that the soul of man, the spirit, had existed from eternity in the bosom of Divinity; and so far as he was intelligible to me, must ultimately return from whence it came."[51]

At the same time, some evidence suggests that Smith was coming to conceive of a process by which God transformed inchoate eternal material into individuated, autonomous spirits. A hint of a possible two-step conception in Smith's language was his recorded statement that spirits "had their existence in an elementary State from eternity," suggesting God may be the Creator of human spirits in the same way he is Creator of the world—as an organizer of elements.[52] This may have been how Lorenzo Snow understood him, since he wrote in an 1842 letter: "Let us indulge our follies at this time and wander a moment into the field of imagination. Some thirteen thousand years ago in Heaven or in Paradise (say) we came into existence or in other words received a spiritual organization according to the laws that govern *spiritual births* in eternity."[53] Pratt later dated to 1840 such a teaching on Smith's part, recording that the prophet told him in private conversations that "the result of our endless union would be an offspring as numerous as the stars of heaven, or the sands of the seashore."⁵⁴ William Clayton also recorded Smith as teaching that marriages which persist in the eternities will include the power to "have children in the celestial glory," implying that we may have been created by a comparable process.⁵⁵ Heber C. Kimball, another of Smith's inner circle, reflected a similar understanding in his journal at the very time Smith was introducing eternal marriage sealings. Kimball wrote of his hope that, enthroned in the worlds to come, he and his wife would continue to "propagate that thare may be no end to us or our Seeds."⁵⁶

Other evidence, however, suggests that Smith considered spirit and intelligence to be synonymous concepts, referring to an eternally existent entity. He referred to "intelligences who surround the throne of Jehovah,"⁵⁷ and in a public meeting on 28 March 1841, he made their equivalence with spirits explicit: "the spirit or the intelligence of men are self-existent principles before the foundation of this earth."⁵⁸ In the Abrahamic text he recorded that spirits "have no beginning" and in his King Follett Discourse, he seemed to disallow a two-tiered scenario: "God never did have power to create the spirit of man at all. God Himself could not create Himself. Intelligence is eternal and exists upon a self-existent principle."⁵⁹ In fact, "spirit, the mind of man—the intelligent Part—is as immortal as, and is coequal [co-eternal] with, God Himself."⁶⁰

At the same time, Smith's reference in the Abraham text to intelligences being "organized" cannot itself be read as referring to spirit formation. His consistent linguistic usage makes it clear the organization was social, not ontological. Smith declared in at least three revelations that the saints "must . . . be organized according to [God's] laws," or his "pattern,"⁶¹ and in another that they should be organized "by a bond or everlasting covenant";⁶² elsewhere he enjoins their organization into a church, into stakes, into High Councils, Quorums, Councils, Presidencies and Societies; into a united order, into Zion's Camp, and into stewardships. Organization is for Smith generally an ordering of people according to priesthood principles. When Abraham saw "the intelligences that were organized," it was doubtless in Smith's mind a deliberate ordering of pre-mortal spirits into priestly or patriarchal organization.⁶³ This is also confirmed by Smith's later reference to a time when "The Father called all spirits before him at the creation of Man & organized them" with Adam as "the head."⁶⁴ Yet again, he appeared to reference the Abrahamic account as an ordering of spirits according to a divine plan when he described "the first organization in heaven [where] we were all present and saw the Savior chosen and appointed."⁶⁵

SPIRIT ADOPTION

Smith clearly referred to intelligences (or spirits) as beings co-eternal with God, forever having inhabited the same universe as God himself. In this primordial populous scenario, God took compassion on what he saw were clearly "inferior," or less progressed, beings: "God saw that those intelegences had Not power to Defend themselves against those that had a tabenicle therefore the Lord Calls them togather in Counsel and agrees to form them tabernacles."[66] This provision is made "for the benefit of inferior intelligences."[67]

Smith expounded this idea in the King Follett Discourse, his most daring theological statement: "The relationship we have with God places us in a situation to advance in knowledge. God Himself found Himself in the midst of spirits and glory. Because He was greater He saw proper to institute laws whereby the rest, who were less in intelligence, could have a privilege to advance like Himself and be exalted with Him."[68] Or, as Young said on the subject, "I view myself as perfectly helpless in [the] beginning." These intelligences were all "as helpless and dependent as any creature can be," but God deigned to "bring them together and mankind is brought forth for nobler purposes to be exalted to Godhead." In other words, "you are planted here an independent arrangement to become Gods."[69] It is a commonplace of Christian orthodoxy that "the drama of salvation began when the Father and Son agreed to redeem the creation from the effects of the fall."[70] In Mormon mythology, however, it is at a moment far more remote in time, before the earth is formed or the first man created, that grace irrupts into the universe.

Smith's word choice, including a "calling together" of preexistence spirits by a superior intelligence whose every act is "for the benifit of inferier inteligences," and is motivated by compassion for their "weaker," vulnerable status, may suggest that the "relationship we have with God" is one that he invites us to enter, rather than one that is organically evolved. In other words, our relationship to a Heavenly Father (and Mother) described by Smith is interpreted by some Mormon scholars as much more like spiritual adoption than primordial birth. In this version, Smith read Job's query, "what is man, . . . that thou shouldst set thy heart upon him?," as containing the seeds of its own reply.[71] God simply *chose* to set his heart upon other beings. Smith thereby goes beyond the simple scenario of a God who has a loving and paternalistic relation to his creation. He reaches toward a scheme in which God invites humankind into a more formalized network of family association, based on an ontological likeness and inherent potential. In B. H. Roberts's terms, "eternities will pass over man's head, . . . with God for guide and teacher."[72]

The impossibility of establishing with certainty Smith's position on spirit birth as opposed to spirit adoption is one of many points of indeterminacy in the Mormon past, and a reminder of how much fog enshrouded a narrative that is at times depicted as clear and unfailingly linear in the modern church. It is possible that Smith was undecided relative to two scenarios of human creation. More likely, perhaps, is the fact that neither adoption nor procreation is an adequate human analogue for the process by which Smith believed eternally existing intelligent element (or beings) to be transformed into individual human spirits. (That might explain why Smith also used the word *emanate* as yet a third metaphor or description of spirit emergence).[73] Hence the ambiguity in Smith's exposition of the idea. In any case, at the very moment of Smith's death, a watershed in the Mormon conception of preexistence develops with the unambiguous literalizing of God's fatherhood of the human spirit, in a procreative process that transforms intelligence or spirit matter into autonomous human spirits. Whether this represents a logical development or the dissemination of an understanding Smith had only taught privately, the shift was decisive. (As we saw, this occurred hand in hand with, and was likely influenced by, the contemporary development of the Mother in Heaven doctrine.) Some Mormon writers have in this regard adopted a scenario similar to that first proposed by the ancient writer Evagrius Ponticus (345–399 CE). He taught that humans began as intelligence (*nous*) that progressed to the acquisition of a nonmaterial form (soul) before becoming incarnate as humans. More recently, Mormonism follows in the wake of Meister Eckhart, who wrote that "something in man . . . is of God's order, . . . by which man is of the genus and species of God."[74] Eckhart seemed to believe that "God's blood flows in our veins," and "we are really in God's family." His editor notes, "No one had ever taken this idea of 'blood relationship' to God so seriously or followed its consequences so radically."[75] At least, not until early Mormonism.

Perhaps Mormonism's first printed reference to man as "the offspring of God" occurs in Orson Pratt's *Prophetic Almanac* of 1845 (already in press before Smith's martyrdom); such a term could be metaphorical (as most Christians take the allusion to humans as "children of God" in Rom. 8), but he also uses the more unambiguous phrase "begotten and born of God," and Pratt also refers in the same context to Christ as "our brother," suggesting an actual, fuller human participation in a heavenly family.[76] Because the notion of a Heavenly Mother was emerging at this same time, and the human and divine anthropology merged by Smith in his King Follett Discourse was coming to be standard doctrine (man's destiny is "to be like God," writes Pratt in the same Almanac, and God's past was to be "like man"), literalizing the parenthood of God would naturally, if not inevitably, follow.[77] And so W. W. Phelps writes in 1845 that man had spent eons as a "spiritual body, while he was a child with his father and mother in heaven."[78] Orson Pratt drew the logical inference in 1852 that "our spirits were formed by generation, the same as the body . . . of flesh and bones."[79]

Initially, Parley P. Pratt endorsed Smith's view of an eternally pre-existing human soul; as "individual intelligences," he wrote, each was already "an organized personage of a proper shape, form, and proportion."[80] But he soon accepted the fuller implications of Smith's radical materialism and a more literal conception of Heavenly

Parenthood. He, like Orson, came to teach that "this individual spirit body was begotten by the heavenly Father, in His own likeness and image, and by the laws of procreation. It was born and matured in the heavenly mansions."[81] He gave a more metaphysical rendering in an 1853 sermon: Imagine, he said, a "spirit liquid invisible," with "a capacity and enjoyment and intellectual power inherent in it." Let it be "organize[d] into an individual being that will see, sense with eye and in the likeness and power that you now see me stand before you with eyes, head, members, mouth, and the gift of hearing, seeing, speaking, thinking with hands, feet, and in short, . . . you have organized it an individual agent a living moving thinking being."[82]

Orson Pratt wrote a highly detailed exposition of preexistence in a series of articles published in *The Seer* that same year. Fired by the same literalist zeal that inspired his brother Parley and other contemporary Mormons, he insisted on moving beyond any possible metaphorical meaning of begetting when he wrote that all spirits were "begotten by a father, and born of a mother in Heaven," and even speculated on the time required for "the formation of the embryo spirit."[83] (The Scottish poet Thomas Campbell, with a vague nod at pre-mortal existence, had popularized the term "embryo spirit" in his widely read 1799 "Pleasures of Hope.") Young differed with Pratt on the origins of spirit bodies; Pratt was an atomist, believing that "there is no substance in the universe which feels and thinks now, but what has eternally possessed that capacity."[84] Young censored Pratt's panpsychism, but otherwise readily adopted a similar two-stage model of spirit birth from some primeval matter, and taught it from the pulpit: "The Father actually begat the spirits, and they were brought forth and lived with him."[85] Later in the century and in the same vein, respected thinkers like Orson Whitney could refer to God as "the Begetter of [the human] spirit in the eternal worlds."[86]

The problem with conceiving of God's begetting of the human spirit as a literal counterpart to human begetting was noted almost immediately upon Joseph Smith's death. As Joseph Robinson wrote in 1845, given that Smith had said that

> our spirits existed eternally with God, the question arose then, How is God the Father of our spirits? . . . I inquired of several of the brethren how that could be—a father and son as old as the father. There was not a person that could or that would even try to explain that matter, but it came to pass that in time a vision opened, the voice of the spirit came to me saying: that all matter was eternal, that it never had a beginning and . . . that the spirits of all men were organized of a pure material or matter upon the principal of male and female so that there was a time when my immortal spirit as well as every other man's spirit . . . was organized or begotten or born so that the spirit has a father and the material or matter [it is] composed of is eternal.[87]

Organized, or *begotten*, or *born*—the stream of near synonyms suggests a process shrouded in mystery whereby primal spirit matter, or in some versions, intelligence(s) comes to be individual spirits, under the operations of Heavenly Parents/Creators.

Even though the transformation or progression of spirit matter or intelligence into spirit through a process analogous to birth has no verifiable basis in Smith's teachings, this interpretation is the logical implication of a heavenly pattern—limned by Smith in his King Follett Discourse and in section 132—whereby exalted men and women become the creators of eternal offspring, in imitation of their own Heavenly Parents. ("God himself was once as we are now;" and exalted women will "bear the souls of men," Smith had said.[88]) Smith may have been heading in the direction of reconciling eternal existence with spirit birth or spirit "organization." He may, in other words, have been working toward a scheme in which primordial intelligence is transformed into spirit corporeality, rather than a familial or societal organizing of pre-existing spirits into priesthood structures (as he suggested in the King Follett Discourse).

For one thing, it is true that although, as we saw above, Smith usually employed that term to suggest social ordering rather than creative process, he did once use the term in the latter way. (Moving from the council of primordial "intelligences," "the Gods went down to *organize* man in their own image" [my emphasis], he wrote in Abraham.[89]) In addition, the concept of human beings as "organized intelligences" was common in Smith's day. As early as 1823, writers refer to the immortal spirit as "organized intelligence."[90] In subsequent years, Spiritualists especially adopted the term as a definition of the human soul ("magnetical science asserts that the soul is an organized intelligence"[91]), as did the Shakers (worlds are "peopled with organized intelligences"; "every soul is an organized substance"[92]). Another writer explicitly employs the term to suggest a process involving divine refinement of a raw material, as Mormons understand spirit birth today: "The wide distinction between spirit and matter which forms the basis of the popular theology of the day, does not in reality, exist; . . . the spirit, contrary to old beliefs, is matter in the highest state of refinement." It has been converted by God from "this grosser matter into refined and organized intelligence."[93]

In any case, Smith's original scheme that suggested God's adoption of spirits/intelligences into his sphere of influence apparently developed into a two-stage primordial existence of eternally existing spirit element that became individuated, begotten, sired, organized, or birthed into human spirits. In another decisive statement, James E. Talmage, the most influential of early twentieth-century theologians, writing one of the few official treatises on LDS theology, called the human spirit "an organized intelligence."[94] A refinement in this two-stage model of human pre-mortality, with a crucial distinction between the two entities, came with B. H. Roberts. When he gave his synthesis final form in his masterwork, *The Truth, the Way, the Life*, its publication was thwarted in part over this issue. Roberts tried to reconcile the language of Smith's teachings, which frequently included the term "intelligence," with the subsequent teachings about spirit birth. He did this by asserting that an "intelligence" was an autonomous, but pre-spirit, being. He may have had scriptural support in mind: Smith had declared that "all truth is independent, . . . to act for itself, *as all intelligence also*" (my emphasis).[95] He may have also thought he was but following Erastus Snow, who had declared that "every individual intelligence is possessed of a will."[96] Nevertheless, the view did not carry the day. The committee reviewing Roberts's work denied the moral autonomy he imputed to intelligence, asserting that "these intelligences . . . may rebel, as Lucifer did" only "after they became spirits."[97] A few years later, Roberts's view reappeared in the work of fellow intellectual John A. Widtsoe, who would become an apostle in 1921. Joseph F. Smith halted the 1914 publication of his *Rational Theology* until Widtsoe eliminated "all that pertained to intelligences before they became begotten spirits as that would only be speculation."[98] A few years later, Charles Penrose, counselor in the First Presidency, confirmed the anti-Roberts position: "intelligences . . . had a beginning when they were born of God as the sons or daughters of God."[99]

Mormon apostle Bruce R. McConkie, the most respected scripture scholar and most doctrinaire leader of his era, invoked the notion of "organization," and reaffirmed the pre-Roberts status quo by using Young's "spirit element" and Smith's "intelligence" as interchangeable. In other words, intelligence, in the singular, is read as some kind of primeval matter or stuff, by contrast with intelligences, which carry the connotation of autonomous beings. McConkie equated "birth" with "organization," perhaps thereby implicitly cautioning against the literal implications of birth that many Mormons are still prone to see there: "We were born as the spirit children of God the Father," McConkie said, then added: "Through that birth process spirit element was organized into intelligent entities."[100] With his contention that "Spirit element . . . is also called intelligence," a kind of synthesis that avoids the individuated nature of pre-spirit existence was achieved that is the dominant model today.[101]

When the language of spirit birth is used in the modern church, it is without the clarification that such begetting may be our best near-equivalent for God's fathering of the human spirit. The First Presidency declared, with an official "Doctrinal Exposition" issued in 1916: "Scriptures embodying the ordinary signification—literally that of Parent—are too numerous and specific to require citation. The purport of these scriptures is to the effect that God the Eternal Father, whom we designate by the exalted name-title 'Elohim,' is the literal Parent of our Lord and Savior Jesus Christ, and of the spirits of the human race."[102] An apostle later declared, "[Man's] spirit as an individual person was begotten unto God in the spirit world," in a typical pronouncement.[103] Or as another official First Presidency statement affirms, "man, as a spirit, was begotten and born of heavenly parents, and reared to maturity in the eternal mansions of the Father."[104]

This theological position, which conceives of God as the Creator/Begetter of human spirits, avoids the clear imputation of individual autonomy or selfhood to the pre-spirit intelligence or matter, which Roberts wanted to embrace. At the same time, the affirmation of a two-tiered pre-mortal existence—as primal matter of some sort, then creation into spirit beings—has the virtue of preserving God's biblical role as our Father/Creator, even as it accords with Smith's claim of a primeval human identity, or at least a primal component, as an uncreated substance, co-eternal with God.

Mormon leaders have embraced this "organizing" version of spirit birth that followed in the wake of Smith's death, even as they maintain the theological force of adoption into God's family. Young's successor John Taylor, described "Man, made in the image of God" as "capable not only of being a son of man, but also a son of God, through adoption." "Through the instrumentality of the atonement and the adoption, it is possible for us to become of the family of God," he emphasized.[105] B. H. Roberts himself acknowledged "the array of evidence that may be massed to prove that it is chiefly through adoption, through obedience to the Gospel of Christ, that man in the scripture is spoken of as being a son of God," even as he emphasized his belief that humans are literally "by nature the [children] of God." Most importantly, he argued, human destiny portends an eventual, full likeness to God. And that process, given human alienation from God through personal sin, requires spiritual rebirth, and hence "adoption" into the heavenly kingdom, and into sonship with God.[106] Adoption is, therefore, renewal of a natural relationship after our estrangement. His voice is especially significant, recognizing the crucial theological point as he does that, as human experience reveals, biological and adoptive fathers are equally and truly parents. And in an age of surrogate mothers and test-tube babies, it is clear that "literal" fatherhood has not yet exhausted its meanings even in a terrestrial sphere.

Whether the human spirit is begotten or adopted by God, its pre-mortal existence leads to the thorough inversion of several elements of the conventional Christian salvation narrative. Most importantly, mortal life does not represent a fall from grace but an ascent; it is not a setback or digression, but the necessary bridge which transitions humans from a primal inadequacy and insufficiency to familial integration and ontological plenitude. This is a novel view, even for partisans of pre-mortal theology. From Origen to Smith's contemporary Edward Beecher, many proponents of human preexistence have seen earth as a purgatory or "moral hospital," where those expelled or fallen from heaven work out their punishment or rehabilitation.[107]

In the LDS view, however, mortality is a step forward in an eternal process of spiritual advancement. In Parley Pratt's language, human spirits are "now in disguise, as it were, in order to pass through the several changes, and the experience necessary to constitute them perfect beings."[108]

The first lesson of the Baltimore Catholic catechism asked, "Why did God make you?" The answer: "God made me to know him, to love him, and to serve him in this world and to be happy with him forever in the next."[109] Mormonism alters the equation, holding that God is not a creator who fashions humans for his own purposes, as much as a guide and heavenly mentor who shepherds a pre-existing intelligence toward its highest potential, or endows spirit matter with the form and conditions conducive to that end: full emulation of a perfect Father and participation in a celestial community. God's declaration that it was his "work and glory to bring to pass the immortality and eternal life of man"[110] suggests just such an eternal program.

SEX AND GENDER

In the vision mentioned above which Joseph Robinson recorded, God created human spirits as male and female. Other traditions were rather vague about the soul's sex, with some exceptions. Plato had hinted at its inherent masculinity; Aristotle denied the soul had an existence independent of the body, but did think all souls possessed greater or lesser degrees of maleness. The Gnostics called it "female in nature and androgynous in form," and Cabbalists thought it dual-gendered.[111] Augustine held that in the spirit "there is no sex";[112] Aquinas wrote that souls were paired to their bodies, in the sense that "the soul of this man cannot possibly enter a body other than its own," but whether that specificity entailed a sexual or gender component he did not say.[113] Sexual differentiation was believed by many in the early church to be a provisional condition of the body only. For Origen, for example, "it was a mere passing phase, . . . a dispensable adjunct of the personality that played no role in defining the essence of the human spirit." Jerome embraced this same view that "bodies endowed with sexual characteristics of men and women were ephemeral things, into which the vibrant spirit had been placed for a short moment."[114] By contrast, Hildegard von Bingen, a twelfth-century mystic, believed that upon resurrection the sexually differentiated body and soul would be eternally integrated.[115] By the eighteenth century, early feminists like Mary Astell and Mary Wollstonecraft argued—largely for reasons of political expediency—for a sexless soul. "All Souls are equal, and alike, and . . . consequently there is no such Distinction as Male and Female Souls," wrote Astell.[116]

For Latter-day Saints, however, the soul itself has always been emphatically sexually differentiated. Orson Pratt affirms Robinson's view, proclaiming spirits "male and female" in 1853.[117] In predictable consistency with nineteenth-century thought and assumptions generally, Mormons of the era spent little time defending what they thought common sense indicated was an essential constituent of human identity. If early Mormon conceptions of gender or sexual identity were distinctive, it was in attaching the category to a pre-mortal spirit and asserting its persistence after death. Christians generally denied the validity of the first claim and differed on the second. (As we saw, some Christians held that in the resurrection, signs of sexual difference would disappear.[118])

As for what today would be labeled gender roles, or the disputed territory of gender differentiation, Smith and Young employed fairly conventional terminology. Smith said women were naturally endowed with charity.[119] Women were inherently more sympathetic and tender, men sterner, said Young.[120] They were also "more ready to do and love the right than men are," with a greater potential for social amelioration than the male.[121] At the same time, even Brigham Young frequently railed against the history of the sexes as one of unremitting oppression and inequality, in which the man has "abused his privilege" and "covered [women] with abuse and dishonor."[122] "The male portion of the human family are the lords of the earth, and they are full of wickedness, evil and destruction, and especially in their acts towards the female sex;"[123] "The female sex have been deceived so long, and been trodden under foot of man so long," that the social order stood in need of reconstitution.[124]

Smith was prepared to extend to women some, though not equal, ecclesiastical roles. "Regarding the female laying on of hands," he said, "there could be no devils in it if God gave his sanction by healing."[125] And he was apparently prepared to ordain his wife to be both an exhorter and a preacher in the early church.[126] And plural marriage itself, as we will see subsequently, can be read as Smith's attempt, among other purposes, to endow women with tremendously significant priestly powers.[127] Young was apparently less progressive regarding women's ecclesiastical roles. And he felt the remedy to a damaged social order, to which he referred, was to be found in deference to righteous patriarchal leadership. Virtually no hint was ever given, however, of any forthcoming change here or hereafter in the roles or essential qualities of the sexes. (Joseph Fielding Smith expressed an exception regarding the procreative capacities of non-celestialized bodies.[128])

Virtually no early dissent emerged from these assumptions about the durability of gender and sexuality. John A. Widtsoe wrote that "Sex, which is indispensable on this earth for the perpetuation of the human race, is an eternal quality which has its equivalent everywhere. It is indestructible. The relationship between men and women is eternal and must continue eternally. In accordance with Gospel philosophy there are males and females in heaven. . . . This simply carries onward the logic of things earthly, and conforms with the doctrine that whatever is on this earth is simply a representation of spiritual conditions of deeper meaning than we can here fathom."[129]

Talmage, too, affirmed the eternity of sexual identity: "There is no accident or chance, due to purely physical conditions, by which the sex of the unborn is determined; the body takes form as male or female according to the sex of the spirit whose appointment it is to tenant that body."[130] He even proposed an explanation for the continuity of sexual identity, which the First Presidency let stand as doctrine: The individual's spirit "shaped for itself a body from the material of earth. . . . In each case the body is formed and fashioned by the power of the immortal spirit."[131]

All of these statements were made in eras when sex and gender were not yet differentiated. Only in recent decades have feminists, social scientists, and gender theorists especially insisted on a clear distinction between sex as biological and essential in nature, and gender as socially constructed and contingent. While many would debate such a rigid polarization, it is common enough in contemporary thought for the World Health Organization to assert it matter of factly: "'Sex' refers to the biological and physiological characteristics that define men and women. 'Gender' refers to the socially constructed roles, behaviours, activities, and attributes that a given society considers appropriate for men and women."[132]

With the close of the twentieth century, in the midst of cultural upheaval regarding gender roles, sexual identity, and the very meaning of those terms, the church issued "The Family: A Proclamation to the World." In this 1995 document, the leadership affirmed that "Gender is an essential characteristic of individual premortal, mortal, and eternal identity and purpose."[133] Given the context and prehistory of this subject in Mormon thought, one can reasonably conclude that the statement is resisting the current social scientific trend, and attributing to gender the essentialist value it had in the past. No one, LDS leaders included, would deny a social aspect to the shape that gender takes; at the same time, the statement appears intended to emphasize that sexual/gender identity encompasses more than either socially acquired habits or differences of the flesh, and that those constants are a feature of the soul's existence from the beginning.

One might argue that the exact meaning of gender is unclear in this statement and in Mormon discourse generally, and that the statement sheds little light on the subject. One Mormon scholar, for instance, writes that "LDS theology faces serious credibility issues by continuing to hold to precritical assumptions about sexual difference."[134] That may be, but given the church's emphatic claim that gender is "eternal," it is not conceivable that Mormon soteriology can dispense with the category. The Proclamation asserts an emphatic position, but leaves undefined the exact nature of what is being defended. It appears to assert that independently of mortal biology, and enduring before and beyond earthly, socially constructed roles and patterns of behavior, human identity is constituted in terms of an eternal binary that the scriptures refer to as man and woman, male and female. Some element of eternal selfhood must in this view underlie and transcend both the physical and the cultural, and exist in a way to constitute mutual complementarity.

In Mormon thought, this eternal differentiation transcends and swallows up earthly echoes, rooted as they are in social roles, acquired habits, and the traditions of the fathers. The differentiation would seem to be necessary to the eternal parenting that has long been part of Mormonism's conception of human anthropology. But there are hints that such difference is also the precondition for an interdependent unity and completion.[135]

PERSONALITY AND LINEAGE

If humans did indeed exist for unnumbered eons in a prior state, it would be natural to conclude that whatever scenes and actions unfolded there have some bearing on present circumstances. In transforming the human condition from cosmic catastrophe to sublime opportunity, preexistence reshapes human identity as something that inherently tends more to divinity than to depravity. But in addition to this reformulation of collective identity, preexistence has bearing on tribal and individual identity as well. Origen thought he had found a crucial clue to the first in the book of Deuteronomy (32:8), when God "fixed the boundaries of the nations, according to the number of the [pre-existent] angels of God." Those souls who progressed to the rank of angels, he wrote, constituted certain "orders" or nations of the earth.[136]

The nation specifically alluded to by the Deuteronomist is of course Israel. Adolf Harnack wrote that borrowing from Jewish precedents, some early Christians adapted the idea to their experience, finding the preexistence of Israel foreshadows the preexistence of a Christian community:

> If the world was created for the sake of the people of Israel, and the Apocalyptists expressly taught that, then it follows, that in the thought of God Israel was older than the world. The idea of a kind of preexistence of the people of Israel follows from this. We can still see this process of thought very plainly in the shepherd of Hermas who expressly declares that the world was created for the sake of the Church. In consequence of this he maintains that the Church was very old, and was created before the foundation of the world.[137]

The idea of pre-mortal existence disappeared from the Christian mainstream, and with it the idea of a lineage who were chosen before birth. Belief in a Christian community as an elect, even a chosen people, would persist, but based on God's foreknowledge or hidden purposes, not His people's prior existence or conduct. And the gathering of the scattered tribes into a redeemed Israel found its modern counterpart in the gathering of spiritual Israel—Christian believers—into the Church (or the body of Christ). Joseph Smith literalized the concept of gathering by calling newly converted Saints to assemble to a geographically identified "Zion"; but he (and more emphatically his successors) also literalized the concept of Israel itself, laying the groundwork for the doctrine, seen in Origen, that a pre-existent group of spirits came to earth through a particular bloodline associated with Jacob or Israel.

It was in his work translating the Book of Mormon that Smith first directly engaged the doctrine of lineage, and of his own lineage in particular. On its very title page, the record identified the Lamanites—or American Indians, in whole or in part[138]—with "the house of Israel," tracing their literal descent from a Manassehite exile from sixth-century Jerusalem. (A connection between American Indians and Israel was commonplace in nineteenth-century thought, though most asserted a linkage through the "lost ten tribes," not a Jerusalem offshoot.)

The Book of Mormon prophesied its own transmission through Gentiles, and the work of the Gentiles in bringing "the remnant" of that people back into the covenant Israel.[139] But the clear ethnic distinction between literal Israel and non-Israel Gentile breaks down when Book of Mormon prophet Nephi asserts that those Gentiles who repent "are [also] the covenant people of the Lord."[140] Thus is set in place an ambiguous template that informs Mormon discourse to the present day. Mormons who have the peculiar habit of referring to non-LDS people—even Jews—as Gentiles are using the label as a signifier of nonbelief, or more specifically, nonparticipation in a covenant they believe Joseph Smith reintroduced. This covenant in Mormon thinking makes assent to the gospel the sign of true membership in the house of Israel, of legitimate status as Abraham's seed. As Orson Whitney explained, "the name Gentile is not with us a term of reproach. It comes from Gentilis, meaning, of a nation, a family or a people not of Israel—that is all. 'Mormon' is a nickname for Latter-day Saint, but 'Gentile' is not a nickname. It simply means, with us, one who does not belong to the Church."[141]

But the Book of Mormon further complicates the issue with a prophecy that Smith took to refer to himself, according to which the Lord promised the Old Testament patriarch Jacob's son Joseph that a "choice seer" would come "out of the fruit of [his] loins" who would perform a powerful ministry among "a branch which was to be broken off" of the house of Israel.[142] Smith doubtless took this to mean that though he was of a Gentile nation, he personally descended from an Israelite. Smith appointed his father to be church patriarch in 1833; one of his prerogatives was to bless individuals and declare their connection to the house of Israel. Some blessings affirmed a literal descent, some an adoptive relationship, and others were ambiguous. So in blessing Hyrum Smith, for instance, Joseph Smith Sr. pronounced him a "true descendant" through the house of Ephraim; another convert, Isa Ames, was "initiated into the family of Joseph"; others, like Orson Pratt, were simply assured that they were "entitled to . . . the blessings of Jacob, who was called Israel," or, like Sarah Harmon, were simply declared "the seed of Israel."[143]

Smith believed that many Latter-day Saints were descended from Israel as he was, for the Abrahamic texts he produced described the Abrahamic covenant as promising that the "literal seed" of Abraham would exercise the priesthood in order to bless "all the families of the earth . . . with the blessings of the gospel."[144] Given that this was the mandate of Restoration missionaries, Smith drew the inevitable conclusion that Latter-day Saints were, by and large, Israelite by blood. Several revelations seemed to confirm this understanding, with their repeated references to the imperative work of Smith and his fellow Saints "to recover my people, who are of the house of Israel."[145]

As Young explained the principle,

> God has had regard to the blood of the covenant for his oath's sake. That promised blood has trickled down through our parents until now we are here. I know who has the right to the Keys—the Prophet has! That blood has been preserved and has been brought down through father to son, and our heavenly Father has been watching it all the time and saw the man that has received the blood pure through descent—that is what Joseph meant the Lord had regard to. . . . Ephraim is the character who has the pure blood of promise in him. The Lord has respect unto it. This doctrine is perfectly plain and simple. Those who have the right will redeem the nations of the Earth.[146]

Mormons were here replicating the language of New England Puritans, who taught that God sent his elect into the world "through the loyns of godly parents," and referred to America as the "New Israel."[147] But the Latter-day Saints went further, believing that the blood of Israel literally flowed in the missionaries—and in their converts as well. In an 1841 sermon, Smith taught that in the last days, "the Lord will begin by revealing the House of Israel among the gentiles."[148] This "revealing" was largely effected by their receptivity to the gospel—those who accepted the message of the Restoration thereby identified themselves as true Israelites. But sometimes Gentiles as well accepted the missionaries' message, though the effects of such conversion were different. Smith taught that

> as the Holy Ghost falls upon one of the Literal Seed of Abraham it is calm & serene & his whole soul & body are only exercised by the pure spirit of

Inteligence; while the effect of the Holy Ghost upon a Gentile is to purge out the old blood & make him actually of the seed of Abraham. That man that has none of the blood of Abraham (naturally) must have a new creation by the Holy Ghost.[149]

That was the renewal promised to the wife of early convert Roswell Blood: "thou art not of Gentile blood but of the seed of Israel yet thy companion is a Gentile. . . . If she will repent and obey the gospel she shall become the seed of Abraham through the law of adoption."[150]

The connection yet to be forged in Mormon thought was the one that linked modern Israel—or the believing blood of the faithful—not just to Abraham but also to a pre-existent past. That step was suggested by Smith himself, in his declaration that "every man who has a calling to minister to the inhabitants of the world, was ordained to that very purpose in the Grand Council of heaven before the world was."[151] From there it was a simple step to conclude that pre-existent conduct entitled one to birth through a blessed lineage. And so Erastus Snow assured the faithful that "the entire lineage of Ephraim" (with which Mormons identified themselves) was called and ordained at the same pre-mortal council Smith had spoken of "to perform a certain work at a certain time of the world's history";[152] in the early twentieth century, Orson F. Whitney would refer to the Latter-day Saints as "a branch of the house of Israel, . . . a preexistent race."[153]

In this view, the faithful who accept the gospel are literal descendants of those tribes which were scattered in the aftermath of the Assyrian defeat of the Kingdom of Israel (circa 720 BCE). Just as the Lord promised to "sift the house of Israel among all nations,"[154] He covenanted to gather them again, and Latter-day Saints are heirs of those promises. As an apostle wrote in the 1960s, Israel is "a group of souls tested, tried, and proven before they were born into the world. . . . Through this lineage were to come the true and tried souls that had demonstrated their righteousness in the spirit world before they came here."[155]

By the twenty-first century, however, the language of universalism was replacing Mormonism's version of special election. Proclamations of special lineage had implications especially troubling in a multi-cultural era and seemed dissonant with New Testament teachings that privilege adoption over bloodlines. In 1991, the church addressed head-on a growing question. As the article in the church magazine queried: "Are Church members literal descendants of Israel, as most patriarchal blessings state? Or are we Gentiles and belong to the house of Israel only by adoption?" Daniel Ludlow answered, "the lineages declared in patriarchal blessings are almost always statements of actual blood lines; they are not simply tribal identifications by assignment."[156] But the paradigm was already by then shifting irrevocably. While some Mormons maintain steadfastly their conviction of literal descent from Israel, the ambivalence about the blood of Israel being literal or figurative has been not so much resolved as tabled. As a current church manual states simply, "Converts to the Church are Israelites either by blood or adoption."[157]

BLACKS AND MORMONISM

"As the promulgators of this extraordinary legend maintain the natural equality of mankind, without excepting the native Indians or the African race, there is little reason to be surprised at the cruel persecution by which they have suffered."[158]

The traveling Englishman Edward Abdy was struck by the brash anomaly of an American church that was so boldly progressive as to impute a special status to American Indians, while inhabiting the frontier in the 1830s, and to welcome black converts, while establishing a church gathering place in pro-slavery Missouri. Mormonism's position on racial difference would soon grow much more complicated and controversial.

In the Old Testament, those peoples who incur God's displeasure generally do so by opposing or corrupting His covenant people. Early in Genesis, however, two particular cursings are described which resonated throughout Christian history with devastating consequences. For the crime of murdering his brother Abel, Cain was cursed and exiled from his homeland as a fugitive and vagabond. Subsequently, "the LORD appointed a sign for Cain" ("set a mark upon him" in the King James Version). Ironically, the mark itself was not a curse; it was an identifier to preserve him from blood vengeance ("lest any finding him should smite him.") Such details tend to get elided in popular theology, however, and some early Christians conflated the mark and the curse, and came to interpret them as a skin of blackness.

A second biblical narrative would become invoked as corollary support for this reading. In the ninth chapter of Genesis, a cryptic tale gives the origin of the Canaanites' subjection to Israelite dominion. Drinking to excess of his own wine, Noah slumbers, naked and uncovered. "And Ham, the father of Canaan, saw the nakedness of his father, and told his two brothers outside." Whether simple mockery or something more sinister is thereby implied, scholars still debate. The resultant cursing, however is less ambiguous: "He said, 'Cursed be Canaan; lowest of slaves shall he be to his brothers.'"[159] Augustine saw in these words the commencement of a practice of human bondage, "introduced by sin"; henceforth, slavery was "penal and . . . appointed by that law which enjoins the preservation of the natural order and forbids its disturbance." ("Happier" in any event "to be the slave of a man than of lust," he consoled.[160])

In 1707, Edward Stillingfleet invokes Augustine's position that a certain people suffered "slavery, disgrace and universal contempt" because "the curse of Cain is upon them"—but surprisingly, Stillingfleet is referring to the Jews, not the blacks.[161] The slave trade introduced a new target of Christian oppression in need of rationalization. The Atlantic African slave trade only gained steam in the seventeenth century and peaked in the eighteenth. One historian notes that "a curse of blackness on Cain," from whom the blacks were thought to descend, "is often noted in European literature of the seventeenth to nineteenth century."[162] In those years slavery engendered widespread debate on the moral and religious legitimacy of the institution, and the stories of Cain and Canaan provided grist for the polemical mills.

At the beginning of the eighteenth century, one finds scattered references that connect the black skin color to the biblical curses. William Whiston wrote a book in 1725 including a section on "the curses denounced against Cain and Lamech . . . proving that the Africans and Indians are their posterity." Cain was born white, he contended, but in consequence of his "most barbarous parricide, God changed him to a perfect Black."[163] A few years later, Augustus Malfert followed with his own *Enquiry into the Origin of the Negroes and the Americans*, claiming that "Cain is the progenitor of the Negroes," and "Blackness of his Body . . . [is] his true Mark."[164] Others mention this theory interpreting the "black complexion" as the effect of Noah's curse upon his second son Ham as common to "some of our pious commentators."[165]

As early as 1764, a *New and Complete Dictionary of Arts and Sciences* could matter of factly trace the institution of slavery to the curse of Canaan.[166] As abolitionism gained steam in succeeding decades, however, such readings came to be hotly disputed. Anti-slavery crusaders were addressing in articles and editorials "the application of the curse of Canaan to the circumstances of modern Negro slavery."[167] One anti-slavery writer conceded Canaan's destiny of servitude, but argued that while it predicted slavery of his descendants, it did not foretell "*uninterrupted* and *interminable* slavery."[168]

Founder of American Methodism John Wesley was uncompromising in his denunciation of slavery, but his church moderated its opposition after 1830. American Baptists famously split over the issue of slavery in 1845. Even when not supporting slavery, writes one religious scholar, "the Puritan heirs of [Calvinist] theology corrupted it into a Protestant theological defense for their racist claim that whites were created superior to blacks." These ideas "influenced racist views of theologians, physicians, and scientists from the post-Colonial years through the Civil War decades."[169]

Initially, the Mormon position on American blacks was relatively egalitarian relative to many other antebellum religious traditions. Regarding contemporary slaves, for example, Joseph Smith wrote, "change their situation with the whites, and they would be like them."[170] Smith put this into religious practice by authorizing the ordination of Elijah Abel, a free black, to the priesthood and office of Elder in March 1836.[171] Unfortunately, at some point in the early years of Mormonism, the pattern was initiated of excluding blacks from the Mormon priesthood, and thus from full participation in the LDS Church and its rituals.

Brigham Young announced a ban on black participation in the priesthood in 1852, during meetings of Utah's first territorial legislature, but this was no abrupt innovation. He did not articulate a rationale at the time, beyond declaring that members of the African race could not bear the priesthood and attributing such denial to the curse of Cain.[172] In thus associating black skin with Cain's posterity, and slavery with Ham's, Young was clearly influenced by nineteenth-century religious thinking about the curses of Cain and Canaan. In addition to these inherited racist readings of the Bible, the misapplication of Mormon scriptural texts provided a convenient ad hoc theological rationale on which to base the ban. Two supports, in particular, were construed from the Book of Abraham, which Smith had produced in 1835–42. First was the doctrine of preexistence itself, with its assertion of a connection between present circumstance and pre-mortal conduct. In the words of that text, some spirits, "noble and great" ones, were accordingly foreordained to leadership roles here on earth.[173] Unfortunately, early Mormons extrapolated from this text to ruinous conclusions. An example from the classical world illustrates how readily a doctrine of preexistence can be appropriated to diverse ends.

Like Origen and many others who developed theories of human preexistence, Plato believed events in a pre-mortal sphere of activity could explain the problematic imbalance in this life of pain and suffering, blessedness and adversity, that seem apportioned with no regard for present merits. And so he fashions a mythology to create a plausible logic behind the apparent injustice of the world. Plato writes of one hero, Er, a soldier who returns from death to narrate to mortals the journey of the soul. This character describes a beautiful meadow which is framed by a pair of portals, a heavenly and an earthly. The spot turns out to be the staging area for reentry into mortal life.

Upon the arrival of Er and his fellow spirits, a prophet comes forward holding "lots and a number of models of lives" and says, "Ephemeral souls, this is the beginning of another cycle that will end in death. Your daemon or guardian spirit will not be assigned to you by lot; you will choose him. The one who has the first lot will be the first to choose a life. . . . The responsibility lies with the one who makes the choice; the god has none." The sample lives exhibit different conditions ranging from royalty to beggary, health to sickness, ugliness to beauty, and encompassing every other quality.

Intuitively, of course, those who pick winning lots would opt for the conditions of life most congenial to comfort and happiness. But, as we learn, the wisest choice may turn out to be other than the obvious one. Only the precipitous would rashly choose the easy and attractive path through mortality. For, as the prophet reminds the assembled spirits, the purpose of life is the acquisition of virtue. Therefore, he admonishes, "a wise soul will consider carefully what the good and bad effects" are of blessedness or adversity, a high-born position or a life of disadvantage. Only with those thoughts in mind, "will [one] be able, by considering the nature of the soul, to reason out which life is better and which worse and to choose accordingly, calling a life worse if it lead[s] the soul to become more unjust, a[nd] better if it leads the soul to become more just."[174]

The beauty of Plato's conception is that it suggests the dangers of simplistic judgment linking anyone's situation in life, one's health or happiness, with any particular worth or standing before God. If anything, Plato suggests, the relationship between one's goodness and one's blessedness may be, ironically, inverse rather than proportional. That was seldom the interpretation that guided the Christian—or the Mormon—world in deciphering the varieties of the human condition. As Job's friends insisted to his chagrin, "think now, who that was innocent ever perished? Or where were the upright cut off?"[175] Longstanding association of Eve's sin with the subservient position of women, the Puritan belief that worldly success was a sign of God's favor, and current versions of prosperity theology are comparable manifestations of the tendency to judge the plight of the oppressed and miserable as deserved or divinely ordained.

Further influencing Mormon doctrinal development on the subject of race was a scripture in the Abrahamic text that mentioned one pharaoh, who was "of that lineage by which he could not have the right of priesthood."[176] Writing in 1845, Apostle Orson Hyde was apparently the first to develop the two Abrahamic passages in combination into a racial doctrine. He opined that some spirits in the pre-mortal realm had been neutral in the "war in heaven," and as a consequence "were required . . . to take bodies in the accursed lineage of Canaan; hence the Negro or African race."[177] Two years later, Parley Pratt took the step of interpreting the "accursed lineage" as the black race, and the curse itself as precluding ordination to the priesthood. In reference to a black member, he stated that he "was a black man with the blood of Ham in him which lineage was cursed as regards the priesthood."[178]

A third scriptural text, the Book of Mormon, provided ambiguous signals. On the one hand, the record recounted that descendants of Israelite voyagers to the New World apostatized from the true knowledge of God and were consequently cursed with "a skin of blackness."[179] And they were promised that, at a future date, they might become "a white and a delightsome people."[180] On the other hand, Joseph Smith changed that wording in 1840 to read "pure and a delightsome people."[181] And a Book of Mormon prophet affirms that God "inviteth them all to come unto him and partake of his goodness; and denieth none that come unto him, black and white, bond and free, male and female ... and all are alike unto God, both Jew and Gentile."[182]

Contemporary events, in which two black Mormons had married white women, outraging the racial sensitivities of Young (and of most other whites in the church), probably were the final catalyst to rapid development of a ban that would preclude black ordination to the priesthood and discourage miscegenation alike.[183] Shortly thereafter, the policy was endorsed by Brigham Young: "What chance is there for the redemption of the Negro?" Young declared, "The Lord had cursed Cain's seed with blackness and prohibited them the Priesthood."[184] By 1852, he had decreed the new policy in a statement to the Territorial legislature, while invoking his status as prophet. "Any man having one drop of the seed of [Cain] ... in him cannot hold the priesthood, and if no other prophet ever spake it before I will say it now."[185] Black women, too, were affected. Though Smith had himself invited a black woman, Jane Manning James, to be adopted into his family, subsequent policy barred both genders from full temple blessings.[186]

Because Brigham Young never supported his policy statement with any claim to special revelation, and there was no unambiguous scriptural basis for the practice, it met increasing resistance and discomfort on the part of many members and leaders by the mid-twentieth century. True, the First Presidency had in 1949 reaffirmed the church's position, insisting it was "not a matter of the declaration of a policy but of direct commandment from the Lord."[187] Still, since there was no official, published scriptural or doctrinal explanation for the commandment, some insisted the LDS position in this regard was more of a culturally conditioned practice than revealed principle and therefore, presumably, amenable to change.

With the growth of the international church in the 1950s, President David O. McKay made the priesthood available to all worthy men unless African ancestry was specifically known (the burden of proof had been the reverse previously). Political pressures against the church mounted in the 1960s, even as important developments were unfolding in Africa. Even without an official missionary presence, congregations of thousands had taken shape, though without any recognition from Salt Lake City.

By 1978, the church was enjoying a relative respite from the political fires of the previous decade. But in that year, a temple in São Paulo, Brazil, was nearing dedication. Work in that country, where extensive racial mixing had followed nineteenth-century emancipation, was especially fruitful. The prospect of a burgeoning national membership denied access to both the priesthood and their own temple was apparently the stimulus that prompted President Spencer W. Kimball to revisit the race proscription with his counselors and the other apostles. As an apostle, as early as 1963 he had referred in ambiguous terms to the policy as a result of "possible error."[188] Now in June of 1978 he announced to a surprised public that he felt divinely directed to lift the priesthood ban. The proclamation, subsequently canonized as scriptural revelation, pronounced that henceforth, "all worthy males" were eligible for priesthood ordination, "regardless of race or color."[189] The momentous shift represented the most dramatic revelation pronounced by an LDS prophet since the ban on plural marriage over a century earlier.

In March 2013, the church acknowledged in a new introduction to the official revocation of the priesthood ban that "Church records offer no clear insights into the origins of this practice."[190] Historians may quibble over the fact that abundant sources indicate a number of cultural prejudices and doctrinal speculations that led to the priesthood ban in the mid-1840s. Presumably, the statement is an acknowledgment by the leadership that evidence is lacking for a decisive verdict as to whether other factors, like unrecorded teachings of Smith, may have played a role. The door is open for an interpretation of this LDS practice as having nothing divine about its implementation; "church leaders believed," notes the new heading, "that a revelation was needed to alter the practice." The church has not explicitly condemned the ban itself as an error or racism pure and simple; however, a subsequent posting on the church's official website comes close, and does unequivocally condemn all rationales that accompanied and followed the policy:

> the Church disavows the theories advanced in the past that black skin is a sign of divine disfavor or curse, or that it reflects actions in a premortal life; that mixed-race marriages are a sin; or that blacks or people of any other race or ethnicity are inferior in any way to anyone else. Church leaders today unequivocally condemn all racism, past and present, in any form.[191]

In any event, as both the new scriptural introduction and the website article note, the words published in the Book of Mormon in 1830 are once again church policy after a painful hiatus: "and all are alike unto God."[192] The universalism of the Book of Mormon in the end trumped the preexistence scenarios of folk tradition.

A man is a moral, responsible, free agent. . . . It was foreordained he should fall.

—JOSEPH SMITH, 5 February 1840

18

The Fall

⌒————————————————————————————

"A SUBSTANTIAL PART of the history of theology in early America," writes Brooks Holifield, "was an extended debate, stretching over more than two centuries, about the meaning and truth of Calvinism."[1] Central to Calvinist theology is a view of human nature in which original sin figures prominently. The doctrine of original sin is fraught with confusion, ambiguity, and equivocation. This is a result of two factors. First is the doctrine's offense to human conceptions of justice. Even the most vigorous proponents of original sin acknowledge that a sin committed by Adam and inherited by succeeding generations cannot be readily reconciled with humankind's intuitive sense of fairness. Many theologians have responded to this fact with theories that rationalize the apparent injustice. We must have sinned before our mortal birth ("fallen preexistence"), Adam acted as our representative ("covenant theology"), we co-participated through a shared metaphysical origin ("seminal nature"), or we were physically present in the eggs of Eve or the sperm of Adam ("ovism" or "animalculism"). A poet summarized the latter explanation: "Thus ADAM's Loins contained his large Posterity, / All People that have been, and all that e'er shall be."[2] When a modern theologian declares the language of original sin has become "a cultural embarrassment,"[3] he could have been referring to the explanations as much as to the doctrine.

Other theologians, on the other hand, have refused to try to mollify our wounded sense of justice, rather relishing the incomprehensibility of the doctrine or praising the unimpeachable sovereignty of God, to which humans must simply acquiesce. Human perplexity in the absence of any theodicy becomes a sign of holy, abject submission. Or original sin is seen to satisfy—if not a sense of justice, a sense of the fractured self, the unsettledness at the heart's core. Pascal's statement is typical in this regard:

> [T]here is nothing so repugnant to the rules of our miserable justice as to damn eternally an infant incapable of will, for a sin in which he seems to have so scanty a share, that it was committed six thousand years before he was in being. Certainly nothing shocks us more rudely than this doctrine, and yet without this mystery, the most incomprehensible of all, we are incomprehensible to ourselves.[4]

The second critical factor in understanding the history of original sin is to recognize the conflation of two distinct principles in the one concept, each with its own history. From its inception, original sin included "both guilt and pollution. The guilt of Adam's sin is imputed to us. Because he sinned as our representative, we are guilty in him. Moreover, we also inherit his pollution, and now have a positive disposition toward sin."[5] But guilt and pollution, of course, are two entirely different things; universal moral culpability, accountability, or guilt for Adam's transgression is quite different from an inherited proclivity to sin, a damaged will, or a depraved nature. For most of Christian history, inherited guilt and inherited nature alike were traced to Adam. "In Adam's Fall, We sinned all," as the New England primer taught generations of schoolchildren. Vicarious guilt inheres in us—or is imputed to us—from our birth, prior to and independently of individual choice. And at the same time, the doctrine asserts a universal predisposition in human nature toward evil rather than good.

In the first Christian centuries, the idea gradually took hold that all humans inherited some ill consequences as a legacy of the transgression in Eden. Tertullian, first to use the term "original sin" in the third century, espoused the notion of some kind of inherited sinfulness, and thought he had found in a particular theory of the soul's creation ("traducianism"), a mechanism whereby an evil nature was transmitted (though he does not say the guilt of Adam was). Traducianism, a view now held by virtually no Western Christians except Lutherans, is the belief that God created only Adam's soul; every successive human soul is engendered by its human parents along with the body. In this model a kind of genetic inheritance, pertaining to physical and spiritual nature alike, explains the Adamic heritage.

Original sin took its decisive step as a doctrine with a commentary on Paul's epistle to the Romans by the early Christian writer known only as Ambrosiaster. Chapter 5, verse 12, of the original reads, "Therefore, as through one man sin entered into the world, and death through sin; and so death passed unto all men, *for that* all sinned." The crucial words here are the Greek *ef 'ho*, rendered as "for that" in the NSRV. The meaning is vague: all men sinned individually at some time? Collectively? Vicariously through Adam? Ambrosiaster rendered *ef 'ho* into Latin as *in quo,* or "in whom, that is, in Adam."[6] With this translation, Ambrosiaster understood that all men sinned "in Adam," making the whole race actual co-participants in Adam's deed, and therefore in Adam's guilt. With this step, a collective human guilt for Adam's sin was cemented to a simple human tendency or disposition to sin. The Vulgate, basis of so many other biblical translations, followed Ambrosiaster's rendering.

Motivated in large measure by external challenges to the church's teachings on Christ and grace, Augustine was by the late fourth century formulating a full-blown doctrine of sin that emphasized absolute human depravity along with unqualified guilt. Augustine was deficient in Greek, and in expounding his view of original sin he relied on what some would call Ambrosiaster's "fatal blunder" as his proof text.[7] With this development, then, Augustine turned Ambrosiaster's reading into the foundation of the doctrine for centuries to come.

Augustine initially found pre-mortal existence the most logical and just explanation for the ills we suffer upon birth. But he eventually adopted something nearer the traducian position of Tertullian because it was less threatening to God's sovereignty while having the virtue of making original sin into a literal, physiological inheritance from one generation to the next. "From the one (primeval) man comes the entire outflow and redundance of men's souls," Tertullian had written. Therefore, it is no empty abstraction to claim that "every soul, then, by reason of its birth, has its nature in Adam." So in addition to any evil introduced into or freely chosen by a morally responsible soul, there is "an antecedent, and in a certain sense natural, evil which arises from its corrupt origin."[8] In Peter Martyr's later, elegantly simple formulation, "originall sinne is by generation traduced by the parentes unto us."[9]

Those who attribute to Augustine an uncompromising assertion of original sin and human depravity seldom note the difficulty with which he came to that position.[10] He certainly was initially appalled by the incomprehensible version of justice the doctrine implied. But Augustine's equivocation on the subject of human depravity and guiltiness was playing into the hands of the gravest threat the church was facing: the teachings of three soon-to-be heretics, Pelagius, Caelestius, and Julian, all of whom emphasized human freedom and rejected original sin as a source of both depravity and guilt. It was in response to this threat that Augustine turned to an uncompromising embrace and defense of inherited human depravity. His teaching endowed humanity with a dual heritage, consisting of both *vitium* or vice, and *reatus* or guilt. We are therefore justly damned, deserving of punishment for an inherited condition and for the sin committed in the Garden of Eden. The guilt of Adam and Eve is ours. "Everyone, even little children, have broken God's covenant, not indeed in virtue of any personal action but in virtue of mankind's common origin in that single ancestor in whom all have sinned. . . . Original sin is common to all men, regardless of the personal sins of each one."[11] And so we find in Augustine the first developed theory that unambiguously assigns actual guilt to, and justifies the infliction of eternal torments upon, creatures who may not even live long enough to make a choice or decision of any kind, who are damned even as they draw their first breath.

Even writers sympathetic to the doctrine find Augustine's embrace of the doctrine so zealous as to be "chilling"; in a final manuscript Augustine wrote, "this is the Catholic view: a view that can show a just God in so many pains and in such agonies of tiny babies."[12] It is no exaggeration to say that Augustine's view of original sin was to "become the center of western Christian tradition."[13] As another cultural historian notes, Augustine "did more than anyone else in the Christian church to convince the world that unbaptized infants, because of the sin they had inherited from Adam, would burn in eternal torment."[14]

Over subsequent centuries, there would be occasional dissents from the Augustinian view. Peter Abelard (1079–1142), for example, denied imputed guilt; he was summarily condemned by the Synod of Sens for teaching "that we did not contract guilt from Adam, but only punishment."[15] The Catholic Church, rather superfluously as the Reformation proved, took occasion in the Council of Trent (1546) to vigorously affirm that baptism was for the remission of *reatus peccati originalis* (the guilt of original sin).[16] With the coming of the Reformation, ironically, came an intensification of Augustine's views. With Luther and Calvin, a compromised will morphs into the concept of "total depravity" and guilt emphatically attaches to original sin, which is depicted as the "the only real sin that exists," any personal sins being only secondary eruptions or manifestations of its presence.[17] Luther had himself declared that "man . . . is with his whole nature and essence not merely a sinner but sin itself."[18] In the 1577 Lutheran Formula of Concord, original sin is defined, not as a "slight corruption of nature, but . . . so deep a corruption that nothing sound or uncorrupted has survived in man's soul or body."[19] Humans inherit a "depraved impulse, filthiness of heart, depraved concupiscences and depraved inclinations."[20] "The damage," in fact, "is so unspeakable that it may not be recognized by a rational process." As for imputed guilt, it receives summary endorsement; to say this "defect and damage is not truly sin" is false. It is frankly acknowledged as "a debt which we owe because of someone else's wrongdoing."[21]

As for Calvin, original sin shifts to "an hereditary depravity extend[ing] to all the faculties of soul." For this condition, "punishment is justly due."[22] Calvin takes

Paul's reference to the "fruits of sin" (Gal. 5:19–21) to imply they derive from a pre-existing state of sin we inherit. This condition of guilt incurred by Adam is justly imputed to us, because Adam is our head ("covenant theology" or "federalism"). And this imputed guilt is actual, blameworthy guilt, he insists because "there could be no condemnation without guilt." Even infants, he adds, are subject to this condemnation, bringing from the womb a nature "odious and abominable to God."[23]

The Church of England likewise endorsed Augustine's views in the Westminster Confession of Faith, in language that explicitly affirmed original sin's two dimensions. Regarding *reatus,* or guilt, Adam and Eve "fell from their original righteousness and communion, with God.... They being the root of all mankind, the guilt of this sin was imputed." As regards *vitium,* or vice, a "corrupted nature [was] conveyed to all their posterity," with the consequence that they are "wholly defiled in all the faculties and parts of soul and body."[24]

In the following centuries, a growing divide seeps into Western Christianity between ecclesiastical dictate and popular belief. Political agitations and revolutions in England, access to English-language Bibles, and the spread of printing and literacy conspired to foment a spirit of independent thought. Most decisive of all, as Norman Williams remarks, "the Reformation, challenging as it did the whole fabric of mediaeval Church life and thought, had the remarkable effect of dragging the doctrines of the fall and of original sin out from the cloister and the lecture-room into the market-place, and of making them issues of the greatest interest and importance for the religious life of hundreds of thousands of ordinary people."[25]

Increasingly in this age, the depravity half of the doctrine gains the upper hand, in a virtual frenzy of universal self-deprecation, while the idea of legalistic accountability for human depravity begins to erode.[26] In seventeenth-century England, a number of English churchmen were resisting an Augustinian reading of human nature and inherited guilt. Latitudinarians, they were called, for their resistance to narrowly defined orthodoxy. These Anglicans included the Cambridge Platonists and other liberal thinkers like Thomas Traherne. They emphasized the "natural light" of reason and its consistency with the light of revelation, resulting in a relatively optimistic assessment of human nature and potential. Traherne poetically expressed his pointed refutation of original depravity in his aptly named "Innocence":

But that which most I wonder at, which most
I did esteem my bliss, which most I boast
And ever shall enjoy, is that within
I felt no stain nor spot of sin.
No darkness then did overshade,

But all within was pure and bright,
No guilt did crush nor fear invade,
But all my soul was full of light.
A joyful sense and purity
Is all I can remember . . .²⁷

By the next century, the dominant figure of American theology was Jonathan Edwards (1703–1758), "the most powerful articulator of the Augustinian doctrine of original sin that America has ever produced."²⁸ At times, he sounded like he was trying to out-Augustine Augustine. "In God's sight," he preached with clear intent to appall, children bearing the heritage of the fall are "infinitely more hateful than vipers."²⁹ His defense of strict Augustinian original guilt was based on the "federalist" logic he inherited from Augustine through Calvin. His pupil Joseph Bellamy argued like a plain-speaking lawyer: "Now it is true we did not Personally rise in Rebellion against God in that first Transgression but he who did do it was *our* Representative. We are Members of the Community he acted for, and God considers us as such; and therefore looks upon us as being legally guilty."³⁰ The problem was that eighteenth-century America was the wrong time and place for that doctrine. As the first generations of Americans increasingly enshrined a ruling ideology in which human freedom and individualism were paramount, the Augustinian heritage held less and less appeal. Edwards's unyielding variety of strict Calvinism eventually led to his expulsion from his church in 1750. He aggressively resisted creeping Arminianism, a theological current that argued for only *partial* human depravity, and for some role of the human will in personal conversion and salvation.

Soon, the controversy over the meaning and extent of original sin consumed New England clergy. The first sustained challenge to the doctrine as creedally defined was John Taylor, published as *The Scripture Doctrine of Original Sin Proposed to Free and Candid Examination* (1757). Taylor thought a major philosophical problem with original sin was that, being the creator of the human spirit, God became the agent responsible for that sin. (Edwards, who was usually a brilliant debater, could only weakly respond that every version of Christianity had that problem.³¹) Taylor argued instead that man always had a power to choose when faced with different options, and human sinfulness was the product of those individual choices, not Adam's sin or predestination. He articulated the most forceful protest against the doctrine it had yet known:

But that any man, without my knowledge or consent, should so represent me, that when he is guilty I am to be reputed guilty, and when he transgresses I shall be accountable and punishable for his transgression, and thereby subjected to the wrath and curse of God, nay further that his wickedness shall give me a sinful nature, and all this before I am born and consequently while I am in no capacity of knowing, helping, or hindering what he doth; surely anyone who dares use his understanding, must clearly see this is unreasonable, and altogether inconsistent with the truth and goodness of God.[32]

Taylor's ideas were widely read and engendered sympathy on the part of many New England clergy. "No one book has done so much towards rooting out . . . the principles and scheme of religion maintained by our pious and excellent forefathers," Edwards would complain of Taylor's assault.[33] Meanwhile, the Anglican cleric and founder of Methodism John Wesley found Taylor's views so alarmingly prevalent among the English that he published his own ringing defense of original sin in 1757. In this work, his endorsement was fairly conventional. A whole section on "imputed guilt" brooked no compromise with Taylor. "God does not look upon infants as innocent," he wrote in strains echoing Augustine, "but as involved in the guilt of Adam's sin." The doctrines of both "personal sin and imputed guilt" are equally "sound and scriptural."[34]

Accordingly, even "infants are guilty of original sin, . . . [and] need to be washed from original sin; therefore they are proper subjects of baptism." Such baptism confers cleansing in the sense of "washing away the guilt of original sin."[35] Writing just a few years later, in 1761, Wesley still insists that there were two foundations to the gospel he preached: "original sin and justification by faith."[36] Pertaining to the first, he announced that "all who deny this—call it 'original sin' or by any other title—are but heathens still."[37] But the doctrine was already undergoing substantial change. By 1786, the American Conference dropped the critical phrase in the baptismal ceremony that referred to the "mystical washing away of sin."[38] Baptismal regeneration was now rejected, but original sin was still affirmed, though redefined. In fact, from 1805, candidates for the ministry were queried on the doctrine of original sin, as a test of theological purity; the 1814 version of the test inquired, "What do you understand by original sin? Are the whole posterity of Adam, in consequence of sin, involved in guilt, and subjects of inherent depravity?"[39] About depravity there was no question. The 1814 document stipulated "total depravity" as demanding "unequivocal consent." What candidates were expected to say about inherited guilt is difficult to determine. If all this sounds hard to sort out, it apparently was to the aspiring ministers undergoing examination as well. As the president of the Methodist conference remarked unhappily of one year's examinations (1839), "Dr. Hannah noticed the discrepancy in some of the statements of the candidates, especially in relation to the transmission of guilt."[40] No wonder, given the fact that the principal of the Wesleyan Academy had claimed two years before that "guilt is not imputed until by a voluntary rejection of the gospel man makes the depravity of his nature the object of his choice."[41]

A few decades later, no confusion remained. Methodists would by then unambiguously affirm that inherited depravity is not inherited guilt, and infants can only sin "so soon as capable of exercising faith." In fact, "No man will ever be condemned for Adam's transgression."[42] Not all Christians were happy with this trend. For the popular George Whitefield (1714–1770), original sin was foundational to the very Christian identity. "If you have never felt the weight of original sin," he thundered, "do not call yourselves Christians."[43]

As indicated in the Methodist panels and Methodism's own shift from Wesley's treatise on the subject, the early decades of the nineteenth century saw increasing challenges to the doctrine of original sin. Harvard at this time came under the control of a liberal faction of ministers, many of whom rejected original sin altogether. By 1819, this liberal wing proclaimed themselves Unitarians and became a major new force in American religious thought. The next year, a pamphlet war erupted between Harvard's Unitarian Henry Ware and Andover Seminary's orthodox Calvinist Leonard Woods over the ramifications of the Augustinian teachings on human nature. Woods conceded early on that "every attempt . . . to prove that God ever imputes to man any sinful disposition to act, which is not strictly *his own*, has, in my judgment, failed of success."[44] Ware saw his opening, and launched an attack not just on the doctrine of imputed sin but of depravity itself, espousing in its place a view of human nature worthy of Jean Jacques Rousseau. "[Man] is by nature no more inclined or disposed to vice than to virtue, and is equally capable, in the ordinary use of his faculties, . . . of either."[45]

A nineteenth-century observer reported the general sentiment that Woods's defense had been a shambles, and put the Calvinist cause back fifty years.[46] More accurately, it was in its last throes. Charles Hodge (1797–1878) would continue to insist that the doctrine "is part of the faith of the whole Christian world."[47] But by 1832, the doctrine of imputed guilt, long under siege, was losing almost its last bit of ground quickly. In that year, Ashbel Green, Presbyterian minister and editor of the *Christian Advocate*, protested what he considered unforgivable revisionism going on by the Methodists to escape the burden of the doctrine of original sin. "We are now to combat the assertion contained in the review by the [Anglican evangelical] *Christian Observer*, . . . that 'he [Calvin] did not hold the doctrine of the imputation of Adam's sin to all his posterity.'"[48] But two years later, liberalizers were making inroads even among Presbyterians. That year, Green wrote to lament that church teaching on original guilt was unambiguous, and yet, "at present, in the Presbyterian church, the imputation of Adam's first sin to his posterity, is absolutely scorned."[49]

Like their seventeenth-century predecessors, eighteenth-century Baptists techni-
cally affirmed original sin (including imputed guilt) in an important defining document, the Philadelphia Confession of 1742.[50] Increasingly, however, Baptists (like
the Methodists) came to emphasize original sin as inherited nature, not inherited
guilt. Reformed Baptists like Campbell and Stone went further, utterly rejecting
original sin. As children could not profess faith, neither could they be culpable for
their sins, until they are able to commit themselves to God; a child "is guilty of no
other sins before that time."[51] Humans are born innocent, not guilty and depraved.
"We are not guilty of Adam's sin. . . . The guilt of sin attaches only to him who com-
mits sin."[52] With this development, we arrive at a doctrinal position that would be
very close to that of Mormonism's founder Joseph Smith.

Unlike many of Mormonism's doctrines, which developed through several
phases, Smith's repudiation of original sin was early and consistent. If Holifield is
correct that subsequent religious movements "had to define themselves in relation
to Calvinist traditions,"[53] Mormonism did so oppositionally. But while the end
result was similar to contemporary movements like the Campbellites (who also rejected original sin and infant baptism), Smith did not simply appropriate the outward forms or end results of the centuries-long evolution of those doctrines. Smith
put into place an elaborate and unprecedented narrative of Adam's sin and human
origins, in light of which the entire picture of human nature, sin, and accountability
was radically altered—though the full implications were not worked out until the
twentieth century.

The theological underpinnings of Smith's rejection of original sin are abundantly
clear in his positing of humankind's prior existence as innocent spirits in the presence of God. Given the Father's plan to fashion an earth for the purpose of human
advancement, human birth into mortality cannot be seen as a fall; it is unmistaka-
ble ascent. And the detritus of the fall—sin and death, especially—is a dark middle
passage, not a point of origin, in humanity's spiritual odyssey. But this elaborate
framework comes a few years after Smith's comprehensive rejection of original sin,
which already appears emphatically in the Book of Mormon.

Repudiation of original sin is perhaps the earliest major divergence from creedal
Christian doctrine (other than the fact of the Book of Mormon itself as canon-
disruptive) that Mormonism unambiguously asserts. In classical Christianity's
reading of the "fortunate fall," the fall is fortunate insofar as the human sin of infinite hubris called forth the unspeakable gift of Christ's infinite grace. The supernal
solution of Christ's incarnation and atonement outshone the perfidious catastrophe
of Adamic rebellion. The fall is divinely mitigated disaster, but it is first and foremost a disaster. Not so in Mormonism, which rewrites the expression to deny the
catastrophe altogether. The fall itself is fortunate, insofar as it unleashes not the

triple specter of sin, death, and depravity but the possibilities of human incarnation and the educative processes of mortality.

> And now, behold, if Adam had not transgressed he would not have fallen, but he would have remained in the garden of Eden. And all things which were created must have remained in the same state in which they were after they were created. . . . And they would have had no children; wherefore they would have remained in a state of innocence, having no joy, for they knew no misery; doing no good, for they knew no sin. But behold, all things have been done in the wisdom of him who knoweth all things. Adam fell that men might be; and men are, that they might have joy.⁵⁴

So the Book of Mormon, with an eye looking forward to Christ's atonement, made what Christians had called "the greatest catastrophe in human history" into an occasion for rejoicing.

Months later, Smith found corroboration for this rewriting of the fall in his redaction of Genesis, with a psalmic celebration of the primordial transgression:

> And in that day Adam blessed God, and was filled, and began to prophesy concerning all the families of the earth, saying: Blessed be the name of God for my transgression, for in this life I shall have joy, and again in the flesh I shall see God. And Eve, his wife, heard all these things and was glad, saying: Were it not for our transgression we never should have had seed, and never should have known good and evil, and the joy of our redemption, and the eternal life which God giveth unto all the obedient.⁵⁵

"Adam and Eve both considered that they had gained, instead of suffered loss, through their disobedience to that law," in church president John Taylor's gloss of the passage.⁵⁶

Mormons do not deny the couple's consequent expulsion from the Garden, but the Book of Mormon interprets that event as mercy, not retribution: "And now behold, if it were possible that our first parents could have gone forth and partaken of the tree of life they would have been forever miserable, having no preparatory state."⁵⁷ As John Jaques's catechism taught generations of Mormon children,

"What would have been the consequence if Adam and Eve had partaken of the tree of life?

A. They would have lived for ever subject to the devil.

But the action that required their expulsion was itself indispensable.

Was it necessary that Adam should partake of the forbidden fruit?

A. Yes, unless he had done so he would not have known good and evil here, neither could he have had mortal posterity. . . .

Did Adam and Eve lament or rejoice because they had transgressed the commandment, and become acquainted with the nature of evil and good?

A. They rejoiced and praised God. . . . We ought to consider the Fall of our first parents as one of the great steps to eternal exaltation and happiness, and one ordered by God in his infinite wisdom."[58]

According to LDS scripture, the fall transpired according to "the wisdom of him who knoweth all things."[59] The fall so-viewed represents the implementation of, not the deviation from, God's original purposes. Eve, not fully knowing what evil was, acquiesced to the enticing of Satan, himself an unwitting instrument of God's design (he "knew not the mind of God"[60]). Consequently, Eve and Adam's action did not bring down God's wrath, upon them or their posterity. As a surprised listener reported of a Smith sermon, "He then entered into some details, the result of which tended to show his total unbelief of what is termed original sin. He believes that it is washed away by the blood of Christ, and that it no longer exists. . . . I believe that a man is a moral, responsible, free agent," he said.[61] His redaction of Genesis included the unambiguous assertion, "The sins of the parents cannot be answered upon the heads of the children."[62] Smith further codified the principle as one of the church's Articles of Faith, second only to affirmation of the godhead.[63]

The great step of Adam and Eve, which was both biblically identified with primal sin and identified by Mormons with divine intent, took many years for LDS thinkers to develop into a coherent and consistent doctrine. One might mitigate Adam and Eve's transgression by pointing out that the biblical story contains the logical difficulty of imputing evil to Adam and Eve for an act committed prior to their knowledge of good or evil. But Smith's solution to the seeming contradiction (why would God intend sin?) went further: "Joseph said in answer to Mr stout that Adam Did Not Comit sin in [e]ating the fruits for God had Decred that he should Eat & fall—But in complyance with the Decree he should Die."[64] Smith's understanding seemed to be that the prohibition in the Garden was actually more in the manner of a warning. Smith gestured in this direction with an editorial insertion in his revision of the Genesis account; after telling Adam, "thou shalt not eat of" the tree, Smith has God add, "nevertheless, thou mayest choose for thyself, for it is given unto thee."[65] As Orson Pratt interpreted Smith, God designed for man to inhabit mortality as a necessary stage in his progression. But "the Lord could not, consistently with his goodness, . . . subject him to death." (Methodist William Law believed the same: "to suppose God to bring any creature into an unnatural state is to suppose Him acting contrary to himself and to that nature which is from Him."[66]) Neither could God entice man to partake of the tree in ignorance. Therefore, God placed the tree in the garden as provocation and allurement, and provided man with a "warning of the consequences which would follow."⁶⁷

However, Smith's suggestion that Adam and Eve may have rejected a warning rather than a prohibition, and acted with independence rather than sinfulness, was not initially embraced by others. Other Mormons adopted the conventional picture of the fall as a sinful act by the first couple, even if they considered it to be intended by God all along. They also affirmed the biblical view that greater wrong inhered in Eve's, not Adam's, decision. "The woman was found in the transgression, and not the man," said Young, invoking the epistle to Timothy.⁶⁸ Still, he hedged, "I will not blame Adam and Eve," unable to reconcile guilt with divine purpose. "Because it was necessary that sin should enter into the world. . . . The Lord knew they would do this, and he had designed that they should."⁶⁹

None of this is to suggest that the disobedience of Adam and Eve was not viewed by Mormons as a transgression, but it seemed a transgression with a difference. A theologically significant distinction eventually evolved in Mormon thought between transgression and sin, with the first a technical violation of a law and the second a morally culpable disobedience deserving punishment. James Talmage tried to minimize Eve's deed by arguing for her ignorance of evil, and for a sin's severity being proportional to the sinner's understanding, and by asserting that regarding the concept of evil, "Eve knew it not." But he certainly did not consider hers to be a valiant choice. She was, he writes, "captivated by [Satan's] representations," and "deceived by the sophistries of the serpent-fiend." Following Young's version of the creation story told in the temple, the hero for Talmage was clearly Adam, his being the nobler choice, the lesser of two contradictory evils forced upon him. He could abstain from the fruit and fail to replenish the earth with his soon-to-be-exiled companion, or he could remain with her to fulfill that command by eating the fruit. "He deliberately and wisely decided to stand by the first and greater commandment, . . . that he might carry out the purposes of his Maker."⁷⁰ This was but an elaboration of the Book of Mormon claim that "Adam fell that man might be."

By mid-twentieth century, Bruce McConkie went further in exonerating both Adam and Eve, asserting that "it is possible to transgress a law without committing a sin, as in the case of Adam and Eve in the Garden of Eden."⁷¹ This distinction was most likely not intended by Smith, but is now read retroactively into the wording of his second Article of Faith, that humans will be punished for their own "sins" and not for Adam and Eve's "transgression." By century's end, this view was developed with regard to Eve in particular. Eve was not simply rehabilitated, but exalted to a position eclipsing even Adam in terms of a decision well considered and well made. In 1821, the controversial poet Lord Byron, allegedly of "the Satanic School" of poetry, had dared suggest as much. Eve had, he enthused, "a mind which made her thirst for knowledge, at the risk of an eternal curse."[72] A writer for the *Woman's Exponent*, an independent Mormon newspaper, proposed this view as serious theology in 1875, acknowledging that "we are taught that Eve was the first to sin. Well, she was simply more progressive than Adam. She did not want to live in the beautiful garden for ever, and be nobody."[73] It took three quarters of a century before a leading church authority, John Widtsoe, intimated that Eve deserved praise, not censure, for her decision, when he wrote, "In life all must choose at times. Sometimes, two possibilities are good; neither is evil. Usually, however, one is of greater import than the other. When in doubt, each must choose that which concerns the good of others—the greater law—rather than which chiefly benefits ourselves—the lesser laws. The greater must be chosen . . . that was the choice made in Eden."[74]

Decades later, leading Mormon intellectual Hugh Nibley returned to the theme. "Eve is the first on the scene, not Adam, who woke up only long enough to turn over to fall asleep again. . . . In all that follows she takes the initiative, pursuing the search for ever greater light and knowledge while Adam cautiously holds back. Who was the wiser for that?"[75] Soon thereafter LDS leaders were picking up that thread. Dallin Oaks noted that "some Christians condemn Eve for her act, concluding that she and her daughters are somehow flawed by it. Not the Latter-day Saints! Informed by revelation, we celebrate Eve's act and honor her wisdom and courage in the great episode called the Fall."[76] Her action was "a planned offense, a formality to serve an eternal purpose." It was the minimum transgression necessary to introduce us to the separation from God necessary for full agency to operate.[77]

So Mormons hold that Adam's (and Eve's) choice, though personally costly in the short term, revealed more nobility than weakness. This is clearly taught today, in one of modern Mormonism's most important sermons on the atonement: "Adam's and Eve's transgression was not really a wrongful act of 'sin' as we usually use that term. While their choice violated the command against partaking of the fruit, that same choice was necessary to enable their obedience to the command to have children. Their 'transgression' was thus a painful but correct, even eternally glorious, choice."[78]

Smith made a further point about the fall in his revision of the Genesis account. After their expulsion from the Garden, Adam and Eve repent, call upon God, offer sacrifice, and find forgiveness.[79] What guilt did inhere in their actions pertained to them alone. It is this point that the Book of Mormon makes most persistently and emphatically. Children are innocent of Adam's sin; therefore, as the Book of Mormon's King Benjamin teaches, "the infant perisheth not that dieth in his infancy."[80] Subsequent passages pointedly condemn infant baptism as "solemn mockery before God."[81] There is here no clear denial of an original Adamic curse, only of its dominion over children. "Little children are not capable of committing sin; therefore the curse of Adam [meaning physical death and separation from God] is taken from them in me," the text reads.[82] In the same text, however, Smith clarified that this was no selective reprieve. The very doctrine of vicarious guilt, the imputation to humans of another's misdeed, is emphatically rejected. Or at least, whatever ill effects follow from the Adamic decision—including death and immersion in a world of sin—are remedied by Christ. "And the Messiah cometh in the fulness of time, that he may redeem the children of men from the fall. And because that they are redeemed from the fall they have become free forever."[83]

Readers of the Book of Mormon were quick to see in such verses an utter repudiation of the position associated with Calvinism. "The doctrine of human depravity is denied," reported one pamphleteer. "Total depravity is denounced. Children are said ... [to] have no sin, and are alive in Christ."[84] Another critic protested that if, as the Book of Mormon taught, "atonement was made for the original transgression of the whole human race, ... then every human being since that event must be born into the world like a sheet of paper; and you may write good or bad upon it as you please." Given this virtual Pelagianism, he chided, "you should have taken care to have kept yourself pure while you was pure."[85] (Pelagianism is the heresy that, among other errors, humans can remain so free of sin that they are able to save themselves without Christ's mediation.) One scholar notes that two of the three heresies Caelestius (who may have been the real theologian behind Pelagianism) advocated were that "Adam's sin harmed only himself, not the human race as a whole," and that "children are born in the same state as Adam before his fall."[86] The Book of Mormon seemed a calculated attempt—and was interpreted by its contemporaries—to baldly embrace both heresies.

It is true that some Book of Mormon passages reflect a dour appraisal of human character, especially the words of King Benjamin that "the natural man is an enemy to God, and will be forever and ever, unless ... he putteth off the natural man."[87] However, moments before, Benjamin had affirmed the automatic salvation of children, and in the next breath, insists it is to the state of a child that the natural man must return to become "a saint." Given the Augustinian view of a child as the clearest evidence of the corrupt Adamic inheritance, the difference between Benjamin's view and a Calvinist position could hardly be starker. In any case, the expression "natural man" is, of course, Pauline.[88] As Paul employs the term, it has reference to an *acquired* worldliness; it is not a statement about human ontology, inherited nature, or innate attributes. In his triple parallelism, the apostle contrasts "the spirit of the world" with the spirit that is "of God"; what "man's wisdom teacheth" with what "the Holy Ghost teacheth"; and "the natural man" with "he that is spiritual."[89] "Natural" is in this formulation clearly a worldly acquisition. Brigham Young understood this point, which is why Smith's (and the Book of Mormon's) occasional Calvinist catch-phrasing notwithstanding, he would preach that men "naturally love and admire righteousness, justice and truth more than they do evil. . . . The natural man [in the literal, non-Pauline sense] is of God."⁹⁰

Smith's mind was often a magnet for catch phrases in the theological lexicon of his day, and they occasionally intrude in ways inconsistent with context. The language of depravity is such a case. In the Book of Mormon's book of Ether, the "brother of Jared" pleads with God not to be angry with him, since "because of the fall our natures have become evil continually." The connotation of the fall, here as elsewhere in Mormon texts, is of separation from God, not inherited or imputed guilt, as the subsequent passage makes clear. The brother is told in the ensuing theophany that he is "redeemed from the fall," and "brought back into [God's] presence."⁹¹ Similarly in Alma, Adam is guilty of a fall, by which all mankind become "lost and fallen." Proof-texting is an unreliable strategy to gauge the standing of any doctrine, especially when Smith is creating mythological narratives in which both human anthropology and the fall as primordial event find substantive redefinition. To the extent one hears a few Calvinist echoes in Smith's texts, they are systematically shorn of their prior theological weight by the larger textual and theological environment of Smith's thought.

This is particularly evident with Smith's Moses material, which allayed any conceivable doubt about the totality of this repudiation of Calvinism and original sin. As full-blown Christianity had appeared in the pre-Columbian history of the Book of Mormon, so did it now appear in a mythic past situated just beyond the borders of Eden itself. In this revised Genesis material Smith produced, an expelled Adam was taught the gospel and versed in the atonement of the Christ to come. In that remote past, the record noted, "the saying [went] abroad among the people that the Son of God hath atoned for original guilt, wherein the sins of the parents cannot be answered upon the heads of the children."⁹² In addition, Adam was personally forgiven his "transgression in the garden," so there was nothing left to transmit in any case.⁹³ As for depravity, the same text reads, it was not until Satan came among the children of Adam and Eve, and they "loved [him] more than God," that "men began *from that time forth* to be carnal, sensual, and devilish."⁹⁴ Humans may be prone to depravity by virtue of bodily weakness and environment, in other words, but individuals must participate in their own alienation from God.

This same post-Adamic lapse into sin is repeated immediately after another passage that sounds Calvinist, but only in isolation from its context. "Thy children are conceived in sin," the Lord tells Adam in language echoing the Davidic psalm, but the explanation that ensues clarifies that "*when they begin to grow up*, sin conceiveth in their hearts." And then the Calvinist narrative is again explicitly displaced by a new one, when the explanation behind such sin is not Adamic inheritance, but providential design with an educative intent: "and they taste the bitter, that they may know to prize the good."[95] Setting the fall of man into an even larger context, as we saw, was Smith's doctrine of pre-mortal existence, in which those born into mortality successfully "kept" their "first estate."[96] These re-invented master narratives that span both dispensational and cosmic history convey a framework utterly incompatible with Calvinist readings of human origins or human depravity.

At the same time, Mormon conceptions of a human nature unencumbered by original sin or inherited depravity comport perfectly with the nineteenth-century zenith of liberal humanism, with its celebration of human potential, sense of boundlessness, and Romantic optimism. But for Smith, those conceptions become grounded in a totally reconfigured human anthropology. As a consequence, he sees God's plan—from the beginning—as being about human elevation rather than remedy, advancement rather than repair. In all this, Smith returns his version of Christian thought to a pre-Augustinian state, starkly different from most of the theology of his day. The early Christian rejection of Origen's doctrines of premortality and *apokatastasis* (restoration to one's primordial position), writes one religious historian, ensured the supremacy "of a Christian theology whose central concerns were human sinfulness, not human potentiality; divine determination, not human freedom and responsibility."[97] Mormon theology comports in this regard with Krister Stendahl's assessment of this development as Augustinian, rather than Pauline.

> The point where Paul's experience intersects with his ... understanding of the faith, furthermore, is not "sin" with its correlate "forgiveness." It is rather when Paul speaks about his weakness that we feel his deeply personal pain. Once more we find something surprisingly different from the Christian language that most of us take for granted: it seems that Paul never felt guilt in the face of this weakness—pain, yes, but not guilt. It is not in the drama of the saving of Paul the sinner, but it is in the drama of Paul's coming to grips with what he calls his "weakness" that we find the most experiential level of Paul's theology.[98]

Christianity's fixation on the "plagued conscience" is a development Stendahl traces to Augustine three centuries after Paul, and then to the Reformers over a thousand years later.

Mormonism's mythology of a premortal cohabitation and consanguinity with God is largely incompatible with this entire Augustinian inheritance. In fact, excepting the dispensability of Christ's atonement (a crucial caveat), which dispensability Mormons do *not* accept, one can see why Mormons have recurrently been accused of Pelagianism, the early Christian heresy of according to man inherent goodness and full self-determination and responsibility for his own salvation. One religious historian describes the entire array of nineteenth-century "deists and free-thinkers, universalists, Stone-Campbell 'Christians,' Adventists, Christian Scientists" as a fractious rebellion against the Augustinian heritage, but he notes that only the "Mormons . . . abandoned predestination's entire substructure in original sin."⁹⁹ Mormonism's conception of a pre-mortal past and kinship with God contributed to this stand.

At the same time, it would be wrong to conclude from the above that the fall does not represent for Mormons, as for other Christians, a radical alteration of the human predicament. Mormonism *does* accept the dominion of sin in the present world, human susceptibility to carnal tendencies, and the need for spiritual regeneration. As the Book of Mormon declares, "all mankind, yea, men and women, all nations, kindreds, tongues and people, must be born again; yea, born of God, changed from their carnal and fallen state, to a state of righteousness, being redeemed of God, becoming his sons and daughters; . . . and unless they do this, they can in nowise inherit the kingdom of God."¹⁰⁰

Smith may have taught the primal innocence of humans, but he was under no illusions about their readiness to choose the evil rather than the good. He unhesitatingly acknowledged that "in this world mankind are naturly selfish ambitious & striving to excell one above another."¹⁰¹ In a church editorial, he complained that "satan was generally blamed for the evils which we did, but if he was the cause of all our wickedness, men could not be condemned."¹⁰² But neither guilt nor corruption of the will follows upon the Adamic fall. The human condition is one of vulnerability to temptation, susceptibility to the natural predispositions of a human body and a soul still untried and untested in the crucible of earthly trial and opposition. In Mormon thought, humans are neither capable of unaided advancement to godliness nor are they accurately described as totally depraved. They are agents made free by Christ's atonement, enticed by evil while yearning for the light.¹⁰³

So the fall and its consequences are real enough. In Mormon thought, the fall entails three distinct effects; consequent to Adam's passage from immortality to mortality, his descendants underwent three kinds of death. The first, almost immediate condition the fall introduced was a universal physical death. Adam and Eve became mortal through their choice and passed such mortality on to the human family. Whether, as James Talmage thought, eating the forbidden fruit introduced an actual substance that altered the human physiology, making mortal that which was immortal; whether God otherwise effected some other transformation of Adam and Eve's immortal condition to human; or whether the story is allegorical of the human family's descent from their pre-mortal abode to earthly, bodily habitations, the fall represents for Mormons the portal though which all humankind pass from God's presence to a state of vulnerability and physical separation from God.

Given Adam and Eve's—and our own—freely made decision to sin, God's act forbidding us the immortality-bestowing fruit becomes an act of mercy, not retribution. Recuperating immortality, while in a sinful, fallen condition, would have been the true catastrophe. "It was in mercy that they were deprived of the means of so doing."[104] Life becomes a condition of exposure to mortal weakness, dissolution, and death; the brute fact of physical death is overcome by virtue of Christ's voluntary death on the cross and His subsequent resurrection. Mormons join with other Christians in celebrating Easter as the occasion of Christ's triumphant conquest of physical death and the extension of that victory to all who have ever lived. Accordingly, "this death . . . which is the temporal, shall deliver up the dead, which death is the grave."[105] Such a gift is unmerited, undeserved, and impossible of repayment. It is a pure act of grace, unconditioned kindness.

The second consequence of the fall was a universal, temporal separation from God, called a "spiritual death," with the result that "all mankind, by the fall of Adam [was] cut off from the presence of the Lord."[106] Mortality necessarily entails departure from God's presence, across the veil and into mortality. The resultant human condition is one of physical isolation from God, and upon death the spirit remains vulnerable and separate in its afterlife limbo, whether in hell or in paradise. If it were to remain there unredeemed and unresurrected, wrote Jacob, "our spirits must become subject to that angel who fell from before the presence of the Eternal God . . . to rise no more."[107] While the Bible suggests Adam and Eve's immediate banishment in the aftermath of transgression, Smith's Moses account records a more subtle exile; from time to time "they heard the voice of the Lord from the way toward the Garden of Eden, speaking unto them, [but] they saw him not."[108] Young also saw this separation as gradual: "When father Adam transgressed the law he did not fall at once from the presence of the Lord but spoke face to face with him a long time afterwards. Men continued to sin and degenerate from generation to generation until they had got so far from the Lord that a veil of darkness sprang up between them so that men could no longer speak with the Lord."[109]

Christ's conquest of death at the same time assures that all humans will be restored to God's presence, overcoming the second consequence of Adam's transgression—temporary separation from God. "And this death . . . which is the spiritual death shall deliver up its dead; which spiritual death is hell."[110] (Hell, as we shall see, is the temporary condition of spiritual separation from God in the spirit world.) This restoration, too, is a universal gift: "this restoration shall come to all, both old and young, both bond and free, both male and female, both the wicked and the righteous; and . . . [all] and shall be brought and be arraigned before the bar of Christ the Son."[111] Such restoration of "all mankind . . . back into the presence of the Lord" preparatory to what the scriptures call judgment is the repair of the temporal breach entailed by Adam's transgression; as such, it too is a universal gift, without condition or exception.

The spiritual alienation from God that Young described constitutes the third, indirect consequence of the fall. This form of "spiritual death" occurs as an accountable individual makes those choices which entail personal sin. The exposure to sin is an essential reason for the passage to mortality. Mormons believe, with Julian of Norwich, that "synne is behovely," that sin is needful.[112] It has an essential part to play in human progress. Brigham Young taught, "Ask a child how a certain fruit that it had never tasted, looks and tastes, he could not tell. It is so with us: If we were not subject to sorrows, sin and affliction, how could we be touched by the infirmities of our children when we become exalted?"[113]

Exposure to the full range of human options, without the overweening presence of God, is also the necessary precondition for genuine freedom. Exposure to sin allows for a knowledge of good and evil that is experiential rather than theoretical or propositional. Christ attained to perfection before ever he was incarnate in the flesh. His embrace of the good was flawless. Mortals, on the other hand, require the hard schooling of mortality. As Meister Eckhart reasoned, in his essay on "How the inclination to sin is always beneficial," "the perfection of virtue comes of struggle."[114] Once children reach the age of accountability (about eight, according to an 1831 revelation),[115] and only at that time, it is possible that "sin conceiveth in their hearts," and being "agents unto themselves," they become responsible for their choices. In their weakness, the willful, deliberate decision to sin inevitably follows. Christ's atonement makes possible the forgiveness and spiritual reconciliation with God of all those whose personal repentance and obedience constitute the choice to accept his grace.

CHOICE AND FREEDOM

Predestination and original sin have closely related histories, and Augustine is the dominant figure in establishing both as influential Christian dogmas. Augustine's thinking in this regard can be seen as pivoting on another one of those scriptural conundrums that comes, not surprisingly, from the book of Romans. "Even before they had been born or had done anything good or bad," Paul wrote, God had determined that "I have loved Jacob, but I have hated Esau."[116] This distressing assertion seems the clearest scriptural example of an entirely and unabashedly capricious God. As Paul has him explain, "'I will have mercy on whom I will have mercy, and I will have compassion on whom I will have compassion.' So it depends not on human will or exertion."[117]

Initially, Augustine made the only sense he could of this scripture, while preserving his attachment to both justice and meaningful human freedom. He explained God's preference as the result of his "foreknowledge, by which he knows what even the unborn will be like in the future."[118] A few years later, however, he disavowed his "feeble reply" to the problem, having by now fastened on predestination as the doctrinal foundation behind the verses.[119] By embracing an uncompromising position on predestination, and man's utter dependence on grace, he managed to fend off the challenges the Pelagians were making to orthodoxy, with their celebration of human dignity and freedom. The cost to Augustine was his abandonment of the two principles he had heretofore defended assiduously, free choice and justice. As he explained regarding the first, "I, indeed, labored in defense of the free choice of the human will; but," he says ("with a shudder," writes his biographer) "the grace of God conquered."[120] And as for the second, he now fully conceded that "God elects us . . . with no consideration whatever of any merits of ours, whether past or foreseen as future. What kind of 'justice,' then, is this? The inscrutable justice proper to God's dealings with human creatures, "Augustine replies," a justice beyond both our understanding and our right of complaint."[121]

Once again, the Reformers would offer little by way of dissent. For Luther, "God foresees nothing contingently, but that He both foresees, determines, and actually does all things, by His unchangeable, eternal, and infallible will. By this thunderbolt the whole idea of free-will is smitten down and ground to powder."[122] ("The very term, free will, was odious to all the Fathers," he adds elsewhere.[123]) Melanchthon went further than Augustine or Luther, insisting that God is "himself the proper agent in all things that happen." So just as the conversion of Paul was his doing, so are "also actions that are bad, like David's adultery." Even this was going too far for Luther's followers, however.[124]

A powerful countercurrent emerged a few years later under the influence of Jacob Arminius (1560–1609), a Dutch Reformed theologian. He argued for a greater role for human will and a more universal atonement. The wholly unmerited gift of grace was still the absolute precondition for regeneration, but any individual, not just the elect, had the freedom of will to accept or reject the gift, to respond or not respond to the movements of the heart initiated by God. His ideas caught fire in America in the fertile ground of the Second Great Awakening. Popular preachers John Wesley (1703–1791), Alexander Campbell (1788–1866), and Charles Finney (1792–1875) all were associated with the Arminian strain, which emphasized individual responsibility and a self-determining will. As one scholar writes, "the liberal Christianity of the new republic would be built around such moral principles."[125]

Arminius's emphasis on free will was liberal only by comparison with Calvin. For in our state as descendants of Adam, he wrote, "the Free Will of man towards the True Good is not only wounded, maimed, infirm, bent, and weakened; but it is also imprisoned, destroyed, and lost: And its powers are not only debilitated and useless unless they be assisted by grace, but it has no powers whatever except such as are excited by Divine grace."[126] The essence of his break with Calvin was his redefinition of the idea of prevenient grace. Augustine had written that the only way humans can choose the good is if God's grace—an irresistible grace at that—allows us to make that choice. No righteous choice, therefore, is of human origin. God is the instigator and enabler. He also elects and chooses.

For Arminius, that prevenient grace activates a real, operative will in humans, which allows them to embrace or resist Christ. So now God is the instigator and enabler, but man is the chooser. Arminius's break with Augustinian Calvinism was therefore a subtle, if theologically pregnant, distinction. He still affirmed predestination and salvation by grace alone. But his gesture in the direction of a greater role for human choice became in the next centuries a bridge to the quasi-Pelagianism of the nineteenth century. Wesley emphatically denied any Pelagian content to his system, though he was accused of the heresy for suggesting in his Articles of Religion that aided and "prevented" (pre-enabled) by the grace of God through Christ, we do have "power to do good works, pleasant and acceptable to God."[127]

A full break with depravity and predestination alike is clear in the immensely popular Charles Finney (1792–1875). He was more renowned as a revivalist than as a theologian, but in both capacities he leveled devastating attacks on old-style Calvinism, with its depiction of a reprobate humanity powerless to choose its own destiny. "The fact is, sin never can consist in having a nature, nor in what nature is; but only and alone in the bad use which we make of our nature," he sermonized. "Our Maker will never find fault with us for what He has Himself done or made; certainly not. He will not condemn us, if we will only make a right use of our powers— of our intellect, our sensibility, and our will. He never holds us responsible for our original nature." In fact, he continued, the espousal of original sin, imputing to man an inherited sinful nature, is a "monstrous dogma" an "infamous libel on Jehovah" and "absurd and utter NONSENSE!"[128]

Mormonism is generally depicted as one more working out of the Arminian impulse, part of what Daniel Walker Howe has called "the rebellion against Calvinist theology which . . . was gradually accepted and followed by mainstream American Protestants in general."[129] But Mormonism is a development with more distinctness from its Arminian predecessors than Arminianism bore to Calvinism. For one thing, Mormons found Arminianism an insufficient corrective to the Calvinist doctrine of total depravity and irresistible grace. God did not just temporarily override depravity by dispensing prevenient grace, the Book of Mormon held. "Because that [humans] are redeemed from the fall they have become free forever."[130] The point was made more emphatic in Smith's 1832 revelation, with his declaration that "every spirit of man was innocent in the beginning; and God having redeemed man from the fall, men became again, in their infant state, innocent before God."[131]

Freedom is man's original condition ("in the day I created them; and in the Garden of Eden, gave I unto man his agency"[132]). And Christ's atonement restores to Adam's descendants, however injured they are by the consequences it brought in its wake, moral freedom and personal accountability. So not only human accountability, in other words, but also the origin—and cost—of moral agency find substantial redefinition in Mormonism. As we saw, Smith had described earlier a primordial divine assembly, where God presented his plan for human advancement in the presence of Jesus, Lucifer, and, he later clarified, the hosts of human spirits.

Elsewhere, Smith had already reached even further back beyond the heavenly council to plumb the history of human agency. In his first, unambiguous profession of humankind's eternal status, as we saw, he said that "Man was also in the beginning with God. Intelligence, or the light of truth, was not created or made, neither indeed can be," adding that "All truth is independent in that sphere in which God has placed it, to act for itself, as all intelligence also; otherwise there is no existence. Behold, here is the agency of man."[133] This predication of human existence itself on moral agency is a striking claim, but it is repeated almost verbatim by a near contemporary theologian who was himself working out a theory of human accountability for sin. Julius Müller likewise finds the only possible ground of moral agency in a human preexistence, and claims that such "self-determination" of "personal beings" is itself "the source of their existence." Müller then quotes the philosopher Friedrich Schelling as writing that "every thing actual, even nature, has its source in activity, life, and freedom," but "Personal beings alone have one ground of their existence in *their own act*" (emphasis in original).[134]

The connection of moral independence to a doctrine of uncreated existence is no coincidence. A longstanding problem in theology and philosophy alike had been that if God created the world and all things in it, *he* should be responsible for the sin in it, not us. (As a Cambridge philosopher put the case, God "could have prevented all sin by creating us with better natures and in more favorable surroundings. . . . Hence we should not be responsible for our sins to God."[135]) Jonathan Edwards in the eighteenth century admitted the problem, but thought "every version of Christianity had the same problem. All Christians taught that there *is* sin in the world and that God created the world."[136] From the seventeenth through the nineteenth centuries, philosophers and theologians in England, America, and Germany especially had found it difficult if not impossible to formulate a theory of free will in the context of a created soul or an omniscient deity. Philosophers Gottfried Leibniz in the seventeenth century, and Kant and his disciples in the eighteenth and nineteenth, invoked various versions of a human soul existing before, or outside of, time, as the necessary precondition for human freedom.

In Smith's writings, the doctrine of preexistence lent theological support to the degree of spiritual autonomy he was developing. Prevenient grace was unnecessary in a system where from the beginning there have existed only two kinds of things: "things to act, and things to be acted upon," and men are reminded that they are of the first type: "free to act for yourselves," "free . . . to act according to their wills and pleasures."[137] And such agency elevated humankind to ethereal company. For in the entire universe, there were but "three independent principles—the spirit of God, the spirit of man, and the spirit of the devil."[138] And even those distinctions were tenuous. As Young characterized the point of such agency, "I put into you intelligence," saith the Lord, "that you may know how to govern and control yourselves, and make yourselves comfortable and happy on the earth; and give unto you certain privileges to act upon as independently in your sphere as I do in the government of heaven."[139]

Joseph Smith's conception of human agency, then, may have been informed by the Arminianism of those Methodists with whom he felt greatest affinity in his young years. Like so many of his peers, Smith was also a product of a zeal for liberty that still fired the hearts and imagination of people only a generation removed from the War for Independence. "It is love of liberty which inspires my soul," Smith wrote, "civil and religious liberty," which was "diffused into my soul by my grandfathers [both Revolutionary War veterans] while they dandled me on their knees."[140] But Smith went beyond a simple celebration of human freedom to inscribe moral agency into a cosmic narrative that makes it the focus of ante-mortal councils, war in heaven, and Satanic stratagems to destroy human happiness. The calamitous cost of that freedom was evident long before Eden was formed; the price to guarantee its implementation in mortal life was a third of the pre-mortal human race. Such was Mormonism's reading of Revelation 12:4: "his tail doth draw the third of the stars of the heaven, and he did cast them to the earth." Even the author of the heavenly rebellion against agency was a casualty whom God and angels mourned. He "was called Perdition," Smith wrote, "for the heavens wept over him."[141]

If our Souls & our bodies are not looking forth for the coming of the Son of Man, . . . we shall be among those who are calling for the rocks to fall upon us.

—JOSEPH SMITH, August 1839

19

Embodiment

⌒───

LACKING THE PREMISE of an eternally existing human spirit, Christianity has no theory of embodiment per se. Physicality is simply the given, the mode of human existence that defines us. Though we may be made in the image and likeness of God, the finitude and materiality of embodiment are themselves powerful differentiators between the human and the divine. This distinction is rendered the more emphatic by the Christian doctrine of creation *ex nihilo*, imposing between Creator and creature an almost infinite ontological gulf. In the context of the soul's prehistory, Mormon thought asserts a clearly defined purposiveness to embodiment. In Talmage's words, "it was the *advancement* from the spirit state to the soul state [united body and spirit] that marked the great gift of God unto man, namely, life here upon the earth."[1] Given God's purported materiality, Mormonism endows an unequivocal value on the physical and bodily.

The position of Christianity in this regard has been mixed. Isaiah compared humans at their best to "filthy rags," and Augustine reputedly went further, lamenting with self-contempt that "we are Born between urine and feces" (*Intra feces et urinas nominem natus est*).[2] The psalmist, on the other hand, considered humans to be "fearfully and wonderfully made," and only "a little lower than God."[3] But by and large, it is the prejudice against the body that has dominated in Christian history. "There is no physical or fleshly pleasure without some spiritual harm," wrote the fourteenth-century German theologian Meister Eckhart in a particularly extreme version of that bias, but not out of harmony with subsequent official pronouncements.[4] "The flesh lusteth always contrary to the spirit," stated the Thirty-Nine Articles, the defining statement of Anglicanism.[5]

The emphatic privileging of the spiritual over the physical has classical roots, and was an integral component of Christian thought from the beginning, although the connection is neither straightforward nor simple. In Plato's dualism, the intellect is primary, and physical reality is ontologically secondary, derivative and therefore inferior. The realm of pure *nous* or intellect is in fact the only reality worthy of the name, he argues in the *Republic*.[6] Philosophy, as he defined it, involved the deliberate distancing of oneself from the world of bodily sense, with its allurements, distortions, and impediments to apprehension of the True, the Good, and the Beautiful. In his metaphor, the soul "is imprisoned in and clinging to the body, and . . . it is forced to examine other things as through a cage."[7]

Hellenic ideas about biology reinforced this philosophy. In Aristotle's fetology it is the woman who provides the gross bodily material which is acted upon and formed by the male principle into something of value. "The contribution which the male makes to the young has to do not with bulk but with specific character," just as milk is curdled by the action of rennet in his famous example.[8] And then he makes the hierarchy emphatic and definitive: "Thus the physical part, the body, comes from the female, and the Soul from the male, since the Soul is the essence of a particular body."[9] Finally, in the Christian theology of the Incarnation, the divine Logos, Christ's supernal spirit consubstantial with the Father, condescends to inhabit a mortal body through the vehicle of the woman. Thus, the gendered hierarchy that privileges the soul over the body has been reinforced through early philosophy, science, and dogma alike.

The Platonic influence on early Christian thought was immense, even if the spirit/duality hierarchy was not adopted unchanged. Christians almost universally have believed that the consequence of the fall is an inherited corrupt nature. But situating that corruption in the will or spirit created theological problems: how could a spirit newly created by God be tainted by sinful inheritance or disposition?[10] One solution was to make the flesh the locus of human degeneracy, which a whole vocabulary of physical depravity reinforced. And as the aspect of humanity most unlike the divine, the body was obviously the most susceptible to corruption. The Methodist mystic William Law believed that "sin alone is the father, first cause, and beginner of all the materiality of the world, and that when sin is removed from nature all its materiality must vanish with it."[11]

Paul is clearly committed to a dualistic picture of human nature ("I know that nothing good dwells within me, that is, in my flesh"[12]), although some scholars now assert that his principal dichotomy, that between the flesh and the spirit, is about the divided inclination of the will, the contest between worldliness and holiness, not between physical body and immaterial spirit.[13] The earliest Christian theologian, Origen, conceived of the body in terms that are unmistakably Platonic in his account of human origins. In *First Principles*, he sees the human body itself as an emblem of fallenness, not because of Adam's transgression but by virtue of our individual expulsions from heaven, where we lived as pre-mortal spirits. As with Plato's myth of a human lapse into mortality, Origen thinks bodily incarnation itself signals a universal fall. "So long as a soul continued to abide in the good it has no experience of union with a body. . . . But by some inclination towards evil these souls lose their wings and come into bodies."[14] In Plato's version, "So long as its wings are in perfect condition it flies high, . . . but a soul that sheds its wings wanders until it lights on something solid, where it settles and takes on an earthly body, which then, owing to the power of this soul, seems to move itself. The whole combination of soul and body is called a living thing, or . . . 'mortal.'"[15]

As many recent historians of theologies of the body are prone to point out, Christianity could not follow Plato in wholesale condemnation of the bodily dimension of the self, for two reasons. One reason was that the anticipation of a physical resurrection meant mortality was not a temporary, degraded condition. The human body would be reconstituted and glorified, not simply abandoned or transcended, as in Plato. Both Job ("in my flesh I shall see God") and Jesus explicitly affirmed bodily, physical resurrection ("a ghost does not have flesh and bones as you see that I have").[16] Humankind's restoration to a physical tabernacle can only be taken therefore as divine affirmation of its eternal value.

A second reason was that God's incarnation itself sanctified the body. True enough, his embodiment was infinite condescension, emptying himself to "tak[e] . . . the form of a slave."[17] Still, some churchmen recognized his incarnation as ennobling the body rather than degrading the divine. As Gregory Nazianzen so poetically rendered the point in imagining a day in Christ's mortal life, "[P]erhaps He goes to sleep, in order that He may bless sleep . . .; perhaps He is tired that He may hallow weariness also; perhaps He weeps that He may make tears blessed."[18]

A final hedge against unqualified Christian condemnation of the body was the fact that God, as author of the material universe, would by virtue of his own nature endow that materiality with goodness. It was the Gnostics and Manicheans who imputed the origin of the physical universe to malignant creator gods. To them, the spiritual world alone was the realm of light and goodness; the material creation was inherently and thoroughly evil. The church father Tertullian wrote his treatise *On the Resurrection of the Flesh*, to refute precisely that argument, with its imputation of "inherent corruption and worthlessness . . . to the flesh, or body of man." But this is a curious defense, in which he doesn't deny the body is "worthless, weak, covered with guilt, laden with misery" and "degradation." He only denies that "it can never be rehabilitated from corruption to integrity, from a shattered to a solid state, and from an empty to a full condition."[19]

At the same time, Tertullian finds a genuine theology of bodily affirmation when he emphasizes human identity not in terms of an encased intelligence, but as a composite creation. "Whatever God has at all purposed or promised to man, is due not to the soul simply, but to the flesh also," he writes.[20] And it is with this step, from the body as mere vehicle or tabernacle to the divinely created form that spirit takes, that Tertullian finds cause to celebrate the bodily, with an exuberance seldom known in subsequent Christian traditions. For Tertullian's creation narrative reverses Origen's. Rather than a pre-existing spirit falling into a newly created body, we have in Tertullian a divinely created body, to which God adds a newly minted spirit. And "so intimate is the union, that it . . . [is] uncertain whether the flesh bears about the soul, or the soul the flesh." Consequently, whatever good the spirit accomplishes or perceives, it does in partnership with a physical body:

> For what enjoyment of nature is there, . . . what relish of the elements, which is not imparted to the soul by means of the body? Is it not by its means that *the soul* is supported by the entire apparatus of the senses—the sight, the hearing, the taste, the smell, the touch? Is it not by its means that it has a sprinkling of the divine power[?] . . . The arts come through the flesh; through the flesh also effect is given to the mind's pursuits and powers.[21]

In this view, "the flesh, which is accounted the minister and servant of the soul, turns out to be also its associate and co-heir."[22] His contemporary Clement of Alexandria agreed: the soul will only attain "its desired end" through the body, its "consort and ally."[23]

Two centuries later, Augustine writes at a time when the Manicheans, like the Gnostics before them, disparage humankind's physical nature. In refuting them, Augustine notes that God, creator *ex nihilo*, could only create a material universe—including human bodies—that is good: "There are no substances not made by You," and "You have made all things good."[24] (The good Augustine perceived in the physical body was not always entirely compelling. "Take away the nipples from the manly breast," he argued, "and see how much beauty you have spoiled."[25])

It is doubtless true, as recent scholars have tended to point out, that Christian theology is rooted in a more nuanced appreciation for the body than popular conceptions of that theology have held.[26] Those less inclined to see the godly virtues of the body have pointed out that the goodness God imputes to his physical creation refers to a state *before* the Adamic fall. And the goodness inherent in a resurrected body pertains to a body transformed and quickened *after* a divine process of physical and spiritual regeneration. As regards the body that falls to the common lot of Adam's posterity, it is a decidedly negative emphasis that Augustine unleashes.

This critical development in theology's treatment of the body comes when Augustine narrows the locus of human depravity to concupiscence, and centers the problem of human evil on sexual appetite. His contributions in this regard have been characterized by one not atypical scholar as a fusion of Christianity "with hatred of sex and pleasure into a systematic unity."[27] While such a judgment may be slightly overstated, its accuracy as a matter of historical perception is evident in the wry definition of a Puritan (an Augustinian descendent through Calvin) as someone who cannot sleep at night, fearing that somewhere, someone may be having fun. Augustine set in motion a reading of Paul that finds in bodily appetites the greatest obstacle to spiritual purity. And here we find the strongest correlation with, if not product of, the Platonic heritage. Nietzsche was only one of the most influential critics who thought Christianity's dominant feature was this animus directed against the body and all its natural inclinations. In his view, the loathing for the body so prominent in Christian history "would perhaps lead the looker-on to infer that our earth is the essentially ascetic star,—a corner of malcontent, conceited and ugly creatures, unable to rid themselves of a deep chagrin at self, at the earth, at all life." Religious asceticism is but the purest form of an attitude wherein "physiological thriving itself,—especially its expression, beauty and joy, is viewed with dark and jealous eye."[28]

Strong countercurrents persisted. Bonaventure wrote of Mary, in the thirteenth century, that "her happiness would not be complete unless she were there . . . as a composite, that is, of soul and body. Otherwise she would not be there [in heaven] in perfect joy."[29] One historian notes that "Franciscan thinkers emphasized the yearning of soul and body for each other after death," and cites Bernard of Clairvaux to this effect: "Do not be surprised if the glorified body seems to give the spirit something, for it was a real help when man was sick and mortal. . . . The sick, dead, and resurrected body is a help to the soul who loves God. . . . Truly the soul does not want to be perfected, without that [body] from whose good services it feels it has benefited . . . in every way."[30] And the fourteenth-century saint Gregory Palamas wrote that "Man, by virtue of the body created in the likeness of God, is higher than the angels."[31]

With the Reformation, these dual currents persist. On the one hand, for instance, Calvin urges Christians to "despise[e] the present life," and "to use the world as if he used it not."[32] At the same time, he urges that God created food "not only for our necessity, but also for our enjoyment and delight," and clothing, "in addition to necessity, comeliness and honor." Sheer beauty and appeal to the senses is part of God's purposes, for in sweet odors and the adornments of nature, "has he not given many things a value without having any necessary use?"[33] And though Calvin does use "the body," and "the flesh" as interchangeable terms describing our subjection to "the power of concupiscence," he reads both terms as metaphorical designations for two sides to our nature. The spirit is that part of the soul "which has been regenerated by God," while the flesh is "the corrupt and polluted [version of] the soul."[34]

Luther could see only Christ's debasement, not man's elevation, in Christ's incarnation. "The body also of Christ Himself was human, like ours. Than which body, what is more filthy?"[35] The Bishop of Salisbury was a kindred spirit who glossed the Anglican Articles as follows: "That *God is without body, parts,* or *passions.* In general, all these are so plainly contrary to the ideas of infinite perfection, and they appear so evidently to be imperfections, that this part of the article will need little explanation. We do plainly perceive that our bodies are clogs to our minds."[36] American theologians of the era were largely in accord. As Jonathan Edwards would put the case, we mortals are weighed down with "a heavy moulded body, a lump of flesh and blood which is not fitted to be an organ for a soul inflamed with high exercises of divine love.... Fain would they fly, but they are held down, as with a dead weight at their feet."[37]

One scholar has even explained the bizarre charismatic manifestations of camp meeting revivalism in terms of a perceived antithesis between the heavenly and earthly that makes up the human self: "The result of the radical disjuncture between the body and the divine for those who participated in charismatic experiences was often painful. As the divine presence, holy, perfect, and entirely Other, filled their bodies, the sinful flesh responded by contorting and jerking to-and-fro."[38] As a consequence of the general suspicion of the body, some Christians condemned pastimes rooted in physical activity. Wesley, for example, extended his disapprobation even to childhood amusements. "For he that plays when he is a child," he said, "will play when he is a man."[39] Not surprisingly, then, the Methodist Episcopal Church in America ruled in 1792, "We prohibit play in the strongest terms."[40] In fact, one American historian notes that Mormonism early developed what he called "an 'ideology' of play at a time when most other American clerics still thought of play as the devil's invention."[41] Those who exhibited a contrary perspective often wrote outside the pale of orthodoxy. Most notable in this regard would have been the English mystic and poet William Blake. He considered the essential Christian error to be its tripartite teaching "1. That Man has two real existing principles Viz: a Body & a Soul. 2. That Energy, call'd Evil, is alone from the Body, & that Reason, call'd Good, is alone from the Soul. 3. That God will torment Man in Eternity for following his Energies." In his anthropology, the body was as divine as the soul, only it happened to be discernible by the senses. And the "energies" it gave rise to were synonymous with "eternal delight."[42]

In its embrace of the eternalism of matter, its explicit rejection of a triune God "without body, parts or passions" in favor of a corporeal deity, and by its association of marital bonds with eternal states and relationships, Mormonism—like Blake— cast the earthly as a sacred sphere and rejected the dichotomies and valuations that necessitated a guarded response to worldly pleasures. It is thus a synthesis that Mormonism effects, and not, as one observer believed, "a repudiation of spirituality in favor of materiality."[43] Here as elsewhere, the polarity that underlies conventional conceptions of sacred distance collapses, and materiality becomes spiritualized. Smith's definitive statement in this regard came in 1833, when he declared that only when spirit is combined with element and "inseparably connected" can humans find "a fulness of joy."[44] As was so often the case, it was Parley Pratt who first elaborated the implications of Smith's conflation of heaven and earth: "In the resurrection, and the life to come, men that are prepared will actually possess a material inheritance on the earth. . . . [T]hey will eat, drink, converse, think, walk, taste, smell and enjoy."[45]

Brigham Young emphatically endorsed Pratt's interpretation, repeatedly expressing a robust appreciation for the eternal value of earthy pleasures. "Our organism makes us capable of exquisite enjoyment," remarked Young.[46] But that condition is more than a threatening distraction; it is very much to the Divine purpose: "We are to learn how to enjoy the things of life," he would later expand,

> how to pass our mortal existence here. There is no enjoyment, no comfort, no pleasure, nothing that the human heart can imagine . . . that tends to beautify, happify, make comfortable and peaceful, and exalt the feelings of mortals, but what the Lord has in store for his people. He never objected to their taking comfort. He never revealed any doctrine, that I have any knowledge of, but what in its nature is calculated to fill with peace and glory, and lift every sentiment and impulse of the heart above every low, sad, deathly, false and groveling feeling. The Lord wishes us to . . . bid farewell to all that gloomy, dark, deathly feeling that is spread over the inhabitants of the earth.[47]

In another discourse given in 1852, Young said "There is the most novelty in 'Mormonism' that there is in anything upon the face of the earth. It is musical, it pleases both the eye and the ear, and I may say, every sense of man."[48] By contrast, he was sure "There is no music in hell."[49]

Sometimes, Mormon inclination to indulge the sensory pleasures created consternation among converts from more abstemious backgrounds. One Mormon immigrant remembered that "after all was settled the ship did plow its way over the briny deep and what did we the Swiss hear and see. Hand organ, violin music and then dancing. We did not like that and asked one another what kind of people is this? One of our elders, . . . [who] could . . . speak English fluently, told us they were all Mormons. We were horror stricken in hearing this. We never expected that Latter-day Saints would indulge in such worldly pleasures. We were disgusted."[50] They would have been a great deal more horrified if they had visited the Mormon temple, holiest edifice in the church, there to find a small orchestra and dancing, as was occasionally the case.[51] Once in Utah, such practices became institutionalized with repercussions that continue to the present. In what *Time* magazine called "the dancingest religion," such church-endorsed bodily expressiveness becomes an emblem, if not a direct outgrowth, of a longstanding commitment to righteous reveling in physicality.[52]

SEXUALITY

Any religion that so valorizes the material and preaches the impossibility of man's being saved alone could hardly be expected to shy away from addressing the eternal implications of human sexuality. Christian tradition had long associated the fall of Adam with the procreative drive and made of human intercourse the means of perpetuating a curse through eons of earthly time. Christ's words that in heaven people "neither marry nor are given in marriage,"[53] together with Paul's suggestion that marriage is only slightly preferable to being "aflame with passion,"[54] satisfied most minds that the congress of the sexes was of temporal duration only and a mark of human concupiscence. Jerome did more than any other early writer to transform Paul's warnings against "the flesh" into a preoccupation with the dark dangers of sexuality.[55] The sexual organs, Augustine sermonized, were the very "site of original sin within us."[56] Marriage mitigated but did not entirely resolve or contain the conundrum of human sexuality. As an early Christian commentary put it, "Remove the utility of being born and the reason for marriage is explained . . . the work of reproduction is characteristically a fleshly act that we share in common with animals."[57]

The association of celibacy with a higher sexual standard, and the Protestant relegation of intercourse to the child-producing function, further nudged marital relations to the far side of spiritual life or eternal purposes. As late as 1851, the Methodist liturgy explicitly characterized sexual relations in those terms: marriage was "ordained for a remedy against sin, and to avoid fornication: that such persons as have not the gift of continency, might marry, and keep themselves undefiled members of Christ's body."[58]

Some dissenters from the Puritan-influenced party line emerged from time to time, like the poet mystic William Blake. For him, as the critic Alfred Kazin wrote, human sexuality "meant enjoyment framed in wonder."[59] In his inversion of the early Christian view, sexuality is not a consequence of fallenness; the shame associated with sexuality is. His dictum that "Shame is Pride's cloak" is not the scandalous provocation of a libertine, but the earnest attempt of a devout Christian mystic to turn back the clock on the Platonization of Christianity, to combat the prudish disdain for God's crowning creation—the human body. To the Augustinian disparagement of the female body, Blake replied stubbornly, "The nakedness of woman is the work of God."[60]

Mormonism's fullest early statement on the sanctity of the marriage relationship and conjugal affection was written by Pratt in 1844. His essay on "Intelligence and Affection" is a celebration of divine physicality. Proceeding from the premise that God—like all divine entities—is embodied (one conclusion of his essay "Immortality of the Body"), Pratt argued that the prejudice of Platonism and Puritanism against the bodily was groundless. Ascribing our natural affections to a fallen and corrupt nature as creedal Christianity does ("wholly defiled in all the parts and faculties of soul and body") mistakes "the source and fountain of happiness altogether."[61] Those true mainsprings are, first, our natural affections and second, our social nature. Pratt held that asceticism does not transcend the carnal but, rather, rejects what is inherently god-like. The direction and cultivation of the passions, not their repression, is God's intention for humans, he wrote. And foremost among these human affections is the reciprocal desire of a man and his wife. There is, in fact, "not a more pure and holy principle in existence than the affection which glows in the bosom of a virtuous man for his companion."[62]

Mormon theology is replete with references to human sexuality as a sacred endowment, as it is for many Christians. Contemplating the choice of a woman to have no children, a character in Kathleen Norris's novel remarks "there's no responsibility like that of decreeing that young lives simply shall not be."[63] The stakes in Mormon parenthood are slightly different. Believing as they do that those human spirits destined for earthly bodies already exist, Mormons see procreation as the conduit through which "noble spirits, that have been waiting for thousands of years" come into mortality, as Pratt taught in 1852.[64] In this view, procreation becomes co-participation with God in the peopling of the earth according to a plan that preceded the earth's creation. Several implications follow: the large families encouraged by Brigham Young were valued not for their own sake but because they represent a kind of spiritual lifeboat for souls that would otherwise founder on the rocks of uncertain family environments and circumstance.[65] Engendering and raising large families in a righteous environment is a gesture of selflessness toward already existing spirit individuals. For much of their history, Mormons therefore followed the Christian tendency to emphasize the priority of procreation in sexual relations, but with these additional theological foundations.

The powers associated with procreation, and the marital institution that Mormons see as instituted *before* the fall, together endow sexuality with an uncompromised status as holy, divine, and in some sense, eternal. Consequently, Mormon doctrine absolutely proscribes sexual relations before or outside marriage. Birth control has a more complicated history. In a church that did not just advocate large families but also theologized the reasons for them, birth control has understandably been discouraged. From Brigham Young past the mid-twentieth century, birth control was condemned as sinful, selfish, and contrary to the purposes of marriage. While the underlying theology remains intact, the church has in recent decades intruded less upon the personal application of those principles. As President Gordon B. Hinckley said in 1984:

> The Lord has told us to multiply and replenish the earth that we might have joy in our posterity, and there is no greater joy than the joy that comes of happy children in good families. But he did not designate the number, nor has the Church. That is a sacred matter left to the couple and the Lord. The official statement of the Church includes this language: "Husbands must be considerate of their wives, who have the greater responsibility not only of bearing children but of caring for them through childhood, and should help them conserve their health and strength."[66]

The most recent version of the handbook also notes that sexual relations in marriage "are divinely approved not only for the purpose of procreation, but also as a way of expressing love and strengthening emotional and spiritual bonds between husband and wife."[67]

The other preventive to birth—abortion—has had a more consistent condemnation in Mormon thought. Nineteenth-century figures—including feminists like Susan B. Anthony and Cady Stanton, used the terms *abortion, foeticide, infanticide*, and *child-murder* as interchangeable or near-equivalents.[68] It was likely in this sense that Mormonism's first oblique reference to abortion comes in 1831. "Thou shalt not . . . kill, nor do anything like unto it."[69] Young and other early Mormon leaders referred to "abortion, infanticide and child-killing" as related crimes, recognizing little distinction from murder.[70] "Infanticide is . . . not so boldly practiced as is the other equally great crime, which no doubt, to a great extent, prevents the necessity of infanticide," said Young in reference to abortion.[71] George Q. Cannon and John Taylor agreed that the practice was a "black art," "a damning evil," and constituted "murder of the unborn," and was so rampant that America had become "a nation of murderers."[72] The modern LDS Church officially treats most abortions as "like unto," rather than "the same as," murder; one may repent and be baptized for the first, but not (without special dispensation) for the latter. Exceptions to the prohibition may be made in cases of dire threat to the mother's health, rape, or incest.

Though the doctrine of pre-mortality has bearing, as we have seen, on Mormon conceptions of procreation generally, it is not typically invoked as having bearing on abortion. Precisely when the soul enters the body is for Mormons, as for Christians generally, a subject of speculation rather than dogma. For a minority of Mormons, the theological emphasis on choice is persuasive rationale for supporting abortion rights. In response, Apostle Dallin Oaks has pointed out the flaw in such reasoning: the sanctity of one agent's choice can never trump the sanctity of the other's life. Given the status of the unborn child as an human individual in Mormon thought, two human agents, and two vested interests, must be weighed accordingly. Oaks's comments also have the virtue of highlighting a particular Mormon understanding of choice. As we saw earlier, a Mormon view of moral freedom assumes the sacrosanct link between choice and consequence. Freedom, in other words, is grounded in a framework of natural law. As Oaks reasons, "the effect in 95 percent of abortions is not to vindicate choice but to avoid its consequences; using arguments of choice to try to justify altering the consequences of choice is a classic case of omitting what the Savior called the 'weightier matters of the law.'"[73] Ironically, in this vision, those who seek to safeguard the human products of conception are the actual defenders of the principle of choice.[74]

MORTALITY'S PURPOSE

Because Mormonism considers embodiment an ascent from ante-mortal existence, but asserts the substantiality of spirit as simply more refined matter, one problem is mitigated even as another appears. Long before Descartes addressed the mind-body problem, Augustine had grappled with the nature of spirit-body interaction. Two ontologically distinct entities would presumably have no means of affecting each other. Leibniz offered one rather inventive solution to the problem. In his scheme, matter and spirit operate in tandem, not through interaction but through a "preestablished harmony." Descartes himself admitted that the mind (or spirit)-body problem was one which "we obscure as we seek to explain."[75] As we saw earlier, in Mormon thought, as for Blake, the dilemma is lessened, if not obviated, by positing a spirit that is itself material. There is no radical ontological divide which introduces the problem of interaction or coordination between the two entities.

Solving one philosophical challenge produces another, however: just what benefit accrues from a specifically physical form of incarnation? A standard teaching in modern Mormonism is that a primary reason for human passage from pre-mortality into earth life is that "our spirits needed to be clothed with physical bodies."[76] But exactly what purpose is accomplished by sheathing "highly refined matter" (spirit) in an impure form (material body)? The criticism that Ann Conway leveled in the seventeenth century against Henry More's defense of spiritual pre-existence seems pertinent to Mormonism as well:

> But if they allege that body and spirit agree in certain attributes, such as extension, motion, and shape, with the result that spirit has extension and is able to reach from one place to another, and also change itself into whatever shape it pleases, in such cases it agrees with the body and the body with it.[77]

Why is the whole scheme of human embodiment, in other words, not redundant? For Joseph Smith, physical tabernacles in some undefined way entail a more empowered mode of existence. Smith insisted the passage into mortality was an ascent in relative power. "The spirits of all men were subject to oppression & the express purpose of God in Giveing it a tabernicle was to arm it against the power of Darkness."[78] He expanded the explanation later: "God is good and all his acts are for the benefit of inferior intelligences." God saw that in their pre-mortal condition, these "intelligences had not the power to defend themselves against those that had a tabernacle, therefore the Lord called them together in Council and agrees to form them tabernacles."[79] Power over all one's enemies is what Smith often equated with salvation, and "no person can have this Salvation except through a tabernacle," he repeated.[80] His thinking may have been prompted by his translation of the Book of Mormon, which held that in the absence of physical resurrection, "our spirits must become subject to [Satan], . . . and we become devils, angels to a devil."[81]

One possibility is that the power he is describing is one that accrues through bodily challenges rather than mere bodily acquisition. He wrote that "We came to this earth that we might have a body and present it pure before God in the Celestial Kingdom. The great principle of happiness consists in having a body. . . . All beings who have bodies have power over those who have not."[82] A reasonable inference is that the process of purifying a recalcitrant physical tabernacle may be the source of a particular kind of strength, but—in distinction from ascetic traditions generally— a strength that is bodily as well as spiritual. Mormonism thus avoids the asceticism that Platonism infiltrated into much of Christianity. As Reinhold Niebuhr points out, the problem is that "Plato does not recognize that the anarchic impulses which the 'soul' brings into subjection are more than mere bodily impulses. They are impulses which have been given their freedom by the fact that man is spirit as well as nature."[83] This view is consistent with the words of Smith, when he intriguingly warned that "If our Souls & our bodies are not looking forth for the coming of the

Son of Man, . . . we shall be among those who are calling for the rocks to fall upon us" (my emphasis).[84] The two must move toward sanctification in tandem.

Mormons, we have seen, do not believe in original sin. They repudiate both inherited guilt and total depravity. But that doesn't mean they deny that we inherit a substantial amount of bodily baggage that moves us toward selfishness and carnality. The commonly drawn inference from this—that the body is inherently base and needs refinement to attain to the spirit's inherent superiority—may be misleading to the point of fundamental error. For one thing, the demarcation between spirit and body is no simple matter. Selfishness may be born of an evolved biological drive for self-preservation, or it might be rooted in what we could call a spiritual disposition toward self-aggrandizement. A violent temper may be an inherited genetic characteristic, or it may be the manifestation of an incapacity for empathy and compassion. If we understand lust to be the failure of the will to control hormonal overdrive, is it the spirit or the body that needs schooling? Niebuhr wrote that "Sin is therefore spiritual and not carnal, though the infection of rebellion spreads from the spirit to the body."[85] Both spirit and body, in other words, are sources of sin and in need of discipline.

It seems self-evident that in the process of disciplining the appetites and passions, the spirit (or the will, seen as a constant of personal identity traceable to the eternal spirit) necessarily grows stronger. Mormonism thus agrees with half of Thomas Aquinas's equation: "the union of soul and body does not take place for the sake of the body, namely, that the body may be ennobled, but for the sake of the soul, which needs the body for its own perfection."[86] More specifically, he thought embodiment somehow enhanced the capacity of the soul to acquire understanding, "which is a soul's essential and principal operation."[87] Brigham Young made the identical point. Our present embodiment, he said, whereby the soul is "clothed upon by tabernacles," was expressly "designed for the attainment of further intelligence."[88]

Unlike Aquinas, Mormonism asserts that the union of body and soul *is* for the sake of the body, too. Through the mortal experience, the body itself is undergoing a process of refinement and improvement. Mormonism emphasizes the literal likeness of the human physical body itself to an embodied God. The human body is held by Mormon scripture to be designedly imitative of a divine model. "Man have I created after the body of my spirit," an unembodied Christ tells an ancient prophet.[89] Parley Pratt elaborated: the physical body corresponds to the spiritual body in every regard. Though "composed of the spiritual elements, [the spirit] possesses every organ after the pattern and in the likeness or similitude of the outward or fleshly tabernacle it is destined to eventually inhabit. Its organs of thought, speech, sight, hearing, tasting, smelling, feeling, etc., all exist in their order as in the physical body; one being the exact similitude of the other."[90]

Those divine attributes are not always apparent in the human species as manifest in the world today. Here, Mormon thinking evokes the remark of the seventeenth-century Henry More: consequent to Adam's fall, we inherit something less than paradisiacal bodies.[91] The eventual destiny of the human body to more fully imitate its divine model suggests it is not just the spirit that is strengthened through its subjugation of the flesh; the body itself must go through a process of sanctification that commences this side of the resurrection. An immortal, glorified body is not simply the reward for a life well lived; it is the fruit of such a life. Mormon adherence to a law of health[92] is sometimes viewed by Mormons as mere deference to the spirit's tabernacle, but it might more accurately be seen as part of an all-encompassing regimen that tends toward the body's apotheosis. As Parley Pratt wrote,

Why came ye to this world of woe? . . .
You came to the earth to be born of flesh,
To fashion and perfect your earthly house. . . .[93]

The Mormon perspective that shuns both asceticism and sensualism is perfectly captured by Stephen Webb, who notes that for Mormons, "salvation is the gradual perfection of the relationship of spirit to matter, not the triumph of the former over the latter."[94]

This principle is confirmed by language in the Mormon tradition that repeatedly asserts a physically manifest transformation of the human body resulting from spiritual discipline. Heber C. Kimball taught that the influence of the Holy Spirit would "enter into every muscle, sinew, and fibre of the body, in proportion to our fitness to receive it. If we render ourselves susceptible of the nourishment that is imparted by the Spirit of God to the spirits that dwell within these mortal bodies, we shall have sufficient light and power to enable our spirits to dictate to our bodies and lead them unto eternal life."[95] Smith died fifteen years before Darwin's famous treatise was published but would doubtless have found his version of evolution amenable to his understanding of human nature. Not metaphysically transmitted sinfulness, but biologically inherited instincts threaten to overwhelm whatever goodness originally inheres in the human spirit.

The theological problem Luther and the traducianists found with Catholic creationism (how can an immediately created soul be tainted with or predisposed toward sin?) is only slightly different for the Mormon belief in pre-existence. (How to reconcile a presumably pure, innocent, and ageless soul with the human propensity toward selfishness and carnality?) Mormons appreciate the purport, if not the theology, behind the waggish observation that original sin is the only Christian dogma that is empirically verifiable. What this means, of course, is that the human condition is one that is demonstrably overridden with tendencies and characteristics readily suggestive of words like *wicked, depraved,* or *fallen.* Denying as Mormonism does an original sin that is bequeathed to posterity, an inherited guiltiness or corrupted will, Mormonism finds alternative explanation for the human condition in the brute fact of a biological inheritance that has yet to be governed and ennobled by a still-developing spiritual self. Here it becomes clear that evolution, if anything, should be even more amenable to Mormon anthropology than to other Christian traditions, since it does the work of original sin without the theological drawbacks.

"When our spirits took possession of these tabernacles," preached Brigham Young, "they were as pure as the angels of God, wherefore total depravity cannot be a true doctrine."[96] On the other hand, virtually substituting evolution for Adam, Young acknowledges that "the body is of the earth, . . . and is under the mighty influence of that fallen nature that is of the earth."[97] The heritage entailed by material, bodily inheritance, not imputed guilt, is the problem. In this context, the mortal condition is not the unfortunate detritus of Adam's catastrophic decision but, rather, a consequence of entirely natural processes and biological forces that bequeath upon us a fraught inheritance. Even so, the very burden of our corporeal humanity, with all its carnal, selfish, and passional attributes, is very much to the divine purpose behind embodiment.

Darwin's contribution in this regard was not just in unfolding a set of laws that explain organic evolution but also in recognizing the correlation between agonistic struggle and perfectibility. In his illuminating discussion of the honeybee, he noted the creature's apparently aborted development; why, he queried, should a honeybee have a stinger that entails self-destruction, when an unserrated stinger would serve the individual and the hive better? Because, he reasoned, evolutionary development halted when the bee achieved supremacy over its immediate environment. If external pressures disappear, so does the progress. The level of resistance one encounters, he explains, will determine "the standard of perfection attained under nature."[98] The Mormon version of this principle appears in the Book of Mormon, where the focus shifts from external to internal obstacles, with the Lord explaining that he "give[s] unto men weakness that they may be humble . . . for if they humble themselves before me, and have faith in me, then will I make weak things become strong unto them."[99] The call to live a godly life while enmeshed in habits and proclivities of the "natural man" produces the dynamic tension productive of self-conquest and sanctification. Or, as the prophet Lehi expresses the principle, "to bring about his eternal purposes in the end of man, . . . it must needs be that there was an opposition; even the forbidden fruit in opposition to the tree of life."[100]

The principal challenge evolution poses for theology (apart from issues unique to literal-minded Creationists) concerns the question of humanity's unique status vis-à-vis ancestral and nonhuman species. Are humans, in other words, the product of blind evolutionary forces, with the rest of the created order? Mormons, along with many Christians, believe there is an unequivocal differentiation of some sort. As Marilynne Robinson recently expresses the problem, "Whatever the shared genetic history of beast and bird, a transformative change occurred over the millennia, . . . a change gradualism could not predict. . . . Language that would have been fully adequate to describe the age before the appearance of the first artifact would have had to be enlarged by concepts like agency and intention, words like creation."[101] G. K. Chesterton had made the same point almost a century earlier. "It sounds like a truism to say that the most primitive man drew a picture of a monkey and it sounds like a joke to say that the most intelligent monkey drew a picture of a man. Something of division and disproportion has appeared; and it is unique."[102]

Some Catholic thinkers explain human exceptionalism by attributing humankind's physical makeup to evolutionary processes, with the addition of a soul at the time of birth as its uniquely differentiating element. Catholic biologist Kenneth Miller, for instance, points out that "All of the Western monotheistic religions maintain that God brought the universe into being, that He intended to create creatures deserving of a soul."[103] But by rejecting a "literal reading of 'image' and 'likeness,'" Catholics like Miller are free to believe that the form such creatures would take is not preordained. Through undirected evolutionary history, he holds, it happened that humans, by pure contingency, "evolved to self-awareness," showing themselves "worthy of a soul," or "the first of these experiments to be ready" for one.[104] That soul, by persisting Catholic dogma, is "created immediately by God."[105]

Mormons likewise maintain that the difference between the human and the animal is not incremental but fundamental, and is centered in an eternal human soul. (Animals have their own as well, according to Smith.[106]) The difference is that for Mormons, the human soul has its own prehistory and its own acquired attributes and character, along with its own moral agency. And the body, we have seen, is made in the literal likeness and similitude of that eternal spirit—and of an anthropomorphic God. So it cannot be the case, as it is for Miller, that the human body acquired its present form by happenstance, or that God waited until any kind of creature evolved with whom he could enter into special relationship. Can Mormonism's view of a foreordained and pre-designed bodily tabernacle be reconciled with Darwin? The question is important, but must be seen in the larger context of Mormonism and science.

SCIENCE AND MORMONISM

The same year that Joseph Smith incorporated a new church in upstate New York, John Murray, the friend and publisher of leading British radicals and revolutionaries (like Lord Byron), published a work that would shake the very foundations of organized religion. That was the year the first volume of Charles Lyell's *Principles of Geology* came off the press. It created major tremors that would anticipate—and amplify—the turbulent upheavals soon to follow in the wake of Darwin's theory of natural selection as the force that drives evolution. Lyell's contribution to orthodoxy's demise had been his compelling geologic evidence for an antiquity of the earth that far exceeded the mere six millennia suggested by Genesis. The overwhelming evidence for an earth age measured in millions of years meant literal readings of the Bible were no longer tenable. "He did more than any other scientist," writes one scholar, "to disturb the religious faith of the 1830s and the century that followed."[107]

Darwin's more famous *Origin of Species* appeared in 1859, but precipitated no immediate crisis in religious circles. The 1860 debate between Thomas Huxley, "Darwin's Bulldog," and the Anglican Bishop Samuel Wilberforce in England, which presaged the prominent "Scopes Monkey Trial" of 1925 featuring Clarence Darrow and William Jennings Bryan in America, typified the studied staging, rather than the natural unfolding, of confrontation and conflict between science and religion. Initially, most Christians were able to accommodate both by embracing a kind of theistic evolution. Books written early on in the Darwin controversy, with titles like *History of the Conflict between Science and Religion* (1875) and *History of the Warfare of Science with Theology* (1896) reaffirmed and exacerbated an invented rather than an inevitable mutual hostility.[108]

At this very time, Mormons were insisting upon the seamless marriage of science and religion. As we saw, Parley Pratt thought the intellectual strength of Mormonism was its unwillingness to claim special exemption from the laws of the scientific world. Even the Father and Son, he declared in his *Key to the Science of Theology*, were part of an eternal and physical universe, and therefore "subject to the laws that govern, of necessity, even the most refined order of physical existence." Because "all physical element, however embodied, quickened, or refined, is subject to the general laws necessary to all existence."[109] Young confirmed this conflation of earthly and heavenly law with a startling image: "When the elements melt with fervent heat, the Lord Almighty will send forth his angels, who are well instructed in chemistry, and they will separate the elements and make new combinations thereof."[110]

Richard Bushman suggests in the same spirit that "The end point of engineering knowledge may be divine knowledge. Mormon theology permits us to think of God and humans as collaborators in bringing to pass the immortality and eternal life of man. Engineers may be preparing the way for humans to act more like gods in managing the world."[111] In this speculation, Mormons ironically find an unlikely (and surely unwilling) ally in the arch-atheist Richard Dawkins. In his controversial critique of religion, he wrote that: "Any creative intelligence of sufficient complexity to design anything comes into existence only at the end product of an extended process of gradual evolution." Elaborating this point, he said that

> you have to have a gradual slow incremental process [to explain an eye or a brain] and by the very same token, God would have to have the same kind of explanation. . . . God indeed can't have just happened. If there are Gods in the universe, they must be the end product of slow incremental processes. If there are beings in the universe that we would treat as Gods, . . . that we would worship . . . as gods, then they must have come about by an incremental process, gradually.[112]

Consistent with scientific understanding of the eternity of matter that had been suggested as early as the eighteenth century with Lavoisier's principle of mass conservation, Smith had already rejected the earth's *ex nihilo* creation, and contested the biblical version of its six-day organization as well. The Book of Abraham, produced by Joseph Smith in 1835–42, substituted indeterminate "times" for twenty-four hour days.[113] And as for the antiquity of the results, Smith's close associate W. W. Phelps recognized that Smith's teachings in this regard conformed to, rather than conflicted with, the new science of geology. Writing to William Smith, he noted that Joseph had learned from his work on the papyri that

> eternity, agreeably to the records found in the catacombs of Egypt, has been going on in this system (not this world) almost two thousand five hundred and fifty five millions of years: and to know at the same time, that deists, geologists and others are trying to prove that matter must have existed hundreds of thousands of years;—it almost tempts the flesh to fly to God, or muster faith like Enoch to be translated.[114]

As for the particular manner of human creation itself, Smith said nothing. Mormonism has no official position on the biblical account of human creation, other than the vague assertion that scripture is "the word of God." Parley Pratt, in his studied repudiation of biblical "spiritualizers" who read the Second Coming in a figurative sense, had set the church on its long trajectory of literalist-inclined exegesis.[115] His influence was especially pronounced in an early church article that attempted "to establish some definite rule for interpretation." Citing Pratt's influence, the author, probably editor Benjamin Winchester, wrote that "the idea of spiritualizing the writings of the prophets and apostles" so that "none but the learned can understand them, is certainly repugnant to the word of God." A "literal" reading, especially as regards prophecies of the millennium was the proper and necessary rule.[116]

Young, however, drew the line at reading the human creation story in that way. He said with some impatience, "I do not believe that portion of the Bible as the Christian world do. I never did, and I never want to. What is the reason I do not? Because I have come to understanding, and banished from my mind all the baby stories my mother taught me when I was a child."[117] His reading, however, did not exactly move in the direction of more palatable allegory. "Mankind are here," he said, "because they are the offspring of parents who were first brought here from another planet."[118] Young's opinion faded from Mormon understanding with the rest of his Adam-God speculations, though a generation later B. H. Roberts cited Lord Kelvin's theory of extra-terrestrial origins for earth life as compatible with Young's view that Adam and Eve were translated beings brought here from another sphere (thereby preserving the scientific validity of evolution while exempting the human family).[119] At the same time, Roberts made Adam head of a dispensation rather than of the human race (thereby allowing for pre-Adamites, while making Adam the "first man" in that particular sense).

In response to Darwin's theory of human evolution, Young himself maintained a careful distance. Coincidentally, just a month after *Origin*'s publication, Young sounded a note the naturalist would have applauded. He "observed that naturalists have divided the kingdom into parts. This is not so," he argued, "as the human species are linked to the animal."[120] He never mentioned Darwin or his theory by name, but more than a decade later he could not restrain a touch of Schadenfreude at the discomfiture of the fundamentalists in the face of scientific developments generally: "I am not astonished that infidelity prevails to a great extent among the inhabitants of the earth," he remarked in 1871, "for the religious teachers of the people advance many ideas and notions for truth which are in opposition to and contradict facts demonstrated by science, and which are generally understood."[121]

Such liberal sentiments, however, did not extend to an embrace of Darwin; most Mormon leaders kept their silence, while Orson Pratt and some others were dismissive.[122] The LDS Church did not declare authoritatively on the subject until 1909, and then with a statement of calculated ambiguity that cautioned against but did not repudiate the theory:

It is held by some that Adam was not the first man upon this earth and that the original human being was a development from lower orders of the animal

creation. These, however, are the theories of men. The word of the Lord declared that Adam was "the first man of all men" (Moses 1:34), and we are therefore in duty bound to regard him as the primal parent of our race.[123]

The real purport of the statement was to sideline the question of human origins as
unimportant and impossible of definitive resolution: only "some of these facts"
touching on human creation are known, it urged. What is certain is that "Man is
the child of God, formed in the divine image and endowed with divine attributes."
Following the Scopes trial, the church softened even that implicit hostility, reissuing
their statement but with the cautionary language about the "theories of men" conspicuously absent.[124]

In the twentieth century, the church continued to emphasize its generally happy
embrace of scientific developments. Eventual apostle John A. Widtsoe continued to
trumpet the unproblematic harmony of science and religion with titles like *Joseph
Smith as Scientist* (1908), *Science and the Gospel* (1908–1909), and his *Rational Theology* (1915), among other writings. The first work was written to prove that "the teachings of Joseph Smith, the Mormon prophet, were in full harmony with the most
advanced scientific thought, and that he anticipated the world of science in the
statement of fundamental facts and theories of physics, chemistry, astronomy and
biology."[125] Consequently, wrote Widtsoe, the miraculous becomes the operating of
higher law (the miracle is but "a law not understood"), and biological processes find
spiritual counterparts. Therefore, though man's biological origin remains in doubt,
what he called "moderate" evolution is but a shadow and type of the law of eternal
progression manifest in Deity and mankind alike ("Joseph Smith taught the law of
evolution as an eternal truth, twenty or more years before Darwin published his
views").[126]

"Science confirms revelation," concurred Orson Whitney in 1927.[127] A few decades
before, the Mormon hierarchy had given to its leading scientist, James E. Talmage
(1862–1933),[128] its first and only authorization to write a compendium of Mormon
doctrine (*Articles of Faith*, 1899). Talmage's scientific credentials sent a powerful
message that secular learning was not only compatible with faith but apparently also
a distinct advantage and qualification in Mormonism's most authoritative voice of
the twentieth century. Two of the century's Mormon intellectual giants, B. H. Roberts and Talmage, both died in 1933. With their passing, the church entered an era of
reaction and biblical literalism. One manifestation was persistent efforts by apostles
Joseph Fielding Smith and Bruce R. McConkie to condemn human evolution as
Mormon heresy. The leadership employed internationally renowned scientist Henry
Eyring to mount a public rebuttal to these developments, while repeatedly invoking
the 1909 and 1925 positions and refusing to adjudicate the issue further.[129]

Some voices in the church leadership continue to the present to speak disparagingly of Darwinian evolution; the wording of some, however, suggests the problem is one of replacing the idea of divine ancestry with a purely materialistic account. That evolution may serve as the vehicle of human bodily creation is not denied. Hence, Talmage would say that "supposing that undeniable proof [of evolution] had been furnished," the theory cannot account for the origin of the "primordial germ" of life, and in any case, "the body is not the *man*" (his emphasis). Such an account of evolution is false, he concludes, if its adherent "gazes upon the inspiring canvas, and says there was no artist."[130] In a similar way, Boyd K. Packer suggests that "the theory of evolution . . . will have an entirely different dimension when the workings of God in creation are fully revealed." We are "the offspring of God," he writes, and not "only advanced animals."[131]

Meanwhile, Mormon Church-owned Brigham Young University has become nationally prominent in the field of molecular evolutionary biology.[132] Neither creationism nor intelligent design find a home in the science departments of the LDS-owned school. How to reconcile the randomness of Darwinian evolution with the dogma of an anthropomorphic God in whose image humans exist is not an issue the church feels compelled to address.

All who would follow the precepts of the Bible, whether Mormon or not, would assuredly be saved.

—JOSEPH SMITH, 5 February 1840

20

Salvation

PHYSICAL INCARNATION, AS a prelude to eventual resurrection with a glorified body, represents a higher, more developed, and more power-laden form of existence than spiritual being in Mormon thought. Embodiment in a corruptible body of flesh and blood does not entail the inheritance of any Adamic sin, though it does entail the physical inheritance of all those traits, conditions, and limitations that tax and enlarge the human soul in its progress toward self-mastery. As Brigham Young proposed, "Why did Father Adam stretch forth his hand for the forbidden fruit? that you and I might drink the bitter cup - and drink the cup of life eternal—... and if we do not descend below all things we could not ascend above all things."[1] Only by choosing the evil ("tasting the bitter") do individuals learn what evil is and why it deserves to be rejected; only by choosing the good do individuals learn to savor and "prize the good" and its consequences.[2] Sin, or a free choice to act contrary to "the truth and natures of things"[3]—to act in a way to contravene eternal moral principles, in other words—is therefore a necessary part of the mortal experience.

Two principles thus come into collision in God's plan for human progression. Moral agency is predicated on a causal connection between choice and consequence. Given the freedom to choose, individuals must be granted the fruits of their choices, good or ill, or such freedom would be only a shadow of genuine agency. And given the uneven playing field called earth, where our untempered spirits contend against bodily weakness, myriad pressures and temptations, and the soul's own imperfect desires, sin is inevitable—and so therefore are its consequences. The inevitability of sin means the inevitability of acquired sinful human natures, and consequent alienation from God and his heaven. But in his infinite love and compassion, God wills the reintegration of every individual into the heavenly family. The freedom to sin thus collides with God's desire to save. The problem of how to reconcile this tragic collision is the problem of atonement.

ALIENATION

The historic doctrine of original sin, as we have seen, conceived as the root cause of human alienation from God, had two traditional dimensions: a universally inherited (or imputed) *reatus* or guilt and a similarly inherited *vitium* or vice. With time many Christian traditions came to downplay or deny any actual guilt accruing to Adam's descendants for his sin; at the same time, some religious traditions emphasized an inherited tendency to sin amounting to total depravity. Mormonism rejects completely the doctrine of original sin as a guilty condition that is either inherited by the human family or imputed to them. At the same time, Mormons recognize that the human condition entails three conditions in need of remedy: universal physical death, departure from God's physical presence, and most damagingly, spiritual alienation from God resulting from choices made by accountable individuals. That we have a human tendency to sin is too readily apparent to deny. However, Mormons do not see this as a necessary condition following from a sinful Adamic heritage; the imperfection of our spirits, the inclination of our wills, in no way accrue as a consequence of Adam and Eve's decision; our predicament is the consequence of our fallible spirits, possessed of imperfectly developed wills, inhabiting tabernacles of flesh, and confronting a world deliberately constructed as an arena of challenge, opposition, and temptation. Humans are born free of sin and therefore of guilt; but they readily succumb to sinful influences. It is after "they begin to grow up [that] sin conceiveth in their hearts."[4] Only when people reach a stage of development at which they are morally accountable are they capable of consciously choosing what is evil, committing sin, and finding themselves spiritually remote from God's spirit and influence.

This separation from God is not a punishment inflicted by God, but an incapacity of those in a state of sin to tolerate his glory, "for no unclean thing can dwell . . . in his presence."[5] A deeply felt guilt is a factor in such isolation, but there is an existential reality at stake: sinfulness is a condition "contrary to the nature of God," explains a Book of Mormon prophet.[6] A subsequent prophet, Samuel, concurs that doing iniquity is "contrary to the nature of that righteousness" which is the root of God's identity and the source of his perfect joy.[7] So the alienation in need of repair is not a product of God's arbitrary decree, of his anger or desire to punish. Neither is it purely a matter of human guilt or shame before the divine presence. It is a product of sinful choices that is incompatible with God's holiness. "For he who is not able to abide the law of a celestial kingdom *cannot abide* a celestial glory" (my emphasis).[8] Consequences are chosen at the time actions are freely committed. To choose to indulge a desire is to choose its fruit—bitter or sweet—assuming, as Lehi did, that "men are instructed sufficiently" to understand what they are choosing.[9]

In this life, instruction may seldom be "sufficient," the playing field is never entirely even, and a host of mitigating circumstances complicate and constrain the agency which humans exercise. In fact, Mormon scripture indicates that utter obliviousness to the nature of what our choices entail precludes moral accountability altogether. Christ's blood, in these cases, "atoneth for the sins of those who have died not knowing the will of God concerning them, or who have ignorantly sinned."[10] But though personal guilt is mitigated by ignorance, all the consequences of sinful conduct are not.

The Book of Mormon relates that humans bear the spiritual traces of every impure thought, unkind word, and hurtful action they have ever committed.[11] The very real detritus of lives tainted by selfishness, carnality, and pride constitute the prison of sin—of a narrowly self-serving nature inconsistent with the divine nature—in which humans entomb themselves. Humanity's damning alienation, then, entails separation from God and his Spirit, which is the most essential and indispensable ingredient in our spiritual health and happiness. But sin also alienates us from our better selves, and from others whose love and intimacy we need and crave.

Mormonism holds that humans are of divine parentage, and as William Wordsworth sensed, their souls resonate with the dim "intimations" of a heavenly past and a more supernal destiny than the one our poor choices foreshadow. As church father Clement wrote, we at some point come to a vague "reminiscence of better things," and desire to "renounce[e] our iniquities" and "speed back to the eternal light, children to the Father."[12] But we cannot ourselves transcend the consequences of our own choices, or suddenly acquire a new human nature unshaped by our own past. The burden of sin that has become habit, the self-perpetuating spiral of choices that further compromise our will and weaken our resolve, a character impaired by the accumulation of soul-damaging decisions—all conspire to make our predicament hopeless without radical intervention by a superior agent.

VICARIOUS ATONEMENT

Historically, the paramount necessity for divine intervention in human fate concerns what some Christian theologies have considered the inexorable decrees of Justice. In Dante's calculus of sin and punishment, humankind's offense against a perfect God was infinitely vile, and so required an infinite payment—which humans cannot provide. "For no obedience, no humility,/he offered later could have been so deep/that it could match the heights he meant to reach/through disobedience."[13] In this view, only the sacrifice of a perfect God can cancel out the incalculable wrong that was committed. Church fathers early taught that sinners were Satan's by right. Christ's death was the ransom Satan demanded for humankind's release. Origen modified this explanation, holding that Satan was deceived into thinking he could hold onto Christ instead; but Christ's sinlessness—and his veiled divinity—made that impossible for Satan. Augustine agreed, comparing Christ to the bait in a mousetrap.

Under St. Anselm, satisfaction theory developed. An infinite offense against a perfect God and his Justice required the satisfaction of an infinite payment. Only Christ, as human, could share in the debt, and only Christ, as God, could pay that infinite penalty. So only Christ as man-God could accomplish atonement. This idea developed further into the penal substitution theory, which emphasized the human affront to moral law and the debt owed to Justice. The similar Governmental Theory emphasized the need to validate the Law of God, by requiring a punishment in accordance with a broken law, maintaining the divine order. In these cases, either an actual entity, Satan, or a reified universal, Justice, requires a payment be made for sin.

Luther and others taught that Christ literally assumed the burden of human sin—either actually transferred or imputed to him—in humankind's place. Calvin, for instance, believed that Christ literally suffered the "the tortures of a condemned and ruined man."[14] In this regard, the philosopher Friedrich Nietzsche's analysis seems accurate: many Christians have treated guilt and mathematical indebtedness as interchangeable, and a prescribed quantity of Christ's suffering seems necessary to zero out the sum total of a human offense, resulting in a state of equilibrium. By the late eighteenth century, Samuel Hopkins and the New Divinity Movement were modifying the Calvinist inheritance, avoiding in the process the later criticism of Nietzsche. New Divinity preachers emphasized the Governmental Theory, in which Christ suffered for sin, but sufferings that were unique to him, not the exact sufferings mankind would have known in the absence of his sacrifice. Additionally, these men emphasized the universal reach of Christ's offering.

The last century and a half has witnessed further developments that reinterpret or move beyond theories grounded in divine appeasement, retribution, or satisfaction. In fact, writes one theologian, "what is most noticeable about the literature on atonement written in the last 150 years is the intense concern with *problems* that the authors (and presumably the readers) have with the traditional doctrines."[15] So it is largely the "embarrassment among Christians" of seeing Christ's sacrifice in terms of Pauline metaphors about ransom, scapegoats, debts, and martyrs that has prompted a range of new atonement theology.[16] One trend has been to shift responsibility for the death on Calvary from God to humans. For René Girard, Christ suffered death "to expose . . . the motivation of the violence-bound *crowd*"; the atonement thus demythologized human craving for sacrifice, it did not fulfill God's.[17] Robert Hamerton-Kelly also "rejects the distortion of blaming God," as does Ted Peters. ("God does not demand sacrifice. We do."[18])

One theory asserts God's role in Christ's sacrifice, but emphasizes its transformative power rather than its satisfaction of abstract categories of justice or debt-holding Satans. Moral influence theory, or the exemplarist view, as it is called, has been popular in recent years, though some writers argue this is actually the oldest version, citing several early church fathers up to and including Augustine.[19] It was further developed by Peter Abelard, whose ethical orientation led him to deny any theology in which God punishes an innocent person. Christ's self-sacrifice is *personally and subjectively* efficacious, calling forth our response to his whole death-culminating ministry of service to mankind. It had the virtue, wrote one theologian, of being "the first . . . doctrine of the atonement . . . which had nothing unintelligible, arbitrary, illogical, or immoral about it."[20] Still others consider the whole project of atonement theology futile: "A compassionate God is . . . incompatible with all atonement theories."[21] Fortunately for those of this mind, "Atonement is not an essential doctrine of Christianity but is in fact derivative."[22]

When asked about the fundamentals of Mormon faith, Smith replied with one doctrine: Christ "died, was buried, and rose again the third day, and ascended up into heaven; and all other things are only appendages to these."[23] The "these" he referred to are those events surrounding the Savior's death whose principal significance lies in the atoning sacrifice he made. Smith affirmed the atonement as a core Mormon doctrine in the Articles of Faith, but used the word only once in his recorded Nauvoo sermons, and never discoursed on the topic in detail.[24] Parley Pratt only fleetingly mentioned the atonement in his major work, and then in thoroughly conventional ways (in baptism "the blood of atonement is applied to the individual, for remission of sins"[25]). Two conclusions are possible: the atonement was not central to Mormon thought in the church's formative years; or atonement theory was absolutely central, but largely adopted without comment from contemporary Christian usage—which was disparate, inconsistent, and often uncritical. That is, Mormon atonement theology did not undergo—or appear to require—thorough reconstruction in the way cosmology (creation *ex materia* rather than *ex nihilo*), human anthropology (pre-existence and radical kinship with the Divine) or divine anthropology (separate, physical, bodily form of God) all did. The evolution of Mormon thinking about atonement, and its indispensability to the entire Mormon theological edifice of human redemption, suggests the latter was the case. Distracted by the need to elaborate and defend its points of radical difference, Mormonism has been slower to fully explore and articulate the doctrine on which all else depends.

Smith's major innovation in atonement theology was more a reconsideration of its place and timing in cosmic history than a reconstitution of the idea itself. One Christian view of Christ's achievement makes of Adam's sin a happy offense, or *felix culpa*, because an unfathomably perverse transgression called forth the universe's most supernal act of love by way of response. As we have seen, Mormonism varies this reading not by denying the atonement's unparalleled goodness or necessity but by emphasizing its anticipatory nature. Other denominations similarly believe Christ was the lamb "slain from the foundation of the world"—that is, foreordained according to God's foreknowledge—hence, his very title of Messiah, or Christ, the [pre-]anointed one. But they see his sacrifice as largely recuperative of a former condition, as the remedy for an unfortunate catastrophe. Smith saw the atonement rather as part of a divinely intended strategy for human progression from pre-mortality into earthly life and onward through endless celestial schooling. ("Father Adam transgressed the law designedly," in Young's words.[26])

Other assumptions further inform Mormonism's version of atonement. Smith saw principles like justice, mercy, and agency as having an existence outside and prior to God.[27] So while other atonement theorists, like the New Divinity School as one example, had to reconcile Christ's sacrifice with conditions and frameworks God himself had ordered, Mormonism had the different task of making sense of Christ's sacrifice in the context of realities which transcended God's institution of a heavenly government—or even creation itself.

Mormons begin with a biblical understanding of sin and redemption, but other materials available for understanding the process of salvation include the Book of Mormon, revelations of Joseph Smith recorded in the Doctrine and Covenants, statements by apostles, and efforts of lay theologians to weave together a coherent theory of atonement. The result is a doctrine that has historically borrowed much from conventional Christian theology, but shows signs of continuing elaboration and exploration in the face of a mystery Mormons devoutly accept but do not pretend to fully understand. What follows is simply one attempt to articulate a coherent version of atonement based on a selection of Mormon sources.

When early Mormons did discuss the atonement, notes one scholar, they "did not think about Christ or atonement in ways much different from nineteenth century Protestants."[28] In the early Utah period, Brigham Young used "atonement" in thoroughly generic ways, often paired with the term "ransom."[29] If any theology of atonement was apparent in early Mormonism, it was conventional penal substitution theory. "There must be an atonement to satisfy the demands of justice," preached apostle Heber C. Kimball pithily.[30] Orson Pratt elaborated: "Would God accept the sacrifice of a corrupted, sinful, degraded, fallen being as an atonement for his own sins? No, that would not satisfy the demands of justice.... The atonement must be an infinite atonement. Hence God sent forth his only begotten Son."[31]

Young's successor John Taylor wrote a treatise on the *Mediation and Atonement*, but it was essentially a compendium of scriptures on the subject with little exposition. His language, however, was also the common language of substitution theory: Christ took "upon Himself their sorrows, assuming their responsibilities, and bearing their transgressions or sins." He "had to take away sin by the sacrifice of Himself, the just for the unjust.... He in His own person bore the sins of all.... He bore the weight, the responsibility, and the burden of the sins of all men."[32]

The major development in Mormon thinking about atonement only came with B. H. Roberts. The significance of Roberts's thought is in his reinterpretation of penal substitution theory through the lens (consistent with both Smithian and Book of Mormon theology) of moral agency. He thus recasts the language of justice, punishment, and retribution into an emphasis on choice, consequence, and human freedom. B. H. Roberts saw the key to understanding atonement in the dominion of law—and specifically in what he called the "inexorableness of law":

> what effect is to cause, in the physical world, so penalty or consequence must be to violation of law in the moral and spiritual kingdom. The inexorableness of law is at once both its majesty and glory; without it neither majesty nor glory could exist in combination with law; neither respect, nor sense of security, nor safety, nor rational faith.... We must postulate such conception of the attributes of God that regularity will result from his personal government, not capriciousness.[33]

Roberts's substitution of "consequence" for "penalty," combined with a teleology or ultimate purpose behind the atonement that emphasizes "security" and "regularity" rather than satisfaction or "capriciousness," is a seismic shift beyond the medieval categories of atonement theology, and represents a genuinely Mormon theology of atonement. One might call it a "consequential substitution" theology, one oriented toward the preservation and validation of agency rather than Divine government or Justice per se. Mormon scripture suggests that "justice" is neither some unimpeachable cosmic universal nor the inflexible standard of a legalistic heavenly monarch. It is, rather, another name for the integrity of human choice. The fact is, the Book of Mormon indicates that genuine moral agency must entail necessary consequences, "else the reign of law is at an end. Its integrity is destroyed."[34] Choice must be choice *of something*. In John Stuart Mills's classic treatment, human liberty requires the freedom "of doing as we like, *subject to such consequences as may follow*" (my emphasis).[35] If choice is to be more than an empty gesture of the will, more than a mere pantomime of decision making, there must be immutable guarantee that any given choice will eventuate in the natural consequence of that choice. As Roberts suggests, what kind of freedom would it be if there were no predictable result attached to any deliberate choice? Second-hand smoke of a thousand types complicates the degree of freedom and accountability behind human choice. But even allowing for the volitional white noise, moral agency clearly requires a stable framework within which choices are rendered meaningful and purposeful. "The quality of regularity that can only come of inexorableness . . . is necessary to a sense of security," in Roberts's words.[36]

Roberts is consistent here with Lehi's sermon in the Book of Mormon, wherein he states, "the law is given to men," and as a result they are "free . . . to act for themselves and not to be acted upon, *save it be by the punishment of the law.*"[37] This point is explicated by one of Joseph Smith's theologically richest revelations. Addressing why God does not simply bestow eternal bliss upon all who die, the revelation explains: "They who remain shall also be quickened; nevertheless, they shall return again to their own place, to enjoy that which they are willing to receive, because they were not willing to enjoy that which they might have received."[38]

Imposing a heavenly reward on those who do not choose heaven, in other words, is just that: an imposition on the "unwilling," and an abrogation of the moral agency on which all human life and earthly existence is predicated. This is neither a thinly veiled Pelagianism (man is capable of unaided self-transcendence) nor Byronic pridefulness (I made my bed and will lie in it). It is, rather, an existential view of what salvation means and entails. Identity—human as well as divine—is constituted as the product of choices freely made. Hell does not exist because of some inflexible ultimatum decreed by an impersonal Justice. Reward or punishment is entailed not simply because that is the "fair" or "just" thing for God to do. For God is also merciful, and if humans can remit a penalty out of compassion or mercy, why cannot God? Because, as Alma continues, such apparent generosity would undermine the essence of that agency on which moral freedom depends. This is the sense in which C. S. Lewis held that hell is the greatest monument to human freedom: for "all that are in Hell, choose it."[39]

To the degree and extent that choices are freely made, "one [must be] raised to happiness according to his desires of happiness, or good according to his desires of good; and the other to evil according to his desires of evil."[40] This view comports with Dante's grim vision of hell, in which God is not present as judge or dispenser of punishments, because choices are allowed, inexorably, to bear their own fruit. In Alma's inferno as well, future states are chosen, not assigned: "For behold," says Alma, "they are their own judges."[41]

Christ's intervention, in assuming the burden of human sin, may operate in accordance with what the Book of Mormon refers to as the Law of Restoration, the cosmic order whereby human agency is guaranteed by the unfolding of consequences in accordance with law. The Book of Mormon emphasizes that the consequences of sin are felt pain and suffering, not an inflicted punishment—and those were the agonies of Christ in Gethsemane. Nephi taught that Christ came into the world not to assume humanity's guilt or deflect God's wrath, but to suffer "the pains of every living creature"; Alma says that in his atonement Christ assumes "their infirmities," and King Benjamin connected Christ's pain to his felt "anguish for the wickedness and abominations of his people."[42]

The incurring of pain in consequence of choice is how the Book of Mormon defines Justice.[43] This is why when one chooses to sin, "justice claimeth the creature and executeth the law, and the law inflicteth the punishment; if not so, the works of justice would be destroyed, and God would cease to be God."[44] The Book of Mormon, as Roberts seems to be reading it, depicts God's intention to assure the enduring operations of moral agency, and that agency requires the continuity between choice and consequence. "God [is] the administrative power in a perfect reign of law," in B. H. Roberts's words.[45]

The historic atonement theory closest to Mormonism's may be the Governmental Theory of Hugo Grotius and later Jonathan Mayhew and Samuel Hopkins, who believed, in Brooks Holifield's phrase, that "having promulgated a moral law, God could not permit its subversion without allowing the destruction of the moral order itself."[46] One difference, as we have seen, is that in the Mormon schema, the moral order may be independent of God (not all Mormons have agreed on this point). The Book of Mormon indicates that Christ voluntarily suffers disastrous but chosen consequences on humankind's behalf, in order to uphold the integrity of the whole system of cause and effect, choice and consequence, whereon agency rests. That relationship is manifest through laws that Christ himself articulates: "Wherefore, the ends of the law [are those] the Holy One hath given, unto the inflicting of the punishment which is affixed . . . to answer the ends of the atonement."[47] Apparently, circumventing those consequences, out of mercy or any other motive, would not only abrogate human agency but also eliminate the very distinctions that make possible a universe of meaningful differences and thus meaningful existence.

In Book of Mormon language, a clear differentiation of alternatives, the ability to choose them, and the stability and expectation of their unfolding in consequence of such choice undergird the cosmic order over which God presides and serves as guarantor. Without a framework of law that reflects these oppositional realities, choice would be uninformed, consequences random, and agency void. As Alma asks, "how could [man] sin if there was no law? How could there be a law save there was a punishment."[48] Or as modern Mormon apostle Russell M. Nelson points out (as did Dallin Oaks in discussing abortion), true agency requires that after we freely make choices we be "tied to the consequences of those choices."[49] Clearly differentiated and predictable possibilities that exist in oppositional relationship are the precondition for a universe in which human beings can function as independent moral agents: "For it must needs be, that there is an opposition in all things. If not so, . . . righteousness could not be brought to pass, neither wickedness, neither holiness nor misery, neither good nor bad." Without contrasting alternatives that are the objects of purposeful choice, "all things must needs be a compound in one."[50]

The challenge of atonement theory—for Mormons as much as other Christians—is to explain how Christ can intervene in the process, to actually suffer the consequences of human choice in humanity's stead. Christ's identification with human suffering originates in his human incarnation. Though a divine "Son, he learned obedience through what he suffered."[51] In his human form, he suffered all the pains and vicissitudes of the mortal condition. "And lo, he shall suffer temptations, and pain of body, hunger, thirst, and fatigue."[52]

To this point, Mormon atonement theology seems consistent with a theology of moral influence, or even governmental atonement. But the Book of Mormon suggests that Christ's perfect compassion and infinite empathy led him to suffer in more than a merely personal way. He endured "even more than man can suffer, except it be unto death; for behold, blood cometh from every pore, so great shall be his anguish for the wickedness and the abominations of his people."[53] "There can be nothing which is short of an infinite atonement which will suffice for the sins of the world," adds another Book of Mormon prophet.[54] So does the Book of Mormon affirm the view that Christ's love, in an infinitely more perfect version of human empathy, displaces the collective pain we suffer onto himself.

As with contemporary theologies of the "moral influence" type, Roberts suggests that the atonement's efficacy on individuals was attributable to its exemplary power as a "love-manifestation." "Shall this suffering for others have no benefitting effect upon those others for whom the suffering is endured?," he asked. He finds its exemplary purpose was "to demonstrate, first of all, God-love for man, by a sacrifice that tasks God that man might be saved; and second, to inspire man-love for God, by the demonstration that God first loved man, and how deeply God loves him; and third, to teach man-love for man."[55]

More recent Mormon writers have sought to further de-emphasize the propitiary aspects of the atonement, and further emphasize Christ's suffering not as substitution but as the suffering of the supremely empathic One. In other words, Christ's willingness to identify with us to the point of experiencing the agonizing effects we feel of our sinfulness motivates us to repent and draw near to God. Influential

Mormon essayist Eugene England espoused a modified version of Abelard's moral theory of atonement, according to which the Justice requiring satisfaction is *our* sense of justice, and witnessing Christ's agony allows us to forgive ourselves and be reconciled to God.[56] England denies atonement's rootedness in some transcendent legal framework that demands ransom or punishment or satisfaction. "Christ's mission was not to straighten out some metaphysical warp in the universe that Adam's taking of the fruit had created. The effects of the Atonement were not metaphysical but moral and spiritual." He propounds a version of the empathy, or moral influence, form of atonement theory, whereby Christ took "into himself the fullness of pain in all human estrangement in some awful awareness of the full force of human evil." His selfless gesture of feeling the full extent of our pain thus inspires and transforms us. His unconditional love "has the power to release man from the barrier of his own guilt." In this way, Christ does not suffer to satisfy Justice, but to satisfy *our* sense of justice (man "feels that every action must bear its consequences; . . . the demands of justice that Amulek is talking about, which must be overpowered, are from *man's own sense of justice*, not some abstract eternal principle"[57]).

One problem with the version propounded by England (and similar influence theories) is that they expound atonement as a powerful, inspiring, sublime catalyst to salvation; but their versions do not establish a convincing rationale for its utter, unqualified, absolute indispensability to human salvation. A stupendous display of sacrificial love does not adequately differentiate Christ's "infinite" atonement from other historical or conceivable human parallels. A lively conversation has ensued among Mormon scholars in the wake of England's attempt to formulate a uniquely Mormon vision of atonement, but little has emanated from the church's leadership.[58] At the same time, apostle Dallin Oaks acknowledged in 1993 that the leadership had been negligent in recent decades in even addressing the doctrine of atonement in both church publications and general conference addresses.[59] In recent discourse, Mormon leaders have reaffirmed the centrality, if they have not explicated the mechanism, of Christ's atoning sacrifice.

Though no official theology articulating the rationale of atonement is in place, one consistent LDS narrative affirms the reality and something of the nature of the suffering Christ experienced. In this view, the full extent of Christ's sacrifice was accomplished by his willed subjection to the most devastating consequence of human sin: absolute alienation from God the Father. Mormon leaders have intimated that the Father's withdrawal of his spirit, and Satan's unleashed assaults, were the vehicles through which Christ's final suffering was effected. The agony in Gethsemane— where Mormon theology centers the principal work of Christ's atonement—was attributed to the withdrawal of God's spirit, at least by implication, in an early 1830 revelation, wherein Christ states that the sufferings he experienced have been known to all, if only in minute degree, "at the time I withdrew my Spirit."[60] Brigham Young preached that "when the crisis came for him to offer up his life, the Father withdrew Himself, withdrew His Spirit, and cast a vail over him. That is what made him sweat blood."[61] John Taylor thought it was such isolation, combined with his full exposure to Satan's enmity, that constituted Christ's suffering. "He had struggled against the powers of darkness that had been let loose upon him there; placed below all things, His mind surcharged with agony and pain, lonely and apparently helpless and forsaken, in his agony the blood oozed from His pores."[62]

Both men were evoking the language of Luke, who likened the Savior's anguished sweat in Gethsemane to "great drops of blood falling down on the ground."[63] The Book of Mormon transformed the simile to physiological literalism, asserting that in Christ's Garden agony, "blood cometh from every pore."[64] The same month the church published that account, a revelation to Joseph Smith had Jesus confirming in a first-person account that the suffering of the atonement "caused myself, even God, the greatest of all, to tremble because of pain, and to bleed at every pore."[65]

Apostle Jeffrey Holland reaffirmed this view of atonement as involving the excruciating withdrawal of the Father's spirit from the Son, but declared it was with God's final abandonment of Christ on Calvary that his suffering culminated, and described his "concluding descent into the paralyzing despair of divine withdrawal, when he cries with ultimate loneliness, 'My God My God, why hast thou forsaken me.'"[66] This view is consonant with the position of Timothy Keller that Christ's physical agony on the cross "was nothing compared to the spiritual experience of cosmic abandonment."[67] Mormon scripture indicates that the divine Presence, sometimes called the Light of Christ, is "the light which is in all things, which giveth life to all things."[68] It enlightens the eyes, quickens the understanding, fills the immensity of space, and infuses the universe with beauty and light. To be deprived of the Light of Christ is to lack the most essential ingredient in human happiness and spiritual nourishment. And yet, our dependence on and love for the Father can be but a feeble shadow of the bonds that unite him to his only begotten Son. Mormons believe that Christ's pain at his Father's abandonment was beyond human reckoning.

Though these scriptural bases suggest the suffering of the atoning Christ was a combination of bodily experience, perfect empathy, and God's abandonment, the essential mystery of the atonement remains for Mormons just that—a mystery. This point deserves emphasis: no Mormon presumes to understand the doctrine of atonement in its entirety. John Taylor, Brigham Young's successor and first Mormon authority to treat the subject comprehensively, wrote that it was "in some mysterious, incomprehensible way, [that] Jesus assumed the responsibility which naturally would have devolved upon Adam; but which could only be accomplished . . . by taking upon himself their sorrows, assuming their responsibilities, and bearing their transgressions or sins. In a manner to us incomprehensible and inexplicable, He bore the weight of the sins of the whole world."[69]

James Talmage, author of the most authoritative and influential Christology in Mormonism, concurred that "Christ's agony in the garden is unfathomable by the finite mind, both as to intensity and cause.... [I]n some manner, actual and terribly real though to man incomprehensible, the Savior took upon Himself the burden of the sins of mankind from Adam to the end of the world."[70]

RECONCILIATION

Joseph Smith wrote, "we know that justification through the grace of our Lord and Savior Jesus Christ is just and true."[71] Through the atonement, the demands of Justice are met, or in the Mormon vocabulary, the consequences of a broken law are fully unfolded. Subject to one's repentance, Christ's merciful gift deflects the full repercussions of sin from the sinner, and clears the way for reconciliation to the Father. But Mormons hold that Christ's suffering on behalf of humans—however effected—cannot of itself impart to humans the fruits of obedience. Only righteous actions yield righteousness, only merciful conduct engenders a merciful character, only pure thoughts produce purity. Only compliance with eternal principles, in other words, creates the exalted condition Mormons associate with salvation. This, and not some calculus of dessert or merit, is what LDS scripture means in stating that "if you will that I give unto you a place in the celestial world, you must prepare yourselves by doing the things which I have commanded you and required of you."[72]

This is why, in an important sense, salvation in Mormon doctrine is not a gift; neither is it a reward that humans earn. Nor is it attainable through the individual's unaided efforts. Self-elevation from an alienated and sinful condition is beyond human reach, and no works mortals perform can make Christ's intervention obligatory or necessary on his part. His intervention is a free gift which is beyond human capacity to deserve or repay. But the salvation it portends is itself equally beyond his capacity to either impose or bestow upon us. Eternal life, the kind and quality of life that God lives, is a natural and inevitable consequence of compliance with eternal principles, just as God's own standing as God is the natural and inevitable consequence of his perfect harmony with eternal law. That God's merciful inclinations are circumscribed and delimited by law is clearly set forth in a revelation of Joseph Smith. "That which is governed by law is also preserved by law and perfected and sanctified by the same. That which breaketh a law, and abideth not by law, but seeketh to become a law unto itself, and willeth to abide in sin, ... *cannot be sanctified by* law, neither by *mercy*, justice, or judgment. Therefore they must remain filthy still."[73] It isn't law itself, but the sanctity of choice (the "will" to *abide* by law or not) that constrains the consequences of Christ's grace. As apostle Erastus Snow reasoned about these constraints:

> it is just as impossible for God to add two and two together and make ten of it as it is for me or you. Mathematical truths are as true with God and angels as they are with man. I understand that what has exalted to life and salvation our Father in heaven and all the Gods of eternity will also exalt us, their children. And what causes Lucifer and his followers to descend to the regions of death and perdition will also lead us in the same direction; and no atonement of our Lord and Saviour Jesus Christ can alter that eternal law, any more than he can make two and two to mean sixteen.[74]

Christ's death and resurrection provide the human race with the gift of their own resurrection and immortality, regardless of their earthly beliefs or conduct. The spiritual fruits of Christ's atonement, on the other hand, salvation itself, can only unfold within the larger framework of human agency's inviolability. Christ's intervention in preventing our permanent spiritual death, or separation from God, is contingent upon an individual's *decision* to embrace the opportunity thus afforded and comply with its conditions. Mormons do not believe that God foreordains a select few to be the beneficiaries of his grace. He desires, and will accomplish, the salvation of virtually the entire human family. (Only those few who never, under any circumstances, will to accept his salvation, will remain sons of perdition, outside the shelter of his grace.)

It is therefore in the realm of the personal and subjective that the fullest effects of the atonement take root and unfold. The Book of Mormon clearly portrays perfect empathy as an aspect of Christ's character and mission, serving as a powerful means for breaking through the calcified human heart. The almost irresistible power of his superabundant love, manifest in his choice to suffer what he suffered, can itself transform the sinner's heart. The Book of Mormon's Amulek says that "all mankind . . . are *hardened*; yea, all are fallen and are lost, and must perish except it be through the atonement,"[75] suggesting that the power of the atonement resides as much in its exemplary love and sacrifice as in its reconciliation of agency and accountability. The atonement is transformative through the magnitude of the gift itself. "For, behold, the Lord your Redeemer suffered death in the flesh; wherefore he suffered the pain of all men, *that all men might repent and come unto him.*"[76] As long as his "sufferings and death, . . . and his mercy and long-suffering, . . . rest in [our] mind[s]," says Moroni, we will be drawn to him, and to repent.[77]

Christ's willing experience of every human pain ever suffered is an unparalleled gesture of love. But according to the Book of Mormon, it also provides the basis for his perfect empathy, that makes it possible for humans to exhibit complete trust and confidence in his comprehension of our pain-filled lives. This is why his role as Savior required that he "take upon him their infirmities, that his bowels may be filled with mercy, according to the flesh, *that he may know according to the flesh how to succor his people according to their infirmities.*"[78] Infinite empathy required the experience of ultimate abandonment, which is why, "that the supreme sacrifice of His Son might be as complete as it was voluntary and solitary, the Father briefly withdrew His Spirit, the support of His personal presence. It was required," Jeffrey Holland said, "that this perfect Son who had never spoken ill nor done wrong nor touched an unclean thing, he had to know how the rest of us humankind—us, all of us—would feel when we commit such sins."[79]

Ultimately, Mormons believe the power of the atonement derives from one's knowledge that Christ can forgive, because whatever pain one has caused or experienced, he has known personally, literally, and comprehensively. He provides the only response possible to the greatest interrogation of the problem of evil in world literature. Ivan, in Dostoevsky's *Brothers Karamazov*, demands to know how the tears of a tortured, innocent child can be expiated:

> They must be atoned for, or there can be no harmony. But how? How are you going to atone for them? Is it possible? By their being avenged? But what do I care for avenging them? What do I care for a hell for oppressors? What good can hell do, since those children have already been tortured? And what becomes of harmony, if there is hell? I want to forgive. I want to embrace. I don't want more suffering. And if the sufferings of children go to swell the sum of sufferings which was necessary to pay for truth, then I protest that the truth is not worth such a price. I don't want the mother to embrace the oppressor who threw her son to the dogs! She dare not forgive him! Let her forgive him for herself, if she will, let her forgive the torturer for the immeasurable suffering of her mother's heart. But the sufferings of her tortured child she has no right to forgive; she dare not forgive the torturer, even if the child were to forgive him! And if that is so, if they dare not forgive, what becomes of harmony? Is there in the whole world a being who would have the right to forgive and could forgive?[80]

Mormon teaching holds that only Christ has the moral authority to forgive all wrongs, because only Christ suffered all wrongs, understands all wrongs, and by his infinite love heals all wrongs. Perhaps it is the knowledge of what Christ suffered, and that he has forgiven humans, that makes it possible for every individual to heal the breach within himself, with God, and with the human family, since love and empathy are the most powerful catalysts to personal transformation. The conditions under which consequent repentance takes place are as generous as Christ can make them, without compromising human agency. The mercy thus freely offered, Christ's supernal grace, cannot extend to the point of *choosing* on behalf of individuals. They must choose, and choose again—that is the essential meaning of repentance in Mormon atonement theology.

Christ's atonement sets up the conditions for humans to demonstrate through ever better and wiser choices, made in accordance with ever nobler and purer desires, that it is their will to live in a way consistent with the eternal principles Christ modeled throughout his exemplary life. Repentance is therefore an ongoing process of repudiating unrighteous choices, acknowledging Christ's role in suffering the consequences of those sins on our behalf, and our choosing afresh to better effect. The process continues—perhaps eons into the future[81]—until in perfect harmony with the laws that underlie the nature of happiness (and thus the nature of God), humans have reached a sanctified condition that permits of perfect at-one-ment with God. God's desire to save is reconciled with the sanctity of human choice. Love and agency, justice and mercy meet. As Smith wrote, "we know also, that sanctification through the grace of our Lord and Savior Jesus Christ is just and true, to all those who love and serve God with all their mights, minds, and strength."[82]

In the ancient temple at Jerusalem, certain offenses required priests to perform the *kpr*, which was "the ritual of restoration and healing." In these cases, the priest carried sacrificial blood into the holy of holies and brought it out again. But "for the great atonement" on the holy day so designated, an Old Testament scholar notes, "a greater ritual was demanded." The high priest on this occasion sprinkled blood on various parts of the temple, then he conveyed the sins of the people onto a scapegoat, and sent it into the desert. "Translated into temple terms," she explains, "this means: The LORD emerged from heaven carrying life, which was given to all parts of the created order as the effects of sin were absorbed and wounds healed."[83] Mormons believe the atonement of Jesus Christ thus foreshadowed is the only act by which the wounds of sin and hurt that rend the world can be repaired. The words of Isaiah 61, which characterize the "suffering servant's" mission "to bind up the brokenhearted, . . . to give unto them beauty for ashes, the oil of joy for mourning," reveal the atonement to be the universe's great "healing power."[84] The atonement is centered on the breach in humankind's relationship with our God. That relationship is the most important one in which humans participate, but in some measure this is because it is the foundation of all human relationships of which we are a part, and which are impaired and crippled by sin.

GRACE AND WORKS

A seminal dispute in Christian thought has been the tension between grace and works. The Protestant Reformation was in large measure a rupture growing out of Luther's differences with Catholic dogma on the subject. The terms are too hotly contested and various in their shades of meaning to adequately survey. In general, however, the doctrine of salvation by grace alone tends to emphasize not just the gratuitous and unmerited nature of God's mercy but also the fact that whatever righteousness the saved obtain is an imputed, not an earned or deserved, righteousness. Frustrated in his efforts to live a life in full compliance with gospel principles, for example, Luther concluded definitively that "No human creature can satisfy the law."[85] If salvation is to occur, it must be in spite of human sinfulness, not by transcendence of such sinfulness. It is the consequence of a freedom from guilt which is entirely granted by God.

At the other end of the theological spectrum is a view of salvation as a recompense earned by merit (with divine assistance). The Catholic Church convened a Council of Trent in order to respond to the onslaught of the Reformation and clarify its own theology of salvation. In a session on the doctrine of justification in 1547, the Catholic Church's position was clearly differentiated from Protestant versions. Canon 11 specifically condemned the idea that "people are justified . . . solely by the attribution of Christ's justice, or by the forgiveness of sins alone," and Canon 12 repudiated the idea that justifying faith is "nothing else but trust in the divine mercy, which pardons sins because of Christ." The role of works was affirmed by Canon 24, which affirmed that "good works" are the "cause of increase" of personal righteousness. The place of grace in Catholic soteriology was explained in Canons 7 and 32.[86]

Those who turn to God, can only do so with "God's grace inciting and helping them." Nevertheless, against Luther's radical pessimism, the council held it false that "all acts done prior to justification, no matter for what reason, are either truly sins or deserve God's hatred." And "the good deeds of a person," though enabled by God's grace, are "also the good merits of the one justified," and therefore that person does "truly merit . . . the obtaining of his own eternal life."[87] Belief that unaided human goodness leading to salvation is possible constituted one of the Pelagian heresies. Virtually all Christians, then, predicate salvation on the grace of Christ. The major point of dispute is whether grace is the direct and sole factor in that salvation or whether grace is what makes possible an individual's choices and works that in turn qualify one for salvation.

Mormonism is hard to situate in the grace vs. works spectrum as traditionally depicted because its doctrine of salvation begins with radically different premises about human pre-mortal participation in the project of human embodiment, about the nature of the fall, about the primacy of human agency, and about what constitutes salvation itself. On the one hand, Smith affirmed that Mormon salvation doctrine centers in Christ and his gift. "Salvation could not come to the world without the mediation of Jesus Christ," he said in 1843.[88] In the Book of Mormon, the term "grace" appears frequently, but in Mormonism's most quoted scripture on the subject, it combines what are often considered the Pauline and Jamesian positions: "for we know that it is by grace that we are saved, *after all we can do*" (emphasis mine).[89] Smith seldom used the term "grace" in any theologically self-conscious way, and Young used it primarily in consistency with Matthew Arnold's observation.[90] Arnold begins his study of the Bible with this statement.

> We have said elsewhere how much it has contributed to the misunderstanding of St. Paul, that terms like grace, ... which he used in a fluid and passing way, as men use terms in common discourse or in eloquence and poetry, ... people have blunderingly taken in a fixed and rigid manner, as if they were symbols with as definite and fully grasped a meaning as the names line or angle, and proceeded to use them on this supposition. Terms, in short, which with St. Paul are literary terms, theologians have employed as if they were scientific terms.[91]

The simplest meaning of the Pauline word for "grace," χαρισ, is graciousness, or goodwill, undeserved favor or gift. In that sense, Mormonism's acceptance of the grace of Christ as the precondition of all human salvation is unambiguous. The Book of Mormon declares both the indispensability of Christ's grace and the particular gesture to which it applies in its most transcendent form. "No flesh can dwell in the presence of God, save it be through the merits, mercy, and grace of the Holy Messiah, who layeth down his life according to the flesh."[92] Only through the utterly undeserved and unearned gift of his willing death and resurrection are humans reborn to immortality. Only through his atonement are the consequences of personal sin remitted, and opportunity renewed to choose the good, as often as we will repent. Only through the empowering influence of his spirit can mortals find their way to holiness through the burdens and impediments that genetics, environment, and bodily weakness entail. Humans can never earn or deserve the gift comprising that death, infinite sacrifice, and spiritual generosity, and they cannot be saved or perfected without them. This is how Young understood Christ's grace: "When we consider how little time we have to spend in this life in comparison to eternity we ought not to consider it a hard matter to be faithful to God and keep his commandments, for when we obtain celestial glory we shall have to explain that it is through the grace of God after all, for the glory far exceeds our suffering in this life."[93]

In the sense that the entire project of human salvation, from creation to mortal incarnation, to ongoing repentance and sanctification, to eventual reunion with God and loved ones, is absolutely predicated on the central and indispensable gesture of Christ's selfless gift of atonement, Mormons emphatically affirm that it is "by grace that we are saved," as Nephi said.[94] In this sense, Mormonism is in accord with the main current of Christian thought on the subject: "the root idea [of grace] is that grace is the undeserved favor of God. The word indicates that God has set His favor up on His people not at all because they merit it, but simply because according to the mysterious counsel of His love He wills to do so."[95] Job asked, "what is man, that thou shouldst . . . set thine heart upon him?"[96] Mormonism asserts that it was this act of setting his heart upon man that constituted the majesty and miracle of God's grace; only in the Mormon conception, when John said, "we love him because he first loved us," he meant that deep in the primeval past when God found himself in the midst of numerous spirit intelligences, before the earth was formed or the first man or woman created, grace irrupted into the universe.[97]

Salvation by grace alone, however, as developed by the Reformers, is not a principle consistent with Mormon thought.[98] Salvation by grace, as Nephi wrote, is "after all that we can do." This is because, again as the Book of Mormon says, "mercy cannot rob justice." God's generosity cannot overwrite the human right to choose. As Brigham Young put the case, "its being the will and design of the Father, Son, and Holy Ghost, . . . that you should be a Saint, will not make you one, contrary to your own choice."[99] In other words, for Mormons, being made a saint, or sanctification, is a process of aligning the self with eternal principles—a process made possible and facilitated by Christ's goodness, but not possible through his goodness alone.

That may explain why, a generation after Young, in Talmage's magisterial treatise on Mormon theology, the term "grace" receives no attention; it is used only in formulaic ways ("the throne of grace," or "full of grace and truth,"), and does not even appear in the index. Talmage addresses the term "justification by faith" only long enough to denounce it as a "pernicious doctrine."[100] Neither do subsequent luminaries like B. H. Roberts devote significant attention to the topic. This reticence reflects no marginalization of Christ or his sacrifice but, rather, the view that, as the discussion of atonement suggests, salvation itself in Mormon doctrine is not a gift that God can bestow or a reward that humans can earn or merit. That is why, as Smith said, Mormons can agree with neither position on the "once saved, always saved" debate.[101] Salvation is a natural consequence of compliance with law, just as God's own standing as God is the natural and inevitable consequence of his compliance with law—*which eventual compliance is made possible by the gift of Christ's atonement*. Mormonism thus assigns grace a foundational role in salvation, but interprets it rather differently from the Protestant tradition, and with greater affinity, though not sameness, to the Catholic view.

One Catholic theologian notes that Smith's soteriology "is siding with that aspect of the Christian tradition best represented by Thomas Aquinas, which says we can and must cooperate with divine grace in order to permit it to actualize our potential for divinization."[102] Mormonism finds congruence, for instance, with the position of Cardinal John Henry Newman, who said, "Good works . . . are required, not as if they had any merit of their own, nor as if they could . . . purchase heaven for us." But through "our acts of charity, self-denial, and forbearance" we will become "charitable, self-denying, and forbearing. . . . These holy works will be the means of making our hearts holy, and of preparing us for the future presence of God."[103] In LDS thought, only conformity to law can sanctify us, because only conformity to law creates the causal conditions under which our character is transformed in accordance with our choices.

The Mormon Seventy (an office just below the Mormon apostles) Bruce Hafen wrote, "Repentance initiates a developmental process that, with the Savior's help, leads us along the path to a saintly character."[104] In this view, only the atonement of Christ can repair the damage done by wrong choices, and create the opportunity to rechoose and rechoose again, in conditions of ever greater moral equilibrium. Hafen emphasizes that the atonement in this regard has a sanctifying, as well as reparative, function: "While much of the perfection process involves a healing from sin and bitterness, the process involves an additional, affirmative dimension through which we may acquire a Christlike nature. . . . His atoning grace can move us beyond the remission of sins to the perfection of a divine nature . . . [because] the Atonement makes possible certain spiritual endowments that actually purify our nature."[105]

By the dawn of the twenty-first century, some Mormon figures were engaged in efforts to effect better relations and discover common ground with Christian evangelicals. To emphasize their shared rootedness in Christian theology, some prominent LDS writers began to highlight a Mormon doctrine of grace. As early as the 1960s, O. Kendall White thought he detected an LDS convergence with recent Protestant emphases on Calvinist depravity and grace, and he called the development "Mormon Neo-Orthodoxy."[106] Donald P. Mangum and Brenton G. Yorgason published *Amazing Grace*.[107] Dean of religion at BYU, Robert Millet trumpeted the shift, boldly and then wryly, in two books, *By Grace We Are Saved* and *Grace Works*.[108] Popular Mormon writers Brad Wilcox and Stephen Robinson made Nephi's passage on grace a focal point of their treatment of Mormon grace.[109] In a bridge-building book, Mormon Stephen Robinson wrote jointly with evangelical Craig Blomberg that "Both Mormons and Evangelicals . . . believe in . . . justification by faith in Christ, and salvation by grace."[110] But even this gesture of consensus was marked by a footnote of qualification. The caveat, like Millet's ambiguity-fraught title, was a sign that nothing had really changed; the shift was more one of emphasis and clarification than substantive redefinition; Mormon Seventy Bruce Hafen wrote that grace—in the sense of a freely offered gift—has always been implicit in Mormon theological understanding, in three particular ways: Christ's offer to sacrifice himself and effect a universal resurrection; Christ's vicarious expiation for personal sins, which requires our repentance to become effective; and Christ's sustaining influence as the repentant and converted strive to "endure to the end."[111]

THE DEAD (A FRAGILE HELL)

To the early Christian Father Origen, as we have seen, even before the earth was formed the heavens were replete with myriad heavenly beings, including the premortal souls of the human family. Given their original high standing before God, Origen thought it made little sense to assume any fall from heaven—or from God's favor—could be of permanent duration. For it was God's pronounced intention to bring all things into subjection under and in harmony with Christ. In God's perfect scheme, "the end is always like the beginning." The restoration of all the damned, therefore, must be a part of God's eternal purposes. "All rational souls" would eventually be "reconciled to God," reaching perfection at differing rates but with none permanently lost along the way.[112]

Origen gave the name of *apokatastasis*, or restoration, to this belief. And it was fiercely condemned by emperors and church councils alike. Emperor Justinian in 543 wrote his "Book Against Origen," appending several condemnations. The ninth fell on those who say or think "that the punishment of demons and of impious men is only temporary, and will one day have an end, and that a restoration (*apokatastasis*) will take place."[113] The Fifth Ecumenical Council of 553 confirmed that "If anyone asserts the fabulous pre-existence of souls, and shall assert the monstrous restoration (*apokatastasis*) that follows from it, let him be anathema. . . . If anyone shall say that the life of spirits shall be like to the life which was in the beginning while as yet the spirits had not come down or fallen, so that the end and the beginning shall be alike, . . . let him be anathema."[114]

An endless hell, in other words, has long been a nonnegotiable part of historic Christianity. Such a view seemed the clear meaning of biblical references to the damned, like John's observation that "the smoke of their torment goes up forever and ever."[115] Belief in perpetual suffering had the benefit of making heaven more heavenly. As Augustine reasoned, "everything is known the more for being compared with its contrary." Therefore, in order "that the happiness of the saints may be more delightful to them and that they may render more copious thanks to God for it, they are allowed to see perfectly the sufferings of the damned."[116] (The rationale was repeated in the late eighteenth century: "God knowing that his little flock cannot be happy any longer than while they see the misery of the wicked, . . . the destruction of hell would be the destruction of heaven."[117]) An eternity of torment, of course, also worked powerfully upon the imagination. It may not be the best motive for a life of virtue, but it is an effective one.

Hell was almost always held to be a more populous venue than heaven. Jesus had declared that "the gate is narrow and the road is hard that leads to life."[118] How few was a matter of recurrent speculation. St. Bernard was reputed to put the number at one in ten.[119] One popular friar of the eighteenth century sermonized on "The Little Number of Those Who are Saved," reviewing the opinions of the church fathers and doctors from Augustine and Thomas up to his day. He finds virtually universal agreement that "the greater number of Christian adults are damned." (Non-Christians and unbaptized children weren't even in the game.) He relates one visionary account that put the proportions at two souls saved and three to purgatory for thirty-three thousand damned to hell. (Another anecdote gave odds of three saved out of sixty thousand.[120])

Such alarming statistics seemed congruent with biblical texts. God only found a single household, Noah's, worth saving from a devastating flood. Abraham bargained with the Lord for the fate of Sodom and Gemorrah, but failed to find ten righteous people within their precincts. Ten lepers were healed by Jesus, but only one received approbation through his gratitude. "There are few who find" that narrow gate, said Jesus.[121] The Reformed tradition maintained that not only would few be saved but also that only a few were even eligible for salvation; God "chose in Christ a definite number of particular people out of the entire human race."[122] Particular Baptists followed suit, whereas General Baptists espoused an atonement making salvation available to all. Until the New Divinity School modified the doctrine, most Calvinists held that for the preordained, and for them alone did Christ die in a "limited atonement."

One of the most widely read books in early America, John Bunyan's *Pilgrim's Progress*, announced the somber verdict, delivered to the "poor sinner, thou [that] readest here, that but a few will be saved."[123] John Wesley reported the horrific vision of a young Alice Miller: "I observed her countenance change, into the form of fear, pity, and distress. Then she burst into a flood of tears, and cried out, 'Dear Lord! They *will* be damned! They will all be damned!'" Queried as to whom she referred to, she replied, "the world; for I saw they were on the brink of hell."[124]

By mid-eighteenth century, two religious titans of the Anglo-Saxon world, erstwhile allies, were at loggerheads over the question of just how many people were destined for an eternity in hell. In 1738, John Wesley delivered an iconoclastic sermon in which he decried the "blasphemy contained in the horrible decree of predestination." The Calvinist teaching on election he rejected for consigning "the greater part of mankind [to] abide in death without any possibility of re-demption."[125] George Whitefield published his response in 1740, attacking Wesley for asserting that "God's grace is free to all." This was tantamount to "propagating the doctrine of universal redemption," he protested, blaming the influence of "arminianism, [which] of late, has so much abounded among us." He stoutly defended his position that a select few were predestined to salvation while "the rest of mankind . . . will at last suffer that eternal death which is its proper wages."[126]

The debate illuminates the historic crisis brewing between those insisting with-out compromise on a God of inscrutable justice and those increasingly inclined to find a more humane interpretation of eternal judgment. Whitefield correctly per-ceived that compromise could not be reached without radical reformulation of foundational precepts. Wesley had agonized over "How uncomfortable a thought is this, that thousands and millions of men, without any preceding offence or fault of theirs were unchangeably doomed to everlasting burnings!"[127] Some in this era, like Francis Okely, simply abandoned the restrictive heaven: "Neither do I thus say, that all that are out of the Pale of the Christian Church will be damned. . . . But what I say is, that God has his own, as well amongst such as are out of the Christian Pale, as amongst the Christians within it. . . . Neither doeth it damn any Man, that he hath not the Word of God, if it is not given to him."[128] And some went on trial for such leniency: Robert Breck was charged with heresy for believing "the heathen who obeyed the light of nature could be saved."[129]

Whitefield accurately replied to Wesley and his ilk that if such a thought both-ered him, he was not a faithful adherent to the doctrine of original sin. For collec-tive culpability for Adam's sin demanded belief in universal human damnation as the justified consequence. Any exceptions to the general rule of damnation, not endless punishment, would be the cause of wonder, he reasoned.[130] Meanwhile, if, as Wesley averred, Christ died for all and not a predestined few, then all must be saved or Christ's purposes will have failed. Wesley was effectively flirting with the heresy of "universal redemption."

The trend toward a more capacious heaven continued into the nineteenth cen-tury. The dominant New England school of theology of the era, the New Divinity Movement, generally held a rather more hopeful estimate of the number of those who would find redemption. Samuel Hopkins advised that "when Satan mutters about . . . the few that are saved, a lively faith says . . . I will trust myself with Christ." In his writings, the "strait and narrow path" is juxtaposed with a "comprehensive view of the extent of the grace of God."[131] Regarding those "who think that but few of mankind, on the whole, will be saved," he protested that "their opinion [was not] founded on any reason or scripture." Christ's words about the few who find salvation, he noted, "are in the present tense: 'Few *are* saved.' He does not say what will be in other ages of the world."[132]

Some in this period were advancing God's generosity even further, as the protest against an irascible God of Justice gained momentum. Conditions were at last ripe for developments that had been brewing for centuries. Catholic purgatory, of course, can be seen as one strategy to increase the number of saved through post-mortal redemption, though it was confined to "those who die in the state of grace, but [are] not yet free from all imperfection."[133] Progress in one's standing after the door of death had closed was precluded by Thomas Cranmer in the 42nd of the first version of the Church of England's Articles (1552). But its framing suggests that background voices were advocating a more expansive universalism than what even purgatory allowed. "All men shall not be saved at the length," read the heading, followed by the anathema: "They also are worthy of condemnation who endeavor at this time to restore the dangerous opinion that all men, be they never so ungodly, shall at length be saved, when they have suffered pain for their sins a certain time appointed by God's justice."[134] That article, however, dropped out of subsequent versions of the Anglican confession.

One universalist voice was Michael Servetus, martyred by John Calvin the year after Cranmer's anathema. He argued that even the pagans were infused with God's spirit and that justification was universal.[135] But real impetus for an expanded salvation was felt in the eighteenth century. Increasingly, the same progressives who rejected Trinitarian formulations repudiated the system whereby humankind was largely a "corrupt mass" doomed to "common ruin" and the endless torments of hell.[136] An early salvo in this new direction was the publication in English in 1753 of the *Everlasting Gospel*.[137] Like so many books of the era, it made its thesis part of its title: "Whereby Devil, Sin, Hell and Death shall at last be abolished, and the whole creation restored to its primitive Purity." Coming out of a radical German tradition, Nicolai Klein argued that all punishment proceeding from a God of love must be based on love, and therefore aimed not at endless torment but at "Melioration and Restoration." And since God wants the wicked to repent and turn to him, his purposes will assure that they do. Based on Origen's doctrine of universal restoration, the book was promulgated in America by the universalist preacher George de Benneville.

A few years later (1770), the preacher John Murray came to America from London preaching universal salvation and turned the doctrine into the basis of a new religious movement. By 1786, the first self-identified Universalists created a charter of compact in Gloucester, Massachusetts,[138] and four years later, Universalists convened in Philadelphia and formulated their Articles of Religion to unite those churches who affirmed their belief "that there is one God, whose nature is Love, revealed in one Lord Jesus Christ, by one Holy Spirit of Grace, who will finally restore the whole family of mankind to holiness and happiness."[139] The prominent preacher Hosea Ballou helped transform the movement into a potent presence on the religious landscape, publishing books and, from 1819, the *Universalist Magazine*.

The logic of Universalist thought proceeded from a few simple premises to radically unorthodox conclusions. Universalists began with belief in God's benevolent and generous character. His love and justice were simply held to be incompatible with widespread condemnation or permanent torment. Original sin was therefore challenged or rejected outright. The influential Charles Chauncy, for example, cites John Taylor's attack on original sin as the principal inspiration for his 1784 work *Mystery Hid from Ages . . . , or, the Salvation of All Men*.[140] God would never have created the human race, he argues, "unless he intended to make them finally happy." And his infinite wisdom would succeed, eventually, in persuading even the most recalcitrant to accept his mercy.

If Universalists had simply argued, in the face of such abundant scriptural evidence to the contrary, that none should go to hell, they would have found little support in a biblical culture. Chauncy's argument, rather, was that while multitudes would, indeed, "be miserable in the next state of existence," that condition would be temporary.[141] Hell, in other words, is but a way station. Murray resolved the apparent contradiction by reasoning that "it is one thing to be punished with everlasting destruction, and another to be everlastingly punished with destruction." The pain of a candle flame, he clarified, is brief, but the pain is still "of everlasting fire."[142]

This left the problem of how the wicked would be fitted for eternal life. Universalists could be vague on the details of the redemption of the unbaptized and unrepentant, but they found one solution to be a future state of instruction and rehabilitation. "'Tis true," Chauncy conceded, God "will not, in *this state*, prevail upon *all* willingly to bow down before him as their *Lord*. . . . May he not, . . . use means with sinners in the *next state*, in order to make them *good subjects* in the *moral* kingdom of God?"[143] Opponents protested that "Now is the accepted time, now is the day of salvation; you may not have another."[144] Murray replied that, indeed, "now" will always be "the accepted time."[145] His views gained currency quickly. By the 1830s, the Scotch church "ejected from its bosom some of the most devout, laborious and able of its preachers" for "their belief in the universal redemption of mankind by Jesus Christ."[146] In America, in 1863, Lyman Beecher's brother Charles was convicted of heresy for these unorthodox positions on the extent and duration of damnation. The ecclesiastical court ruled that "He weakens and undermines the doctrine of future punishment by teaching that the offers of salvation are made to men after death; that God, to affect men, overstates the reality of future punishment in his threatenings of it."[147]

At present, the future and composition of hell is decidedly uncertain in Christian thought. John Paul II alluded to a "universal salvation" a number of times, and in Pope Benedict XCI's 2007 document, "The Hope of Salvation for Infants Who Die Without Being Baptized," faith was expressed "that unbaptized infants who die will be saved."[148] On the other hand, one of the most popular Christian apologists today insists upon the reality of final judgment, hell, and the damnation of the unsaved, even as he insists that "hell is simply one's freely chosen identity apart from God on a trajectory into infinity."[149] He considers it a travesty to imagine God "casting people into a pit who are crying 'I'm sorry! Let me out!'"; but he does not address the elephant in the room: what of the billions who lived and died outside the orbit of Christian teachings about salvation? How is their unsaved condition "freely chosen?" Yet another twenty-first-century evangelical created controversy when he refuted the theological notion that "of all the billions of people who have ever lived, only a select number will 'make it to a better place' and every single other person will suffer in torment and punishment forever."[150] As for the fate of those who die uncatechized, he asks, "what if the missionary gets a flat tire?"[151] Claiming support from Origen and other universalists, he argues that "No one can resist God's pursuit forever."[152] Even his critics (who are numerous) acknowledge, "there is a pervasive uneasiness both about the nature of hell and about who is relegated to it,"[153] but they are reluctant to so readily relinquish hell, citing its motivational function, its assurance of freedom's reality, and its satisfaction of "our sense of what is humanly [im]permissible."[154] Mormonism's belief in a hell of limited duration and scope emerged out of those same personal motivations and historical forces that inspired the rise of Universalism, but Smith would add a further layer of theological reasoning and concreteness to that movement's vague hope.

REDEEMING THE DEAD

Nineteenth-century Americans were steeped in the experience of death. Warren Foote recorded in his journal the same dread of death that always lurked in mournful proximity to those where fear of losing a loved one so often came to fuition: "1 January, 1838. Thousands, who on last New Year's day, rejoiced and made merry in the dance were looking forward with fond anticipation, to behold this day. Where are they? Alas! disease and death has preyed upon them, and they are now mouldering beneath the cold clods, and naught remains of them on earth except in the memories of their kindred and friends." And those kindred, Foote knew, were tied to us by bonds most tenuous. His sister Dorcas died before his own birth. Older brother Harrison passed when Foote was a toddler. His sister Nancy died when he was six, and Laura when he was seven. Less than two months after his New Year's entry, consumption took his sister Malinda. Barely out of his adolescence, Foote had been a visitor to the graves of five siblings.[155]

Just weeks before six-year-old Nancy Foote died, and just across the Finger Lakes from the Groton Cemetery, Joseph Smith's family was laying their eldest son to rest. Alvin died November 19 from a toxic dose of calomel (mercurous chloride) administered by a physician for a stomach ailment. "Taken from us in the vigor of life, in the bloom of youth," mourned his father.[156] "A youth of singular goodness of disposition—kind and amiable, so that lamentation and mourning filled the whole neighborhood in which he resided," recalled his mother.[157] A powerful young man, Alvin was a pillar of his family, bearing the brunt of physical labor on the farm and working strenuously to build a frame home for his overtaxed parents. But more than that, he was the spiritual center of the home. "I remember well the pangs of sorrow that swelled my youthful bosom and almost burst my tender heart, when he died," remembered his younger brother Joseph.[158] "It has been hard for me to live on earth & see those young men upon whome we have leaned upon as a support & comfort taken from us in the midst of their youth, yes it has been hard to be reconciled to these things."[159]

Untimely death, with the damnation often held to follow in its wake, was something to which the Universalists refused to be reconciled. Universalism was rife in Joseph Smith's background and environs, and fiercely debated in print and pulpit. Smith's grandfather Asael was impressed enough with the doctrines to form his own Universalist society in 1797 with oldest sons Jesse and Joseph Sr. and thirteen others.[160] Joseph Jr.'s grandfather on his mother's side was likewise a Universalist most of his life.[161] Many other first-generation Mormons had Universalist sympathies or backgrounds, including stalwarts and leaders like the Joseph Knight family and Martin Harris, but also several converts of those years like Nancy Tracy, Lorenzo Hill Hatch, Benjamin Ashby, Leonard E. Harrington, and Stephen H. Goddard.[162] For Howard Coray, the text, "For as in Adam all die, even so in Christ shall all be made alive" [1st Cor. 15:22] clinched the case;[163] Benjamin Brown was similarly logical: "The Universalist system appeared to me the most reasonable of the various denominations I came in contact with. The horrible hell and damnation theories of most of the other parties, in my idea, being inconsistent with the mercies and love of God."[164] Benjamin Ashby agreed: he couldn't help but reject "the doctrines of the Orthodox churches that held to the everlasting punishment of all who did not embrace their peculiar dogmas."[165]

Smith was obviously deeply moved by the same considerations that activated the Universalist movement, and he acted to develop more concretely the problems they raised but did not fully resolve: the nature and duration of hell, and the opportunity provided in the "next state" to better qualify for salvation. The Book of Mormon provided only the hint of a solution, which Smith would be some years fully unfolding.

HELL, PARADISE, AND SPIRIT PRISON

In the Book of Mormon, hell is often formulaically invoked as the conventional abode of the devil and the damned, but also refers to intense remorse in this life— the acute pangs of conscience. A more rigorous explication of the concept occurs when Alma preaches on the "space between the time of death and the resurrection." He indicates that the righteous will abide in a paradise while the wicked "shall be cast into outer darkness." Alma emphasizes that these are not discrete places, but separate "states" of the soul. The "righteous are received into a state of happiness, which is called paradise, a state of rest, a state of peace, where they shall rest from all their troubles and from all care, and sorrow." By contrast, "this is the state of the souls of the wicked, yea, in darkness, and a state of awful, fearful looking for the fiery indignation of the wrath of God upon them; thus they remain in this state, as well as the righteous in paradise, until the time of their resurrection."[166]

Nephi had similarly referred to two pre-judgment realms; the first he also named paradise, but he called the second state hell rather than outer darkness.[167] At least one meaning of hell, therefore, is defined by the Book of Mormon as the temporary condition of the wicked, prior to judgment. It is principally a state of being. Those terms generally associated with lakes of brimstone or a lightless underworld, this usage suggests, are metaphors for the spiritual, emotional, and psychological condition in which the wicked who die *initially* find themselves. "Hades, shaole paradise, spirits in prison is all one it is a world of spirits," said Smith.[168] And, he indicated, spirits of the departed "are not far from us."[169] Young agreed on this point. Speaking at a funeral of one Sister Ivins, he asked, "Where is she gone? She is in Paradise in the world of spirits. Where is it? It is in this world & on this Earth. I do not think sister Ivins is far off."[170]

Smith emphasized that the partition between departed wicked and departed righteous was largely a matter of self-selection: "The words Prison Paradise & Hell are different translations of the Greek Hades which answers to the Hebrew Shaole the true translation of which is 'The world of spirits where the righteous & the wicked dwell together.'"[171] Implicit in this conception of the afterlife is the shock of self-judgment.[172] Paul's most famous epistle on charity did not refer to seeing through a dark glass, but looking into a dim mirror that would one day reflect our image with startling clarity, for good or ill.[173] The Book of Mormon is replete with this idea: "They are their own judges," writes Alma; some will have a "perfect knowledge of their guilt," while others will rejoice in "a perfect knowledge of their enjoyment." For the wicked, it will be "their own guilt and abominations" that "doth cause them to shrink from the presence of the Lord," preaches King Benjamin.[174] But it was Smith's discovery of what transpires in that spirit world that answered to his Universalist impulses.

EVANGELIZING THE DEAD

Although Christians were generally accepting of the categorical damnation of the uncatechized and unbaptized, biblical scripture did suggest there may have been important exceptions to what was seen as a general rule. The first epistle of Peter made provocative reference to Christ having gone, in the spirit after his death, to "the spirits in prison" where he preached to those who were disbelievers "in the days of Noah." This was so that hearing the "gospel . . . proclaimed" to them, they could "live in the spirit as God does."[175] Some Christians, like Bishop Hilary of Arles (403–499) and Andreas (563–637), took "the dead" to refer to the Gentiles, "who are dead in sin."[176] But other early Christians took these verses to refer to a literal descent of Christ into hell, inscribing the doctrine in both the Apostles' Creed and the Athanasian Creed (though some Christians were uncomfortable with the notion of a Christ fully present in Satan's realm. Clement of Alexandria thought it safer to hold that the spirits "did not see his form, but they heard the sound of his voice"[177]). There, Jesus announced his victory over sin and death, and—as the idea acquired more detail—liberated the righteous who died before his advent in a victorious "harrowing of hell." The apocryphal gospel of Nicodemus rendered a dramatic account of Christ's storming of hell, where he broke "the gates of brass, and cut the bars of iron asunder," and rescued "Adam and his sons."[178] The idea achieved widespread currency in the Middle Ages, as described by poets and depicted by myriad artists. Not all the righteous were so liberated, according to church father Tertullian. This special act of clemency pertained to "the patriarchs and prophets" only.[179] Cyril of Alexandria thought the opportunity extended to "all those who would believe on him." Augustine was unsure, thinking the ark of Noah mentioned in Peter's epistle might have been a metaphor for the entire human race.[180]

Thomas Aquinas believed Christ's descent into hell was a figurative redemption of the biblical Fathers who waited in an area designated Limbo for the moment of their release. This "Limbo of the Fathers" was distinct from the "Limbo of Children."[181] The poet Dante gave the idea enduring currency in his guided tour of hell called the *Inferno*, written in the early fourteenth century. The Roman poet Virgil tells Dante that he was denied heaven for failing to "duly worship God." But he recalls the day he saw

A Great Lord enter here;
The crown he wore, a sign of victory,
He carried off the shade of our first Father,
Of his son Abel, and the shade of Noah,
Of Moses, the obedient legislator,
Of father Abraham, David the King,
Of Israel, his father and his sons,
And Rachel, she for whom he worked so long,
And many others—and he made them blessed;
And I should have you know that, before them,
There were no human souls that had been saved.[182]

In 2007, Pope Benedict approved the dismissal of the centuries-old idea that unbaptized infants perish eternally, calling it an "unduly restrictive view of salvation."[183] But the forty-one-page document did not directly address the fate of adults who died outside the faith. More recently, Catholics and Lutherans have their "Common Statement" on eternal life, which traces "the impetus for a discussion of a hope for universal salvation" to Reformed theologian Karl Barth, who asked, "if God's . . . saving will is supreme, how is eternal loss possible? . . . Barth concludes that the possibility of final loss cannot be ruled out, but also that the final *reality* that some will be lost also cannot be affirmed."[184]

Long before Benedict's decision, the Reformers were already casting doubt on the reality of Limbo—in some cases not as an overly restrictive doctrine but as an overgenerous one. Calvin flatly denied a literal descent of Christ to a place of entombed spirits as "nothing but a fable."[185] According to the Geneva Catechism, Christ's descent into hell means Christ's "soul was pierced with amazing anguish."[186] As for his preaching to the dead there, Calvin argued that "the purport of the context [for the words in 1 Peter] is, that believers who had died before that time were partakers of the same grace with ourselves."[187] In what sense uncatechized pre-Christians could be believers, he did not explain. But in any case, he concludes that Peter, in reference to both godly and ungodly souls of earlier eras, "only means to intimate, that the death of Christ was made known to both."[188] As he insisted elsewhere, "it is an indubitable doctrine of Scripture, that we obtain no salvation in Christ except by faith; then there is no hope left for those who continue to death unbelieving."[189] The creed of Reformed doctrine, the Westminster Confession, accordingly modified the language of the Apostles' Creed. That Christ "was crucified, died, and was buried [and then] he descended to the dead" became "He was buried, and remained under the power of death for a time." A modern Reformed theologian explains, "as the words stand in our Bible they afford no ground for the doctrine that Christ after death went into hell and preached to the spirits there confined."[190]

The Lutheran Formula of Concord had no problem taking Christ's descent literally: in "simplicity of faith," Lutherans are enjoined to know "that Christ went to hell, destroyed hell for all believers, and has redeemed them from the power of death, of the devil, and of the eternal damnation of the hellish jaws."[191] But regarding Jesus's preaching to the spirits, the great reformer confessed he was stumped. "I do not know for a certainty just what Peter means," he said, calling it "a more obscure passage than any other in the New Testament."[192] Wesley explained the episode away by taking Peter to mean that Christ *effectively* preached to the souls of the flood era "through the ministry of Noah."[193] Accordingly, the Methodists removed the allusion to Christ's descent into hell from their version of the Apostles' Creed. The popular commentary of Adam Clarke adopted the same tack, considering that "the Gospel [was] preached by Noah to them also who are dead."[194]

On the nineteenth-century American religious landscape, Christ's preaching to the dead seems to have been largely abandoned with other vestiges of what went by the name of "popery religion." The teaching was largely relegated to apocryphal works that circulated in edited compilations. One exception was the Shakers. Mother Ann Lee "uniformly taught the doctrine of a free offer of the gospel to *all souls*, whether in this world, or in the world of spirits." She recounted numerous visions in which departed Shakers, or she herself, ministered to the dead, "like claps of thunder among them, waking them up." She also taught that the righteous in this life could "travail and suffer" on behalf of the dead, at times effecting their release from hell.[195] Smith may have known of these Shaker teachings; he may also have encountered the idea through the Apocryphal New Testament (which he owned), or he may simply have been more open to a plain reading of Peter's description. In any case, in 1832 he described a vision which explicitly referenced the evangelizing of the uncatechized dead as the lynchpin of a near Universalist view of salvation.

In the contemporary LDS Church, Mormons tend to consider Smith's greatest experience of the divine to be his 1820 theophany, or "First Vision." But in the nineteenth century, it was his 1832 experience that loomed the largest in his prophetic resume, known simply and tellingly as "The Vision." Smith had been pondering the evangelist John's allusion to the hard dichotomy of judgment day: "all that are in the graves . . . shall come forth; they that have done good, unto the resurrection of life; and they that have done evil, unto the resurrection of damnation."[196] Believing the reality must be less simplistic than what was intimated, he—along with colleague Sidney Rigdon—found an expansive vision of heaven opened up to them. And almost the first words he heard confirmed his Universalist inclinations, dispelling the Christian notion of hell before explicating the realms of heaven: hell was indeed a temporary abode, from which virtually all humans would be redeemed. Only those who insistently rejected Christ, who "suffered themselves ... to be overcome," would not be redeemed. They were "the only ones," repeated twice for emphasis. "All the rest," "all ... whom the Father had put into [Christ's] power," "all except" the intractable would be saved.[197] As W. W. Phelps wrote under Smith's name, "The Savior will save all his Father did give, Even all that he gave in the regions abroad." Only the "Sons of Perdition ... are ever lost, and can never return to the presence of God."[198] And even those few "sons of perdition" were returned to outer darkness for a period of indefinite duration. "The end thereof ... no man knows."[199]

Next, Smith and Rigdon saw in the vision the inhabitants of heaven, which was subdivided into three realms: the celestial, the terrestrial, and the telestial. The celestial was occupied by "an innumerable company of angels"; the terrestrial by throngs of the uncatechized, the honorable, and the deceived; and the telestial by inhabitants "as innumerable as the stars."[200] So the Universalists were (almost) correct. Hell was largely a place of limited duration. Salvation came to virtually everyone. And the explanation, Smith learned, was much as Chauncy and Murray had speculated. Those numerous men, women, and children who died without exposure to the Christian message would hear it in "the next state." Peter had indeed, in this view, been referring to a literal ministry to the numberless dead who perished before the days of Christ. As the vision revealed, heaven contained those "whom the Son visited, and preached the gospel unto. . . . Who received not the testimony of Jesus in the flesh, but afterward received it."[201]

Parley Pratt took up this visionary gloss on Peter's epistle, insisting the dead "not only live, move, and think but might hear the gospel." "We reason from what we know," Pratt matter-of-factly said. In the "spirit world societies are made up of all kinds." Many presumably "have lived in part of the spirit world ... where the key has not yet been turned nor the gospel preached." The sinful, "being left in their darkness," wait in a hell of uncertainty, "without even a clear idea of hope of resurrection. . . . Yes, they [are waiting]." Pratt extended the ministry of Christ even further, surmising that faithful "modern saints that have departed this earth clothed upon with ... priesthood go to the world of spirits not to sorrow but as joyful messengers with glad tiding of eternal truth anointed to preach the gospel."[202]

In 1918, church president Joseph F. Smith confirmed Pratt's inferences with a detailed vision that was eventually canonized in 1976. Like a modern Virgil, Smith described "the hosts of the dead, both small and great," and the appearance in that realm of the Son of God, "declaring liberty to the captives who had been faithful." Then Smith watched as, "from among the righteous, he organized his forces and appointed messengers, clothed with power and authority, and commissioned them to go forth and carry the light of the gospel to them that were in darkness, even to all the spirits of men; and thus was the gospel preached to the dead."[203]

With Smith's vision, the distance separating Mormonism from Universalism had shrunk drastically. As Brigham Young's shocked brother characterized the vision, "why the Lord was going to save everybody."[204] Smith did indeed preach that "God hath made a provision that every spirit can be ferretted out in that world that has not sinned the unpardonable sin."[205] Earlier he had told a Washington crowd "that all who would follow the precepts of the Bible, whether Mormon or not, would assuredly be saved."[206] Young himself noted that the capacious heaven was too much for the hard-core Calvinists in their midst: "When God revealed to Joseph Smith and Sidney Rigdon that there was a place prepared for all, according to the light they had received and their rejection of evil and practice of good, it was a great trial to many, and some apostatized because God was not going to send to everlasting punishment heathens and infants, but had a place of salvation, in due time, for all, and would bless the honest and virtuous and truthful, whether they ever belonged to any church or not. It was a new doctrine to this generation, and many stumbled at it."[207]

No wonder that Lucy Smith noted the opposition to Mormonism of the Universalists in particular, who were "alarmed lest their religion should suffer loss."[208] Important distinctions from the Universalists existed, however. One involved the small but very real exceptions to universal clemency. As Lorenzo Snow protested, "[apostates] adopt the doctrine of universalism and think none too wicked for a complete and unconditional salvation."[209] One observer knew better, who noted, while imposing on Mormonism the terminology of the universalists: "They believe in the final restoration of all men except apostate Mormons."[210] He wasn't exactly correct.

In light of Smith's teachings about agency, it appears that the apostasy associated with the unpardonable sin is a matter of freedom and law, not loyalty or gravity per se. The only mortals beyond redemption, according to Smith's 1843 revelation on marriage, are those who commit "the blasphemy against the Holy Ghost, which shall not be forgiven in the world nor out of the world."[211] As Smith explained in D&C, section 88, all choices made by freely choosing agents must be honored, and Christ's atonement makes it possible for the repentant to re-choose life and salvation. But repentance is predicated on the desire to correct a decision made in error, in weakness, or with deficient will or understanding—which is virtually always the case with mortals. However, it is possible to imagine a choice made with an uncompromised will. A choice, in other words, made with perfect clarity and understanding. This sin committed with untainted deliberation, in full and utter knowledge of its meaning and repercussions, may be what Smith meant by the sin against the Holy Ghost, which the scripture also equated with "assent[ing] to [Christ's] death." It is unforgiveable not because it is so grievous or offensive, but because it is the only sin a human can make with no mitigating circumstances that could be the basis of re-choosing under different conditions. This is why, as Smith taught, receiving the Holy Ghost was a precondition for committing "the unpardonable sin."[212] All other sins are performed "through a glass darkly," as it were, without a perfect understanding, on an uneven playing field, where to greater or lesser degree the weakness of the flesh, of intellect, or of judgment intrudes. In all such cases, regret and reconsideration are conceivable. Only the choice of evil made in the most absolute and perfect light of understanding admits no imaginable basis for reconsideration or regret. "He has got to say that the sun does not shine while he sees it," in Smith's words.[213] And for this sin, an act of fully self-aware rebellion comparable to Lucifer's, there can be, in other words, no possibility of repentance. Such sin is unforgivable because it is unrepentable. That is why, as the vision revealed, those who deny the Holy Ghost "after having received it" cannot "be redeemed in the due time of the Lord."[214]

Both Brigham Young and Lorenzo Snow imbibed Smith's Universalist bent. Young preached, "Every faithful Methodist that has lived up to and faithfully fulfilled the requirements of his religion, . . . will have as great a heaven as he ever anticipated in the flesh, and far greater. Every Presbyterian, and every Quaker, and every Baptist, and every Roman Catholic member,—. . . that lives according to the best light they have, . . . will have and enjoy all they live for. . . . This is the situation of Christendom after death. You may go among the Pagans, or among all the nations there are . . . and if they have lived according to what they did possess, so they will receive hereafter. And will it be glory? you may inquire. Yes. Glory, glory, glory."[215] Wilford Woodruff, in encouraging an all-encompassing project of genealogical research and family sealing back to Adam, justified it in terms of his vision of a Universalist salvation. "There will be very few, if any, who will not accept the Gospel."[216] Lorenzo Snow concurred: "very, very few of those who die without the Gospel will reject it on the other side of the veil."[217] Snow, too, believed God would persist in his salvific efforts until he succeeded.

> The antediluvians rejected the word of God; but they were the sons and daughters of God, and . . . after twenty-five hundred years had passed away the Lord revealed himself to them again and gave them another opportunity. Then they no doubt accepted. . . . The people of this generation may not receive our testimony here, but they will receive it at some future time, from us or from some other servants of God.[218]

A mere eight years after Snow's statement, the church printed an article headed "Salvation Universal," noting that "we hold out the hope that all may be saved, excepting the sons of perdition—a class that willfully rejects the atonement of the Savior: for the Lord intends to save all the workmanship of his hands." Even so, the author qualified salvation as "in some degree of glory."[219] (Not that a universal salvation "in some degree of glory" is any small thing.) A few generations later, however, under the harsh doctrinal conservatism of Mormonism's mid-twentieth century, such a liberal view of universal salvation as pertaining to virtually all souls diminished in Mormon consciousness. Certainly the persistent LDS rhetoric of the "one true church," Amulek's emphasis on this life being "the time for men to prepare to meet God,"[220] and the general Jonah-like tendency to want to see Ninevah burn—all conspired to move Mormon cultural understanding in a less generous direction.

If Joseph Smith had any fears about the fate of his brother Alvin's soul, he at least knew after his 1832 vision that it was not in hell. In any case, Smith had learned two years earlier that the hell, or the spirit prison which the Book of Mormon described, was a temporary state. As he wrapped up translation of that record, a revelation came to him that the "endless torment" spoken of biblically was not without end. Echoing the language he may have read in John Murray's volume, Smith wrote that "it is not written that there shall be no end to this torment; but it is written endless torment."[221] Murray had differentiated everlasting destruction from destruction that is everlasting, when he distinguished the everlastingness of a candle's flame from the everlastingness of the pain it can cause.[222] Smith later argued as a matter of logical principle, that "every thing which had a *beginning* must have an *ending*; and consequently if the punishment of man *commenced* in the next world, it must, according to his logic and belief have an *end*."[223]

In January 1836, Smith had a vision of the celestial world that brought further salve to his grieving heart. He "saw Father Adam and Abraham; and my father and my mother; my brother Alvin, that has long since slept; And marveled how it was that he had obtained an inheritance in that kingdom, seeing that he had departed this life before the Lord had set his hand to gather Israel the second time, and had not been baptized for the remission of sins."[224] The consolation was emphatic, but the theology was still incomplete. Unlike the Universalists, in other words, Smith considered a third conundrum complicated the desired outcome of a universal salvation. Granting a temporary hell, and the evangelizing of the dead in the next state, the problem remained of reconciling God's mercy with what seemed the nonnegotiable price of admission to heaven: not just a life of virtue and holiness but also the satisfaction of gospel ordinances stipulated by Jesus Christ. If "believe and be baptized" was the formula, and evangelizing in the spirit world as intimated by Peter and now confirmed by revelation was taking place, only baptism persisted as the obstacle.

In August 1840, Smith closed the theological loop in the Universalist dream of a comprehensive salvation: when, where, and how would the uncatechized by brought to Christ? Not only would they be proselytized in the spirit world, taught Smith; the baptism that betokened acceptance of Christ would be vicariously performed for such spirit converts by those still living. Thus, the dead could comply with an essential Christian ordinance through the ministrations of their living descendants, uniting the children and the fathers in the same gospel covenant. He "set forth the glory" of the doctrine at a funeral for Seymour Brunson. Soon, to the flocks of Mormon converts were added legions of those converts' deceased relatives.[225]

Thou hast made me, and given unto me a right to thy throne, and not of myself, but through thine own grace.

—MOSES 7:59, PGP

21

Theosis

KIERKEGAARD REFERRED TO the "infinite qualitative difference" between the human and the divine, which idea found historical grounding in the doctrine of creation *ex nihilo*. Emil Brunner claimed there is "no greater sense of distance than that which lies in the words Creator-Creation. . . . Man . . . is separated by an abyss from the Divine manner of being. The greatest dissimilarity between two things which we can express at all . . . is that between the Creator and that which is created."[1]

Joseph Smith's cosmological monism, his radical materialism, and his assertion of an eternally pre-existing human identity profoundly diminish that distance as it pertains to human origins. And the literal kinship thus established leads almost inexorably to a collapse of that distance in the domain of human destinies as well. This is why human pre-existence has historically been so often linked with theories of human theosis (the idea that man may become godlike), eliciting orthodox resistance to both. As Reinhold Niebuhr says, "Man is mortal; that is his fate. Man pretends not to be mortal; that is his sin."[2]

Nevertheless, the subversive idea that the human may have a kinship with the gods occurs in the oldest religious texts known. The unsettling sense that such a recognition can be dangerous and destabilizing occurs in those same texts. In *Atra-Hasis*, a Mesopotamian creation narrative, the gods decide to create a race of humans to take over the burdensome task of working the earth.[3] To animate this new creation and make it capable of fulfilling work previously performed by gods, they recognize the need for a divine element. So they slay a god named We-ila, and mix his spirit with clay to create man. At the same time they fear that if he knows he has a divine ancestry, then man will claim eternal life as his due. So they hide from their human creation the truth about his origins "so that he would never seek immortality further."[4]

The importance of this story lies in the twin preoccupations it illustrates that are a part of human consciousness at the very dawn of recorded history. On the one hand, the writer senses that human identity is a hybrid, a mixture of earthly clay and divine essence, and that our roots lie in the realm of the gods. On the other hand, the conduct of the gods in the myth reflects the storyteller's awareness that danger lurks in such knowledge, that to know our divine ancestry and aspire to attain those ancient heights is an invitation to disaster. In its treatment of humankind's divine potential, *Atra-Hasis* foreshadows both the timeless appeal and the undeniable hazards of theosis.

Western history records multiple versions of this tension between divine nature and human limitations, between portentous origins and dangerous presumption. Classical thought repeated the pattern of the Mesopotamian text. A veritable pantheon of Greek heroes found elevation to divine status, Hercules being the most famous. Dionysus, Helen of Troy, Asclepius, and dozens of others also achieved immortality or the heights of Mt. Olympus after their mortal lives. At the same time, many Greek characters suffered horrible fates for their pretentions. Arachne challenged Athena to a weaving contest. She was punished not for losing but because she won. In Ovid's version of the tale, Athena beats her with a shuttle and turns her into a spider. The satyr Marsyas challenges Apollo to a flute-playing contest. For his presumption, he is skinned alive before he plays a note. Icarus is not the only other character to suffer for flying too close to the sun. Niobe, Phaeton, and a dozen more similarly suffer the repercussions of their hubris, which is usually defined as pride, but these cases could more accurately be construed as attempts to transcend the human station in the Great Chain of Being and ascend to the ranks of divinity.

At the same time, such lofty aspirations for human potential were part of the Hellenistic world out of which Christianity arose. If you asked any well-educated citizen of antiquity "to name the official moral goal, or *telos*, of each major current philosophical system," writes one scholar, "you will hear that Plato's is *homoiosis theoi kata to dunaton*, 'becoming like god so far as is possible.' "[5] Implicit in several of Plato's dialogues, including the *Timaeus*, the ideal is most explicitly stated in the *Theaetetus*, where Socrates tells Theodorus, "a man should make all haste to escape from earth to heaven, and escape means becoming as like God as possible."[6] Adolf Harnack considered the whole idea of deification a disastrous intrusion into Christian thought of mystery cult ideas. Others have agreed that the doctrine is "a disastrous flaw in Greek Christian thought."[7]

The Old Testament reflects the same ambiguity about the pursuit of theosis. Three biblical stories involve the motif of godlike aspirations. The fall of King Nebuchadnezzar is described in Isaiah: "How you are fallen from heaven.... You said in your heart, I will ascend to heaven; above the stars of God I will set my throne on high.... I will make myself like the Most High. But you are brought down to Sheol, to the depths of the Pit."[8] Commentators from Origen and Jerome to Augustine saw the passage as a clear allusion to Lucifer. Jerome summed up the moral most simply: "Lucifer fell from heaven because he wanted to be like God."[9]

Augustine finds a close parallel between this morality tale of godlike ambition and the fall of Adam. Both Lucifer and Adam, he wrote in his *Explanations of the Psalms*, were "robbers," for seizing what did not belong to them. In Adam's case, he and Eve ate the fruit of the tree of knowledge, apparently because it offered the prospect of becoming "as the gods"; and indeed, the Lord remarked that their action had had just that effect, making them "as one of us." For Augustine, this was proof that humankind, specifically, "wanted to make a grab at divinity."[10]

Finally, we have the story of the Tower of Babel:

> And the whole earth had one language, and the same words. And as they migrated from the east, they came upon a plain in the land of Shinar, and settled there. And they said to one another, "Come, let us make bricks, and burn them thoroughly ... [and] build a tower with its top in the heavens, and let us make a name for ourselves."[11]

That is the New Revised Standard Version of the Bible. The King James translation is significant in its difference, as it makes the episode more evocative of Adam's sin. "And they said, Go to, let us build us a city and a tower, *whose top may reach unto heaven;* and let us make us a name. . . ." The subtle shift from a visual description (with its top in the heavens) to an aspirational description ("whose top may reach unto heaven") is potent. The KJV wording emphasizes the hubris of the action, lending logic to the divine wrath that follows.

At the same time, there are biblical echoes of a fully countenanced ascent to godhood. God's words in the aftermath of Adam and Eve's sin, that the man and woman have become "as one of us," acknowledge a process of approaching godhood that is already under way. Some scholars read Daniel as describing "a 'deification,' as it were, of the 'saints of the most high,'"[12] and in at least one instance, the Old Testament suggests that God has given to Moses some kind of godlike status. "I have made thee a god to Pharaoh," he says.[13] Although the usage there seems figurative,

Jewish traditions accord to Moses and others a literal elevation to godhood. "Moses is actually deified" in one second-century BCE text, and the Hellenized Jew Philo of Alexandria also calls Moses a god. In fact, Philo taught that others besides Moses are "changed into the divine, . . . become kin to God and are truly divine."[14] The Essenes also wrote that some humans would "draw near to [God]" and "be counted with Him in the com[munity of the g]ods."[15] Given the prevalence of the concept in Jewish thought, it is not surprising that Norman Russell would claim that "The idea of human beings becoming 'gods' entered Christian thought from Rabbinic Judaism."[16]

So the fall of Icharus, of Lucifer and myriad angels, the tragedy of Eden, the Faustian yearning for transcendence—all can be read as the playing out of this millennia-long contest between simple *apokatastasis,* or restoration to glory, on the one hand, and "vaulting ambition" and the path to perdition, on the other. The mortal striving for deification has been seen as both natural destiny and supreme blasphemy. The human spirit has repeatedly been invoked as that which distinguishes mortals from other varieties in the created order of things and makes him nearer the gods than all other beings. The spark of divinity in the human breast beckons to a heavenly home, even as it is a temptation to pride, to step beyond the assigned link in the Great Chain of Being and incur divine displeasure, or even wrath.

In the book of Job, the trial-weary man likens himself to the ephemeral nature of a cloud, which today is, but tomorrow "is consumed and vanisheth away: so he that goeth down to the grave shall come up no more."[17] Jews maintained the perseverance of the soul in some sense, but the exact nature of that survival was disputed. (Debates between the Sadducees and the Pharisees over resurrection was one echo of the lingering debate.) In the Christian story, it is the promise of resurrection that first bridges the gulf between the mortal and the immortal. The good news of Christ was that his resurrection did away with the ambiguity of Sheol's dominion. Jesus "rose again the third day" after his crucifixion, and by so doing brought everlasting life to all the human family; as a consequence, "all will be made alive in Christ." Not figuratively, but in glorified form, as evidenced by his own physical resurrection. The mortal body, Paul taught, "is sown a physical body; it is raised a spiritual body. . . . This mortal body [then] puts on immortality." With that event, "Death has been swallowed up in victory."[18]

But what then? What does that access to immortality encompass? Jesus encouraged his disciples to be perfect, as God is, and prayed for his disciples to become one with him and the Father.[19] The second epistle of Peter refers to the Savior's "precious and very great promises" that we might become "participants of the divine nature."[20] Other passages emphasize a familial relationship to God that has been variously interpreted. Paul insisted that "we are God's offspring,"[21] and his epistle to the

Romans taught that we are "children of God; and if children, then heirs; heirs of God, and joint heirs with Christ."[22] He admonishes his Christian audience to imitate God (*mimetai tou theou/estote ergo imitatores Dei*).[23] With these encouragements, it is no wonder, then, that scholars have referred to the "ubiquity of the doctrine of deification" in the early Christian centuries.[24]

One early expression of an ideal oriented toward theosis or deification was the assertion of Irenaeus (died ca. 202) that "Jesus Christ . . . did, through His transcendent love, become what we are, that He might bring us to be what He is Himself."[25] Irenaeus saw such likeness to God as a heavenly gift, not the unfolding of an innate human capacity: man should not err in thinking a capacity to theosis "is his own naturally, . . . as if he were naturally like to God." Rather, it is God who is "immortal and powerful to such a degree as to confer immortality upon what is mortal, and eternity upon what is temporal." These and other attributes humans receive through "adoption."[26] In other words, Irenaeus affirmed an unbreachable divide between an eternal God and his adopted, merely mortal children. The inherently mortal nature of humans meant there could be no full parallel between God's status and our capacity to be like him. "The things established are distinct from Him who established them. . . . For He is Himself uncreated, both without beginning and end, and lacking nothing. . . . So that He indeed who made all things can alone . . . properly be termed God and Lord: but the things which have been made cannot have this term applied to them."[27]

This context is important, because it suggests significant limitations on the way deification was understood by many in these years. The general parameters of the concept were given formulation by Dionysius in the sixth century: "Deification (theosis) is the attaining of likeness to God and union with him *so far as is possible*."[28] A principal limitation on how far that likeness could extend was the doctrine of creation *ex nihilo*, and the consequent difference between a self-existing, eternal God and a created, inherently mortal human. When the theme of theosis was repeated by several of the church fathers, it was often with adoption or "participation" as the operative terms that delimit the scope of divinization, ensuring the ontological distance between God and humans always remained intact. Still, the degree to which these church fathers understood all allusions to theosis as metaphorical is contested.[29]

Some scholars have resisted the metaphorical renderings of early expressions of the doctrine, insisting we should "envy [Clement's] optimism," even while recognizing his blatant challenge to "our conception of the godhead."[30] At times early writers seem to be reaching beyond metaphor. Clement (ca. 150–215 CE), for example, echoes Irenaeus's formula, writing that "The Word of God became man, that thou mayest learn from man how man may become God."[31] Then he turns possible figure of speech to literal destiny, when he writes that "those who have become perfect . . . are called by the appellation of gods, being destined to sit on thrones with the other gods that have been first put in their places by the Saviour."[32] Basil the Great (330–379) also celebrated the prospect not just of "being made like to God" but, "highest of all, the being made God," as did Gregory Nazianzen (ca. 329–390).[33]

The theme was developed by their older contemporary Athanasius (293–373), who made deification central to his theology. As a principal opponent of the Arians, who denied the full divinity and equality of Christ, Athanasius in fact based his Trinitarian conception—that God and Christ were fully equal and of the same substance—on his commitment to human theosis. He reasoned that Christ could not make humans divine, unless he was himself fully divine. If God had merely granted Christ his divinity, in his words, then Christ "would not deify [human-kind], . . . since what He has is not His own, but the Giver's."[34] For this church father human theosis is a participation in the divine nature that is made possible by God's act of uniting the human and the divine in the person of Christ. Christ is united with us through his humanity, and then "by partaking of Him, we partake of the Father."[35] This is the meaning of his famous formulation, that "He was made man that we might be made God."[36]

In similar fashion, many treatments of theosis emphasized a kind of mystical union through grace, rather than an achievement of divinity through effort or birthright. (Being created and ontologically distinct, man is granted union, or "participation in God's energies," but not in his essence.[37]) Others were uncomfortable with the doctrine on any terms. "To modern ears the word *deification* sounds not only strange but arrogant and shocking" wrote William Ing, Archbishop of Canterbury, though he defended the doctrine.[38] The expressions of church father Clement of Alexandria on the subject are especially "startling to Western ears," agrees a contemporary historian of the idea.[39]

Not surprisingly, then, the term faded in Western Christianity, though it continues to the present as a key element in Eastern Orthodoxy. Orthodox Christians, who recognize that "Protestants, and even some Catholics, might find the Orthodox concept of theosis unnerving," clarify that by theosis they mean "human beings can have real union with God, and so become like God to such a degree that we participate in the divine nature." We do not, however, share in his essence: "intrinsic divinity is never ascribed to humankind . . . and no created thing is confused with the being of God. Most certainly, humans are not accorded ontological equality with God."[40]

Luther is not generally associated with the idea, but a recent article by Kurt Marquart referred to "the rediscovery of neglected elements in Luther's theology," in particular his emphasis on theosis.[41] Christ "becomes completely humanified (*vermenschet*) and we become completely deified (*gantz und gar vergottet*, 'Godded-through')," he said in a 1526 sermon.[42] Even as he affirmed the patristic doctrine, he emphasized its particular meaning as pertaining to participation, not essence. "We . . . are made Word not by being substantially changed into the Word, but by taking it on and uniting it to ourselves."[43]

A modern flowering of theosis occurred with another group of clergymen philosophers—the Cambridge Platonists. They were motivated by admiration for Plato—and his belief in theomorphism, or becoming like God—and for church father Origen, who along with championing human pre-existence had alluded to some form of human divinization ("we have presented these comments that we may flee being men with all our strength and hasten to become 'gods.'"[44]). Aharon Lichtenstein goes so far as to call deification the idea that governs the "whole ethical and theological thought" of Henry More, the group's foremost figure.[45] Some of their group followed precedent in emphasizing mystical union as the end of human striving. "This indeed is such a θέωσις [*theosis*, or] Deification as is not transacted merely upon the Stage of *Fancy* by Arrogance and Presumption, but in the highest Powers of the Soul by a living and quickening Spirit of true Religion there uniting God and the Soul together in *the Unity of Affections, Will* and *End*," insisted the group's John Smith.[46] "Do not stumble at the use of *the Word* [deification]," wrote Benjamin Whichcote in a sermon devoted to the topic. "For, we have Authority for the use of it, Scripture. 2 Pet. 1:4. *Being made Partakers of the Divine Nature;* which is in effect our *Deification*."[47] Others emphasized human potential over divine grace. Man, these philosopher theologians will assert time and again, is "deiform," borrowing the phrase from "Plato's school."[48] Thomas Vaughan, in this strain, quoted precedent: Arius Montanus makes

> the creation of man a little Incarnation, as if God in his worke had multiplyed Himself. . . . St Luke also tells us the same thing, for he makes Adam the son of God, not in respect of the exterior act of creation, but by way of descent, and this St Paul confirms in the words of Aratus. "For we also are his generation."[49]

Like their predecessors, however, the Cambridge group accepted the doctrine of creation *ex nihilo*, and so did not develop the idea far beyond its early Christian forms.

John Wesley appears to have studied Eastern Orthodoxy, and he developed the concept of theosis into the doctrine of perfectibilism. In his book on the subject (*A Plain Account of Christian Perfection*), he equates perfection with sanctification, or salvation "from all sin" and "evil desires," and perfect unity with Christ.[50]

Some noted that the upper limit to godly striving would seem to be established by a Christian monotheism that holds one (triune) God to be the true, absolute, and sole God of the universe. As the nineteenth-century Ethan Smith argued, "the question is, can real divinity be derived or propagated? Is not a conception of the affirmative a vast absurdity? . . . Can there exist a real God, beside the one only true and living God?" Can it be possible, he continued, that "because many creatures do propagate their species, and communicate their own specific natures; therefore the infinite God must be supposed to have a power in like manner to propagate his species? . . . The reasoning appears to me but little short of blasphemy."[51]

In the mid-nineteenth century, the Oneida Community's blend of perfectionist theology and open marriage did little to enhance the doctrinal reputation of the first. But the most pervasive shifts in thinking about humanity's divine potential were found in the Unitarian movement. Born of an antipathy to Calvinist emphasis on human depravity, Unitarianism quickly slid to the opposite extreme. If Universalism held that God was too good to damn humans, Thomas Starr King said only half-jokingly, Unitarians thought humans were too good to be damned.[52] William Ellery Channing, the movement's dominant minister, turned "Humanity's Likeness to God" into one of its central tenets. "Likeness to God is a good so unutterably surpassing all other good," he wrote two years before Mormonism's founding, "that whoever admits it as attainable, must acknowledge it to be the chief aim of life, . . . the highest and happiest office of religion." Where he broke with earlier Christians was in the literalism of this ideal. "It may be said, that there is danger from too literal an interpretation, that God is an unapproachable being," he noted. But he insisted on an actual, "like nature" to the Divine. "God does not sustain a figurative resemblance to man. It is the resemblance of a parent to a child, the likeness of a kindred nature."[53]

Later in the century, George MacDonald (who influenced C. S. Lewis's pronouncements on this and other subjects) noted some Christians were uncomfortable with his own vocabulary of perfectionism, feeling that "I do not want to be perfect; I am content to be saved." But "they little think," he wrote, "that without perfection there is no salvation—that perfection is salvation: they are one."[54] Lewis's version was without theological explication. He simply asked, "Is it so very difficult to believe that the travail of all creation which God Himself descended to share, at its most intense, may be necessary in the process of turning finite creatures (with free wills) into—well, into Gods."[55] In the later twentieth century, the title of an article in *Christianity Today* captured the fractious history of the doctrine: "How the Strange Yet Familiar Doctrine of Theosis Can Reinvigorate the Christian Life."[56] In it, the author notes that "In the ancient Hellenistic world in which the church was born, divinization in some form or another was a common way of describing humanity's ultimate goal." Sounding more like Wesley than Plato, he encouraged divinization, "a project of becoming like God," "conformity to Christ at every point," and urged that "salvation [be] viewed in terms of deification."

MORMON THEOSIS

Q. Are there more Gods than one?

A. Yes, many. 1 Cor. 8: 5. Repeat the passage.

"There be that are called gods, whether in heaven or on earth (as there be gods many, and lords many)."

Q. Must we worship more than one God?

A. No. To us there is but one God, the Father of mankind, and the Creator of the earth. 1 Cor. 8: 6. Matt. 4:10.

Repeat the passages.

"But to us there is but one God, the Father, of whom are all things."[57]

When Joseph Smith introduced the concept of theosis or deification in the first years of Mormonism, he did so in the context of a radically different conception of God, humans, and the universe than was typical in Christian thought. And the contours of deification would differ accordingly. In Joseph Smith's thought, humans are inherently more godlike, God is more anthropomorphic, and God's purposes are more oriented toward human theosis than is the case with earlier Christian conceptions. That explains why, rather than assert solidarity with Methodist conceptions of perfectionism, for instance, Mormons distanced themselves from it. "We have often heard individuals, who advocate the Arminian doctrine, talking about perfection," wrote an ungenerous LDS editorialist in a twice-published essay, "when indeed, they are not only ignorant of the principle, but destitute of the necessary qualifications."[58] In any case, while early Methodists were prone to "exhort believers to go on to perfection," by the rise of Mormonism they were preaching far less on the subject; it was already coming to mean much less "to most American Methodists," notes one historian of the movement, "than it had to Wesley."[59]

For the Babylonians and Plato, Origen and the Cambridge Platonists, human existence was believed to be traceable to an origin before temporal creation. And humanity's primordial roots in a heavenly home were taken to intimate an eventual return to a heavenly fullness of glory as a generously conveyed birthright. The same linkage may have been at work in early Mormon development of the idea of theosis, for both pre-existence and theosis took initial shape in the earliest years of the church, and derived from the same texts. The first intimations of theosis were present in the Enoch prophecy Smith produced in 1830. After learning that God "made the world, and men before they were [in the flesh]," Enoch proclaims to God, "Thou hast made me, and given me a right to thy throne."[60] The juxtaposition of pre-existence with theosis is then followed by a magnificent, if harrowing, *imitatio dei*—Enoch experiences his own moment of infinite, godly compassion and suffering.

In July 1832, the church published a revelation of Smith in which he uses the language of theosis more explicitly. Those saved in the highest kingdom of glory, he says, will be "gods, even the sons of God."[61] Months later, Smith received a revelation that declared "the saints shall be filled with his glory, and receive their inheritance and be made equal with him."[62] A few years later (1836), future Church President Lorenzo Snow was promised in what he took to be a "dark parable" expressed through a blessing by Joseph Smith Sr. that he "would become as great as you can possibly wish—EVEN AS GREAT AS GOD." It was four years before, through what he called an "extraordinary manifestation," he saw "with wonder and astonishment, the pathway of God and man," learning that "As God now is, man may be."[63]

Meanwhile, the published references to becoming gods and to equality with Christ were too much for the anti-Mormon crusader editor La Roy Sunderland, who produced in 1838 a multi-part attack on the faith in his *Zion's Watchman*. Parley Pratt responded to the criticisms with his own pamphlet. Pratt could easily have made recourse to the language of biblical scripture, since Christians found nothing offensive in Paul's reference to "joint-heirship" in his epistle to the Romans. Pratt ignored the innocuous readings of precedent and pushed possible metaphor into a literal reference to theosis. Indeed, he proclaimed, the saved will "have the same knowledge that God has, [and] they will have the same power. . . . Hence the propriety of calling them 'Gods, even the sons of God.' " Other Christians may call this blasphemy, Pratt suggested, yet he would not retreat from "this doctrine of *equality*."[64] Five years before, two revelations had referred to human pre-existence in terms of emanation.[65] Pratt now invokes that concept to link premortality in God's presence to eventual divinization: "The redeemed . . . return to the fountain, and become part of the great all, from which they emanated."[66]

These affirmations of a robust Mormon version of theosis were the first to appear in print, a full six years before the doctrine's elaboration in Smith's King Follett Discourse. While Pratt's language resonates with Neoplatonism, it is most notable for its intimations of a divine origin that betokens a divine future. As Pratt memorably captures the essential feature of this anthropology, "God, angels and men are all of one species,"[67] thus diminishing the ontological distinction between the human and the divine. Pratt was quick to develop the seeds of this theosis further than Smith's first public teachings on the subject, into the planet-peopling, world-shaping, system-building model of deification known to nineteenth-century

Mormonism. It is important, however, to sort out just what it means in Mormon thought to become "gods, even the sons of God."

In explaining the divine motives behind creation, the Platonic dialogue *Timaeus* envisions a deity of particular generosity. "He who framed this whole universe . . . was good, and one who is good can never become jealous of anything. And so, being free of jealousy, he wanted everything to become as much like himself as was possible."[68] Such a formulation is similar in spirit to the Mormon conception of theosis. However, it raises two questions. First, what is God—the ultimate goal of human striving and emulation—"*like*"; and to return to the principle of Dionysius, what degree of "attaining of likeness to God . . . *is possible*?"

For Mormons, eternal life means not merely a life everlasting, but a destiny modeled on the existence, character, and nature of God himself. This follows from the fact that "eternal" or "endless" is God's name;[69] eternal life is therefore the life that God lives. Anything that Mormonism has to say about the nature of salvation, exaltation, or theosis must therefore be grounded and understood in the context of what Mormonism has to say about the divine nature, which they adore and seek to emulate. Mormons associate at least three conditions with the divine nature, and orient their own quest for salvation around them: (1) God is primarily a relational being—that is, his perfect happiness arises primarily from his loving relationship to other beings. (2) God is perfectly good and virtuous. His name, Elohim, means "Man of Holiness."[70] (3) God is a dynamic, infinitely wise, and infinitely creative being. As the Genesis creation story illustrates, his divine activity consists in converting an infinite universe of chaos into a system of physical and moral order.

Mormons believe that before the world's creation, when God himself entered into fatherly relationship with his spirit children, he had in mind their eventual emulation of his own fully perfected divine nature. His very work and glory, he declared to Moses, was "to bring to pass the immortality and eternal life."[71] And such eternal life would involve eternal relationships, a gradually acquired holiness of character, knowledge of all things, and co-participation in God's ongoing work of creation, with an eternity of progression, stage by stage, into more perfect harmony with the divine nature.

ETERNAL RELATIONSHIPS

"Divine families encircled by his fire and light are the very essence of life and eternal life; without them this earth—indeed this cosmos—will have missed the measure of its creation."[72]

The end of all Christian striving is heaven. But heaven has meant many things to many people, from the beatific vision, to pearly gates and streets of gold, to eternal rest. Generally, however, preachers and poets alike have been much more effective at portraying the torments of the damned than the felicities of the blessed. Dante's visualizations of the citizens of hell are unsurpassed. The lustful are wafted on eternal currents of passion, while the vengeful gnaw on the skulls of those who betrayed them. Heaven, by contrast, he lamely describes an "exalted Light," "three circles" of "three different colors," like a "rainbow is [reflected] by rainbow" before lamenting "how incomplete is speech, how weak, when set against my thought."[73]

Dante, like most poets and mystics before and since, envisioned a theocentric heaven. God's presence makes heaven the consummate end of all human striving; full and perfect communion with God is the essence of heavenly rapture. Even Jonathan Edwards sounded the mystic when he described heaven: "When they see God so glorious, and at the same time see how greatly this God loves them, what delight will it not cause in the soul! Love desires union. They shall therefore see this glorious God united to them, and see themselves united to him."[74]

The century after Edwards, however, saw a growing domestication of heavenly society, one consequence of "the feminization of American culture" that Ann Douglas views as a central dynamic in the Victorian era. In Congregationalist minister George Cheever's version, heaven "is not the dim incomprehensibility of omnipresence merely, but a place for our abode, as determinate as place is for us now, and with as intimate a home circle, as the dearest fireside on this earth can have."[75] Unitarians like Andrew Peabody, F. W. P. Greenwood, Henry Ware, Charles Follen, and William Channing were particularly prone to preach "that heavenly life satisfied the human heart as presently constituted, that it offered homes restored, families regathered, and friends reunited."[76]

The massive casualties of the American Civil War only lent impetus to an already vast literature of consolation, spurring bestsellers like Elizabeth Stuart Phelps's *Gates Ajar* (1868), whose protagonist Mary loses her brother in that conflict. Refusing to believe that all mortal loss is swallowed up in Christ, Phelps took seriously the sentimental poetic protest, "O mother, mother, what is heaven? O mother what is Hell? To be with Wilhelm—that's my Heaven, Without him, that's my Hell."[77] Accordingly, *The Gates Ajar* is a self-conscious dismantling of an orthodox heaven, a "shockingly heterodox" treatise masquerading as sentimental fiction. Mary learns from a wise aunt that while conventional clergy like the pompous Deacon Quirk may preach otherwise, the beloved dead "will meet you at the door in this other home." There we will see the smiles and clasp the hands of family, in a "very material kind of heaven." Dismissing even the learned Dr. Bland's abstractions and "glittering generalities" ("Heaven is an eternal state, . . . a state of holiness" where "we shall study the character of God"), Aunt Winifred describes a familiar, domestic setting where relatives laugh and joke, work and worry, and enjoy "life and activity."[78] Sequels to the bestseller added family pets to the heavenly hearth.[79]

Such a reconstructed heaven becomes commonplace in the literature of late Victorian England and America.[80] Mormonism participated in the first wave of this new orientation, of a domestic rather than a theocentric heaven, but with an elaborate underlying theology. In the Mormon view, God is first and foremost a relational being, and the condition toward which all righteous endeavor leads is one of participation in heavenly relationships that are eternal. *He* chose to "set his heart" upon the human family. God's title as Father is universally acknowledged throughout the Judeo-Christian traditions. For Mormons, the relationship is literal; God is (along with a Heavenly Mother) construed as the begetter (or adoptive parent in one reading of Smith's earlier view) of the human soul, along with that of the Christ. Jesus is the firstborn in the world of spirits, and thus elder brother as well as savior to the human family.

In this view, the divine order is one of extended filiation, loving relationships that extend in every direction. Heaven is not merely an abode in God's presence; it is a continuation and sacralization of human relationships in an eternal sphere—but those human relationships are rooted in an even older order. The central fact of our existence common to both Smith's original teachings and subsequent developments is the reality of human participation in a pre-mortal, heavenly family.

Smith said little of the pre-mortal organization of human spirits, but the gist of a visionary conversation Young described having with Smith accords with the fragments in the historical record. "The brethren have a great anxiety to understand the law of adoption or sealing principles; and if you have a word of counsel for me I should be glad to receive it," Young recalled asking the Mormon prophet in his vision. Smith replied that the people

> were organized by our Father in Heaven before they came into the world. Our Father in Heaven organized the human family but they are all disorganized and in grate confusion. Joseph then showed me the pattern, how they were in the beginning. This I cannot describe but I saw it, and saw where the Priesthood had been taken from the earth and how it must be joined together, so that there would be a perfect chain from Father Adam to his latest posterity.[81]

Smith's construction of heaven was based on his conviction that earthly forms of association—friendship and family—are but carryovers from an eternal past, as well as portents of an eternal future. They are the product, not the source, of an eternal template, and their continuation in heaven therefore represents the eternalizing of pre-existent forms. "The earthly is the image of the Heavenly," he said.[82] By which he meant, "that which is earthly conform[s] to that which is heavenly," or "that which is temporal [is] in the likeness of that which is spiritual," not the other way around.[83] This may have been what Young referred to a few years later, preaching that "all things were created spiritual, then temporal," where they are "disorganized and wait for a *reorganization*."[84] Orson Spencer, whose theology Young considered authoritative, wrote that the family order instituted by God with the patriarchs "was the order observed among celestial beings, in the celestial world. . . . When God sets up any portion of his kingdom upon the earth, it is patterned after his own order in the Heavens. When he gives to men a pattern of family organization on earth, that pattern will be just like his own family organization in the heavens. The family of Abraham was a transcript of a celestial pattern."[85]

John Taylor believed the organization specific to each individual, not just the general template, was foreordained. Under his editorial direction, an article addressed to the women of the church declared, "thou made a covenant with . . . two others, male and female spirits, that thou wouldst come and take a tabernacle through their linage, and become one of their offspring. You also chose a kindred spirit whom you loved in the spirit world . . . to be your . . . husband, and protection on earth."[86] Young's counselor confirmed the pattern, teaching that we are born of parents "through whom we doubtless chose to come before we were born into this world."[87] Though going further than Smith, these views were but elaboration of what he had publicly affirmed in 1839, declaring that "The Father called all spirits before him at the creation of Man & *organized* them," with Adam as "the head,"—using the word *organization* as he did in the Abrahamic revelation, to signify a social ordering.[88] In 1843, Smith again sermonized on the "organization of spirits" in the pre-mortal world, but details are lacking.[89] In any case, Smith's teachings and the 1847 vision had profound impact on Young, who made adoption theology the nucleus of his gospel understanding. In this grand scheme, for the organization limned in the pre-existence to be rendered eternal, spirits must be embodied, families formed, and those relations solemnized in temple rituals through priesthood power to seal and bind. Or as Smith said, it is in this life that God "organiz[es] us to prepare us for the Eternal world."[90]

If one life event was seminal in the shaping of Smith's cosmic vision of the family, it was the boyhood loss of his idol, elder brother Alvin. As he wrote a full two decades later, "There is a thought more dreadful than that of total annihilation That is the thought that we shall never again meet with those we loved here on earth."[91] Elsewhere he remarked that "If I had no expectation of seeing my mother Brother & Sisters & friends again my heart would burst in a moment."[92] The theme was a constant one in his life. "Let me be resurrected with the saints, whether to heaven or hell or any other good place . . . what do we care if the society is good?"[93] The consolidation of his own family into an eternal order was both the catalyst for his grand project and a microcosm of its fulfillment.

Only weeks before Alvin's 1823 death, Smith had received his first visitation from the angel Moroni. Mormons herald the occasion as the effective annunciation for the Book of Mormon, which Moroni first described on this occasion. But of more immediate importance to Smith, though cryptic and years in coming to fruition, were the words the messenger quoted from the Old Testament prophet Malachi. "Behold, I will reveal unto you the Priesthood, by the hand of Elijah the prophet, before the great and dreadful day of the Lord. . . . And he shall plant in the hearts of the children the promises made to the fathers, and the hearts of the children shall turn to their fathers. If it were not so, the whole earth would be utterly wasted at his coming."[94]

The prophecy Moroni had quoted contained both a dire warning and a promised blessing. The curse upon the wicked was that they would have neither "root nor branch"—"What better way to say they would be left without connection to their ancestors or to their descendants," notes one historian.[95] And the promise to come was of a power associated with Elijah, the prophet who never tasted of death and who thus bridges the realms of the living and the dead. This power associated with him suggested a more durable connection of those alive (the children) to those departed (the fathers).

As such a possibility took shape in Smith's mind over subsequent years, it was evident that two separate ideas were involved in the preservation of kinship across the veil of death. First was the necessity for those who had died outside gospel covenants to have access to those truths in the realm of the departed. As we saw above, Smith's 1836 vision of his brother in the Celestial Kingdom, followed by the unfolding theology of vicarious salvation, gave him assurance that the great gulf separating Lazarus from the rich man (Luke 16:26) would not divide his own family. The second need was for a binding power that would actually perpetuate kinship in the life to come, making of earthly associations something eternally durable. By 1842, Smith had come to see the key to both was to be found in the intergenerational binding power associated with this prophet Elijah, as Moroni had intimated those many years previous.

Smith declared this link between vicarious salvation and the preservation of family relationships in an 1842 epistle. Fully divining the meaning of Malachi's prophecy almost two decades after he first heard it, he wrote, "it is sufficient to know, in this case, that the earth will be smitten with a curse unless there is a welding link of some kind or other between the fathers and the children, upon some subject or other—and behold what is that subject? It is the baptism for the dead."[96]

Baptism itself does not form us into families, of course; family sealings were yet to come. But baptism of deceased ancestors unites them to the same family of Christ to which believers belong, erasing a major transgenerational gulf.

The priesthood authority "to seal on earth and on heaven" was necessary both to enable a wider humanity to be adopted into Christ's covenantal family and to preclude the threatened curse of family dissolution across the generations. The term "seal" did double duty, reflecting both the traditional Christian meaning of assured salvation and the now common Mormon usage of binding individuals together.[97] The conflation of meanings was no coincidence; Smith's salvational vision emphasized the inseparability of the two concepts. Baptism for the dead was a concrete instance of this fact: the same ordinance that connects the deceased to Christ by baptismal adoption is itself integrally related to the welding together of "children" to "fathers." This is so because, in Mormon thought, there is only one Heavenly Family, and Christ is its head. To take his name upon oneself through baptism is at the same time to become numbered as his progeny. The ultimate end of those sealing and binding powers is "a whole and complete and perfect union, and welding together of dispensations, and keys, and powers, and glories."[98]

The roots of this doctrine were in a conception of pre-mortal life that made of humans primordial members of God's family, and of earth life the means for that family to be fully eternalized; the result was a conception of the eternal family as one that extended temporally in both directions and became a literal enactment and expansion of belief in God's literal fatherhood of the human family. Theologians have recurrently warned against an all too human tendency to project merely earthly paradigms upon an eternal world. Renée Haynes has put the case most simply: "The more detailed pictures of life after death are, the less acceptable they seem to be."[99] Or as a recent Catholic scholar writes, in criticizing another writer, "he makes the boundary between heaven and earth much too permeable. So much so that here, for example, he assumes . . . that we will have bodily needs, like thirst, in heaven."[100] A Mormon prophet, by contrast, declared that "I picture heaven to be a continuation of the ideal home."[101]

Young's counselor Jedediah Grant gave a detailed account of family organization as it exists in the hereafter, as reported at Grant's funeral by his fellow apostle Heber C. Kimball.

[Grant] said to me, brother Heber, I have been into the spirit world two nights in succession, and, of all the dreads that ever came across me, the worst was to have to again return to my body, though I had to do it. But O, says he, the order and government that were there! When in the spirit world, I saw the order of righteous men and women; beheld them organized in their several grades, and there appeared to be no obstruction to my vision; I could see every man and woman in their grade and order. I looked to see whether there was any disorder there, but there was none; neither could I see any death nor any darkness, disorder or confusion. He said that the people he there saw were organized in family capacities; and when he looked at them he saw grade after grade, and all were organized and in perfect harmony. He would mention one item after another and say, "Why, it is just as brother Brigham says it is."[102]

The consolidation of these relationships represents what Smith called "the order and organization of the Spirits of the just made perfect."[103] As those words suggest, the lines separating friends and kin blur in Smith's conception of a heavenly network of loved ones. "Thou shalt have all of thy friends" in the Celestial World, Smith promised one woman, contingent on her faithfulness.[104] It is in this expansive sense of human connectivity that his claim must be understood, that "friendship is the grand fundamental principle of Mormonism."[105] As he said in April 1843, "the same sociality which exists among us here will exist among us there, only it will be coupled with eternal glory, which glory we do not now enjoy."[106] Within this larger context of the "everlasting covenant," Smith decreed a special ritual of greeting practiced by those in the School of the Prophets. Members received one another "to fellowship in a determination that is fixed, immovable, and unchangeable, to be your friend and brother through the grace of God in the bonds of love, . . . forever and ever."[107] Or as Brigham Young commented, the dead "are [in the spirit world] together, and . . . associate together, and collect together in clans and in societies as they do here."[108] As Pratt wrote the year after Smith's death, in "the celestial glory," one is restored to an association with "his family, friends, and kindred," as part of "the chain which connects the great and royal family of heaven and earth, in one eternal bond of kindred affection, and association."[109]

This doctrine radically concretized the construction of Mormon salvation as a communal enterprise. Attending to the spiritual needs of others both living and dead became more than a matter of charity, and more than a precondition for personal blessedness. It became the substance and hope of that blessedness. And creating this eternal community became the driving preoccupation of the church. "It is necessary to have a regular chain clear back to Adam, and if we have commenced it and if we are faithful we shall accomplish it."[110] This was an insistent theme with Young. There "must be a connection from Adam to the last man born of woman the same as in the priesthood in eternity, like Nephi's iron rod. If you let go 'tis the same as though the rod was taken away. If men are not saved together they cannot be saved at all."[111] And again, "as soon as the time comes I shall form a chain to Father Adam. That is the business of this church."[112]

The precise manner in which these celestial lineages are constituted has changed with time and evolving understanding of the nature of the "Heavenly Family."[113] In nineteenth-century Mormonism, the key concept in this regard was adoption. The language of adoption appears in the New Testament, where baptism is the symbol of the New Covenant; as circumcision emphasized procreation and blood filiation as the mechanism of chosen status, baptism signified the means by which a convert was buried and reborn—that is, adopted, into God's family—in symbolic membership or in expectation of a closer spiritual kinship yet future.[114] Mormons embraced the ordinance, its symbolism, and its indispensability, like most other Christians. Parley Pratt first emphasized adoption theology as comprising the "laws and ordinances"— especially baptism—that qualified one for membership in the Kingdom of God. "When we speak of the kingdom of God," he clarified in 1837, "we wish to be understood as speaking of his organized government on earth."[115] But consistent with New Testament usage, Pratt emphasized that this adoption also fully qualified one to be "son" of God. He was here doubtless influenced by his mentor Alexander Campbell, who had described baptism as the means by which the adopted were "born into the Divine family, enrolled in Heaven."[116]

This was the trajectory that Joseph Smith—and later Brigham Young—developed consistently. By 1840, the editor of the church newspaper had outlined the comprehensive picture: explicating Pauline teachings on the subject, he preached that before the world was even created, the Father chose his pre-mortal children unto himself, and put in place a plan whereby—through Jesus Christ—"mankind should become his sons through adoption."[117] The next year, Smith was referring to Abraham as the line through which the covenant of adoption passed, and the Latter-day Saints as those who would possess the priesthood, enabling them to administer this adoption theology—that is, the laws and ordinances of the gospel—to the rest of the human family in extension of Christ's mission.[118] Smith used the word sparingly, but others employed adoption with greater frequency in ensuing years, taking the fatherhood of God, and the joint-heirship with Christ alluded to by Paul,[119] to be literal truths. In this view, humans proceed from the pre-existence as God's progeny, progressing in accordance with what Pratt called the "doctrine of equality," to become fully and "conjointly with Christ the sons of God."[120]

Soon LDS writers were referring to their vision of "a society of men and women, that had as it were, . . . been born by the great law of adoption into the family of Heaven."[121] Adoption would suggest the lack of an inherent connection to God as Father, but the LDS editor Thomas Ward clarified that adoption implied not the creation but the restoration of a "natural and legitimate claim of heirship" lost through transgression. By sin we cut ourselves off from our celestial inheritance. Compliance with gospel laws and ordinances, he wrote, gives us our claim to become sons of God, "children beloved, approved, and whose claims to the heritage and glory of their parent none can dispute."[122]

As one follower wrote (probably John Taylor), there was "a depth, a dignity, and glory connected with this subject that very few have any idea of," and a literal purport to this "adoption of sons" that radically distinguished it from what "professing Christians" meant by becoming "sons of God."[123] Specifically, it meant an everlasting destiny "with [one's] family, friends, and kindred, as one of the necessary links of the chain which connects the great and royal family of heaven and earth, in one eternal bond of kindred affection and association."[124] Primary in this web of eternal relationships that Joseph Smith envisioned was marriage.

MARRIAGE

The theology taught in the seminaries and popular belief of the masses are seldom fully in sync. From the Catholic Rite of Marriage to the Book of Common Prayer, the language of marriage ceremonies affirms the bond's cessation upon the death of one of the married. Churchmen have found little room to challenge the plain reading of Matthew 22:30, wherein Jesus says "in the resurrection they neither marry nor are given in marriage." "Idiots!" fumes one anonymous ancient commentator at the Sadducees for even asking the question. For the purpose of marriage is reproduction, he reasons. "Remove the utility of being born and the reason for marriage" disappears. When we live chastely, by contrast, we imitate the angels rather than animals.[125] Only those with "crude, fleshly ideas about the state of humanity after the resurrection" would ask such a question, agreed Augustine.[126] Clement of Alexandria similarly associated marriage with both procreation and physical desire; in heaven, the need for the first and the burden of the second will be lifted, rendering marriage purposeless.[127] Irenaeus struggled to find theological room for a heavenly kingdom where "Christians could bear and raise children," but confined his hopes to the millennial kingdom of the Messiah.[128]

Two dissents were heard in the seventeenth and eighteenth centuries by those two religious radicals, John Milton and Emanuel Swedenborg. "Love not the Heavenly Spirits," asks Milton's Adam of the angel Raphael, "and how their love express they?" To which the angel replied, "Whatever pure thou in the body enjoy'st/ (And pure thou wert created) we enjoy / In eminence, and obstacle find none / Of membrane, joynt, or limb, exclusive barrs: / Easier then Air with Air, if Spirits embrace, / Total they mix, Union of Pure with Pure."[129] Swedenborg, the Swedish mystic, posed the question of whether married couples "will be parted after death or live together," and insisted by way of reply that "marital love persists. Two partners usually meet after death, recognize each other, associate again, and for a time live together. . . . If they can live together, they remain partners. . . . Partners enjoy an intercourse like that in the world, but pleasanter and more blessed; but without prolification [offspring]."¹³⁰

Swedenborg's views might have been heretical, but they have been seconded by countless men and women who feel in their own fierce love a power to survive the grave. The trope of lovers, both star-crossed and married, who expect to be reunited in heaven is a staple of Western literature, and always has been. From the dying words of Shakespeare's Cleopatra to the dead Antony, "Husband, I come"; to Dante Gabriel Rossetti's "Blessed Damozel," who observes "lovers newly met" in heaven and prays that she, too, may live there with her lover "as once on earth"; to Elizabeth Barrett Browning, who shall only love her Robert "better after death," the expectation is that a heaven without the beloved, no heaven is.¹³¹ So, too, in the personal letters of untold thousands, men and women both profess their faith in being "reunited never to part again."¹³² A plaque erected in 1636 in York Minster by Phineas Hodson to his departed wife expresses his hope "to be re-united with her in bliss who now hears not when he calls."¹³³

Some preachers of the nineteenth century made the same predictions. Taught one,

> Parents will there meet their children, and husbands their wives, after a long and painful separation. Brothers and sisters will rush into each other's arms and exclaim, "Have I found you at last? This is far unlike the parting hour when I closed your eyes, and far unlike the solitary evenings in which I have visited your grave and wept over your dust."—Those blessed spirits will enjoy the most perfect friendship, with every distrust and rival interest banished; each loving the other as his own soul, and not a thought nor a joy but what is common.¹³⁴

But with the possible exception of Swedenborgianism, Mormonism was alone among Christian faiths in explicitly exalting the marriage relation to a status reserved in the eternities for the inhabitants of the highest heaven. (Perhaps more striking yet, the church has countenanced the possibility of a married Christ.¹³⁵) In endowing marital love with the highest spiritual as well as eternal value, Joseph Smith followed in a line that stretches at least from Milton, through Swedenborg, and to the eighteenth-century poet-mystic William Blake.

Preachers of the era continued, somewhat tentatively, to revise the earlier hostility to a sociable heaven. True, acknowledged Henry Harbaugh in mid-century, there would be no need for reproduction and hence sexual intercourse in heaven. Still, "this does not, in the least, intimate that the affections begotten, and the friendships formed in this relation, shall not be renewed and continue in the heavenly social life."[136] Authors Colleen MacDannell and Bernard Lang survey an array of like-minded Protestant and Catholic writers of the period, from the Presbyterian John Kerr who affirmed the continuation of marriage's "pure and heavenly" dimension, to the bishop Wilhelm Schneider, who likewise covered his theological bases by limiting his view of heavenly union to a "pure and holy" relationship as chaste as "the ideal love of a betrothed couple before marriage."[137]

Mormons push the social heaven further than precedents, based on their view that the relationships we live by and cherish here on earth are modeled on a prior, divine pattern, a heavenly family. Baptism, living and vicarious, is the portal through which disciples gain admission into the family of Christ. And eternal marriage was developed by Joseph Smith as the ritual that established important lines of family associations in the hereafter. In 1835, just months after taking up temporary residence with Smith, W. W. Phelps made one of the first public references to the idea that marriage bonds could survive the grave. "New light is occasionally bursting in to our minds," he wrote in the *Messenger and Advocate,* which he edited. "We shall by and by learn that we were with God in another world, . . . that we came into this world and have our agency, in order that we may prepare ourselves for a kingdom of glory; become archangels, even the sons of God where the man is neither without the woman, nor the woman without the man in the Lord: A consummation of glory, and happiness, and perfection so greatly to be wished."[138] Pratt wrote that it was during his time with Smith in Philadelphia, in early 1840, that he first learned of "the heavenly order of eternity. It was at this time that I received from him the first idea of eternal family organization, and the eternal union of the sexes."[139]

One of the earliest attestations to Smith's conception of the eternity of the marriage relationship is a record of a marriage ceremony in which Smith was himself wed to a plural wife, Sarah Whitney, in 1842. According to the ceremony, the couple agreed to preserve themselves "for each other and from all others, and also throughout all eternity."[140] But the first records of Smith teaching the doctrine to an expanding circle do not appear until 1843, just months after his epistle on baptism for the dead. Benjamin Johnson recorded that in the spring, Smith visited him and "called me and my wife to come and sit down, for he wished to marry us according to the Law of the Lord. I thought it a joke, and said I should not marry my wife again, unless she courted me, for I did it all the first time. He chided my levity, told me he was in earnest, and so it proved, for we stood up and were sealed by the Holy Spirit of Promise."[141]

By May 1843, Smith was teaching that to obtain the highest heavenly glory, a person "must enter into this order of the priesthood" ["meaning the new and everlasting covenant of marriage," added Orson Pratt to the canonical version of the statement].[142] Now, Smith began performing temple rituals for several other couples, binding them together for time and eternity.[143] As with baptisms, the ritual was performed to eternally bind together, or "seal," companions both living and dead. The widower Joseph Kingsbury, for instance, was promised in the ceremony,

> thy Companion Caroline who is now dead thou shalt have in the first Reserection . . . and She Shall be thine and no one shall have power to take her from thee. And you both Shall be Crowned and enthroned to dwell together in a Kingdom in the Celestial Glory in the presents of God, And you Shall Enjoy each other's Society & Embraces . . . worlds without End.[144]

By the year after Smith's death, the church newspaper was trumpeting "the irresistible conclusion, that the love and union of a man and his wife should extend into, and even be more perfect in eternity."[145]

At this point it was becoming clear in Mormon theology that eternal marriage was not a requirement or blessing incidental to eternal life; rather it was the essential feature of that life. The celestial sociality of which Smith had spoken constituted the nature of heavenly existence. And as Orson Spencer taught in 1848, these "federative unions of the whole family of heaven and earth" could only be "organized according to the law of adoption."[146]

The bonds of marriage represented only one means of building links between individuals and families, and between the living and the dead across generations, but others were conceivable.[147] By 1845, Joseph Smith was dead, and John Bernheisel participated in another temple ritual that reflected an underlying principle and logic to adoptive sealings that was more rooted in priesthood lines of heirship than in simple familial connectedness: Bernheisel "gave himself to Prest. Joseph Smith (martyred) to become his son by the law of adoption and to become a legal heir to all the blessings bestowed upon Joseph Smith."[148] The apostles Paul and John considered their converts to be spiritual progeny, their "children." But in the Mormon conception, adoption was part of a larger and literal enterprise of family building organized along priestly lines that must reach back ultimately to the father of the human race himself. Samuel Brown has called this a "sacerdotal genealogy," meaning "a pedigree or family tree dependent upon priesthood rather than biology for its connections."[149]

With the death of Joseph Smith, Brigham Young inherited the leadership, but not the title of prophet.[150] His principal task was the implementation of Smith's theology, and its expansion and adaptation to a radically different environment and challenges. And the most immediate challenge was physical survival. In this regard, Smith's adoption theology revealed its practical dimensions. In the Nauvoo

Temple, couples continued to be sealed to church leaders and their wives as their adoptive children. In addition to their eternal significance, these sealings established a web of reciprocal responsibilities between the adoptive parents and children; some of the children even took the last names of their parents. During the winter of 1846–47, Young and the other apostles in Winter Quarters organized the Mormon emigration along the theological principle of adoption, with the emigration divided into two adoptive families, those of Brigham Young and of Heber Kimball. In the absence of a temple, church members organized themselves into family networks around prominent leaders. Not all adoptions were formalized by temple ritual, but the temple theology of adoption was the basis for these expanding family networks.

After settlement in Utah, such associations continued to receive temple sanction, defended by Young. "It is the privilege of a man who wishes to be sealed, to be sealed to who he chooses.... For instance, a man says, 'I want to be sealed to you Brigham Young,' if he is a good man and obeys my council that proves him a good man, I have no right to reject him or thousands."[151]

We saw that Joseph Smith, at least in Young's description of a vision, characterized the pre-mortal world as one in which a family organization prevailed, and may have served as a template for mortality. In Smith's conception, these family structures were organized along priesthood lines, in a "patriarchal" order that merged the domestic and the priestly, even as it interwove the mortal and the heavenly. So adoption begins with one's adoption into the family and Kingdom of Christ. Through baptism for the dead (and posthumous sealings of couples and families) individuals qualify ancestors to unite in that same group, joining them to Christ and themselves. Finally, the family begun on earth acquires both the bonds of permanence, solidifying pre-existence associations into eternity, and priestly power, forging the power to increase and extend family members into that same eternal future. In Pratt's poetic treatment, earth was the fulcrum where pre-mortal associations and eternal organization met:

"To My Wife"[-es]
I know ye now; and knowing can but love.
O my father in Heaven! Thine they were,
And Thou gavest them to me—Precious gifts!
Endear'd by long acquaintance in the heavens ...
Secur'd
By the spirit and power of Elijah ...
... Enliven'd by the hope
Of endless union ...

And earthly posterity was a shadow of a heavenly posterity to come:

> There dwell my family,—my bosom friends,—
> The precious lambs of my Redeemer,—my
> Best of Heaven's gifts to man,—my germs of
> Life and immortality,—my hope of Heaven,—
> My principality on earth began,—
> My kingdom in embryo . . .
> My kindred spirits from worlds celestial!
> Offsprings of Deity!¹⁵²

Joseph Smith and Brigham Young envisioned the celestial world as one character-ized by the continuance of relationships based on marital love, profound friend-ship, and extended kinships. Only in the context of such enthusiasm for multiple ties and connections that unite individuals and families alike does Mormonism's most innovative social and theological experiment make sense. But the institu-tion would continue to evolve, both socially and theologically, under subsequent leaders.

PLURAL MARRIAGE

No Mormon doctrine has been subject to more opacity, controversy, and revision than the doctrine of plural marriage. No one disputes that polygyny was practiced by Old Testament figures, most notably Abraham, Jacob, David, and Solomon, and well over a dozen others mentioned by name. The Deuteronomic law acknowledges the practice (21:15–17), and Jewish understanding is that "polygamy was theoreti-cally still possible, though discouraged" and seldom practiced by the Rabbinic Era (200–500 CE).¹⁵³ It met with formal prohibition by the eleventh century. Luther's attitude toward polygamy was that, for a Christian, there was "no necessity for it, no benefit for it, and no special word of God commanding it."¹⁵⁴ However, he acknowl-edged that he could not forbid what was not contradicted by scripture and granted Landgrave Phillip of Hesse a dispensation to marry a second wife.

The next century, the poet John Milton wrote the most extensive apologies for polygamy in the English language up to that time, included in his work *Treatise on Christian Doctrine*, first published in English in 1825. After discussing extensive Old Testament examples, he concludes, "Let therefore the rule received among theolo-gians have the same weight here as in other cases: 'The practice of the saints is the best interpretation of the commandments.'"¹⁵⁵ In subsequent centuries, other spo-radic defenses emerged, including those of the Methodist Martin Madan, who in

the 1700s defended plural marriage on several grounds. It was not proscribed biblically, and, as he quoted theologian Bishop Gilbert Burnet, "what God made necessary in some cases [of the Mosaic Law] to any degree, can in no case be sinful in
itself."[156] In addition, he reasoned, "many Gentiles and Turks . . . might come over to
the Christian faith if polygamy were not prohibited among us."[157] His co-religionist
(and brother-in-law of John Wesley) Reverend Westley Hall defended the principle
on the grounds of natural inclination. He preached the doctrine in at least one
sermon—and practiced what he preached.[158] To the Christian world as a whole, a
general prohibition is suggested by Paul's admonition to Timothy that bishops and
deacons should be the husband of one wife.[159] The Catholic Church considers that
the practice "is not in accord with the moral law."[160] Like stoning and pork prohibitions, Old Testament polygamy is seen by many Christians as pertaining to a pre-
Christian dispensation only.

Because plural marriage was never publicly taught (or acknowledged) by Joseph
Smith, the origins of the practice and theology behind it are shrouded in darkness.
Smith believed God had directed him to initiate the practice. But what rationale did
Smith have in mind for God's command that he defy convention, reputation, and
his own conscience? In the 1842 Sarah Whitney marriage ceremony, the authority
of "holy progenitors" like Melchizedek and Jethro was invoked, based on "revelation
and commandment," to "concentrate" in the couple and their posterity holy
"powers."[161] The only canonized revelation on the subject (1843) came in response to
Smith's questions about the practice of Abraham and other Old Testament characters of taking plural wives, presumably raised at the time he was "translating" the
Bible beginning in 1830.[162] Helen Mar Whitney, one of his wives, wrote that the
doctrine was revealed to him in 1831,[163] and it was a few years thereafter that he entered into relationship with his first alleged plural wife, Fanny Alger (though no
record of an actual ritual has appeared).

Whitney traced his first public intimations on the subject to an 1841 address in
which he preached "on the restoration of all things, and said that as it was anciently
with Abraham, Isaac, and Jacob, so it would be again." Seeing the shock and "astonishment" of his wife and others, he found it necessary to console them, saying "the
time of which he had spoken might be further off than he anticipated."[164] The general practice was indeed a few years removed, but Smith had already contracted marriages to Lucinda Harris in 1838 and several others followed in the early 1840s. Obviously sensitive to the explosive reception the teaching would elicit, Smith was also
aware of the potential for abuse by even the faithful. "This order would damn more
than it would save, because it was a holy principle that could not be trifled with," he
was remembered to have said.[165] He clearly believed instituting the practice was
imperative.[166]

Rationales given after the fact run a wide gamut: frequent invocations of an Abrahamic test, polygamy's touted benefits as a mechanism of sexual control, and an expedient for quickly amassing a "righteous seed" color the commandment as a temporary suspension of conventional moral norms or as an improvement over prevailing societal arrangements. But in the context of Smith's social heaven and the Pratts' cosmic system-building, plurality of wives clearly presupposed an eternal arrangement. As a consequence, Mormon understanding and public defense of the principle alike alternated between sociological and theological explanations. The earliest Mormon text on plural marriage comes from the Book of Mormon and is strongly condemnatory. In that scripture, God declares that "there shall not any man among you have save it be one wife; and concubines he shall have none," then adds the qualifier, "if I will, saith the Lord of Hosts, raise up seed unto me, I will command my people; otherwise they shall hearken unto these things [i.e., monogamy]."[167] Two important caveats emerge from this prohibition. The need to "raise righteous seed" may justify the practice, and a heavenly mandate can override the scriptural ban.

When Smith first explicated the principle in his 1843 revelation, he invoked the language of righteous seed (132:63), but the multiplication of Mormon progeny was not a consequence in his case. Of his thirty or so alleged plural wives, none is known definitely to have borne him a child, though reports existed. Still, as we saw, family relationships, construed as an almost infinitely expansive sociality, were at the heart of Smith's cosmic vision. From its inception, polygamy was referred to as "doing the works of Abraham," and Smith clearly understood the practice as involving the same promises that were associated with Abraham: a righteous, numerous, and blessed posterity, and special status as a conduit of God's blessings to those multitudes. Smith and, later, Young saw themselves in the tradition of the biblical patriarchs, heads of celestial tribal dynasties, whose blessedness would extend to those who came within their orbit of kinship (the 1843 revelation had even indicated that Smith was "of Abraham"). As Smith elaborated, "A measure of this sealing is to confirm upon their head . . . the doctrine of election or the covenant with Abraham—which when a Father & mother of a family have entered into[,] their children who have not transgressed are secured by the seal wherewith the Parents have been sealed. And this is the Oath of God unto our Father Abraham and this doctrine shall stand forever."[168]

At times Smith's remarks reveal a kind of voracious appetite to expand his relations exponentially, far beyond his immediate family: "If you have power to seal on earth & in heaven then we should be Crafty, the first thing you do go & seal on earth your sons & daughters unto yourself, & yourself unto your fathers in eternal glory, & go ahead and not go back, but use a little Craftiness & seal all you can. . . . I will walk through the gate of heaven and Claim what I seal & those that follow me and my council."[169] At least some of his marriages were almost certainly seen by him as something more like dynastic alliances than procreative opportunities. (Many of his sealings apparently involved no sexual relations.[170]) As one of Smith's wives recalled, her father, Heber C. Kimball, consented to his daughter's marriage because of his "great desire to be connected with the Prophet Joseph."[171]

Smith's motivation or understanding was clearly moving in the direction of eternalizing human bonds of affection and kinship in multiple levels and directions. This is what many scholars of Mormon polygamy increasingly depict, confirming George Q. Cannon's vision of the practice as constituting a "new order of society"; writers emphasize the "ties of loyalty," the "dynastic" system it generated, the female priestly "empowerment" that resulted, and other nonsexual and nonmarital dimensions in plumbing the principle's underlying philosophy.[172] In Samuel Brown's words, the practice expanded "a sacerdotal genealogy, . . . strenuously protested the shrinking nucleus of the Victorian family, and attempted to overcome the social alienation of death."[173] The great consummation toward which all Saints strove was to employ the powers of the temple to "gather together their living relatives," along with "all our Progenitors who are dead" and unite them in "the chain that binds the hearts of the fathers to the Children, & the Children to the Fathers which fulfills the mission of Elijah."[174]

In the aftermath of Joseph Smith's martyrdom and the Saints' exile from Illinois, Brigham Young quickly expanded plural marriage from an esoteric teaching shared with Smith's intimates to a more general practice.[175] Obviously, polygamous Mormons had to reconceptualize nineteenth-century notions of romantic love and companionate marriage if they were to succeed in these unconventional arrangements. The rationale developed accordingly, shaped in large measure by an emphasis on public justification. In 1852, Young assigned Orson Pratt to publicly announce and defend the principle. In his 29 August sermon from the Tabernacle, effectively an official manifesto, he set forth "some of the causes why the Almighty has revealed such a doctrine." There were three principal justifications. First, Pratt argued, like the mathematician he was, a plurality of wives facilitated the Abrahamic promise of a posterity literally as numerous as the sand upon the seashore.

Second, he employed a rather Pauline justification. The New Testament apostle had considered divinely authorized marriage a condition preferable to burning in lust. With similar reasoning, Pratt said that given the "fallen nature" men have "to grapple with, . . . a plurality of wives" is an inspired preventative against the "whoredom, adultery, and fornication" plaguing the non-Mormon world. This became a favorite defense, since it turned polygamy into a remedy rather than a problem.

Finally, he advanced the "righteous seed" rationale; given the number of righteous spirits God has held in reserve to send to earth, the Saints needed to maximize the opportunities for those spirits to "be raised up among the righteous."[176] Plural marriage suggested just such an expanded pool of available tabernacles. A variant of this "righteous seed" explanation persists to this day in Mormon ways of validating the nineteenth-century practice and its cost. A substantial number of Mormons born into the church hail from polygamous backgrounds, members are frequently reminded.[177]

To many Saints, and to any familiar with the vast progeny of a Young or a Pratt or a Kimball (about 60, 34, and 65 children, respectively), a primary purpose of polygamy seemed to be production of a *numerous* righteous seed in the here and now. As the church newspaper declared, "polygamy . . . was the most effectual means of rapidly multiplying a righteous seed upon the earth."[178] And indeed, the system did involve proportionately more women in marriage than was the norm. In a study of one nineteenth-century Mormon community, in the frontier period 99 percent of Mormon women who resided in Manti eventually married while only 92 to 93 percent of their U.S. peers did.[179] Even so, the net effect of polygamy on Utah's birthrate was not dramatically higher as a consequence. More frequently invoked as explanation, however, was the notion of a righteous, rather than a numerous, seed. As Young exhorted the men, "if the Latter-day Saints wish to have more wives than one to live holy, and raise up Holy Seed unto the Lord, let them enjoy that privilege."[180] In other words, since only the most worthy males were capable of living the law of plurality, the result was a "divinely ordained species of eugenics," according to B. H. Roberts.[181]

For most plural wives (and the men as well), the practice was a costly burden, a form of "sacred loneliness," in one scholar's phrase.[182] Some women thrived under "the principle." And a surprising number rose to defend plural marriage when it was under attack, revealing a stalwart solidarity under siege, but also giving insight into their own understanding of its foundations and purposes. Here as never before or since, gender informed theological rationales to a degree without parallel in Mormon history. Mormon leaders seldom invited women to share the theological platform, and those women who presumed to do so risked public chastisement when they did. So Young censured Eliza R. Snow's speculations on resurrection;[183] and though Wilford Woodruff referred to Snow's "revelation" on a Mother in Heaven, Joseph F. Smith publicly insisted she had but cribbed the truth from Joseph Smith. When it came to polygamy, however, Mormon leaders were anxious to let women speak in defense of the principle, to counter the picture of female oppression and coercion widely promulgated in the press and popular fiction.[184] Not surprisingly, their justifications often took a different approach from those of their priesthood leaders and husbands.

The male narrative of Smith and Young especially emphasized the dynastic dimension to eternal families. Much nineteenth-century rhetoric about plurality emphatically positioned plural wives as instrumental to male exaltation and kingdom-building. Women, by contrast, often emphasized the benefits to society and posterity; for themselves, it was more a crucible than a blessing. "I find that Polygamists were the friends of God,—that the family and lineage of a polygamist was selected, in which all nations should be blessed," wrote Belinda Marden Pratt, a vocal defender of the practice.[185] She also saw its practical and social benefits. Since sexual relations were "mainly for the purpose of procreation," it should not be indulged in during pregnancy, as it might "disturb, irritate, weary, or exhaust" the female body. A man, however, "has no such draw back upon his strength," Belinda reasoned. "Polygamy then, as practiced under the Patriarchal law of God, leads directly to the chastity of women, and to sound health and morals in the constitutions of their offspring." Furthermore, polygamy allowed all women to marry "virtuous men," rather than "a drunkard, a man of hereditary disease, a debauchee, an idler, or a spendthrift."[186]

Eliza R. Snow's defense also emphasized that "we are a practical, not a theoretical people." Polygamy tended toward "the elevation and redemption, morally and physically, of fallen human nature, and laying a foundation for the prolongation of life." Those who qualified for the higher marriage law, in this view, tended to pass on the best characteristics, both moral and physical. Her view gave priority to polygamy's impact on the world, not its preparation for, or status in, the eternities. It held the promise of "renovating the earth and in regenerating the human family," working "to stem the torrent of evils," presumably of a largely sexual nature, "with which the inhabitants of the earth are being inundated."[187]

As the practice grew and its immense challenges became manifest, a common objective of plural marriage hypothesized by its female adherents in particular was that it represented a higher spiritual practice, a refiner's fire that purified rather than thwarted emotional attachment. Though it seems self-evidently to devalue women, Whitney argued rather counter-intuitively—and unpersuasively to most—that "the ones who practice and advocate it will be the first to stand as man's equal."[188] Smith had reportedly called plural marriage "a celestial law that would eventually redeem and exalt the human family."[189] Romania Pratt Penrose, an accomplished physician and plural wife, believed of the practice that "though it be a fiery furnace at some period in our life, it will prove the one thing needful to cleanse and purify our inmost soul of selfishness, jealousy, and other mundane attributes."[190] If marital love survived, it was not the love of Victorian companionate marriage, with two soul mates caught up in a unitary bond to the exclusion of all else. And if romantic love had to die in the process, as it did,[191] it must be because a higher form of love awaited the faithful practitioners of plural marriage. "Their souls will be expanded, and in the place of selfishness, patience and charity will find place in their hearts," insisted one long-time plural wife.[192]

Novelistic accounts of Utah polygamy, which abounded throughout the nineteenth century, depicted women as duped, deluded, or coerced into the practice, in which men reveled. In actual fact, recognizing that few of either gender were happy with the practice, Young and his successors increasingly turned to the language of trial and spiritual refining to characterize plural marriage—which validated the women in their experience of the practice and shaped their understanding of its purpose accordingly. On one such occasion, Young declared, "I wish here to say to the Elders of Israel, and to all the members of this Church and kingdom, that it is in the hearts of many of them to wish that the doctrine of polygamy was not taught and practiced by us. It may be hard for many, and especially for the ladies, yet it is no harder for them than it is for the gentlemen."[193] His successor John Taylor remarked, "We complain sometimes about our trials: we need not do that. These are things that are necessary for our perfection."[194]

Exactly how necessary plural marriage was for celestial perfection was never clear. In 1866, Young famously asserted that "the only men who become Gods . . . are those who enter into polygamy."[195] But in the same remarks, he said the faithful must "be polygamists at least in your faith," and reaffirmed that position in 1871, saying that "a Man may Embrace the Law of Celestial Marriage in his heart & not take the Second wife & be justified before the Lord."[196] Such seemed to be his general belief; in 1870 he declared that "there would be men saved in the Celestial Kingdom of God with one wife with Many wives & with No wife at all."[197]

By 1890, mounting federal pressure against the practice had become irresistible. Leaders were imprisoned or underground, church properties had been confiscated, and the church itself disincorporated. In October conference, Wilford Woodruff revealed to a shocked congregation that he intended to submit to federal prohibitions and urged his followers "to refrain from contracting any marriage forbidden by the law of the land."[198] Some members thought they discerned in his words a strategy of ostensible compliance but tacit resistance. And indeed, some plural marriages were performed by church leaders for a number of years thereafter. But eventually it became clear that the era of plural marriage was, for faithful members of the church, finally at an end. Woodruff's successor Joseph F. Smith issued a second manifesto in 1904, making clear that those contracting or performing plural marriages would be excommunicated.

The ban on the practice was not in doubt. But for Mormons, the status of the principle itself was and the doctrine currently exists in a theological limbo. Probably reflecting the uncertainty of thousands, a member queried the First Presidency in 1912, "Is plural or celestial marriage essential to a fulness of glory in the world to come?" He was answered that "Celestial marriage is essential to a fulness of glory in the world to come, as explained in the revelation concerning it; but it is not stated that plural marriage is thus essential."[199] The form of the question and its response perfectly capture the shift in terminology already under way. To the questioner, celestial marriage was another name for plural marriage. Those terms had been used interchangeably for much of the nineteenth century. Celestial marriage *was* plural marriage, for time and all eternity. But the church leadership was now making a distinction between marriage for eternity, which they called celestial marriage, and marriage to more than one wife, which was now only referred to, uneuphemistically, as plural marriage.

From a contemporary Mormon perspective, this distinction is interpreted as a clarification of a longstanding confusion, rather than as a doctrinal shift. The nineteenth-century confounding of the two terms was traceable to two facts: first, the two principles of eternity and plurality had developed at the same time. As we saw above, William Phelps had first referred to Smith's doctrine of the eternity of marriage in 1835, the same period of Smith's likely involvement with Fanny Alger in a plural arrangement, suggesting the ideas of plurality and eternity were evolving more or less in tandem. Second, the two principles were elaborated jointly in the only published revelation on the subject of plurality—section 132 of the Doctrine and Covenants. Smith's wife Emma alternately resisted and acceded to his taking of plural wives, while his close brother Hyrum disbelieved the growing rumors of the practice. Under pressure from both to justify polygamy with a revelation, Smith dictated one on 12 July 1843, though it would not be published until shortly after the public announcement of the practice in 1852. (It was canonized as scripture in 1876.)

Section 132 is one of those seminal texts that is read in very different ways even today. Confusion arises from the fact that the revelation ranges over a few interrelated principles, using vocabulary that is fraught with ambiguity and multiple meanings. It opens with a promise to address the question of polygamy practiced by some of the patriarchs and kings of Israel. And the revelation eventually stipulates that Abraham was justified because he was so commanded. But in the interim, the revelation espouses a doctrine of a new and everlasting covenant, in which a man and woman may be sealed in such a way that death will not sever the bond, and they will come forth jointly in the resurrection to inherit eternal life.

Because the practice was suspended but the revelation never superseded, the significance of plural marriage in the eternities hovers in indeterminacy. However, the association of polygamy in Mormon rhetoric with Abrahamic sacrifice, and the explicit juxtaposition of those topics in section 132, suggests an answer: "Abraham was commanded to offer his son Isaac; nevertheless, it was written, thou shalt not kill. Abraham, however, did not refuse, and it was accounted to him for righteousness."

In the logic of Abrahamic sacrifice, as in the historical case of polygamy, the essence of the test is in a person's willingness to *provisionally* suspend a moral imperative (do not practice human sacrifice) in deference to a divine mandate to perform an ethically repugnant act. Abraham had to choose between the ethical requirements of his surroundings (the "social morality") and what he regarded as his absolute duty to God ("duty is simply the expression of God's will," wrote Kierkegaard[200]). But of course God does not require us to actually violate an ethical law. In V. H. Cassler's words, an Abrahamic sacrifice is "always temporally bounded and there is always a ram in the thicket, whether that be in this life or the next life. . . . Outside of a commandment to perform an Abrahamic sacrifice, an Abrahamic sacrifice is always an abomination."[201]

In the case of polygamy, the association with the Abrahamic offering of Isaac would be perverse if the act in question were transformed into a supernal principle, rather than a costly and agonizing trial. Even its most fervent defenders persisted, in the final analysis, in seeing the practice as a wrenching schooling, a test of faith, and the means to a greater end, not the blessed end itself: "In obeying this law it has cost [us] a sacrifice nearly equal to that of Abraham. . . . There is nothing that would induce me to . . . lose my hold upon that crown which awaits all those who have laid their willing but bleeding hearts upon the altar," said one plural wife.[202] Young's second wife Mary Ann concurred: "God will be very cruel if he does not give us poor women adequate compensation for the trials we have endured in polygamy."[203] Lorena Bent found nothing to praise in a "principle which had caused so much sacrifice, heartache, and trial."[204] Heavenly continuation of those trials would hardly constitute compensation.

That view of polygamy as a temporary purgatory was apparently prevalent enough among Utah women that Heber C. Kimball tried to squelch it. "The principle of plurality of wives never will be done away although some sisters have had revelations that, when this time passes away and they go through the veil, every woman will have a husband to herself."[205] But he was swimming against the tide. Although Mormon discourse at times invoked the logic of a "higher law" and the need to overcome "selfishness," the decades-long acknowledgment of the principle's difficulty, pervasive, wrenching heartache, consistent practice by a small minority, incompatibility with contemporary expressions of companionate marriage, and a dominant view of polygamy as a trial not a blessing make polygamy's eternal perpetuation unlikely and undesirable to most Latter-day Saints (with the possible exception of those involved in remarriage after decease of a spouse).

Only in very recent times has the church in fact come to clarify that the practice was a temporary diversion from an otherwise immutable law. An official press statement proclaims that

The standard doctrine of the Church is monogamy, as it always has been, as indicated in the Book of Mormon (Jacob, chapter 2): "Wherefore, my brethren, hear me, and hearken to the word of the Lord: For there shall not any man among you have save it be one wife; and concubines he shall have none. . . . For if I will, saith the Lord of Hosts, raise up seed unto me, I will command my people; otherwise they shall hearken unto these things." In other words, the standard of the Lord's people is monogamy unless the Lord reveals otherwise. Latter-day Saints believe the season the Church practiced polygamy was one of these exceptions.[206]

In spring 2013, the church elevated that position to the status of virtual scripture, introducing the canonized manifesto ending plural marriage with a new introduction that uses similar language: "Monogamy is God's standard for marriage unless He declares otherwise."[207]

In spite of the practice's demise around the turn of the twentieth century, it has not gone unnoticed that in Mormon temples, widowers are frequently married eternally to a second wife—and deceased widows may be sealed to more than one deceased husband—thus seemingly perpetuating a form of plural marriage, or at least tacitly reflecting an abiding faith in the possibility of plural marriage in the hereafter.[208] And indeed, some Mormons affirm their personal belief that, in such cases, both spouses will be their eternal marriage companions. However, the trend of church teachings on the subject, through the 2013 scriptural emendations, is toward greater reticence even regarding the eternal significance of such modern remarriages. As church president Spencer W. Kimball counseled a troubled widower on the subject of eternal remarriage in the 1970s, "he did not know exactly how these relationships will be worked out, but he did know that through faithfulness all will be well."[209] A more recent church leader concurred in this sentiment: "We are not concerned about who will be sealed to whom. We simply trust in the Lord's wisdom and love and try to live righteously."[210]

The end of plural marriage as a social practice, and its consequent demise as a theological principle, was accompanied by other major shifts in the theology of adoption. Interpreted liberally, "adoption" had been taken to mean just that: temple rituals joined members into priestly lines without regard for blood relationship. Not just women were sealed to men, but also men to men, in great priesthood chains—frequently based on the prominence of the individual. Joseph Smith and Brigham Young were principal figures to whom myriad Saints were sealed in adoptive sealing rituals.

In 1894, as members began to come to terms with the dissolution of the plural marriage system, President Woodruff announced another sweeping doctrinal change.

Asserting an ongoing evolution in adoption theology, consistent with the principle of continuing revelation ("Young . . . did not receive all the revelations that belong to this work"), Woodruff set the parameters of future practice: "When a man receives the endowments, adopt him to his father; not to Wilford Woodruff. . . . We want the Latter-day Saints from this time to trace their genealogies as far as they can, and to be sealed to their fathers and mothers. Have children sealed to their parents, and run this chain through as far as you can get it."[211] At last, it would seem, the organizational structure indicated by Brigham Young a half century before became the template for Mormon sealing endeavors. "The human family . . . must be joined together, so that there would be a perfect chain from Father Adam to his latest posterity," he had reported as Smith's original vision.[212]

So from 1894 to the present, celestial organization is conceived in terms of nuclear families linked trans-generationally. The shift was immediately registered in treatments of celestial marriage by two of the major figures of the era, James Talmage and B. H. Roberts. Talmage explicitly defines celestial marriage in terms wholly divorced from plurality. It involves "covenants as to time and eternity," and is "the order of marriage that exists in the celestial worlds." Larger and more expansive theological implications are not ignored, but the emphasis has clearly shifted from infinite chains of belonging to durable pairings of righteous individuals.

A similar move is evident in Roberts's major work. Though himself a polygamist, he concludes his theological tome with a discussion not of plural, but of "companionate marriage," in terms that ignore if they do not preclude an eternal role for plurality. "Completed man," he writes, "is man-woman. Each is but half of a necessary whole." Duality, not multiplicity, appears in his vision as the eternal as well as the social pattern. (As for the practice of plural marriage, we don't know what "may become of it" in the future. But it has played its part as a sacrificial offering of God's people, attested by their "suffering."[213]) The 1995 Proclamation on the Family reaffirmed the distinctness and eternal duration of gendered identity, and the consummation of human purposes here and hereafter to be the linking of heterosexual individuals in a sacred bond, united eternally to each other and their offspring.[214]

It would be perhaps naïve to read into these conceptions of sealing a set of eternal domestic arrangements typical of Victorian America or of twenty-first-century extended families. Ultimately, the point is about the connection that such sealings establish with Christ. This is so because, in Mormon thought, there is only one heavenly family, and Christ is its head. The significance of those temple sealings was interpreted by Orson Whitney and reaffirmed with increasing frequency in recent years:

Joseph Smith declared . . . that the eternal sealings of faithful parents and the divine promises made to them for valiant service in the Cause of Truth, would save not only themselves, but likewise their posterity. Though some of the sheep may wander, the eye of the Shepherd is upon them, and sooner or later they will feel the tentacles of Divine Providence reaching out after them and drawing them back to the fold. Either in this life or in the life to come, they will return.[215]

EVOLVING MARRIAGE DEFINITIONS

For two generations, Mormonism managed to reconcile its theological underpinnings with a system of plurality. With the advent of the twentieth century, however, Mormons came to match, and then outstrip, the American ideal of domesticity and companionate marriage. If the contemporary American family is undergoing paroxysms of realignment, of which the iconoclastic sixties now seem tame precursor rather than culmination, Mormonism from a distance looks like a ship passing in the opposite direction, having moved from radical outlier to ultra-conventional (and heterosexually) monogamist. It is perhaps surprising that an institution so firmly associated in the public mind with the defense of the traditional family has itself been so variable in its conception of just what the family's ideal form is. The shifting configurations of the Mormon family, however, only throw into stark relief the underlying principles of Mormon thinking about the family which have never changed—the eternal nature of those bonds that constitute family organization and gender as a binary of eternal origin and duration.

A small minority of Mormons urges a reconsideration of the theological, as well as sociological, support for the single ideal of a heterosexual couple presiding over a nuclear family. Does Mormon theology itself contain a space for alternative configurations of the family? Some may point not only to polygamy as precedent but also to a period in LDS history when voluntary affiliation, rather than sexually determined relationships, was the basis for building extending families. Richard Bushman has referred to Joseph Smith's "lust for kin"[216] as a motivating factor in his quest for establishing such large and complex networks of filiation through temple ordinances. That explains why, in addition to matrimonial alliances, for a considerable time in Mormon history men were sealed to other men, in a kind of dynastic chain of being. In Christ's great intercessory prayer, Jesus petitioned God to bless his disciples with a friendship, a love and unity, that paralleled his own relationship to his Father. "The glory that you have given me I have given them," he prayed, "so that they may be one, as we are one."[217] Given the emphasis, seen above, that Smith placed on friendship, it is obvious that relationships other than heterosexual unions constitute important, and eternal, modes of connection in the eternities.

Two considerations are relevant to evolving notions of kinship. First, gender and gender roles are viewed by most scholars as social constructs rather than essential elements of human identity. And second, family organization and government have themselves undergone significant transformation in Mormon teaching and culture, as they have in the larger world. Additionally, Mormon conceptions of patriarchy have continued to evolve in substantial ways, moving in the past generations from a masculinist conception of family government toward a more egalitarian model. Smith's early project envisioned a remarkably equitable place for women, the problems raised by polygamy notwithstanding; no man could be saved without the woman, he encouraged female healing practices, he designated his wife as an exhorter and teacher, and he structured the women's Relief Society as a counterpart to the male priesthood. And modern scholars of plural marriage have emphasized the extent to which the system of plurality empowered women by conferring upon them priestly powers and prerogatives.[218] Not only did they acquire a greater degree of independence than their monogamous counterparts (they "seem to have the entire management, not only of their families, but their households, even outside business affairs, as if they were widows," remarked one astonished observer[219]); they also came with their husbands to participate in "mutually interdependent, priestly identity," a shared authority that descended to both from "Holy Progenitors."[220]

Within this larger context, twenty-first-century developments represent a return to some aspects of Smith's progressivism, even if these developments have been triggered by modern feminist sensibilities. President Ezra Taft Benson in 1985 referred to patriarchy as "family government,"[221] Robert L. Millet in the church magazine the *Ensign* defined the Melchizedek Priesthood as the "new and everlasting covenant of marriage," which itself is a patriarchal order of "family government presided over by a father and mother, patterned after what exists in heaven."[222] Apostle James E. Faust taught that "every father is to his family a patriarch and every mother a matriarch as coequals in their distinctive parental roles," and Elder Russell M. Nelson declared that "Eve served in a matriarchal partnership with the patriarchal priesthood."[223] Apostle L. Tom Perry emphasized that "there is not a president and vice-president in a family" but "co-presidents working together eternally for the good of their family . . . united in word, in deed, and in action, as they lead, guide, and direct their family unit. They are on equal footing."[224] Finally, in reading the Genesis account of woman's presumed curse of subordination, Elder Bruce Hafen says the account actually indicates an ideal of Adam "ruling *with*, not ruling *over* [Eve]. . . . The concept of interdependent equal partners is well-grounded in the doctrine of the restored gospel. . . . Eve was adequate for, or equal to, Adam. She wasn't his servant or his subordinate."[225] If there is a consistent direction in Mormon conceptions of the family, it is in the direction of a more fully egalitarian, companionate view of marriage.

Given these reconfigurations of patriarchal marriage, some voices in the LDS faith consider the time ripe for accommodating gay marriage itself as an acceptable form of the family. Some would compare the current LDS opposition to that development with the church's nineteenth-century ban on black priesthood holders. In that case, civil rights–era critics were eventually vindicated in their opposition to a practice which the church now treats more as an unfortunate policy than as inspired doctrine. So does a vocal minority within the church today assert that the barriers in Mormon culture to gay marriage will similarly fall, as cultural bias gets weeded out from doctrinal essentials.

Such a scenario is possible, but not likely. The priesthood ban arose under murky circumstances, abruptly intruding into a culture that under Smith's leadership had been moving in the opposite direction (he supported emancipation and ordained blacks to the priesthood). The ban had no identifiable moment of revelatory origins. Nor was it indissolubly connected—as heterosexual marriage is—to Mormon conceptions of the divine. V. H. Cassler argues that Mormon theology erects three powerful barriers to a post-heterosexual theology.

First, Mormonism finds in corporeality a step toward, rather than away, from the divine. C. S. Lewis, in the tradition of Milton and Blake, denied that in the resurrection, "the distinction of sexes will disappear," though he doubted their continued biological purposefulness. "What is no longer needed for biological purposes may be expected to survive for splendour," he wrote.[226] But while embodied procreation in the afterlife is not a given, neither can it be simply dismissed as superfluous or absurd. Cassler suggests that the female role in human creation is emblematic if not absolutely constitutive of her indispensability.

Second, consistent with the bodily nature of all sacraments, physical union is itself "an ordinance rife with meaning, . . . the sacrament of peace between men and women."[227] More particularly, following the feminist philosopher Sylviane Agacinski, Cassler argues that "sexual union between a man and a woman in marriage is an admission that self-love, or love of what one is, is sterile." As she quotes feminist philosopher Sylviane Agacinski, sexual difference is "the foundation of ethics": "If humanity is mixed, and not single, all individuals are confronted with their own insufficiency and cannot fully claim to be full human beings. . . . There is indeed a lack essential to every human being, which is neither the lack of a penis nor some other attribute of men, or women, but stems from being only male or only female."[228] The creation account of Genesis seems to confirm this foundational status of difference. Differentiation is, in fact, the common factor in the six creative periods of divine activity, culminating in the final, crowning gesture. God separates, differentiates woman from man, then restores them to a union which he blesses and sanctifies in its complementarity.

Third, the feminine divine is in Mormonism an embodied, essential, indispensable participant in creation. Since "God" in Mormonism means an exalted woman and man, "Eve was not created in the image of a male god; she was created in the image of her Heavenly Mother." Thus both the institution of marriage and godhood itself are grounded in a celestial model of heterosexuality. Contrary to social constructionist models of gender, Mormon thought maintains that male and female "are woven into the fabric of the universe, a vital, foundational element of eternal life and divine nature."[229]

POSTERITY TO COME

"What will I do if I gets there? . . . I tell you, believe I'll just do the town—walkin and runnin' all roun' to see the home whitch Jesus done bult for His people. . . . Then I would cut roun' to the back streets and look for the litte home where my Saviour's set my mother up to housekeepin' when she got there. I 'spect to know the house by the roses in the yard and the vine on the porch. Look there; mighty sweet house, ain't it lovely?"
—JOHN JASPER

Like the popular preacher John Jasper, Mormonism has always emphasized the radical continuities, rather than the discontinuities, between earth and heaven. Crossing the veil, two LDS prophets predicted, will elicit the surprise of recognition. "When I meet the God I worship I expect to [meet a] personage with whom I have been acquainted upon the same principle that I would to meet with my Earthly Father after going upon a Journey & returning home," said Young.[230] Ezra Taft Benson concurred: "Nothing is going to startle us more when we pass through the veil to the other side than to realize how well we know our Father and how familiar His face is to us."[231]

Smith's early emphasis on heaven as perpetuation of earthly sociality met initial opposition. Warren Cowdery protested that a non-Mormon observer "must be mistaken if he has imbibed the idea that we consider the kingdom of heaven will be composed of real estate, houses or lands, flocks or herds. . . . In short, we disclaim and disavow any and all definitions of the kingdom of God, except as Paul explained it."[232] But Cowdery's view was soon overwhelmed in the emphatically material heaven of Parley Pratt, who rejected a "heaven beyond the bounds of time and space," a "fairy world of spirits, some heaven without substance."[233] Cowdery's protests notwithstanding, Pratt wrote, "in the resurrection and the life to come, men . . . will actually possess a material inheritance on the earth. They will possess houses, and cities, and villages." And where is heaven located? It comprises "an eternal inheritance on earth."²³⁴ There, men and women of "immortal flesh and bones . . . will eat, drink, converse, reason, love, walk, sing, [and] play on musical instruments."²³⁵

Here as elsewhere, Mormonism's collapse of sacred distance is pronounced, its vision of heaven one of almost seamless continuation of the quotidian. Families continue, homes and gardens continue, bodily existence (on a glorified plane) continues, education continues. Mormonism is of all religions perhaps the most relentlessly incompatible with traditional Christian conceptions of heaven, connected as those conceptions are to sublimity, incomprehensibility, immaterialism, and other flights from the conditions of our fallen, mortal habitation. Pratt insisted that "the difference between our world and a Heavenly one, consists, not in the diversity of the elements, for they are the same, but in the difference of the organization of these elements."²³⁶

But Mormonism tends toward explicit projections of the substance of heavenly *activity* itself. Most historic versions of the heaven have emphasized rest, contemplation, and praise—eternal enjoyment as a perpetual bliss of state rather than activity. Mormonism holds out the promise of a salvation in which any rest is purely metaphorical. Joseph's crowned Saints are no angelic choirs passively basking in the glory of their God, but Faustian strivers endlessly seeking to shape themselves into progressively better beings, "This is a wide field for the operation of man," said Brigham Young, "that reaches into eternity."²³⁷ Those "operations" were developed in heady ways in Mormonism's early years, but were rooted in an unusually literal reading of one biblical concept in particular. Mormonism, as we have seen, views its theology as a restoration and recuperation not just of New Testament Christianity but also of Old Testament priesthoods and principles (as well as doctrines and ordinances traceable to an Adamic dispensation). Central to Old Testament theology is the Abrahamic Covenant. In one of the covenant's iterations, God promises the patriarch that he "will make your offspring as numerous as the stars of heaven and as the sand that is on the seashore."²³⁸

The status of that Abrahamic covenant, and the place of the Jews in the universal scheme of Christian salvation, has been a matter of dispute in the Christian world. The view that long dominated (though currently in retreat) was supersessionism, or the belief that the Christian covenant, the "new testament," replaces or supersedes God's covenant with the house of Israel. Mormonism reverses the equation, considering the Abrahamic covenant to be an early adumbration of, rather than distinct from or anticipatory of, the fullness of the gospel of Jesus Christ. In Smith's restored version of the original pact, Jehovah says to the patriarch,

I will make of thee a great nation, and . . . thou shalt be a blessing unto thy seed after thee, that in their hands they shall bear this ministry and Priesthood

unto all nations; And I will bless them through thy name; for as many as receive this Gospel shall be called after thy name, and shall be accounted thy
seed, and shall rise up and bless thee, as their father; . . . and in thy seed after
thee (that is to say, the literal seed, or the seed of the body) shall all the families
of the earth be blessed, even with the blessings of the Gospel, which are the
blessings of salvation, even of life eternal.[239]

One of the oft-repeated elements of this covenant was the promise of "seed" as numerous as the stars in the sky or the sand upon the shore. When Smith inaugurated
the practice of celestial marriage, it was explicitly done in the context of the promises God had made to Abraham. And Smith took the decisive step of extending the
promise of bountiful posterity beyond this life. The new order of marriage, he said,
was "to fulfil the promise which was given by my Father before the foundation of
the world, and for their exaltation in the eternal worlds, that they may bear the
souls of men; for herein is the work of my Father continued, that he may be glorified."[240] As Orson Pratt expressed the doctrine, "when male and female are restored
from the fall, by virtue of the everlasting and eternal covenant of marriage, they
will continue to increase and multiply to all ages of eternity, to raise up beings after
their own order, and in their own likeness and image, germs of intelligence, that are
destined, in their times and seasons, to become not only sons of God, but Gods
themselves."[241]

In 1840, a pamphlet dispute erupted over the question of procreation in the resurrection. Mormon elder Samuel Bennett took exception to a Methodist antagonist's
claim that Mormons anticipated a "carnal paradise." Elder Erastus Snow joined the
debate, seconding Bennett's contention that only Saints alive at the Second Coming
of Christ would continue to enjoy procreative powers.[242] In any case, they did not
yet envision the possibility of continuing posterity in an eternal setting. With
Smith's 1843 declaration, however, Mormonism began to envision heaven as a place
where God's own creative powers were mirrored in his exalted children. As ever,
Parley Pratt was quick to embrace the radical expansion of heavenly being. "I might
also tell you of the continued exertions of creative power by which millions of new
worlds will yet be formed and peopled," Pratt wrote, not just by God the Father, but
also "by king Adam and his descendants."[243]

Mormon Joseph Holbrook shared in this sense that Mormon salvation, like
nineteenth-century America, was steeped in boundlessness: in a vision he saw "endless suns and planets moving in their orbits, vast systems waiting only to be filled
and governed."[244] Smith may not have mentioned world creation publicly, but it
followed quickly, doubtless from the anticipation of begetting generations through

the ages of eternity if not from private remarks. As one satirist rendered the idea in Smith's own lifetime,

> A TENFOLD glory—that's the prize!
> Without it you're undone!
> But with it you will shine as bright
> As the bright shining sun.
> There you may shine like mighty Gods,
> Creating worlds so fair—
> At least a WORLD for every WIFE
> That you take with you there."[245]

The Scottish minister George MacDonald had speculated on the subject with more delicate lyricism:

> [I]n the perfect time, O perfect God,
> When we are in our home, our natal home,
> When joy shall carry every sacred load,
> And from its life and peace no heart shall roam,
> What if thou make us able to make like thee—
> To light with moons, to clothe with greenery,
> To hang gold sunsets o'er a rose and purple sea![246]

Mormons quickly turned such poetry into speculative theology, and rumors that Mormons believed they would "create worlds" were extant already in 1841.[247] By the Utah period, Young was teaching such ideas from the pulpit. "When we are resurrected," he preached, "they turn around and beget spirit, they organize a world—and begin to bring forth their progeny upon it—when they are brought into existence we then have power to form a world."[248] Pratt found the idea culminated a sweeping vision of salvation rooted in Smith's first intimations of pre-mortal existence: "men are the offspring or children of the Gods, and destined to advance by degrees, and to make their way by a progressive series of changes, till they become like their father in heaven, and like Jesus Christ their elder brother. Thus perfected, the whole family will . . . continue to organize, people, redeem, and perfect other systems which are now in the womb of Chaos."[249]

In this version of futurity, as God took pre-existent matter and shaped it into the earth, so does he take primordial intelligences, father them into spirits, and mentor them into divinity. As the chaos of matter becomes earth, planets, and star systems, the scattered children of God are assimilated into eternal marriages, families, and heavenly dynasties. They then become co-participants with God in his ongoing purposes: fashioning worlds and creating endless posterity, eternally working to impose order and form on an infinitely malleable cosmos.

Like all faith traditions, Mormonism has evolved and continues to refine and reshape its teachings, guided—as the LDS devout believe—by continuing revelation. The early decades of Mormonism were marked by unfettered exuberance and speculative riot—and by a propensity to view the eternal through the prism of the present. The Restoration found its fullest expression in the temple and its ordinances, whereby a pre-mortal pattern of human relationships found recuperation and eternal formulation within a vast heavenly family. Smith and early LDS leaders understood the Law of Adoption to create the conditions for a person fully to "comprehend the things of God, enter into the designs of Jehovah, unravel the mysteries of the kingdom of God, and contemplate the future designs of the great I Am."[250] The details of how those relations were to be articulated went through several iterations, involving eternal marriage, polygamous sealings (and some polyandrous), and tribal adoptions before Wilford Woodruff admitted the limitations of revealed knowledge and focused the celestial program of eternal relations on the nuclear family.

In the twentieth and twenty-first centuries, critical approaches to gender and sexuality have thrown suspicion on theologies that argue, as Mormonism does, for the eternity of gender or for the man-woman union as the apotheosis of nature's—or the cosmos's—highest purposes. When it comes to the subject of engendering an eternal posterity, it may be useful to recall the imprecision of Smith's own language on the subject. As adoption theology suggests in its very terminology, God's fatherhood, like his counterpart's motherhood, tells us nothing about the process of divine engendering, or parenting. Literalizing the eternal procreation of posterity was fully in harmony with the nineteenth-century propensities we have seen, but modern leaders have been more circumspect on the subject. Similarly, it does not appear to be coyness that explains Mormon reluctance to canonize King Follett, to defend world creation, or to celebrate planetary dominions. Such doctrines are today simply left to occupy that space of theological indeterminacy, which may be a mark of Mormonism's growing theological maturity.

One principle, however, does continue to occupy hallowed status in Mormon thought. Pratt wrote that "Our natural affections are planted in us by the Spirit of God," and "are the very main-springs of life and happiness—they are the cement of all virtuous and heavenly society."[251] Ultimately, Mormons understand God's nature, and human salvation, to be the simple preservation and expansion of that which is most elemental, and most worthwhile, about our life here on earth. However rapturous or imperfect, fulsome or shattered, our knowledge of love has been, Mormons believe it is the very basis and purpose of our existence. For Mormons, heaven holds out the promise of a belonging that is destined to extend and surpass any which any have ever known in this wounded world.

HOLINESS AND SANCTIFICATION

The great mystic William Law explained theosis using the familiar language of God's indwelling, even as he emphasized the creaturely nature of the human:

> God himself cannot make a creature to be in itself, or as to its own nature, any-thing else but a state of emptiness, of want, of appetite, etc. He cannot make it to be good and happy, in and from its natural state. . . . The highest life, there-fore, that is natural and creaturely can go no higher than this; it can only be a bare capacity for goodness and happiness and cannot possibly be a good and happy life, but by the life of God dwelling in, and in union with it.[252]

Those writers are correct who see Mormon theosis as essentially different in kind from its Catholic and Protestant counterparts; for Mormonism sees the human primeval nature as ontologically of a kind with God; its original condition is not creaturely, but eternal. As such, one's growth into godliness is a process directed and enabled by God, but in accord with an inherent potential, not a borrowed or imputed nature.

In a cosmos split ontologically between the self-existent Creator, on the one hand, and the infinitude of derivative creatures, on the other, any perfection or deification must be understood in light of that essential difference. Only a divine bestowal of sanctifying grace can make the creature fit for a celestial glory, compensating for an eternal and irremediable difference. Mormonism denies the ontological divide, even as it acknowledges the indispensability of grace in the process of sanctification. In the Mormon conception, grace is requisite, and subordination is eternal. Brigham Young said "you are not going to have a separate kingdom; I am not going to have a separate kingdom; it is not our prerogative . . . ; if we are ever prepared for an eternal exaltation, we must be concentrated in the head of the eternal Godhead . . . and all of our interest must centre in the Godhead in eternity."[253]

Even so, the *imitatio dei* enacted by Christ is one in which Mormons believe they are called upon to participate. As Brigham Young described the process, "The gospel . . . causes men and women to reveal that which would have slept in their disposi-tions until they dropped into their graves. The plan by which the Lord leads this people makes them reveal their thoughts and intents, and brings out every trait of disposition lurking in their [beings]. . . . Every fault that a person has will be made manifest, that it may be corrected by the Gospel of salvation, by the laws of the Holy Priesthood."[254]

The Book of Mormon's restatement of the New Testament promise of eventual likeness to God emphasizes the literal force of that promise in Mormon thought:

> Wherefore, my beloved brethren, pray unto the Father with all the energy of heart, that ye may be filled with this love, which he hath bestowed upon all who are true followers of his Son, Jesus Christ; that ye may become the sons of God; that when he shall appear we shall be like him, for we shall see him as he is; that we may have this hope; that we may be purified even as he is pure.[255]

In Oliver Cowdery's 1834 version of Mormonism's articles of faith, he wrote that "We believe that God is the same in all ages; and that it requires the same holiness, purity, and religion, to save a man now, as it did anciently."[256] In Joseph's final version, that article drops out, to be replaced by "a man must be called of God . . . by the laying on hands, by those who are in authority, to . . . administer in the ordinances" of the gospel.[257] There is no question that by disposition and by pronouncement, Smith was a legalist. A legalistic vocabulary dominated his religious thought: Authority, priesthood, laws, and ordinances were crucial. "There is no salvation," he declared, "without a legal administrator." That title he applied to John the Baptist but also to Jesus Christ;[258] the prophet is whoever holds "keys," and the exact "order and ordinances of the Kingdom" were nonnegotiable, set in stone "by the Priesthood in the council of heaven before the world was."[259] His emphasis on correct ordinances and authority could at times suggest that form trumped substance, and he personally disavowed any personal piety. "I am not so much of a christian as many suppose I am, when a man undertakes to ride me I am apt to kick him off," he frankly admitted.[260] Months later, he repeated the point: "I do not want you to think that I am very righteous, for I am not."[261]

None of this, however, is to say that holiness and purity were not the point of it all. It may be helpful to view Smith's words and actions in the context of contemporary developments that he was reacting against. First, Mormons suffered recurrent persecution, especially in the Missouri years, frequently under the instigation of clerics, making Smith and other suffering Saints particularly sensitive to religious hypocrisy. Genuine piety, Smith knew, was evident in right action. "I love that man better," he said, "who swears a stream as long as my arm, and administer[s] to the poor and divide[s] his substance, than the long, smooth-faced hypocrite."[262] In this regard, he was fully in harmony with the century's turn away from theology's privilege over ethics. Methodism was the first great movement to make religion more experiential than theological. The year of Smith's death, the Presbyterian Robert Baird noted that theological problems were no longer of much public interest.[263]

"By the beginning of the twentieth century," writes Daniel Howe with only slight exaggeration, "most respectable American clergymen had little to say about the Trinity, atonement, or predestination."[264]

Second, early nineteenth-century suspicions against organized religion generally were part of the larger Romantic cultural revolution. Nathan Hatch has written of the era as one in which a heightened sense of individualism and common sense combined to challenge the institutional power of the church and its monopolistic control by "classically educated and university trained clergymen."[265] One consequence—persisting to the present day—was the displacement of religiosity by spirituality, a substitution of interiority for external observance, with the result that a kind of self-absorbed subjectivity became a new, cheapened version of Christian discipleship. As William Blake preached the new Romantic sensibility with mesmerizing appeal, the point was:

> To see the world in a grain of sand,
> and heaven in a wildflower
> hold infinity in the palm of your hand,
> and eternity in an hour.[266]

But as Terry Eagleton notes with some impatience, the Gospel of Matthew teaches: "Eternity lies not in a grain of sand but in a glass of water. The cosmos revolves on comforting the sick."[267]

Mormon scriptures frequently enjoin the people to "sanctify" and "purify" themselves, but the emphasis at times seems to be more on obedience than on grace as the key to such holiness. Clearly, in Mormon thought, the two operate in tandem. In the Book of Mormon's telling formulation, persons are saved "in and through the grace of God," but "after all we can do."[268] God's generosity undergirds the multi-stage process of embodiment, salvation, and exaltation; Christ's unmerited gift makes personal repentance and resurrection possible; and the Holy Spirit works its transformation in the heart of the penitent. This salvific synthesis is captured in Smith's reworking of Genesis, wherein Adam learns that "by the water ye keep the commandment; by the Spirit ye are justified, and by the blood ye are sanctified."[269] In Christian theology generally, as in Mormon thought, the Spirit sanctifies and the blood of Christ justifies. Smith's reversal in this formulation only suggests his general inattentiveness to theological nomenclature, at the same time it emphasizes the primacy in his thought of obedience, Christ's sacrifice, and the work of the Spirit. As he said the year before his death, "through the atonement of Christ and the resurrection and obedience in the Gospel we shall again be conformed to the image of his Son Jesus Christ, then we shall have attained to the image glory and character of God."[270]

COMMUNITY

For Mormons, this process of sanctification is communal. Christianity, in its very roots, is other-oriented. Service to others, the church as the body of Christ, and the Heavenly City are all Christian ideas. Mormonism actually conceives of holiness in collective terms, and makes these collectivities actual functioning entities in both the process and the end result of Christian striving. The concept of solitary salvation does not exist in Mormon thought. Participating in the divine nature means first and foremost developing a sanctified partnership, in the form of eternal marriage described above. To fail to pursue or develop such a partnership is to be limited, eternally, to the saved but subordinate role of ministering angel.[271]

This communal salvation operates on other levels. Smith's first recorded angelic visitation inculcated the essential link between the fathers and the children, which he eventually developed into the ideas of baptism for the dead, temple sealings, and a vast Heavenly Family. When he preached in reference to the dead that "without us they could not be made perfect, nor we without them,"[272] he captured the essential interdependence of Mormon salvation. Such interdependence assumed a more practical form in the laboratory of Mormon communitarian experiments, and the ideal of a Zion society.

ZION

Christians have long employed the term that first appeared in scripture as the Jerusalem stronghold captured by David.[273] Church fathers read *Zion* to mean "every holy and godly person" who "is lifted above this life."[274] Augustine saw the related expression, the New Jerusalem, as a metaphor for the universal church to which all righteous saints belonged. Puritans used *Zion* to refer to the godly society they hoped to form in the New World, and by Smith's day Methodists and others employed the term to suggest a godly people or project. The cause of Zion was simply the work or kingdom of God (as when the Methodists named a new paper, *Zion's Herald* in 1823, or *Zion's Watchman* in 1835). At times, however, visionaries and eccentrics alike turned their efforts to the task of literally constructing a New Jerusalem in the shape of a religious utopia in the American wilderness. John Hartwick, Jemima Wilkinson ("the Publick Universal Friend"), and Robert Matthews ("Matthias") all launched such enterprises in upstate New York.[275]

The impractical quest for a literal Zion by these dreamers and idealists, on the one hand, and the persistent invocation of the word in church hymns, religious newspapers, and Sunday sermons, on the other, reveal something of the idea's powerful and enduring appeal in America's religious history. For most Christians, the New

Jerusalem, Zion, the Heavenly City—all reflect men's and women's deepest spiritual yearning. This longing takes many forms: the repair of a damaged relationship with God, the healing of a sick and sinful society, the dramatic triumph of good over evil, or the transition into the eternal of all that is mortal, transient, and temporary. The several Zion-oriented enterprises of the era reflected the various ways in which Christians expected to find their spiritual yearnings fulfilled.

In September 1830, Smith records his first revelation pertaining to a city that is to be a gathering place for the Latter-day Saints. Then, a few months later, he receives the theologically rich prophecy of Enoch. There, for the first time, he learns that "Enoch built a city that was called the City of Holiness, even Zion." He learns that this people were "of one heart and one mind, and dwelt in righteousness; and there was no poor among them"; he learns that the people of Enoch were so righteous, the entire city "was taken up into heaven." From this point on, Smith transforms his repeated admonitions to "bring forth and establish Zion" into a project of literal community building.[276]

By 1831, the location for Smith's version of Zion had been identified as northern Missouri. It was to be "the New Jerusalem, a land of peace, a city of refuge, a place of safety for the saints of the Most High God."[277] "The building up of Zion," Smith believed, "is a cause that has interested the people of God in every age; it is a theme upon which prophets, priests and kings have dwelt with peculiar delight; they have looked forward with joyful anticipation to the day in which we live; and fired with heavenly and joyful anticipations they have sung and written and prophesied of this our day; but they died without the sight; we are the favored people that God has made choice of to bring about the Latter-day glory."[278]

Soon a temple site was dedicated, and a plat for erecting the Holy City designed. Smith enunciated principles of communalism and consecration which were called "The Law of Enoch."[279] The Saints were soon gathering by hundreds and thousands, to the accompaniment of poems of praise, hymns of celebration, and expectations of the Lord's imminent return. The Saints' hopes were dashed when conflict with old settlers led to the Mormons' expulsion in 1833. Smith led a paramilitary expedition to reclaim their land, but it disbanded in failure. Smith pronounced a revelation that indicated a fundamental reorientation. The quest for Zion, he was told, the grand project of building and sanctifying a godly people in preparation for the Savior's return, could not be accomplished in isolation from the sacrifice, worship, and ordinances associated with a temple they would build in Ohio. Only then would they find the "power ... to accomplish all things pertaining to Zion." Zion, in other words, would be accomplished as the product of a sanctified community, rather than a consecrated place. Enoch represented the possibility of something more durable than a loose agglomeration of the righteous *or* of a more inspired ecclesiastical institution. Enoch embodied the idea of a covenant *people*. "It is the testimony that I want," Joseph said, "that I am God's servant, and this people his people."[280] Or as he told a group in March 1842, he would succeed where Moses and a number of Eliases had failed. "He was going to make of this society a kingdom of priests—as in Enoch's day."[281] He saw the forging of this community as his true prophetic task.

Smith's efforts to accomplish an earthly Zion in Missouri ended in bloodshed, expulsion, and failure. But the dream of a brick-and-mortar Zion has never disappeared completely from Mormon thought. As in the Book of Mormon, the concept of Zion continued some time as a geographical idea, though the location was mutable. Kirtland, Ohio; various locations in Missouri; Nauvoo, Illinois; and the intermountain West—all became in turn the Mecca to which members and immigrant converts streamed, while maintaining in the background a belief in Independence, Missouri, as the eventual site of the New Jerusalem of scripture. Although the physical gathering to Zion had tapered off by the end of the nineteenth century, the First Presidency formally reversed the decades-old immigration policy in 1907, urging those Latter-day Saints still in Europe to remain in the homelands.[282] From that time to the present, church members around the globe have been counseled to build up spiritual Zion in their native lands. "Zion [is] the pure in heart," not "Missouri . . . is the land which I have appointed," is the scripture most commonly invoked in contemporary discussion of the topic.[283] The language of millennial imminence is still heard occasionally. Meanwhile, Saints continue the project of creating Zion in their hearts, and in the communal arrangements, the tent pegs of Zion, known appropriately as stakes (comparable to the diocese) and wards (the parish).

In the contemporary logic of Zion building, Saints must build heaven where they find themselves gathered; they do not go in search of the heavenly city—or a more heavenly congregation. Thus, Zion building continues to have precisely determined geographical referents. Mormons wards are constituted by strict geographical boundaries, with virtually no exceptions, no church shopping. The seeking out of more satisfying spiritual nourishment has long been a heritage of the Protestant Reformation. So much so that in 1559, the Act of Uniformity required all English people to attend their own parish church. Mormon practice has fully achieved what the English Parliament could not.

It would be hard to overestimate the impact this physical boundedness has on the shaping of Mormon culture. Like the family into which one is born, wards become the inescapable condition of a Mormon's social and spiritual life. Just as, ironically, siblings forge fiercer bonds of loyalty and love to those with whom they never freely choose to associate, so does the arbitrariness of ward boundaries create a virtual inevitability about the LDS ward's cohesion. Congregations and their bishops do not audition for the adherent's willful association. They are instantaneously designated a new congregant's adoptive family, without the member's right of dissent or appeal. While not all family relations are idyllic, most are remarkably strong and a primary source for the individual's identity. And like Crusoe on his island, Mormons implicitly recognize that any resources they need to employ for the erection of Zion must be found within themselves or their immediate environs, not among more congenial fellow Saints or under the tutelage of more inspiring leaders the next block over. These wards and stakes thus function as laboratories and practicums for the heavenly Zion of promise. Like Christians generally, Mormons see their churches as preparatory to the celestial church, the "general assembly and church of the firstborn."[284]

The crowning attribute of a Zion people, one that creates the bond of brotherhood, the absence of the poor and needy, and the joy of human intimacy, is the attribute most characteristic of God himself. As we saw in Enoch's encounter with God, the most conspicuous attribute of the Divine turns out to be love—costly love, a love that manifests itself as full participation in and vulnerability to the epic of human suffering.

So the most sobering aspect of Mormon conceptions of theosis is that the "weight of glory" described by Paul is a glory whose cost is, in some sense, eternal to all who follow in God's footsteps. This is made clear in the LDS scripture that comes closer to any other in modeling exactly what the principle of deification will entail.

And Enoch said unto the Lord: How is it that thou canst weep, seeing thou art holy, and from all eternity to all eternity? And were it possible that man could number the particles of the earth, yea, millions of earths like this, it would not be a beginning to the number of thy creations; . . . how is it thou canst weep? The Lord said unto Enoch: Behold these thy brethren; they are the workmanship of mine own hands, and I gave unto them their knowledge, in the day I created them; and in the Garden of Eden, gave I unto man his agency; And unto thy brethren have I said, and also given commandment, that they should love one another, and that they should choose me, their Father; but behold, they are without affection, and they hate their own blood; . . . and among all the workmanship of mine hands there has not been so great wickedness as among thy brethren . . . wherefore should not the heavens weep, seeing these shall suffer? . . . And it came to pass that the Lord spake unto Enoch, and told Enoch all the doings of the children of men; wherefore Enoch knew, and looked upon their wickedness, and their misery, and wept and stretched forth his arms, and his heart swelled wide as eternity; and his bowels yearned; and all eternity shook.[285]

In this magnificent, if harrowing, *imitatio dei*—Enoch experiences his own moment of infinite, godly compassion and empathy. Enoch is drawn into the divine nature—his heart swells wide as eternity—through a shared act of vicarious pain for the spectacle of a suffering humanity. Through this mentoring in the cosmic perspective, the divine potential of man and the divine nature of God are shown to be the same. Godliness turns out to be more about infinite empathy than infinite power; the divine nature constitutes infinite capacity for pain as well as for joy. Humans can become partakers of the divine nature through full integration into God's Heavenly Family, but that implies a love that has its wrenching costs as well as supernal blisses. Brigham Young apparently viewed the crucible of life through this lens of an eventual perfect empathy, daunting in its cost. "Ask a child how a certain fruit that it had never tasted, looks and tastes, he could not tell. It is so with us: If we were not subject to sorrows, sin and affliction, how could we be touched by the infirmities of our children when we become exalted?"[286]

Enoch's vision is not all about pain. His vision ends with a foretaste of a happier destiny in store, in a celestial reunion. The heaven that was revealed to Joseph Smith in his vision of Enoch was essentially an extension of the Zion community forged on earth. God's righteousness will "sweep the earth as with a flood, to gather out" those that will have Him to be their God. Then, the Lord says to Enoch, "thou and all thy city [shall] meet them there, and we will receive them into our bosom, and they shall see us; and we will fall upon their necks, and they shall fall upon our necks, and we will kiss each other; And there shall be mine abode, and it shall be Zion."[287] God and his people, the living and the departed, heaven and earth, embrace. The immense distance between the spiritual and the mundane collapses, and it becomes clear that the project of Zion building is the project of fashioning the heaven mortals will themselves inhabit.

In Mormonism's first few generations, Smith and Young emphasized Mormonism's ultimate end as the creation of a chain of belonging linking all of humanity in a Heavenly Family. The mechanics of that chain of belonging went through numerous iterations. Smith emphasized literal kinship with God, even as he considered adoption a metaphor for formal integration into God's kingdom after the alienation of sin.[288] Plural marriage theology developed in measure as a way of consolidating and expanding lines of eternal kinship. And to some extent, the practice was understood as a means of creating a vast and endless posterity related to world creation. As Samuel Brown and Jonathan Stapley have documented, under Young especially, adoption theology enabled the construction of extensive sacerdotal families.[289] Mormon theology underwent its greatest transformation in the years surrounding the abandonment of plural marriage. Making natural kinship lines, rather than priesthood dynasties, the focus of temple sealing rituals placed the Mormon nuclear family front and center in the newly articulated gospel vision. One consequence of the old adoption theology had been a predisposition toward what George Q. Cannon called "clannishness and divisions."[290] Unfortunately, the practice invited unseemly orientation around prestige and dynasty building; as Woodruff commented, "men would go out and electioneer and labor with all their power to get men adopted to them."[291]

In a related way, the project of salvation frequently found emphasis in notions of expansiveness and dominion; early writers like the Pratts in particular found heady appeal in the possibilities of boundless posterity and godlike sovereignty over new worlds. With the abandonment of polygamy in the nineteenth century's closing decade, Mormonism underwent profound change. The cessation of a practice that had long been a wrenching social experiment, a political bone of contention, and a focus of Mormon theologizing created substantive shifts in Mormon thought. In particular, the language and aspirations of Mormon soteriology underwent a two-pronged contraction. The first, as we saw, shifted much of the focus from the heavenly family, for all practical purposes, to the orbit of the nuclear family. Mormons successfully became exemplars, rather than subverters, of the domestic ideal. Though genealogical work continued apace, in tandem with language about intergenerational bonds, the focus was undoubtedly on the nuclear unit, and on its preservation and perfection here as much as hereafter.

The second development was a shift in emphasis from world building to character sanctifying. Church programs and sermons alike aimed to cultivate a practical ethic of self-discipline, self-improvement, and moral living. Both these shifts were explicitly manifest in the two major works of the era's two greatest Mormon theologians, Talmage and Roberts.

In 1899, even before polygamy had fully ceased as a practice, Talmage was already shifting the Mormon focus from the many to the one, and from eternal dynasties to social benefits. Talmage describes marriage not in the context of endless posterity in the eternities but as a principle of "proper social organization," for "the perpetuation of the human family," and as a model of "strictest personal purity."[292] He introduces his section on marriage by invoking "the necessity of proper social organization," and the institution of marriage as "essential to the stability of society."[293] In the same final chapter, Talmage concludes his treatise with a deliberate gesture of theological modesty rather than audacity. "Practical Religion," he called the last chapter. Ironically, but one could say pointedly, it is under that rubric that he invokes the Mormon doctrine of theosis. "As God is, man may become," he quotes, using Snow's famous couplet. But the key to this *imitatio dei* immediately follows: "charity," he writes, "is the love that saves."[294] Benevolence, through active participation in works and gifts of charity, round out his discussion. The work of becoming God, in Talmage's hands, is indistinguishable from the work of simply being a good Christian.

As Roberts brings *The Truth, The Way, The Life* to a close, he mirrors Talmage's twin emphases. His last chapter is on "The Marriage Institution." And here, like Talmage, his emphasis shifts from the post-mortal to the this worldly, from the theological to the practical. Roberts begins his discussion with the words, "The unity of society—the family," defending its benefits to civilization. Plural marriage he relegates to an "appendage." More central to his concerns, marriage is "the chief cornerstone of the temple of human existence," the basis of "the family [and] the home."[295] And the central concern in presenting these doctrines, as with Talmage, is expressed as a "hope to see . . . this ethic of sex relations and marriage . . . become—by the grace of God—the sex and marriage ethic of the world."[296]

Finally, Roberts considers the final meaning of Mormon theology, with conclusions much like those of Talmage. According to his book's tripartite division, "life" refers to the life of Christ, and the attainment of the kind and quality of life he embodied. Roberts writes two chapters elaborating what he calls "The Christian Character." Forsaking discussions of new worlds or endless posterity, he recenters adoption in a more conventional Christian way: "the new birth into fellowship by union with these—the Father and the Son—and the indwelling of God in the human soul." He continues, "the true disciple of the Christ is born of God, and by that birth men participate in the divine nature."[297] As for how we understand the final result of this gradual transformation, "a matter of growth as well as of birth," he quotes the epistle of John: "Now are we the sons of God, and it doeth not yet appear what we shall be; but we know that, when he shall appear, we shall be like him."[298]

This early twentieth-century reorientation from the communal to the individual, and from other-worldly bonds to this-worldly character formation, was further enhanced by important developments in the social context of the era. The key influence in this regard was the mania for progressivism that swept the period—a philosophy that emphasized the amelioration of social conditions and the blossoming of human potential through the improvement of technology, government, and education. Progress became the mantra across the social and cultural spectrum. As a prominent voice of the movement declared, "democracy must stand or fall on a platform of human perfectibility." "Human nature" itself, he argued, was improvable "by institutions."[299] The convergence of such optimism about human potential with Mormon theologies of eternal progress was fortuitous, coming as it did on the heels of polygamy's abandonment. As Matthew Bowman has argued, "the early twentieth century was a time of rehabilitation for Mormons, when they worked to reinvent a religion shorn of polygamy and forced into American ways of being, and progressivism gave them the concepts, language, and tools to preserve their distinctiveness within adaptation."[300]

The practical consequence of these developments, in and outside the church, was a new emphasis on individual perfectibility. In Smith's thought, humankind's role in the process of sanctification centers on his submission to divine law. It is this submission, Smith declared, that makes Christ's freely offered sacrifice personally efficacious, allowing individuals to become "perfected and sanctified."[301] For this reason, Mormons hold, obedience is "the first law of heaven." That phrase frames Sunday School lessons, is recognized in LDS temple worship, and is repeated in conference addresses often enough to be a Mormon mantra.[302] Church emphasis on the demonstration of faithfulness is evident across a spectrum that reveals a seamless synthesis of progressivist impulses with Mormon institutional life: going back to 1875, Mormon young men participated in a "mutual improvement association." Since 1913, Mormons have participated officially in the Boy Scouts of America organization; here young men progress through the ranks, earning both merit badges and a "duty to God" award in a way that blurs the spiritual and civic completely. With a similar mind to Christian life as an upward-leaning ladder, young men are said to "progress" through the ranks of the priesthood, from deacon at age twelve, through teacher and priest and on to elder at age eighteen. Young women have their own "Personal Progress" program that measures goal setting against achievement. Even the women of the church were presented with a "pursuit of excellence" program in the 1970s. All of these initiatives can be seen as giving corporate form to the Mormon ideal of "eternal progression," an idea rooted in Joseph Smith's teachings, but which only "moved to the center of the Mormon lexicon" in the Progressive Era.[303]

Perfection is a goal which Mormons unabashedly espouse and pursue. "We also need to remember that the Lord gives no commandments that are impossible to obey," a modern apostle chided in reference to Christ's injunction to be perfect, in a book titled *Perfection Pending*.[304] "Preparing for Exaltation" is the name of the Sunday School lesson manual targeting young teens. And the preparation is long term. It may be, as the Book of Mormon teaches, that "This life is the time for men to prepare to meet God; yea, behold the day of this life is the day for men to perform their labors."[305] But in the quest for the repose of the righteous, death brings no respite even to the valiant. Fourth president of the church Wilford Woodruff recorded how, years after the martyrdom of Smith, "by and by I saw the Prophet again, and I got the privilege to ask him a question. 'Now,' said I, 'I want to know why you are in a hurry. I have been in a hurry all through my life but I expected my hurry would be over when I got into the kingdom of heaven, if I ever did.' Joseph said, 'I will tell you, Brother Woodruff, . . . so much work has to be done and we need to be in a hurry in order to accomplish it.'"[306] Tellingly, Mormons measure their commitment to their church not in terms like "devout," "lapsed," or "believing," but as "active" or "inactive." The beehive was the state symbol chosen by the

Utah Mormons, and frenetic activity in the pursuit of salvation is their hallmark. In this regard, Mormons conspicuously take to heart Paul's admonition to "work out" their salvation. Doubtless this is one reason why Harold Bloom called Mormons, "perhaps the most work-addicted culture in religious history."[307]

ETERNAL BECOMING

"It is reasonable to anticipate that the life of the world to come will not be focused in a timeless moment of illumination, as some eschatological traditions have suggested (the beatific vision), but it will take the form of an evolving salvific process, involving judgment and purgation and leading to the endless exploration of the inexhaustible riches of the divine nature as they are progressively unveiled. If finite creatures are truly to encounter the infinite reality of the divine, it must surely be through such a 'temporal' process of this kind. The finite cannot take in the Infinite at a glance."
—J. C. POLKINGHORNE, Theology in the Context of Science[308]

The dynamic cosmos first directly viewed by William Herschel provided an emphatic challenge to the centuries-old model of a Great Chain of Being, a scale of static hierarchy into which each element of creation fit securely and snugly. But as long ago as the Renaissance, the great humanist Pico della Miradola had insisted that Adam—first human—was exempt from the fixity proper to the "universal Chain," because only he was given no "fixed abode." "The nature of all other beings is limited and constrained," his Creator told him. Only "thou, constrained by no limits, in accordance with thine own free will, . . . shalt ordain for thyself the limits of thy nature." Beasts, Pico continued, "bring their nature with them from the womb. Spiritual beings, by contrast, 'become what they are to be.' "[309]

Such "becoming" has been variously characterized in Christian thought as event or process. In the eighteenth century, John and Charles Wesley had contended, as many fellow Christians have, over the timing of salvation: "We sang and fell into dispute," Charles recorded in his journal, "whether conversion was gradual or instantaneous. My brother was very positive for the latter and very shocking. . . . I insisted a man need not know when he first had faith."[310] Joseph Smith effectively sidestepped one of the primary theological controversies of his age by reframing the issue, situating salvation in a distant future and defining it as an eternal process of transformation rather than an earthly state of justification or sanctification. In this sense, Smith's views were consistent with nineteenth-century liberal humanism generally, which accorded to the human soul unfettered potential and a dynamic future.

The evolutionary bent to views of human destinies were common in the century after Darwin. "There could be nothing inherent in the act of dying which caused instantaneous perfection. . . . Only the continuous development of the soul in heaven would accomplish spiritual perfection," as one Methodist writer saw the case.[311] Mormon salvation differed in one essential regard from Christian precedent. Common to all versions of Christian salvation was the qualitative divide believed to exist between Creator and creature, a divide that could only be bridged by an endowment of sanctifying grace. Hostility to Origen's belief in pre-mortal existence was largely a fear, as Tertullian expressed it, that such heavenly origins, like the divine destiny it intimated, "put [the human soul] on a par with God." In the modern, more secular, age, such fears dissipated in the face of optimism about human potential. Joseph Addison, for example, believed there was not

a more pleasing and triumphant Consideration in Religion than this of the perpetual Progress which the Soul makes towards the Perfection of its Nature, without ever arriving at a Period in it. To look upon the Soul as going from Strength to Strength, to consider that she is to shine for ever with new Accessions of Glory, and brighten to all Eternity; that she will be still adding Virtue to Virtue, and Knowledge to Knowledge; carries in it something wonderfully agreeable to that Ambition which is natural to the Mind of Man. . . . We know not yet what we shall be.[312]

By the French Revolution, faith in human progress became a virtual religion unto itself. So Pierre Cabanis could assert that "the only true religion is that which ennobles man by giving him a sublime idea of the dignity of his being and of the great destinies to which he is called by the designer of the human condition."[313] Enlightenment thought considered human reason, properly educated, the engine of personal and collective progress. In the early Republic, practical philosophers like Thomas Dick believed such intellectual values were perfectly conformable, rather than threatening, to Christian conceptions of salvation. At a bare minimum, Dick argued, men and angels in a future state would continue their intellectual progress in mathematics and astronomy, as a simple precondition for understanding the glory and majesty of the heavens they inherit. But he also enumerated natural philosophy, anatomy, physiology, and history as "some of those branches of science which will be recognized [and studied] by the righteous in a future state."[314]

Smith found in Dick a kindred spirit, excerpting his writings in his own church newspaper, but he expanded and canonized their intellectual thrust. The consequence of this current is evident in the overstatement of an observer like Harold Bloom, who calls Mormonism a Gnostic religion,[315] a debatable appellation but one that recognizes the religion's unusually heavy emphasis on knowledge. "The principle of knowledge is the principle of salvation," Smith declared.[316] And "the relationship we have with God places us in a situation to advance in knowledge."[317] Together these statements provide a key to understanding Mormonism's conception of human destiny: salvation is an incremental process rather than event or static condition, and it involves the perpetual acquisition of greater understanding. "Salvation" Smith at one time defined as "being placed beyond the powers of all [ones's] enemies," and the key to that superior power was knowledge. "Knowledge is power and the man who has the most knowledge has the greatest power." This was why he deemed it "impossible for a man to be saved in ignorance."[318] Damnation was anything short of such an eternal journey; for the damned, "there is an end of his career in knowledge, he cannot obtain all knowledge for his has sealed up the gate."[319] Life is not so much a probation as an educative experience: "Whatever principle of intelligence we attain unto in this life, it will rise with us in the resurrection. And if a person gains more knowledge and intelligence in this life through his diligence and obedience than another, he will have so much the advantage in the world to come."[320]

Unsurprisingly, this Gnostic bent finds expression in Smith's understanding of Deity itself: "These two facts do exist, that there are two spirits, one being more intelligent than the other; there shall be another more intelligent than they; I am the Lord thy God, I am more intelligent than they all."[321] By clear implication, a central component in the ongoing process by which humans participate in the divine nature is the steady progress through eons of time in the acquisition of knowledge. "When you climb a ladder," said Smith, "you must begin at the bottom rung. You have got to . . . go on until you have learned the last principle of the Gospel. It will be a great while after the grave before you learn to understand the last, for it is a great thing to learn salvation beyond the grave and it is not all to be comprehended in this world."[322]

The process of eternal education began before physical bodies were even acquired. Mosiah Hancock's vision of the pre-mortal world is not canonical. But it reflects, if it does not establish, a Mormon sense of education's primordial roots as well as its eternal future. He saw innumerable spirits, "arranged in classes," where "they were taught in the arts and sciences, and everything necessary to make the heart happy. The teachers . . . received the instruction they imparted from certain notable ones, who in turn got their directions from the Father and the Son. . . . I also saw Joseph, Brigham, and many others engaged in this work of education."[323]

Mormonism thoroughly merges the spiritual and the material, the heavenly and the earthly, into one eternal continuum. So it is not surprising that in the Mormon conception of eternal learning, facile dichotomies evaporate. "Man may advance by effort and by obedience to higher and yet higher laws as he may learn them through the eternities to come, until he attains the rank and status of Godship. 'Mormonism' is so bold as to declare that such is the possible destiny of the human soul."[324]

The striking emphasis here is on the acquisition of knowledge pertaining to successively higher forms of law, with which humans learn to comply—without distinction between the laws of physics and the laws of holiness. Arts and sciences do not typically suggest the spiritual knowledge that Gnosticism—or any conventional *Imitatio Christi*—implies. But in a cosmos where heaven and earth merge, where angels are resurrected humans, and all spirit is matter, other dichotomies collapse as well.

The consequences can at times be disconcerting: We saw Young's vision of an earth transformed by angelic chemists; Orson Pratt would elaborate this view a few years later. "The study of science is the study of something eternal. If we study astronomy, we study the works of God. If we study chemistry, geology, optics, or any other branch of science, every new truth we come to the understanding of is eternal; it is a part of the great system of universal truth. It is truth that exists throughout universal nature; and God is the dispenser of all truth—scientific, religious, and political."[325] Young elaborated the principle further, in an eloquent celebration of the eternal quest for knowledge, framing it as not just an ingredient in salvation but also one of salvation's principal joys:

> All men should study to learn the nature of mankind, and to discern that divinity inherent in them. A spirit and power of research is planted within, yet they remain undeveloped. . . . What will satisfy us? If we understood all principles and powers that are, that have been, and that are to come, and had wisdom sufficient to control powers and elements with which we are associated, perhaps we would then be satisfied. If this will not satisfy the human mind, there is nothing that will. . . . If we could so understand true philosophy as to understand our own creation, and what it is for . . . and could understand that matter can be organized and brought forth into intelligence, and to possess more intelligence, and to continue to increase in that intelligence; and could learn those principles that organized matter into animals, vegetables, and into intelligent beings; and could discern the Divinity acting, operating, and diffusing principles into matter to produce intelligent beings, and to exalt them—to what? Happiness. Will [anything] short of that fully satisfy the spirits implanted within us? No.[326]

Man and God, building bridges and creating worlds, practicing chemistry and endowing the earth with its celestial glory—the mundane and the miraculous are but different degrees on an eternal scale of knowledge acquisition.

This unending process, a favorite doctrine with Mormons, is referred to as "eternal progression," and can be an idea both debilitating and bracing. Perpetual, painful self-revelation, and inadequacies ameliorated only through eons of schooling, stand in stark tension with confidently expressed certainties about theological truths and spiritual realities. Latter-day Saints presume to know positively where they came from, why they are here, and where they are headed. But such confidence is paired with the sometimes disheartening personal recognition that salvation itself must wait upon complete personal transformation into a godly individual, the laborious acquisition of an unfathomable scope of knowledge.

The principle of eternal progression in a framework of discrete degrees of glory (seen in Smith's 1832 vision) has led Mormons to ponder whether progress is confined to those spheres where judgment initially places the individual. Joseph Smith's brother Hyrum saw Joseph's universalism as meaning no salvific state was static: "Hiram said Aug 1st. Those of the Terrestrial Glory either advance to the Celestial or recede to the Telestial or else the moon would not be a type, [because] it 'waxes & wanes.'" Contemporary Charlotte Haven thought Joseph's Nauvoo sermons were even more optimistic in this regard, understanding him to say that a spirit in the lowest kingdom "constantly progresses in spiritual knowledge until safely landed in the Celestial."³²⁷ The Mormon temple ritual itself recapitulates this form. In its most basic outline, temple ritual charts the progress of the individual from pre-mortal life through mortality and into the beyond, passing through the lower two kingdoms and culminating with entry into a representation of the celestial kingdom itself.

B. H. Roberts also explicitly interpreted Smith's universalism to imply a steadfast progression through the kingdoms of glory. Though scripture was vague, he argued, the ministry alluded to in each kingdom seemed meaningless "unless it be for the purpose of advancing our Father's children along the lines of eternal progress." However, whether "after education and advancement without those spheres" all could "at last emerge from them and make their way to the higher degrees of glory" was not revealed.³²⁸ Talmage thought the answer was implicit in the principle of eternal progression itself: "advancement from grade to grade within any kingdom, and from kingdom to kingdom, will be provided for. . . . Eternity is progressive."³²⁹

Apparently balancing faithfulness to Smith's original vision and liberality with a fear of the spiritual slackness a misunderstood universalism could invite, the church leadership has refrained from officially endorsing one version over the other, as one First Presidency communication indicates:

Dear Brother,

The brethren direct me to say that the Church has never announced a definite doctrine upon this point. Some of the brethren have held that it was possible in the course of progression to advance from one glory to another, invoking the principle of eternal progression; others of the Brethren have taken the opposite view. But as stated, the Church has never announced a definite doctrine on this point.

Sincerely your brother,

Joseph L. Anderson, Secretary to the First Presidency.[330]

Still, voices of influential individuals like J. Reuben Clark maintained a sympathetic continuity with the line from Smith through Talmage:

It is my belief that God will save all of His children that he can; and while, if we live unrighteously here, we shall not go to the other side in the same status, so to speak, as those who lived righteously; nevertheless, the unrighteous will have their chance, and in the eons of the eternities that are to follow, they, too, may climb to the destinies to which they who are righteous and serve God, have climbed.[331]

With its virtual universalism, Mormonism comes close to reenacting the heresy of the first Christian theologian Origen.

Origen's claim of a universal salvation for the human family, along with his assertion of pre-mortal existence, was put under anathema in the sixth century.[332] Both teachings became closely if not exactly replicated in Mormonism. Two of the teachings of Pelagius condemned in the early fifth century accorded humankind exemption from original sin and an unprecedented degree of free will. Mormonism embraced both, and the LDS people have sometimes been accused of Pelagianism as a consequence. The twin condemnation of Pelagius and Origen, writes one scholar, ensured the supremacy in the Christian tradition of a "theology whose central concerns were human sinfulness, not human potentiality; divine determination, not human freedom and responsibility."[333] LDS thought is rooted in a conception of human potential born of a filiation with God that extends infinitely backward in time. God, in this schema, is a kindred Being, who invites the human family to share his condition and nature. Christ facilitates an ongoing process of divinization, by an atonement that enlarges the scope of human freedom and possibility, even as it balances those goods with the costs of human accountability for choice.

Pelagius and Origen, in other words, represent a Christian road not taken, but one that might have led to a Christianity in which Mormonism would find a more congenial place, though doubtless with important caveats. Like the Protestants who preceded them, Mormons found compelling reasons to drastically change the shape of Christian doctrine they encountered in their contemporary world. But

Mormonism would locate the need for major church reform backwards almost a millennium from the theses of Luther and the Geneva experiment of Calvin. This is because Mormon Restoration, in many cases, finds greater theological kinship with the ancient Christian past than with the great age of reform. This fact may account in large measure for the dissonance contemporary Christians experience in the face of Mormonism's unique body of teachings.

NOTES

—

SOURCE ABBREVIATIONS

ANF Alexander Roberts and James Donaldson, eds., *The Ante-Nicene Fathers* (Grand Rapids, MI: Eerdmans, 1977).

BC Book of Commandments for the Government of the Church of Jesus Christ of Latter-day Saints Christ (Independence, MO: W. W. Phelps, 1833).

C&C Jaroslav Pelikan and Valerie Hotchkiss, *Creeds and Confessions of Faith in the Christian Tradition* (New Haven: Yale University Press, 2003).

CHL Church History Library, The Church of Jesus Christ of Latter-day Saints

CD *The Complete Discourses of Brigham Young*, ed. Richard S. Van Wagoner (Salt Lake City: Smith-Petit Foundation, 2009).

D&C Doctrine and Covenants of the Church of Jesus Christ of Latter-day Saints. Revelations now in this scripture will generally be cited according to the edition in which they were first published, or in the church newspaper where they first appeared, since those published forms and not the MS copy would usually be the most disseminated and influential version. The early editions subsequent to the Book of Commandments (1833) were the 1835 Doctrine and Covenants (Kirtland, OH: F. G. Williams), the 1844 edition (Nauvoo: John Taylor), and the 1876 edition (Salt Lake City: Deseret News). The current 1981 LDS version, also known as the Doctrine and Covenants, will always be indicated parenthetically, unless the 1876 version is cited, whose numbering is the same as in the 1981.

EMS *The Evening and Morning Star*

JD	*Journal of Discourses*, 26 vols., reported by G. D. Watt et al. (Liverpool: F.D. and S. W. Richards, et al., 1851–1886). (Reprint Salt Lake City: n.p., 1974.)
JSP-H1	*Joseph Smith Papers: Histories, Volume 1*, ed. Dean C. Jessee, Ronald K. Esplin, and Richard L. Bushman (Salt Lake City: Church Historian's Press, 2012).
JSP-J1	*Joseph Smith Papers: Journals Volume 1:1832–1839*, ed. Dean C. Jessee, Mark Ashurst-McGee, and Richard L. Jensen (Salt Lake City: Church Historians Press, 2008).
JSP-J2	*Joseph Smith Papers: Journals, Volume 2*, ed. Andrew H . Hedges, Alex D. Smith, and Richard Lloyd Anderson (Salt Lake City: Church Historian's Press, 2011).
Key	Parley P. Pratt, *Key to the Science of Theology* (Liverpool: F. D. Richards, 1855).
KJV	King James Version of the Bible
MA	*The Messenger and Advocate*
MHC	Manuscript History of the Church, Church History Library
MS	*The Latter-day Saints Millennial Star*
NPNF1	*Philip Schaff, Nicene and Post-Nicene Fathers of the Christian Church*, First series (Edinburgh: T&T Clark, 1993).
NPNF2	Philip Schaff, ed., *Nicene and Post-Nicene Fathers of the Christian Church*, Second series (Peabody, MA: Hendrickson, 1999).
NRSV	New Revised Standard Version of the Bible
NT	New Testament
NYPL	New York Public Library
OT	Old Testament
PGP	The Pearl of Great Price (Salt Lake City: Deseret, 1981). Earlier editions noted by date.
TS	*Times and Seasons*
WJS	Andrew F. Ehat and Lyndon W. Cook, eds., *The Words of Joseph Smith* (Orem, UT: Grandin Book Company, 1991).

Biblical quotations are from the New Revised Standard Version (NRSV), unless otherwise indicated. When the King James Version (KJV) is cited, it is generally because Smith and subsequent Mormons relied upon that edition.

PREFACE

1. Sydney Ahlstrom, *A Religious History of the American People* (New Haven: Yale University Press, 1972), 508. Ahlstrom's study won the National Book Award in 1973.

2. Catholics, Methodists, Presbyterians, and Baptists all passed resolutions to that effect in the early twenty-first century. See references in "Striving for Acceptance," *Washington Post*, 9 February 9, 2002, p. B9.

3. Emblematic of the intellectual energy characterizing younger Mormon scholars are numerous substantive blogs and podcasts addressing Mormon Studies, as well as a journal launched in 2005, *Element*, produced by the Society for Mormon Philosophy and Theology. Not all the contributors in this field are from the rising generation; Truman Madsen in the 1970s, and David Paulsen in subsequent decades, successfully developed significant dialogue with theologians from other faith traditions. As two examples, see Madsen, ed., *Reflections on Mormonism: Judaeo-Christian Parallels* (Provo: Religious Studies Center, 1978), a product of a Brigham Young University symposium involving luminaries from Jacob Milgrom to David Noel Freedman to Krister Stendahl. Paulsen, with David Musser, produced *Mormonism in Dialogue with*

Contemporary Christian Theologies (Macon, GA: Mercer University Press, 2007), involving such names as Clark Pinnock, David Tracy, and David Griffin.

CHAPTER 2

1. Stephen Webb, *Jesus Christ, Eternal God: Heavenly Flesh and the Metaphysics of Matter* (New York: Oxford, 2011), 6.

2. Hugh Nibley, "Paths That Stray: Some Notes on the Sophic and Mantic," in *The Ancient State*, ed. Donald W. Parry and Stephen D. Ricks (Salt Lake City and Provo: Deseret and Foundation for Ancient Research and Mormon Studies, 1991), 381. See also his essay in the same collection, "Three Shrines: Mantic, Sophic, and Sophistic," 311–79.

3. Though better known as the Lectures on Faith, in the Manuscript History of the Church they are first referred to as "the lectures on theology" (B-1, 562) and are so denominated in the 1835 Doctrine and Covenants.

4. Elements of the Articles of Faith had appeared in earlier iterations of a Mormon creed, including versions by Oliver Cowdery (1834), Joseph Young (1836), and others. See John W. Welch and David Whittaker, "'We Believe…': Development of the Articles of Faith," *Ensign* 9. 9 (September 1979):51–55.

5. David Whitmer objected to publication of revelations as tantamount to "a creed." "An Address to all Believers in Christ" (Richmond, MO: D. Whitmer, 1887), 51.

6. 1835 D&C, section iii.

7. Gary J. Bergera, *Conflict in the Quorum: Orson Pratt, Brigham Young, Joseph Smith* (Salt Lake City: Signature, 2002).

8. Notable exceptions would be several additions to the Doctrine and Covenants in 1876; the Pearl of Great Price [hereafter PGP] (primarily a compilation of Smith's additions to Genesis, purported writings of Abraham, and extracts from Smith's personal history), added to the canon in 1880; a vision each recorded by Joseph Smith and Joseph F. Smith were canonized in 1976.

9. Theology Lecture First, Q&A 1.1, in 1835 D&C 9. Smith cited Charles Buck, *A Theological Dictionary* (Philadelphia: Joseph Woodward, 1830), 582. Sidney Rigdon apparently wrote the bulk of the lectures, under Smith's supervision.

10. Origen, *De Principiis*, trans. Frederick Crombie, Preface, 3, in *ANF*, 4: 239.

11. "Theology," in *Oxford Dictionary of the Christian Church*, ed. F. L. Cross and E. A. Livingstone (Oxford: Oxford University Press, 1997), 1604.

12. John Milton, *Paradise Lost*, Book 1, ll. 15–16, in *The Complete Poetry and Essential Prose of John Milton*, ed. William Kerrigan, John Rumrich, and Stephen M. Fallon (New York: Modern Library, 2007), 294.

13. Milton, *Paradise Lost*, Book 8, ll. 167–77, pp. 502–503.

14. Augustine, *Confessions* XI: 12, trans. F. J. Sheed (Indianapolis: Hackett, 1993), 218.

15. Milton, *Paradise Lost*, Book 7, ll. 182–91, p. 482.

16. Thomas Dick, *The Philosophy of a Future State* (Philadelphia: Biddle, 1845 [first published in 1829]), v.

17. Terryl L. Givens, *When Souls Had Wings: Premortal Life in Western Thought* (New York Oxford University Press, 2010), 147–87.

18. E. Brooks Holifield, *Theology in America* (New Haven: Yale University Press, 2003), 335.

19. Rodney Stark, "The Rise of a New World Faith," *Review of Religious Research* 26.1 (September 1984):19.

20. Gerald E. Smith, *Schooling the Prophet: The Influence of the Book of Mormon on Joseph Smith and the Early Restoration.* Unpublished ms.

21. A mob destroyed the Mormon printing press and scattered the printed pages of the work in progress. Several signatures survived to be bound and distributed as the Book of Commandments, containing some 65 revelations of an intended 77. See *Joseph Smith Papers: Revelations and Translations; Vol. 2: Published Revelations*, ed. Robin Scott Jensen, Richard E. Turley Jr., and Riley M. Lorimer (Salt Lake City: Church Historian's Press, 2011), 173–93.

22. Fred C. Collier and William S. Harwell, eds., *Kirtland Council Minute Book*, 21 April 1834 (Salt Lake City: Collier's, 1996), 62–63.

23. MHC A-1, 172; "History of Joseph Smith," *TS* 5. 9 (1 May 1844):512. In CHL.

24. See Noel B. Reynolds, "The Case for Sidney Rigdon as Author of the 'Lectures on Faith,'" *Journal of Mormon History* 31.2 (Fall 2005):1–41.

25. MHC B-1, 562.

26. Lecture 1.14, 2.2, 5.3 in 1835 D&C, 7, 12, 54.

27. "Lecture Seventh," 1835 D&C, 67.

28. "Lecture Second," 1835 D&C, 35.

29. Joseph Smith, "To the Elders of the Church of Latter Day Saints," *MA* 1.12 (September 1835):179.

30. Young acquired the designation of prophet some three years later.

31. *New York World*, 25 September 1870, cited in Stanley P. Hirshson, *The Lion of the Lord: A Biography of Brigham Young* (New York: Knopf, 1969), 323.

32. See Benjamin E. Park, "(Re)Interpreting Early Mormon Thought," *Dialogue: A Journal of Mormon Thought* 45.2 (Summer 2012):59–88.

33. Proclamation, *MS* 5 (March 1845):152.

34. Annie Clark Tanner, *A Mormon Mother: An Autobiography* (Salt Lake City: Tanner Trust Fund, 1991), 12, 14.

35. Cited in Parley P. Pratt, *A Voice of Warning* (Edinburgh: H. Armour, 1847), v. "Standard work" did not have the contemporary Mormon meaning of scriptural or canonical, but meant a writing "established as a rule or model." Noah Webster, *American Dictionary of the English Language* (New York: S. Converse, 1828).

36. Brigham Young to a "Gentleman in New York," 31 October 1864. In CHL.

37. *Deseret News*, 22 April 1875; *Deseret News,* 26 May 1875.

38. Brigham *CD*, 1: 498.

39. David Whittaker discusses Joseph Keeler's role as director there in 1902–1903. See "Joseph B. Keeler, Print Culture, and the Modernization of Mormonism, 1885–1918," in *Religion and the Culture of Print in Modern America*, ed. Charles L. Cohen and Paul S. Boyer (Madison, WI: University of Wisconsin Press, 2008), 105–27.

40. *The Seer* 1.1 (January 1853): 1.

41. John Taylor, *JD*, 5: 240.

42. Parley P. Pratt, *The Millennium, and Other Poems: To Which Is Annexed, A Treatise on the Regeneration and Eternal Duration of Matter* (New York: Molineux, 1840), 137.

43. Wilford Woodruff, *MS* 57.23 (6 June 1895):355–56.

44. An account of this episode is given by Richard Sherlock, "'We Can See No Advantage to a Continuation of the Discussion': The Roberts/Smith/Talmage Affair," *Dialogue: A Journal of Mormon Thought* 13.3 (Fall 1980):63–76.

45. See Terryl L. Givens, *People of Paradox: A History of Mormon Culture* (New York: Oxford University Press, 2007), 205–209.

46. J. Reuben Clark, "The Charted Course of the Church in Education," *Improvement Era* 41.9 (September 1938):521, 572.

47. From a meeting of the Twelve, 7 January 1930. Cited in James B. Allen, "The Story of *The Truth, The Way, The Life*," in B. H. Roberts, *The Truth, the Way, the Life*, ed. John W. Welch (Provo: BYU Studies, 1994), clxxviii.

48. Bruce R. McConkie, *Mormon Doctrine* (Salt Lake City: Bookcraft, 1958), 5.

49. Gregory A. Prince and William Robert Wright, *David O. McKay and the Rise of Modern Mormonism* (Salt Lake City: University of Utah Press, 2005), 50–52.

50. Prince and Wright, *David O. McKay*, 53.

51. Harold B. Lee, who oversaw correlation, pointed to Dunn's study as particular influential. Prince and Wright, *David O. McKay*, 144.

52. Bruce R. McConkie, personal letter widely reproduced and cited in many sources, including Philip L. Barlow, *Mormons and the Bible* (New York: Oxford University Press, 1991), 190.

53. Tanner, *Mormon Mother*, 12, 14.

54. James E. Faulconer, "Why a Mormon Won't Drink Coffee but Might Have a Coke: The Atheological Character of The Church of Jesus Christ of Latter-day Saints," *Element* 2.2 (Fall 2006):21.

55. MHC D-1, 1433.

56. Robert L. Millet, "What Do We Really Believe? Identifying Doctrinal Parameters Within Mormonism," in *Discourses in Mormon Theology: Philosophical and Theological Possibilities*, ed. James M. McLachlan and Loyd Ericson (Salt Lake City: Kofford, 2007), 265–81.

57. See the excellent overview of Mormon models including Millet's, with criticisms, by Loyd Ericson, "The Challenges of Defining Mormon Doctrine," *Element* 3.1 & 2 (Spring and Fall 2007):69–85.

58. Mark A. Noll, *America's God: From Jonathan Edwards to Abraham Lincoln* (New York: Oxford University Press, 2002), 233. The Dwight quotation, cited by Noll, is from *Theology: Explained and Defended* (London: William Baynes, 1819), 5:233.

59. On the evils of spiritualizing scripture, see *EMS* 1.2 (July 1832):11, 14; *EMS* 2.19 (April 1834):145; *EMS* 2.20 (May 1834):153.

60. *EMS* 1.5 (October 1832):3 (D&C 68:4).

61. Though not strictly speaking a priesthood office in Mormon ecclesiology, like deacon, elder, high priest, or apostle, for example, the president of the LDS Church is sustained as "prophet, seer, and revelator" by the membership.

62. "The sealing power is always vested in one man," Young remembered Smith teaching, "& Joseph told [Hyrum] if he did not stop it he would go to hell." Brigham Young to William Smith, 10 August 1845, Brigham Young Collection, in CHL.

63. *WJS*, 183–84.

64. Terryl L. Givens and Matthew Grow, *Parley P. Pratt: The Apostle Paul of Mormonism* (New York: Oxford University Press, 2011), 119, 125.

65. A rare exception was Smith's complaint about the theft of some of his ideas by the "great big elders" of the church, including the Pratts. "Nauvoo Relief Society Minutes," 28 April 1842, *WJS*, 116.

66. Parley P. Pratt, "Regulations for the Publishing Department of the Latter–day Saints in the East," *The Prophet*, reprinted in *TS* 6.1 (15 January 1845):778.

67. Jessee W. Crosby, in Hyrum L. Andrus and Helen Mae Andrus, *They Knew the Prophet: Personal Accounts from over 100 People Who Knew Joseph Smith* (Salt Lake City: Bookcraft, 1974), 140.

68. For early publication, see Peter Crawley, *A Descriptive Bibliography of the Mormon Church* (Provo: Religious Studies Center, 1997), 1:309–12. For subsequent publishing history, see Donald Q. Cannon, "The King Follett Discourse: Joseph Smith's Greatest Sermon in Historical Context," *BYU Studies* 18.2 (Winter 1978):191–92. George Albert Smith apparently endorsed its position that God was once as man and man could become as God ("Mormon View of Life's Mission," *Deseret Evening News*, June 27, 1908, Church section, p. 2); doubts apparently centered on other aspects of the sermon, such as the condition of children in the resurrection. My thanks to Don Bradley for this information and source.

69. David Van Biema, "Kingdom Come," *Time*, 4 August 1997.

70. "You need not worry that I do not understand some matters of doctrine. I think I understand them thoroughly, and it is unfortunate that the reporting may not make this clear." http://www.lds.org/general-conference/1997/10/drawing-nearer-to-the-lord?lang=Eng&clang=eng.

71. To give but one example, *Teachings of Presidents of the Church: Joseph Smith* (Salt Lake City: Church of Jesus Christ of Latter-day Saints, 2007), 40.

72. Woodruff's words were spoken in General Conference, 6 October 1890, and canonized as "Excerpts from Three Addresses," D&C Official Declaration 1 in the 1981 edition.

73. 1 Nephi 15:24; 1 Nephi 19:24.

74. BC 58:4 (D&C 56:4).

75. John C. Murray, *The Problem of God Yesterday and Today* (New Haven: Yale University Press, 1964), 53; cited in Jaroslav Pelikan, *Development of Christian Doctrine. Some Historical Prolegomena* (New Haven: Yale University Press, 1969), 1.

76. George MacDonald, "The Higher Faith," *Unspoken Sermons*, First Series (Whitehorn, CA: Johannesen, 2004), 35–37.

77. The revelation recorded as 1876 D&C 132 gave scriptural foundation for plural marriage. In ending it, Wilford Woodruff used language of revelatory authority: "The Lord has told me," "the Lord showed me," and "the God of heaven commanded me to do what I did do . . . and I wrote what the Lord told me to write." Cache Stake Conference, 1 November 1891. Canonized as "Excerpts," D&C Official Declaration 1.

78. Brown's position and McKay's pronouncement are discussed in Gregory A. Prince, "David O. McKay and Blacks: Building the Foundation for the 1978 Revelation," *Dialogue: A Journal of Mormon Thought* 35.1 (Spring 2002):145–53.

79. "Official Declaration 2," http://www.lds.org/scriptures/dc-testament/od?lang=eng.

80. Gary Wills, *Papal Sin: Structures of Deceit* (New York: Image Books, 2004), 7.

81. Wills, *Papal Sin*, 1.

82. 1844 D&C 103:1 (D&C 124:1). The phrase, and idea, recurs frequently in the D&C, as it does in the biblical story of Gideon, where the leader is required to pare his army of thousands down to 300, so divine might and not human strength will be seen as the source of salvation.

83. D. Todd Christofferson, "The Doctrine of Christ," *Ensign* 42.5 (May 2012):88.

CHAPTER 3

1. William Bradford, *Bradford's History of Plymouth Plantation, 1606–1646*, ed. William T. Davis (New York: Scribner's, 1908), 1:23; cited in Richard T. Hughes and C. Leonard Allen, *Illusions of Innocence: Protestant Primitivism in America, 1630–1875* (Abilene, TX: Abilene Christian University Press, 2008), 13.

2. The term is a translation of *depositum fidei*, and is rooted in the epistles to Timothy, which admonish him to "keep the deposit" (*depositum custodi* in the Vulgate, 1 Tim. 6:20 and 2 Tim. 1:14). The idea of balancing the development of doctrine with the church's responsibility to guard this original deposit is generally attributed to the fifth-century Vincent of Lerins.

3. John Henry Newman, "Essay on the Development of Christian Doctrine." This discussion borrows much from the overview of these developments in Alister McGrath, *Heresy: A History of Defending the Truth* (New York: HarperOne, 2009), 66–68.

4. Hughes and Allen, *Illusions,* 21.

5. Hughes and Allen, *Illusions,* 7, 4.

6. John Calvin uses the term, usually in phrasing alluding to "the restoration of the Church" its purity, etc. See *Institutes of the Christian Religion*, trans. Henry Beveridge (Peabody, MA: Hendrickson, 2008), 84, 296, 826, etc.

7. Lavina Fielding Anderson, ed., *Lucy's Book: A Critical Edition of Lucy Mack Smith's Family Memoir* (Salt Lake City: Signature, 2001), 230–31.

8. Anderson, *Lucy's Book,* 467. The emphasis on NT parallels does not appear in Lucy's draft; it may be an interpolation by the transcribers Martha Coray and Howard Coray, or subsequent editor Orson Pratt. In either case, the same Restorationist impulse is evident.

9. Sidney E. Mead, *The Lively Experiment: The Shaping of Christianity in America* (New York: Harper and Row, 1963), 108.

10. *JSP-H1,* 214.

11. *JSP-H1,* 11–12.

12. Charles Buck, *A Theological Dictionary* (Philadelphia: Joseph Woodward, 1830), 28.

13. "To N. C. Saxton," 4 January 1833, in *Personal Writings of Joseph Smith,* ed. Dean C. Jessee (Salt Lake City: Deseret, 2002), 296.

14. "Millennium," *EMS* 2.17 (February 1834):131.

15. Parley P. Pratt, *Voice of Warning and Instruction to all People* (New York: Sandford, 1837), 147.

16. The motto is attributable to Thomas Stone, who made it a principle of his 1809 manifesto, "Declaration and Address": "Nothing ought to be received into the faith or worship of the Church . . . that is not as old as the New Testament" (Washington, DC: Brown and Sample, 1809). See W. A. Morris, ed., *The Writings of Alexander Campbell* (Austin, TX: von Boeckmann, 1896), vii.

17. Ethan Smith, *View of the Trinity* (Poultney, VT: Smith & Shute, 1824), vii.

18. John H. Wigger, *Taking Heaven by Storm: Methodism and the Rise of Popular Christianity in America* (New York: Oxford University Press), 115. See 106ff for several examples.

19. "To the Most Vertuous and Noble Queen," Geneva Bible. Facsimile of the 1560 edition (Madison: University of Wisconsin Press, 1969), iii.

20. Thomas Russell, ed., *Works of John Owen* (London: Richard Baynes, 1826), 15:33.

21. Parley P. Pratt, "Fountain of Knowledge," in *An Appeal to the Inhabitants of the State of New York; Letter to Queen Victoria; The Fountain of Knowledge; Immortality of the Body; and Intelligence and Affection* (Nauvoo, IL: John Taylor, [1844]), 17.

22. To William W. Phelps, 27 November 1832, in Jessee, *Personal Writings*, 287.

23. "Ordinances of the gospel," in Buck, *Theological Dictionary*, 418.

24. 1835 D&C 4:3 (D&C 84:20–21).

25. *JSP-H1*, 214.

26. Cited in Wigger, *Taking Heaven*, 23.

27. Christopher C. Jones, "The Power and Form of Godliness: Methodist Conversion Narratives and Joseph Smith's First Vision," *Journal of Mormon History* 37.2 (Spring 2011):89. Jones's article shows the substantial influence of Methodism on Joseph Smith and early Mormon understanding and rhetoric of conversion.

28. Wigger, *Taking Heaven*, 16. As an example of this contrasting emphasis, Wesley wrote of the need to "build [members] up to that Holiness, without which they cannot see the Lord." For Smith, purity of heart was requisite (1835 D&C 81:4 [D&C 97:16]), but he also recorded that without "the ordinances . . . and the authority of the priesthood . . . no man can see the face of God" (1835 D&C 4:3 [D&C 84:21–22]).

29. Benjamin Winchester, *The History of the Priesthood from the Beginning of the World to the Present Time* (Philadelphia: Brown, Bicking & Guilpert, 1843), iii, 17, 74.

30. 1844 D&C 103:13 (D&C 124:40).

31. Orson Pratt, *An Interesting Account of Several Remarkable Visions* (Edinburgh: Ballantyne and Hughes, 1840).

32. Smith described in various sources his receipt of priesthood keys at the hands of John the Baptist, Peter, James, and John, and a host of Old Testament figures.

33. See in this regard Richard L. Bushman, "The Visionary World of Joseph Smith," *BYU Studies* 37.1 (1997–98):183–204.

34. *JSP-H1*, 222.

35. Pratt, "Fountain of Knowledge," 17.

36. To William W. Phelps, 27 November 1832, in Jessee, *Personal Writings*, 287.

37. Alexander Campbell, "Delusions: An Analysis of the Book of Mormon," *Millennial Harbinger* II (7 February 1831):85–96. Reprinted in part in Francis W. Kirkham, *A New Witness for Christ in America*, 2 vols. (Independence, MO: Zion's, 1951), 2:101–109.

38. Mario S. De Pillis, "The Quest for Religious Authority and the Rise of Mormonism," *Dialogue: A Journal of Mormon Thought* 1 (Spring 1966):68–88.

39. David Holland employs this term in his groundbreaking study, *Sacred Borders: Continuing Revelation and Canonical Restraint in Early America* (New York: Oxford, 2011), 6, 209.

40. Walt Whitman, *Notebooks and Unpublished Prose Manuscripts*, ed. Edward F. Grier, 6 vols. (New York: New York University Press, 1984), 6:2046, 1:353.

41. David M. Robinson, *The Spiritual Emerson* (Boston: Beacon, 2003), 78.

42. Richard L. Bushman, *Believing History*, ed. Reid L. Neilson and Jed Woodworth (New York: Columbia University Press, 2004), 274.

43. Francis J. Bremer, *John Winthrop: America's Forgotten Founding Father* (New York: Oxford University Press, 2003), 199.

44. *Retractions*, 1.13. Cited in Gerald R. McDermott, "Jonathan Edwards, John Henry Newman, and Non–Christian Religions," paper delivered at the American Society of Church History Meeting, Yale University, New Haven, CT, 31 March 2001.

45. *Matthew Henry's Commentary* (Grand Rapids, MI: Zondervan, 1961), 1914. The glossed verse is Heb. 4:2. The commentary on the epistles was written by a board of non-Conformist ministers after Henry's death in 1714.

46. Although the idea is an old one, D. P. Walker claims to have "launched" the term *prisca theologia*. See his *Ancient Theology: Studies in Christian Platonism from the 15th to the 17th Century* (London: Duckworth, 1972), 1.

47. "To the Elders of the Church," *EMS* 2.18 (March 1834):143.

48. Parley P. Pratt, Meeting, 25 April 1847, Miscellaneous Minutes from 25 April 1847 Meeting; cited in Terryl L. Givens and Matthew J. Grow, *Parley P. Pratt: The Apostle Paul of Mormonism* (New York: Oxford University Press, 2010), 242.

49. *EMS* 1:10 (March 1833):73; *EMS* 1.11 (April 1833):81.

50. *EMS* 1.11 (April 1833):81; *EMS* 1.10 (March 1833):73 (Moses 6:52, 65, PGP).

51. "To the Elders of the Church," *EMS* 2.18 (March 1834):143.

52. *WJS*, 39.

53. *WJS*, 41.

54. 1844 D&C 106:20–21 (D&C 128:20–21).

55. BC 6, 1835; D&C 82 (D&C 7, 93).

56. Dean C. Jessee, ed., *The Papers of Joseph Smith. Volume 1: Autobiographical and Historical Writings* (Salt Lake City: Deseret, 1989), 372. The vision was published in *EMS* 1.2 (July 1832):2–3 and in 1835 D&C 91 (D&C 76).

57. Richard L. Bushman, *Mormonism: A Very Short Introduction* (New York: Oxford University Press, 2008), 5-6.

58. Rev. 12:6, 14.

59. Alexander Fraser, *Key to the Prophecies of the Old and New Testaments, which are not yet accomplished* (Philadelphia: John Bioren, 1802 [1795]), 157, 159.

60. Joseph Milner, *The History of the Church of Christ,* vol. 1 (London: R. B. Seeley and W. Burnside, 1834), v; vol. 2 (Boston: Farrand, Mallory, 1809), v. On early Mormon familiarity with Milner, see Matthew Bowman, "Biblical Histories and Joseph Smith," paper delivered at 2013 Church History Conference, Provo, Utah.

61. Milner, *History*, 2:538.

62. Fraser, *Key to the Prophecies*, 164, This image of the church coming out of the wilderness, terrible as an army with banners, combining the language of Solomon and Revelation, appears in Matthew Henry's early eighteenth-century commentary on Joshua's invasion of Canaan. Matthew Henry, *An Exposition of the Old and New Testaments* (London: Joseph Ogle Robinson, 1828), 531.

63. 1835 D&C 32:3 (D&C 5:14).

64. "The Early Degeneracy of the Methodists," *The Telescope* 1.48 (30 April 1825):189.

65. David L. Rowland, "An Epitome of Ecclesiastical History," broadside engraved and printed by Amos Doolittle (1806), in Rare Book and Special Collections Division, Library of Congress. http://www.loc.gov/exhibits/religion/rel07.html.

66. W. Coldwell, "Europe in the Summer of 1831," *The Imperial Magazine* (London: Fisher, Son, & Jackson, 1831), 380.

67. Most exegetes read the 1260 days as figurative for years. For Edwards, see E. Brooks Holifield, *Theology in America* (New Haven: Yale University Press, 2003), 122.

68. The Book of Mormon's typesetter, John H. Gilbert, confirmed his understanding that Smith saw the Book of Mormon initially "not [as] establishing a new religion, but confirming the Old Testament." John H. Gilbert to James T. Cobb, at Salt Lake City, from Palmyra, NY, 10 February 1879, in Theodore Schroeder Papers, Manuscript Division, NYPL; microfilm copy in CHL. Reference courtesy of Don Bradley.

69. BC 4:5.

70. 1835 D&C 32:3 (D&C 5:14).

71. BC 35:4 (D&C 33:5); D&C 109:73.

72. Rev. 12:1, 3, 4, 6 (KJV).

73. BC 9:13–14 (D&C 10:52–55).

74. The architectural parallel was pointed out to me by Joseph Spencer. Personal correspondence. Smith's typology was expressed in *JSP-J2,* 208.

75. 1835 D&C 6 (D&C 86).

76. 2 Nephi 3:24.

77. John Calvin, *Institutes* 4.1.7, p. 677; Letter 46 in Robin Waterfield, ed., *Jacob Boehme* (Berkeley: North Atlantic Books, 2001), 16.

78. BC 9:13–14 (D&C 10:52–55).

79. *EMS* 1.6 (November 1832):7 (D&C 49:8).

80. *EMS* 1.4 (September 1832):2 (D&C 29:32).

81. Matthew Stewart, *The Courtier and the Heretic: Leibniz, Spinoza, and the Fate of God in the Modern World* (New York: Norton, 2006), 38.

82. Jessee, *Personal Writings,* 457–58.

83. MHC D-1, 1433.

84. The text is corrupt, but the sense is plain: "Presbyterians any truth. embrace that. Baptist. Methodist &c. get all the good in the world. come out a pure Mormon." *WJS,* 234.

85. "To Isaac Galland," in Jessee, *Personal Writings,* 458.

86. *WJS,* 159. For extended treatment of this theme in Smith's thought, and his adaptation of Masonic ritual in particular, see Don Bradley, "'The Grand Fundamental Principles of Mormonism': Joseph Smith's Unfinished Reformation," *Sunstone* 141 (April 2006):32–41.

87. 1844 D&C 103:1 (D&C 124:1).

88. 8 February 1843, *JSP-J2,* 256.

89. *MS* 3.11 (March 1843):177.

90. *WJS,* 381–82. Smith was certainly correct, from a Mormon perspective. Contrary to a popular Mormon narrative that sees the Reformation as paving the way for the LDS Restoration, Luther, Calvin, and others in fact shaped Reformation theology in a direction much further removed from the teachings Smith would propound than Catholicism ever was. They did this by emphasizing a God "without body, parts, or passions," human depravity, the Bible as the only source of authority, and salvation by faith alone.

91. Benjamin F. Johnson, *My Life's Review* (np: Johnson Family Organization, 1997), 85.

92. Augustine, *On Christian Doctrine* II.xl.60, trans. J. F. Shaw, in *NPNF1 of the Christian Church,* First series, ed. Philip Schaff (Edinburgh: T&T Clark, 1993), 2:554.

93. For Buck's appropriation in early Mormonism, see Benjamin E. Park, "'Reasonings Suffi-cient': Joseph Smith, Thomas Dick, and the Context(s) of Early Mormonism," *Journal of Early Mormon History* 38 (Summer 2012):210–24.

94. Joseph Smith to L. Daniel Rupp, 5 June 1844. MHC F-1, 70.

95. *JSP-H1*, 218.

96. *WJS*, 367.

97. *WJS*, 382.

98. H. E. W. Turner, *The Pattern of Christian Truth: A Study in the Relations Between Ortho-doxy and Heresy in the Early Christian Church* (London: Mowbray, 1954), 9. Cited in McGrath, *Heresy*, 57.

99. *TS* 2.24 (15 October 1841):578.

100. "No one shall be appointed to receive commandments and revelations in this church excepting my servant Joseph Smith." BC 30:2 (D&C 28:2).

101. "History of Joseph Smith," *MS* 20.49 (4 December 1858):774.

102. *JSP-J2*, 164.

103. "The Religion of the Ancients," *TS* 4.9 (15 March 1843):136.

104. Not the Prophet, S.T.P., "To the Editor," *TS* 5.8 (15 April 1844):503. Samuel Brown em-phasizes that what Charles Buck pointed out in his theological dictionary as early Christian heresies, Mormons were glad to claim as some of these lost fragments. (See Brown and Matthew Bowman, *Joseph Smith and Charles Buck: Heresy and the Living Witness of History*, unpublished ms.) This view has been propounded before, though it has never gained much traction in con-temporary Mormon culture. Probably with the above article in mind, Joseph F. Smith said "if we find truth in broken fragments through the ages, it may be set down as an incontrovertible fact that it originated at the fountain, and was given to philosophers, inventors, patriots, reformers, and prophets by the inspiration of God." Using the same language, Hugh Nibley made this view his guiding hermeneutic, writing that Smith "recognized a primal archaic order which had pro-duced all manner of broken fragments and scattered traditions." (Joseph F. Smith, *Gospel Doc-trine* [Salt Lake City: Deseret News, 191], 38). Hugh W. Nibley, *Temple and Cosmos*, ed. Don E. Norton (Salt Lake City and Provo: Deseret and Foundation for Ancient Research and Mormon Studies, 1992), 82.

105. In a Catholic theologian's words, Mormons "pick up the detritus that was jettisoned" along the way to the ecumenical creeds and "recycle these discarded beliefs into a shining, novel creation of their own." Stephen Webb, *Jesus Christ, Eternal God* (New York: Oxford University Press, 2012), 245.

CHAPTER 4

1. B. H. Roberts, *Mormon Doctrine of Deity: The Roberts-Van Der Donckt Discussion* (np: B. H. Roberts, 1903), 167.

CHAPTER 5

1. William Herschel, "On the Construction of the Heavens," *Philosophical Transactions of the Royal Society of London* 75 (1785):216.

2. Richard Holmes, *Age of Wonder* (London: Harper, 2008), 191–92.

3. William Blake, "The Marriage of Heaven and Hell," *Complete Poetry and Selected Prose of John Donne and the Complete Poetry of William Blake* (New York: Random House, 1941), 651.

4. 1835 D&C 82:5 (D&C 93:29, 33).

5. B. H. Roberts would give the name "eternalism" to the larger theology implied by the eternal materiality of all that exists. See "Nature of the Universe," chapter 7 in B. H. Roberts, *The Truth, the Way, the Life*, ed. John W. Welch (Provo: BYU Studies, 1994), 69–76.

6. *WJS*, 9.

7. *WJS*, 37.

8. Pratt wrote his Treatise in 1837–38 while confined in a Missouri prison but only published it two years after his release. Parley P. Pratt, *The Millennium, and Other Poems: To Which Is Annexed, a Treatise on the Regeneration and Eternal Duration of Matter* (New York: Molineux, 1840), 105.

9. Karen Armstrong, *The Case for God* (New York: Anchor, 2010), 105.

10. Stephen Webb, *Jesus Christ, Eternal God: Heavenly Flesh and the Metaphysics of Matter* (New York: Oxford University Press, 2012), 243.

11. Blake Ostler, "The Mormon Concept of God," *Dialogue: A Journal of Mormon Thought* 17.2 (Summer 1984):67.

12. Justin Martyr, *The First Apology* X, in *ANF*, 1:165.

13. The characterization of creation *ex nihilo* as a doctrine that primitive Christianity found "ready-made in the Jewish tradition" and simply adopted or assumed for itself "can today no longer be sustained." Most scholars would agree with David Winston: "no explicit theory of creation *ex nihilo* had ever been formulated either in Jewish or Greek tradition before Philo," and the case for Philo is ambiguous but unlikely. Gerhard May, *Creation Ex Nihilo*, trans. A. S. Worrall (Edinburgh: T. & T. Clark, 1994), xi; Philo of Alexandria, *The Contemplative Life, The Giants, and Selections*, ed. and trans. David Winston (New York: Paulist Press, 1981), 11.

14. May, *Creation ex Nihilo*, 57.

15. Athanansius, *On the Incarnation of the Word* 2.4, in *NPNF2 of the Christian Church*, ed. Philip Schaff and Henry Wace, Second series (Peabody, MA: Hendrickson, 1994), 4:37.

16. John Mason Good, *The Book of Nature* (New York: Harper, 1830), 26. In Rick Grunder, *Mormon Parallels: A Bibliographic Source* (LaFayette, NY: Rick Grunder Books, 2008), digital version, 613–14.

17. Richard Watson et al., *On the Evidences of Christianity* (London: William Baynes, 1824), 468.

18. *The Farmer's Diary, or Beers' Ontario Almanack* . . . (Canandaigua, NY: J. D. Bemis, [1823]), 18. In Grunder, *Mormon Parallels*, 567.

19. Thomas Dick, *The Christian Philosopher; or, the Connection of Science and Philosophy with Religion* (Hartford: Robinson, 1833), 165.

20. Thomas Dick, *The Philosophy of a Future State* (Philadelphia: Biddle, 1845), 88–90.

21. Lord Byron, "Cain," II, ii, ll. 281–86, 325–30, in *Complete Poetical Works* (Boston: Houghton Mifflin, 1905), 640–41.

22. Dick, *Future State*, 88. Cited in *MA* 3.3 (December 1836):423.

23. *TS* 4.5 (16 January 1843):73 (Moses 1:38, PGP).

24. See the excellent treatment of this topic by Benjamin E. Park, "Salvation though a Tabernacle: Joseph Smith, Parley P. Pratt, and Early Mormon Theologies of Embodiment," *Dialogue: A Journal of Mormon Thought* 43.2 (Summer 2010):1–44.

25. *WJS* 60, 61.

26. See Terryl L. Givens, *When Souls Had Wings: Premortal Life in Western Thought* (New York: Oxford University Press, 2010).

27. Adolf Harnack, *History of Dogma*, 7 vols., trans. from 3rd German edition by Neil Buchanan (London: Williams & Norgate, 1894), 1:318–19.

28. Augustine, *Confessions* IV.15, trans. F. J. Sheed (Indianapolis: Hackett, 1993), 63.

CHAPTER 6

1. Matthew Steward, *The Courtier and the Heretic: Leibniz, Spinoza, and the Fate of God in the Modern World* (New York: Norton, 2006), 167.

2. Thomas Hobbes, *Leviathan* I.iv (London: Routledge, 1887), 26.

3. Not all who considered Hobbes an atheist thought he denied God's existence. Asserting his materiality amounted to the same thing, in the views of many. "That the universe is body, that God is part of the world and therefore body" were part of a list of his heresies that brought the atheist epithet down on him. See Samuel I. Mintz, *The Hunting of Leviathan* (Cambridge: Cambridge University Press, 1962), 45.

4. Joseph Glanvill [and George Rust], *Two Choice and Useful Treatises: The One Lux Orientalis . . . The Other, A Discourse on Truth* (New York: Garland, 1978), 49. (Reprint of London: James Collins and Samuel Lowndes, 1682.)

5. Anatole France, *The Revolt of the Angels* (New York: Gabriel Wells, 1924), 93.

6. Stephen Fallon, *Milton Among the Philosophers* (Ithaca: Cornell University Press, 1991), 80–81.

7. William Blake, "The Marriage of Heaven and Hell," *Complete Poetry and Selected Prose of John Donne and the Complete Poetry of William Blake* (New York: Random House, 1941), 652.

8. Samuel T. Coleridge, "Notebooks," *Samuel Taylor Coleridge*, ed. H. J. Jackson (Oxford: Oxford University Press, 1985), 555.

9. Parley P. Pratt, *The Millennium, and Other Poems: To Which Is Annexed, A Treatise on the Regeneration and Eternal Duration of Matter* (New York: Molineux, 1840), 111, 124, 125, 142.

10. "Try the Spirits," *TS* 3.11 (1 April 1842):745. Unsigned, but generally attributed to Joseph Smith.

11. 1876 D&C 131:7.

12. Parley P. Pratt, "Materiality," *MS* 6.2 (1 July 1845):19. (Originally published in *The Prophet*, 24 May 1845.)

13. *Key*, 43–44.

14. Rom, 8:13, for example.

15. For an example of Gnostic cosmology that sees the material world as inherently antithetical to divine perfection, see the Apocryphon of John in James M. Robinson, ed., *The Nag Hammadi Library* (San Francisco: Harper & Row, 1977), 98–116. On the emergence of creation *ex nihilo*, see Gerhard May, *Creation ex Nihilo: The Doctrine of "Creation out of Nothing" in Early Christian Thought*, trans. A. S. Worrall (Edinburgh: T&T Clark, 1994).

16. Jane Benett, *The Enchantment of Modern Life: Attachments, Crossings, and Ethics* (Princeton: Princeton University Press, 2001), 64.

17. Stan Larson, "The King Follett Discourse: A Newly Amalgamated Text," *BYU Studies* 18.2 (Winter 1978):203.

18. *TS* 3.10 (15 March 1842):721 (Abraham 4:18, PGP).

19. Orson Pratt, "Great First Cause," in *A Series of Pamphlets* (Liverpool: R. James, 1851), 10.

20. Pratt, "Great First Cause," 9.

21. Orson Pratt, "Mormon Philosophy," *New York Messenger* (3 September 1845):82. Cited in Breck England, *The Life and Thought of Orson Pratt* (Salt Lake City: University of Utah Press, 1985), 100.

22. *Key*, 43.

23. *CD*, 2:1075.

24. Sterling McMurrin, *The Theological Foundations of the Mormon Religion* (Salt Lake City: University of Utah Press, 1965), 7.

25. David Ray Griffin, "Process Theology: What It Is and Is Not," in *Mormonism in Dialogue with Contemporary Christian Theologies*, ed. Donald W. Musser and David L. Paulsen (Macon, GA: Mercer University Press, 2007), 170.

26. John A. Widtsoe, *Joseph Smith as Scientist* (Salt Lake City: Young Men's Mutual Improvement Associations, 1908), 62–65.

27. John A. Widtsoe, *A Rational Theology* (Salt Lake City: General Boards of the Mutual Improvement Association, 1932), 13.

CHAPTER 7

1. Frank Farrell, *Subjectivity, Realism, and Postmodernism* (Cambridge: Cambridge University Press, 1996), 2.

2. This is true of Process Theology a la Alfred North Whitehead and Charles Hartshorne. David Ray Griffin, "Process Theology: What It Is and Is Not," in *Mormonism in Dialogue with Contemporary Christian Theologies*, ed. Donald W. Musser and David L. Paulsen (Macon, GA: Mercer University Press, 2007), 161–62.

3. Terry Eagleton, *The Meaning of Life: A Very Short Introduction* (New York: Oxford University Press, 2008), 73.

4. Thomas Aquinas, *Summa Theologica* 1 Q.13 Art. 2 (Chicago: Encyclopedia Britannica, 1980), 1:64.

5. Timothy Keller, *The Reason for God* (London: Hodder, 2009), 71.

6. Parley P. Pratt, *The Millennium, and Other Poems: To Which Is Annexed, A Treatise on the Regeneration and Eternal Duration of Matter* (New York: Molineux, 1840), 124, 125, 142.

7. *WJS*, 60.

8. Pratt, *Millennium*, 110.

9. *Key*, 37. Whereas Parley Pratt emphasized God's subjection to scientific law, Orson Pratt differed from his own brother's interpretation, saying in 1880 that the law of gravity, for instance, "some will tell us is merely a law of materials, that God has nothing to do with it. But I dispute it. I say that God is the author of this law, and were it not for this infinitely wise provision, there would not be such a thing as one particle of matter being drawn to another." *JD*, 21:235.

10. Keller, *Reason for God*, 85, 95.

11. "A miracle is emphatically not an event without cause or without results. Its cause is the activity of God: its results follow according to Natural law." C. S. Lewis, *Miracles* (New York: HarperCollins, 2009), 95.

12. John A. Widtsoe, *A Rational Theology* (Salt Lake City: General Boards of the Mutual Improvement Association, 1932), 175, 23–24.

13. Alma 41:11.

14. Alma 42:13.

15. Mormon 9:19.

16. D&C 88:42. Cited in B. H. Roberts, *The Truth, the Way, the Life*, ed. John W. Welch (Provo: BYU Studies, 1994), 418n.

17. *CD*, 1:376.

18. Kent Robson, "Omnis on the Horizon," *Sunstone* 8.4 (July–August 1983):21.

CHAPTER 8

1. "United Methodists claim LDS not really Christian," *Idaho Statesman*, 11 May 2000, A2.

2. "Striving for Acceptance," *Washington Post*, 9 February 9, 2002, B9. In this same period, the author was present at a hearing of the Faith and Order board of a state affiliate of the National Council of Churches, listening to an LDS petition for a shift from observer status to membership (more by way of testing the issue, than in earnest presumably). During the proceedings, a Methodist representative concluded, "based on our own criteria" (according to the WCC constitution, members constitute "a fellowship of churches which confess the Lord Jesus Christ as God and Saviour according to the scriptures"), "Mormons are as Christian as any here." However, he was overruled by another member who insisted repeatedly and vehemently, "but they don't accept the Trinity." The meeting was in Charlottesville, Virginia.

3. G. H. Joyce, "Trinity, Blessed," *Catholic Encyclopedia* (New York: Encyclopedia Press, 1913), 15:49; R. L. Richard, "Trinity, Holy," *New Catholic Encyclopedia* (New York: McGraw-Hill, 1967), 14:299.

4. Jouette M. Bassler, "God Most High," in *Anchor Bible Dictionary*, ed. David Noel Friedman (New York: Doubleday, 1992), 2:1055.

5. Irenaeus, *Proof of the Apostolic Preaching*, in Linwood Urban, *A Short History of Christian Doctrine* (New York: Oxford University Press, 1995), 53.

6. Arius, "Statement of Belief to Alexander of Alexandria," in *C&C,* 1:77.

7. Edward Peters, *Heresy and Authority in Medieval Europe* (Philadelphia: University of Pennsylvania Press, 1980), 41.

8. "The Creed of Nicaea," *C&C,* 1:159.

9. Alexander of Alexandria, "Letter to Alexander of Constantinople," *C&C,* 1:80.

10. Urban, *Short History*, 66.

11. "The Athanasian Creed," *C&C,* 1:676–77.

12. William Ellery Channing, *Unitarian Christianity* (Boston: American Unitarian Association, 1819).

13. Channing, *Unitarian Christianity* (Hong Kong: Forgotten Books, 2007), 11.

14. *JSP-H1*, 218.

15. Lesson 3, "I had Seen a Vision," *Doctrine and Covenants and Church History Gospel Doctrine Teacher's Manual*, https://www.lds.org/manual/doctrine-and-covenants-and-church-history-gospel-doctrine-teachers-manual/lesson-3-i-had-seen-a-vision?lang=eng&query=%22separate+beings%22.

16. *EMS* 1.1 (June 1832):1 (D&C 20:5).

17. Many scholars (and critics) have read this account as an unambiguous reference to one personage, which changes to two in subsequent accounts. Dean Jessee argues that since all hearsay and official accounts subsequent to this version mention two beings, "Lord" can plausibly be read here as referring to first the Father, and then to the Son in its second mention. See his "Earliest Documented Accounts of Joseph Smith's First Vision," in *Opening the Heavens: Accounts of Divine Manifestations, 1820–1844,* ed. John W. Welch with Erick B. Carlson (Provo and Salt Lake City: Brigham Young University Press and Deseret, 2005), 1–33.

18. *JSP-H1*, 214. Jones notes the important influence of Methodist formulations of conversion experiences on Smith's language in "Power and Form," 88–114.

19. *WJS*, 378.

20. *WJS*, 214.

21. Lecture 2.2 in 1835 D&C, 12.

22. Lecture 5.1–2, in 1835 D&C, 51–53.

23. *WJS*, 63.

24. Benjamin Huff, "Unity in Action and the Unity of God," *Element* 2.1 (Spring 2006):17–18.

25. Orson Pratt, "Great First Cause," in *A Series of Pamphlets* (Liverpool: R. James, 1851), 16.

26. Orson Pratt to Brigham Young, 4 November 1853. In Gary James Bergera, *Conflict in the Quorum: Orson Pratt, Brigham Young, Joseph Smith* (Salt Lake City: Signature, 2002), 107–108. Bergera treats in detail the prolonged tensions between Pratt and his priesthood superior over his speculative theology.

27. For a detailed analysis of how "mainstream Social Trinitarian and the Mormon view of the Trinity are close but . . . not the same," see Stephen T. Davis, "The Mormon Trinity and Other Trinities," *Element* 2.1 (Spring 2006):1–14.

28. *WJS*, 64.

29. *WJS, 87.*

30. B. H. Roberts, *Mormon Doctrine of Deity: The Roberts-Van Der Donckt Discussion* (np: B. H. Roberts, 1903), 168.

CHAPTER 9

1. *JSP-H1*, 218. The description of Smith's interaction with his mother was added to the 1838 account in 1842. See *JSP-H1*, 215.

2. Avery Dulles, *Models of Revelation* (Maryknoll, NY: Orbis, 1992).

3. William Abraham, *Divine Revelation and the Limits of Historical Criticism* (New York: Oxford University Press, 1982), 24.

4. Jaroslav Pelikan, *The Emergence of the Catholic Tradition* (Chicago: University of Chicago Press, 1971), 100.

5. Eve LaPlante, *American Jezebel: The Uncommon Life of Anne Hutchinson, the Woman Who Defied the Puritans* (New York: HarperCollins, 2004), 118.

6. LaPlante, *American Jezebel*, 124–25.

7. E. Brooks Holifield, *Theology in America* (New Haven: Yale University Press, 2003), 34.

8. Leonard W. Levy, *Blasphemy: Verbal Offense against the Sacred, from Moses to Salman Rushdie* (Durham: University of North Carolina Press, 1995), 246.

9. Jonathan Edwards, cited in David Holland, *Sacred Borders: Continuing Revelation and Canonical Restraint in Early America* (New York: Oxford University Press, 2011), 47.

10. Review of Frederick Lucas, "Reasons for Becoming a Roman Catholic," *Christian Examiner and General Review* 30.34 (March 1841):110.

11. David Holland, *Sacred Borders: Continuing Revelation and Canonical Restraint in Early America* (New York: Oxford University Press, 2011), 10.

12. Clarke Garrett, *Spirit Possession and Popular Religion: From the Camisards to the Shakers* (Baltimore: Johns Hopkins University Press, 1987), 195–96. Cited in Holland, *Sacred Borders*, 14.

13. Gilbert Wardlaw, *The Testimony of Scripture to the Obligations and Efficacy of Prayer* (Boston: Peirce and Williams, 1830), 8, 59, 97n.

14. Alan Taylor surveys Hartwick's career and several kindred examples in "The New Jerusalem of the Early American Frontier," *Visions of the Future: Collective and Individual; Secular and Sacred*, 117–26. Quaderno V, Quaderni online, http://www.library.vanderbilt.edu/Quaderno/Quaderno5/quaderno5.html.

15. Extract of a Letter from Rev. Ira Chase to the Secretary of the Massach[usetts]. Bap[tist]. Miss[ionary]. Society, Clarksburg, Virginia, 6 January 1818, in *American Baptist Magazine*, 1818. In Rick Grunder, *Mormon Parallels: A Bibliographic Source* (Lafayette, NY: Rick Grunder Books, 2008), digital version, 80–82.

16. Charles Mayo Ellis, "An Essay on Transcendentalism" and William C Cannett, "Ezra Stiles Gannett," quoted in Philip F. Gura, *American Transcendentalism: A History* (New York: Hill and Wang, 2007), 10, 14.

17. Holland refers to the Transcendentalist goal of "freeing revelation from the moorings of a church," and cites Bradley Dean's image of Thoreau bringing others to Mt. Sinai. Holland, *Sacred Borders*, 174.

18. A. S. Hayden, *Early History of the Disciples in the Western Reserve, Ohio* (Cincinatti: Chase & Hall, 1875), 121. (Reprint, n.d.)

19. David M. Robinson, *The Spiritual Emerson* (Boston: Beacon, 2003), 78.

20. For examples see Richard L. Bushman, "The Visionary World of Joseph Smith," *BYU Studies* 37.1 (1997–98):183–204.

21. *JSP-H1*, 220.

22. "The Book of Mormon fully engages familiar nineteenth-century scriptural forms, terms, and categories, only to subvert them and constitute them into an utterly new American Bible; for instance, a few of these themes are revelation, Christology, Zion, and scripture." See Terryl Givens, "Joseph Smith's American Bible: Radicalizing the Familiar," *Journal of the Book of Mormon and Other Restoration Scripture* 18.2 (2009):4–17.

23. See Terryl L Givens, *By the Hand of Mormon: The American Scripture that Launched a New World Religion* (New York: Oxford University Press, 2003), 209–39.

24. "Prophecy," in *Oxford Dictionary of the Christian Church,* ed. F. L. Cross and E. A. Livingstone (Oxford: Oxford University Press, 1997), 1336.

25. One notable exception is Rebekah, who "went to inquire of the LORD. And the LORD said to her, "Two nations are in your womb, . . ." (Gen. 25:23–24).

26. 1 Nephi 11:6.

27. Moroni 10:4–5.

28. Alexander Campbell, "Delusions: An Analysis of the Book of Mormon," *Millennial Harbinger* 2 (7 February 1831):85–96.

29. Eliza R. Snow, *The Personal Writings of Eliza Roxcy Snow*, ed. Maureen Ursenbach Beecher (Salt Lake City: University of Utah Press, 1995), 9.

30. See the "Peter, Apostle St.," in *New Catholic Encyclopedia* (Detroit: Thomson Gale, 2003), 11:175, for a typical discussion of the passage as affirming "the bestowal of the primacy" to Peter.

31. *WJS*, 158.

32. Fred C. Collier and William S. Harwell, eds., *Kirtland Council Minute Book*, 21 April 1834 (Salt Lake City: Collier's, 1996), 37.

33. *WJS*, 5.

34. Kathleen Flake, "The Mormons," PBS documentary, aired 2007. "Joseph Smith was the Henry Ford of revelation. He wanted every home to have one, and the revelation he had in mind was the revelation he'd had, which was seeing God." Interview recorded April 27, 2006.

35. Parley P. Pratt to John Taylor, 27 November 1836, in John Taylor Collection, CHL.

36. BC 30:2, 6 (D&C 28:2, 7).

37. In reference to the extensive revelation known as "the Vision" (1835 D&C 91 [D&C 76]), Philo Dibble recorded that "during the time that Joseph and Sidney were in the spirit and saw the heavens open, there were other men in the room, perhaps twelve, among whom I was one during a part of the time—probably two-thirds of the time, —I saw the glory and felt the power, but did not see the vision." *Juvenile Instructor* 27 (15 May 1892):303–304.

38. *MS* 16.46 (18 November 1854):721–22.

39. BC 8:3 (D&C 9:8).

40. Ezra Taft Benson, "Seek the Spirit of the Lord," *Ensign* 18.4 (April 1988):2.

41. BC 7:1 (D&C 8:2).

42. Richard L. Bushman, "Joseph Smith's Visions and Revelations," in *The Oxford Handbook to Mormonism*, ed. Terryl L. Givens and Philip Barlow (New York: Oxford University Press, forthcoming).

43. Besides the Brigham Young revelation canonized as D&C 136, and the Joseph F. Smith vision added as D&C 138, a few other revelations to John Taylor were disseminated and even printed in some nineteenth-century foreign editions of the Doctrine and Covenants. See Richard Neitzel Holzapfel and Christopher C. Jones, "'John the Revelator': The Written Revelations of John Taylor," in *Champion of Liberty: John Taylor*, ed. Mary Jane Woodger (Provo: Religious Studies Center, Brigham Young University, 2009), 273–308. I thank Don Bradley for this reference.

44. B. H. Roberts, *Defense of the Faith* (Salt Lake City: Deseret News, 1907), 535.

45. For a study of personal revelation in the Mormon Church, see Tom Mould, *Still, the Small Voice* (Logan: Utah State University Press, 2011).

46. Harold Bloom, *The American Religion* (New York: Simon & Schuster, 1992) and John Brooke's *The Refiner's Fire* (Cambridge: Cambridge University Press, 1996) are only two of the more famous treatments associating Mormonism with Gnosticism.

47. Alma 32:26; Moroni 10:5.

48. "To some it is given by the Holy Ghost to know that Jesus Christ is the Son of God, and that he was crucified for the sins of the world; to others it is given to believe on their words." *EMS* 1.3 (August 1832):1 (D&C 46:13–14).

49. "Joseph Smith and others to the Church at Quincy, Illinois," 20 March 1839. In *Personal Writings of Joseph Smith,* ed. Dean C. Jessee (Salt Lake City: Deseret, 2002), 437 (1876 D&C 121:33).

50. The expression is found in George MacDonald, "The Eloi," *Unspoken Sermons,* Second Series (Whitehorn, CA: Johannesen: 2004), 110.

51. *JSP-H1*, 218.

52. *EMS* 1.1 (June 1832):6.

CHAPTER 10

1. Sigmund Freud, *Civilization and Its Discontents* (New York: Norton, 1989), 33.

2. C. S. Lewis, *The Great Divorce: A Dream* (New York: Simon and Schuster, 1946), 115–16.

3. Marcel Sarot, *God, Passibility, and Corporeality* (Kampen, Netherlands: Pharos, 1992), 1–2. Sarot gives more than a half dozen examples of defenses of impassibilism by contemporary theologians, suggesting the doctrine may be experiencing a revival.

4. Richard Bauckham, "'Only the Suffering God Can Help': Divine Passibility in Modern Theology," *Themelios* 9.3 (April 1984):6.

5. Bauckham, "The Suffering God," 7.

6. *Origen: Homilies 1–14 on Ezekiel 6.6,* trans. Thomas P. Scheck (New York: Newman Press, 2010), 92–93.

7. Augustine, *De Diversis Quaestionibus Ad Simplicianum* n.2, in Nicholas Wolterstorff, "Suffering Love," ed. William E. Mann, *Augustine's Confessions: Critical Essays* (Lanham, MD: Rowman and Littlefield, 2006), 122.

8. Thomas Aquinas, *Summa Theologica* 1 Q.21 Art. 3 (Chicago: Encyclopedia Britannica, 1980), 1:126.

9. Martin Luther, *Bondage of the Will,* trans. Henry Cole (New York: Feather Trail Press, 2009), 33.

10. Plato, *Republic* II.381, trans. G. M. A. Grube, rev. C. D. C. Reeve, in *Plato: Complete Works,* ed. John M. Cooper (Indianapolis: Hackett, 1997), 1021–22.

11. *C&C,* 3:202.

12. *Book of Common Prayer* (London: W. Bulmer, 1801), np.; Philip Schaff, *Creeds of Christendom: The Evangelical Protestant Creeds* (New York: Harper & Brothers, 1877), 3:486.

13. *The Doctrines and Discipline of the Methodist Episcopal Church,* 14th ed. (New York: John Wilson and Daniel Mitt, for the Methodist Connection, 1808), iii.

14. *Wesleyan-Methodist Magazine* 37 (1814):169.

15. Isaac C. Goff, *A Faithful Report of the Theological Debate Held at Milford, New Jersey, December, 1830, by Rev. W. L. M'Calla of the Presbyterian, and Elder W. Lane, of the Christian Connexion* (New York: Mitchell, 1831), 39.

16. Thomas G. Weinandy, "Does God Suffer?" *First Things* 117 (November 2001):35.

17. Ronald Goetz, "The Suffering God: The Rise of a New Orthodoxy," *Christian Century,* 16 April 1986, 385.

18. Paul L. Gavrilyuk, *The Suffering of the Impassible God: The Dialectics of Patristic Thought* (New York: Oxford University Press, 2006), 1.

19. Heschel uses the term in *Between God and Man: An Interpretation of Judaism* (New York: Simon & Schuster, 1997), 25. See also Clark Pinnock, *Most Moved Mover: A Theology of God's*

Openness (Grand Rapids, MI: Baker Academic, 2001); and John Sanders, *The God Who Risks: A Theology of Divine Providence* (Westmont, IL: IVP Academic, 2007).

20. Jacob 5:41.

21. *EMS* 1.3 (August 1832):19 (Moses 7:28–29, PGP). Moses 6:57 and 7:35 identify the speaker as "Man of Holiness," the Father of Christ.

22. *EMS* 1.3 (August 1832):19 (Moses 7:29–37, PGP).

23. See Daniel C. Peterson, "On the Motif of the Weeping God in Moses 7," in *Revelation, Reason, and Faith: Essays in Honor of Truman G. Madsen,* ed. Donald W. Parry, Daniel C. Peterson, and Stephen D. Ricks (Provo: Foundation for Ancient Research and Mormon Studies, 2002), 285–318. See also Jeffrey M. Bradshaw, Jacob Rennaker, and David A. Larson, "Revisiting the Forgotten Voices of Weeping in Moses 7: A Comparison with Ancient Texts," *Interpreter: A Journal of Mormon Scripture* 1.2 (2012):41–71.

24. Pisqa 29, cited by Michael Fishbane, *The Exegetical Imagination: On Jewish Thought and Theology* (Cambridge, MA: Harvard University Press, 1998), 78.

25. BC 2:1 (D&C 3:1).

26. BC 45:4 (D&C 43:4).

27. 2 Nephi 2:2.

28. *EMS* 1.2 (July 1832):2 (D&C 76:26).

29. *TS* 4.5 (16 January 1843):73 (Moses 1:39, PGP).

CHAPTER 11

1. Largely informed by nineteenth-century Protestant historical narratives, Mormon scholars like James Talmage tended to downplay those reformation theologies emphatically hostile to Joseph Smith's thought, in creating a Whig, or unfailingly progressive, interpretation of post-apostolic church history. While acknowledging some Reformation "fallacies," Talmage attributed the growth of religious freedom to the generation of Luther and Calvin. See his *The Great Apostasy* (Salt Lake City: Deseret News, 1909), especially 152ff.

2. Philip Schaff, *The Creeds of Christendom: The Evangelical Protestant Creeds* (New York: Harper & Brothers, 1877), 487.

3. George Foote Moore, *Judaism in the First Centuries of the Christian Era* (Cambridge, MA: Harvard University Press, 1927), 1:438.

4. Marcel Sarot, *God, Passibility, and Corporeality* (Kampen, Netherlands: Kok Pharos, 1992), 9.

5. Ronald Goetz, "The Suffering God," *Christian Century* 103 (1986):386, in Sarot, *Passibility*, 9–10.

6. Sarot, *Passibility*, 244.

7. Sarot, *Passibility*, 209–42.

8. Stephen Webb, *Jesus Christ, Eternal God: Heavenly Flesh and the Metaphysics of Matter* (New York: Oxford University Press, 2011), 78.

9. John Norton, *The Orthodox Evangelist* (London: John Mocock, 1654), 5, 23. In E. Brooks Holifield, *Theology in America* (New Haven: Yale University Press, 2003), 36.

10. Karen Armstrong, *The Case for God* (New York: Anchor Books, 2009), 15.

11. Gen. 5:3; Exod. 24:10; Exod. 33:23; Num. 14:14.

12. "Anthropomorphism," in *Encyclopedia Judaica* (Jerusalem: Keter, 1971–72), 3:51.

13. Stephen Finlan, *Problems with Atonement* (Collegeville, MN: Liturgical Press, 2005), 13.

14. "Anthropomorphism," 3:51.

15. Mark S. Smith, *The Early History of God* (Grand Rapids, MI: Eerdmans, 2002), 140.

16. Smith, *Early History*, 144.

17. John 4:24.

18. É. Des Places, "Anthropomorphism," in *New Catholic Encyclopedia* (Detroit: Thomson Gale, 2003), 1:510.

19. James Morgan, *The Importance of Tertullian in the Development of Christian Doctrine* (London: Kegan Paul, 1928), 182. Cited in David L. Paulsen, "Divine Embodiment: The Earliest Christian Understanding of God," in *Early Christians in Disarray*, ed. Noel B. Reynolds (Provo: Foundation for Ancient Research and Mormon Studies, 2005), 270–71.

20. Stephen Webb, *Jesus Christ, Eternal God: Heavenly Flesh and the Metaphysics of Matter* (New York: Oxford University Press, 2011), 249. For Paulsen, see "Early Christian Belief in a Corporeal Deity: Origin and Augustine as Reluctant Witnesses," *Harvard Theological Review* 83.2 (1990):105–16.

21. John A. McGuckin, "Cyril of Alexandria: Bishop and Pastor," in *The Theology of St Cyril of Alexandria: A Critical Appreciation*, ed. Thomas Gerard Weinandy and Daniel A. Keating (London: T&T Clark, 2003), 213.

22. Isaac Sharpe, *An Historical Account of the Rise and Growth of Heresie in the Christian Church, to the Sixteenth Century and Farther* (London: R. Wilkin, 1718), 46.

23. Stephen Charnock, *Discourses Upon the Existence and Attributes of God* (New York: Robert Carter and Brothers, 1874), 193.

24. John Hargrove, *A Sermon, on the True Object and Nature of Christian Worship . . .* (Baltimore: New Jerusalem Church, 1800), 16, in Richard Lyman Bushman, "The Archive of Restoration Culture, 1997–2002," *BYU Studies* 45.4 (2006):101.

25. "The Atheist has no God. The sectarian has a God without body or parts. Who can define the difference?" Parley P. Pratt, "Materiality," *MS* 6.2 (1 July 1845):19. (Originally published in *The Prophet*, 24 May 1845.)

26. William Kinkade, *The Bible Doctrine of God, Jesus Christ, The Holy Spirit, Atonement, Faith, and Election* (New York: H. R. Piercy, 1829), 160.

27. Kinkade, *Bible Doctrine*, 157–58.

28. Isaac C. Goff, *A Faithful Report of the Theological Debate Held at Milford, New Jersey, December, 1830, by Rev. W. L. M'Calla of the Presbyterian, and Elder W. Lane, of the Christian Connexion* (New York: Mitchell, 1831), 28.

29. Goff, *Faithful Report*, ix–x.

30. Goff, *Faithful Report*, 35.

31. Rev. H. Mattison, *A Scriptural Defence of the Doctrine of the Trinity* (New York: Lewis Colby, 1846).

32. William Ellery Channing, *Unitarian Christianity* (Boston: American Unitarian Association, 1819), 26.

33. James Freeman Clarke, William Henry Channing, and James Handasyd Perkins, *The Western Messenger* (Louisville: T. H. Shreve, 1838), 5:351.

34. Goff, *Faithful Report*, 26.

35. 3 Nephi 11.

36. Ether 3:15–16.

37. Kinkade, *Bible Doctrine*, 162.

38. Moses 6:8–9, PGP. These passages first appeared in the 1878 edition of the PGP, eleven years after publication by the Reorganized Church of Jesus Christ of Latter-day Saints.

39. David Paulsen, "The Doctrine of Divine Embodiment: Restoration, Judeo–Christian, and Philosophical Perspectives," *BYU Studies* 35.4 (1995–1996):21.

40. 1835 D&C 82:5 (D&C 93:35).

41. *MA* 2.17 (February 1836):265.

42. Truman Coe, "Mormonism," *Ohio Observer*, 11 August 1836, in Milton V. Backman Jr., "Truman Coe's 1836 Description of Mormonism," *BYU Studies* 17.3 (1977):5–6.

43. Lecture 5.2, in 1835 D&C, 53.

44. *Gospel Reflector* 1.1 (1 January 1841):3.

45. Parley P. Pratt, *Mormonism Unveiled: Zion's Watchman Unmasked* (New York: Pratt and Fordham, 1838), 31.

46. Parley P. Pratt, An Answer to Mr. William Hewitt's Tract Against the Latter-day Saints (Manchester, England: Thomas, 1840), 9.

47. *WJS*, 60.

48. *WJS*, 64.

49. *WJS*, 370.

50. *WJS*, 173. Canonized as D&C 130:22, in 1876.

51. *WJS*, 74.

52. *CD*, 4:2125.

53. "The organization of man, embracing all the attributes and powers of his physical and mental constitution, is considered a mystery." And the "attributes" like "wisdom, intelligence, honor, excellence, power, glory, might, and dominion, . . . fill eternity." *CD*, 2:613, 634.

54. 1835 D&C 82:5 (D&C 93:33).

55. Parley P. Pratt, *The Millennium and Other Poems; to Which is Annexed a Treatise on the Regeneration and Eternal Duration of Matter* (New York: Molineux, 1840), 141.

56. Orson Spencer, *Letters Exhibiting the Most Prominent Doctrines of the Church of Jesus Christ of Latter-day Saints* (Salt Lake City: George Q. Cannon, 1891), 92. Spencer's Letters were highly enough regarded to earn a place in the capstone of the Salt Lake Temple (*Church News*, 4 April 1992).

57. John Jaques, *Catechism for Children Exhibiting the Prominent Doctrines of the Church of Jesus Christ of Latter-day Saints* (Liverpool: F. D. Richards, 1855), 18.

58. "Conference Minutes," *TS* 5.14 (1 August 1844):598.

59. Donald Q. Cannon, "The King Follett Discourse: Joseph Smith's Greatest Sermon in Historical Context," *BYU Studies* 18.2 (Winter 1978):191.

60. *CD*, 4:2396.

61. See, for example, Francis J. Beckwith, "Moral Law the Mormon Universe, and the Nature of the Right We Ought to Choose," in Beckwith et al., *The New Mormon Challenge* (Grand Rapids, MI: Zondervan, 2002), 219–41.

62. See, for example, Blake Ostler's position, quoted in Beckwith, "Moral Law," 233.

63. Blake Ostler, "Moral Obligation and Mormonism: A Response to Francis Beckwith," http://www.fairlds.org/reviews_of_the_new-mormon-challenge/moral-obligation-and-mormonism-a-response-to-francis-beckwith#en19.

64. David L. Paulsen, cited in *Mormonism at the Crossroads of Philosophy and Theology: Essays in Honor of David L. Paulsen,* ed. Jacob T. Baker (Salt Lake City: Kofford, 2012), xxxix.

65. The classic statement of incompatibility of omniscience and free will is Nelson Pike, "Divine Omniscience and Voluntary Action," *The Philosophical Review* 74.1 (1965): 27–46.

66. Boethius, *The Consolation of Philosophy* Book 5, ed. and trans. Scott Goins and Barbara H. Wyman (San Francisco: Ignatius, 2012), 147–73.

67. Boethius, *Consolation*, 160.

68. Thomas Aquinas, *Summa Theologica* 1 Q.57 Art. 3 (Chicago: Encyclopedia Britannica, 1980), 1:297.

69. W. S. Anglin, *Free Will and the Christian Faith* (Oxford: Oxford University Press, 1990), 74.

70. Christopher Smart, *On the Omniscience of the Supreme Being* (Cambridge: J. Bentham, 1756), 6–7.

71. Thomas Brown, *Lectures on the Philosophy of the Human Mind* (Philadelphia: John Grigg, 1824), 3: 384.

72. Anglin, *Free Will*, 72. See Anglin's extensive defense of Christian free will in his chapter "Omniscience," 72–103.

73. Lecture 2.2 in 1835 D&C 12.

74. 1 Nephi 9:5.

75. Believing enemies would alter his translation to compare unfavorably with a second effort, Smith was unwilling to retranslate the lost portion.

76. *WJS*, 8, 33.

77. *CD*, 2:732–33

78. A number of contemporary theologians have dissented from the traditional position of God's eternity, i.e., the belief that he created and transcends time. Note especially in this regard Nicholas Wolterstorff, who argues the eternal nature of God is unbiblical and a product of Greek philosophy. "Given that all human actions are temporal," he reasons, "those actions of God which are 'response' are temporal as well." "God is Everlasting," in *God and the Good: Essays in Honor of Henry Stob*, ed. Clifton Orlebeke and Lewis Smedes (Grand Rapids, MI: Eerdmans, 1975), 197.

79. Austin Farrer, "Images and Inspiration," in *The Truth Seeking Heart*, ed. Ann Loades and Robert MacSwain (Norwich: Canterbury Press, 2006), 24–25.

80. Orson Pratt, *The Seer* 1.8 (August 1853):117; Young twice declared Pratt's views in this regard "not true." *Deseret News* 10.21 (25 July 1860):162–63 and *Deseret News* 14.47 (23 August 1865):372–73.

81. *CD*, 2: 832.

82. Jaques, *Catechism*, 18.

83. B. H. Roberts, *Mormon Doctrine of Deity: The Roberts-Van Der Donckt Discussion* (np: B. H. Roberts, 1903), 65.

84. B. H. Roberts, *The Truth, the Way, the Life*, ed. John W. Welch (Provo: BYU Studies, 1994), 418.

85. James E. Talmage, "The Philosophical Basis of Mormonism," in *The Essential Talmage*, ed. James Harris (Salt Lake City: Signature, 1997), 147.

86. James E. Talmage, "Timeliness," conference address delivered 9 April 1933. In Harris, *Essential Talmage*, 265.

87. David L. Paulsen, "Omnipotence of God; Omnipresence of God; Omniscience of God," in *Encyclopedia of Mormonism*, ed. Daniel H. Ludlow, 4 vols. (New York: Macmillan, 1992), 3:1030.

88. These words were reported in a now lost letter of the Washington correspondent Mathew L. Davis to his wife Mary, 6 February 1840. *WJS*, 33.

89. Sterling McMurrin, *The Theological Foundations of the Mormon Religion* (Salt Lake City: University of Utah Press, 1977), 39.

90. Kent Robson, "Omnis on the Horizon," *Sunstone* 8.4 (July August 1983):23.

91. William James, *A Pluralistic Universe* (Lincoln, NE: University of Nebraska Press, 1996), 305.

92. James, *Pluralistic Universe*, 111.

93. Stephen E. Robinson, in Craig L. Blomberg and Robinson, *How Wide the Divide: A Mormon and an Evangelical in Conversation* (Downers Grove, IL: InterVarsity Press, 1997), 92. Eugene England traces the history of the Mormon debate about God's finitism (including this reference) in "The Weeping God of Mormonism," *Dialogue: A Journal of Mormon Thought* 35.1 (Spring 2002):63–80.

94. Alfred North Whitehead, *Process and Reality* (New York: Macmillan, 1941), 526. In McMurrin, *Theological Foundations*, 24.

95. McMurrin, *Theological Foundations*, 34.

96. McMurrin, *Theological Foundations*, 35.

97. "We also envisaged God making a world, the future of which was not yet completely settled, again to make room for the input of significant creatures." Clark H. Pinnock, *Most Moved Mover: A Theology of God's Openness* (Grand Rapids, MI: Baker Academic, 2001), 3.

98. "We are simple examples of minds, and . . . the existence of mind is certainly a *datum* for the construction of any world picture: At the very least, its *possibility* must be explained. And it hardly seems credible that its appearance should be a natural accident, like the fact that there are mammals." Thomas Nagel, *The Last Word* (New York: Oxford University Press, 1997), 132.

99. Stan Larson, "The King Follett Discourse: A Newly Amalgamated Text," *BYU Studies* 18.2 (Winter 1978):201.

100. *WJS*, 378.

101. *TS* 3.10 (25 March 1842):720. (Abraham 3:18, PGP).

102. *WJS*, 380.

103. *WJS*, 60.

104. *WJS*, 84.

105. *EMS* 1.2 (July 1832):2 (D&C 76:58).

106. The view of Nauvoo theology as a radical rupture with preceding theology has been the majority view. For example, Andrew Ehat and Lyndon Cook assert that "Clearly the Nauvoo era was distinct from its Kirtland underpinnings." *WJS*, 84. For a summary view of my dissent from this position, see Terryl Givens, "The Prophecy of Enoch as Restoration Blueprint," Leonard J. Arrington Lecture, Utah State University, 16 September 2012.

107. Orson Pratt, *JD*, 18:292.

108. This is the reading of Blake Ostler, "God the Eternal Father," in *Exploring Mormon Thought: The Problems with Theism and the Love of God* (Salt Lake City: Kofford, 2006). Ostler's series represents the most prolonged and rigorous engagement with Mormon theology in recent decades.

109. Larson, "King Follett," 201.

110. Orson Pratt, "Great First Cause," in *A Series of Pamphlets* (Liverpool: R. James, 1851), 16.

111. John A. Widtsoe, *Joseph Smith as Scientist* (Salt Lake City: Young Men's Mutual Improvement Associations, 1908), 9.

112. John A. Widtsoe, *A Rational Theology* (Salt Lake City: General Boards of the Mutual Improvement Association, 1932), 23. See Blake Ostler, "The Idea of Pre-existence in the Development of Mormon Thought," *Dialogue: A Journal of Mormon Thought* 15.1 (Spring 1982):69.

113. Widtsoe, *Rational Theology*, 23–24.

114. Anthon Lund, Journal, 11 December 1914. Cited in Ostler, "Idea of Pre-existence," 69.

115. "Origin of Man," *Messages of the First Presidency*, comp. James R. Clark (Salt Lake City: Bookcraft, 1971), 4:205–206"(Originally published in *Improvement Era* 13.1 [1909].)

116. James E. Talmage, *Jesus the Christ* (Salt Lake City: Deseret News, 1915), 143.

117. James E. Talmage, "The Son of man," conference address delivered 6 April 1915. In Harris, *Essential Talmage*, 137.

118. James E. Talmage, journal entry, 10 May 1915. Cited in Harris, *Essential Talmage*, xxviii.

119. Heb. 7:1; "God," in LDS Bible Dictionary, published with the LDS version of the Bible (Salt Lake: Church of Jesus Christ of Latter-day Saints, 1979).

120. David Van Biema, "Kingdom Come," *Time*, 4 August 1997.

121. "Musings of the Main Mormon," *San Francisco Sunday Examiner and Chronicle*, 13 April 1997.

CHAPTER 12

1. Paul Hoskisson, "William Dever. Did God Have a Wife," *BYU Studies* 45.2 (2006):186.

2. 1 Kings 18.

3. Saul M. Olyan, *Asherah and the Cult of Yahweh in Israel* (Atlanta: Scholars Press, 1988), 73. Cited in Daniel Peterson, "Nephi and his Asherah," *Journal of Book of Mormon Studies* 9.2 (2000):16–25.

4. *Bengal Catholic Herald* 5:21 (18 November 1843):287; M. Hobart Seymour, *Mornings Among the Jesuits at Rome* (New York: Harper & Brothers, 1849), 55; *The Catholic Magazine* 2 (1 July–1 December 1843):241. For a study of the Virgin Mary/Heavenly Mother connection, see Margaret Barker, *The Mother of the Lord, Volume 1: The Lady in the Temple* (London: Bloomsbury, 2012).

5. "Hevenly Moder" appears in Julian of Norwich *The Showings*, XIV, chap. 63 (New York: Norton, 2005), 99. Julian of Norwich refers variously to God, the Trinity, and Jesus, as "our Moder" in chaps. 57–62. For background into this motif, see Caroline Walker Bynum, *Jesus as Mother: Studies in the Spirituality of the High Middle Ages* (Berkeley: University of California Press, 1982).

6. Isaac Penington, *Works* (London: Samuel Clark, 1761) 2:139, 517.

7. Calvin Green and Seth Y. Wells, *A Summary View of the Millennial Church, or United Society of Believers* (Albany: Packard & Benthuysen, 1823), 218.

8. F. W. Evans, *Short Treatise on the Second Appearing of Christ* (Boston: Bazin and Chandler, 1853), 14–15.

9. Paulina Bates, *The Divine Book of Holy and Eternal Wisdom*, cited in *Eve and Adam: Jewish, Christian, and Muslim Readings on Genesis and Gender*, ed. Kristen E. Kvam, Linda S. Schearing, and Valarie H. Ziegler (Bloomington: Indiana University Press, 1999), 361.

10. Bates, *Divine Book*, 360.

11. Green and Wells, *Summary View*, 228–29.

12. Mario de Pillis, *The Development of Mormon Communitarianism, 1826–1846*. Ph.D. dissertation, Yale University, 1960, p. 66.

13. *EMS* 1.6 (November 1832):7 (D&C 49:22).

14. Spencer Fogleman, *Jesus Is Female: Moravians and Radical Religion in Early America* (Philadelphia: University of Pennsylvania Press, 2007), 2.

15. Theodore Parker, *The Collected Works*, ed. Frances Power Cobbe (London: Trubner, 1867), 2:45, 63, 66–67, 108–109, 125, etc.

16. Parker, *Collected Works*, 88.

17. 1876 D&C 132:63.

18. B. H. Roberts, for one, read "bearing of the souls of men" to refer to "'replenishing the earth' with the race of men." *The Truth the Way, the Life*, ed. John W. Welch (Provo: BYU Studies, 1994), 555.

19. 1876 D&C 132:19.

20. See, for example, Joseph Fielding Smith, who interprets "continuation of the seeds" to mean "the power of procreation" in the Celestial Kingdom. *Doctrines of Salvation* (Salt Lake City: Bookcraft, 1955), 2: 287–88. Jonathan Stapley, who considers "viviparous spirit birth" a "wildly popular folk belief," argues that the "continuation of the seeds" refers to a retention of kinship rather than continuing child-creation. The strong biblical connotations of seeds with procreation, however, makes that reading unlikely.

21. *WJS*, 293.

22. W. W. Phelps, "The Answer," [to William Smith], *TS* 5.24 (1 January 1844):758.

23. Samuel Brown, *In Heaven as It Is on Earth* (New York: Oxford University Press, 2012), 11–12.

24. Jer. 44.

25. The hymn was reported as being sung on that occasion in *TS* 6.2 (1 February 1845):794; the hymn was reprinted as W. W. Phelps, "A Voice from the Prophet. Come to Me," *TS* 6.1 (15 January 1845):783.

26. "Joseph's Speckled Bird" [W. W. Phelps], "Paracletes," *TS* 6.8 (1 May 1845):892.

27. Linda P. Wilcox, "The Mormon Doctrine of a Mother in Heaven," in *Sisters in Spirit: Mormon Women in Historical and Cultural Perspective*, ed. Maureen Ursenbach Beecher and Lavina Fielding Anderson (Urbana: University of Illinois Press, 1992), 65–66.

28. First published in *TS* 6.17 (15 November 1845):1039.

29. [McNemar, Richard (or Rufus Bishop)], *The Orthodox Trinity* [Watervliet, (O[hio]), March 1, 1835], 2–3. In Rick Grunder, *Mormon Parallels: A Bibliographic Source* (Lafayette, NY: Rick Grunder Books, 2008), digital version, 229.

30. Orson Pratt, *JD*, 14:241.

31. Orson Pratt, *JD*, 18:292.

32. George Q. Cannon, "Mr. Can[n]on's Lecture," *Salt Lake Daily Herald*, 15 April 1884, 8. Cited in David Paulsen and Martin Pulido, "A Survey of Historical Teachings About Mother in Heaven," *BYU Studies* 50.1 (2011):77. Paulsen and Pulido's is the most comprehensive survey of the subject.

33. Erastus Snow, *JD*, 26:214.

34. Erastus Snow, *JD*, 19:266.

35. V. H. Cassler, "Plato's Son, Augustine's Heir: '"A Post–Heterosexual Mormon Theology"'? *Square Two* 5.2 (Summer 2012), online at http://squaretwo.org/Sq2ArticleCasslerPlatosSon.html.

36. "Origin of Man," *Messages of the First Presidency*, comp. James R. Clark (Salt Lake City: Bookcraft, 1971), 4:205–206. (Originally published in *Improvement Era* 13.1 [1909].)

37. "The Father and the Son: A Doctrinal Exposition by the First Presidency and the Twelve," Clark, *Messages* 5:34. (First published in pamphlet form, 30 June 1916.)

38. Paulsen and Pulido, "Mother There," 76.

39. Orson F. Whitney, "What Is Education?" *Contributor* 6.9 (1885):347; John A. Widtsoe, "Everlasting Motherhood," *MS* 90 (10 May 1928):298. Cited in Paulsen and Pulido, "Mother There," 77–78.

40. George Q. Cannon, "Topics of the Times: The Worship of Female Deities," *Juvenile Instructor* 30 (15 May 1895):314–17. Cited in Paulsen and Pulido, "Mother There," 78.

41. Susa Young Gates, "The Vision Beautiful," *Improvement Era* 23 (April 1920):542. Cited in Paulsen and Pulido, "Mother There," 78.

42. *CD*, 4:3086; Milton R. Hunter, *Will a Man Rob God? The Laws and Doctrine of Tithing, Fast Offerings, and Observance of Fast Day* (Salt Lake City: Deseret News, 1952), 183–84. In Paulsen and Pulido, "Mother There," 80.

43. "The Family: A Proclamation to the World" was first read by Church President Gordon B. Hinckley to the General Relief Society Meeting, 23 September 1995. It is available on the church website, https://www.lds.org/topics/family-proclamation.

CHAPTER 13

1. *EMS* 1.11 (April 1833):81; *EMS* 1.10 (March 1833):73 (Moses 6:52, 65, PGP).

2. 1835 D&C 50:2 (D&C 27:11).

3. *WJS*, 8.

4. 1876 D&C 116:1.

5. *WJS*, 8.

6. *WJS*, 39.

7. "History of Brigham Young," *MS* 25.28 (11 July 1863):439.

8. L. John Nuttall, Journal, 7 Februrary 1877. In David John Buerger, *The Mysteries of Godliness: A History of Mormon Temple Worship* (Salt Lake City: Signature, 2002), 73.

9. Buerger, *Mysteries*, 80.

10. William Kinkade, *Bible Doctrine of God . . .* , cited in Bernard Whitman, *A Discourse on Denying the Lord Jesus* (Boston: Bowles and Dearborn, 1827), 45–46.

11. Kenneth W. Godfrey, "A Note on the Nauvoo Library and Literary Institute," *BYU Studies* 14 (Spring 1974):386–89.

12. "The first of all men have I called Adam, which is many." *TS* 4.5 (16 January 1843):73 (Moses 1:34, PGP).

13. For elaboration of the link between adoption theology and Adam-God teachings, see Jonathan Stapley, "Adoptive Sealing Ritual in Mormonism," *Journal of Mormon History* 37.3 (Summer 2011):53–118.

14. *CD*, 1:180.

15. *CD*, 1:276.

16. Wilford Woodruff recorded his understanding that, following a line of priesthood delegation, Joseph Smith would say to Brigham Young, "now go Brother Brigham & resurrect your wives & children & gather them together." Wilford Woodruff, *Journal*, ed. Scott G. Kenney (Midvale, UT: Signature, 1983), 4:389.

17. *CD*, 1:518.

18. *MS* 15.50 (10 December 1853):801–802.

19. *CD*, 2:740.

20. *CD*, 2:763.

21. *CD*, 2: 832.

22. *CD*, 2:851–52.

23. *CD*, 2: 845.

24. *CD*, 1:553.

25. *CD*, 1:560.

26. *CD*, 3:1533.

27. Nuttall, Journal, 7 February 1877, BYU Special Collections.

28. *The Instructor* 80.6 (June 1945):259, written on 17 January 1878. Cited in David John Buerger, "The Adam–God Doctrine," *Dialogue: A Journal of Mormon Thought* 15.1 (Spring 1982):34–35.

29. See the sources gathered and cited by Craig L. Tholson, *Adam-God: Doctrines of the Restoration* (np: Publishment, 1994), 153.

30. Tholson, *Adam-God*, 156.

31. Charles W. Penrose, "Our Father Adam," *Improvement Era* 5.1 (September 1902):879–80.

32. Spencer W. Kimball, "Our Own Liahona," *Ensign* 6.11 (November 1976):77.

CHAPTER 14

1. Martin Rose, "Names of God in the OT," in *Anchor Bible Dictionary,* ed. David Noel Freedman (New York: Doubleday, 1992), 4:1002; Henry O. Thompson, "Yahweh," 6:1011.

2. Rose, "Names," 4:1006.

3. Mark S. Smith, *The Early History of God: Yahweh and the Other Deities in Ancient Israel* (San Francisco: Harper & Row, 1990), 32.

4. Helmer Ringgren, *Israelite Religion*, trans. David E. Green (Philadelphia: Fortress, 1966), 44. He places their consolidation in David's reign.

5. Daniel C. Peterson, "Nephi and His Asherah," *Journal of Book of Mormon Studies* 9.2 (2000):19; Peterson cites Smith, Frank Moore Cross Jr., Raphael Patai, Margaret Barker, and others in support.

6. Margaret Barker, *The Great Angel: A Study of Israel's Second God* (Louisville: John Knox, 1992), 192–93.

7. Edward Andrews, *Lectures on the Doctrine of the Trinity* (London: Palmer, 1828), 7, 11.

8. Richard Watson, *Theological Institutes* (London: John Mason, 1829), 544.

9. Ethan Smith, *View of the Trinity* (Poultney, VT: Smith & Shute, 1824), 35.

10. Smith, *Trinity*, 41, 68–70, 72.

11. Smith, *Trinity*, 69.

12. E[rastus] Snow and B[enjamin] Winchester, "An Address to the Citizens of Salem," *TS* 3.1 (15 November 1841):578.

13. *JSP-J2,* 117.

14. In his King Follett Discourse, he refers to "the Great Elohim" and to the "Head One of the Gods." Stan Larson, "The King Follett Discourse: A Newly Amalgamated Text," *BYU Studies* 18.2 (Winter 1978):199, 202. George Laub remembered him defining "Eloheam" as "the God of all gods." "George Laub's Nauvoo Journal," ed. Eugene England, *BYU Studies* 18.2 (Winter 1978):171.

15. In his final Sermon in the Grove, Smith was defending the plurality of Gods. "The heads of the Gods appointed one God for us," he preached. *WJS*, 379.

16. George D. Smith, ed., *An Intimate Chronicle: The Journals of William Clayton* (Salt Lake City: Signature, 1995), 210.

17. *CD*, 5:2856.

18. John Taylor, *The Mediation and Atonement* (Salt Lake City: Deseret News, 1882), 138, 151.

19. *Juvenile Instructor* 6 (30 September 1871):155. Cited in the useful overview of the subject, Boyd Kirkland, "Jehovah as Father: The Development of the Mormon Jehovah Doctrine," *Sunstone* 9.2 (Autumn 1984):36–44.

20. James E. Talmage, *Jesus the Christ* (Salt Lake City: Deseret News, 1915), 40.

21. "The Father and the Son," *Messages of the First Presidency*, comp. James R. Clark (Salt Lake City: Bookcraft, 1971), 5:31–34.

22. Bruce R. McConkie, *The Promised Messiah* (Salt Lake City: Deseret, 1995), 351–52.

23. *WJS*, 212.

24. 1835 D&C 82:2 (D&C 93:13–14).

25. "Fourth Ecumenical Council," *C&C*, 1:181.

26. Talmage, *Jesus the Christ*, 119.

27. "The Father and the Son," 5:31–32.

28. "He is the image of the invisible God, the firstborn of all creation" Col. 1:15; see also Heb. 1:6, "when he brings the firstborn into the world, he says, 'Let all God's angels worship him.'"

29. 1835 D&C 82:4 (D&C 93:21).

30. John 1:1, *Joseph Smith's "New Translation" of the Bible* (Independence, MO: Herald House, 1970), 442.

31. Blake Ostler, for instance, argues that "the view that man originated when spirit matter was organized into an individual though literal spirit birth seems to have been the *only* view consistently elucidated from 1845–1905." Ostler, "The Idea of Pre–Existence in the Development of Mormon Thought," *Dialogue: A Journal of Mormon Thought* 15.1 (Spring 1982):68.

32. Smith referred to a vision of "Jesus, the Son of God, our elder brother." Salt Lake City School of the Prophets Minutes, in *Joseph Smith Papers: Documents 3: February 1833–March 1834*, ed. Gerrit J. Dirkmaat et al. (Salt Lake City: Church Historians Press, 2014), v.

33. *CD*, 1:61; "Firstborn of the spirit children of our Heavenly Father," the LDS Bible Dictionary reads (appended to the 1981 LDS edition of the Holy Bible).

34. The Doctrinal Exposition declared "no impropriety, therefore, in speaking of Jesus Christ as the Elder Brother of the rest of human kind." "The Father and the Son," 5:34.

35. "The Father and the Son," 5:33.

36. Talmage, *Jesus the Christ*, 143.

37. Talmage, *Jesus the Christ*, 10.

38. For an extended treatment of shifts in the doctrinal emphases of Mormon Christology, see Matthew Bowman, "The Crisis of Mormon Christology: History, Progress, and Protestantism," *Fides Et Historia* 40.2 (Fall 2008):1–25.

39. 1835 DC 82:5 (D&C 93:33).

40. 3 Nephi 12:48.

41. *TS* 3.10 (25 March 1842):720 (Abraham 3:27, PGP). A second account was produced by Smith in 1830 but not published until 1867: "Satan . . . came before me, saying—Behold, here am I, send me, I will be thy son, and I will redeem all mankind, that one soul shall not be lost, and

surely I will do it; wherefore give me thine honor. But, behold, my Beloved Son, which was my Beloved and Chosen from the beginning, said unto me—Father, thy will be done, and the glory be thine forever." Moses 4:1–2, PGP.

42. See Camille Fronk, "Mary, Mother of Jesus," in *Encyclopedia of Mormonism,* 4 vols. (New York: Macmillan, 1992), 2:863–64.

43. Luke 1:35; Matthew 1:18.

44. *CD* 1:321; Joseph Fielding Smith followed suit in his personal views, but Lee did not. See Harold B. Lee, *Teachings of Harold B. Lee* (Salt Lake City: Bookcraft, 1996), 14.

45. "The Father and the Son," 5:27.

CHAPTER 15

1. Alistair McGrath, *Christian Theology: An Introduction* (Chichester: Wiley-Blackwell, 2011), 228.

2. The Nicene Creed and the Athanasian Creed can be found in *C&C,* 1:159 and 676–77.

3. Matt. 28:19.

4. Isa. 63:10; Ps. 51:11.

5. Luke 4:1.

6. Luke 12:12.

7. Acts 2:4.

8. John 14:26. "Comforter" is the term in the KJV.

9. 1 Cor. 12.

10. Rom. 15:16; 2 Thess. 2:13; 1 Cor. 6:11, etc.

11. In 1844, Smith was reported to say the Holy Ghost was "in a state of probation," and "is yet a Spiritual body and waiting to take to himself a body," but he never developed the idea further, and the idea found little subsequent support. *WJS,* 245, 305.

12. *WJS,* 170.

13. *CD,* 3:1377.

14. 1876 D&C 130:22.

15. "I spake unto him as a man speaketh; for I beheld that he was in the form of a man; yet nevertheless, I knew that it was the Spirit of the Lord." (1 Nephi 11:11). Some Mormons read the reference as an allusion to a pre-mortal Christ, but in Book of Mormon usage the spirit of the Lord seems to always refer to the Holy Ghost.

16. *Key,* 45.

17. Orson Pratt, "Great First Cause," in *A Series of Pamphlets* (Liverpool: R. James, 1851), 10.

18. *Key,* 39.

19. Philip Sidney, "Defence of Poesie," in *The Complete Works of Sir Philip Sidney* (London: William Ponsonby, 1595), 34; John Foxe, *Fox's Book of Martyrs* (Philadelphia: J. J. Woodward, 1830), 534.

20. Edward Burrough, *Truth, the strongest of all . . .* (London: Giles Calvert, 1657), 25; George Whitehead, *The Divine Light of Christ in Man* (London: Thomas Northcott, 1692).

21. 1835 D&C 7:2–3 (D&C 88:7–12).

22. *Key,* 40.

23. Stewart Goetz and Charles Taliaferro, *A Brief History of the Soul* (Chichester: Wiley-Blackwell, 2011), 147.

24. *Key*, 39.

25. *Key*, 105–106.

26. Lorenzo Snow, "Submission to the Divine Will," *JD*, 7:353.

27. B. H. Roberts, *The Gospel: An Exposition of Its First Principles* (Salt Lake City: Deseret News, 1901), 191.

28. James Talmage, *Articles of Faith* (Salt Lake City: Deseret News, 1899), 166.

29. Talmage noted in his journal that "the First Presidency" agreed that it was imperative "to make plain that the Church does not refuse to recognize the discoveries and demonstrations of science." James Harris, ed., *The Essential Talmage* (Salt Lake City: Signature, 1997), 239.

30. John A. Widtsoe, *Joseph Smith as Scientist* (Salt Lake City: Young Men's Mutual Improvement Associations, 1908), 24.

31. Orson Pratt, "The Holy Spirit and the Godhead," *JD*, 2:345–46.

32. James R. Clark, comp., *Messages of the First Presidency* (Salt Lake City: Bookcraft, 1971), 2:214–23 and 235–40.

33. *CD*, 3:1614, 3:1466, 1:291, etc.

34. *CD*, 3:1617, 4:1993, 4:2080.

35. *CD*, 1:532, 1:350.

36. James E. Talmage Diary, January 5, 1894. In *Minutes of the Apostles of the Church of Jesus Christ of Latter-day Saints 1894-1899* (Salt Lake City: Privately Printed, 2010), 1.

37. Talmage, *Articles of Faith* 165. Not all church leaders agreed with Talmage's reading of that Book of Mormon passage, though by way of precedent Orson Pratt did. "The Holy Spirit," *A Series of Pamphlets by Orson Pratt*, 56, cited in Harris, *Essential Talmage*, xxxvii.

38. Young, *CD*, 5:2821.

39. Talmage, *Articles of Faith*, 167.

40. Joseph F. Smith, *Gospel Doctrine*, ed. John A. Widtsoe (Salt Lake City: Deseret, 1919), 60–61.

41. *True to the Faith: A Gospel Reference* (Salt Lake City: Church of Jesus Christ of Latter-day Saints, 2004), 96.

42. Joseph Fielding Smith, *Doctrines of Salvation* (Salt Lake City: Bookcraft, 1954), 1:52.

43. John Wesley, "The Means of Grace," *Sermons on Several Occasions* (New York: Carlton and Phillips, 1855), 1:140.

44. Though Arminians emphasized prevenient grace, the concept is traceable to Augustine and was confirmed at the Council of Trent, where it was stated that a "predisposing grace of God" turns the sinful toward God, his "grace inciting and helping them." *C&C*, 2:828.

45. John Wesley, "The Scripture Way of Salvation," *Sermons*, 2: 236.

CHAPTER 16

1. Rev. 12:7–8

2. Luke 10:18.

3. Philo of Alexandria, Quis Rerum Divinarum Heres Sit [Who is the Heir of Divine Things] XLIX (239–240), in *The Contemplative Life, The Giants, and Selections*, trans. David Winston (New York: Paulist Press, 1981), 118–19.

4. Origen, *De Principiis* 1.3.8, *ANF*, 4:255.

5. Origen, *De Principiis* 1.5.5, *ANF*, 4:259.

6. John Milton, *Paradise Lost*, Book 4, ll. 58–56, in *The Complete Poetry and Essential Prose of John Milton*, ed. William Kerrigan, John Rumrich, and Stephen M. Fallon (New York: Modern Library, 2007), 386.

7. Isa. 14:12–15.

8. Adam Clarke, *Clarke's Commentary* (Nashville: Abingdon, 1977), 4:82.

9. Charles Buck, *A Theological Dictionary* (Philadelphia: Joseph Woodward, 1830), 147.

10. 2 Nephi 2:17.

11. Smith referred to his work on the papyri as "translation"—the same term he employed when working with the Book of Mormon and when reworking an English version of the Bible. Fragments of the papyri, long out of the public eye and rediscovered in 1966, appear to correspond to Egyptian funerary texts, not Smith's "Book of Abraham." Various explanations have been offered, with the church's official position being that "Little is known concerning the process JS employed in bringing forth the Book of Abraham." http://josephsmithpapers.org/intro/introduction-to-book-of-abraham-manuscripts.

12. In 1944, H. Wheeler Robinson published a groundbreaking paper on the divine council in antiquity: "The Council of Yahweh," *Journal of Theological Studies* 45 (1944):151–57. See also E. Theodore Mullen, *The Divine Council in Canaanite and Early Hebrew Literature.* Harvard Semitic Monographs, no. 24 (Missoula, MT: Scholars Press, 1986).

13. *TS* 3.10 (25 March 1842):720 (Abraham 3:22–28, PGP).

14. Moses 4:1–4, PGP, first appearing in the 1867 PGP. Smith produces a second, similar but shorter, account at about the same time: "the devil . . . rebelled against me, saying, Give me thine honor, which is my power; and also a third part of the hosts of heaven turned he away from me." *EMS* 1.4 (September 1832):2 (D&C 29:36).

15. Joseph Smith [W. W. Phelps], "The Answer," *TS* 4.6 (1 February 1843):83.

16. *EMS* 1.2 (July 1832):2 (D&C 76:26).

17. 2 Nephi 2:5, 26.

18. John Taylor, *The Mediation and Atonement* (Salt Lake City: Deseret News, 1882), 97.

19. Edward Beecher, *Concord of the Ages* (New York, Derby & Jackson, 1860), 98.

20. Alma 1:4.

21. Alma 11:36–37.

22. W. W. Phelps, "The Answer," *TS* 5:24 (1 January 1845):758.

23. *The Seer* 1.4 (April 1853):52.

24. Orson Pratt, *JD*, 21:288.

25. George Q. Cannon, "Foreknowledge of God," *Collected Discourses*, ed. Brian H. Stuy (np: B. H. S. Publishing, 1999), 2:228.

26. J. Reuben Clark, "Power in Unity," Conference Report of the Church of Jesus Christ of Latter-day Saints (October 1949), 193.

27. Maura R. O'Connor, "Exorcism Makes a Comeback," *EnlightenNext Magazine* (September-November 2005), http://www.enlightennext.org/magazine/j30/exorcism.asp.

28. In 1935 only 19% of BYU students believed in a literal devil. Harold T. Christensen and Kenneth L. Cannon, "The Fundamentalist Emphasis at Brigham Young University: 1935–1973," *Journal for the Scientific Study of Religion* 17.1 (March 1978):55.

29. Moses 4:4, PGP.

30. 2 Nephi 28:20–22.

31. Sterling McMurrin, *The Theological Foundations of the Mormon Religion* (Salt Lake City: University of Utah Press, 1965), 52.

32. The hymn (with its strident Arminianism) was taken from an 1805 camp-meeting collection. Michael Hicks, *Mormonism and Music: A History* (Urbana: University of Illinois Press, 1989), 21.

33. "They are free to choose liberty and eternal life, through the great Mediator of all men, or to choose captivity and death, according to the captivity and power of the devil." 2 Nephi 2:27.

34. Rev. 12:9.

35. P. W. Coxon, paraphrasing Moses Aberbach, in "Nephilim," in *Dictionary of Deities and Demons in the Bible*, ed. Karel van der Toorn, Bob Becking, and Pieter W. van der Horst (New York: E. J. Brill, 1995), 619.

36. The connection of these two traditions, from the last and first biblical books, is suggested by P. W. Coxon. "The NT notion of the fallen angels who like Satan (Luke 10:18) plummeted to earth because they failed to recognize their position in the divine hierarchy (2 Pet. 2:4; Jude 6) has clear allusions to the Nephilim.... Etymologically, the basis of Nephilim is transparent. This explains the wealth of allusions which exploits the *fall* from heaven." "Nephilim," in van der Toorn et al., *Dictionary*, 619.

37. 2 Pet. 2:4; Jude 1:6.

38. Tertullian, *Apology* XXII, trans. S. Thelwall, *ANF*, 3:36.

39. Dante Alighiere, *Inferno* VIII.83, trans. Allen Mandelbaum (New York: Bantam, 1982), 73.

40. Milton, *Paradise Lost*, Book 10, ll. 464, 617–18, pp. 566, 570–71.

41. Dee E. Andrews, *The Methodists and Revolutionary America, 1760–1800* (Princeton: Princeton University Press, 2002), 82.

42. *WJS*, 60.

43. "History of Joseph Smith," *TS* 4.1 (15 November 1842):13.

44. 2 Nephi 28:22.

45. Ps. 82:1–7.

46. John 10:34–36.

47. Cyrus Gordon long ago disputed the effort to translate the offending term Elohim as "rulers" or "judges" in "Elohim in its Reputed Meaning of Rulers, Judges," *Journal of Biblical Literature* 54 (1935):139–44. More recently, Michael Heiser provides reasons for reading the word as "gods" or "heavenly beings," in "Deuteronomy 32:8 and the Sons of God," *Bibliotheca Sacra* 158.629 (January–March 2001):52–74.

48. Job 38:4, 7.

49. 1 Kings 22:19–22.

50. Isa. 6:8.

51. Deut. 33:2–3.

52. E. Theodore Mullen, *The Assembly of the Gods: The Divine Council in Canaanite and Early Hebrew Literature*. Harvard Semitic Monographs, no. 24 (Missoula, MT: Scholars Press, 1986), 192–93.

53. E. Theodore Mullen Jr., "Divine Assembly," in *Anchor Bible Dictionary*, ed. David Noel Freedman, 6 vols. (New York: Doubleday, 1992), 2:214.

54. Mullen, "Divine Assembly," 2:216.

55. Moshe Halbertal and Avishai Margalit, *Idolotry*, trans. Naomi Goldblum (Cambridge, MA: Harvard University Press, 1992), 4.

56. Clement of Rome, *The Apostolic Constitutions* VIII, in *The Clementine Homilies; The Apostolic Constitutions,* ed. James Donaldson (Edinburgh: T. and T. Clark, 1870), 226, 230; *Testament of Adam* 4.1–4.8, trans. S. E. Robinson, in James H. Charlesworth, *The Old Testament Pseudepigrapha* (Garden City: Doubleday, 1983), 1:995.

57. Thomas Aquinas, *Summa Theologica* Q.108 Art. 1–6 (Chicago: Encyclopedia Britannica, 1980), 1:552–60.

58. *Concerning the Holy Angels and their Ministry* (Sheffield: John Blackwell, 1826), 4.

59. *Holy Angels*, 43, 45.

60. Margaret Barker, *An Extraordinary Gathering of Angels* (London: MQ, 2004), 10.

61. Barker, *Gathering*, 19.

62. "I have been laboring in this cause for eight years," he wrote in a letter published in *MA* 1.12 (September 1835):179. Of course, Smith's earlier 1820 theophany had also included the appearance of "many angels."*JSP-J1*, 88.

63. *JSP-H1*, 222.

64. John Taylor, *JD*, 21:94.

65. Joseph Noble, reported in Mark L. McConkie, *Remembering Joseph* (Salt Lake City: Deseret, 2003), 24. The Taylor and Noble reports are cited in Brian L. Smith, "'Taught From On High': The Ministry Of Angelic Messengers To The Prophet Joseph Smith," in *Joseph Smith and the Doctrinal Restoration* (Provo: Brigham Young University, Religious Studies Center, 2005), 332–45.

66. William Mulder, "'Essential Gestures': Craft and Calling in Contemporary Mormon Letters," *Weber Studies* 10.3 (Fall 1993):7.

67. *JSP-H1*, 222.

68. Rudolf Otto, *The Idea of the Holy*, 2nd ed., trans. J. W. Harvey (London: Oxford University Press, 1950), 27.

69. *WJS*, 171.

70. *WJS*, 253, 77.

71. *WJS*, 44.

72. *WJS*, 77.

73. *JSP-H1*, 222.

74. *WJS*, 8.

75. 1835 D&C 3:10 (D&C 107:20). The ministering of angels is identified as pertaining to the Aaronic Priesthood, to which virtually all Mormon men are ordained as youth. 1835 D&C 4:15 (D&C 84:88).

76. Wilford Woodruff, *Journal*, ed. Scott G. Kenney (Midvale, UT: Signature, 1983), 2:200.

77. Joseph F. Smith, Gospel Doctrine, ed. John A. Widtsoe (Salt Lake City: Deseret, 1919), 435–36.

78. Heber C. Kimball to John Taylor, 9 November 1840, in *WJS*, 49.

79. "Ministering Spirits," in James Lyman Merrick, *The Pilgrim's Harp* (Boston: Crocker and Brewster, 1847), 493.

80. "Omnipotence of God," in Benjamin Beddome, *Hymns Adapted to Public Worship or Family Devotion* (London: Burton, 1818), 30.

81. Socrates invoked his belief in a personal *daimon* as evidence of his religiosity. It warned him away from danger and moral wrong, he told the court.

82. Gen. 28–29, 32; Matt. 18:10.

83. Jerome, *Commentary on Matthew* 3.18.10, trans. Thomas P. Scheck (Washington, DC: Catholic University of America Press, 2008), 209.

84. *Testament of Adam*, 4.1, Charlesworth, *Old Testament*, 1:995.

85. John Calvin, *Institutes of the Christian Religion*, trans. Henry Beveridge (Peabody, MA: Hendrickson, 2008), 93.

86. "St. Michael and all Angels," *The Collects of the Book of Common Prayer* (Boston: Dutton, Church of England, 1883), 435.

87. Anatole France, *Revolt of the Angels* (New York: Gabriel Wells, 1924), 41.

88. *WJS*, 10.

89. The account is published in Joseph Smith Jr., *History of the Church of Jesus Christ of Latter-day Saints*, 7 vols., ed. James Mulholland et al. (Salt Lake City: Deseret, 1951), 6:461. However, the story is not found in Smith's own papers, but in a reminiscence, "Miles Romney Report, circa 1854–1856," in CHL. My thanks to Steven Harper and Andrew Hedges for this information.

90. *TS* 6.21 (February 1845): 796.

91. *Key*, 120.

92. *CD*, 5:2607.

93. "Angels shall guard thy head," said one. "They whose Spirits are in heaven will prove unto thee a guardian angel," promised another. (One living correspondent's blessing [1975] similarly promised her that her deceased relatives had been assigned to watch over her [copy in author's possession]). Many other nineteenth-century blessings promised the attendance of "ministering" or unspecified angels, and Alva West was promised *he* would be a ministering angel. *Early Patriarchal Blessings of the Church of Jesus Christ of Latter-day Saints*, comp. H. Michael Marquardt (Salt Lake City: Smith-Pettit Foundation, 2007), 421, 429, 15, 17, 19 etc.; 430.

94. Heber C. Kimball, *JD*, 8:258.

95. Orson Hyde, *JD*, 6:16.

96. John Taylor, "Origin and Destiny of Woman." *The Mormon* 3.28 (29 August 1857). (Reprinted in *Deseret News,* 26 May 1899.)

97. Orson Pratt, *JD*, 2:343–34. Pratt does not identify the other speaker.

98. George Q. Cannon, *Gospel Truth: Discourses and Writings of President George Q. Cannon*, comp. Jerreld L. Newquist (Salt Lake City: Deseret, 1987), 65.

99. *Messages of the First Presidency*, comp. James R. Clark (Salt Lake City: Bookcraft, 1971), 6: 134.

100. John A. Widtsoe, *Improvement Era* (April 1944):225.

101. 1835 D&C 4:6 (D&C 84:42); see also D&C 109:22.

102. The McConkie quotation is from *Mormon Doctrine* (Salt Lake City: Bookcraft, 1960), 341. Cited in several versions of the church's magazine feature, "I have a Question." See, for instance, Dean Jarman, *Tambuli* (April 1984):22–23, the September 1988 issue of the *Liahona*, and the March 1988 issue of the *Ensign*.

103. "Are there guardian angels? Do I have one assigned to me?" *New Era* (January 2012):37.

104. Jeffrey R. Holland, "The Ministry of Angels," *Ensign* 38.11 (November 2008):29.

CHAPTER 17

1. Karen Armstrong, *The Case for God* (New York: Anchor, 2010), 105.

2. Andrew Louth, *The Origins of the Christian Mystical Tradition: From Plato to Denys* (Oxford: Oxford University Press, 2007), 77.

3. Cornelius Van Til, *An Introduction to Systematic Theology* (Phillipsburg, NJ: Presbyterian and Reformed, 1974), 12.

4. *Prayer of Joseph* fragment A 2–3, trans. J. Z. Smith, in James H. Charlesworth, *The Old Testament Pseudepigrapha* (Garden City: Doubleday, 1983), 2:713. Charlesworth notes that while not widespread, Jewish claims that "the patriarchs or Moses were pre-existent" were not uncommon (713n).

5. *Apocalypse of Abraham* XXI.7–XX.5, trans. R. Rubinkiewicz, in Charlesworth, *Old Testament* 1:699–700.

6. Wisd. of Sol. 8:19–20 Still included in the Apocryphal/Deuterocanonical section of the NRSV, but not the KJV or most other versions.

7. This at least is Adolf Harnack's explanation for the widespread belief in preexistence. Adolf Harnack, *History of Dogma*, 7 vols., trans. from 3rd German ed. by Neil Buchanan (London: Williams & Norgate, 1894), 1:324.

8. Origen, *De Principiis* 1.8, trans. G. W. Butterworth, in *Origen on First Principles, Being Koetschau's Text of the De Principiis* (New York: Harper & Row, 1966), 67.

9. Tertullian, *Treatise on the Soul* XXIV, trans. Peter Holmes, *ANF*, 3:203.

10. In E. Brooks Holifield, *Theology in America* (New Haven: Yale University Press, 2003), 112.

11. Arnobius, *Against the Heathen* 1.28, trans. Hamilton Bryce and Hugh Campbell, *ANF*, 6:420.

12. R. T. Wallis, *Neo-Platonism* (London: Duckworth, 1995), 103.

13. Arnobius, *Against the Heathen* 1.29, *ANF*, 6:420.

14. Arnobius, *Against the Heathen* 2.47, 51, *ANF*, 6:451–53.

15. Augustine, Letter 143 (to Marcellinus), in *The Works of Saint Augustine: A Translation for the 21st Century. Letters 100–155,* trans. Roland Teske (Hyde Park: New City Press, 1990), Part II, 2:305.

16. Augustine, *On Free Choice of the Will* III.21, trans. Thomas Williams (Indianapolis: Hackett, 1993), 111.

17. Augustine, *Confessions* X.21, trans. F. J. Sheed (Indianapolis: Hackett, 1993), 189.

18. Jerome, Letter 126.1 (to Marcellinus and Anapsychia), in *Jerome: Letters and Select Works*, in *NPNF2 of the Christian Church*, ed. Philip Schaff, Second series *[NPNF2]* (Peabody, MA: Hendrickson, 1999), 6:252. Fremantle gives the date as 412; other sources assign the date 410.

19. Leo the Great, Letter 15 ("To Turribius, Bishop of Asturia, Upon the Errors of the Priscillianists"), XI (10), trans. Charles Lett Feltoe, in *The Letters and Sermons of Leo the Great, NPNF2* 12:23. This letter is considered spurious by some scholars. See K. Künstle, *Antepriscilliana* (Freiburg, 1905). See also the broader condemnation in Leo the Great, Letter 35 (To Julian, Bishop of Cos), *NPNF2* 12:48.

20. Henry R. Percival, *The Seven Ecumenical Councils of the Undivided Church* (New York: Scribner's, 1900), 320.

21. Eadmer, *The Life of St Anselm: Archbishop of Canterbury*, trans. R. W. Southern (Oxford: Clarendon Press, 1972), 142.

22. Hildegard of Bingen, *Scivias* 1.4.1–8, trans. Columba Hart and Jane Bishop (New York: Paulist Press, 1990), 109–16; Julian of Norwich, *Showings* XIV.51, ed. Denise N. Baker (New York: Norton, 2005).

23. Henry More, "Preface General," *A Collection of Several Philosophical Writings of Dr. Henry More* (New York: Garland, 1978) xxi. (Reprint of London: James Flesher, 1662.)

24. More, "Preface General," xx.

25. Abraham Tucker [Edward Search], *Freewill, Foreknowledge and Fate: A Fragment* (Bristol: Thoemmes, 1990, 169–71. (Reprint of London: 1763.)

26. Benjamin Franklin to Jane Mecom, *The Works of Benjamin Franklin*, 10 vols., ed. Jared Sparks (Boston: Hilliard, Gray, 1840), 7:58–59. Sparks does not date the letter.

27. See Terryl L. Givens, *When Souls Had Wings: Premortal Life in Western Thought* (New York: Oxford University Press, 2010), 200–206.

28. Wilhelm Benecke, *An Exposition of St. Paul's Epistle to the Romans*, trans. Friedrich Wilhelm (London: Longman, Brown, Green, and Longmans, 1854), 455–56.

29. Julius Müller, *The Christian Doctrine of Sin*, 2 vols., trans. William Urwick (Edinburgh: Clark, 1868), 2:72–73.

30. Charles Hodge, *Systematic Theology*, 3 vols. (Grand Rapids, MI: Eerdman's, 1970), 2:215.

31. Samuel Taylor Coleridge, "Sonnet" (London: Edward Moxon, 1863), 270.

32. Letter to John Thelwall (19 November 1796), in *Collected Letters of Samuel Taylor Coleridge*, ed. E. L. Griggs, 6 vols. (Oxford: Clarendon Press, 1956), 1:260–261.

33. William Wordsworth, "Ode: Intimations of Immortality," in *Poems* (London: Longman, 1815), 2:349.

34. Jared Curtis, ed., *The Fenwick Notes of William Wordsworth* (London: Bristol Classical Press, 1993), 61–62. These Fenwick Notes derive from oral commentary Wordsworth delivered on his poetry to his friend Isabella Fenwick in 1843.

35. Green's article appeared in *The Christian Advocate* 3 (1825):530. The delayed reaction protest took fifteen years to hit the pages of the *Christian Observer* 19.32 (6 August 1840), which printed excerpts of the article.

36. Duffield's words, from his *Spiritual Life, or, Regeneration* (Carlisle, PA: George Fleming, 1832), 395, were cited in the *Christian Observer* article, along with the editor's and a reader's response.

37. Orson Pratt, *JD*, 199.

38. Moses 3:5, PGP, first appearing in the 1878 PGP.

39. *EMS* 1.4 (September 1832):2 (D&C 29:45).

40. *EMS* 1.10 (March 1833):73 (Moses 6:51, PGP).

41. EMS 1.6 (November 1832):7 (D&C 49:17).

42. "A Sample of Pure Language Given by Joseph the Seer," *Kirtland Revelation Book 1* (ca. March 1832), in *Joseph Smith Papers: Revelations and Translations; Manuscript Revelation Books*, ed. Robin Scott Jensen, Robert J. Woodward, and Steven C. Harper (Salt Lake City: Church Historian's Press, 2009), 265.

43. "Mysteries of God," Broadside, Special Collections, Harold B. Lee Library, Brigham Young University, Provo, Utah.

44. "Sang by the gift of Tongues and Translated," *Kirtland Revelation Book 2* (27 February 1833), in *Manuscript Revelation Books*, 509.

45. Frederick G. Williams makes the case that his ancestor and namesake wrote the hymn. See "Singing the Word of God: Five Hymns by President Frederick G. Williams," *BYU Studies* 48.1 (2009):57–88.

46. 1835 D&C 82:5 (D&C 93:29).

47. *EMS* 1.12 (May 1833):96. The poem may be a Mormon re-rendering of a contemporary poem with a line identical to one in Phelps's poem: "Before the mountains rais'd their heads," called "Metrical Paraphrase of the 90th Psalm," by "Cinsurenete," *Calcutta Christian Observer* (Calcutta: Thacker, 1836), 5:482–83 Phelps invokes the same psalmic description of a time before creation, but to point to human, rather than Divine preexistence.

48. Parley P. Pratt, *Mormonism Unveiled: Zion's Watchman Unmasked* (New York: Pratt and Fordham, 1838), 27.

49. *TS* 3.10 (25 March 1842):720 (Abraham 3:18–23, PGP).

50. *WJS*, 9.

51. Mathew L. Davis to Mary Davis, 6 February 1840, in *WJS*, 33.

52. *WJS*, 9.

53. Lorenzo Snow, Letterbook, cited in Van Hale, "The Origin of the Human Spirit in Early Mormon Thought," in, *Line Upon Line*, ed. Gary James Bergera (Salt Lake City: Signature, 1989), 119–20.

54. Parley P. Pratt, *Autobiography*, ed. Scot Facer Proctor and Maurine Jensen Proctor (Salt Lake City: Deseret, 2000), 361.

55. George D. Smith, *An Intimate Chronicle: The Journals of William Clayton* (Salt Lake City: Signature, 1995), 102.

56. Journal entry for 23 June 1843. Cited in Brian C. Hales, who argues that Smith was clearly teaching a version of spirit birth by celestial parents by 1843. See his "'A Continuation of the Seeds': Joseph Smith and Spirit Birth," *Journal of Mormon History* 38.4 (Fall 2012):105–30.

57. Joseph Smith to Orson Hyde and John E. Page, 14 May 1840, Nauvoo, Illinois. Joseph Smith Papers, Letterbook 2, 146–47, in CHL.

58. *WJS*, 68.

59. Stan Larson, "The King Follett Discourse: A Newly Amalgamated Text," *BYU Studies* 18.2 (Winter 1978):204.

60. Larson, "King Follett," 196. It is important to note that the *Oxford English Dictionary* gives as one definition of *coequal*, "of the same age, coeval." (London: Oxford University Press, 1980). This was quite probably Smith's meaning.

61. 1835 D&C 23:1 (D&C 51:2); 1876 D&C 109:15; 1835 D&C 5:7 (D&C 102:12).

62. 1835 D&C 75:2 (D&C 78.11).

63. *TS* 3.10 (25 March 1842):720 (Abraham 3:22, PGP).

64. *WJS*, 9.

65. *WJS*, 60.

66. *WJS*, 68.

67. *WJS*, 67–68.

68. Larson, "King Follett," 204.

69. *CD*, 1:350, 532.

70. Holifield, *Theology*, 36.

71. Job 7:17, KJV.

72. B. H. Roberts, *Mormon Doctrine of Deity: The Roberts-Van Der Donckt Discussion* (np: B. H. Roberts, 1903), 93.

73. "Adam . . . emenated and came down from God." "A Sample of Pure Language Given by Joseph the Seer," in *Joseph Smith Papers: Revelations and Translations; Manuscript Revelation*

Books, ed. Robin Scott Jensen, Robert J. Woodward, and Steven C. Harper (Salt Lake City: Church Historian's Press, 2009), 265.

74. Meister Eckhart, "The Book of Divine Comfort," in *Meister Eckhart*, ed. and trans. Raymond B. Blakney (New York: Harper Torchbooks, 1941), 44–45.

75. Eckhart, "Divine Comfort," xx.

76. Orson Pratt, *Prophetic Almanac for 1845* (New York: The Prophet, 1844), 4, 3.

77. Pratt's Almanac has a heading, "The Mormon Creed," under which he writes "Let every body mind their own business," before he begins a catechism including the cited words (3). If readers assumed, as many scholars have, that the catechism and not just the unrelated motto was part of the Mormon Creed, it would have had even greater normative influence. In other places, however, only the "Mind Your Own Business" constituted the "Creed." See, for example, *MS* 4.2 (June 1843):29.

78. "Joseph's Speckled Bird" [W. W. Phelps], "Paracletes," *TS* 6.8 (1 May 1845):892.

79. Orson Pratt, *JD*, 1:55.

80. Parley P. Pratt, "Immortality and Eternal Life of the Material Body," in *An Appeal to the Inhabitants of the State of New York; Letter to Queen Victoria; The Fountain of Knowledge; Immortality of the Body; and Intelligence and Affection* (Nauvoo, IL: John Taylor, [1844]), 31.

81. *Key*, 50.

82. Parley P. Pratt, Sermon, 7 April 1853, papers of George D. Watt, transcribed by LaJean Purcell Carruth, CHL.

83. Pratt saw no reason that heavenly gestation should vary in length from earthly. *The Seer* 1.2 (March 1853):37–38.

84. *The Seer* 1.7 (July 1853):102.

85. *CD*, 3:1227.

86. Orson F. Whitney, "Man's Origin and Destiny," *Contributor* 3.9 (June 1882):269–70.

87. Joseph Lee Robinson Journal, 21. Cited in Charles Harrell, "The Development of the Doctrine of Preexistence, 1830–1844," *BYU Studies* 28.2 (Spring 1988):87.

88. 1876 D&C 132:63.

89. *TS* 3.10 (15 March 1842):721 (Abraham 4:27, PGP). This creation narrative mirrors the Genesis version, but consistently uses the word *organize* rather than *create* for the divine activity.

90. *The Investigator* 7 (July and October 1823):110.

91. *New Age and Concordium Gazette* 16.1 (1 April 1844):203.

92. F. W. Evans, *A Short Treatise on the Second Appearing of Christ* (Boston: Bazin & Chandler, 1853), 3, 5.

93. *The Spirit Messenger,* 10 August 1850, 4. Thomas Dick also used the expression in his *Practical Astronomer* (London: Seeley, Burnside, and Seeley, 1845), 2.

94. James E. Talmage, *The Vitality of Mormonism* (Boston: Gorham, 1919), 241.

95. 1835 D&C 82:5 (D&C 93:30).

96. Lorenzo Snow, "Submission to the Divine Will," *JD*, 7:351–52.

97. See the Roberts review committee documents cited in Blake Ostler, "The Idea of Pre-existence in the Development of Mormon Thought," *Dialogue: A Journal of Mormon Thought* 15.1 (Spring 1982):71–72.

98. Anthon H. Lund, Journal, 11 December 1914. Cited in Ostler, "Idea of Preexistence," 69.

99. Charles Penrose, "Religious Problems Solved," 1029–30, cited in Kenneth W. Godfrey, "The History of Intelligence in Latter-day Saint Thought," in *The Pearl of Great Price:*

Revelations from God, ed. H. Donl Peterson and Charles D. Tate Jr. (Provo: Religious Studies Center, Brigham Young University, 1989), 230.

100. Bruce R. McConkie, *Mormon Doctrine* (Salt Lake City: Bookcraft, 1966), 750.

101. McConkie, *Mormon Doctrine*, 751.

102. "The Father and the Son," *Messages of the First Presidency*, comp. James R. Clark (Salt Lake City: Bookcraft, 1971), 6:26.

103. Marion G. Romney, *Conference Report,* April 1964, 123.

104. "'Mormon' View of Evolution," in Clark, *Messages,* 5:244.

105. John Taylor, *The Mediation and Atonement* (Salt Lake City: Deseret News, 1882), 141, 145–46.

106. Roberts, *Doctrine of Deity*, 102, 165.

107. See especially Edward Beecher, *The Conflict of Ages: or, the Great Debate on the Moral Relations of God and Man* (Boston: Phillips, Sampson, 1853).

108. Parley P. Pratt, "Materiality," *MS* 6.2 (1 July 1845):20. (Originally published in *The Prophet,* 24 May 1845.)

109. *The Catechism of Christian Doctrine, Prepared and Enjoined by Order of the Third Council of Baltimore* became the standard catechism in American Catholic schools (Philadelphia: Cunningham and Son, 1885).

110. *TS* 4.5 (16 January 1843):73 (Moses 1:39, PGP).

111. Givens, *When Souls*, 36, 143–44.

112. Prudence Allen, *The Concept of Woman: The Aristotelian Revolution, 750 BC–AD 1250* (Grand Rapids, MI: W.B. Eerdmans, 1997), 219.

113. Thomas Aquinas, *Summa contra Gentiles* 2.73.4, cited in Stewart Goetz and Charles Taliaferro, *A Brief History of the Soul* (Chichester: Wiley and Blackwell, 2011), 50.

114. Peter Brown, *Body and Society: Men, Women, and Sexual Renunciation in Early Christianity* (New York: Columbia University Press, 1988), 168, 373.

115. Allen, *Concept of Woman*, 301. Rachael Givens Johnson surveys many of these views in "'Equal Portions of Heavenly Fire': Mary Wollstonecraft's Sexless Soul." *Religion in the Age of Enlightenment*, forthcoming.

116. Mary Astell, *An Essay in Defense of the Female Sex: A Letter to a Lady* (Columbia, NY: 1721), 10, cited in Givens, *"Equal Portions"*.

117. *The Seer* 1.3 (March 1853):37.

118. In Peter Brown's words, "from the age of Valentinus and Origen to that of Jerome and Evagrius, the delicious suspicion that even the rigid boundaries between the sexes might trickle away in the liquid gold of a 'spiritual' body, caused disturbing gusts of freedom to blow, intermittently, among the intelligentsia of the church." Brown, *Body and Society*, 442.

119. *WJS*, 117.

120. *CD*, 4: 2084.

121. *CD*, 5: 2547.

122. *CD*, 5: 2547.

123. *CD*, 5: 3038.

124. *CD*, 5: 2358.

125. *WJS*, 116.

126. BC 26:6 (D&C 25:7). Charles Buck considered exhortation "a great branch of preaching." (*A Theological Dictionary* [Philadelphia: Joseph Woodward, 1830], 176.) However, the language of the revelation seemed to invoke contemporary Methodist categories and distinctions,

suggesting that Emma's role was to both edify the congregation and expound upon scripture, roles associated by the Methodists with exhorting and preaching respectively. See Wigger, *Taking Heaven*, 29. Emma's ordination may have been effected in her ordination to head the women's Relief Society.

127. Kathleen Flake, "The Emotional and Priestly Logic of Plural Marriage," Leonard J. Arrington Lecture, 1 October 2009 (Logan: Utah State University Press, 2009).

128. "In both of these kingdoms [i.e., the terrestrial and telestial] there will be changes in the bodies and limitations. . . . Some of the functions in the celestial body will not appear in the terrestrial body, neither in the telestial body, and the power of procreation will be removed." Joseph Fielding Smith, *Doctrines of Salvation* (Salt Lake City: Bookcraft, 1954), 2:287–88.

129. John A. Widtsoe, *A Rational Theology* (Salt Lake City: General Boards of the Mutual Improvement Association, 1932), 64–65.

130. "The Eternity of Sex," *Young Women's Journal* 25 (October 1914):600.

131. James E. Talmage, "Earth and Man," 9 August 1931. (Reprinted in *Deseret News,* 21 November 1931.)

132. http://www.who.int/gender/whatisgender/en/.

133. "The Family: A Proclamation to the World," https://www.lds.org/topics/family-proclamation.

134. Taylor Petrey, "Towards Post-Heterosexual Theology," *Dialogue: A Journal of Mormon Thought* 44.4 (Winter 2011):129.

135. For a Mormon elaboration of the proposition that man is fundamentally "incomplete by himself," as is woman, see Hugh W. Nibley, "Patriarchy and Matriarchy," in *Old Testament and Related Studies*, in *Collected Works of Hugh Nibley*, ed. John W. Welch, Gary P. Gillum, and Don E. Norton (Salt Lake City: Deseret, 1986–), 1:87–113.

136. Origin is quoting the Septuagint in his reading. Human beings are organized in "certain different orders," he wrote, with some pre-mortal "souls of men [being] assumed in consequence of their moral progress into the order of angels." And some nations are in turn "called a part of the angels" is how Origen glossed the passage. Origen, *De Principiis* 1.8.4, 1.5.2, *ANF,* 4:266, 257.

137. Harnack, *History of Dogma*, 1:103n.

138. Smith and his contemporaries equated Lamanites with the Native Americans of North and South America as a whole. In more recent years, LDS scholars have argued that the Book of Mormon itself makes no such sweeping claims, and a revised introduction (2007) declares the Lamanites to be "among the ancestors" of the American Indians.

139. 1 Nephi 15:14.

140. 2 Nephi 30:2.

141. Orson F. Whitney, *Conference Report,* April 1928, 59–60.

142. 2 Nephi 3:5–7.

143. *Early Patriarchal Blessings of the Church of Jesus Christ of Latter-day Saints*, comp. H. Michael Marquardt (Salt Lake City: Smith-Pettit Foundation, 2007), 12, 23, 26, 65.

144. *TS* 3.9 (1 March 1842):706 (Abraham 2:11, PGP).

145. BC 41:10 (D&C 39:11); see also BC 12:5 (D&C 14:10), BC 15:5 (D&C 18:6), *EMS* 1.2 (July 1832):1 (D&C 42:39), etc.

146. *CD*, 1:66.

147. Holifield, *Theology*, 68; Conrad Cherry, ed., *God's New Israel: Religious Interpretations of American Destiny* (Chapel Hill, NC: University of North Carolina Press, 1998).

148. *WJS*, 67.

149. *WJS*, 4.

150. *Early Patriarchal Blessings*, 71.

151. *WJS*, 367.

152. Erastus Snow, *JD*, 23:185. Cited in Armand Mauss, *All Abraham's Children: Changing Mormon Conceptions of Race and Lineage* (Urbana: University of Illinois Press, 2003), 25. Mauss provides a comprehensive treatment of early to modern LDS ideas about Mormonism's relationship to the house of Israel.

153. Cited in Mauss, *Abraham's Children*, 17.

154. Amos 9:9.

155. Melvin J. Ballard, "The Three Degrees of Glory," cited in Robert Millet, *Power of the Word: Saving Doctrines from the Book of Mormon* (Salt Lake City: Deseret, 1994), 211.

156. Daniel H. Ludlow, "Of the House of Israel," *Ensign* 21.1 (January 1991):52.

157. *Gospel Principles* (Salt Lake City: Church of Jesus Christ of Latter-day Saints, 2009), 273.

158. Edward Strutt Abdy, *Journal of a Residence and Tour in the United States of North America, from April 1833 to October 1834* (London: Murray, 1835), 3:59.

159. Gen. 9:22, 25.

160. Augustine, *The City of God* 19.15, trans. Marcus Dods, in *NPNF1 of the Christian Church*, First series, ed. Philip Schaff (Edinburgh: T&T Clark, 1993), 2:411.

161. Edward Stillingfleet, *Fifty Sermons Preached Upon Several Occasions* (London: J. Heptinstall, 1707), 109. For more on the curse of Cain as applied to Jews, see Benjamin Braude, "Michelangelo and the Curse of Ham: From a Typology of Jew–Hatred to a Genealogy of Racism," in *Writing Race across the Atlantic World: 1492–1763,* ed. Gary Taylor and Phil Beidler (New York: Palgrave, 2002).

162. David M. Goldenberg, *The Curse of Ham: Race and Slavery in Early Judaism, Christianity, and Islam* (Princeton: Princeton University Press, 2003), 179.

163. William Whiston, *A Supplement to the Literal Accomplishment of Scriptural Prophecies* (London: T. Longman, 1725). Cited in Michel de la Roche, *New Memoirs of Literature* (London: William and John Innys, 1725), 348–51.

164. Augustus Malfert, "An Enquiry into the Origin of the Negroes and the Americans." Cited in *The Present State of the Republick of Letters for July 1734* (London: Innys and Manby, 1734), 60–65.

165. Thomas Salmon, *Modern History or the Present State of All Nations* (London: T. Longman, 1744), 1:102.

166. *New and Complete Dictionary of Arts and Sciences* (London: W. Owen, 1764), 4:2979.

167. "To the Editor," *The Christian Observer* 27 (London: J. Hatchard and Son, 1828), 343.

168. "Abednego," "West Indian and Old Testament Slavery Considered," in *Imperial Magazine* 1, Second Series, ed. Samuel Drew (London, Fisher, Son, & Jackson, 1831), 407.

169. Paul R. Griffin, "Protestantism and Racism," in Alister E. McGrath and Darren C. Marks, *The Blackwell Companion to Protestantism* (Malden, MA: Blackwell, 2004), 357.

170. Scott H. Faulring, ed., *An American Prophet's Record: The Diaries and Journals of Joseph Smith* (Salt Lake City: Signature, 1989), 269.

171. D. Michael Quinn, "LDS 'Headquarters Culture' and the Rest of Mormonism: Past and Present," *Dialogue: A Journal of Mormon Thought* 34:3–4 (Fall–Winter 2001):141.

172. The closest thing to an authoritative declaration from a Church leader would be Young's comment recorded by Wilford Woodruff on 16 January 1852: "Any man having one drop of the seed of [Cain] . . . in him cannot hold the priesthood, and if no other prophet ever spake it before I will say it now." Matthias Cowley, *Wilford Woodruff* (Salt Lake City: Deseret News Press, 1909), 351.

173. *TS* 3.10 (25 March 1842):720 (Abraham 3:22, PGP).

174. Plato, *Republic* X.618, in *Plato: Complete Works,* ed. John M. Cooper (Indianapolis: Hackett, 1997), 1221.

175. Job 4:7.

176. *TS* 3.9 (1 March 1842):705 (Abraham 1:27, PGP).

177. Orson Hyde, *Speech of Elder Orson Hyde . . .* (Liverpool: James and Woodburn, 1845), 30.

178. General Minutes, April 25, 1847, Brigham Young Papers, CHL.

179. 2 Nephi 5:21.

180. 2 Nephi 30:6.

181. Book of Mormon, trans. Joseph Smith (Nauvoo, IL: Robinson and Smith, 1840), 115. Because subsequent modern editions were based on the 1837 text, the change did not become permanent until the 1981 edition of the Book of Mormon.

182. 2 Nephi 26:33.

183. The men were Enoch Lewis and William McCarey. Connell O'Donovan did important work on this episode, reported in "I would confine them to their own species: LDS Historical Rhetoric and Praxis Regarding Marriage Between Whites and Blacks," 28 March 2009, Sunstone West Conference, Cupertino, California. See also John Turner, *Brigham Young: Pioneer Prophet* (Cambridge, MA: Harvard University Press, 2012), 220–23.

184. William S. Harwell, ed., *Manuscript History of Brigham Young 1847–1850* (Salt Lake City: Collier's, 1997), 156.

185. Wilford Woodruff, *Journal,* ed. Scott G. Kenney (Midvale, UT: Signature, 1983), 4:97.

186. James declined the Smiths' offer to be spiritually adopted as a family member. After several petitions to do so years later, she was shamefully permitted to be adopted into the deceased Smiths' family, but with a proxy representing her in the Mormon temple, and as a servant, not daughter. See Max Perry Mueller, "Playing Jane," *Harvard Divinity Bulletin* 39.1&2 (Winter/Spring 2011). http://www.hds.harvard.edu/news-events/harvard-divinity-bulletin/articles/playing-jane.

187. First Presidency Statement, 17 August 1949. Quoted in *"Neither White Nor Black": Mormon Scholars Confront the Race Issue in a Universal Church,* ed. Lester Bush and Armand Mauss (Midvale, UT: Signature, 1984), 221.

188. Edward L. Kimball, ed., *Teachings of Spencer W. Kimball* (Salt Lake City: Bookcraft, 1982), 448–49. The context leaves it unclear if the possible error refers to the ban, or to an unnamed offense by pre-mortal blacks that precipitated the ban.

189. "Official Declaration 2," D&C.

190. "Official Declaration 2," http://www.lds.org/scriptures/dc-testament/od?lang=eng.

191. http://www.lds.org/topics/race-and-the-priesthood.

192. 2 Nephi 26:33.

CHAPTER 18

1. E. Brooks Holifield, *Theology in America* (New Haven: Yale University Press, 2003), 10.

2. Henry Baker, *The Universe: A Poem* (London, [1734?]), 23. Cited in Dennis Todd, "'One Vast Egg': Leibniz, the New Embryology, and Pope's *Dunciad*," in *English Language Notes* 26.4 (June 1989):28.

3. Gabriel Daly, "Theological Models in the Doctrine of Original Sin," *Heythrop Journal* 13.2 (April 1972):121.

4. Blaise Pascal, *Thoughts*, trans. C. Kegan Paul (London: George Bell, 1905), 108.

5. Louis Berkhof, *Summary of Christian Doctrine* (Grand Rapids, MI: Eerdmans, 1938), 76.

6. Norman Powell Williams, *The Ideas of the Fall and of Original Sin* (London: Longmans, Green, 1927), 308.

7. Williams, *Ideas of the Fall*, 379. Augustine relies upon Ambrosiaster in his *Treatise Against Two Letters of the Pelagians*.

8. Tertullian, *On the Soul,* XXVII, XL, XLI, *ANF,* 3:208, 220.

9. Pietro Vermigli, *Most Learned and Fruitfull Commentaries . . . upon the Epistle of S. Paul to the Romanes* 85b (London: Daye, 1568). Cited in "Traduce," in *Oxford English Dictionary*, 2nd ed. (Oxford: Clarendon Press, 1989), 18:355.

10. Terryl L. Givens, *When Souls Had Wings: Premortal Life in Western Thought* (New York: Oxford University Press, 2010), 120 ff.

11. *City of God*, 16.27; *Against Julian* 6.7.21. Both citations from *Ancient Christian Commentary on Scripture,* ed. Gerald Bray (Downers Grove, IL: InterVarsity, 1998), New Testament 6:132.

12. Alan Jacobs, *Original Sin: A Cultural History* (San Francisco: HarperOne, 2008), 63.

13. Elaine Pagels, *Adam, Eve, and the Serpent* (New York: Vintage, 1988), 99.

14. Jacobs, *Original Sin*, 64.

15. *C&C,* 1:734.

16. *C&C,* 2:826.

17. Williams, *Ideas of the Fall*, 433.

18. J. A. Quenstedt, *Theologia didactico-polemica* (Wittenberg, 1691), 134 f. Cited in Williams, *Ideas of the Fall*, 429.

19. Formula of Concord: Epitome, in *C&C*, 2:170.

20. Williams, *Ideas of the Fall*, 430.

21. Formula of Concord: Epitome, in *C&C*, 2:170–71.

22. John Calvin, *Institutes of the Christian Religion*, trans. Henry Beveridge (Peabody, MA: Hendrickson, 2008), 147, 152.

23. Calvin, *Institutes*, 153.

24. John H. Leith, ed., *Creeds of the Churches: A Reader in Christian Doctrine from the Bible to the Present*, 3rd ed. (Atlanta: John Knox, 1982), 201.

25. Williams, *Ideas of the Fall*, 419.

26. The Catholic Church itself has abandoned the idea of inherited guilt, now declaring in its catechism that "original sin does not have the character of a personal fault in any of Adam's descendants." *Catechism of the Catholic Church*, 2nd ed. (New York: Doubleday Religion, 2003), 114.

27. Thomas Traherne, "Innocence," in *Selected Writings of Thomas Traherne*, ed. Dick Davis (Manchester: Fyfield, 1980), 24–26.

28. Jacobs, *Original Sin*, 135.

29. Jacobs, *Original Sin*, 142.

30. Joseph Bellamy, *True Religion Delineated* (Boston, 1750), 256. Cited in H. Shelton Smith, *Changing Conceptions of Original Sin* (New York: Scribner's, 1955), 7.

31. George M. Marsden, *Jonathan Edwards: A Life* (New Haven: Yale University Press, 2003), 453.

32. John Taylor, *The Scripture Doctrine of Original Sin, Proposed to Free and Candid Examination, and the Supplement* (Newcastle: J. Barker, 1845), 177.

33. Marsden, *Edwards*, 451.

34. John Wesley, *The Doctrine of Original Sin according to Scripture, Reason, and Experience: in Answer to Dr. John Taylor* (New York: J. Soule and T. Mason, 1817), 171–73. (Orig. Bristol: F. Farley, 1757.)

35. John Wesley, "On Baptism," in *John Wesley*, ed. Albert Outler (New York: Oxford University Press, 1980), 324–26. The sermon was written in 1756.

36. John Wesley, *Letters* 4:243. Cited in Roy Hattersley, *The Life of John Wesley: A Brand from the Burning* (New York: Doubleday, 2003), 301.

37. John Wesley, "Original Sin," *Sermons* (Nashville: Abingdon, 1985), 2:183, 185.

38. Mathew Simpson, *Cyclopedia of Methodism: Embracing Sketches of its Rise, Progress, and Present Condition* (Everts & Stewart, 1878), 478.

39. George Smith, *History of Wesleyan Methodism* (London: Longman, Green, Longman, and Roberts, 1862), 2:710.

40. Benjamin Gregory, *Sidelights of the Conflicts of Methodism, 1827–1852* (London: Cassell, 1898), 280.

41. Wilbur Fisk, *Calvinistic Controversy: Embracing a Sermon on Predestination and Election* (New York: T. Mason and G. Lane, 1837), 45.

42. Simpson, *Cyclopedia of Methodism*, 683–84.

43. Jacobs, *Original Sin*, 133.

44. Leonard Woods, *Letters to Unitarians Occasioned by the Sermon of the Reverend William E. Channing...* (Andover: Flagg and Gould, 1820), 45. Cited in Smith, *Changing Conceptions*, 75.

45. Henry Ware, *Letters Addressed to Trinitarians and Calvinists, Occasioned by Dr. Woods' Letters to Unitarians* (Cambridge: Hilliard and Metcalf, 1820), 20–21. Cited in Smith, *Changing Conceptions*, 76.

46. Bennet Tyler, *Letters on the Origin and Progress of the New Haven Theology* (New York: Carter and Collier, 1837), 6.

47. Charles Hodge, *Systematic Theology* (Grand Rapids, MI: Eerdmans, 1970), 2:192.

48. Ashbel Green, ed., *Christian Advocate* 10 (Philadelphia: A. Finley, 1832), 312.

49. Ashbel Green, ed., *Christian Advocate* 12 (Philadelphia: A. Finley, 1834), 31.

50. It stated that "Our first parents by this sin fell from their original righteousness and communion with God, and we in them.... The guilt of sin was imputed (and corrupt nature conveyed) to all their posterity descending from them." *Philadelphia Confession of Faith* (Lafayette, IN: Sovereign Grace, 2002), 27.

51. Charles Ready Nichol, *Sound Doctrine* (Clifton, TX: Nichol, 1920), 5:65.

52. Nichol, *Sound Doctrine*, 1:35.

53. Holifield, *Theology*, 10.

54. 2 Nephi 2:22–25

55. *EMS* 1.11 (April 1833):81 (Moses 5:10–11, PGP [1851]). In 1878, the wording was changed slightly to "Blessed be the name of God, for because of my transgression my eyes are opened, and in this life I shall have joy."

56. John Taylor, *The Mediation and Atonement* (Salt Lake City: Deseret News, 1882), 130.

57. Alma 12:26.

58. John Jaques, *Catechism for Children Exhibiting the Prominent Doctrines of the Church of Jesus Christ of Latter-day Saints Jesus Christ of Latter-day Saints* (Liverpool: F. D. Richards, 1855), 31.

59. 2 Nephi 2:24.

60. Moses 4:6, PGP, first appearing in the 1878 edition.

61. *WJS*, 33.

62. *EMS* 1.10 (March 1833):73 (Moses 6:54, PGP).

63. "We believe that all men will be punished for their own sins, and not for Adam's transgression." Article of Faith 2, PGP.

64. *WJS*, 63.

65. Moses 3:17, PGP, first appearing in the 1878 edition.

66. William Law, *The Spirit of Love,* in *A Serious Call to a Devout and Holy Life; The Spirit of Love*, ed. Paul G. Stanwood (New York: Paulist, 1978), 372.

67. Orson Pratt, *The Seer* 1.6 (June 1853):84.

68. "Adam was not deceived, but the woman was deceived and became a transgressor." 1 Tim. 2:14.

69. *CD*, 4:2197.

70. James Talmage, *Articles of Faith* (Salt Lake City: Deseret News, 1899),, 67–69, 72.

71. Bruce R. McConkie, *Mormon Doctrine* (Salt Lake City: Bookcraft, 1966), 804.

72. Lord Byron, *Cain* 1.i, in *Complete Poetical Works* (Boston: Houghton Mifflin, 1905), 630.

73. E. N. B., "Woman's Rights," *Woman's Exponent* 3.16 (15 January 1875):122.

74. John A. Widtsoe, *Evidences and Reconciliations* (Salt Lake City: Bookcraft, 1947), 2:78.

75. Hugh Nibley, "Patriarchy and Matriarchy," in *Old Testament and Related Studies*, ed. John W. Welch, Gary P. Gillum, and Don E. Norton (Salt Lake City: Deseret and Foundation for Ancient Research and Mormon Sudies, 1986), 92. Nibley first gave the paper on 1 February 1980.

76. Dallin H. Oaks, "The Great Plan of Happiness," *Ensign* 23.11 (November 1993):72–75.

77. Oaks, "Great Plan," 72.

78. Bruce C. Hafen, "Beauty for Ashes: The Atonement of Jesus Christ," *Ensign* 20.4 (April 1990):9.

79. *EMS* 1.11 (April 1833):81 (Moses 5, PGP).

80. Mosiah 3:18.

81. Moroni 8:9.

82. Moroni 8:8.

83. 2 Nephi 2:26.

84. Samuel Haining, *Mormonism Weighed in the Balances of the Sanctuary . . .* (Douglas: Robert Fargher, 1840), 31.

85. R. Clarke, *Mormonism Unmasked, or, The Latter-day Saints in a Fix* (London: Banks, 1849), 7–8.

86. Alister McGrath, *Heresy: A History of Defending the Truth* (New York: HarperOne, 2009), 161.

87. Mosiah 3:19.

88. 1 Cor. 2:14 (KJV).

89. 1 Cor. 2:12–15.

90. *CD*, 4: 2020.

91. Ether 3:2, 13.

92. *EMS* 1.10 (March 1833):73 (Moses 6:54, PGP).

93. *EMS* 1.10 (March 1833):73 (Moses 6:53, PGP).

94. *EMS* 1.11 (April 1833):81 (Moses 5:13, PGP).

95. *EMS* 1.10 (March 1833):73 (Moses 6:55, PGP). The language is an echo of Ps. 51:5: "I was born guilty, a sinner when my mother conceived me." Or "in sin did my mother conceive me" (KJV).

96. *TS* 3.10 (25 March 1842):720 (Abraham 3:26–28, PGP).

97. Elizabeth A. Clark, *The Origenist Controversy: The Cultural Construction of an Early Christian Debate* (Princeton: Princeton University Press, 1992), 250.

98. Krister Stendahl, *Paul Among Jews and Gentiles* (Philadelphia: Fortress, 1979), 40–41, 85.

99. Peter J. Thuesen, *Predestination: The American Career of a Contentious Doctrine* (New York: Oxford University Press, 2009), 103.

100. Mosiah 27:25–26.

101. *WJS*, 200–201.

102. *TS* 2.15 (1 June 1841):429.

103. "Because that [humans] are redeemed from the fall they have become free forever, knowing good from evil; to act for themselves and not to be acted upon." 2 Nephi 2:26; "The Lord God gave unto man that he should act for himself. Wherefore, man could not act for himself save it should be that he was enticed by the one or the other." 2 Nephi 2:16.

104. Talmage, *Articles of Faith*, 69.

105. 1 Nephi 9:11.

106. Helaman 14:16.

107. 2 Nephi 9:8.

108. *EMS* 1.11 (April 1833):81 (Moses 5:4, PGP).

109. *CD*, 1:135–136

110. 1 Nephi 9:12.

111. Alma 11:44.

112. Julian of Norwich, *The Showings* 13.27 (New York: Norton, 2005), 39–40.

113. *CD*, 5: 2741.

114. *Meister Eckhart*, trans. Raymond B. Blakney (New York: Harper & Row, 1941), 12.

115. *EMS* 1.5 (October 1832):3 (D&C 68:27).

116. Rom. 9:11–13.

117. Rom. 9:15–16.

118. Augustine, *On Romans*, in *Ancient Christian*, New Testament 6:242. Written about 394; See also Serge Lancel, *St Augustine*, trans. Antonia Nevill (London: SCM, 2002), 181.

119. Lancel, *Augustine*, 429.

120. The expression was *sed vicit Dei gratia*, in Augustine, *Retractions* 2.27, trans. Mary Inez Bogan (Washington, DC: Catholic University of America Press, 1968), 120; Robert J. O'Connell, *Images of Conversion in St. Augustine's Confessions* (New York: Fordham University Press, 1996), 305.

121. *De diversis quaestionibus ad Simplicianum*. Paraphrased by Robert J. O'Connell, *The Origin of the Soul in St. Augustine's Later Works* (New York: Fordham University Press, 1987), 91.

122. De Servo Arbitrio. in Williams, *Ideas of the Fall*, 434.

123. "Of Free Will," CCLIX, in Martin Luther, *Table Talk*, trans. William Hazlitt (Gainsville, FL: Bridge-Logos, 2004), 165.

124. The passage comes from Melancthon's pupil Martin Chemnitz, cited in Williams, *Ideas of the Fall*, 435.

125. Marsden, *Edwards*, 439.

126. Jacob Arminius, *The Works of Arminius,* 3 vols., trans. James Nichols and William Nichols (Grand Rapids, MI: Baker Book House, 1991), 3:192.

127. Article 8, "The Articles of Religion 1784/1804," in *C&C*, 3:203.

128. Charles G. Finney, *Sermons on Gospel Themes* (Oberlin, OH: E.J. Goodrich and New York: Dodd, Mead & Company, 1876), 79.

129. Daniel Walker Howe, *The Unitarian Conscience: Harvard Moral Philosophy, 1805–1861* (Cambridge, MA: Harvard University Press, 1970), 7.

130. 2 Nephi 2:26.

131. 1835 D&C 82:6 (D&C 93:38).

132. *EMS* 1.3 (August 1832):19 (Moses 7:32, PGP).

133. 1835 D&C 82:5 (D&C 93:29–30).

134. Julius Müller, *The Christian Doctrine of Sin*, 2 vols., trans. William Urwick (Edinburgh: Clark, 1868), 2:157.

135. J. Ellis McTaggart, *Some Dogmas of Religion* (London: Edward Arnold, 1906), 165.

136. Marsden, *Edwards*, 453.

137. 2 Nephi 2:14, 2 Nephi 10:23, Alma 12:31.

138. *WJS*, 74.

139. *CD*, 2:890.

140. *WJS*, 229.

141. *EMS* 1.2 (July 1832):2 (D&C 76:26).

CHAPTER 19

1. "Our Bodies, Gifts from God," Conference address, 6 October 1913, in *The Essential Talmage*, ed. James Harris (Salt Lake City: Signature, 1997), 108.

2. Isa. 64:6, KJV; Sigmund Freud is only one of several writers who attribute the phrase to Augustine. *Civilization and its Discontents* (New York: Norton, 1989), 43. It may in fact originate much later, with Bernard of Clairvaux.

3. Ps. 139:14; 8:5.

4. Meister Eckhart, "About Disinterest," in *Meister Eckhart*, trans. Raymond Blakney (New York: Harper and Row, 1941), 90.

5. *C&C*, 2:531.

6. Plato, *Republic* X.596–599, in *Plato: Complete Works*, ed. John M. Cooper (Indianapolis: Hackett, 1997), 1200–203.

7. Plato, *Phaedo* 82, trans. G. M. A. Grube, in *Plato: Complete Works*, 72.

8. Aristotle, *On the Generation of Animals* I.19.30 (727b); I.21.13–20 (729b–730a); II.4 (739b), trans. A. L. Peck (Cambridge, MA: Harvard University Press, 1943), 101, 113–14, 117, 191.

9. Aristotle, *Generation of Animals* II.4.25 (738b), 185.

10. This was a principal argument against the almost universally held doctrine of creationism. See Terryl L. Givens, *When Souls Had Wings: Premortal Life in Western Thought* (New York: Oxford University Press, 2010), 2–3, 156. Augustine located sin in both a corrupt will and a lust-ridden body.

11. William Law, *The Spirit of Love,* in *A Serious Call to a Devout and Holy Life; The Spirit of Love*, ed. Paul G. Stanwood (New York: Paulist Press, 1978), 370.

12. Rom. 7:18.

13. Some scholars and theologians insist that "the personal origin of sin in the flesh does not have reference to the physical flesh. That was the mistake of the Greek philosophy of Plato and much of Eastern Christianity. . . . [In Paul] flesh has reference to man's self-centered life as he turns away from God." That may be the case on occasion, but Paul's privileging of what is spiritual over what is physical is also undeniable. Dale Moody, *The Word of Truth: A Summary of Christian Doctrine* (Grand Rapids, MI: Eerdmans, 1990), 284–85.

14. Origen, *De Principiis* 1.8, trans. G. W. Butterworth, in *Origen on First Principles, Being Koetschau's Text of the De Principiis* (New York: Harper & Row, 1966), 72–73.

15. Plato, *Phaedrus* 246, trans. Alexander Nehamas and Paul Woodruff, in *Plato: Complete Works*, 524.

16. Job 19:26; Luke 24:39.

17. Phil. 2:7.

18. Gregory Nazianzen, "Oration 37," trans. Charles Gordon Browne and James Edward Swallow, in *NPNF2 of the Christian Church*, ed. Philip Schaff (Peabody, MA: Hendrickson, 1999), Second series 7:338.

19. Tertullian, *On the Resurrection of the Flesh*, trans. Dr. Holmes, *ANF*, 3:545, 548.

20. Tertullian, *On the Resurrection*, 549.

21. Tertullian, *On the Resurrection*, 551.

22. Tertullian, *On the Resurrection*, 551.

23. Clement of Alexandria, *The Instructor* I.13, *ANF*, 2:235.

24. Augustine, *Confessions*, trans. F. J. Sheed (Indianapolis: Hackett, 1993), 7:12, 119.

25. Augustine, *Sermons*, 243:6, ed. John E. Rotelle and Edmund Hill (New York: New City Press, 1993), 91.

26. A strongly revisionist reading is Ronald H Nash, "Paul and Platonism," in his *Christianity and the Hellenistic World* (Grand Rapids, MI: Zondervan, 1984).

27. Uta Ranke-Heinemann, *Eunuchs for the Kingdom of Heaven: Women, Sexuality, and the Catholic Church* (New York: Penguin, 1991), 75.

28. Friedrich Nietzsche, *A Genealogy of Morals*, trans. William A. Hausemann (New York: Macmillan, 1897), 160–61.

29. Cited in Caroline Bynum, "The Female Body and Religious Practice in the Later Middle Ages," in *Fragments for a History of the Human Body*, ed. Michel Feher, Ramona Naddaff, and Nadia Tazi (New York: Zone, 1989), 1:192.

30. Bynum, "Female Body," 193.

31. Gregory Palamas, cited in *The Cambridge Platonists,* ed. C. A. Patrides (London: Edward Arnold, 1969), 19.

32. John Calvin, *Institutes of the Christian Religion*, trans. Henry Beveridge (Peabody, MA: Hendrickson, 2008), 471.

33. Calvin, *Institutes,* 470.

34. Calvin, *Commentaries on the Epistle of Paul to the Romans*, trans. John Owen (Edinburgh: Calvin Translation Society, 1849), 271.

35. Martin Luther, *The Bondage of the Will*, trans. Henry Cole (New York: Feather Trail Press, 2009), 22.

36. Gilbert Burnet, *An Exposition of the Thirty Nine Articles of the Church of England* (Edinburgh: W. Sands, A. Murray, & J. Cochran, 1745), 32. Burnet's popular work was in its third edition by 1705.

37. Jonathan Edwards, *Heaven is a World of Love*, cited in George M. Marsden, *Jonathan Edwards: A Life* (New Haven: Yale University Press, 2003), 191.

38. Amanda Hendrix-Komoto, "Wallowing in the Mud and Snorting like Beasts: The Problem of the Body in Early Mormon Spiritual Experiences." Unpublished ms.

39. G. Smith, ed., *History of the Methodist Church in Great Britain* (London: Longman, 1862), 4:649.

40. H. D. Lehman and Paul A. Witty, *Psychology of Play Activities* (New York: A. S. Barnes, 1927), 1–2. Cited in Leona Holbrook, "Dancing as an Aspect of Early Mormon and Utah Culture," *BYU Studies* 16.1 (Autumn 1975):119.

41. R. Lawrence Moore, "Learning to Play: The Mormon Way and the Way of Other Americans," *Journal of Mormon History* 16 (1990):91.

42. William Blake, "The Marriage of Heaven and Hell," in *Complete Poetry and Selected Prose of John Donne and the Complete Poetry of William Blake* (New York: Random House, 1941), 651–52.

43. Thomas O'Dea, *The Mormons* (Chicago: University of Chicago, 1957), 150.

44. 1835 D&C 82:5 (D&C 93:33).

45. Parley P. Pratt, "Immortality and Eternal Life of the Material Body," in *An Appeal to the Inhabitants of the State of New York; Letter to Queen Victoria; The Fountain of Knowledge; Immortality of the Body; and Intelligence and Affection* (Nauvoo, IL: John Taylor, [1844]), 30.

46. *CD*, 3:1529.

47. *CD*, 3:1620.

48. *CD*, 1:576.

49. *CD*, 4:1973.

50. "Autobiography of Johann Lebrecht Baer, Mormon Immigrant," cited in Terryl L. Givens, *People of Paradox: A History of Mormon Culture* (New York: Oxford University Press, 2007), 117.

51. Givens, *People of Paradox*, 129ff.

52. The 1959 *Time* article is cited in Dennis L. Lythgoe, "The Changing Image of Mormonism," *Dialogue: A Journal of Mormon Thought* 3.4 (Winter 1968):48.

53. Matt. 22:30.

54. 1 Cor. 7:9.

55. This is the judgment of Peter Brown, *Body and Society: Men, Women, and Sexual Renunciation in Early Christianity* (New York: Columbia University Press, 1988), 376.

56. Augustine, *On Concupiscence*, Book 2. Quoted in Alan Jacobs, *Original Sin: A Cultural History* (San Francisco: HarperOne, 2008), 61.

57. "Incomplete Work on Matthew," in *Ancient Christian Commentary on Scripture*, ed. Manlio Simonetti (Downers Grove, IL: InterVarsity Press, 1998), New Testament 1b: 153–54.

58. Robert Emory, *History of the Discipline of the Methodist Episcopal Church* (New York: Lane & Scott, 1851), 205.

59. Alfred Kazin, ed., *The Portable Blake* (New York: Viking, 1946), 40.

60. Blake, "Marriage of Heaven and Hell," 653.

61. "Westminster Confession of Faith," in *Creeds of the Churches: A Reader in Christian Doctrine from the Bible to the Present*, ed. John H. Leith, 3rd. ed. (Atlanta: John Knox, 1982); Pratt, "Intelligence and Affection," in Pratt, *An Appeal*, 37.

62. Pratt, "Intelligence and Affection," 37.

63. Kathleen Norris, *Mother: A Story* (New York: Grosset and Dunlap, 1911), 180.

64. Orson Pratt, *JD*, 1:63.

65. This is explicitly argued by Orson Pratt in his August 1852 sermon. Young admonishes that "large families" are a right unique to the LDS, in *CD*, 4:2424.

66. Gordon B. Hinckley, *Cornerstones of a Happy Home* (Salt Lake City: The Church of Jesus Christ of Latter-day Saints, 1984), 6. The official statement he refers to is from the church's *General Handbook of Instructions* (Salt Lake City: Church of Jesus Christ of Latter-day Saints, 1983), 77.

67. *General Handbook of Instructions 2* (Salt Lake City: Church of Jesus Christ of Latter-day Saints, 2010), 21.4.4.

68. In Susan B. Anthony's newsletter, *The Revolution*, abortion was described as "child murder," "infanticide" and "foeticide" (9 April 1868, 8 July 1869). Elizabeth Cady Stanton, who in 1848 organized the first women's rights convention in Seneca Falls, New York, condemned the "murder of children, either before or after birth." *Revolution,* 5 February 1868.

69. *EMS* 1.2 (July 1832):1 (D&C 59:6).

70. Erastus Snow referred to "destructive medicines" to effect "abortion, infanticide; child murder." *JD,* 25:111.

71. Young, *CD*, 4:2476.

72. George Q. Cannon and John Taylor, *JD*, 25:315–16.

73. Oaks makes the point that safeguarding choice is no more valid as a defense of abortion than as a defense of other crimes where a second party suffers, naming child abuse, animal cruelty, and fraud as examples. "Weightier Matters," *Ensign* 31.1 (January 2001):13–15.

74. The inherent moral consistency of Mormonism's opposition to abortion based on choice is further evident in the church's granting of an exception in the case of rape, where no choice was made by the mother of the child. A church video affirms Oaks's view: "if we choose to use that [procreative] power we have to deal with the consequences of that choice." http://www.lds.org/media-library/video/doctrine-and-covenants-visual-resources?lang=eng#2010-2007-12-the-plan-of-salvation.

75. René Descartes, letter to Arnault, cited in Stewart Goetz and Charles Taliaferro, *A Brief History of the Soul* (Chichester: Wiley-Blackwell, 2011), 81.

76. *Gospel Principles* (Salt Lake City: Church of Jesus Christ of Latter-day Saints, 2009), 10.

77. Ann Conway, *The Principles of the Most Ancient and Modern Philosophy concerning God, Christ and the Creatures*, ed. and trans. Allison P. Coudert and Taylor Corse (Cambridge: Cambridge University Press, 1996), 49.

78. *WJS*, 62.

79. *WJS*, 68.

80. *WJS*, 200.

81. 2 Nephi 9:8–9.

82. *WJS*, 60.

83. Reinhold Niebuhr, *The Nature and Destiny of Man* (New York: Scribner's Sons, 1955), 30–31.

84. *WJS*, 10–11.

85. Niebuhr, *Nature and Destiny*, 20–21.

86. Thomas Aquinas, *On Spiritual Creatures* VI, in Goetz and Taliaferro, *Brief History*, 63.

87. Aquinas, *Questions on the Soul* VIII.ad 15, in Goetz and Taliaferro, *Brief History*, 63.

88. *CD*, 3:1518.

89. Ether 3:16.

90. *Key*, 50.

91. Henry More, "Preface General," in *A Collection of Several Philosophical Writings of Dr. Henry More* (New York: Garland, 1978), xxv. (Reprint of London: James Flesher, 1662.)

92. The Word of Wisdom, revealed in 1833, prohibits coffee, tea, alcohol, and tobacco, and enjoins a quasi-vegetarianism. 1835 D&C 80 (D&C 89).

93. Parley P. Pratt, *Autobiography*, ed. Scot Facer Proctor and Maurine Jensen Proctor (Salt Lake City: Deseret, 2000), 443.

94. Stephen Webb, *Jesus Christ, Eternal God: Heavenly Flesh and the Metaphysics of Matter* (New York: Oxford University Press, 2011), 259.

95. Heber C. Kimball, *JD*, 9:126–27

96. *CD*, 4:2125.

97. *CD*, 2:922.

98. Charles Darwin, *Origin of Species* (New York: Collier, 1909), 213–14.

99. Ether 12:27.

100. 2 Nephi 2:15.

101. Marilynne Robinson, *Absence of Mind: The Dispelling of Inwardness from the Modern Myth of the Self* (New Haven: Yale University Press, 2010), 134–35.

102. G. K. Chesterton, *Everlasting Man* (San Francisco: Ignatius, 1993), 34.

103. Kenneth R. Miller, *Finding Darwin's God* (New York: HarperCollins, 1999), 249.

104. Miller, *Finding*, 273, 274.

105. The Catholic doctrine of "immediate creation," that God creates each human soul "at the very moment of conception" or soon thereafter, stands in opposition to traducianism and pre-existence. J. E. Royce and E. J. Furton, "Soul, human, origin of," in *New Catholic Encyclopedia* (Detroit: Thomson Gale, 2003), 13:357–58

106. Animal bodies are in the likeness of their spirits, according to 1876 D&C 77:2, and will be resurrected. *EMS* 1.4 (September 1832):2 (D&C 29:24–25).

107. A. N. Wilson, *God's Funeral* (New York: Norton, 1999), 178–79.

108. John W. Draper, *History of the Conflict between Religion and Science* (New York: Appleton, 1881); Andrew D. White, *History of the Warfare of Science with Theology in Christendom* (New York: Appleton, 1896).

109. *Key, 37*.

110. *CD*, 5:2910.

111. A. Scott Howe and Richard L. Bushman, eds., *Parallels and Convergences: Mormon Thought and Engineering Vision* (Salt Lake City: Greg Kofford, 2012), foreword.

112. Richard Dawkins, *The God Delusion* (New York: Houghton Mifflin, 2008), 52; "Richard Dawkins Explains 'The God Delusion,'" *Fresh Air with Terry Gross*, 28 March 2007, http://www.npr.org/templates/story/story.php?storyId=9180871.

113. *TS* 3.10 (15 March 1842):721–22 (Abraham 4:5–31, PGP).

114. *TS* 5.24 (1 January 1845):758.

115. Terryl L. Givens and Matthew J. Grow, *Parley P. Pratt: The Apostle Paul of Mormonism* (New York: Oxford University Press, 2010), 105, 110–11.

116. "Spiritualizing the Scriptures," *TS* 3.5 (1 January 1842):644–46. (Reprinted from *The Gospel Reflector*.)

117. *CD*, 2:731.

118. *CD*, 3:1518.

119. Further segregating Mormon theology from fundamentalist conflicts with science, Roberts argued that the earth was constructed of "pre–existing world–stuff" (implicitly acknowledging the fossil record while making it irrelevant to the dating of creation). He asserted that a cataclysm had annihilated earthly life before Eden (thus life and death pre-existed Adam, but he was needed to "*replenish* the earth"). B. H. Roberts, *The Truth, the Way, the Life,* ed. John W. Welch (Provo: BYU Studies, 1994), 238.

120. *CD*, 3:1531.

121. *CD*, 5:2835.

122. Erastus Snow in 1878 opined that "There is a theory put forth by Mr. Darwin, and others, that is the school of modern philosophers, which is termed in late years, the theory of Evolution," but "they fail to demonstrate their theories, simply because they are not demonstrateable" (*JD*, 19:271, 325–26); the same year, Orson Pratt referred to "the evolution theory; in other words, that which you learn from books, [as] the creation of man's folly and foolishness" (*JD*, 20:76).

123. "Origin of Man," in *Messages of the First Presidency*, comp. James R. Clark (Salt Lake City: Bookcraft, 1971), 4:205.

124. "'Mormon' View of Evolution," in Clark, *Messages*, 5:243–44.

125. John A. Widtsoe, *Joseph Smith as Scientist: A Contribution to Mormon Philosophy* (Salt Lake City: Young Men's Mutual Improvement Associations, 1908), 9.

126. ¹ Widtsoe, *Joseph Smith*, 35, 109, 154.

127. Orson F. Whitney, "Latter–Day Saint Ideals and Institutions," *Improvement Era* 30.10 (August 1927):854

128. Talmage was a geologist who had studied at Lehigh, Johns Hopkins, and Wesleyan (and was the first Mormon, in 1896, to receive a doctorate). He gained an international reputation, and was made a fellow of several elite, learned societies, including the Royal Society of Edinburgh.

129. Henry Eyring rebutted Joseph Fielding Smith's position in his talk, "The Age of the Earth," reported in *Deseret News* (21 November 1931):7–8. In response to a disagreement between B. H. Roberts and Joseph Fielding Smith on the related issue of pre-Adamic death, the First Presidency declared, "We can see no advantage to be gained by a continuation of the discussion to which reference is here made, but on the contrary are certain that it would lead to confusion, division and misunderstanding if carried further." First Presidency, Memorandum to General Authorities, April 1931, 6–7. See the review of the subject in Richard Sherlock, "'We Can See No Advantage to a Continuation of the Discussion': The Roberts/Smith/Talmage Affair," *Dialogue: A Journal of Mormon Thought* 13.3 (Fall 1980):63–78.

130. James E. Talmage, "The Theory of Evolution," in Harris, *Essential Talmage*, 20, 28, 29.

131. Boyd K. Packer, *Ensign* 14.11 (November 1984):66; *Ensign* 35.1 (January 2005):48.

132. Keith Crandall, Michael Whiting, and Jack Sites are best known for molecular evolution. All three are major players in the National Science Foundation's "Tree of Life" project. A particularly powerful case for human evolution comes from then BYU professor Daniel Fairbanks, *Relics of Eden: The Powerful Evidence of Evolution in Human DNA* (Amherst, NY: Prometheus, 2007).

CHAPTER 20

1. *CD*, 1:357.

2. *EMS* 1.10 (March 1833):73 (Moses 6:55, PGP).

3. Samuel Johnson, quoted in E. Brooks Holifield, *Theology in America* (New Haven: Yale University Press, 2003), 89.

4. *EMS* 1.10 (March 1833):73 (Moses 6:55, PGP).

5. *EMS* 1.10 (March 1833):73 (Moses 6:57, PGP).

6. Alma 41:11.

7. Helaman 13:38.

8. 1835 D&C 7:5 (D&C 88:22).

9. 2 Nephi 2:5.

10. Mosiah 3:16.

11. Alma 12:14.

12. Clement of Alexandria, *Instructor*, I.6 (*ANF*, 2:217).

13. Dante Alighiere, *Paradiso* VII.97–101, trans. Allen Mandelbaum (New York: Bantam, 1984), 61.

14. John Calvin, *Institutes of the Christian Religion*, trans. Henry Beveridge (Peabody, MA: Hendrickson, 2008), 331.

15. Stephen Finlan, *Problems with Atonement* (Collegeville, MN: Liturgical Press, 2005), 1.

16. Finlan, *Problems*, 84.

17. Finlan, *Problems*, 91. Rene Girard's mimetic theory of violence is presented in several places, including *I Saw Satan Fall Like Lightening* (Maryknoll, NY: Orbis, 2001).

18. Finlay, *Problems*, 94–95. See Robert Hamerton-Kelly, *Sacred Violence: Paul's Hermeneutic of the Cross* (Minneapolis: Augsburg Fortress, 1992); Ted Peters, "Atonement and the Final Scapegoat," *Perspectives in Religious Studies* 19 (1992):181.

19. A. J. Wallace and R. D. Rusk, *Moral Transformation: The Original Christian Paradigm of Salvation* (New Zealand: Bridgehead, 2011).

20. Hastings Rashdall, *The Idea of Atonement in Christian Theology* (London, 1919), 357–62. Cited in Peter Abelard, *Commentary on the Epistle to the Romans*, trans. Steven R. Cartwright (Washington, DC: CUA Press, 2011), 44.

21. Jack Nelson-Pallmeyer, *Jesus Against Christianity: Reclaiming the Missing Jesus* (Harrisburg: Trinity, 2001), 222–24. Cited in Finlay, *Problems*, 101.

22. Finlay, *Problems*, 104.

23. *Elders' Journal* 1.3 (July 1838):44.

24. *WJS*, 231.

25. *Key*, 95.

26. *CD*, 1:357.

27. Some Mormons have seen God as the author of law, reading D&C 132:5 as referring to the establishment of universal law rather than the articulation or enunciation of those laws: "For all who will have a blessing at my hands shall abide the law which was appointed for that blessing, and the conditions thereof, as were instituted from before the foundation of the world." As we saw above, D&C 88:42 ("he hath given a law unto all things") was quoted to similar effect by apostles disagreeing with B. H. Roberts.

28. Matthew Bowman, "The Crisis of Mormon Christology: History, Progress, and Protestantism," *Fides Et Historia* 40.2 (Fall 2008):3.

29. *CD*, 2:690, *CD*, 2:1004, *CD*, 3:1479, etc.

30. Heber C. Kimball, *JD*, 4:120.

31. Orson Pratt, *JD*, 7:256.

32. John Taylor, *Mediation and Atonement* (Salt Lake City: Deseret News, 1882), 149–50.

33. B. H. Roberts, *The Truth, the Way, the Life*, ed. John W. Welch (Provo: BYU Studies, 1994), 404.

34. Roberts, *The Truth*, 425.

35. John Stuart Mill, *On Liberty* (Boston: Ticknor and Fields, 1863), 28.

36. Roberts, *The Truth*, 405.

37. 2 Nephi 2:5, 26.

38. 1835 D&C 7:6 (D&C 88:32).

39. C. S. Lewis, *The Great Divorce: A Dream* (New York: Simon and Schuster, 1946), 72.

40. Alma 41:5.

41. Alma 41:7.

42. 2 Nephi 9:21; Alma 7:12; Mosiah 3:7.

43. "All sin against moral law is followed by suffering," wrote Roberts (*The Truth*, 448).

44. Alma 42:22.

45. Roberts, *The Truth*, 408.

46. Holifield, *Theology*, 133.

47. 2 Nephi 2:10.

48. Alma 42:17.

49. Russell M. Nelson, "Addiction or Freedom," *Ensign* 18.10 (November 1988):7.

50. 2 Nephi 2:11.

51. Heb. 5:8.

52. Mosiah 3:7.

53. Mosiah 3:7.

54. Alma 34:12.

55. Roberts, *The Truth*, 453–54.

56. Eugene England, "That They Might Not Suffer: The Gift of Atonement," *Dialogue: A Journal of Mormon Thought* 1.3 (Autumn 1966):141–55.

57. England, "Gift of Atonement," 149–50.

58. Blake Ostler, Dennis Potter, and Adam Miller, for example, have propounded their own versions of atonement theology.

59. Dallin H. Oaks, "Another Testament of Christ." Address at Brigham Young University, 6 June 1993, http://speeches.byu.edu/?act=viewitem&id=574.

60. BC 16:21 (D&C 19:20).

61. *CD*, 2:1046–47.

62. Taylor, *Mediation and Atonement*, 45.

63. Luke 22:44. As is well known in biblical studies, many ancient manuscripts omit verses 43–44, with their reference to the drops of blood. Mormon corroborating scripture implicitly accepts the inclusion as legitimate.

64. Mosiah 3:7.

65. BC 16:18 (D&C 19:18).

66. Jeffrey R. Holland, "None Were with Him," *Ensign* 39.5 (May 2009):87.

67. Timothy Keller, *The Reason for God* (London: Hodder, 2009), 30.

68. 1835 D&C 7:3 (D&C 88:13).

69. Taylor, *Mediation and Atonement*, 148–49.

70. James E. Talmage, *Jesus the Christ* (Salt Lake City: Deseret News, 1915), 613.

71. *EMS* 1.1 (June 1832):1 (D&C 20:30). Smith seldom used technical theological terms like "justification" and "sanctification." When he did, he used them inconsistently. E.g., he referred

in one instance to sanctification by the spirit (1835 D&C 4:6 [D&C 84:33]) and in another wrote that "by the Spirit ye are justified, and by the blood ye are sanctified." *EMS* 1.10 (March 1833):73 (Moses 6:60, PGP).

72. 1835 D&C 75:1 (D&C 78:77).

73. 1835 D&C 7:8 (D&C 88:34–35).

74. Erastus Snow, *JD*, 7:354–55.

75. Alma 34:9.

76. BC 15:13 (D&C 18:11).

77. Moroni 9:25.

78. Alma 7:12.

79. Holland, "None Were with Him," 88.

80. Fyodor Dostoevsky, *Brothers Karamazov*, trans. Constance Garnett (New York: New American Library, 1999), 238.

81. "It will be a great while after the grave before you learn to understand the last.... Salvation ... is not all to be comprehended in this world." Stan Larson, "The King Follett Discourse: A Newly Amalgamated Text," *BYU Studies* 18.2 (Winter 1978):202.

82. *EMS* 1.1 (June 1832):1 (D&C 20:31).

83. Margaret Barker, *The Great High Priest: The Temple Roots of Christian Liturgy* (Edinburgh: T&T Clark, 2003), 50.

84. Bruce C. Hafen, "Beauty for Ashes: The Atonement of Jesus Christ," *Ensign* 20.4 (April 1990):7.

85. Martin Luther, *Table Talk* CCLX, trans. William Hazlitt (Gainesville, FL: Bridge-Logos, 2004), 166.

86. *C&C*, 2: 836–39.

87. *C&C*, 2:828.

88. *WJS*, 244.

89. 2 Nephi 25:23.

90. He desired grace "to lead the people" (*CD*, 1:282), to "sustain me in the hour of darkness" (1:387); our blessings come "through His grace" (1:140), etc.

91. Matthew Arnold, *Literature and Dogma* (New York: Macmillan, 1873), 10. Biblical scholar Stephen Finlay makes the same implicit point by consistently referring to "the *generosity* of God," rather than the theologically fraught term "grace," in his study of atonement. Finlay, *Problems with Atonement*, 9 and *passim*.

92. 2 Nephi 2:8.

93. *CD*, 1:276.

94. 2 Nephi 25:23.

95. John Lawson, *Comprehensive Handbook of Christian Doctrine* (Englewood Cliffs: Prentice-Hall, 1967), 206.

96. Job 7:17 (KJV).

97. I John 4:19 (KJV); Terryl Givens and Fiona Givens, *The God Who Weeps* (Salt Lake City: Ensign Peak, 2012), 53.

98. In apparent deference to Luther, whose translation he admired, Smith followed the reformer in his own version of Rom. 3:28: "a man is justified by faith *alone*." *Joseph Smith's "New Translation" of the Bible* (Independence, MO: Herald House, 1970), 471. Nothing in Smith's preaching or writing, however, reflects any deeper influence of the idea on his own thought.

99. *CD*, 3:1378.

100. James Talmage, *Articles of Faith* (Salt Lake City: Deseret News, 1899), 447, 123, 109, 120.

101. "The prespetary says once in grace always in grace, the methodist says once in grace can fall from grace and be renewed again. there is some truth in both of these statements," though "both are wrong." *WJS*, 333, 330.

102. Stephen Webb, *Jesus Christ, Eternal God: Heavenly Flesh and the Metaphysics of Matter* (New York: Oxford University Press, 2011), 256.

103. John Henry Newman, *Selection, Adapted to the Seasons of the Ecclesiastical Year* (London: Longmans, Green, 1895), 282.

104. Bruce Hafen, *The Broken Heart* (Salt Lake City: Deseret, 1989), 149.

105. Hafen, "Beauty for Ashes," 8.

106. See his *Mormon Neo-Orthodoxy: A Crisis Theology* (Salt Lake City: Signature, 1987).

107. Donald P. Mangum and Brenton G. Yorgason, *Amazing Grace: The Tender Mercies of the Lord* (Salt Lake City: Bookcraft, 1996).

108. Robert L. Millet, *By Grace We Are Saved* (Salt Lake City: Bookcraft, 1989); Robert Millet, *Grace Works* (Salt Lake City: Deseret, 2007).

109. Brad Wilcox, *The Continuous Atonement* (Salt Lake City: Deseret, 2009), 103–20; Stephen E. Robinson, *Believing Christ* (Salt Lake City: Deseret, 1992).

110. Craig L. Blomberg and Stephen E. Robinson, *How Wide the Divide: A Mormon and an Evangelical in Conversation* (Downers Grove, IL: Intervarsity Press, 1997), 186–87.

111. Bruce C. Hafen, "Grace," in *Encyclopedia of Mormonism,* 4 vols. (New York: Macmillan, 1992), 2:560–63

112. Origin, *De Principiis* 3.6.6, *ANF,* 4:347.

113. Henry R. Percival, *The Seven Ecumenical Councils of the Undivided Church* (New York: Scribner's, 1900), 320.

114. Percival, *Seven Ecumenical Councils*, 318–19; Percival also reprints the eleven anathemas of the Council and the nine "anathematisms" of Justinian (312–20).

115. Rev. 14:11.

116. Thomas Aquinas, *Summa Theologia* III Q94 A1 (Chicago: Encyclopedia Britannica, 1980), 2:1041.

117. John Murray, *Letters and Sketches of Sermons* (Boston: Joshua Belcher, 1812), 2: 39.

118. Matt. 7:14.

119. Louis de Granada, *The Sinner's Guide* (New York: P. O'Shea, 1890), 297.

120. St. Leonard of Port Maurice, "The Little Number of Those Who Are Saved," http://olrl.org/snt_docs/fewness.shtml.

121. Matt. 7:14.

122. Canons of Synod of Dort, *C&C*, 2:572.

123. John Bunyan, "The Strait Gate; or, Great difficulty of Going to Heaven," in *Works* (Edinburgh: Sands, Murray, Cochran, 1769), 6:375.

124. John Wesley, *An Extract of the Rev. Mr. John Wesley's Journal,* August 1759 (London, 1788), 10:75.

125. John Wesley, "Free Grace," *Sermons on Several Occasions* (London: J. Kershaw, 1825), 2:10–11, 3.

126. George Whitefield, *Works* (London: Edward and Charles Killy, 1771), 4:55–58

127. Wesley, "Free Grace," 2:6

128. Francis Okely, *The Divine Visions of John Engelbrecht* (Northhampton: Thomas Dicey, 1780), 2:53–54

129. Holifield, *Theology*, 83.

130. Whitefield, *Works*, 4:67–72

131. Samuel Hopkins, *Lessons at the Cross: or Spiritual Truths* (Boston: Gould and Lincoln, 1864), 55, x.

132. Samuel Hopkins, *Twenty-one Sermons on a Variety of Interesting Subjects . . .* (Salem: Joshua Cushing, 1803), 369.

133. J. F. X. Cevetello, "Purgatory," in *New Catholic Encyclopedia* (Detroit: Thomson Gale, 2003), 11:824.

134. Edmund Gibson, *Codex Juris Ecclesiastici Anglicani* (Oxford: Claredon, 1761), 1: 324.

135. Jerome Friedman, *Michael Servetus: A Case Study in Total Heresy* (Geneva: Librairie Droz, 1978), 60.

136. William Ellery Channing, *Unitarian Christianity* (Boston: American Unitarian Association, 1819), 24.

137. Paul Siegvolck [Georg Klein-Nicolai], *The Everlasting Gospel*, trans. John S. (Germantown: Christopher Sower, 1753).

138. http://universalistchurch.net/universalist-history/1786-charter-of-compact-independent-christian-church/.

139. Profession of Faith of the 1803 General Convention of Universalists, article II, Winchester, New Hampshire. Cited in I. Daniel Rupp, *An Original History of the Religious Denominations* (Philadelphia: J. Humphreys, 1844), 727.

140. Charles Chauncy, *The Mystery Hid from Ages and Generations Made Manifest . . . , or, the Salvation of All Men* (Bedford: Applewood, 2009), xi. (Reprint of London: Charles Dilly, 1784.)

141. Chauncy, *Mystery*, 9.

142. Murray, *Letters and Sketches*, 2:253.

143. Chauncy, *Mystery*, 191.

144. An unnamed disputant quoted by Murray, *Letters and Sketches*, 2:40.

145. Murray, *Letters, and Sketches,* 2:254.

146. Frederick Denison Maurice, *Kingdom of Christ* (Norwich: SCM Press, 1958), 1: 152.

147. *New York Times*, 26 July 1863. (Reprinted from the *Boston Journal*, 23 July 1863), http://www.nytimes.com/1863/07/26/news/the-trial-of-rev-charles-beecher-he-is-convicted-of-heresy-result.html?pagewanted=all.

148. International Theological Commission, "The Hope of Salvation for Infants Who Die Without Being Baptized," 1.7.41, http://www.ewtn.com/library/CURIA/itclimbo.HTM 3.6.102.

149. Keller, *Reason for God*, 78.

150. Rob Bell, *Love Wins* (New York: HarperOne, 2012), 2.

151. Bell, *Love Wins*, 9.

152. Bell, *Love Wins*, 108.

153. James Davison Hunter, *American Evangelicalism: Conservative Religion and the Quandary of Modernity* (New Brunswick: Rutgers University Press, 1983). Cited in Edward T. Oaks, "Bell's Present Heaven," *First Things* 216 (October 2011):24.

154. Oakes cites Peter Berger, *A Rumor of Angels* (New York: Anchor, 1970), on hell as a necessary response to moral outrage. Oaks, "Bell's Present Heaven," 24.

155. Warren Foote, *Autobiography* (Mesa, AZ: Dale Foote, 1997), 15.

156. "Blessing by Joseph Smith Sr. dated December 9, 1834," in *Early Patriarchal Blessings of the Church of Jesus Christ of Latter-day Saints*, comp. H. Michael Marquardt (Salt Lake City: Smith-Pettit Foundation, 2007), 11.

157. Lavina Fielding Anderson, ed., *Lucy's Book: A Critical Edition of Lucy Mack Smith's Family Memoir* (Salt Lake City: Signature, 2001), 73.

158. Dean C. Jessee, ed., *The Papers of Joseph Smith. Volume 1: Autobiographical and Historical Writings* (Salt Lake City: Deseret, 1989), 2:440.

159. *WJS*, 112.

160. See the document of membership they signed in Dan Vogel, *Early Mormon Documents* (Salt Lake City: Signature, 1996), 1:633.

161. Vogel, *Early Mormon*, 1:57, n.9.

162. Those converts all left autobiographies, journals, or personal histories, in which they mention universalism as a factor in their background or conversion. Most may be found in CHL.

163. "Biographical Sketch of Howard Coray," 3. In CHL.

164. Benjamin Brown, *Testimonies for Truth: A Record of Manifestations of the Power of God . . .* (Liverpool: S. W. Richards, 1853), 1. In CHL.

165. "Autobiography of Benjamin Ashby," 2. In CHL.

166. Alma 40:11–14.

167. 1 Nephi 9:12.

168. *WJS*, 213.

169. *WJS*, 253.

170. *CD*, 4:2170.

171. *WJS*, 215.

172. By comparison, NDE researchers say the common experience the deceased have of a "life review" entails no external judgment; "the life review is not an expression of divine wrath but a requirement that they experience the true outcomes of their choices." and "the reports appear to be in agreement that all judgment comes from within the individual." Mario Beauregard and Denyse O'Leary, *The Spiritual Brain* (New York: Harper Perennial, 2007), 158, 164.

173. "For now we see through a glass darkly," is the KJV rendering of 1 Cor. 13:12. The "glass" (esoptron) is of course a mirror, as the NRSV less ambiguously translates the word.

174. Alma 41:7; 2 Nephi 2:14; Mosiah 3:25.

175. 1 Pet. 3:20, 4:6.

176. Hilary, *Introductory Commentary on 1 Peter*; Andreas, *Catena*, in *Ancient Christian Commentary on Scripture*, ed. Gerald Bray (Downers Grove, IL: InterVarsity Press, 1998), New Testament 11:113.

177. Clement of Alexandria, *Adumbrations*, in Bray, *Ancient Christian*, New Testament 11:107.

178. *Apocryphal New Testament*, 3rd ed. (London: William Hone, 1821), 64.

179. Tertullian, *On the Soul*, LV, *ANF*, 3:231.

180. Cyril of Alexandria, *Catena*; Augustine, Letter 164, in Bray, *Ancient Christian*, New Testament 11:107–109

181. P. J. Hill and K. Stasiak, "Limbo," in *New Catholic Encyclopedia* (Detroit: Thomson Gale, 2003), 8:590.

182. Dante Alighiere, *Inferno*, IV.53–63, trans. Allen Mandelbaum (New York: Bantam, 1982). 33.

183. International Theological Commission, "Hope of Salvation," introduction, 2.

184. Karl Barth, *Church Dogmatics* (Edinburgh: T. & T. Clark, 1956–1975), 2:486–96 In "The Hope of Eternal Life: Common Statement of the Eleventh Round of the U.S. Lutheran–Roman Catholic Dialogue," 33. http://www.lutherANForum.org/extras/The-Hope-of-Eternal-Life.pdf.

185. Calvin, *Institutes*, 331.

186. *C&C,* 2:327.

187. Calvin, *Institutes*, 331.

188. Calvin, *Institutes*, 331.

189. John Calvin, "Commentaries on the First Epistle of Peter," in *Calvin's Commentaries* (Grand Rapids, IA: Baker, 2005), 22:113.

190. Charles Hodge, *Systematic Theology* (Grand Rapids, MI: Eerdmans, 1970), 2:619.

191. *C&C,* 2:195.

192. Martin Luther, *Commentary on Peter and Jude,* trans. and ed. John Nichols Lenker (Grand Rapids, MI: Kregel, 2005), 166.

193. John Wesley, *Explanatory Notes Upon the New Testament* (London: Thomas Cordeux, 1813), 2: 314.

194. Adam Clarke, *Clarke's Commentary* (Nashville: Abingdon, 1977), 3:864.

195. *Testimonies of the Life, Character, Revelations and Doctrines of our Ever Blessed Mother Ann Lee . . . ,* ed. Rufus Bishop and Seth Y. Wells (Albany: Weed, Parsons, 1888), 185–92. Cited in Ryan Tobler, *Saviors on Mt. Zion: Mormon Sacramentalism, Mortality, and "The Baptism for the Dead."* Unpublished ms.

196. John 5:28–29 (KJV).

197. *EMS* 1.2 (July 1832):2 (D&C 76:37, 38, 42, 44).

198. Joseph Smith [W. W. Phelps], "The Answer," *TS* 4.6 (1 February 1843):83.

199. *EMS* 1.2 (July 1832):2 (D&C 76:45).

200. *EMS* 1.2 (July 1832):2 (D&C 76:31–45).

201. *EMS* 1.2 (July 1832):2 (D&C 76:73–74).

202. Parley P. Pratt, sermon, 7 April 1853, papers of George D. Watt, transcribed by LaJean Purcell Carruth. In CHL.

203. 1981 D&C 138:11, 18, 30. Though approved as scripture in 1976 (as an insert in the PGP), this revelation was added to the D&C only in 1981.

204. Joseph Young, *Deseret News* (18 March 1857):11. Cited in Casey Paul Griffiths, "Universalism and the Revelation of Joseph Smith," in *The Doctrine and Covenants, Revelations in Context: The 37th Annual Brigham Young University Sidney B. Sperry,* ed. Andrew H. Hedges, J. Spencer Fluhman, and Alonzo L. Gaskill (Provo: Brigham Young University, Religious Studies Center, 2008), 168–87. Griffiths provides a good overview of Universalist/Mormon connections.

205. *WJS,* 360.

206. *WJS,* 34.

207. *CD,* 5:2960. Warren Foote recorded that "Landon and others had been cut off for rejecting the vision concerning the three glories." Foote, *Autobiography,* 5.

208. Anderson, *Lucy's Book,* 467.

209. Eliza R. Snow, *Biography and Family Record of Lorenzo Snow* (Salt Lake City: Deseret News, 1884), 31.

210. Truman Coe, "Mormonism," *Ohio Observer,* 11 August 1836.

211. 1876 *D&C* 132:27.

212. "No man can commit the unpardonable sin, until he receives the Holy Ghost." *WJS,* 347.

213. *WJS,* 353.

214. *EMS* 1.2 (July 1832):2 (D&C 76: 35, 38).

215. *CD,* 1:569.

216. Brian H. Stuy, ed., *Collected Discourses* (np: B. H. S. Publishing, 1999), 4:74.

217. Abraham H. Cannon, Journal, 5 April 1894. Cited in Stuy, *Collected Discourses,* 4:68.

218. Lorenzo Snow, *Conference Report,* April 1901, 3.

219. Joseph Fielding Smith, "Salvation Universal," *Improvement Era* 13.44 (November 1909):43–44.

220. Alma 34:32.

221. BC 16:7 (D&C 19:6).

222. Murray, *Letters and Sketches,* 2:253.

223. *WJS,* 33.

224. This vision was recorded in Smith's journal for 21 January 1836. *JSP-J1,* 167–68. It was canonized as D&C 137:5–6 in 1981, after forming part of the PGP in 1976.

225. Heber C. Kimball, letter, cited in *WJS,* 49.

CHAPTER 21

1. Emil Brunner, *Man in Revolt,* trans. Olive Wyon (London: Lutterworth Press, 1953), 90.

2. Reinhold Niebuhr, *Beyond Tragedy* (New York: Scribner's, 1937), 28.

3. W. G. Lambert and A. R. Millard, *Atra-hasis: The Babylonian Story of the Flood* I.2–6 (Winona Lake, IN: Eisenbrauns, 1999), 43.

4. Jean Bottéro, *Religion in Ancient Mesopotamia,* trans. Teresa Lavender Fagan (Chicago: University of Chicago, 2001), 100.

5. David Sedley, "The Ideal of Godlikeness," in *Plato: Ethics, Politics, Religion, and the Soul,* ed. Gail Fine, 2 vols. (Oxford: Oxford University Press, 1999), 2:309.

6. Plato, *Theaetetus* 176, trans. M. J. Levett, rev. Myles F. Burnyeat, in *Plato: Complete Works,* ed. John M. Cooper (Indianapolis: Hackett, 1997), 195.

7. Norman Russell, *The Doctrine of Deification in the Greek Patristic Tradition* (New York: Oxford University Press, 2006), 3.

8. Isa. 14:12–15.

9. Cited in Steven A. McKinion, ed., *Ancient Christian Commentary on Scripture* (Downers Grove, IL: InterVarsity Press, 1998), Old Testament 10:120–21.

10. Cited in McKinion, *Ancient Christian,* OT 10:124.

11. Gen. 11:1–4.

12. Matthew Black, quoted in Russell, *Deification,* 67.

13. Exod. 7:1.

14. Exagoge, quoted in Russell, *Deification,* 68. Russell quotes a number of studies of "Philo's treatment of Moses as a god" (62n.); Philo, quoted in Russell, *Deification,* 61.

15. Russell, *Deification,* 69.

16. Russell, *Deification,* 112.

17. Job 7:9.

18. 1 Cor. 15:22, 54.

19. John 17:23.

20. 2 Pet. 1:4.

21. Acts 17:29.

22. Rom. 8:16–17.

23. Eph. 5:1.

24. Russell, *Deification*, 6.

25. Irenaeus, *Against Heresies* 5, preface, *ANF*, 1:526.

26. Irenaeus, *Against Heresies* 3.20.1–2 and 3.191, *ANF*, 1:450, 448–49.

27. Irenaeus, *Against Heresies* 3.8.3, *ANF*, 1:422.

28. Dionysius the Areopagite, EH 1.3, in Russell, *Deification*, 1.

29. The most comprehensive study of theosis is Russell's *Deification*, but he rather blithely asserts the fundamentally metaphorical nature of all early usage of the term. "The implications of the metaphor were clear to its first hearers," he claims (1).

30. Russell, *Deification*, 121, quoting R. B. Tollington, *Clement of Alexandria* (London: Willam and Norgate, 1914), 2:91–92.

31. Clement of Alexandria, *Exhortation to the Heathen* 1, *ANF*, 2:174.

32. Clement of Alexandria, *Stromata* 7.10, *ANF*, 2:539.

33. Saint Basil the Great, *On the Spirit* 9.23, in *NPNF2* 8:16; Gregory Nazianzen believed that through the incarnation Christ would "make me God." "Fourth Theological Oration" [Oration XXX] XIV, *NPNF2* 7:315.

34. Athanasius, *On the Councils of Ariminum and Seleucia* 51, *NPNF2* 4:477.

35. Athanasius, *On the Councils* 51, *NPNF2* 4:477.

36. Athanasius, *Incarnation of the Word* 54.3, *NPNF2* 4:65.

37. Andrew Louth, "The Reception of Dionysius in the Byzantine World," in *Re-Thinking Dionysius the Areopgagite,* ed. Sarah Coakley and Charles M. Stang (New York: Wiley, 2011), 66.

38. William Ralph Inge, *Christian Mysticism* (London: Metheun, 1948[1899]), 356.

39. Russell, *Deification*, 121.

40. Mark Shuttleworth, "Theosis: Partaking of the Divine Nature," Antiochian Orthodox Christian Archdiocese of North American, http://www.antiochian.org/node/16916.

41. Kurt E. Marquart, "Luther and Theosis," *Concordia Theological Quarterly* 64.3 (July 2000): 183.

42. *Martin Luthers Werke* 20:229–230, cited in Marquart, "Luther," 185.

43. Luther 1.28:25–32, 39–41, cited in Marquart, "Luther," 187.

44. Origen, *Commentary on the Gospel of John Books 13–32* 20.266, trans. Ronald Heine (Washington, DC: Catholic University of America Press, 1993), 261.

45. Aharon Lichtenstein, *Henry More: The Rational Theology of a Cambridge Platonist* (Cambridge, MA: Harvard University Press, 1962), 45.

46. John Smith, "The Excellency and Nobleness of True Religion," in *The Cambridge Platonists*, ed. C. A. Patrides (London: Edward Arnold, 1969), 167.

47. Benjamin Whichcote, "The Manifestation of Christ and the Deification of Man," in Patrides, *Cambridge Platonists*, 70.

48. Henry More, *Antimonopsychia* XXV, cited in Patrides, *Cambridge Platonists*, 18.

49. Thomas Vaughan, *Anthroposophia Theomagica*, in *The Magical Writings of Thomas Vaughan,* ed. Arthur Edward Waite (London: George Redway, 1888), 23.

50. John Wesley, *A Plain Account of Christian Perfection* (New York: Lane and Sanford, 1844), 7–12.

51. Ethan Smith, *View of the Trinity* (Poultney, VT: Smith & Shute, 1824), 55. Smith, in this instance in particular, was unwilling to grant such multiplying of divinity even to the person of Christ.

52. Thomas Starr King, *Socrates: An Oration* (San Francisco: Harr Wagner, 1924), 20.

53. William Ellery Channing, "Humanity's Likeness to God," in *The American Transcendentalists: Essential Writings*, ed. Lawrence Buell (New York: Modern Library, 2006), 13–15.

54. George MacDonald, "The Hardness of the Way," in *Unspoken Sermons*, Second series (Whitehorn, CA: Johannesen: 2004), 191.

55. C. S. Lewis, To Bellen Allen, 1 November 1954, in *Collected Letters* (New York: Harper-Collins, 2007), 3:520.

56. James R. Payton Jr., "Keeping the End in View: How the Strange Yet Familiar Doctrine of Theosis Can Reinvigorate the Christian Life," *Christianity Today*, 27 October 2008.

57. John Jaques, *Catechism for Children Exhibiting the Prominent Doctrines of the Church of Jesus Christ of Latter-day Saints Jesus Christ of Latter-day Saints* (Liverpool: F. D. Richards, 1855), 13.

58. "On Perfection," *TS* 3.6 (15 January 1842):655. (Reprinted from an earlier version in the *Gospel Reflector*.)

59. Preacher William Watters believed any sermon incomplete without the exhortation. John H. Wigger, *Taking Heaven by Storm: Methodism and the Rise of Popular Christianity in America* (New York: Oxford University Press), 20.

60. *EMS* 1.10 (March 1833):73; *EMS* 1.3 (August 1832):19 (Moses 6:51; 7:59, PGP).

61. *EMS* 1.2 (July 1832):2 (D&C 76:58).

62. 1835 D&C 7:33 (D&C 88:107). Before appearing in the Doctrine and Covenants, allusion to Saints being made "equal with [God]" occurred five times in a church editorial. *EMS* 2.17 (February 1834):135–36.

63. Eliza R. Snow, *Biography and Family Record of Lorenzo Snow* (Salt Lake City: Deseret News, 1884), 10, 46–47.

64. Parley P. Pratt, *Mormonism Unveiled: Zion's Watchman Unmasked* (New York: Pratt and Fordham, 1838), 27.

65. Members of the human family are "the greatest parts of Awman Son"; and "Enoch 'saw the begining the ending of man he saw the time when Adam his father was made and he saw that he was in eternity before a grain of dust in the ballance was weighed he saw that he emenated and came down from God.'" "A Sample of Pure Language Given by Joseph the Seer," in *Joseph Smith Papers: Revelations and Translations; Manuscript Revelation Books,* ed. Robin Scott Jensen, Robert J. Woodward, and Steven C. Harper (Salt Lake City: Church Historian's Press, 2009), 265. The second, "Sang by the gift of Tongues and Translated," held that Adam "emenated and came down from God." Kirtland Revelation Book 2 (27 February 1833), in *Manuscript Revelation Books*, 509.

66. Pratt, *Mormonism Unveiled*, 27.

67. *Key*, 33.

68. Plato, *Timaeus* 29e, trans. Donald J. Zeyl, in Cooper, *Plato: Complete Works*, 1236.

69. BC 16 (D&C 19); *EMS* 1.3 (August 1832):19 (Moses 7:35, PGP).

70. *EMS* 1.10 (March 1833):73 (Moses 6:57, PGP).

71. "Behold this is my work to my glory, to the immortality and eternal life of man," reads the original version. *TS* 4.5 (16 January 1843):73 (Moses 1:39, PGP).

72. Truman G. Madsen, "Are Christians Mormon?" *BYU Studies* 15.1 (Autumn 1974):89.

73. Dante, *Paradiso* XXX:115–22, trans. Allen Mandelbaum (New York: Bantam, 1986), 303.

74. Jonathan Edwards, "Sermon 8 on Romans 2:20," in Carol Zaleski and Philip Zaleski, *The Book of Heaven* (New York: Oxford University Press, 2010), 174.

75. From Cheever's *The Powers of the World to Come* (1857). Cited in Ann Douglas, *The Feminization of American Culture* (New York: Knopf, 1977), 222.

76. Douglas, *Feminization,* 223.

77. Gottfried Burger, "Lenore," quoted by the main character in Elizabeth Stuart Phelps, *Gates Ajar* (Boston: James R. Osgood, 1878), 10.

78. Phelps, *Gates Ajar,* 110, 53, 124, 69.

79. Phelps, *Beyond the Gates.* Cited in Douglas, *Feminization,* 225.

80. For several examples in the genre, see Douglas, *Feminization,* 374–75.

81. *CD,* 1:188.

82. *WJS,* 232.

83. Smith quotes Paul (1 Cor. 15:46–48) to this effect, in 1876 D&C 128:13; 1876 D&C 77:2.

84. *CD,* 1:350.

85. Spencer had in mind that this family organization was polygamous. Orson Spencer, *Patriarchal Order, or Plurality of Wives!* (Liverpool: 1853?), 1. See also *Letters Exhibiting the Most Prominent Doctrines of the Church of Jesus Christ of Latter-day Saints* (Liverpool: Orson Spencer, 1848), 55.

86. John Taylor, "Origin and Destiny of Woman," *The Mormon* 3.28 (29 August 1857). (Reprinted in *Deseret News,* 26 May 1899.)

87. George Q. Cannon, in *Collected Discourses,* ed. Brian H. Stuy (np: B. H. S. Publishing, 1999), 4:68.

88. *WJS,* 9.

89. *WJS,* 205.

90. *WJS,* 205. Both remarks about organization take place in the context of a discussion about the necessity for embodiment.

91. *WJS,* 239.

92. *WJS,* 196.

93. *WJS,* 234.

94. *JSP-H1,* 224. The verses, an alteration of Mal. 4:5–6, were later canonized as 1876 D&C 2:1–3.

95. Richard E. Turley Jr., "BYU Family History Fireside," Provo, Utah (9 November 2001), https://docs.google.com/viewer?url=http%3A%2F%2Ffamilyhistory.byu.edu%2Fpdf%2Ffiresides%2F2001-2011-09.pdf.

96. 1844 D&C 106:18 (D&C 128:18).

97. For a history of the term in Christian and then Mormon usage, see Samuel Brown, *In Heaven as it is on Earth* (New York: Oxford University Press, 2012).

98. 1844 D&C 106:18 (D&C 128:18).

99. Colleen McDannell and Bernhard Lang, *Heaven: A History* (New Haven: Yale University Press, 1988), 322.

100. Edward T. Oakes, "Bell's Present Heaven," *First Things* (October 2011):24.

101. David O. McKay, *Gospel Ideals: Selections from the Discourses of David O. McKay* (Salt Lake City: Deseret, 1953), 490.

102. Heber C. Kimball, *JD*, 4:135–36

103. *WJS*, 240.

104. *Early Patriarchal Blessings of the Church of Jesus Christ of Latter-day Saints*, comp. H. Michael Marquardt (Salt Lake City: Smith-Pettit Foundation, 2007), 87. Cited in Brown, *In Heaven*, 18.

105. *WJS*, 234.

106. 1876 D&C 130:2.

107. *EMS* 1.10 (March 1833):6 (D&C 88:133).

108. *CD*, 2:888.

109. Parley P. Pratt, "Celestial Family Organization," *The Prophet* [New York City], 1 March 1845,1.

110. *CD*, 1:277.

111. *CD*, 1:183.

112. *CD*, 1:184.

113. The most comprehensive account of the early years of this theology is Brown, *In Heaven*.

114. Calvin is fairly representative in calling baptism "the symbol of adoption," which replaces circumcision. See his *Institutes of the Christian Religion*, trans. Henry Beveridge (Peabody, MA: Hendrickson, 2008), 872ff. Rom. 8:15 associates adoption with a spiritual recognition that we are God's children. Rom. 8:23 associates adoption with a future "redemption of our body."

115. Parley P. Pratt, *Voice of Warning and Instruction to all People* (New York: Sandford, 1837), 29–31, 96, 107.

116. Alexander Campbell, *Christian Baptism: With the Antecedents and Consequences* (Bethany, VA: Alexander Campbell, 1852). Cited in Samuel Brown, "Early Mormon Adoption Theology and the Mechanics of Salvation," *Journal of Mormon History* 37.3 (Summer 2011):11. Brown indicates that Campbell had expressed this view in print as early as 1829.

117. *TS* 2.1 (1 November 1840):199–200.

118. *TS* 2.15 (1 June 1841):430. See also, for a reference to gospel administrations like blessing or laying on of hands as "the ordinances of adoption," *TS* 4:20 (1 September 1843):315.

119. Rom. 8:17.

120. See, for example, in *TS* 3.1 (15 November 1841):578; *TS* 3.6 (15 January 1842):656; *TS* 3.7 (1 February 1842):676, etc. The Pratt expression is from Pratt, *Mormonism Unveiled*; *TS* 4.5 (16 January 1843):74.

121. *MS* 2.12 (April 1842):178. The expression is repeated on p.180.

122. "The Law of Adoption," *MS* 4.2 (June 1843):17.

123. "Sons of God," *TS* 4.5 (16 January 1843):74. (Reprinted in *MS* 4.4 [August 1843]: 56–60.)

124. Parley P. Pratt, "Celestial Family Organization," *New York Prophet* (1 March 1845):1.

125. "Incomplete Work on Matthew," in *Ancient Christian Commentary on Scripture*, ed. Manlio Simonetti (Downers Grove, IL: InterVarsity Press, 1998) New Testament 1b, 153.

126. Augustine, Sermon 362, in *Ancient Christian Commentary*, ed. Arthur A. Just Jr., New Testament 3:312.

127. Clement of Alexandria, "Stromateis," in Just, *Ancient Christian*, New Testament 3:313.

128. McDannell and Lang, *Heaven*, 53.

129. Milton, *Paradise Lost*, Book 8, ll. 615–27, in *The Complete Poetry and Essential Prose of John Milton*, ed. William Kerrigan, John Rumrich, and Stephen M. Fallon (New York: Modern Library, 2007), 515.

130. Emanuel Swedenborg, *Marital Love: Its Wise Delights*, trans. William Frederic Wunsch (New York: Swedenborg Publishing Association, 1938), 73–74.

131. William Shakespeare, *Antony and Cleopatra* 5.2.281 (Cambridge: Cambridge University Press, 1990), 254; Dante Gabriel Rossetti, "The Blessed Damozel," in *Collected Poetry and Prose* (New Haven: Yale University Press, 2003), 4–6; Elizabeth Barrett Browning, "Sonnet 43," in *Complete Poetical Works* (Boston: Houghton Mifflin, 1900), 223.

132. This is from a letter of Peggy Dow to her brother Lorenzo, in 1813. Rick Grunder, *Mormon Parallels: A Bibliographic Source* (Lafayette, NY: Rick Grunder Books, 2008), digital version, 121. Grunder gives several other examples of similar epistolary expressions from the early and mid-nineteenth century, including "Mary" in 1854 (242), William Wilcox in 1807 (471), and "M.K." in the 1820s (157).

133. The plaque was translated from the Latin by "Mr T. Young." The translation is presently on display in the Minster.

134. Edward D. Griffin, "Heaven," in *Sermons* (Albany, NY: Packard, Van Benthuysen, 1838), 2:437.

135. Ogden Kraut, in *Jesus Was Married* (n.p., 1969), documents a number of early LDS leaders who taught Christ was married, including Orson Hyde, Orson Pratt, and Orson Spencer. In 1912, the First Presidency declared "the Church has no authoritative declaration on the subject." *Improvement Era* 15.11 (1912):1042.

136. McDannell and Lang, *Heaven*, 259.

137. McDannell and Lang, *Heaven*, 260–61.

138. *MA* 1.9 (June 1835):130.

139. Parley P. Pratt, *Autobiography*, ed. Scot Facer Proctor and Maurine Jensen Proctor (Salt Lake City: Deseret, 2000), 361.

140. "Revelation Regarding Plural Marriage to Sarah Whitney," 27 July 1842. "Revelations Collections, circa 1831–1876," *MS* 4583, in CHL. Reproduced in *Unpublished Revelations,* comp. Fred C. Collier (Salt Lake City: Collier's, 1981), 1:95.

141. Benjamin F. Johnson, *My Life's Review* (np: Johnson Family Organization, 1997), 85–86.

142. 1876 D&C 131:2.

143. Scott H. Faulring, ed., *An American Prophet's Record: The Diaries and Journals of Joseph Smith* (Salt Lake City: Signature, 1989), 381.

144. Brown, *In Heaven*, 235.

145. Pratt, "Celestial Family Organization," 1.

146. Orson Spencer, *Letters Exhibiting the Most Prominent Doctrines of the Church of Jesus Christ of Latter-day Saints* (Liverpool: Orson Spencer, 1848), 170.

147. The three major works on the subject are Jonathan Stapley, "Adoptive Sealing Ritual in Mormonism," *Journal of Mormon History* 37.3 (Summer 2011):53–118; Brown, "Early Mormon Adoption Theology," and Brown, *In Heaven*.

148. Devery Anderson and Gary Bergera, eds., *The Nauvoo Endowment Companies, 1845–1846* (Salt Lake City: Signature, 2005), 566. Samuel Brown cites the above sources in his discussion of Bernhisel as an instance of the Mormon "Chain of Belonging," in *In Heaven*, 203ff.

149. Brown, "Early Mormon Adoption," 5.

150. Sidney Rigdon made a pitch to be sustained as the Saints' "guardian" after Smith's death. Young asked the crowd, "do you, as individuals, at this time, want to choose a Prophet or a guardian to lead you?. . . If 10,000 men rise up and say they have the Prophet Joseph's shoes, I know they are imposters." The quorum was instead sustained as "the head." *CD*, 1:40–42

151. *CD*, 1:277.

152. Pratt, *Autobiography*, 440.

153. "Marriage," in *Encyclopedia Judaica* (Jerusalem: Keter, 1971–72), 11:1027.

154. Martin Luther to Joseph Levin Metzsch, 9 December 1526, in *Letters of Spiritual Comfort*, ed. and trans. Thoedore G. Tappert (Louisville: Westminster John Knox Press, 2006), 276.

155. John Milton, *A Treatise on Christian Doctrine* (Cambridge: Cambridge University Press, 1825), 243.

156. Martin Madan, *Thelyphthora: or, A Treatise on Female Ruin . . .* (London: J. Dodsley, 1780), 1:262.

157. Madan, *Thelyphthora*, 2:82.

158. Luke Tyerman, *The Oxford Methodists* (New York: Harper & Brothers, 1873), 400.

159. 1 Tim. 3:2, 12.

160. *Catechism of the Catholic Church*, 2nd ed. (New York: Doubleday Religion, 2003), par. 2387, 633.

161. "Revelation Regarding Plural Marriage," in Collier, *Unpublished Revelations*, 1:95.

162. Smith connected his 1830–33 redaction of the Bible to his first consideration of plural marriage. *Nauvoo Neighbor* 2 (17, 19 June 1844). Noted in Brown, *In Heaven*, 231.

163. Helen Mar Whitney, *Why We Practice Plural Marriage* (Salt Lake City: Juvenile Instructor, 1884), 53.

164. Helen Mar Whitney, *Plural Marriage as Taught by the Prophet Joseph* (Salt Lake City: Juvenile Instructor, 1882), 11.

165. Whitney, *Plural Marriage as Taught*, 27.

166. For the most comprehensive treatment of Joseph Smith and polygamy, see Brian C. Hales, *Joseph Smith's Polygamy* (Salt Lake City: Greg Kofford, 2013).

167. Jacob 2:27–30.

168. *WJS*, 241.

169. *WJS*, 331.

170. The question of Smith's sexual involvement with his wives is much debated. His biographer notes that in case of his marriages to already-married women in particular, "there is no certain evidence" of such relations. Richard L. Bushman, *Joseph Smith, Rough Stone Rolling, A Cultural Biography of Mormonism's Founder* (New York: Alfred A. Knopf, 2005), 439. Evidence of sexual relations with plural wives exists, but DNA testing of several alleged descendants has failed to confirm any polygamous offspring from any relationship other than his marriage to Emma. See a summary in Michael De Groote, "DNA Solves a Joseph Smith Mystery," *Deseret News,* 9 July 2011.

171. Helen Mar Whitney, *A Woman's View: Helen Mar Whitney's Reminiscences of Early Church History*, ed. Richard N. Holzapfel (Provo: BYU Religious Studies Center, 1997), 482.

172. George Q. Cannon referred to the "new order of society." Kathryn Daynes mentions "ties of loyalty," and Tod Compton writes of "the dynastic nature" of Smith's marriages. See references in Matthew Bowman, "The Crisis of Mormon Christology: History, Progress, and

Protestantism," *Fides Et Historia* 40.2 (Fall 2008):6. For female empowerment, see Kathleen Flake, "The Emotional and Priestly Logic of Plural Marriage," Leonard J. Arrington Lecture, 1 October 2009 (Logan: Utah State University Press, 2009).

173. Brown, *In Heaven*, 228.

174. *WJS*, 318.

175. Polygamy never became the practice of the majority of Mormons, but was very high among priesthood leaders. Estimates (and means of gauging the number) vary widely, but are generally in the 20–30% range before the cessation of polygamy.

176. Orson Pratt, *JD*, 1:61–63.

177. "Their descendants, tens of thousands of whom are living, worthy citizens of the land, are proud of their heritage." John A. Widtsoe, *Evidences and Reconciliations* (Salt Lake City: Deseret, 1943), 390. "Their descendants are prominent throughout the Intermountain West," says the *Encyclopedia of Mormonism,* 4 vols. (New York: Macmillan, 1992), 3:1095.

178. *MS* 19.27 (4 July 1857):432.

179. Kathryn Daynes, in *More Wives than One: The Transformation of the Mormon Marriage System 1840–1910* (Urbana: University of Illinois Press, 2001), 93–94.

180. *CD*, 1:419.

181. B. H. Roberts, *Comprehensive History of the Church of Jesus Christ of Latter-day Saints* (Provo: Brigham Young University Press, 1965), 5:297. (First published in 1912.)

182. Todd Compton, *In Sacred Loneliness: The Plural Wives of Joseph Smith* (Salt Lake City: Signature, 1997).

183. Snow printed her speculations as "Mortal and Immortal Elements of the Human Body," *Woman's Exponent* 2.13 (1 December 1873):99. The essay was popular enough to be reprinted (4.7 [1 September 1875]:54), but the leadership came down immediately and emphatically after the reprint. The *Woman's Exponent* editors placed Young's rebuke at the middle section of their April issue, with the obituaries. The church, however, reprinted it as the lead article on the front page of the *Deseret News*, along with an extensive critique Young directed apostle John Taylor to write. *Woman's Exponent* 4.8 (15 September 1875):60; *Deseret News,* 22 September 1875, 1. Snow published a perfunctory retraction—but only after six months had passed, and on the fourth page of the women's journal. Eliza R. Snow, "To Whom It May Concern,"March 19, 1876 *Woman's Exponent* 4.21 (1 April 1876):164; reprinted in *Deseret News Weekly*, 5 April 1876, 152. For an extended discussion, see Jill Mulvay Derr, "The Lion and the Lioness: Brigham Young and Eliza R. Snow," *BYU Studies* 40.2 (2001):54–101.

184. See Terryl L. Givens, *Viper on the Hearth: Mormons, Myths, and the Construction of Heresy*, rev. ed. (New York: Oxford University Press, 2013), for depictions of polygamy as the product of both mental and physical coercion.

185. "Belinda Marden Pratt to Her Sister," 12 January 1854, http://jared.pratt-family.org/parley_family_histories/belinda_marden_defense.html.

186. Belinda Marden Pratt, "Defence of Polygamy, by a Lady in Utah," in a letter to her sister in New Hampshire, Salt Lake City, 1854.

187. Eliza R. Snow to M. L. Holbrook, 30 November 1866 and 2 December 1869. In Jill Mulvay Derr and Matthew J. Grow, "Letters on Mormon Polygamy and Progeny: Eliza R. Snow and Martin Luther Holbrook, 1866–1869," *BYU Studies* 48.2 (2009):157, 159, 163.

188. Helen Mar Whitney, "Life Incidents," *Woman's Exponent* (15 October 1883):74. Cited in Donna Hill, *Joseph Smith: The First Mormon* (Salt Lake City: Signature, 1999), 360.

189. Whitney, *Plural Marriage as Taught*, 16.

190. Romania B. Pratt Penrose, "Memoir of Romania B. Pratt, M.D." (1881), in Flake, "Emotional and Priestly Logic."

191. "A successful polygamous wife must regard her husband with indifference, and with no other feeling than that of reverence, for love we regard as a false sentiment; a feeling which should have no existence in polygamy." *New York World*, 19 November 1869, as cited in Richard S. Van Wagoner, *Mormon Polygamy: A History* (Salt Lake City: Signature, 1986), 102.

192. Whitney, *Plural Marriage as Taught*, 27.

193. *CD,* 4:2357.

194. *JD,* 25:344.

195. *CD,* 4:2357.

196. Wilford Woodruff, *Journal*, ed. Scott G. Kenney (Midvale, UT: Signature, 1983), 7:31.

197. Woodruff, *Journal*, 6:527.

198. Official Declaration-1, D&C.

199. Charles Penrose, "Editor's Table," *Improvement Era* 15.11 (September 1912):1042.

200. "Fear and Trembling," in *The Essential Kierkegaard,* ed. Howard V. Hong and Edna H. Hong (Princeton: Princeton University Press, 2000), 99–100.

201. V. H. Cassler, "The Two Trees," FAIR Conference, Sandy, Utah, 6 August 2010; online version, http://www.fairlds.org/fair-conferences/2010-fair-conference/2010-the-two-trees.

202. Whitney, *Plural Marriage*, 48.

203. Quoted in Richard S. Van Wagoner, *Polygamy: A History* (Salt Lake City: Signature, 1992), 100.

204. Autobiography of Lorena Eugenia Washburn Larsen, quoted in Paula Kelly Harline, *The Polygamous Wives Writing Club* (New York: Oxford University Press, 2014).

205. *JD,* 3:125.

206. http://www.mormonnewsroom.org/article/polygamy-latter-day-saints-and-the-practice-of-plural-marriage.

207. https://www.lds.org/scriptures/dc-testament/od/1?lang=eng.

208. As confirmed in a 1988 First Presidency letter, deceased women may be sealed to multiple husbands. See circular letter, Ezra Taft Benson, Gordon B. Hinckley, and Thomas S. Monson, 8 December 1988. In *The Development of LDS Temple Worship,* ed. Devery S. Anderson (Salt Lake City: Signature, 2011), 456. The technical implication is that polyandry as well as polygyny are eternal possibilities. However, the stated understanding is that such multiple sealings, in the absence of a known preference, are a preferable alternative to eternalizing the wrong one. Only one will presumably be countenanced in the eternities, but "these determinations must, of necessity, be made beyond the veil."

209. The Kimball story is recounted by Jake Garn, *Why I Believe* (Salt Lake City: Aspen, 1992), 13. Cited in Robert E. Wells, "Uniting Blended Families," *Ensign* 27.8 (August 1997):28.

210. Wells, "Uniting," 28.

211. Stuy, *Collected Discourses*, 4:72–73

212. *CD,* 1:188.

213. B. H. Roberts, *The Truth, The Way, the Life*, ed. John W. Welch (Provo: BYU Studies, 1994), 559.

214. "The Family: A Proclamation to the World," https://www.lds.org/topics/family-proclamation.

215. Orson F. Whitney, Conference Report, April 1929,p.11; The quotation has been cited frequently in General Conference addresses. See in other Conference Reports, Boyd K. Packer (April 1992), Robert D. Hales (April 1999, April 2004), James E. Faust (April 2003), and Richard H. Winkel (May 2006).

216. Busham, *Rough Stone Rolling*, 440.

217. John 17:22.

218. Flake, "Emotional and Priestly Logic."

219. Elizabeth Wood Kane, *A Gentile Account of Life in Utah's Dixie, 1872–1873* (Salt Lake City: University of Utah Press, 2001), 39. Cited in Flake, "Emotional and Priestly Logic," 8.

220. Flake, "Emotional and Priestly Logic," 12–13.

221. Ezra Taft Benson, "What I Hope You Will Teach Your Children About the Temple," *Ensign* 15 (August 1985):9.

222. Robert L. Millet, "The Ancient Covenant Restored," *Ensign* 28 (March 1998):38.

223. Russell M. Nelson, "The Prophetic Voice," *Ensign* 26 (May 1996):6; "Lessons from Eve," *Ensign* 17 (November 1987):87.

224. L. Tom Perry, "Fathers' Role in Anchoring Families," *LDS Church News* (10 April 2004):15.

225. Elder Bruce C. Hafen and Marie K. Hafen, "Crossing Thresholds and Becoming Equal Partners," *Ensign* 37.8 (August 2007):24–29.

226. C. S. Lewis, *Miracles* (New York: HarperCollins, 2009), 261.

227. V. H. Cassler, "Plato's Son, Augustine's Heir: "'A Post–Heterosexual Mormon Theology'"? *Square Two* 5.2 (Summer 2012), http://squaretwo.org/Sq2ArticleCasslerPlatosSon.html.

228. Sylviane Agacinski, *Parity of the Sexes* (New York: Columbia University Press, 2001), 39. Cited in Cassler, "Plato's Son."

229. Bruce D. Porter, "Defending the Family in a Troubled World," *Ensign* 41.6 (June 2011). Quoted in Cassler, "Plato's Son."

230. Young, *CD*, 3:1533.

231. Ezra Taft Benson, "Jesus Christ—Gifts and Expectations," in *Speeches of the Year, 1974* (Provo: Brigham Young University Press, 1975), 313.

232. Warren Cowdery, "Editorials," *MA* 3.7 (April 1837):489.

233. Parley P. Pratt, "Immortality and Eternal Life of the Material Body," in *An Appeal to the Inhabitants of the State of New York; Letter to Queen Victoria; The Fountain of Knowledge; Immortality of the Body; and Intelligence and Affection* (Nauvoo, IL: John Taylor, 1844), 21, 29.

234. Pratt, "Immortality," 30, 35.

235. Parley P. Pratt, "Materiality," *MS* 6.2 (1 July 1845):20. (Originally published in *The Prophet*, 24 May 1845.)

236. Pratt, *The Seer* 1.2 (February 1853):23.

237. *CD*, 4:1972.

238. Gen. 22:17.

239. *TS* 3.9 (1 March 1842):706 (Abraham 2:9–11, PGP).

240. 1876 D&C 132:63.

241. Orson Pratt, *JD*, 1:59.

242. The Methodist pamphlet is referred to, but not by name, in Samuel Bennett, "A few remarks by way of reply to an anonymous scribbler, calling himself a philanthropist, disabusing the Church of Jesus Christ of Latter Day Saints of the slanders and falsehoods which he has attempted to foist upon it" (Philadelphia: Brown, Bicking & Guilbert, 1840); Erastus Snow,"E. Snow's reply to the Self-Styled Philanthropist, of Chester County" (Philadelphia: n.p., 1840). The debate is discussed in Blair Hodges, " 'My Principality on Earth Began': Millennialism and the Celestial Kingdom in the Development of Mormon Doctrine," *Dialogue* 46.2 (Summer 2013).

243. Pratt, "Celestial Family Organization," 1–2.

244. "Life of Joseph Holbrook," 1:40. Cited in Bowman, "Crisis of Mormon Christology," 6.

245. "Buckeye's Lamentation for Want of More Wives," *Warsaw Message* (February 7, 1844). Cited in Roger D. Launius, *Joseph Smith III: Pragmatic Prophet* (Urbana: University of Illinois Press, 1995), 193.

246. George MacDonald, "March 3," *Diary of an Old Soul* (Minneapolis: Augsburg, 1975), 27.

247. Sharpe was apparently relying upon materials collected by William Harris, *Mormonism Portrayed: its errors, absurdities, etc.* The report could have been a misinterpretation or based on oral teachings. See Benjamin E. Park and Jordan Watkins, "The Riches of Mormon Materialism: Parley Pratt's 'Materiality' and Early Mormon Theology," *Mormon Historical Studies* 11.2 (Fall 2010):159–72.

248. *CD*, 1:351

249. Pratt, "Materiality," 21.

250. "Sons of God," 74.

251. Pratt, *Intelligence and Affection*, 37.

252. William Law, "The Spirit of Love," in *A Serious Call to a Devout and Holy Life; The Spirit of Love*, ed. Paul G. Stanwood (New York: Paulist Press, 1978), 400.

253. *CD*, 2:1152–53.

254. *CD*, 2:1009.

255. Moroni 7:48. Compare 1 John 3:2.

256. "Address," *MA* 1.1 (October 1834):2.

257. Article of Faith 4, PGP.

258. *WJS*, 160.

259. *WJS*, 215.

260. *WJS*, 178.

261. *WJS*, 204.

262. *WJS*, 204.

263. Robert Baird, *Religions in America* (New York, 1844), 291. Cited in Daniel Walker Howe, The Unitarian Conscience: Harvard Moral Philosophy, 1805-1861 (Cambridge: Harvard University Press, 1970), 7.

264. Howe, *Unitarian*, 7.

265. Nathan O. Hatch, *The Democratization of American Christianity* (New Haven: Yale University Press, 1989), 162.

266. William Blake, "Auguries of Innocence," *Complete Poetry and Selected Prose of John Donne and the Complete Poetry of William Blake* (New York: Random House, 1941), 597.

267. Terry Eagleton, *A Very Short Introduction to the Meaning of Life* (New York: Oxford University Press, 2008), 95.

268. 2 Nephi 10:24; 25:23.

269. *EMS* 1.10 (March 1833):73 (Moses 6:60, PGP).

270. *WJS*, 231.

271. 1876 D&C 132:16.

272. *WJS*, 329. Smith was glossing Heb. 11:40, which reads, "God having provided some better thing for us, that they without us should not be made perfect" (KJV).

273. 2 Sam. 5.

274. Chrysostom, *Proof of the Gospel* 6.24, in *Ancient Christian,* ed. Erik M. Heen and Philip D. W. Krey, New Testament 10:223.

275. Alan Taylor overviews these and other examples in "The New Jerusalem of the Early American Frontier," *Visions of the Future: Collective and Individual; Secular and Sacred,* 117–126. Quaderno V, Quaderni Online, http://www.library.vanderbilt.edu/Quaderno/Quaderno5/quaderno5.html.

276. *EMS* 1.3 (August 1832):19 (Moses 7:19, 18, 27, PGP).

277. *EMS* 1.1 (June 1832):2 (D&C 45:66).

278. "The Temple," *TS* 3.13 (2 May 1842):776.

279. "The Law" of the church, which first pointed toward consecration in the context of a Zion society, came in 9 February 1831: *EMS* 1.2 (July 1832):1 (D&C 42). Orson Pratt said the allusion to Enoch was removed from printed versions of the law. *JD,* 16:156.

280. *WJS*, 367.

281. *WJS*, 110.

282. *Messages of the First Presidency,* comp. James R. Clark (Salt Lake City: Bookcraft, 1971), 4:165.

283. 1835 D&C 81: 5 (D&C 97:21); 1835 D&C 27:1 (D&C 57:1).

284. Heb. 12:23 (KJV). The expression is repeated in 1835 D&C 91:5 (D&C 76:67), first published in *EMS* 1.2 (July 1832):2, and in 1835 D&C 3:9 (D&C 107:19).

285. *EMS* 1.3 (August 1832):19 (Moses 7:29–41, PGP).

286. *CD,* 5:2741.

287. *EMS* 1.3 (August 1832):19 (Moses 7:64, PGP).

288. In Smith's lifetime, when Mormon editors noted "the greatest importance" assumed by the "great law of adoption," and commented on its promulgation to the point of "weary[ing] the people by the monotony of the subject," they were using the term in the New Testament sense. After "alienation of our race from God," one must be spiritually reborn, and receive "the spirit of adoption, whereby he can call Abba, Father." "Law of Adoption," *MS* 4.2 (June 1843):17 and "Editorial" *MS* 4.2 (June 1843):31.

289. Brown, "Early Mormon Adoption Theology"; Jonathan A. Stapley, "Adoptive Sealing Ritual in Mormonism," *Journal of Mormon History* 37.3 (Summer 2011):53–117.

290. Stuy, *Collected Discourses,* 4:68.

291. Stuy, *Collected Discourses,* 4:72.

292. James Talmage, Articles of Faith (Salt Lake City: Deseret News, 1899),, 455–58.

293. Talmage, *Articles of Faith,* 455–58.

294. Talmage, *Articles of Faith,* 444.

295. Roberts, *The Truth,* 539–59.

296. These ideas first appeared in Roberts's article "Complete Marriage," *Improvement Era* 31 (January 1928):189–92; Roberts, *The Truth*, 554.

297. Roberts, *The Truth*, 526–27.

298. Roberts, *The Truth*, 527–28. Roberts is quoting 1 John 3:2.

299. Herbert Croly, *The Promise of American Life* (New York: Macmillan, 1914), 400. (First published in 1909.)

300. Matthew Bowman, "Eternal Progression: Mormonism and American Progressivism," in *Mormonism and American Politics Since 1945,* ed. Jana Reiss and Randall Balmer (New York: Columbia University Press, forthcoming). Indeed, Thomas Alexander has characterized the theology of Roberts, Widtsoe, and Talmage as "progressive theology"; see his "The Reconstruction of Mormon Doctrine," *Sunstone* 5.4 (July-August 1980):24–33.

301. 1835 D&C 7:8 (D&C 88:34).

302. The phrase is the title of lesson 23 in the Sunday School manual, *Preparing for Exaltation* (Salt Lake City: Church of Jesus Christ of Latter-day Saints, 1998); it may have been used first by Joseph F. Smith, *JD*, 16:247–48

303. Bowman, "Eternal Progression," 1. He cites the study by Gordon and Gary Shepherd, *A Kingdom Transformed: Themes in the Development of Mormonism* (Salt Lake City: University of Utah Press, 1984), 237–42.

304. Russell M. Nelson, *Perfection Pending, and Other Favorite Discourses* (Salt Lake City: Deseret, 1998), 3.

305. Alma 34:32.

306. Wilford Woodruff, "The Administration of Angels," in Stuy, *Collected Discourses*, 5:237–38.

307. Harold Bloom, *The American Religion* (New York: Simon & Schuster, 1992), 90–91.

308. J. C. Polkinghorne, *Theology in the Context of Science* (New Haven: Yale University Press, 2009), 156.

309. Pico della Miradola, "On the Dignity of Man," in *Renaissance Philosophy of Man*, ed. Ernst Cassirer et al. (Chicago: University of Chicago, 1967), 224–25.

310. Roy Hattersley, *The Life of John Wesley: A Brand from the Burning* (New York: Doubleday, 2003), 132–33.

311. This is how McDannell and Lang characterize a common view from Longfellow to Leslie Weatherhead. McDannell and Lang, *Heaven*, 276.

312. Joseph Addison, *The Spectator* 1.111 (7 July 1711), in *Addison's Spectator*, ed. George Washington Greene (New York: Derby & Jackson, 1860), 302–303.

313. Quoted in Charles Taylor, *A Secular Age* (Cambridge, MA: Harvard University Press, 2007), 52.

314. Thomas Dick, *The Philosophy of a Future State* (Philadelphia: Biddle, 1845), 166.

315. Bloom, *American Religion,* 123. Bloom had in mind primarily the esoteric and hermetic associations with the word, but the Greek term also refers to a species of higher knowledge as the key to salvation.

316. *WJS*, 200.

317. Stan Larson, "The King Follett Discourse: A Newly Amalgamated Text," *BYU Studies* 18.2 (Winter 1978):204.

318. *WJS*, 202.

319. *WJS*, 379.

320. 1876 D&C 130:19.

321. *TS* 3.10 (25 March 1842):720 (Abraham 3:19, PGP).

322. Larson, "King Follett," 202.

323. "A Vision Given to Mosiah Hancock," *Levi and Mosiah Hanock Journals* (Genola, UT: Pioneer, 2006), 188.

324. James E. Talmage, "The Philosophical Basis of Mormonism," 1915, in *The Essential Talmage,* ed. James Harris (Salt Lake City: Signature, 1997), 153.

325. *JD,* 7:157.

326. *JD,* 7:3.

327. Franklin D. Richards, "Words of the Prophets," in CHL; Charlotte Haven, "A Girl's Letters from Nauvoo," 26 March 1843, *The Overland Monthly* 16.96 (December 1890):626, http://www.olivercowdery.com/smithhome/1880s-1890s/havn1890.htm. I thank Michael Reed for these sources.

328. Brigham Henry Roberts, *Outlines of Ecclesiastical History: A Textbook* (Salt Lake City: Cannon, 1893), 427.

329. Talmage, *Articles of Faith,* 421. The passage was dropped from subsequent editions.

330. Letter from the Office of The First Presidency, 5 March 1952, and again on 17 December 1965. Cited in George T. Boyd, "A Mormon Concept of Man," *Dialogue: A Journal of Mormon Thought* 3.1 (Spring 1968):72.

331. *Church News* (23 April 1960):3. In subsequent years, Bruce McConkie dissented from those liberal views, condemning them as a "deadly heresy." McConkie, "The Seven Deadly Heresies," in *Devotional Speeches of the Year 1980* (Provo: Brigham Young University Press, 1981). Spencer W. Kimball shared McConkie's stricter soteriology. "No progression between kingdoms," he said. *Teachings of Spencer W. Kimball,* Edward L. Kimball, ed. (Salt Lake City: Bookcraft, 1995), 50. However, McConkie's condemnation of organic evolution in the same sermon, a position the church presidency steadfastly refused to take, reflected the dogmatism into which his theology could slip. The church publisher recently ceased publication of his doctrinal compendium (*Mormon Doctrine*) .

332. Terryl L. Givens, *When Souls Had Wings: Premortal Life in Western Thought* (New York Oxford University Press, 2010), 124.

333. Elizabeth A. Clark, *The Origenist Controversy: The Cultural Construction of an Early Christian Debate* (Princeton: Princeton University Press, 1992), 250.

INDEX